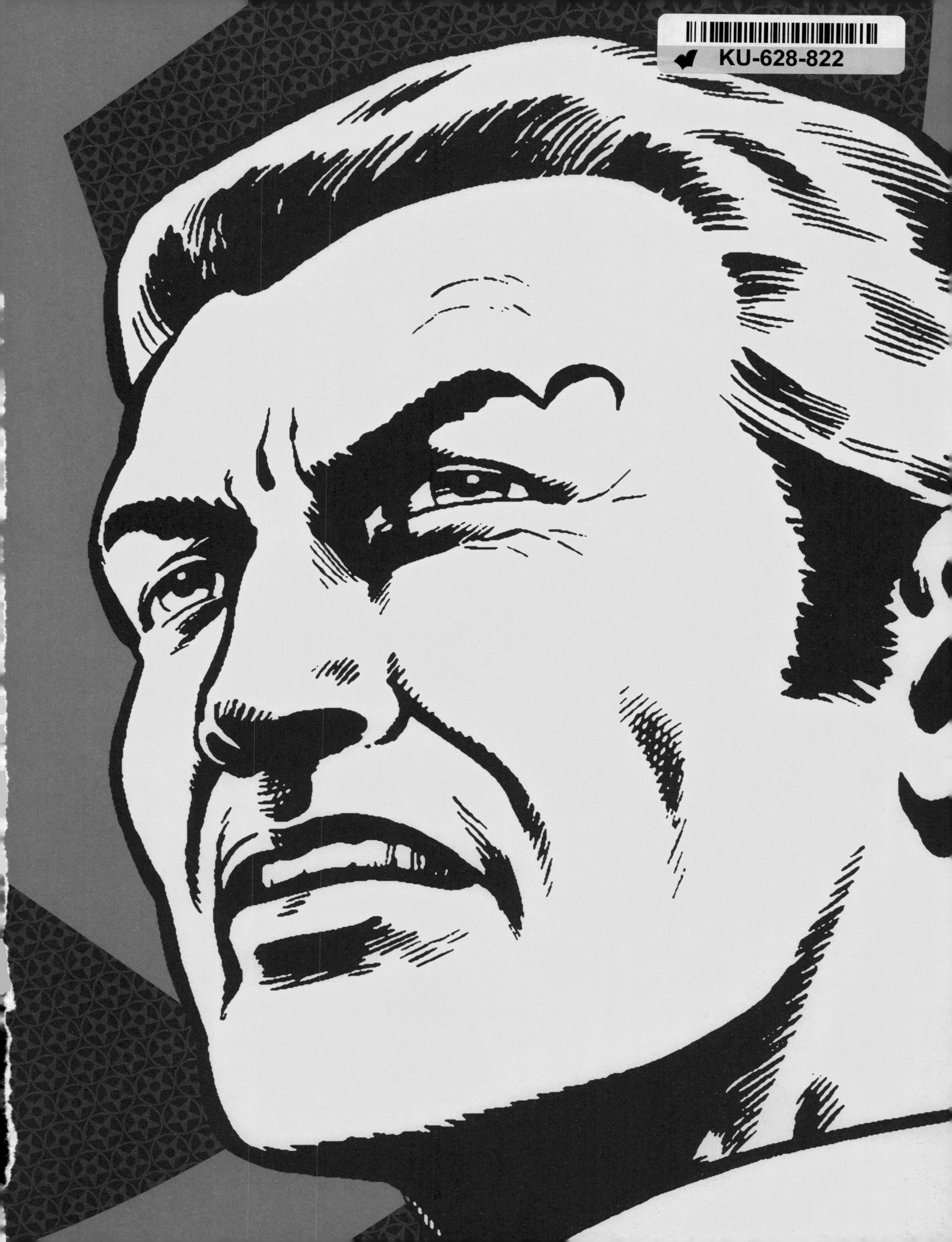

DAN

THE 2000
VOLUM

DARE

AD YEARS

E   O   N   E

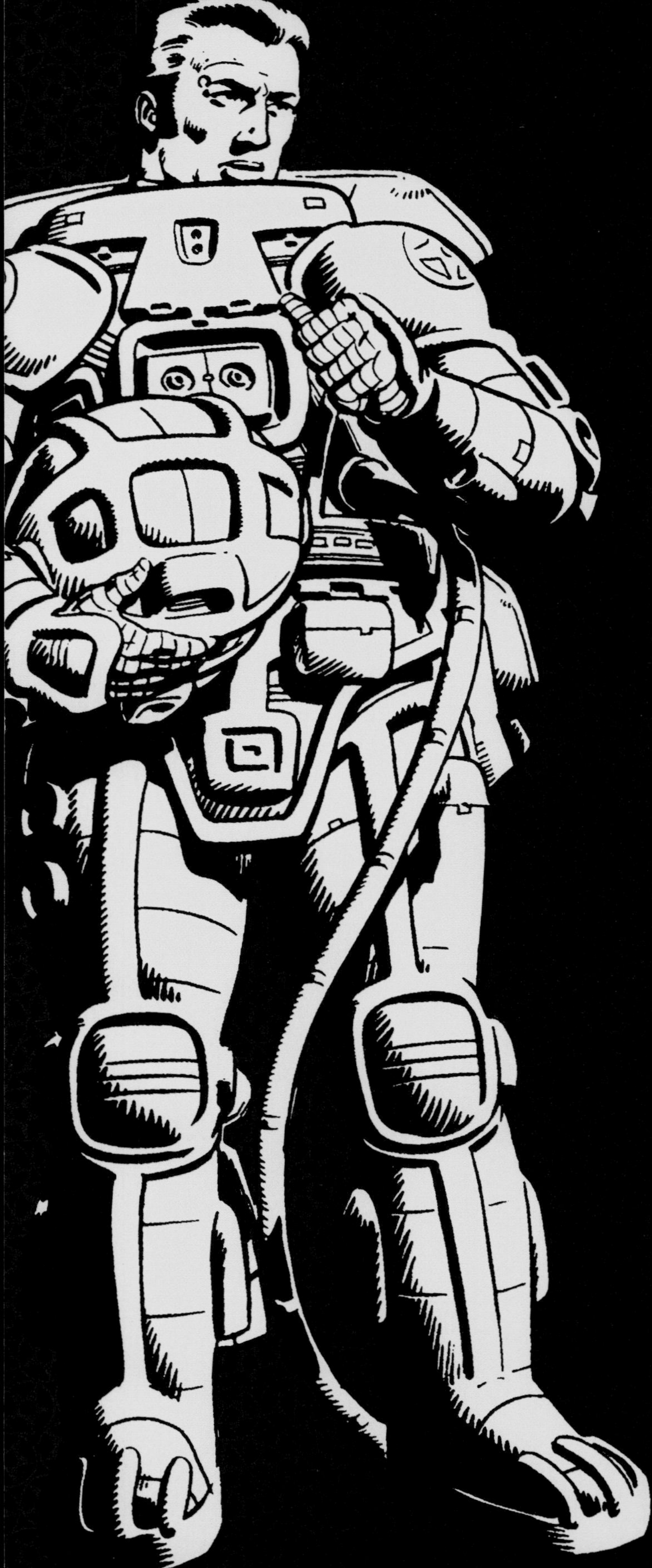

INTR

This was our Dan Dare.

By which I mean, this is the *Dan Dare* that awaited the readers of *2000 AD* when it first appeared in February of 1977. It is not Frank Hampson's original creation from the 1950's *Eagle*, far from it. This is a different beast, featuring a harder man in a harsher world, a long way from the good-natured stoicism and stalwart, stiff upper lip of the original: but for anyone who was a kid in the late seventies, it was the one we read and the one we knew. Speaking personally, it's what I immediately think of when anyone says "Dan Dare". It was ours.

When I first looked in detail at Hampson's work on the character, I was highly impressed. Beautiful artwork combined with straightforward narrative to tell the story of a decent and honest man, who faced unspeakable evil and dreadful odds- and triumphed. I couldn't reconcile this with the tough-minded dirty fighter of *2000 AD*, who blasted his way across the galaxy with a legion of devils at his back and a starship whose devastating firepower he was only too ready to unleash. I didn't even try. Yet to fully understand the *Dan Dare* you're about to read, it's necessary to compare and contrast it with what it replaced.

Eagle was cancelled in 1969. Quality had nosedived and sales had gone with it; "two and a half vicars wrote in to complain", as one wag later opined. All the same, the comic's lead character was fondly remembered, and when Pat Mills was putting *2000 AD* together he seemed like an obvious fit. Dan Dare was brought out of Limbo and updated for the grimmer, post-*Battle* and *Action* world of British comics. He looked and dressed differently, said "gonna" instead of "going to", and killed anyone who crossed him stone dead. Indignant observers at the time said he'd been changed beyond recognition, and it's here that we get to the crux of the matter. Because whatever anyone else might have said of the new *Dan Dare*, we simply lapped it up.

Telling a seven year-old that what he's reading is a travesty will get you nowhere. You can't tell him the original Dare was a true hero, the embodiment of traditional English values; he's too busy marveling at the guy carrying the psychotic living axe. You won't get very far talking about the wonderful clean lines of the *Anastasia*; he's transfixed by the battle of Jupiter, with men drowning in acid and living spaceships throwing

...moons like rocks, and a Martian giant on the cover of Prog 11 beckoning us into the blazing hell of the sun. And you can guess what mentioning a gentler, more compassionate time will mean to him; what price compassion next to a squad of space commandos pouring automatic fire into that week's alien freak?

A child enjoying whatever entertainment he encounters will do so with an emotional honesty that is all but lost to adults. That's why we remember the stories we liked as kids with the fondness we do, and that's why we love reading them again later- especially if they stand the test of time. A reader of the fifties *Dan Dare* can no more relate to the *2000 AD* version than I can the one he loved; we may be able to appreciate each others' favourites technically, but not emotionally, for the simple reason that we didn't discover them as children. They might get us in the head, but not in the heart. They aren't ours.

In considering the *Dan Dare* I read in 1977, where else can I start but with Massimo Belardinelli? There are not superlatives enough in the language to describe the sheer alien beauty of the man's art. The scripts for those first two dozen episodes asked for visuals that ranged from stupendous to demented, but Belardinelli took them all in his stride. One eye-popping image followed another: the Biogs and their Shepherd servants, the lethal landscape of Jupiter, a fleet of iron ships engaging another of sentient flesh, the London of 2177, the Two of Verath (who gave me nightmares), Dare belly-landing the *Titan* in smashing, grinding, ten-mile hops, so much and so many more. One wonders what Steve Moore and the other writers thought of the imagery their words had inspired; it must surely have been beyond their wildest dreams.

So it was more than a little surprising that Belardinelli was immediately followed by Dave Gibbons. Two more different art styles it would be difficult to imagine, but Dan Dare- like all truly classic characters- was strong enough to survive the change. Gibbons' flawless storytelling and carefully considered design have always been well suited to stories involving the military, and that was exactly the look he brought to the strip. His Space Fort and Eagle craft seem like superbly functional war machines; the Fort's initial tussle with two Starslayer cruisers remains one of my favourite sequences

as Pilot Polanski's insane battle orbit puts the huge vess... right where the gun crews need her to be. And a glance at th... cover of Prog 51- one of the comic's all-time greatest- revea... a sense of drama and character second to none. Bravo, Sir.

The scripts on this second phase of the story were provide... by British comics veteran Gerry Finley-Day, who as an idea... man has few equals- in fact, he seems to come up with mo... notions in five pages than many modern writers do in fift... His characters are always memorable; the *Legion* stories sa... Dare joined by Polanski, Hitman (who I liked best) and th... enjoyably thuggish Great Bear. He knows how to ratchet u... the tension, too, as demonstrated by the increasingly blea... last episodes of the Starslayer story. I still recall a sense o... genuine dread when I first read those pages; I couldn't for th... life of me see how our heroes could escape dreadful orbit... crucifixion, or how their last stand would prove anything oth... than fatal. But the sky over the Space Fort burned with fla... and the Earthmen fought bulkhead by bulkhead and hand... hand for their ship, and... well, wait and see.

Framed on my office wall is a Dave Gibbons page fro... the vampire two-parter, specifically page three of the secor... episode, featuring Hitman in a rather sticky situation. Mo... than one visitor has asked me what happens next, and m... answer is always the same: guess. But if he couldn't han... load six loose rounds in less than a second, he'd hardly b... called "Hitman", would he? This fantastic first book of Da... Dare's *2000 AD* adventures closes an important gap in th... record of the comic's early history- perhaps the final piec... of the puzzle, as far as the collected *2000 AD* is concerne... These stories are hugely enjoyable, filled with countless na... biting moments like the one on my much-prized Gibbor... original. They won't leave you smiling warmly as you pull c... your slippers and light your pipe, content in the knowledg... that there'll always be an England and that we'll take th... old ways and values with us when we go to the stars. The... absolutely will not do that.

But if this is your *Dan Dare*, they'll have you grinning a... over your chops.

Garth Enn...
New York City, March 20...

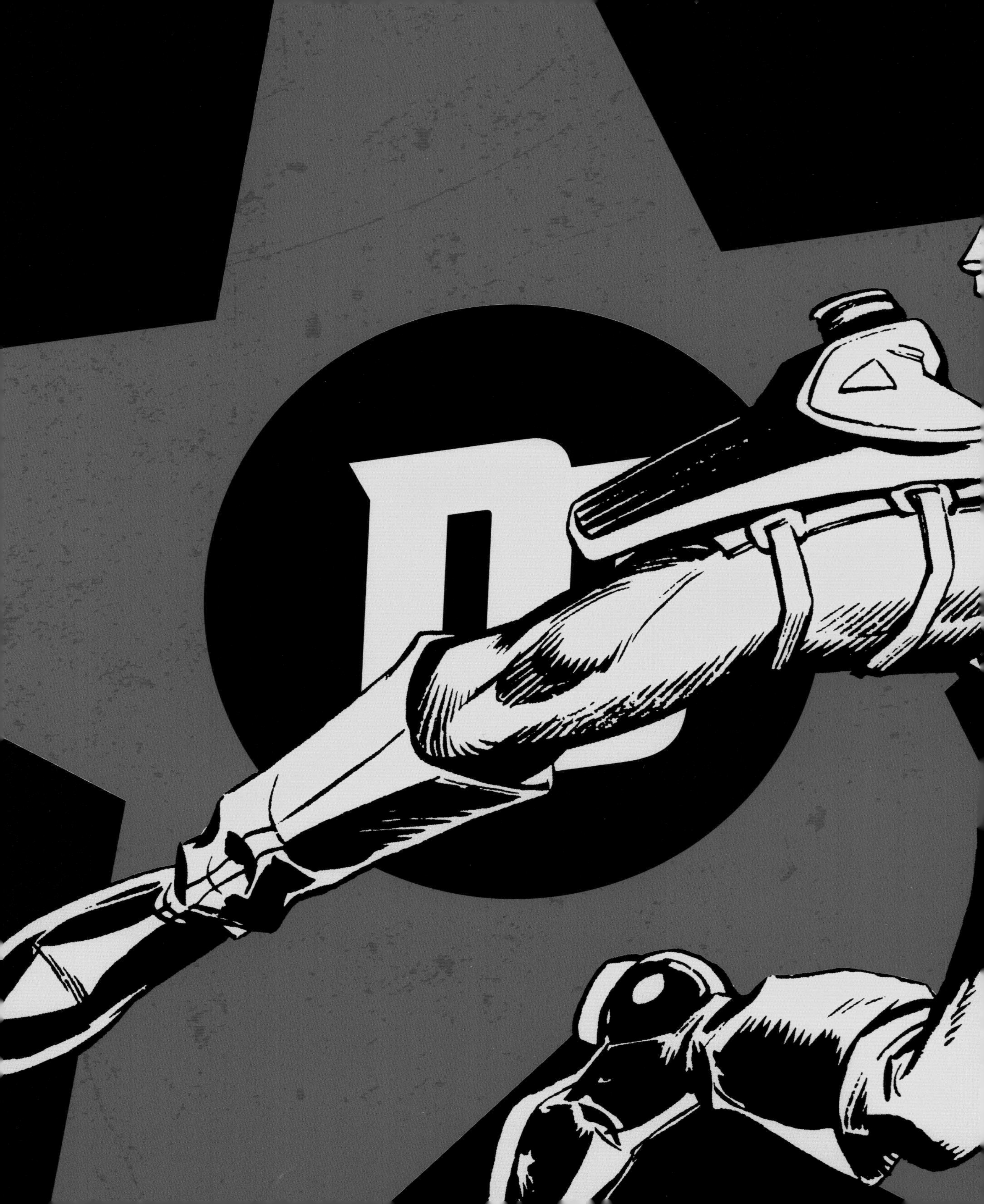

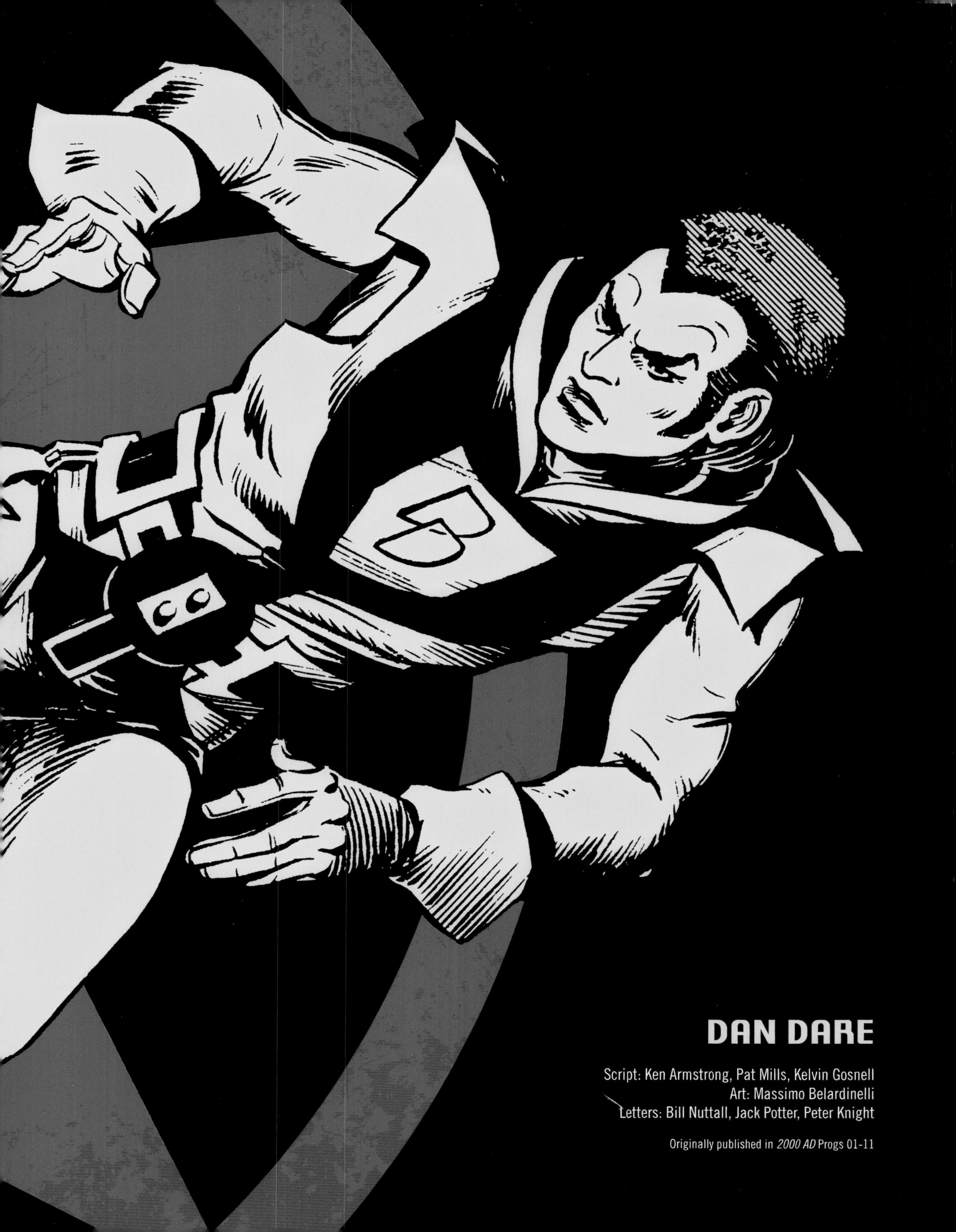

DAN DARE

Script: Ken Armstrong, Pat Mills, Kelvin Gosnell
Art: Massimo Belardinelli
Letters: Bill Nuttall, Jack Potter, Peter Knight

Originally published in *2000 AD* Progs 01-11

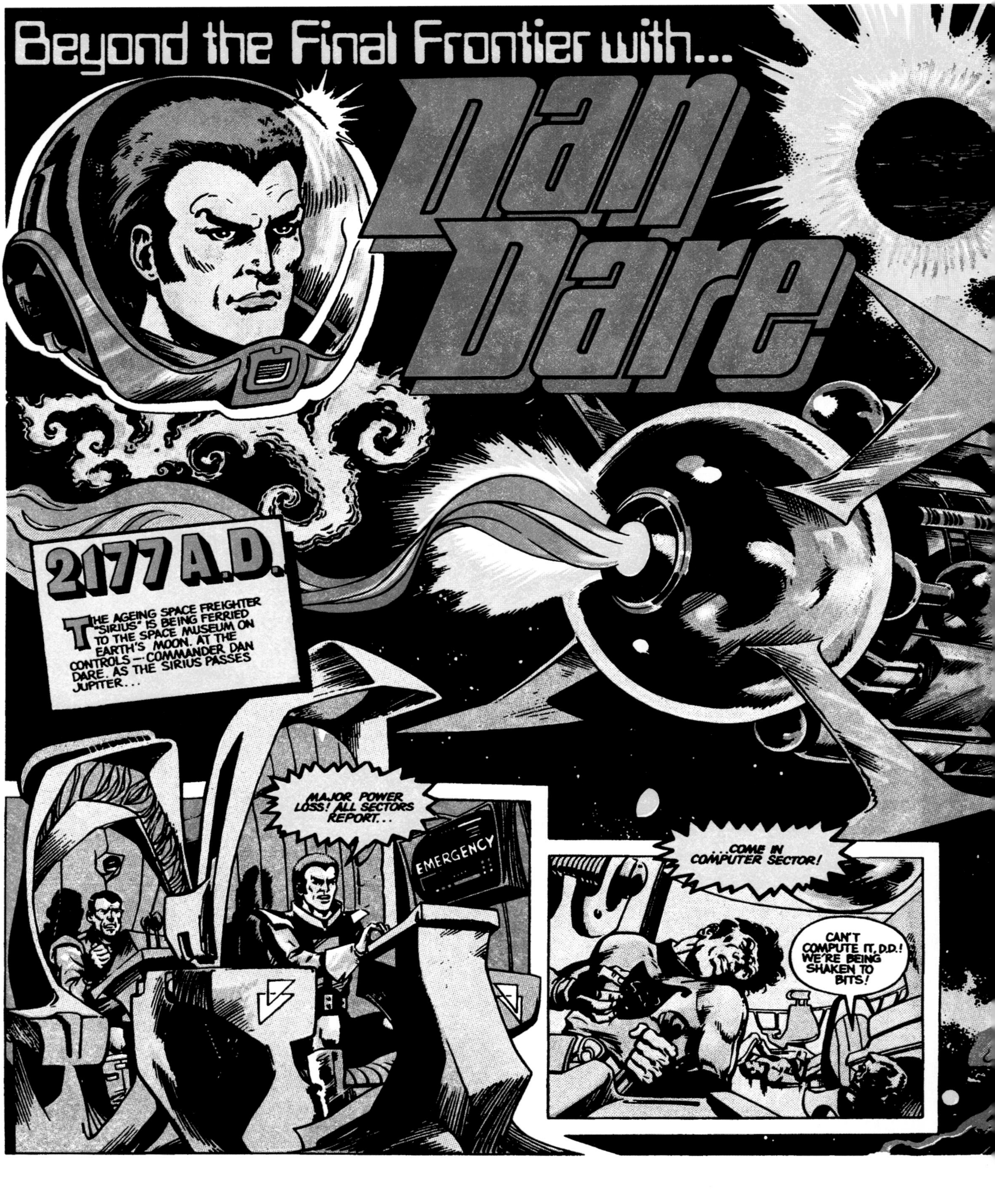
Beyond the Final Frontier with...
Dan Dare
2177 A.D.
THE AGEING SPACE FREIGHTER "SIRIUS" IS BEING FERRIED TO THE SPACE MUSEUM ON EARTH'S MOON. AT THE CONTROLS — COMMANDER DAN DARE. AS THE SIRIUS PASSES JUPITER...
MAJOR POWER LOSS! ALL SECTORS REPORT...
EMERGENCY
...COME IN COMPUTER SECTOR!
CAN'T COMPUTE IT, D.D.! WE'RE BEING SHAKEN TO BITS!

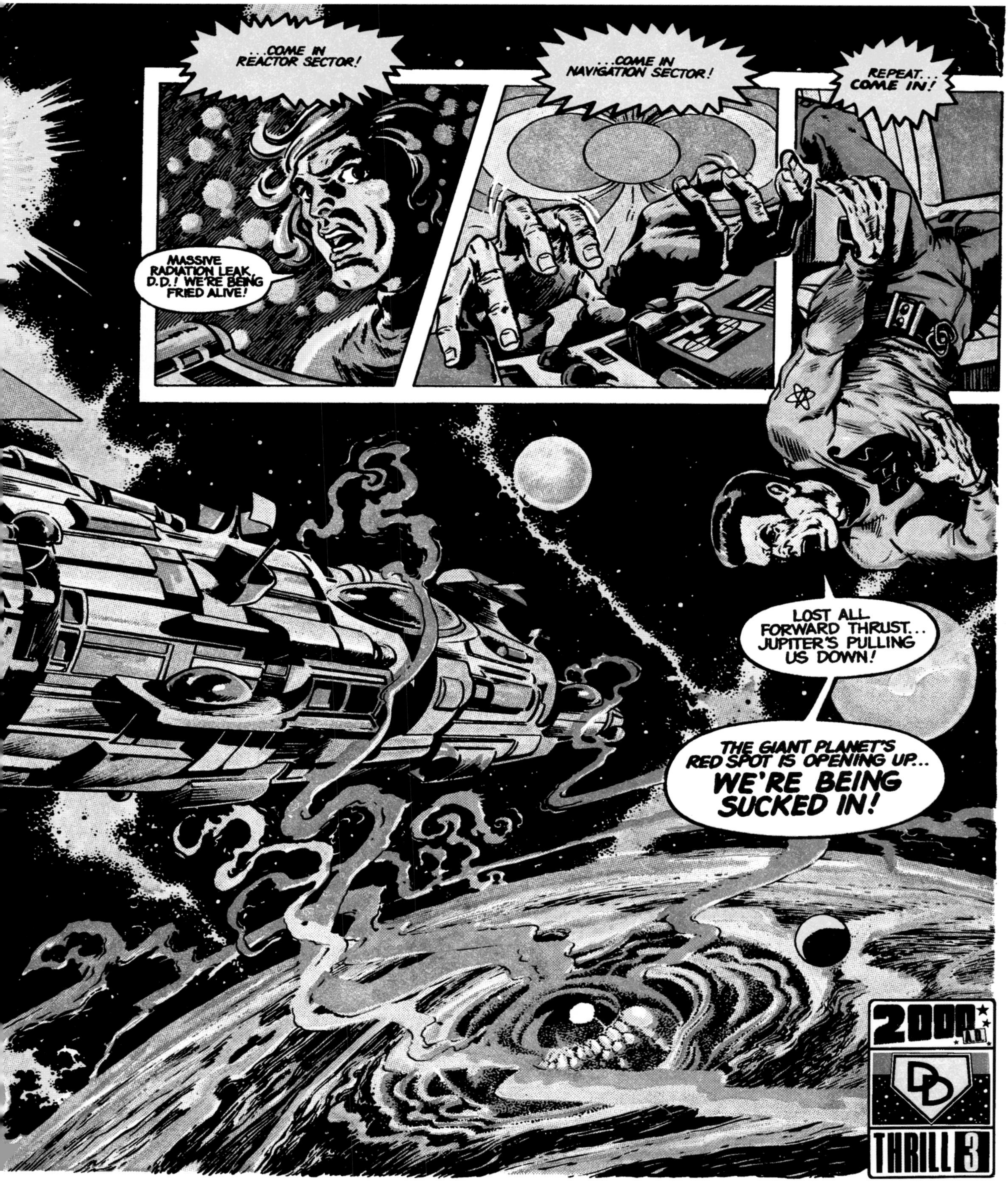
...COME IN REACTOR SECTOR!
MASSIVE RADIATION LEAK, D.D.! WE'RE BEING FRIED ALIVE!
...COME IN NAVIGATION SECTOR!
REPEAT... COME IN!
LOST ALL FORWARD THRUST... JUPITER'S PULLING US DOWN!
THE GIANT PLANET'S RED SPOT IS OPENING UP... WE'RE BEING SUCKED IN!
2000 A.D.
DD
THRILL 3

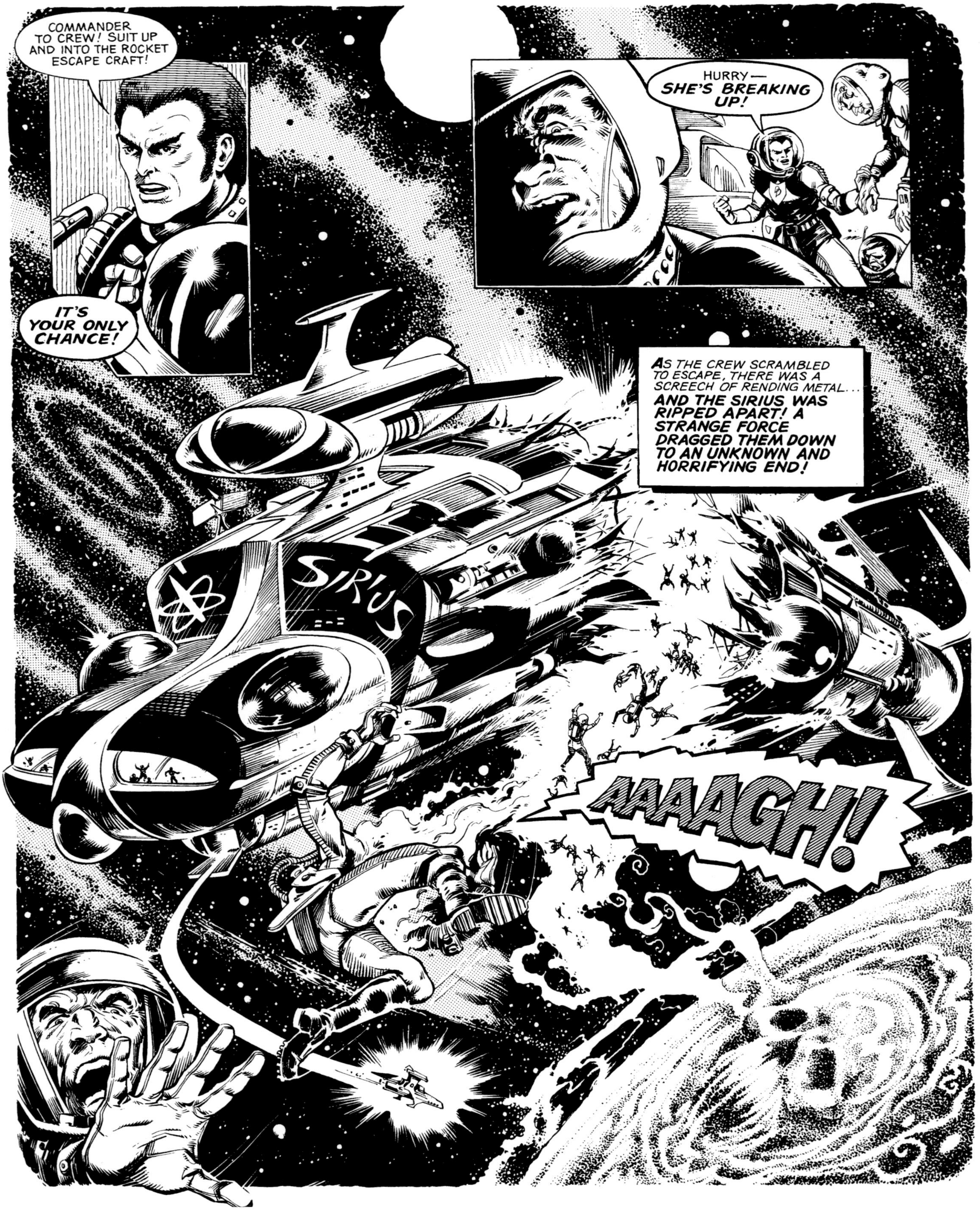
COMMANDER TO CREW! SUIT UP AND INTO THE ROCKET ESCAPE CRAFT!
IT'S YOUR ONLY CHANCE!
HURRY— SHE'S BREAKING UP!
AS THE CREW SCRAMBLED TO ESCAPE, THERE WAS A SCREECH OF RENDING METAL... AND THE SIRIUS WAS RIPPED APART! A STRANGE FORCE DRAGGED THEM DOWN TO AN UNKNOWN AND HORRIFYING END!
SIRIUS
AAAAGH!

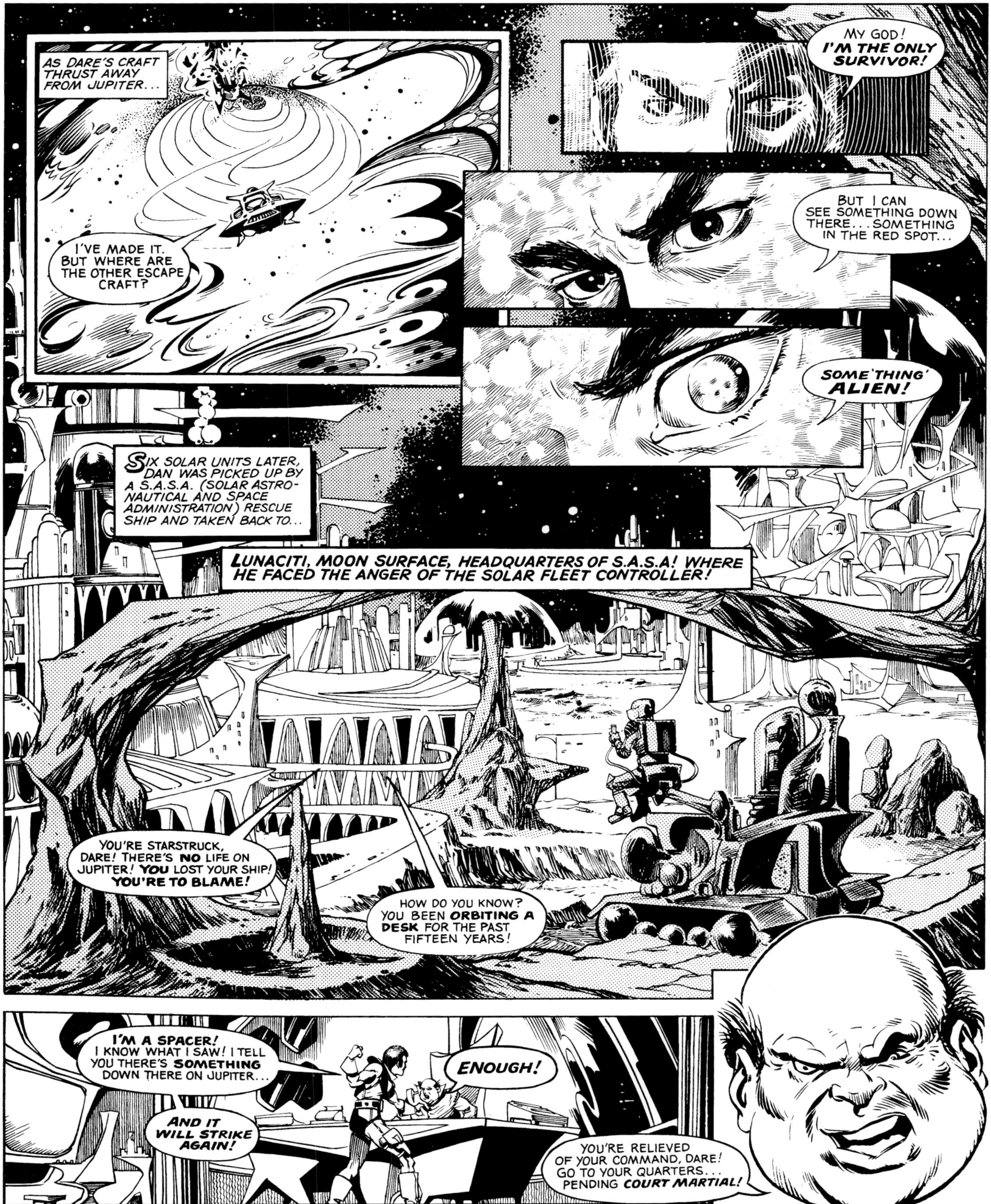
AS DARE'S CRAFT THRUST AWAY FROM JUPITER...
I'VE MADE IT. BUT WHERE ARE THE OTHER ESCAPE CRAFT?
MY GOD! I'M THE ONLY SURVIVOR!
BUT I CAN SEE SOMETHING DOWN THERE... SOMETHING IN THE RED SPOT...
SOME'THING' ALIEN!
SIX SOLAR UNITS LATER, DAN WAS PICKED UP BY A S.A.S.A. (SOLAR ASTRONAUTICAL AND SPACE ADMINISTRATION) RESCUE SHIP AND TAKEN BACK TO...
LUNACITI, MOON SURFACE, HEADQUARTERS OF S.A.S.A! WHERE HE FACED THE ANGER OF THE SOLAR FLEET CONTROLLER!
YOU'RE STARSTRUCK, DARE! THERE'S NO LIFE ON JUPITER! YOU LOST YOUR SHIP! YOU'RE TO BLAME!
HOW DO YOU KNOW? YOU BEEN ORBITING A DESK FOR THE PAST FIFTEEN YEARS!
I'M A SPACER! I KNOW WHAT I SAW! I TELL YOU THERE'S SOMETHING DOWN THERE ON JUPITER...
AND IT WILL STRIKE AGAIN!
ENOUGH!
YOU'RE RELIEVED OF YOUR COMMAND, DARE! GO TO YOUR QUARTERS... PENDING COURT MARTIAL!

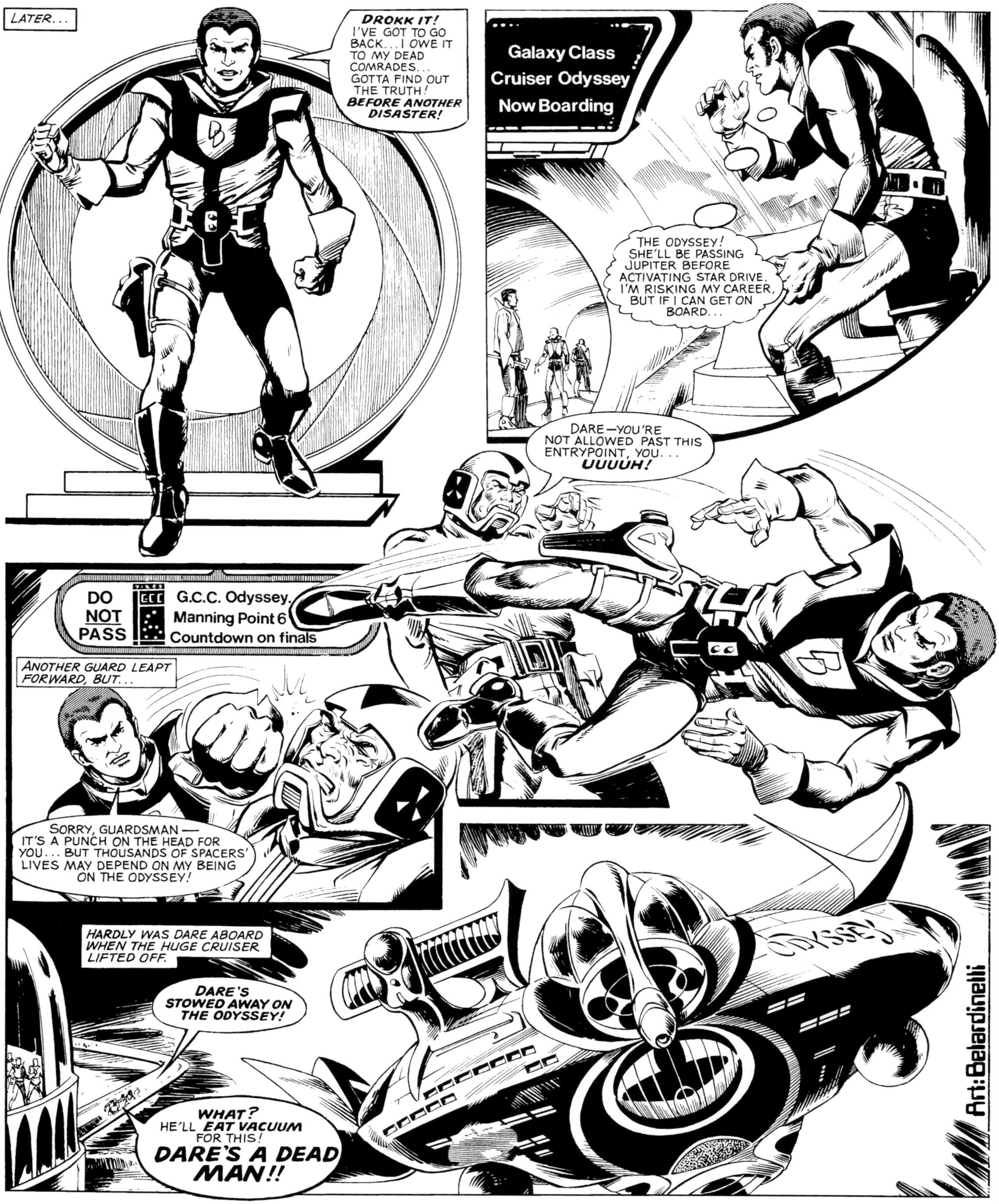
LATER...
DROKK IT! I'VE GOT TO GO BACK... I OWE IT TO MY DEAD COMRADES... GOTTA FIND OUT THE TRUTH! BEFORE ANOTHER DISASTER!
Galaxy Class Cruiser Odyssey Now Boarding
THE ODYSSEY! SHE'LL BE PASSING JUPITER BEFORE ACTIVATING STAR DRIVE. I'M RISKING MY CAREER, BUT IF I CAN GET ON BOARD...
DARE—YOU'RE NOT ALLOWED PAST THIS ENTRYPOINT, YOU... UUUUH!
DO NOT PASS
G.C.C. Odyssey. Manning Point 6 Countdown on finals
ANOTHER GUARD LEAPT FORWARD, BUT...
SORRY, GUARDSMAN — IT'S A PUNCH ON THE HEAD FOR YOU... BUT THOUSANDS OF SPACERS' LIVES MAY DEPEND ON MY BEING ON THE ODYSSEY!
HARDLY WAS DARE ABOARD WHEN THE HUGE CRUISER LIFTED OFF.
DARE'S STOWED AWAY ON THE ODYSSEY!
WHAT? HE'LL EAT VACUUM FOR THIS! DARE'S A DEAD MAN!!
ODYSSEY
Art: Belardinelli

DAN DARE

MY PART IN HIS REVIVAL
PART ONE

THIS IS AN EDITED VERSION OF AN ARTICLE WRITTEN BY PAT MILLS FOR *SPACESHIP AWAY* – THE CLASSIC **DAN DARE** FAN MAGAZINE, AND KINDLY REPUBLISHED WITH THE PERMISSION OF PAT MILLS.

1976. I realize that the science fiction comic I'm creating, *2000 AD*, needs a space hero. I think about bringing back **Dan Dare** – the publisher, John Sanders, is agreeable, he tells me not to worry about the original fans and I study the bound *Eagle* volumes. I'm hugely impressed by the original *Venus* adventure. I commission writer Ken Armstrong (he wrote *Hook Jaw* in *Action*) to write a NASA-style version, with something of the realistic tone of the original.

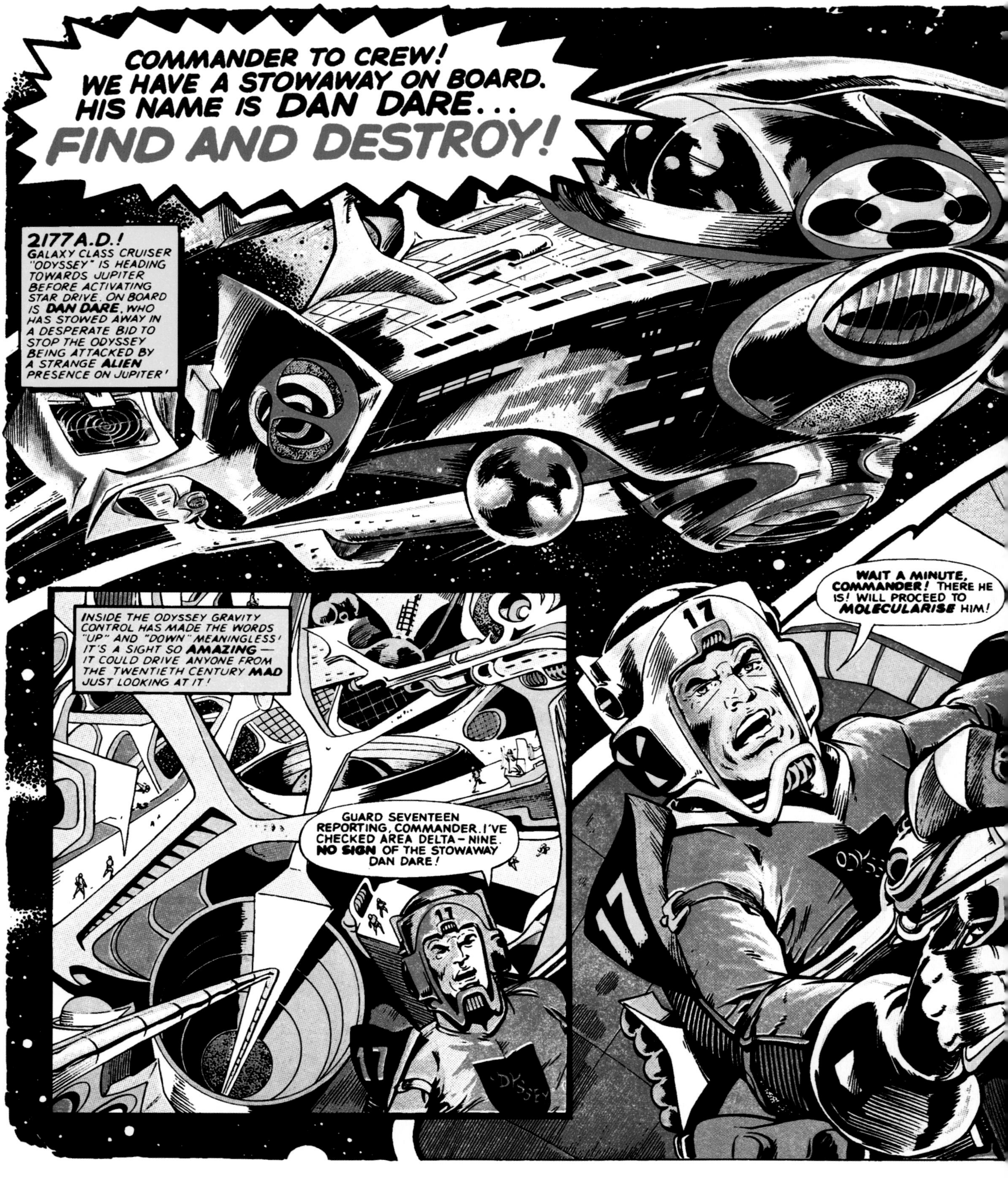
COMMANDER TO CREW! WE HAVE A STOWAWAY ON BOARD. HIS NAME IS DAN DARE... FIND AND DESTROY!
2177 A.D.! GALAXY CLASS CRUISER "ODYSSEY" IS HEADING TOWARDS JUPITER BEFORE ACTIVATING STAR DRIVE. ON BOARD IS DAN DARE, WHO HAS STOWED AWAY IN A DESPERATE BID TO STOP THE ODYSSEY BEING ATTACKED BY A STRANGE ALIEN PRESENCE ON JUPITER!
INSIDE THE ODYSSEY GRAVITY CONTROL HAS MADE THE WORDS "UP" AND "DOWN" MEANINGLESS! IT'S A SIGHT SO AMAZING — IT COULD DRIVE ANYONE FROM THE TWENTIETH CENTURY MAD JUST LOOKING AT IT!
GUARD SEVENTEEN REPORTING, COMMANDER. I'VE CHECKED AREA DELTA-NINE. NO SIGN OF THE STOWAWAY DAN DARE!
WAIT A MINUTE, COMMANDER! THERE HE IS! WILL PROCEED TO MOLECULARISE HIM!

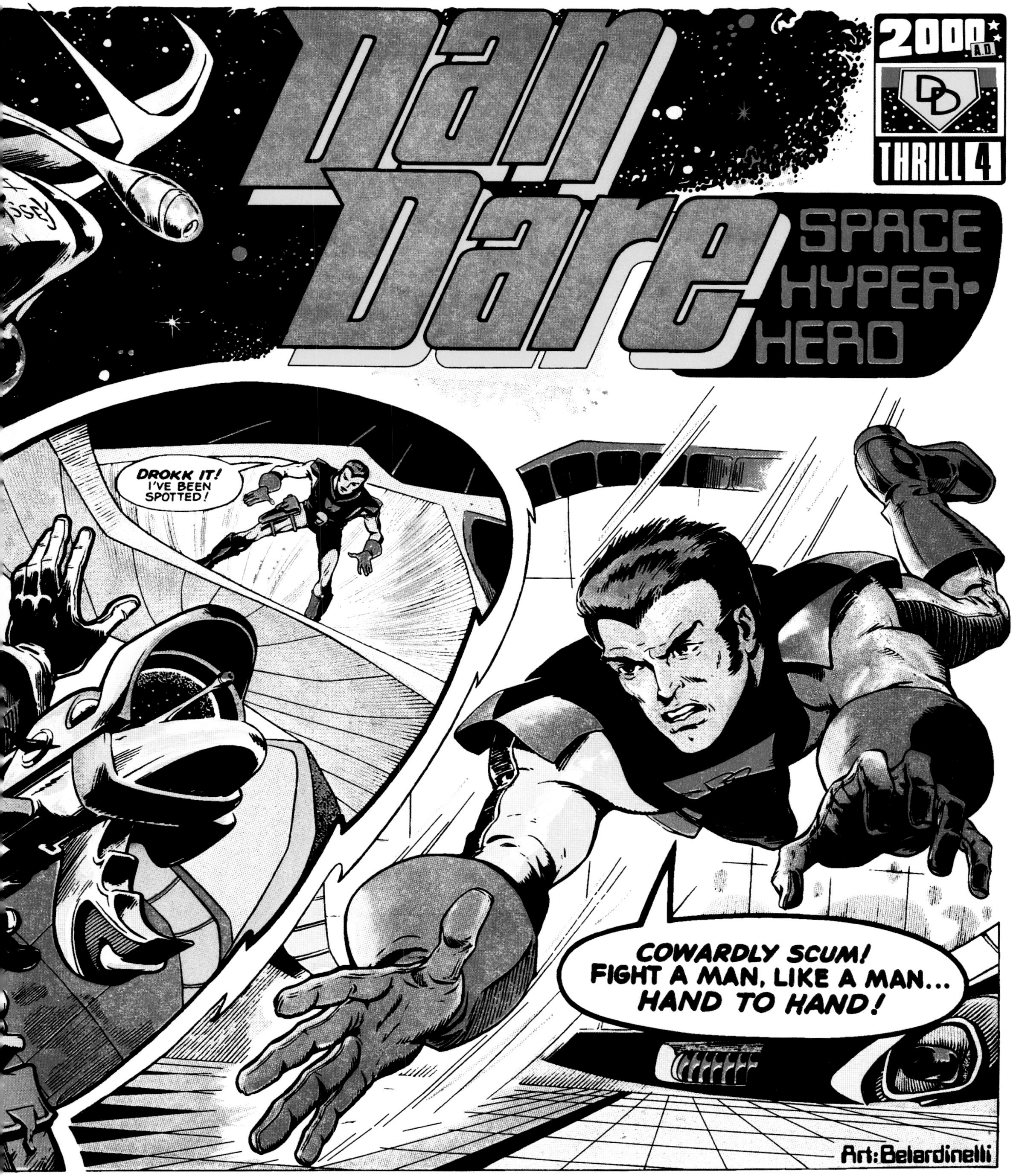

2000 A.D.
THRILL 4
DAN DARE
SPACE HYPER-HERO
DROKK IT! I'VE BEEN SPOTTED!
COWARDLY SCUM! FIGHT A MAN, LIKE A MAN... HAND TO HAND!
Art: Belardinelli

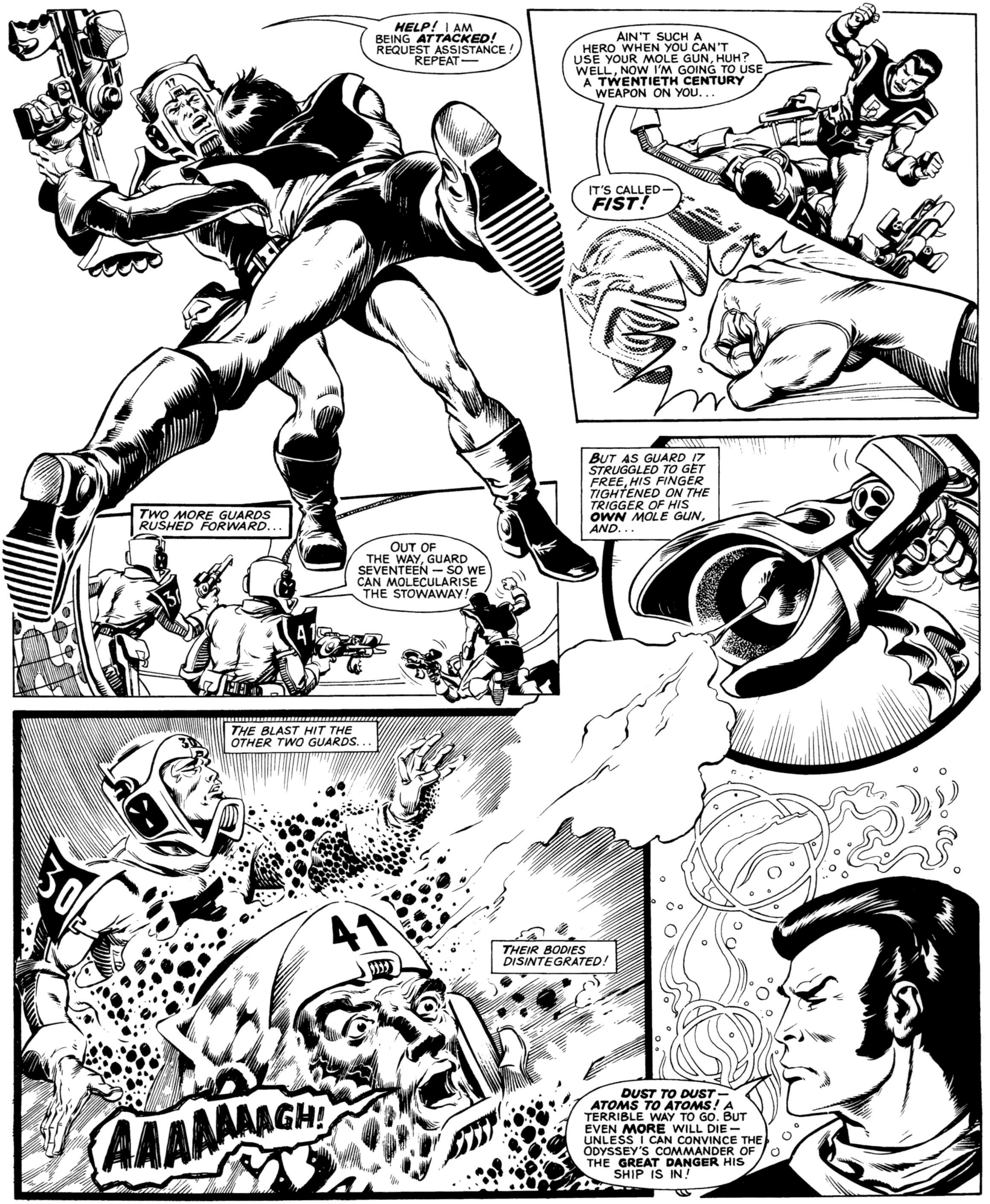

HELP! I AM BEING ATTACKED! REQUEST ASSISTANCE! REPEAT—
AIN'T SUCH A HERO WHEN YOU CAN'T USE YOUR MOLE GUN, HUH? WELL, NOW I'M GOING TO USE A TWENTIETH CENTURY WEAPON ON YOU...
IT'S CALLED— FIST!
TWO MORE GUARDS RUSHED FORWARD...
OUT OF THE WAY, GUARD SEVENTEEN — SO WE CAN MOLECULARISE THE STOWAWAY!
BUT AS GUARD 17 STRUGGLED TO GET FREE, HIS FINGER TIGHTENED ON THE TRIGGER OF HIS OWN MOLE GUN, AND...
THE BLAST HIT THE OTHER TWO GUARDS...
THEIR BODIES DISINTEGRATED!
AAAAAAAGH!
DUST TO DUST— ATOMS TO ATOMS! A TERRIBLE WAY TO GO. BUT EVEN MORE WILL DIE— UNLESS I CAN CONVINCE THE ODYSSEY'S COMMANDER OF THE GREAT DANGER HIS SHIP IS IN!

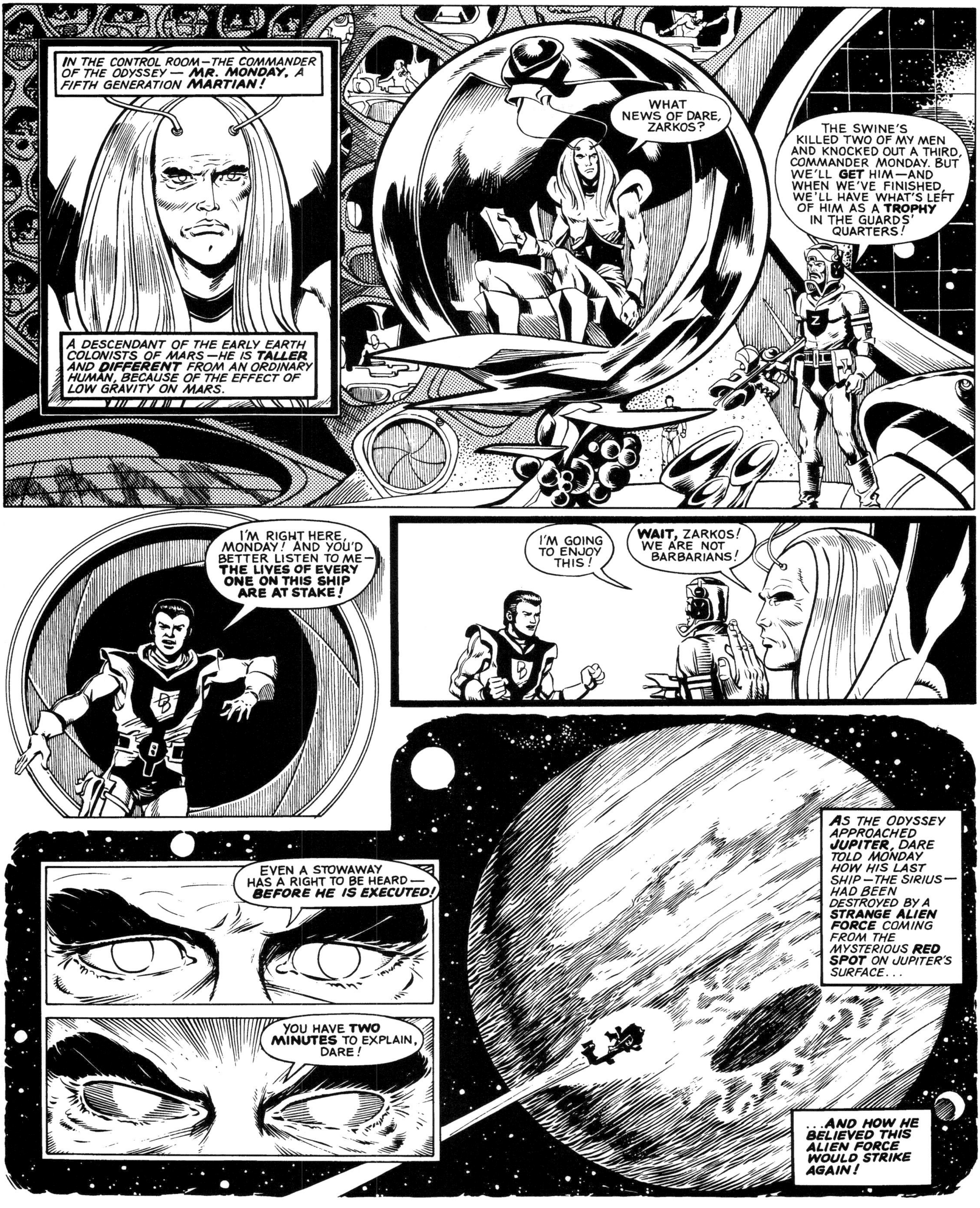
IN THE CONTROL ROOM—THE COMMANDER OF THE ODYSSEY — MR. MONDAY, A FIFTH GENERATION MARTIAN!
A DESCENDANT OF THE EARLY EARTH COLONISTS OF MARS—HE IS TALLER AND DIFFERENT FROM AN ORDINARY HUMAN, BECAUSE OF THE EFFECT OF LOW GRAVITY ON MARS.
WHAT NEWS OF DARE, ZARKOS?
THE SWINE'S KILLED TWO OF MY MEN AND KNOCKED OUT A THIRD, COMMANDER MONDAY. BUT WE'LL GET HIM—AND WHEN WE'VE FINISHED, WE'LL HAVE WHAT'S LEFT OF HIM AS A TROPHY IN THE GUARDS' QUARTERS!
I'M RIGHT HERE, MONDAY! AND YOU'D BETTER LISTEN TO ME— THE LIVES OF EVERY ONE ON THIS SHIP ARE AT STAKE!
I'M GOING TO ENJOY THIS!
WAIT, ZARKOS! WE ARE NOT BARBARIANS!
EVEN A STOWAWAY HAS A RIGHT TO BE HEARD— BEFORE HE IS EXECUTED!
YOU HAVE TWO MINUTES TO EXPLAIN, DARE!
AS THE ODYSSEY APPROACHED JUPITER, DARE TOLD MONDAY HOW HIS LAST SHIP—THE SIRIUS— HAD BEEN DESTROYED BY A STRANGE ALIEN FORCE COMING FROM THE MYSTERIOUS RED SPOT ON JUPITER'S SURFACE...
...AND HOW HE BELIEVED THIS ALIEN FORCE WOULD STRIKE AGAIN!

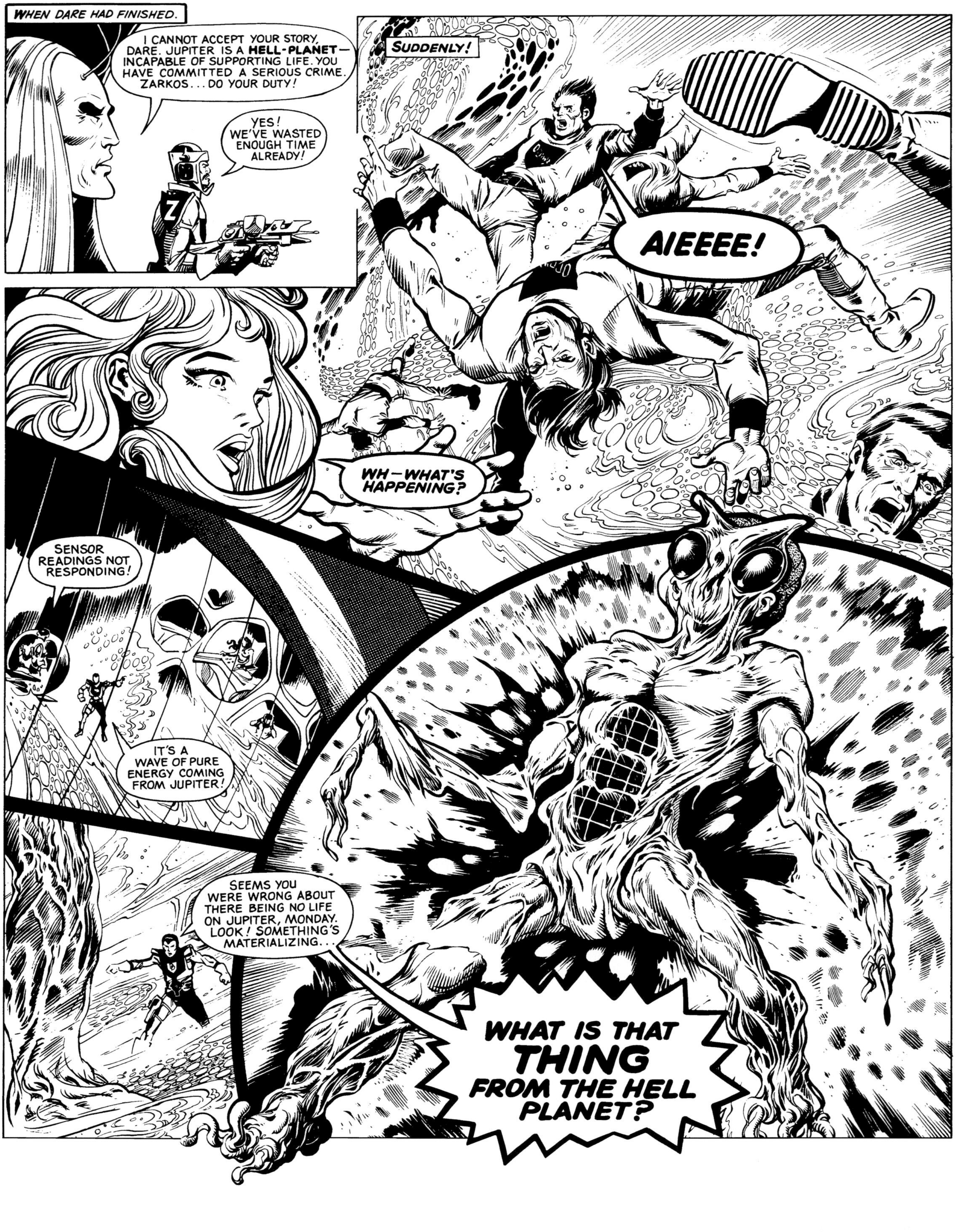
WHEN DARE HAD FINISHED.
I CANNOT ACCEPT YOUR STORY, DARE. JUPITER IS A HELL-PLANET— INCAPABLE OF SUPPORTING LIFE. YOU HAVE COMMITTED A SERIOUS CRIME. ZARKOS... DO YOUR DUTY!
YES! WE'VE WASTED ENOUGH TIME ALREADY!
SUDDENLY!
AIEEEE!
WH-WHAT'S HAPPENING?
SENSOR READINGS NOT RESPONDING!
IT'S A WAVE OF PURE ENERGY COMING FROM JUPITER!
SEEMS YOU WERE WRONG ABOUT THERE BEING NO LIFE ON JUPITER, MONDAY. LOOK! SOMETHING'S MATERIALIZING...
WHAT IS THAT THING FROM THE HELL PLANET?

DAN DARE

MY PART IN HIS REVIVAL
PART TWO

2000 AD's paper won't be web offset, which takes 'fair' colour, it will be 'pulp' letterpress with rudimentary colour. This could be a real problem for **Dan Dare**. Ken designs a superb, authentic NASA style-spaceship with lots of projecting bits and pieces, based on modern orbiting spaceships. I commission an Argentine artist to draw it – in black and white.

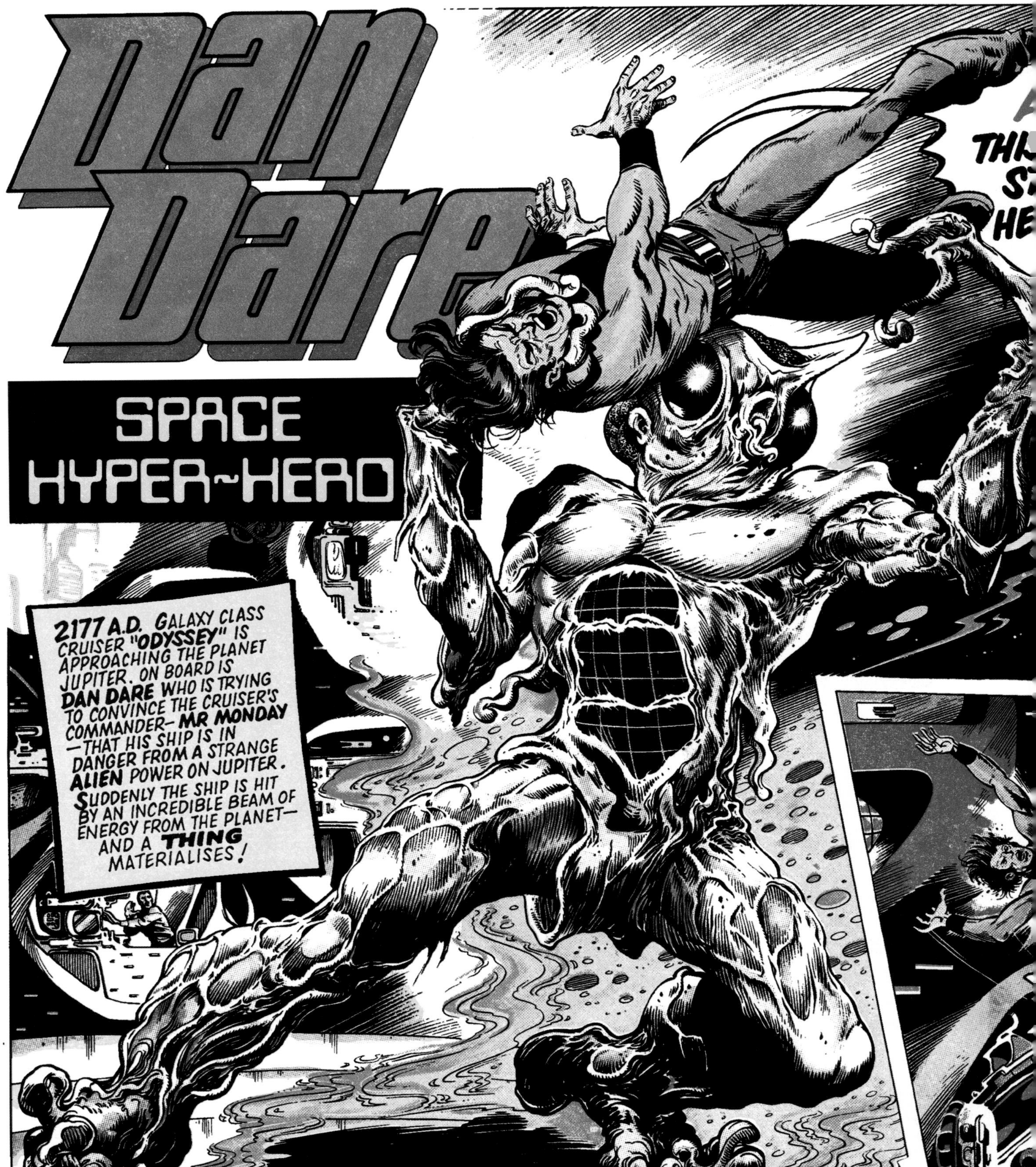
DAN DARE
SPACE HYPER~HERO
2177 A.D. GALAXY CLASS CRUISER "ODYSSEY" IS APPROACHING THE PLANET JUPITER. ON BOARD IS DAN DARE WHO IS TRYING TO CONVINCE THE CRUISER'S COMMANDER– MR MONDAY –THAT HIS SHIP IS IN DANGER FROM A STRANGE ALIEN POWER ON JUPITER. SUDDENLY THE SHIP IS HIT BY AN INCREDIBLE BEAM OF ENERGY FROM THE PLANET– AND A THING MATERIALISES!
Art: Belardinelli

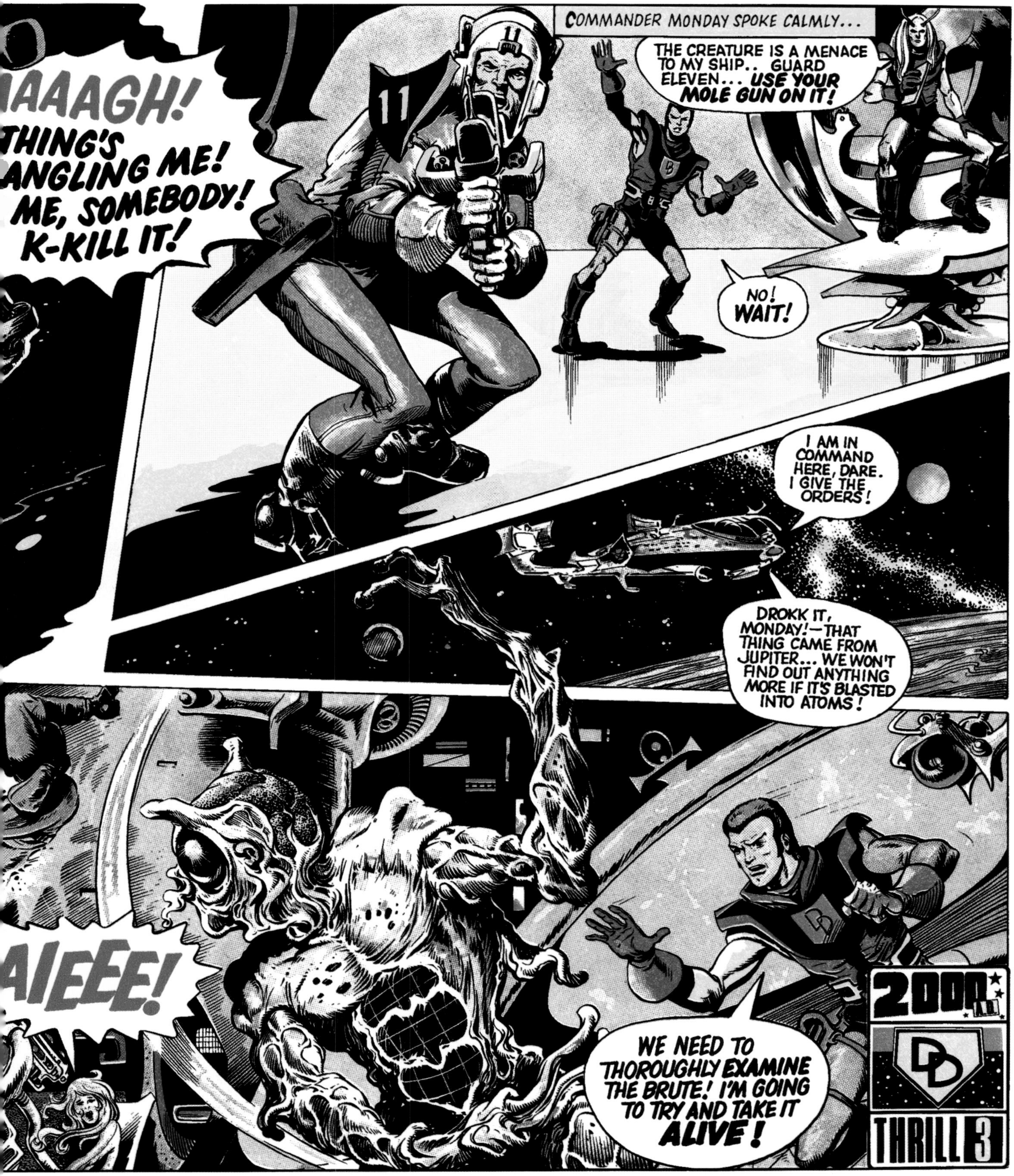
AAAAGH! THING'S ANGLING ME! ME, SOMEBODY! K-KILL IT!
COMMANDER MONDAY SPOKE CALMLY...
THE CREATURE IS A MENACE TO MY SHIP.. GUARD ELEVEN... USE YOUR MOLE GUN ON IT!
NO! WAIT!
I AM IN COMMAND HERE, DARE. I GIVE THE ORDERS!
DROKK IT, MONDAY!—THAT THING CAME FROM JUPITER... WE WON'T FIND OUT ANYTHING MORE IF IT'S BLASTED INTO ATOMS!
AIEEE!
WE NEED TO THOROUGHLY EXAMINE THE BRUTE! I'M GOING TO TRY AND TAKE IT ALIVE!
2000 A.D.
THRILL 3

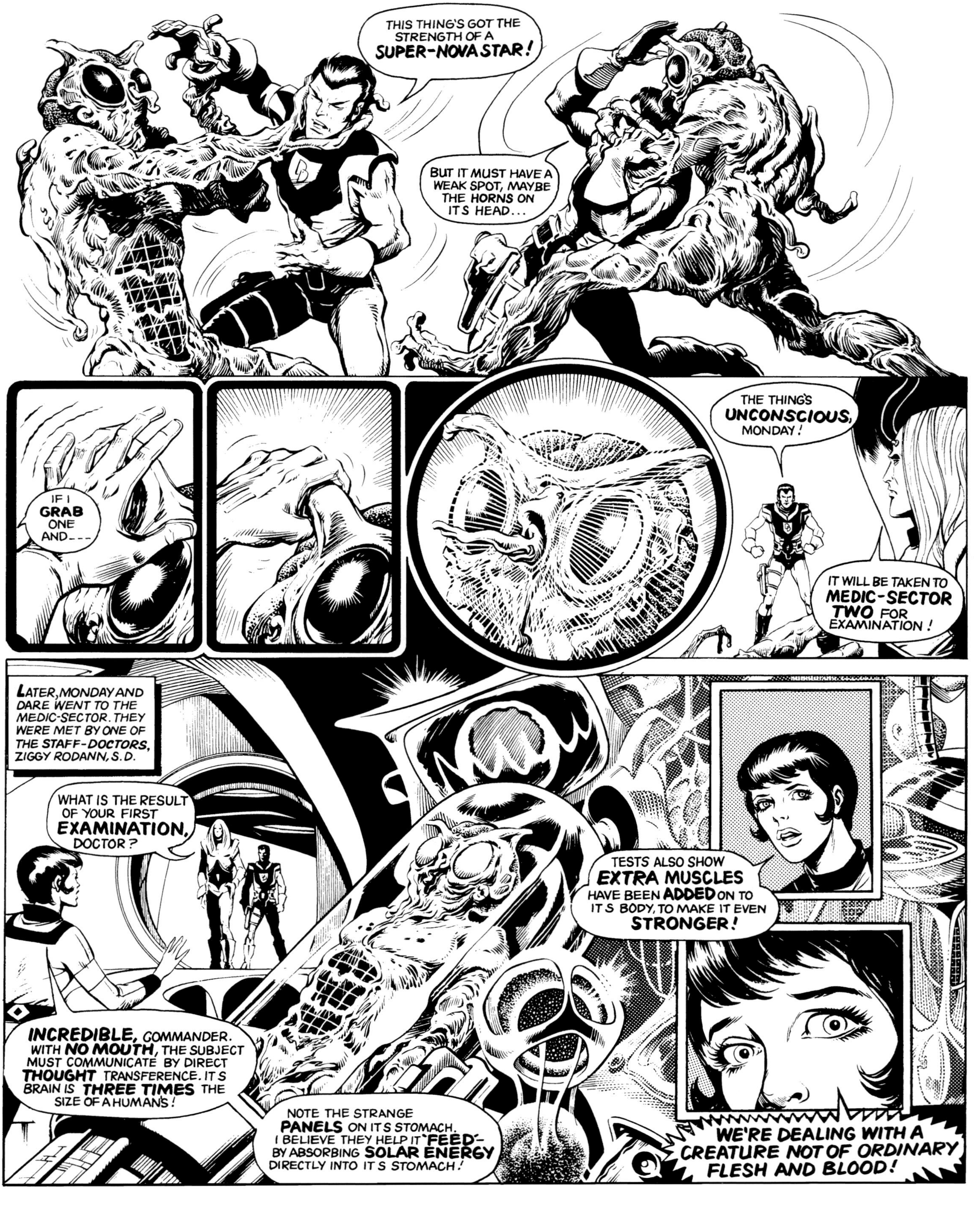
THIS THING'S GOT THE STRENGTH OF A SUPER-NOVA STAR!
BUT IT MUST HAVE A WEAK SPOT, MAYBE THE HORNS ON ITS HEAD...
IF I GRAB ONE AND---
THE THING'S UNCONSCIOUS, MONDAY!
IT WILL BE TAKEN TO MEDIC-SECTOR TWO FOR EXAMINATION!
LATER, MONDAY AND DARE WENT TO THE MEDIC-SECTOR. THEY WERE MET BY ONE OF THE STAFF-DOCTORS, ZIGGY RODANN, S.D.
WHAT IS THE RESULT OF YOUR FIRST EXAMINATION, DOCTOR?
INCREDIBLE, COMMANDER. WITH NO MOUTH, THE SUBJECT MUST COMMUNICATE BY DIRECT THOUGHT TRANSFERENCE. IT S BRAIN IS THREE TIMES THE SIZE OF A HUMAN'S!
NOTE THE STRANGE PANELS ON IT S STOMACH. I BELIEVE THEY HELP IT "FEED"- BY ABSORBING SOLAR ENERGY DIRECTLY INTO IT S STOMACH!
TESTS ALSO SHOW EXTRA MUSCLES HAVE BEEN ADDED ON TO IT S BODY, TO MAKE IT EVEN STRONGER!
WE'RE DEALING WITH A CREATURE NOT OF ORDINARY FLESH AND BLOOD!

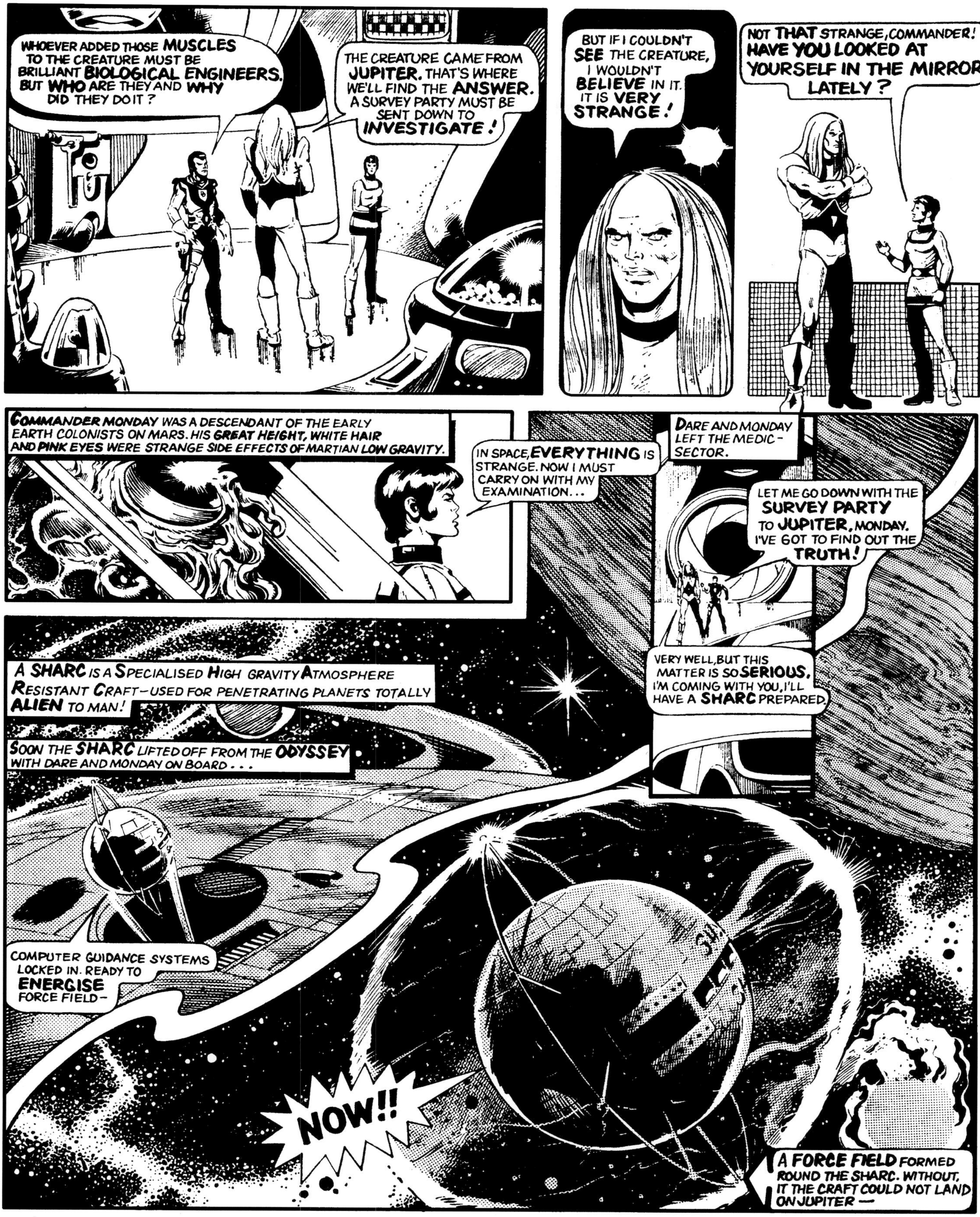
WHOEVER ADDED THOSE MUSCLES TO THE CREATURE MUST BE BRILLIANT BIOLOGICAL ENGINEERS. BUT WHO ARE THEY AND WHY DID THEY DO IT?
THE CREATURE CAME FROM JUPITER. THAT'S WHERE WE'LL FIND THE ANSWER. A SURVEY PARTY MUST BE SENT DOWN TO INVESTIGATE!
BUT IF I COULDN'T SEE THE CREATURE, I WOULDN'T BELIEVE IN IT. IT IS VERY STRANGE!
NOT THAT STRANGE, COMMANDER! HAVE YOU LOOKED AT YOURSELF IN THE MIRROR LATELY?
COMMANDER MONDAY WAS A DESCENDANT OF THE EARLY EARTH COLONISTS ON MARS. HIS GREAT HEIGHT, WHITE HAIR AND PINK EYES WERE STRANGE SIDE EFFECTS OF MARTIAN LOW GRAVITY.
IN SPACE, EVERYTHING IS STRANGE. NOW I MUST CARRY ON WITH MY EXAMINATION...
DARE AND MONDAY LEFT THE MEDIC-SECTOR.
LET ME GO DOWN WITH THE SURVEY PARTY TO JUPITER, MONDAY. I'VE GOT TO FIND OUT THE TRUTH!
VERY WELL, BUT THIS MATTER IS SO SERIOUS, I'M COMING WITH YOU. I'LL HAVE A SHARC PREPARED.
A SHARC IS A SPECIALISED HIGH GRAVITY ATMOSPHERE RESISTANT CRAFT—USED FOR PENETRATING PLANETS TOTALLY ALIEN TO MAN!
SOON THE SHARC LIFTED OFF FROM THE ODYSSEY WITH DARE AND MONDAY ON BOARD...
COMPUTER GUIDANCE SYSTEMS LOCKED IN. READY TO ENERGISE FORCE FIELD—
NOW!!
A FORCE FIELD FORMED ROUND THE SHARC. WITHOUT IT THE CRAFT COULD NOT LAND ON JUPITER—

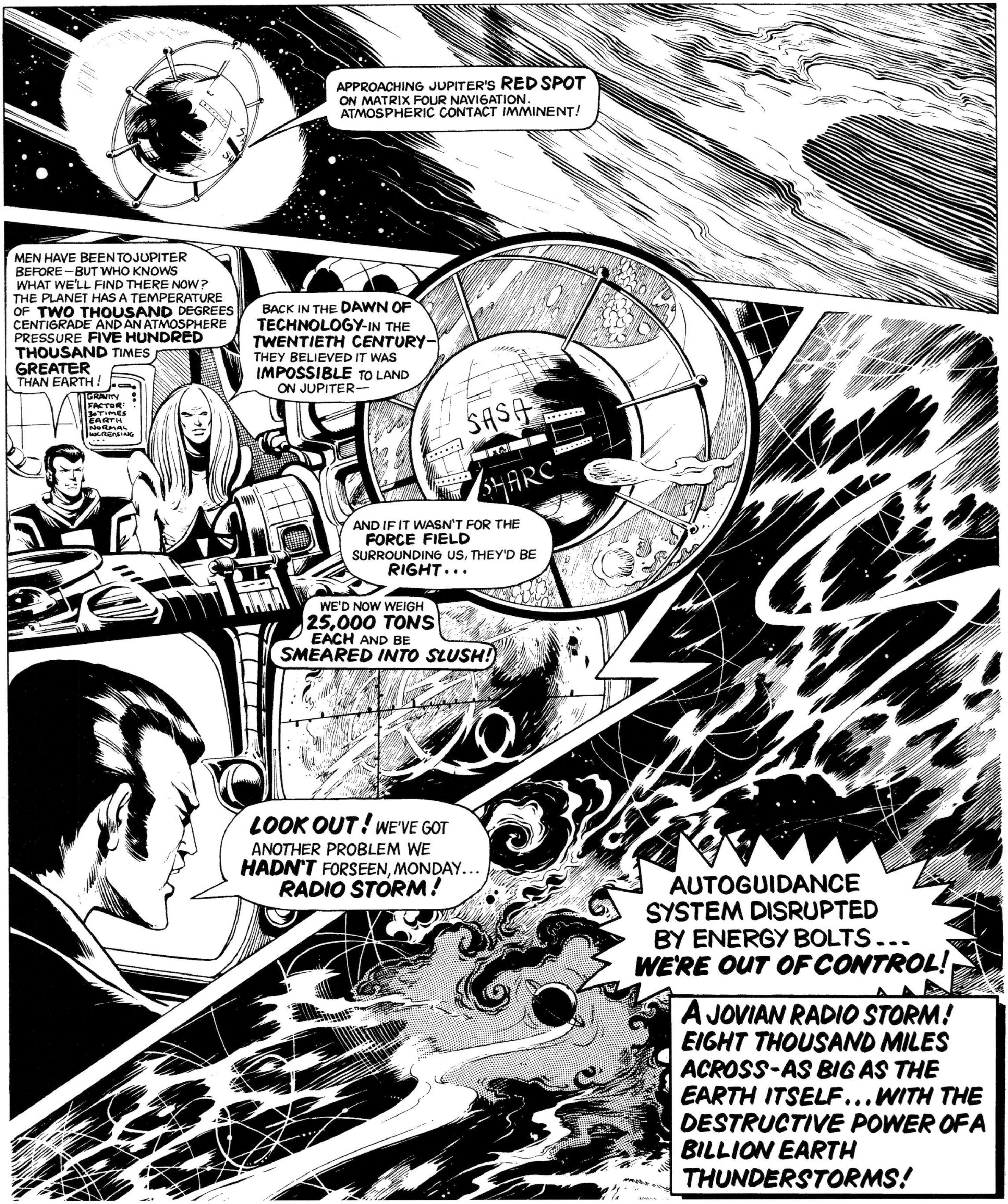
APPROACHING JUPITER'S RED SPOT ON MATRIX FOUR NAVIGATION. ATMOSPHERIC CONTACT IMMINENT!
MEN HAVE BEEN TO JUPITER BEFORE—BUT WHO KNOWS WHAT WE'LL FIND THERE NOW? THE PLANET HAS A TEMPERATURE OF TWO THOUSAND DEGREES CENTIGRADE AND AN ATMOSPHERE PRESSURE FIVE HUNDRED THOUSAND TIMES GREATER THAN EARTH!
BACK IN THE DAWN OF TECHNOLOGY—IN THE TWENTIETH CENTURY—THEY BELIEVED IT WAS IMPOSSIBLE TO LAND ON JUPITER—
AND IF IT WASN'T FOR THE FORCE FIELD SURROUNDING US, THEY'D BE RIGHT...
WE'D NOW WEIGH 25,000 TONS EACH AND BE SMEARED INTO SLUSH!
GRAVITY FACTOR: 30 TIMES EARTH NORMAL INCREASING
SASA
SHARC
LOOK OUT! WE'VE GOT ANOTHER PROBLEM WE HADN'T FORSEEN, MONDAY... RADIO STORM!
AUTOGUIDANCE SYSTEM DISRUPTED BY ENERGY BOLTS... WE'RE OUT OF CONTROL!
A JOVIAN RADIO STORM! EIGHT THOUSAND MILES ACROSS-AS BIG AS THE EARTH ITSELF... WITH THE DESTRUCTIVE POWER OF A BILLION EARTH THUNDERSTORMS!

DAN DARE

MY PART IN HIS REVIVAL
PART THREE

Paul Da Savary has film rights to **Dan Dare** and shows me his fantastic artwork for a movie and also a retro TV series featuring the Treens. His producer, who has worked on *Space 1999*, thinks our spaceship would not make good merchandising because of all the projecting solar panels. I formed the impression they weren't keen on us reviving **Dan Dare**.

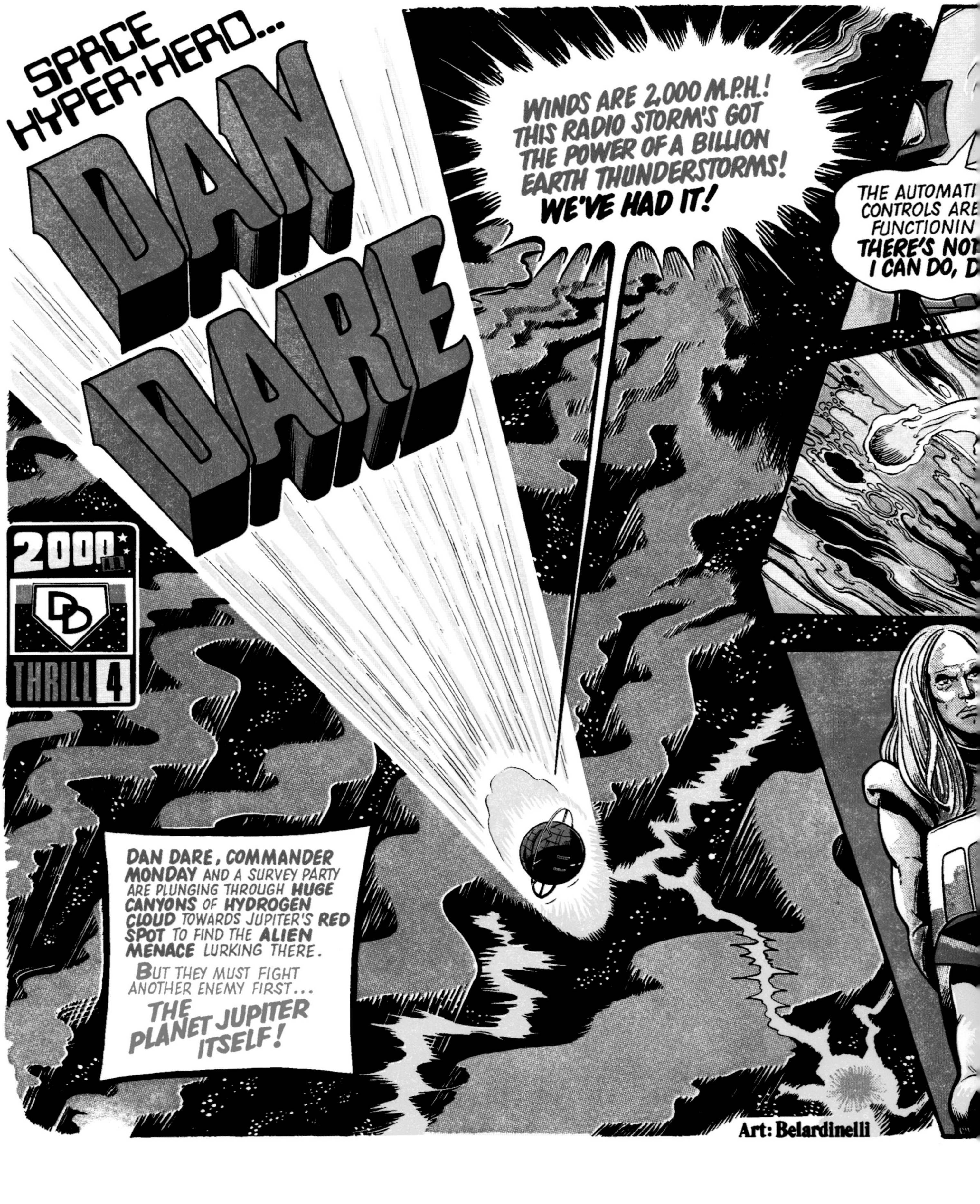

SPACE HYPER-HERO...
DAN DARE
2000 A.D.
THRILL 4
WINDS ARE 2,000 M.P.H.! THIS RADIO STORM'S GOT THE POWER OF A BILLION EARTH THUNDERSTORMS! WE'VE HAD IT!
THE AUTOMATI CONTROLS ARE FUNCTIONIN THERE'S NOT I CAN DO, D
DAN DARE, COMMANDER MONDAY AND A SURVEY PARTY ARE PLUNGING THROUGH HUGE CANYONS OF HYDROGEN CLOUD TOWARDS JUPITER'S RED SPOT TO FIND THE ALIEN MENACE LURKING THERE.
BUT THEY MUST FIGHT ANOTHER ENEMY FIRST...
THE PLANET JUPITER ITSELF!
Art: Belardinelli

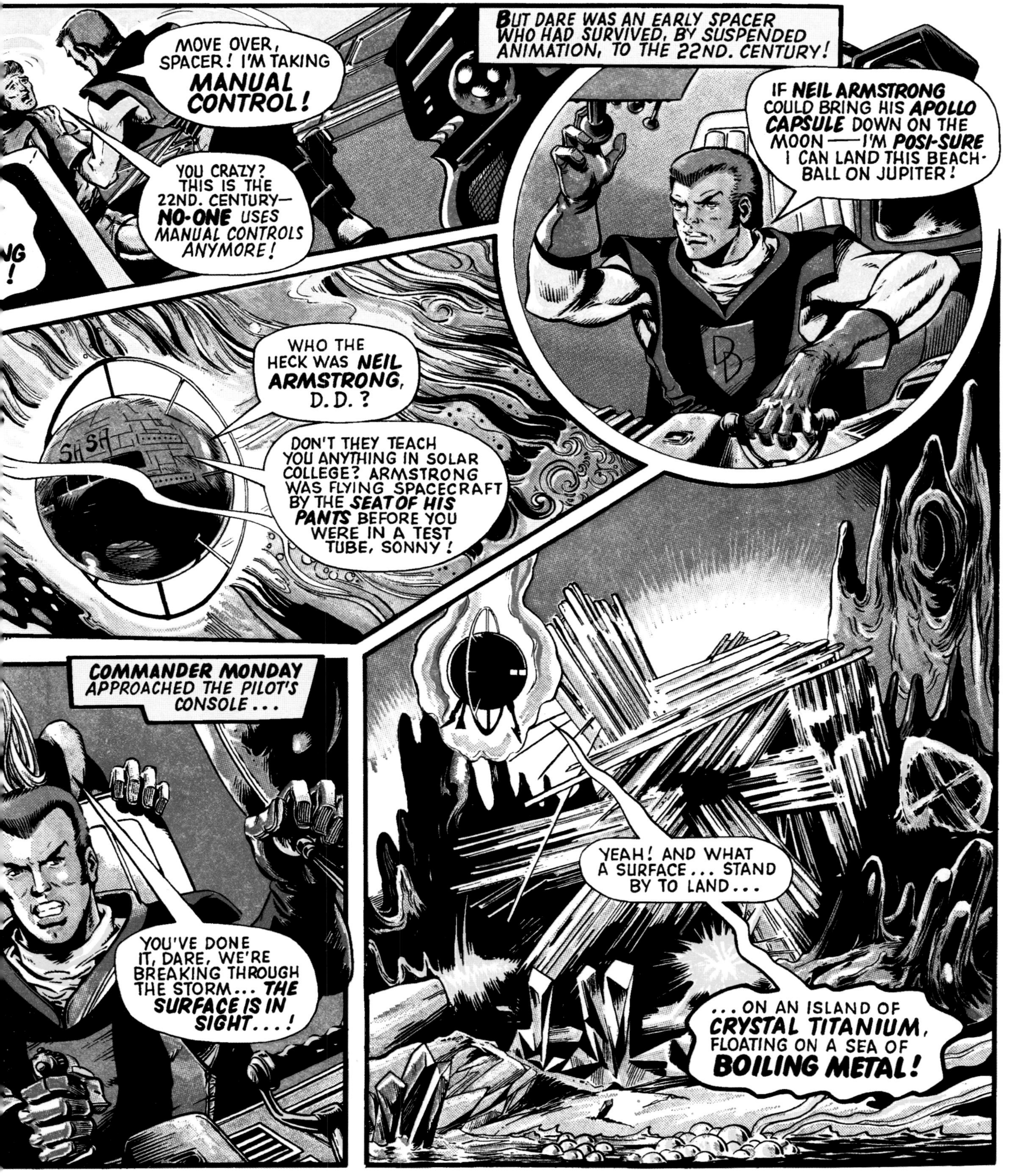
MOVE OVER, SPACER! I'M TAKING MANUAL CONTROL!
YOU CRAZY? THIS IS THE 22ND. CENTURY— NO-ONE USES MANUAL CONTROLS ANYMORE!
BUT DARE WAS AN EARLY SPACER WHO HAD SURVIVED, BY SUSPENDED ANIMATION, TO THE 22ND. CENTURY!
IF NEIL ARMSTRONG COULD BRING HIS APOLLO CAPSULE DOWN ON THE MOON —— I'M POSI-SURE I CAN LAND THIS BEACH-BALL ON JUPITER!
WHO THE HECK WAS NEIL ARMSTRONG, D.D.?
DON'T THEY TEACH YOU ANYTHING IN SOLAR COLLEGE? ARMSTRONG WAS FLYING SPACECRAFT BY THE SEAT OF HIS PANTS BEFORE YOU WERE IN A TEST TUBE, SONNY!
COMMANDER MONDAY APPROACHED THE PILOT'S CONSOLE...
YOU'VE DONE IT, DARE, WE'RE BREAKING THROUGH THE STORM... THE SURFACE IS IN SIGHT...!
YEAH! AND WHAT A SURFACE... STAND BY TO LAND...
...ON AN ISLAND OF CRYSTAL TITANIUM, FLOATING ON A SEA OF BOILING METAL!

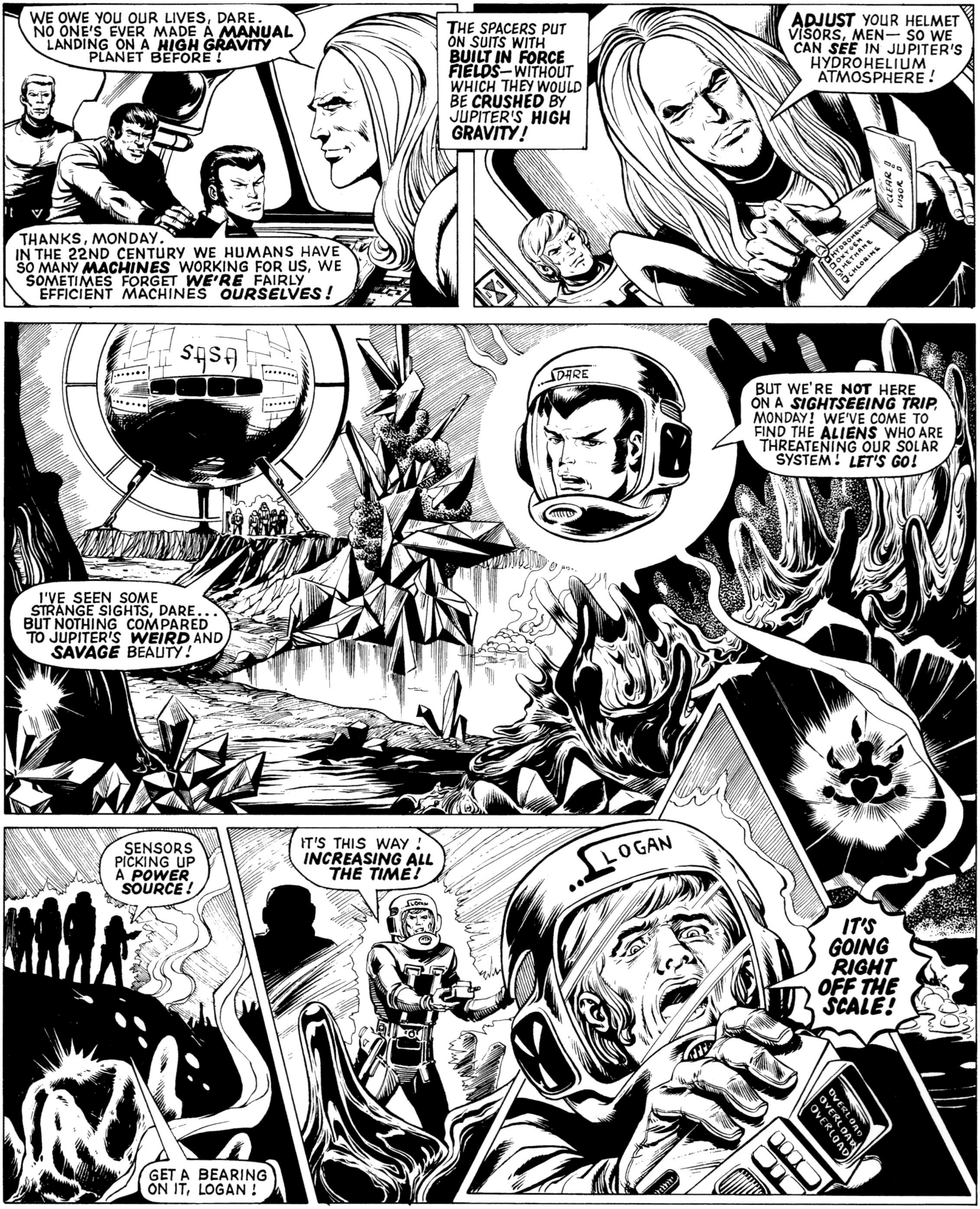
WE OWE YOU OUR LIVES, DARE. NO ONE'S EVER MADE A MANUAL LANDING ON A HIGH GRAVITY PLANET BEFORE!
THANKS, MONDAY. IN THE 22ND CENTURY WE HUMANS HAVE SO MANY MACHINES WORKING FOR US, WE SOMETIMES FORGET WE'RE FAIRLY EFFICIENT MACHINES OURSELVES!
THE SPACERS PUT ON SUITS WITH BUILT IN FORCE FIELDS—WITHOUT WHICH THEY WOULD BE CRUSHED BY JUPITER'S HIGH GRAVITY!
ADJUST YOUR HELMET VISORS, MEN— SO WE CAN SEE IN JUPITER'S HYDROHELIUM ATMOSPHERE!
CLEAR VISOR
SASA
DARE
BUT WE'RE NOT HERE ON A SIGHTSEEING TRIP, MONDAY! WE'VE COME TO FIND THE ALIENS WHO ARE THREATENING OUR SOLAR SYSTEM! LET'S GO!
I'VE SEEN SOME STRANGE SIGHTS, DARE... BUT NOTHING COMPARED TO JUPITER'S WEIRD AND SAVAGE BEAUTY!
SENSORS PICKING UP A POWER SOURCE!
GET A BEARING ON IT, LOGAN!
IT'S THIS WAY! INCREASING ALL THE TIME!
LOGAN
IT'S GOING RIGHT OFF THE SCALE!
OVERLOAD
OVERLOAD
OVERLOAD

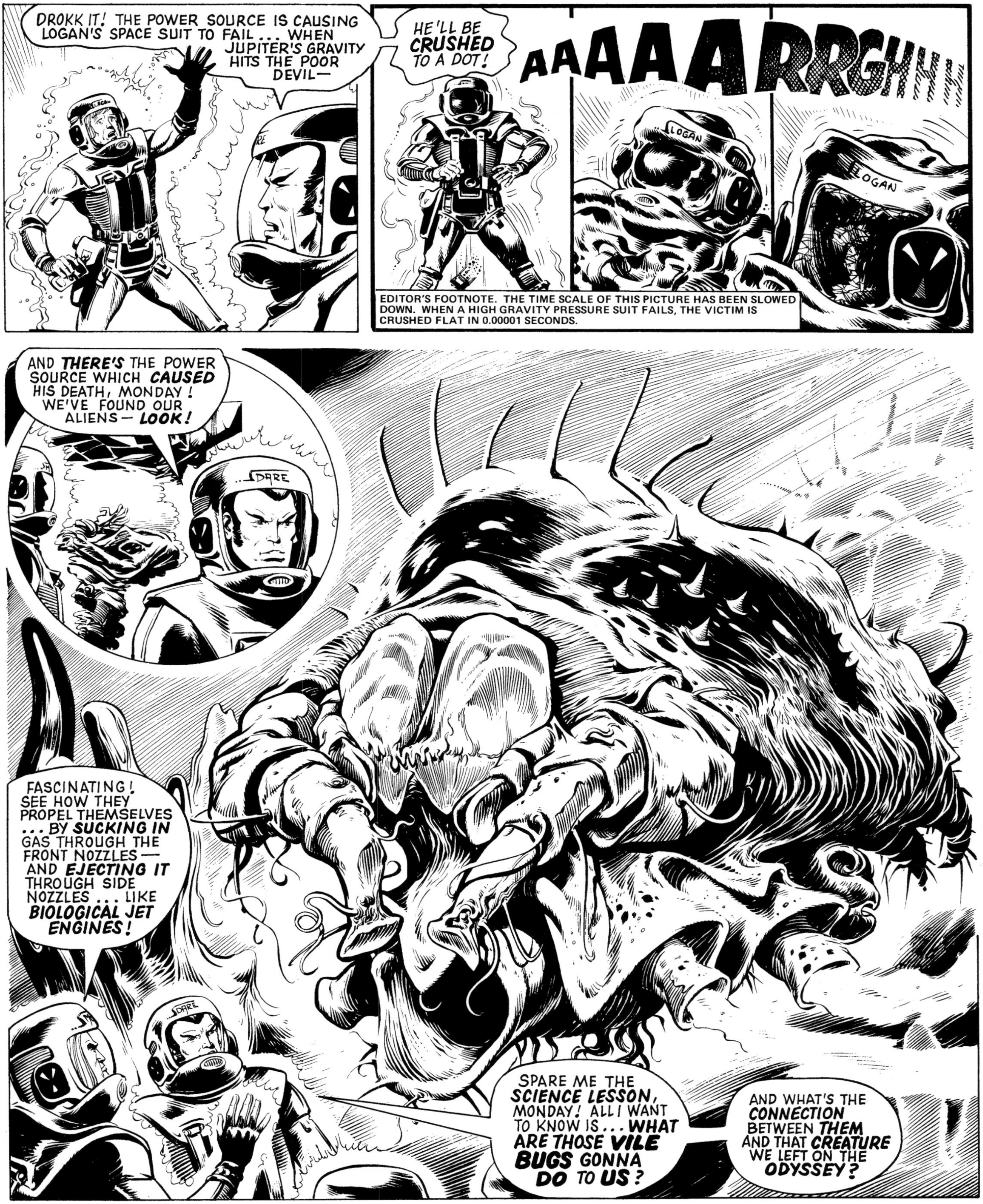
DROKK IT! THE POWER SOURCE IS CAUSING LOGAN'S SPACE SUIT TO FAIL ... WHEN JUPITER'S GRAVITY HITS THE POOR DEVIL—
HE'LL BE CRUSHED TO A DOT!
AAAAARRGHH!!
EDITOR'S FOOTNOTE. THE TIME SCALE OF THIS PICTURE HAS BEEN SLOWED DOWN. WHEN A HIGH GRAVITY PRESSURE SUIT FAILS, THE VICTIM IS CRUSHED FLAT IN 0.00001 SECONDS.
AND THERE'S THE POWER SOURCE WHICH CAUSED HIS DEATH, MONDAY! WE'VE FOUND OUR ALIENS— LOOK!
FASCINATING! SEE HOW THEY PROPEL THEMSELVES ... BY SUCKING IN GAS THROUGH THE FRONT NOZZLES— AND EJECTING IT THROUGH SIDE NOZZLES ... LIKE BIOLOGICAL JET ENGINES!
SPARE ME THE SCIENCE LESSON, MONDAY! ALL I WANT TO KNOW IS ... WHAT ARE THOSE VILE BUGS GONNA DO TO US?
AND WHAT'S THE CONNECTION BETWEEN THEM AND THAT CREATURE WE LEFT ON THE ODYSSEY?

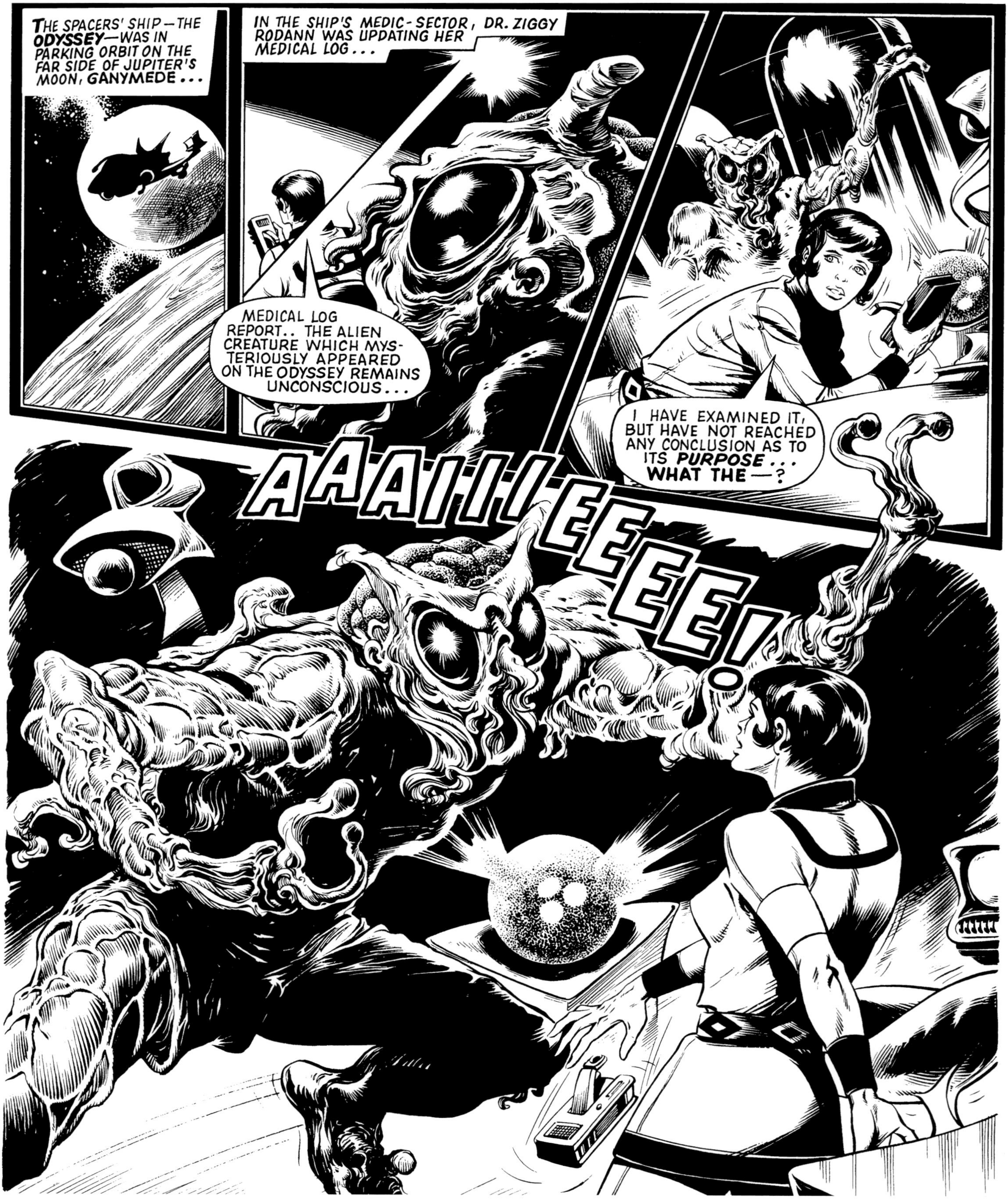
THE SPACERS' SHIP — THE ODYSSEY — WAS IN PARKING ORBIT ON THE FAR SIDE OF JUPITER'S MOON, GANYMEDE...
IN THE SHIP'S MEDIC-SECTOR, DR. ZIGGY RODANN WAS UPDATING HER MEDICAL LOG...
MEDICAL LOG REPORT.. THE ALIEN CREATURE WHICH MYSTERIOUSLY APPEARED ON THE ODYSSEY REMAINS UNCONSCIOUS...
I HAVE EXAMINED IT, BUT HAVE NOT REACHED ANY CONCLUSION AS TO ITS PURPOSE... WHAT THE —?
AAAIIIIEEEEE!

DAN DARE

MY PART IN HIS REVIVAL
PART FOUR

1977. The Argentine version of **Dan Dare** is very good – but only from a purist pov. It was in a semi-Sidney Jordan style with a cool inking style. I know SF fans will like it – but I also know that it won't appeal to the mass audience I'm aiming for. The artist's figures are small, under-characterised, and his storytelling is hard work. Given that the story was also a realistic slow burn, I just know it won't appeal to kids. I decide to dump it. Awed by the Da Savary version, I decide to write a new, less NASA and more compelling version myself with my editor designate Kelvin Gosnell.

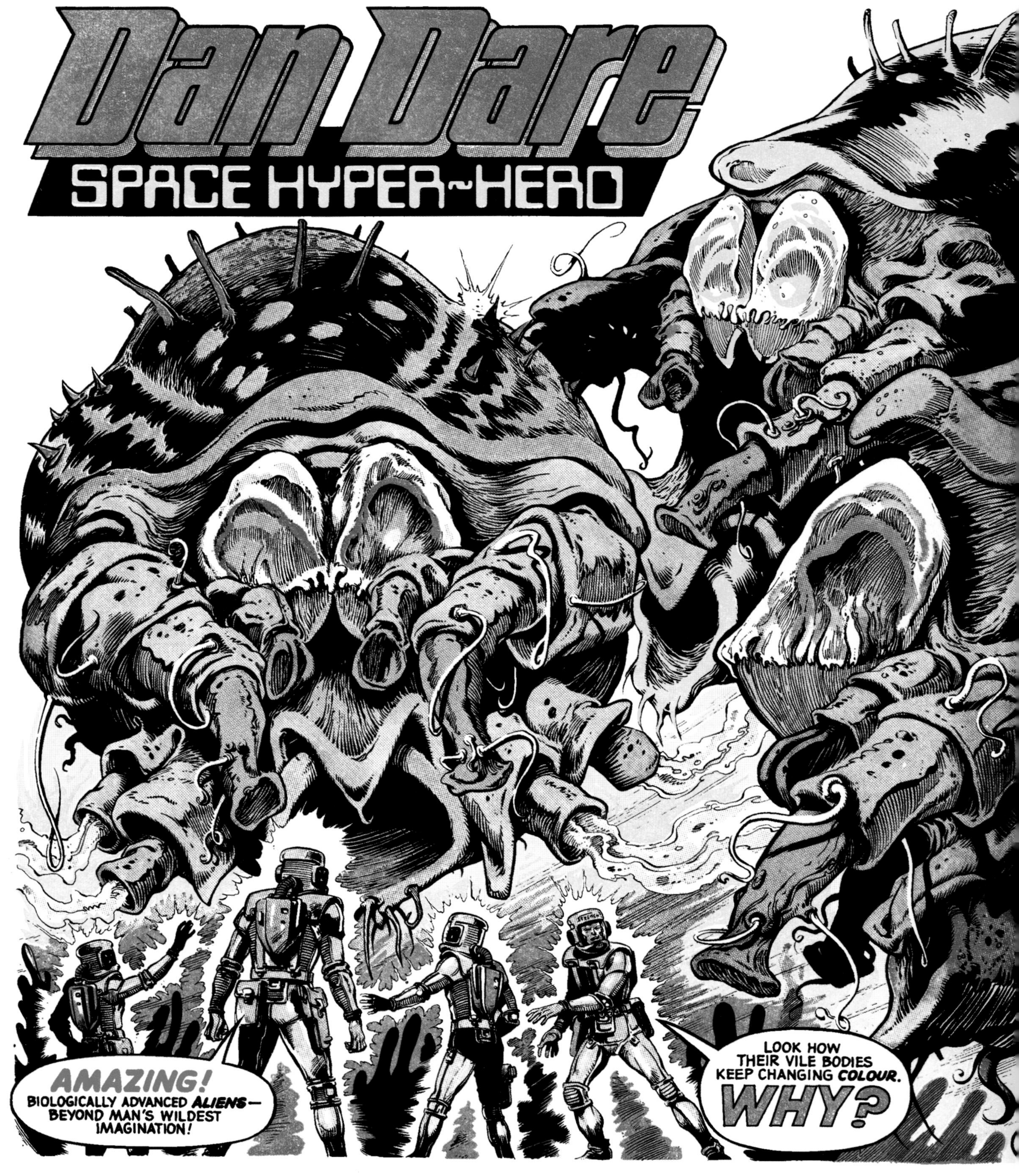
Dan Dare
SPACE HYPER~HERO
AMAZING! BIOLOGICALLY ADVANCED ALIENS— BEYOND MAN'S WILDEST IMAGINATION!
LOOK HOW THEIR VILE BODIES KEEP CHANGING COLOUR. WHY?

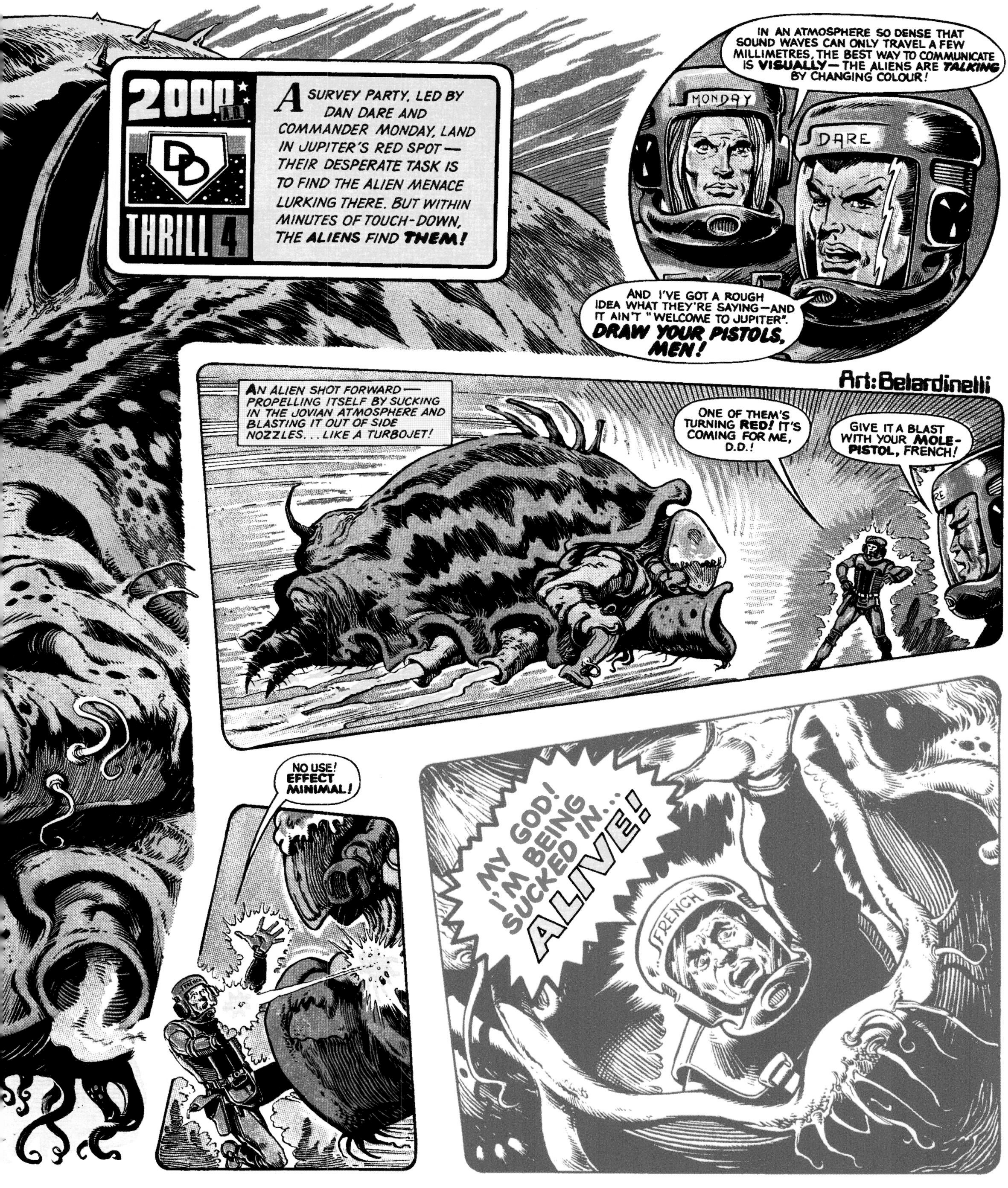

2000 A.D.
DD
THRILL 4
A SURVEY PARTY, LED BY DAN DARE AND COMMANDER MONDAY, LAND IN JUPITER'S RED SPOT — THEIR DESPERATE TASK IS TO FIND THE ALIEN MENACE LURKING THERE. BUT WITHIN MINUTES OF TOUCH-DOWN, THE ALIENS FIND THEM!
IN AN ATMOSPHERE SO DENSE THAT SOUND WAVES CAN ONLY TRAVEL A FEW MILLIMETRES, THE BEST WAY TO COMMUNICATE IS VISUALLY — THE ALIENS ARE TALKING BY CHANGING COLOUR!
MONDAY
DARE
AND I'VE GOT A ROUGH IDEA WHAT THEY'RE SAYING — AND IT AIN'T "WELCOME TO JUPITER". DRAW YOUR PISTOLS, MEN!
Art: Belardinelli
AN ALIEN SHOT FORWARD — PROPELLING ITSELF BY SUCKING IN THE JOVIAN ATMOSPHERE AND BLASTING IT OUT OF SIDE NOZZLES... LIKE A TURBOJET!
ONE OF THEM'S TURNING RED! IT'S COMING FOR ME, D.D.!
GIVE IT A BLAST WITH YOUR MOLE-PISTOL, FRENCH!
NO USE! EFFECT MINIMAL!
MY GOD! I'M BEING SUCKED IN... ALIVE!
FRENCH

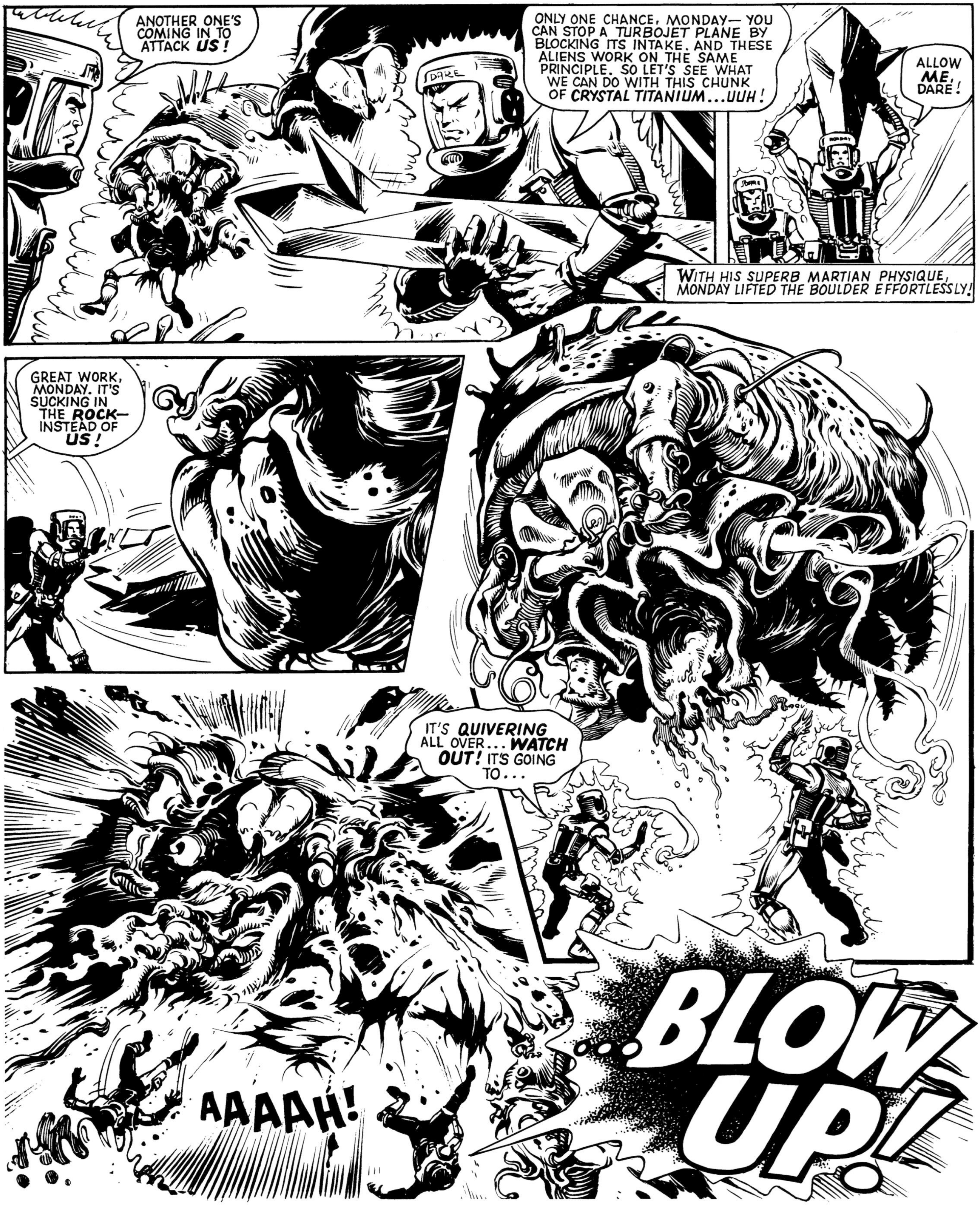

ANOTHER ONE'S COMING IN TO ATTACK US!
ONLY ONE CHANCE, MONDAY— YOU CAN STOP A TURBOJET PLANE BY BLOCKING ITS INTAKE. AND THESE ALIENS WORK ON THE SAME PRINCIPLE. SO LET'S SEE WHAT WE CAN DO WITH THIS CHUNK OF CRYSTAL TITANIUM...UUH!
ALLOW ME, DARE!
WITH HIS SUPERB MARTIAN PHYSIQUE, MONDAY LIFTED THE BOULDER EFFORTLESSLY!
GREAT WORK, MONDAY. IT'S SUCKING IN THE ROCK— INSTEAD OF US!
IT'S QUIVERING ALL OVER... WATCH OUT! IT'S GOING TO...
...BLOW UP!
AAAAH!

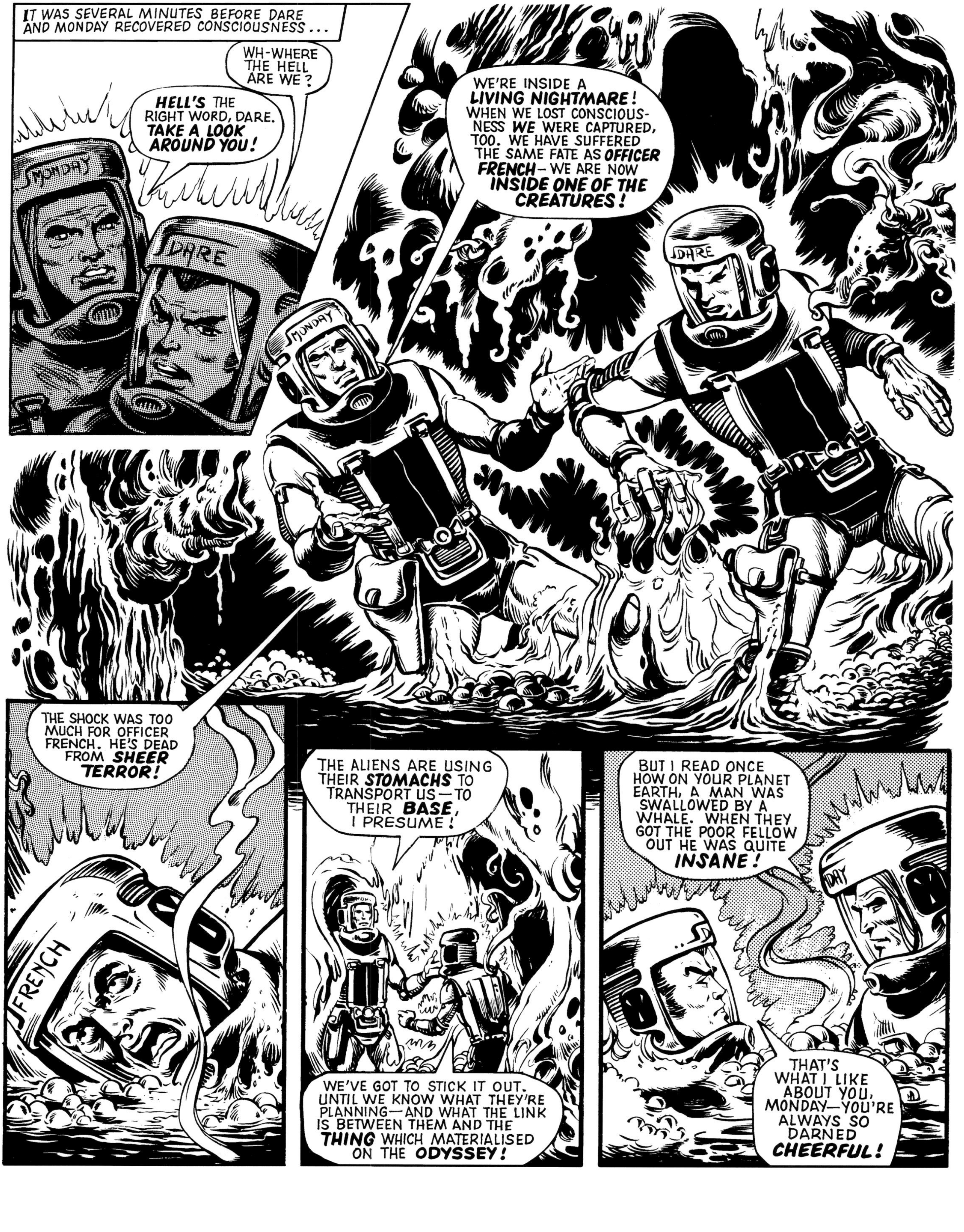
IT WAS SEVERAL MINUTES BEFORE DARE AND MONDAY RECOVERED CONSCIOUSNESS ...
WH-WHERE THE HELL ARE WE?
HELL'S THE RIGHT WORD, DARE. TAKE A LOOK AROUND YOU!
WE'RE INSIDE A LIVING NIGHTMARE! WHEN WE LOST CONSCIOUSNESS WE WERE CAPTURED, TOO. WE HAVE SUFFERED THE SAME FATE AS OFFICER FRENCH— WE ARE NOW INSIDE ONE OF THE CREATURES!
THE SHOCK WAS TOO MUCH FOR OFFICER FRENCH. HE'S DEAD FROM SHEER TERROR!
FRENCH
THE ALIENS ARE USING THEIR STOMACHS TO TRANSPORT US — TO THEIR BASE, I PRESUME!
WE'VE GOT TO STICK IT OUT. UNTIL WE KNOW WHAT THEY'RE PLANNING — AND WHAT THE LINK IS BETWEEN THEM AND THE THING WHICH MATERIALISED ON THE ODYSSEY!
BUT I READ ONCE HOW ON YOUR PLANET EARTH, A MAN WAS SWALLOWED BY A WHALE. WHEN THEY GOT THE POOR FELLOW OUT HE WAS QUITE INSANE!
THAT'S WHAT I LIKE ABOUT YOU, MONDAY — YOU'RE ALWAYS SO DARNED CHEERFUL!

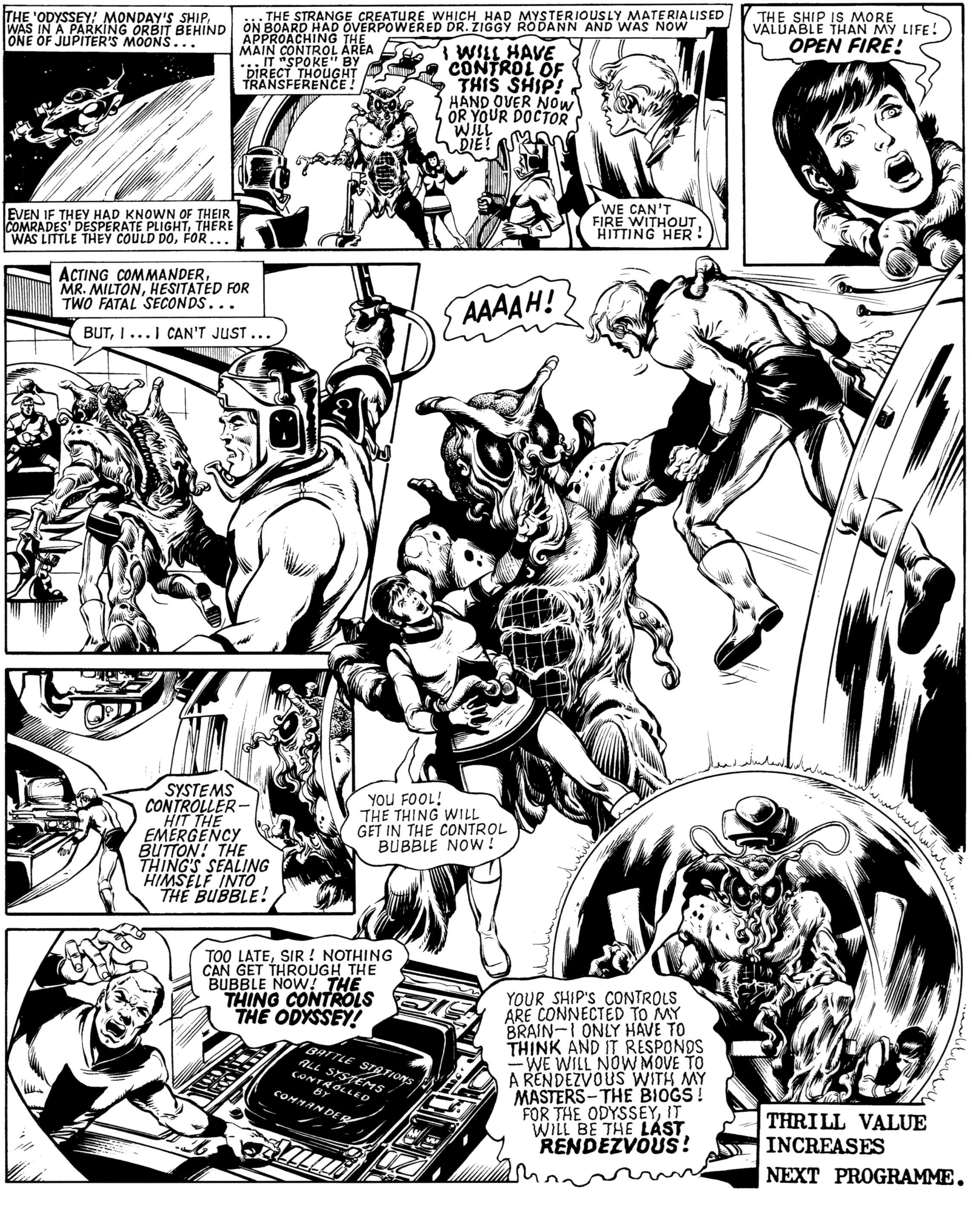
THE 'ODYSSEY,' MONDAY'S SHIP, WAS IN A PARKING ORBIT BEHIND ONE OF JUPITER'S MOONS...
EVEN IF THEY HAD KNOWN OF THEIR COMRADES' DESPERATE PLIGHT, THERE WAS LITTLE THEY COULD DO, FOR...
...THE STRANGE CREATURE WHICH HAD MYSTERIOUSLY MATERIALISED ON BOARD HAD OVERPOWERED DR. ZIGGY RODANN AND WAS NOW APPROACHING THE MAIN CONTROL AREA ...IT "SPOKE" BY DIRECT THOUGHT TRANSFERENCE!
I WILL HAVE CONTROL OF THIS SHIP! HAND OVER NOW OR YOUR DOCTOR WILL DIE!
WE CAN'T FIRE WITHOUT HITTING HER!
THE SHIP IS MORE VALUABLE THAN MY LIFE! OPEN FIRE!
ACTING COMMANDER, MR. MILTON, HESITATED FOR TWO FATAL SECONDS...
BUT, I...I CAN'T JUST...
AAAAH!
SYSTEMS CONTROLLER— HIT THE EMERGENCY BUTTON! THE THING'S SEALING HIMSELF INTO THE BUBBLE!
YOU FOOL! THE THING WILL GET IN THE CONTROL BUBBLE NOW!
TOO LATE, SIR! NOTHING CAN GET THROUGH THE BUBBLE NOW! THE THING CONTROLS THE ODYSSEY!
BATTLE STATIONS ALL SYSTEMS CONTROLLED BY COMMANDER
YOUR SHIP'S CONTROLS ARE CONNECTED TO MY BRAIN— I ONLY HAVE TO THINK AND IT RESPONDS —WE WILL NOW MOVE TO A RENDEZVOUS WITH MY MASTERS— THE BIOGS! FOR THE ODYSSEY, IT WILL BE THE LAST RENDEZVOUS!
THRILL VALUE INCREASES NEXT PROGRAMME.

DAN DARE

MY PART IN HIS REVIVAL

PART FIVE

Kelvin and I then write an exploration of Jupiter's red spot with astronauts wearing anti-grav suits and alien life forms based on microscopic life in the *National Geographic*. Story-wise I think its basic plot is valid in Dare terms. We try out one or two artists – I believe two Italian brothers, one of whom drew *Death Game 1999* for *Action* – but their version looks dull to me and I turn them down. I want **Dan Dare** to be special.

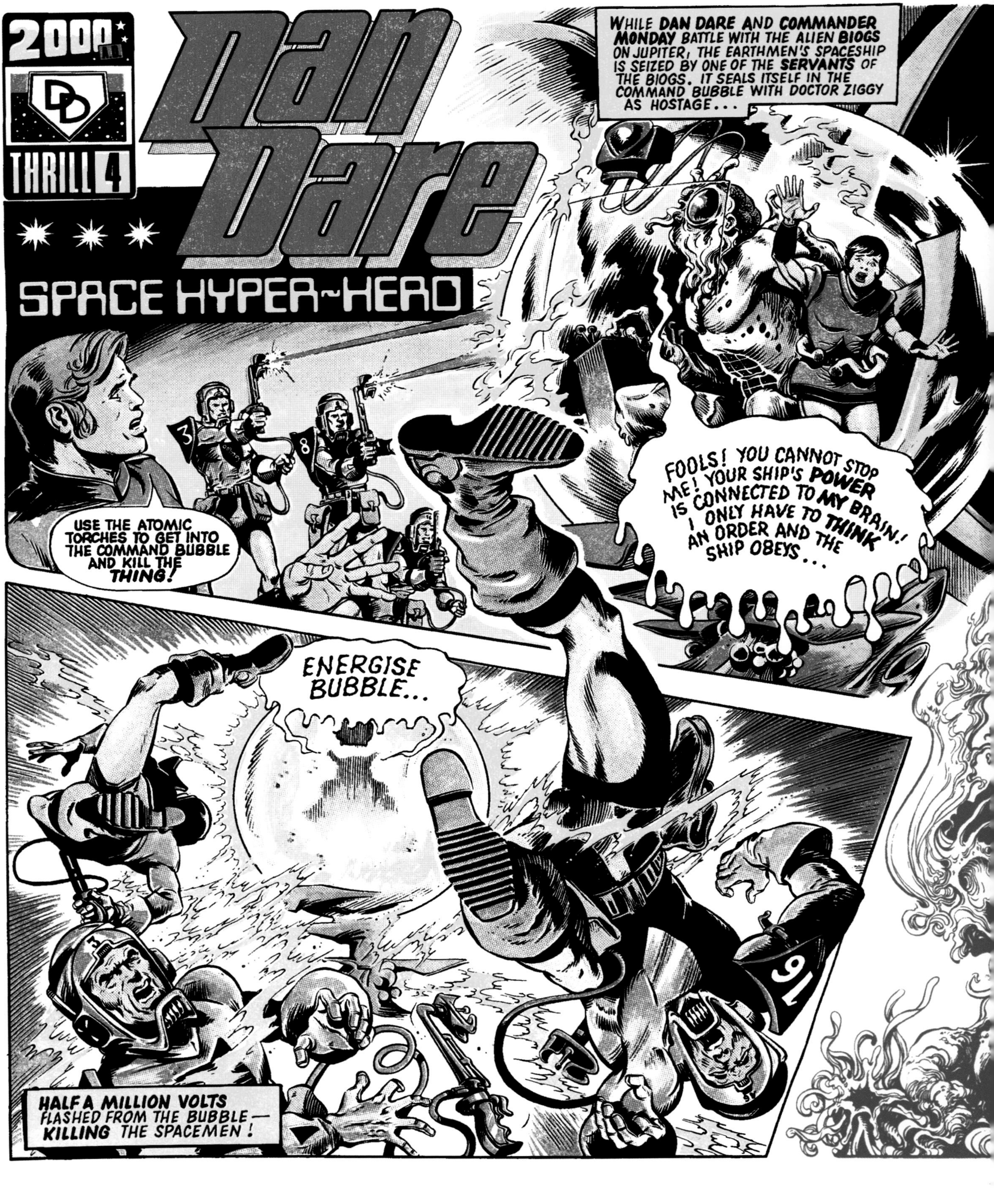
2000 AD
THRILL 4
DAN DARE
SPACE HYPER~HERO
WHILE DAN DARE AND COMMANDER MONDAY BATTLE WITH THE ALIEN BIOGS ON JUPITER, THE EARTHMEN'S SPACESHIP IS SEIZED BY ONE OF THE SERVANTS OF THE BIOGS. IT SEALS ITSELF IN THE COMMAND BUBBLE WITH DOCTOR ZIGGY AS HOSTAGE...
USE THE ATOMIC TORCHES TO GET INTO THE COMMAND BUBBLE AND KILL THE THING!
FOOLS! YOU CANNOT STOP ME! YOUR SHIP'S POWER IS CONNECTED TO MY BRAIN! I ONLY HAVE TO THINK AN ORDER AND THE SHIP OBEYS...
ENERGISE BUBBLE...
HALF A MILLION VOLTS FLASHED FROM THE BUBBLE— KILLING THE SPACEMEN!

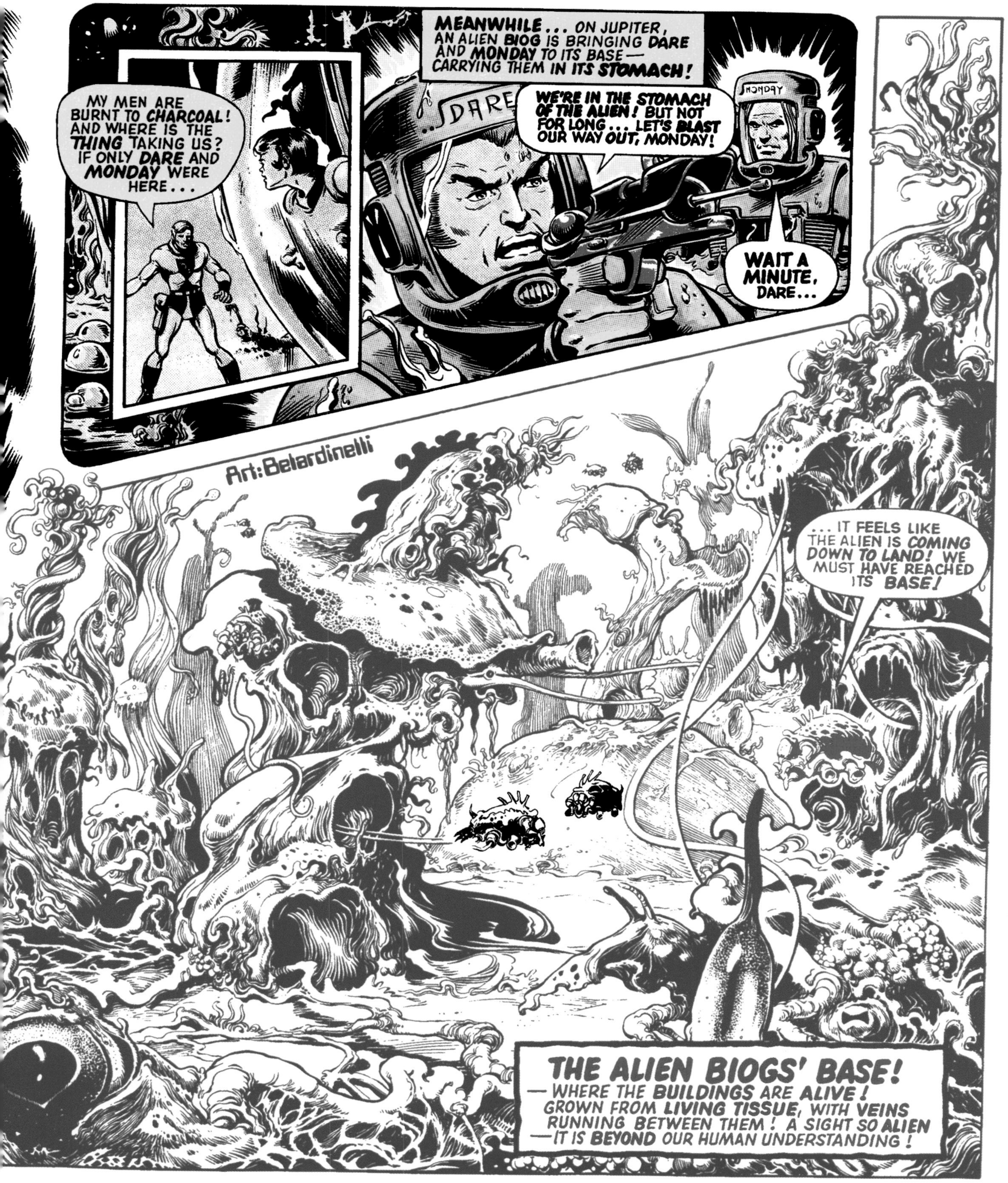
MEANWHILE... ON JUPITER, AN ALIEN BIOG IS BRINGING DARE AND MONDAY TO ITS BASE— CARRYING THEM IN ITS STOMACH!
MY MEN ARE BURNT TO CHARCOAL! AND WHERE IS THE THING TAKING US? IF ONLY DARE AND MONDAY WERE HERE...
DARE
MONDAY
WE'RE IN THE STOMACH OF THE ALIEN! BUT NOT FOR LONG... LET'S BLAST OUR WAY OUT, MONDAY!
WAIT A MINUTE, DARE...
Art: Belardinelli
...IT FEELS LIKE THE ALIEN IS COMING DOWN TO LAND! WE MUST HAVE REACHED ITS BASE!
THE ALIEN BIOGS' BASE!
—WHERE THE BUILDINGS ARE ALIVE! GROWN FROM LIVING TISSUE, WITH VEINS RUNNING BETWEEN THEM! A SIGHT SO ALIEN —IT IS BEYOND OUR HUMAN UNDERSTANDING!

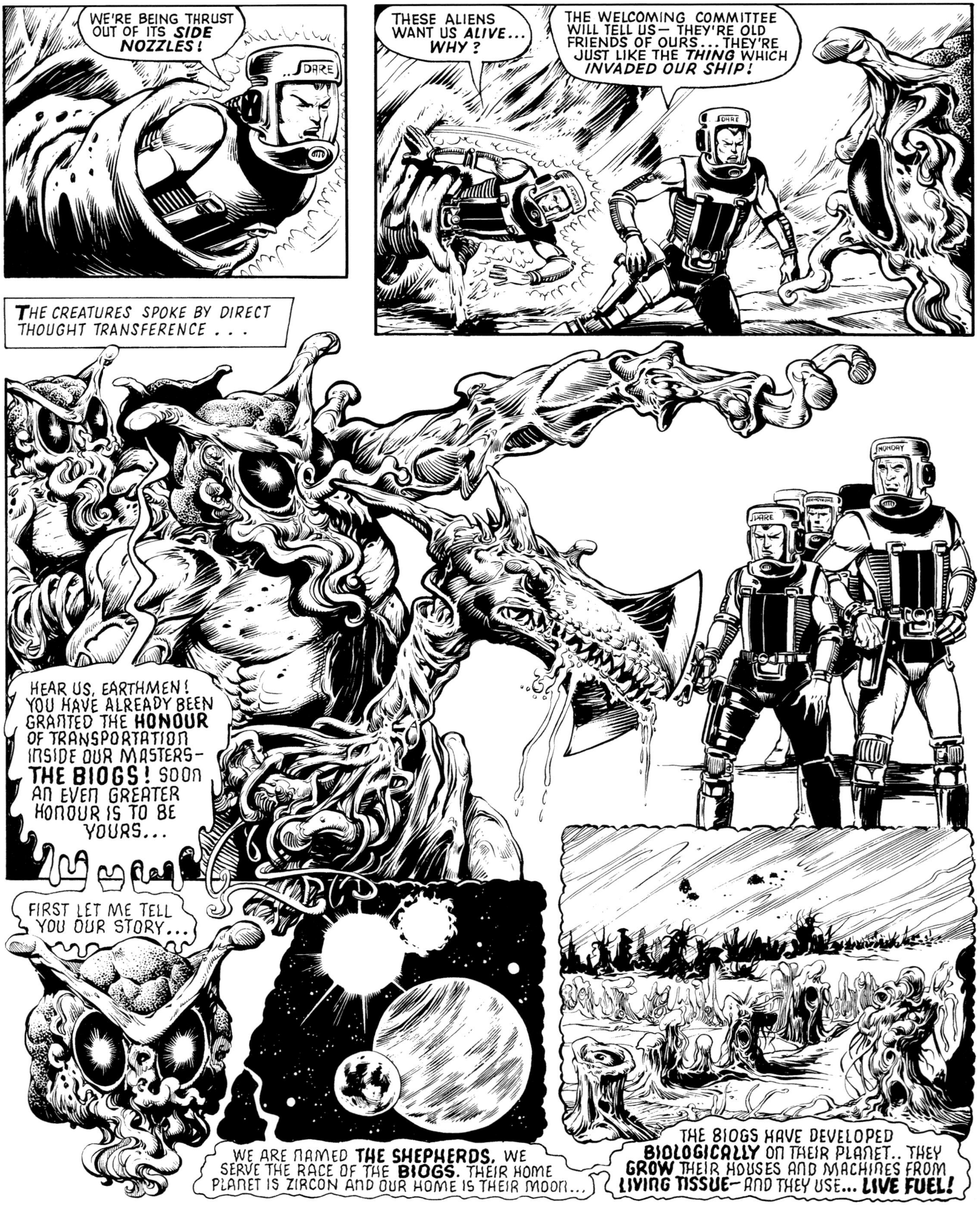

WE'RE BEING THRUST OUT OF ITS SIDE NOZZLES!
THESE ALIENS WANT US ALIVE... WHY?
THE WELCOMING COMMITTEE WILL TELL US— THEY'RE OLD FRIENDS OF OURS... THEY'RE JUST LIKE THE THING WHICH INVADED OUR SHIP!
THE CREATURES SPOKE BY DIRECT THOUGHT TRANSFERENCE . . .
HEAR US, EARTHMEN! YOU HAVE ALREADY BEEN GRANTED THE HONOUR OF TRANSPORTATION INSIDE OUR MASTERS— THE BIOGS! SOON AN EVEN GREATER HONOUR IS TO BE YOURS...
FIRST LET ME TELL YOU OUR STORY...
WE ARE NAMED THE SHEPHERDS. WE SERVE THE RACE OF THE BIOGS. THEIR HOME PLANET IS ZIRCON AND OUR HOME IS THEIR MOON...
THE BIOGS HAVE DEVELOPED BIOLOGICALLY ON THEIR PLANET.. THEY GROW THEIR HOUSES AND MACHINES FROM LIVING TISSUE— AND THEY USE... LIVE FUEL!

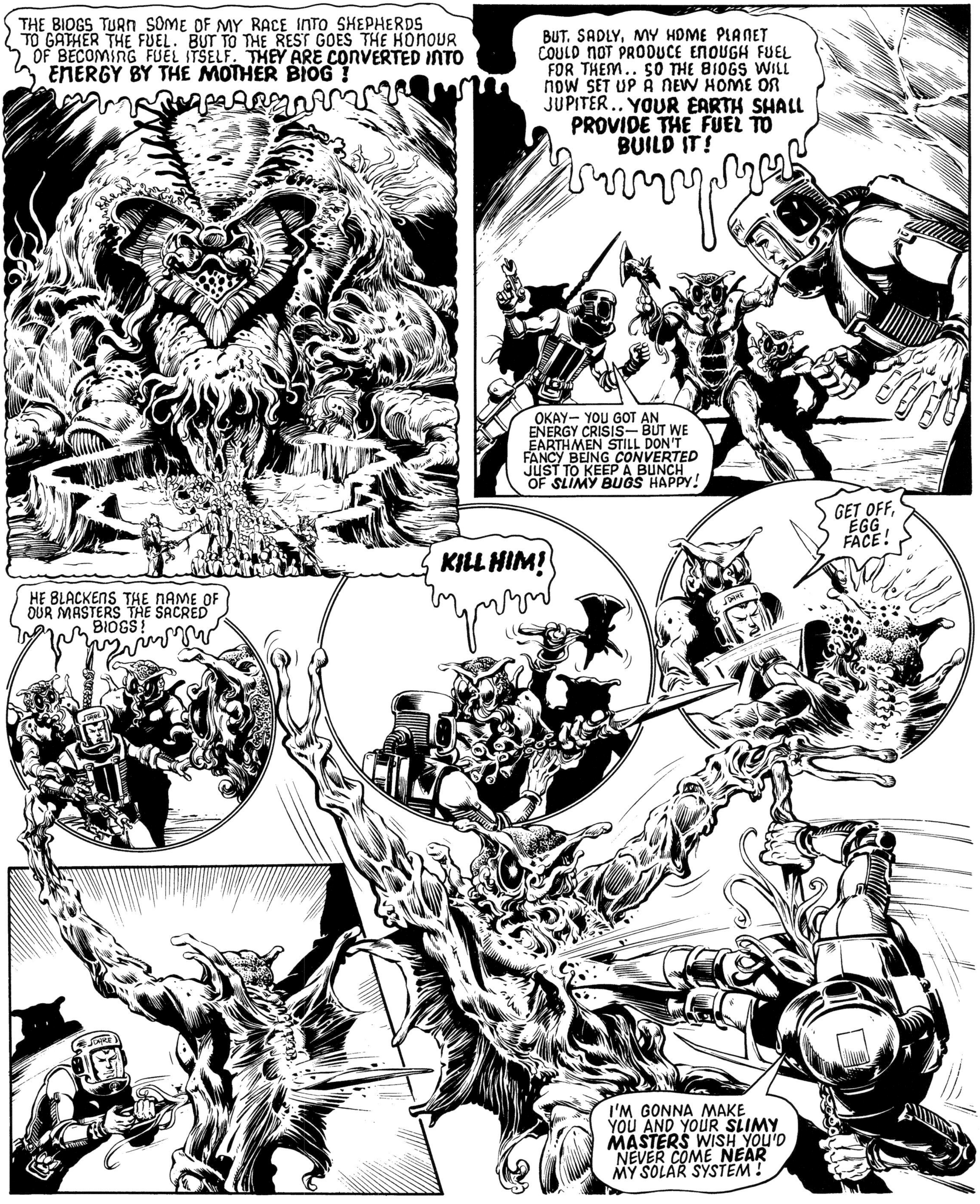
THE BIOGS TURN SOME OF MY RACE INTO SHEPHERDS TO GATHER THE FUEL. BUT TO THE REST GOES THE HONOUR OF BECOMING FUEL ITSELF. THEY ARE CONVERTED INTO ENERGY BY THE MOTHER BIOG!
BUT, SADLY, MY HOME PLANET COULD NOT PRODUCE ENOUGH FUEL FOR THEM.. SO THE BIOGS WILL NOW SET UP A NEW HOME ON JUPITER.. YOUR EARTH SHALL PROVIDE THE FUEL TO BUILD IT!
OKAY— YOU GOT AN ENERGY CRISIS— BUT WE EARTHMEN STILL DON'T FANCY BEING CONVERTED JUST TO KEEP A BUNCH OF SLIMY BUGS HAPPY!
HE BLACKENS THE NAME OF OUR MASTERS THE SACRED BIOGS!
KILL HIM!
GET OFF, EGG FACE!
I'M GONNA MAKE YOU AND YOUR SLIMY MASTERS WISH YOU'D NEVER COME NEAR MY SOLAR SYSTEM!

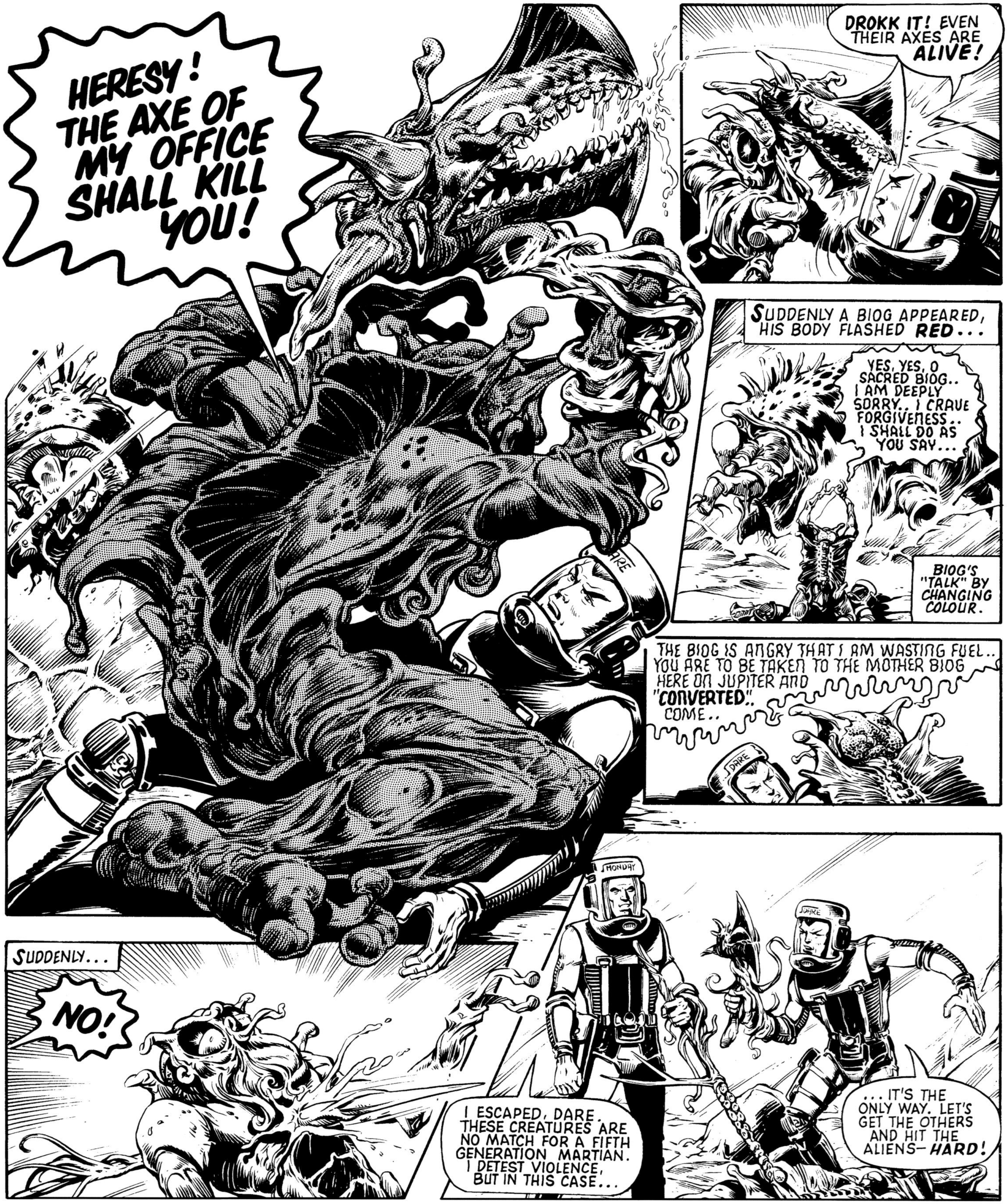
HERESY! THE AXE OF MY OFFICE SHALL KILL YOU!
DROKK IT! EVEN THEIR AXES ARE ALIVE!
SUDDENLY A BIOG APPEARED, HIS BODY FLASHED RED...
YES, YES, O SACRED BIOG.. I AM DEEPLY SORRY.. I CRAVE FORGIVENESS.. I SHALL DO AS YOU SAY...
BIOG'S "TALK" BY CHANGING COLOUR.
THE BIOG IS ANGRY THAT I AM WASTING FUEL.. YOU ARE TO BE TAKEN TO THE MOTHER BIOG HERE ON JUPITER AND "CONVERTED".. COME..
DARE
SUDDENLY...
NO!
MONDAY
DARE
I ESCAPED, DARE. THESE CREATURES ARE NO MATCH FOR A FIFTH GENERATION MARTIAN. I DETEST VIOLENCE, BUT IN THIS CASE...
...IT'S THE ONLY WAY. LET'S GET THE OTHERS AND HIT THE ALIENS—HARD!

DAN DARE

MY PART IN HIS REVIVAL
PART SIX

Artist (Massimo) Belardinelli submits a wild
version on spec. At least it's exciting and eye-
catching and – most important – helps us over
the poor quality paper. Belardinelli's black line
is the best in the business. I know his work
from the past on *Battle* and *Action* and there
his figure work is not bad. Distinctive, but not
weak anatomy.

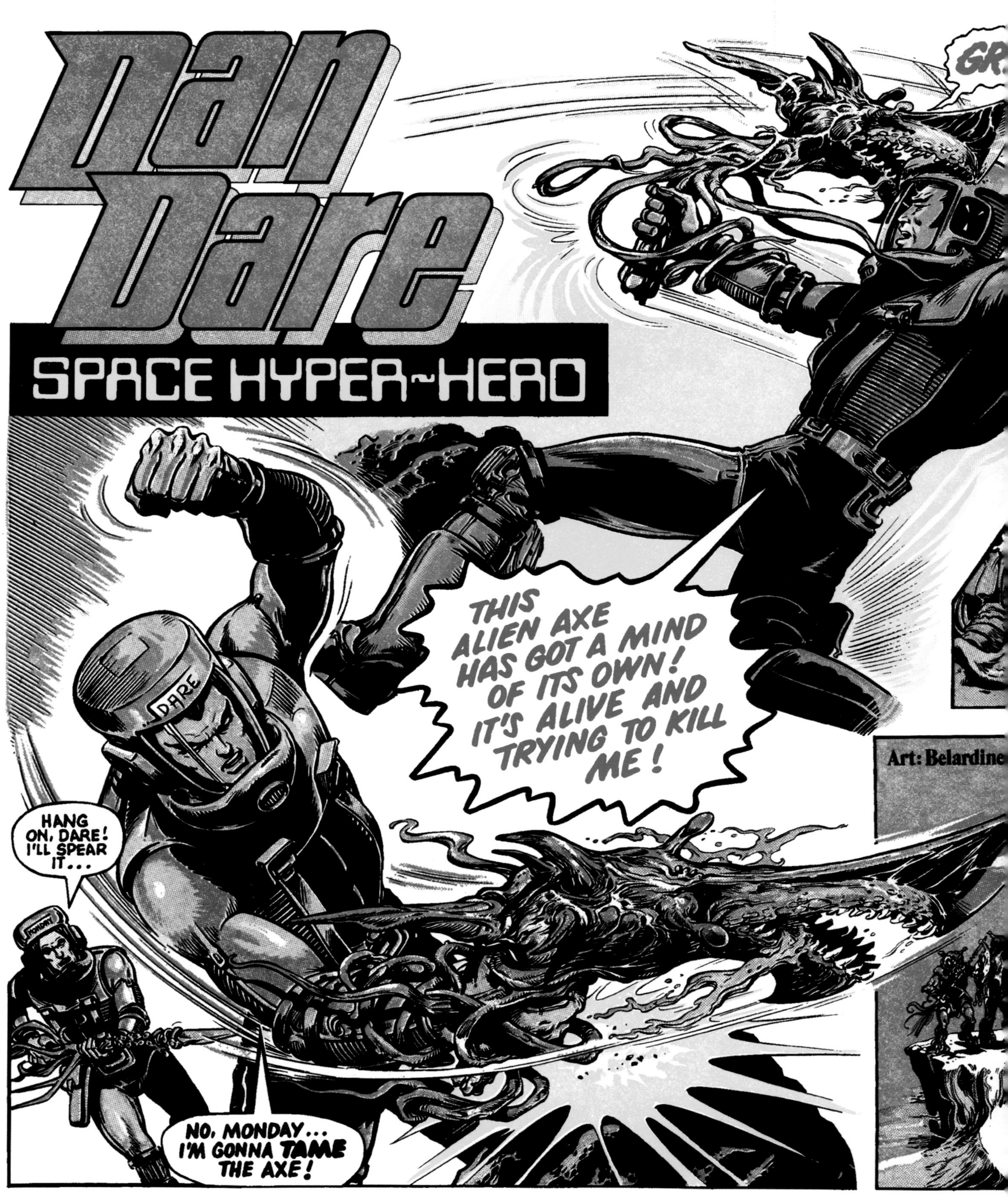

DAN DARE
SPACE HYPER~HERO
THIS ALIEN AXE HAS GOT A MIND OF ITS OWN! IT'S ALIVE AND TRYING TO KILL ME!
HANG ON, DARE! I'LL SPEAR IT...
NO, MONDAY... I'M GONNA TAME THE AXE!
Art: Belardine

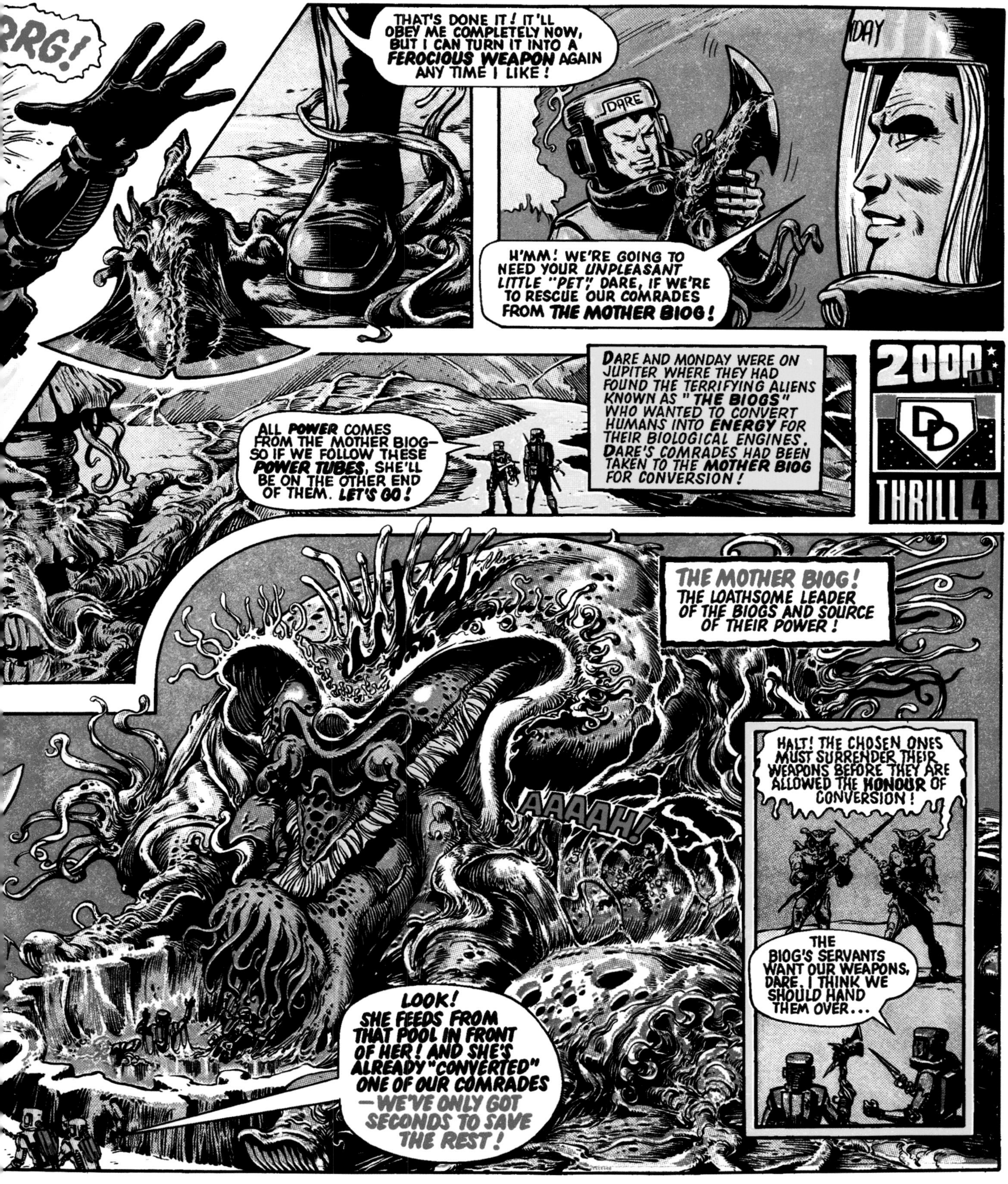

RRG!
THAT'S DONE IT! IT'LL OBEY ME COMPLETELY NOW, BUT I CAN TURN IT INTO A FEROCIOUS WEAPON AGAIN ANY TIME I LIKE!
DARE
H'MM! WE'RE GOING TO NEED YOUR UNPLEASANT LITTLE "PET", DARE, IF WE'RE TO RESCUE OUR COMRADES FROM THE MOTHER BIOG!
DARE AND MONDAY WERE ON JUPITER WHERE THEY HAD FOUND THE TERRIFYING ALIENS KNOWN AS "THE BIOGS" WHO WANTED TO CONVERT HUMANS INTO ENERGY FOR THEIR BIOLOGICAL ENGINES. DARE'S COMRADES HAD BEEN TAKEN TO THE MOTHER BIOG FOR CONVERSION!
ALL POWER COMES FROM THE MOTHER BIOG— SO IF WE FOLLOW THESE POWER TUBES, SHE'LL BE ON THE OTHER END OF THEM. LET'S GO!
2000 AD
THRILL 4
THE MOTHER BIOG! THE LOATHSOME LEADER OF THE BIOGS AND SOURCE OF THEIR POWER!
AAAAH!
HALT! THE CHOSEN ONES MUST SURRENDER THEIR WEAPONS BEFORE THEY ARE ALLOWED THE HONOUR OF CONVERSION!
THE BIOG'S SERVANTS WANT OUR WEAPONS, DARE. I THINK WE SHOULD HAND THEM OVER...
LOOK! SHE FEEDS FROM THAT POOL IN FRONT OF HER! AND SHE'S ALREADY "CONVERTED" ONE OF OUR COMRADES —WE'VE ONLY GOT SECONDS TO SAVE THE REST!

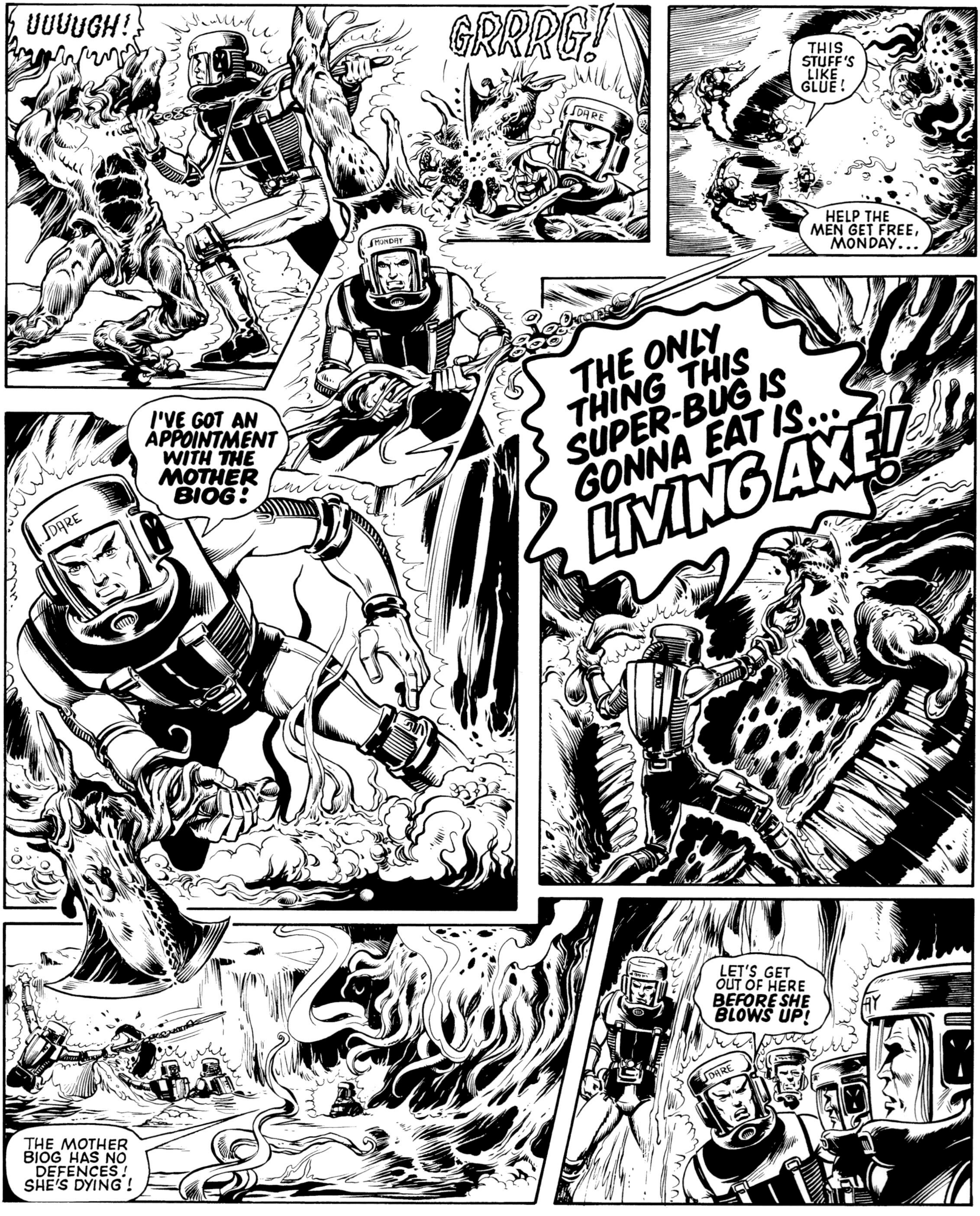
UUUUGH!
GRRRG!
THIS STUFF'S LIKE GLUE!
HELP THE MEN GET FREE, MONDAY...
THE ONLY THING THIS SUPER-BUG IS GONNA EAT IS... LIVING AXE!
I'VE GOT AN APPOINTMENT WITH THE MOTHER BIOG!
THE MOTHER BIOG HAS NO DEFENCES! SHE'S DYING!
LET'S GET OUT OF HERE BEFORE SHE BLOWS UP!

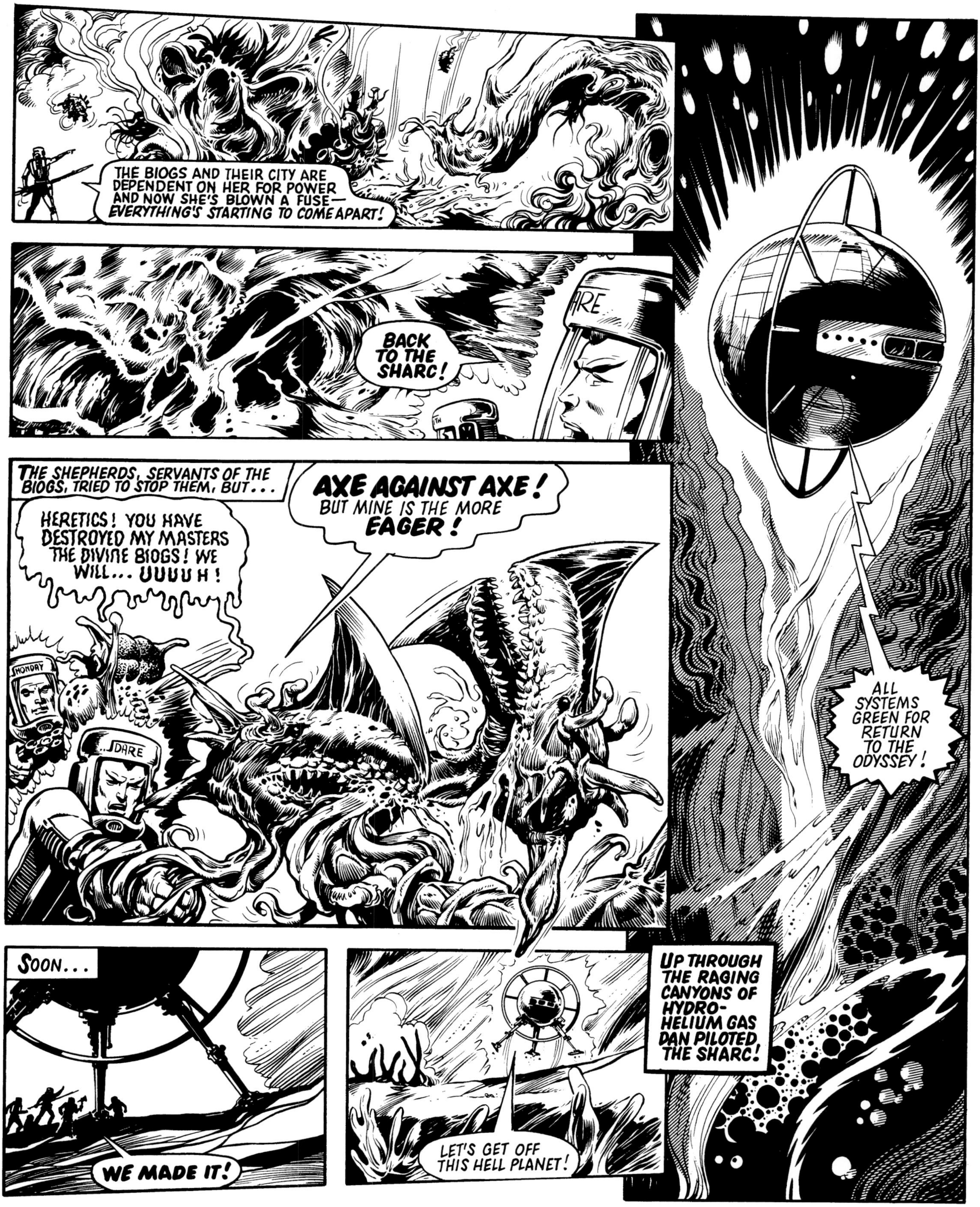
THE BIOGS AND THEIR CITY ARE DEPENDENT ON HER FOR POWER AND NOW SHE'S BLOWN A FUSE— EVERYTHING'S STARTING TO COME APART!
BACK TO THE SHARC!
THE SHEPHERDS, SERVANTS OF THE BIOGS, TRIED TO STOP THEM, BUT...
HERETICS! YOU HAVE DESTROYED MY MASTERS THE DIVINE BIOGS! WE WILL... UUUUH!
AXE AGAINST AXE! BUT MINE IS THE MORE EAGER!
SOON...
WE MADE IT!
LET'S GET OFF THIS HELL PLANET!
UP THROUGH THE RAGING CANYONS OF HYDRO-HELIUM GAS DAN PILOTED THE SHARC!
ALL SYSTEMS GREEN FOR RETURN TO THE ODYSSEY!

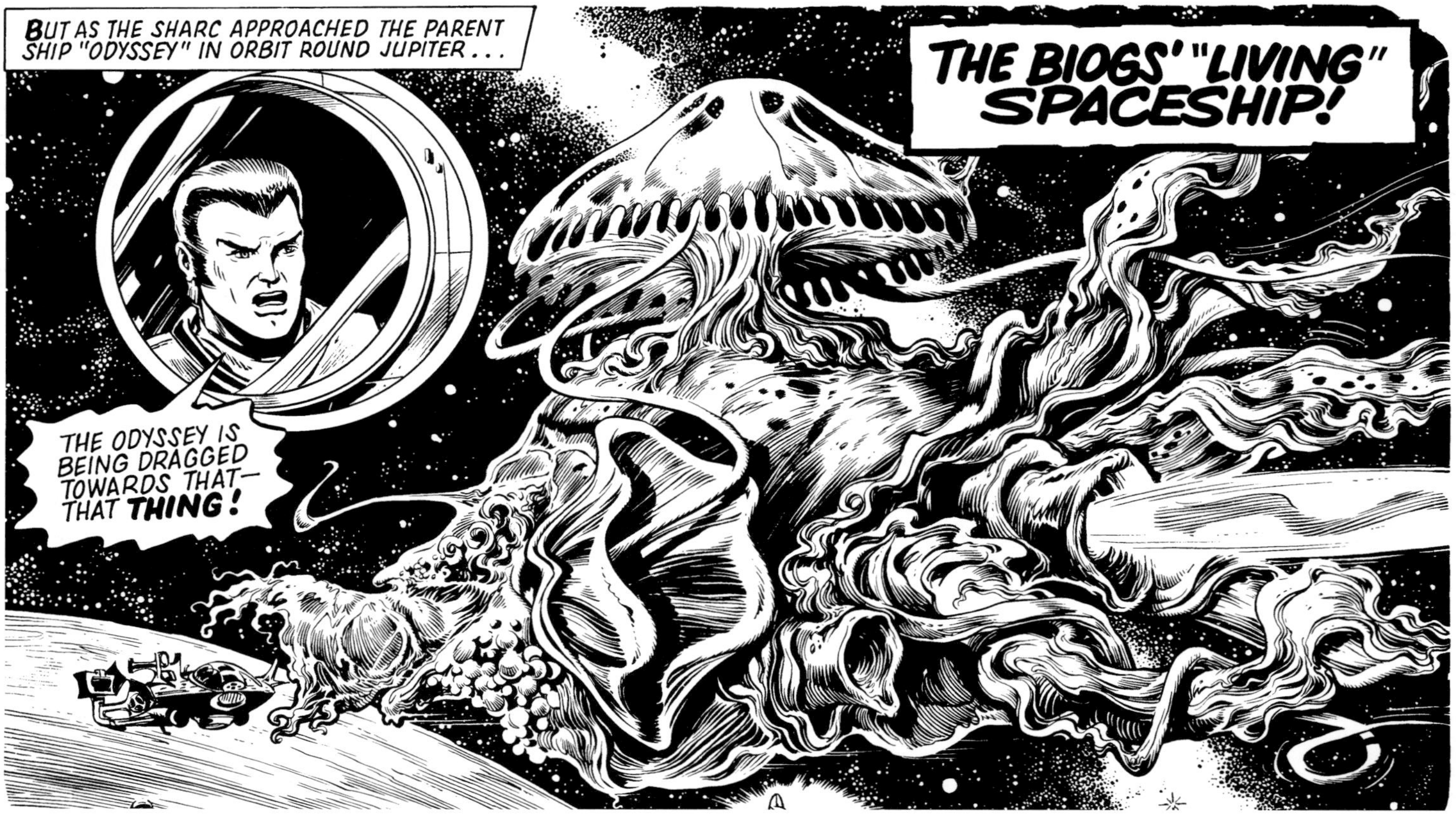
BUT AS THE SHARC APPROACHED THE PARENT SHIP "ODYSSEY" IN ORBIT ROUND JUPITER . . .
THE BIOGS' "LIVING" SPACESHIP!
THE ODYSSEY IS BEING DRAGGED TOWARDS THAT— THAT THING!

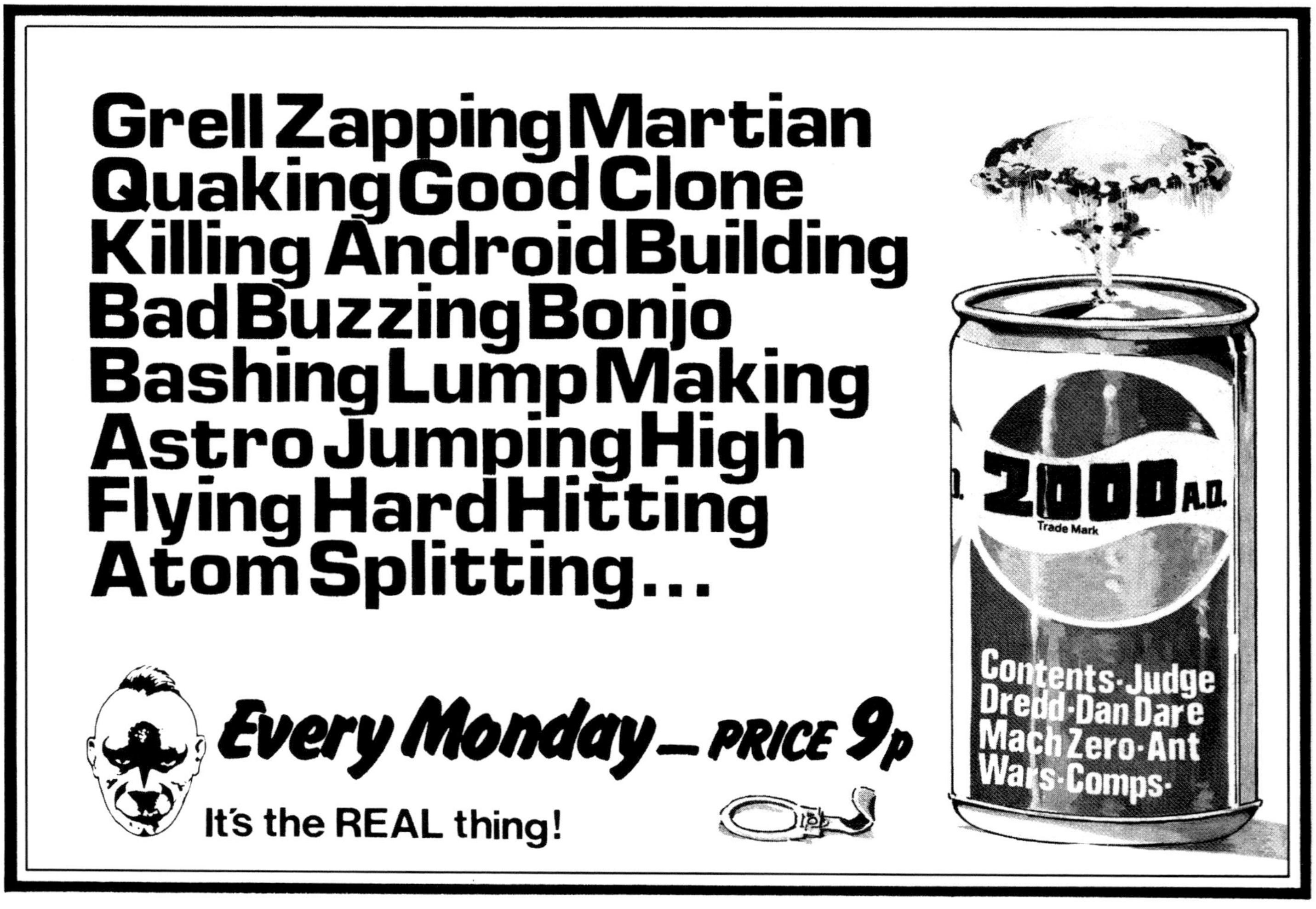
Grell Zapping Martian
Quaking Good Clone
Killing Android Building
Bad Buzzing Bonjo
Bashing Lump Making
Astro Jumping High
Flying Hard Hitting
Atom Splitting...
2000 A.D.
Trade Mark
Contents·Judge Dredd·Dan Dare Mach Zero·Ant Wars·Comps·
Every Monday — PRICE 9p
It's the REAL thing!

DAN DARE

MY PART IN HIS REVIVAL
PART SEVEN

The basic (**Dan Dare**) character design is wrong
– an over-reaction against the old Dan images.
Kevin O'Neill, my art editor, points this out
to me and I arrange a straw poll to see what
everyone in IPC juveniles think: some thirty
or more people. If they agree with Kevin, I'm
still prepared to dump it – even at this horribly
late date. But my straw poll really liked it apart
from the managing editor who thought it was
a bit "fantasmagoric". It's now two weeks to
press date and encouraged by the straw poll, I
decide to go for it.

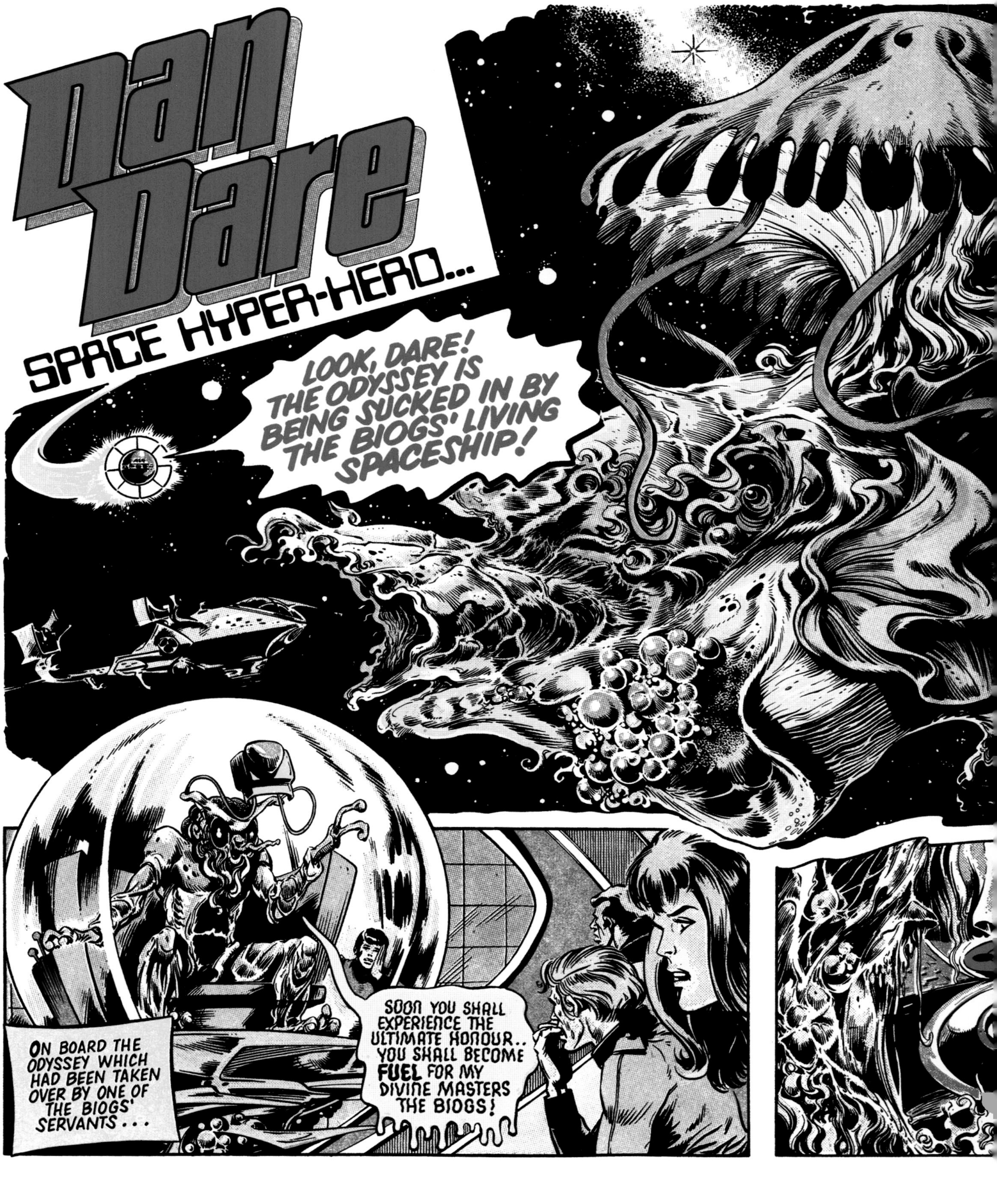
DAN DARE
SPACE HYPER-HERO...
LOOK, DARE! THE ODYSSEY IS BEING SUCKED IN BY THE BIOGS' LIVING SPACESHIP!
ON BOARD THE ODYSSEY WHICH HAD BEEN TAKEN OVER BY ONE OF THE BIOGS' SERVANTS . . .
SOON YOU SHALL EXPERIENCE THE ULTIMATE HONOUR.. YOU SHALL BECOME FUEL FOR MY DIVINE MASTERS THE BIOGS!

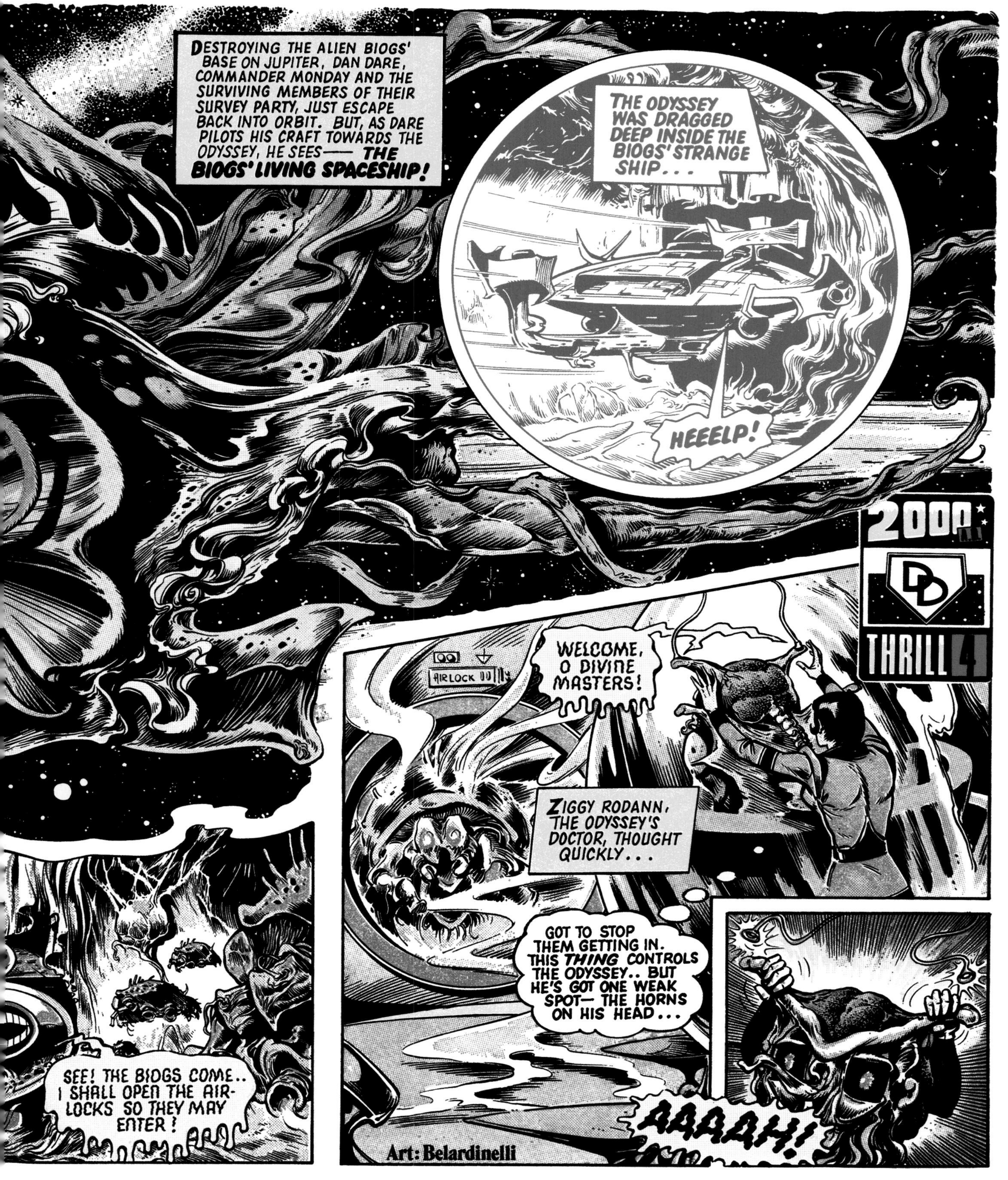
DESTROYING THE ALIEN BIOGS' BASE ON JUPITER, DAN DARE, COMMANDER MONDAY AND THE SURVIVING MEMBERS OF THEIR SURVEY PARTY, JUST ESCAPE BACK INTO ORBIT. BUT, AS DARE PILOTS HIS CRAFT TOWARDS THE ODYSSEY, HE SEES— THE BIOGS' LIVING SPACESHIP!
THE ODYSSEY WAS DRAGGED DEEP INSIDE THE BIOGS' STRANGE SHIP...
HEEELP!
2000 AD
DD
THRILL 4
AIRLOCK
WELCOME, O DIVINE MASTERS!
ZIGGY RODANN, THE ODYSSEY'S DOCTOR, THOUGHT QUICKLY...
SEE! THE BIOGS COME.. I SHALL OPEN THE AIR-LOCKS SO THEY MAY ENTER!
GOT TO STOP THEM GETTING IN. THIS THING CONTROLS THE ODYSSEY.. BUT HE'S GOT ONE WEAK SPOT— THE HORNS ON HIS HEAD...
AAAAH!
Art: Belardinelli

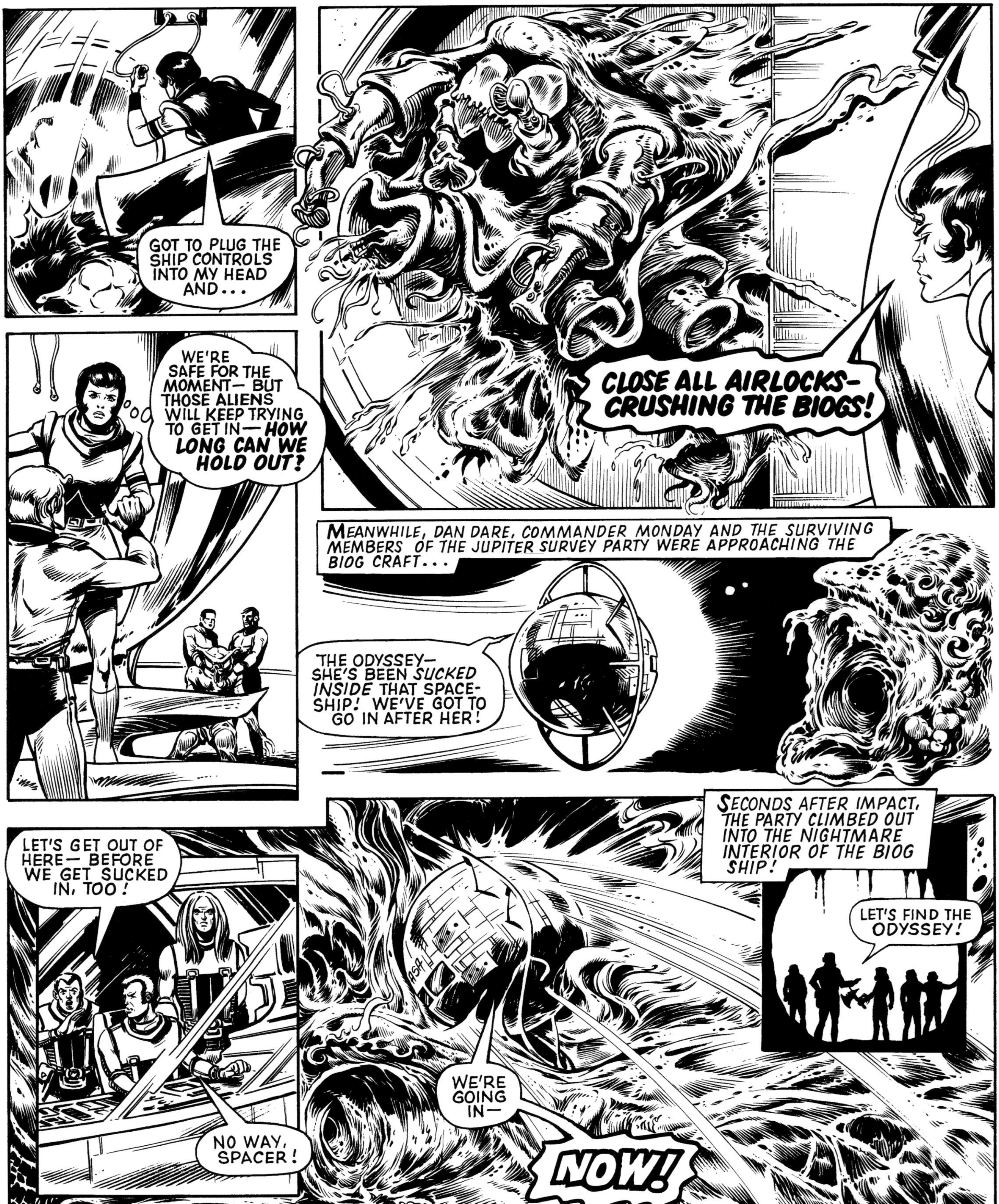
GOT TO PLUG THE SHIP CONTROLS INTO MY HEAD AND...
CLOSE ALL AIRLOCKS- CRUSHING THE BIOGS!
WE'RE SAFE FOR THE MOMENT— BUT THOSE ALIENS WILL KEEP TRYING TO GET IN— HOW LONG CAN WE HOLD OUT?
MEANWHILE, DAN DARE, COMMANDER MONDAY AND THE SURVIVING MEMBERS OF THE JUPITER SURVEY PARTY WERE APPROACHING THE BIOG CRAFT...
THE ODYSSEY— SHE'S BEEN SUCKED INSIDE THAT SPACE-SHIP! WE'VE GOT TO GO IN AFTER HER!
LET'S GET OUT OF HERE— BEFORE WE GET SUCKED IN, TOO!
NO WAY, SPACER!
WE'RE GOING IN—
NOW!
SECONDS AFTER IMPACT, THE PARTY CLIMBED OUT INTO THE NIGHTMARE INTERIOR OF THE BIOG SHIP!
LET'S FIND THE ODYSSEY!

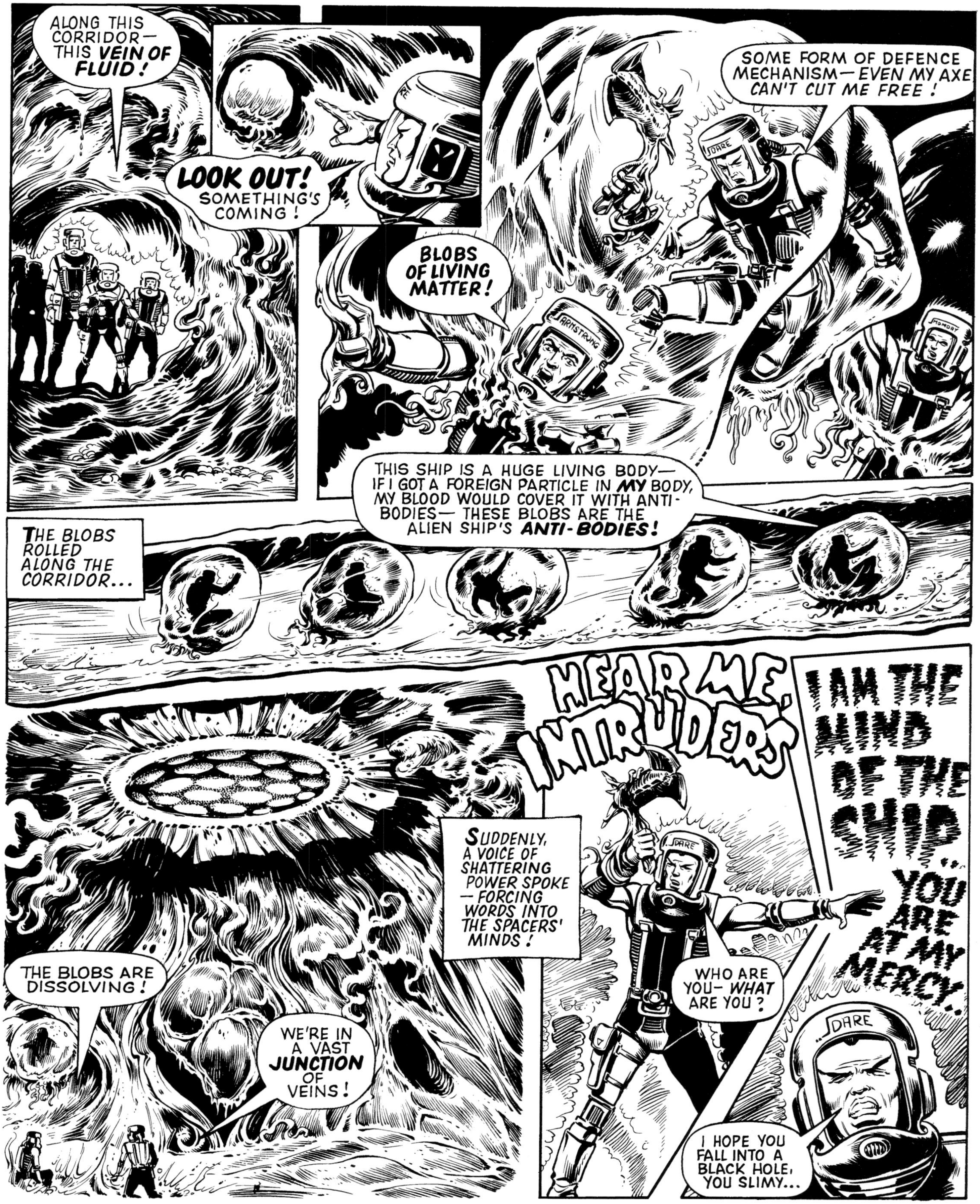

ALONG THIS CORRIDOR— THIS VEIN OF FLUID!
LOOK OUT! SOMETHING'S COMING!
BLOBS OF LIVING MATTER!
SOME FORM OF DEFENCE MECHANISM— EVEN MY AXE CAN'T CUT ME FREE!
THIS SHIP IS A HUGE LIVING BODY— IF I GOT A FOREIGN PARTICLE IN MY BODY, MY BLOOD WOULD COVER IT WITH ANTI-BODIES— THESE BLOBS ARE THE ALIEN SHIP'S ANTI-BODIES!
THE BLOBS ROLLED ALONG THE CORRIDOR...
THE BLOBS ARE DISSOLVING!
WE'RE IN A VAST JUNCTION OF VEINS!
SUDDENLY, A VOICE OF SHATTERING POWER SPOKE —FORCING WORDS INTO THE SPACERS' MINDS!
HEAR ME, INTRUDERS!
I AM THE MIND OF THE SHIP... YOU ARE AT MY MERCY...
WHO ARE YOU— WHAT ARE YOU?
I HOPE YOU FALL INTO A BLACK HOLE, YOU SLIMY...

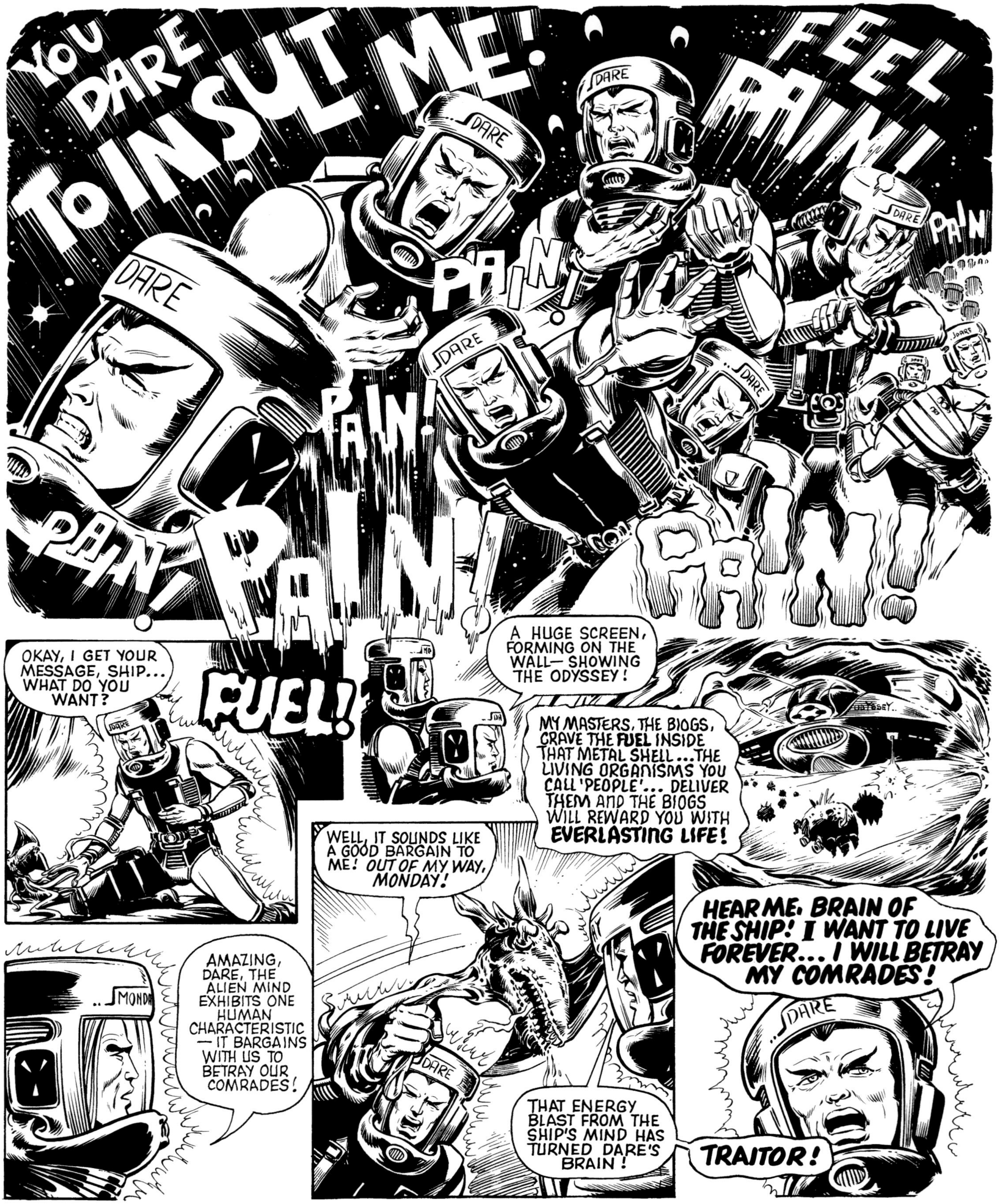

YOU DARE TO INSULT ME! FEEL PAIN!
PAIN
PAIN!
PAIN!
PAIN!
PAIN!
PAIN!
OKAY, I GET YOUR MESSAGE, SHIP... WHAT DO YOU WANT?
FUEL!
A HUGE SCREEN, FORMING ON THE WALL— SHOWING THE ODYSSEY!
MY MASTERS, THE BIOGS, CRAVE THE FUEL INSIDE THAT METAL SHELL... THE LIVING ORGANISMS YOU CALL 'PEOPLE'... DELIVER THEM AND THE BIOGS WILL REWARD YOU WITH EVERLASTING LIFE!
AMAZING, DARE, THE ALIEN MIND EXHIBITS ONE HUMAN CHARACTERISTIC — IT BARGAINS WITH US TO BETRAY OUR COMRADES!
WELL, IT SOUNDS LIKE A GOOD BARGAIN TO ME! OUT OF MY WAY, MONDAY!
THAT ENERGY BLAST FROM THE SHIP'S MIND HAS TURNED DARE'S BRAIN!
HEAR ME, BRAIN OF THE SHIP! I WANT TO LIVE FOREVER... I WILL BETRAY MY COMRADES!
TRAITOR!

DAN DARE

MY PART IN HIS REVIVAL

PART EIGHT

2000 AD appears, it's a success and **Dan Dare** is popular – about 3rd or 4th in the popularity charts. Certainly not at the bottom in a comic where the readers liked all the stories. I don't recall any critical letters apart from things along the lines of "my dad doesn't like it, but I do". And sometimes, "my dad likes it, too." Lot of criticism in the press, however, but we don't care about annoying them. In fact we quite like it.

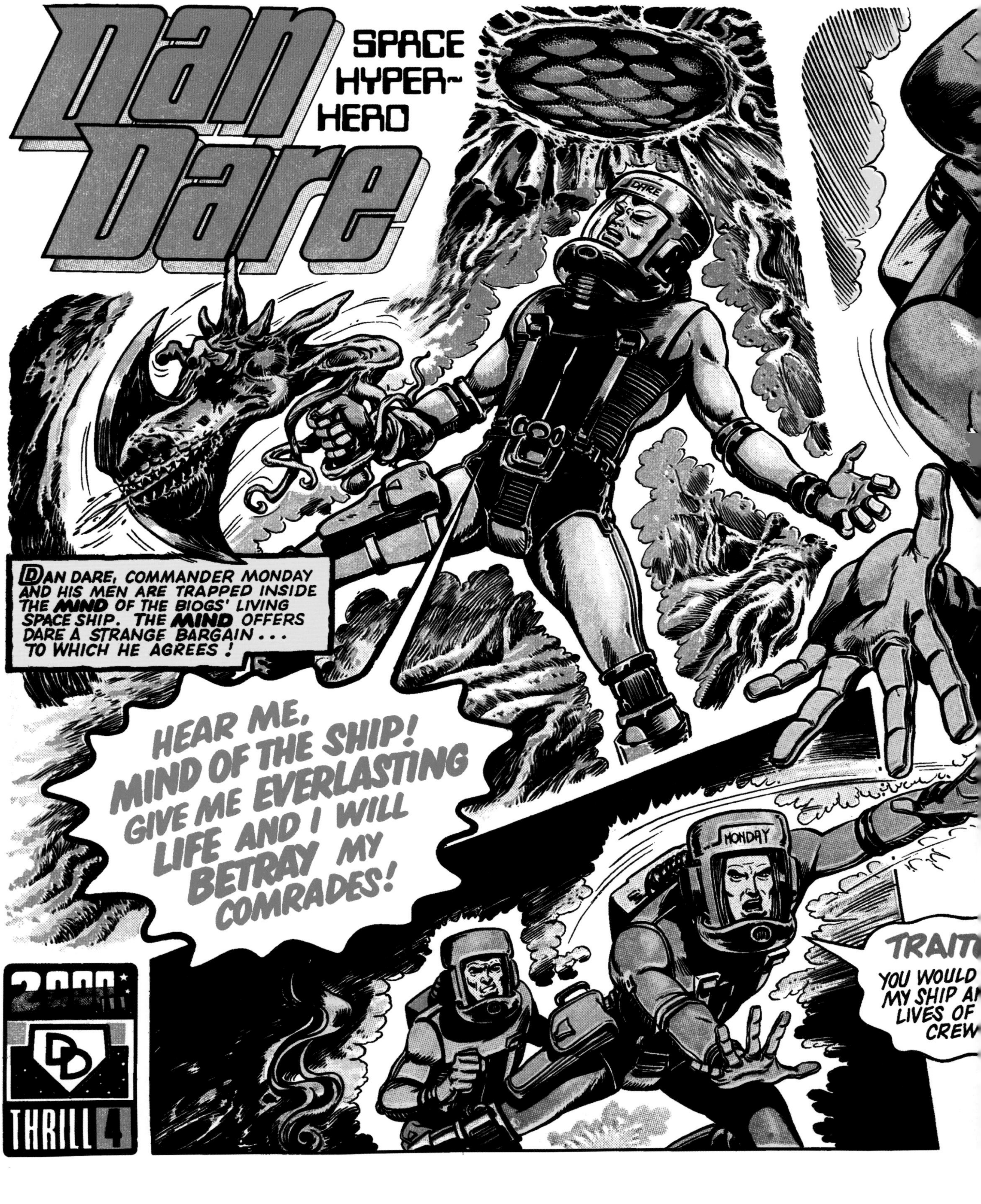
DAN DARE
SPACE HYPER-HERO
DARE
DAN DARE, COMMANDER MONDAY AND HIS MEN ARE TRAPPED INSIDE THE MIND OF THE BIOGS' LIVING SPACE SHIP. THE MIND OFFERS DARE A STRANGE BARGAIN . . . TO WHICH HE AGREES!
HEAR ME, MIND OF THE SHIP! GIVE ME EVERLASTING LIFE AND I WILL BETRAY MY COMRADES!
MONDAY
2000 AD
THRILL 4

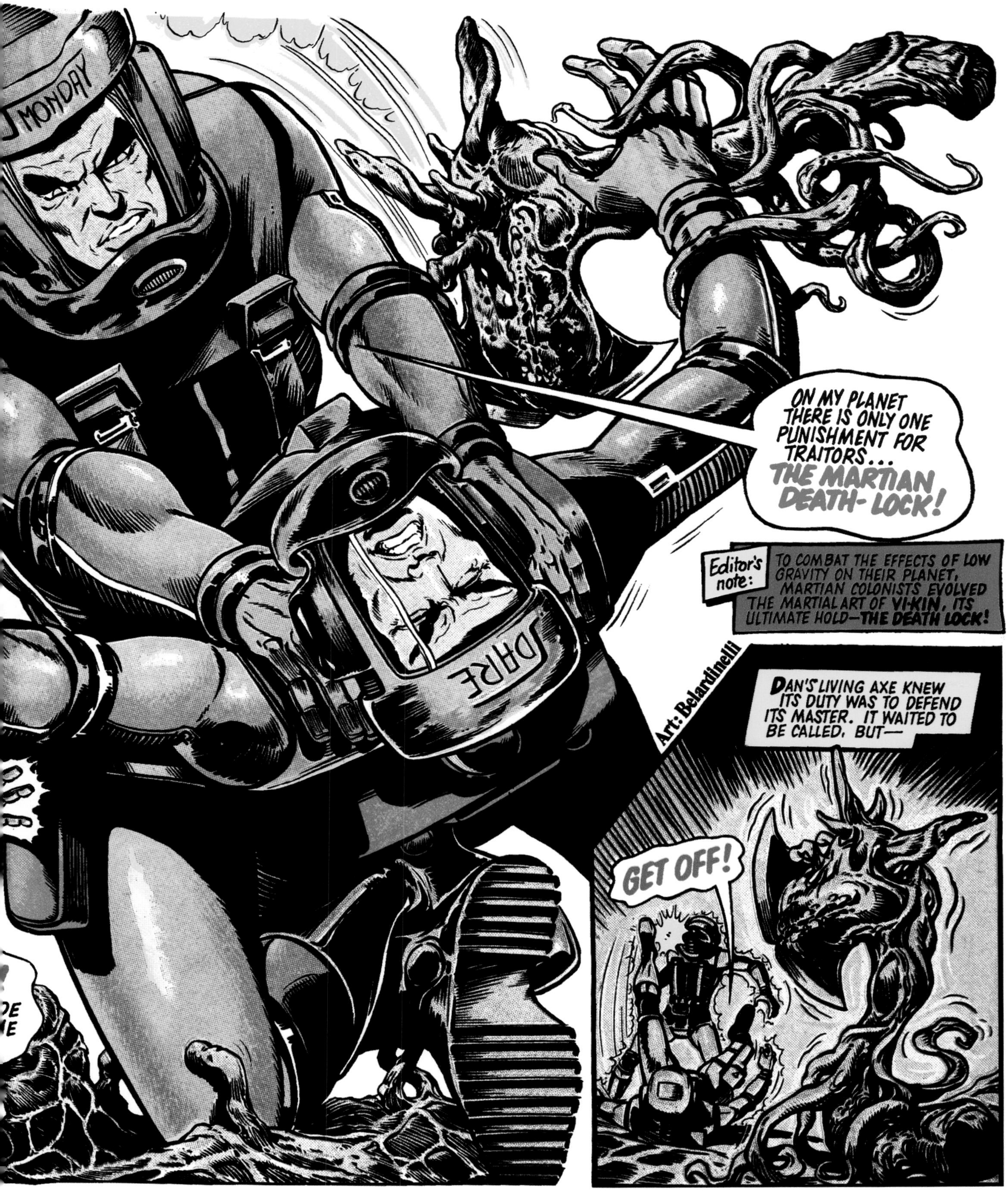

ON MY PLANET THERE IS ONLY ONE PUNISHMENT FOR TRAITORS... THE MARTIAN DEATH-LOCK!
Editor's note: TO COMBAT THE EFFECTS OF LOW GRAVITY ON THEIR PLANET, MARTIAN COLONISTS EVOLVED THE MARTIAL ART OF VI-KIN, ITS ULTIMATE HOLD—THE DEATH LOCK!
Art: Belardinelli
DAN'S LIVING AXE KNEW ITS DUTY WAS TO DEFEND ITS MASTER. IT WAITED TO BE CALLED. BUT—
GET OFF!

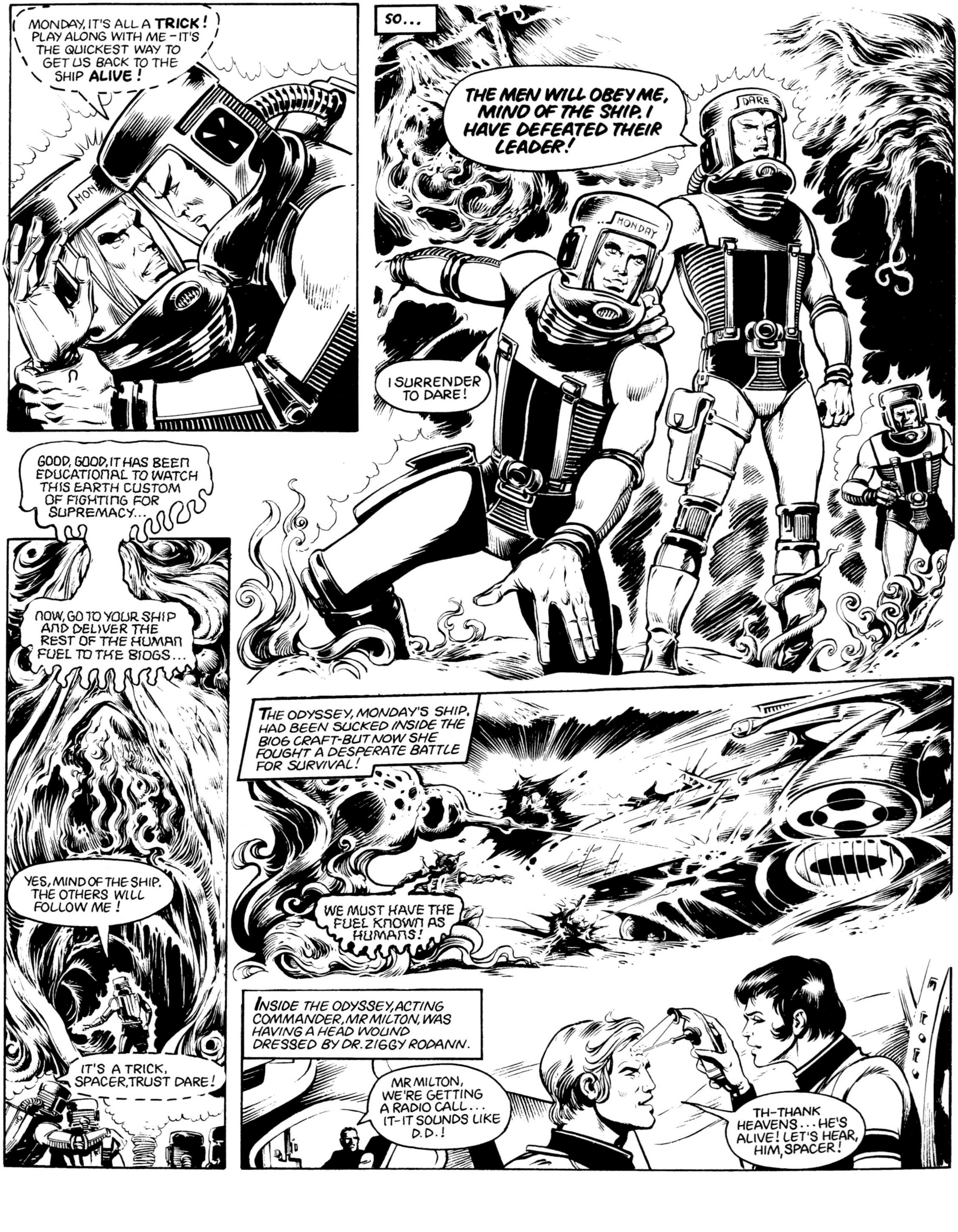
MONDAY, IT'S ALL A TRICK! PLAY ALONG WITH ME – IT'S THE QUICKEST WAY TO GET US BACK TO THE SHIP ALIVE!
MON
SO...
THE MEN WILL OBEY ME, MIND OF THE SHIP. I HAVE DEFEATED THEIR LEADER!
DARE
MONDAY
I SURRENDER TO DARE!
GOOD, GOOD, IT HAS BEEN EDUCATIONAL TO WATCH THIS EARTH CUSTOM OF FIGHTING FOR SUPREMACY...
NOW, GO TO YOUR SHIP AND DELIVER THE REST OF THE HUMAN FUEL TO THE BIOGS...
YES, MIND OF THE SHIP. THE OTHERS WILL FOLLOW ME!
IT'S A TRICK, SPACER, TRUST DARE!
THE ODYSSEY, MONDAY'S SHIP, HAD BEEN SUCKED INSIDE THE BIOG CRAFT-BUT NOW SHE FOUGHT A DESPERATE BATTLE FOR SURVIVAL!
WE MUST HAVE THE FUEL KNOWN AS HUMANS!
INSIDE THE ODYSSEY, ACTING COMMANDER, MR MILTON, WAS HAVING A HEAD WOUND DRESSED BY DR. ZIGGY RODANN.
MR MILTON, WE'RE GETTING A RADIO CALL... IT-IT SOUNDS LIKE D.D.!
TH-THANK HEAVENS... HE'S ALIVE! LET'S HEAR, HIM, SPACER!

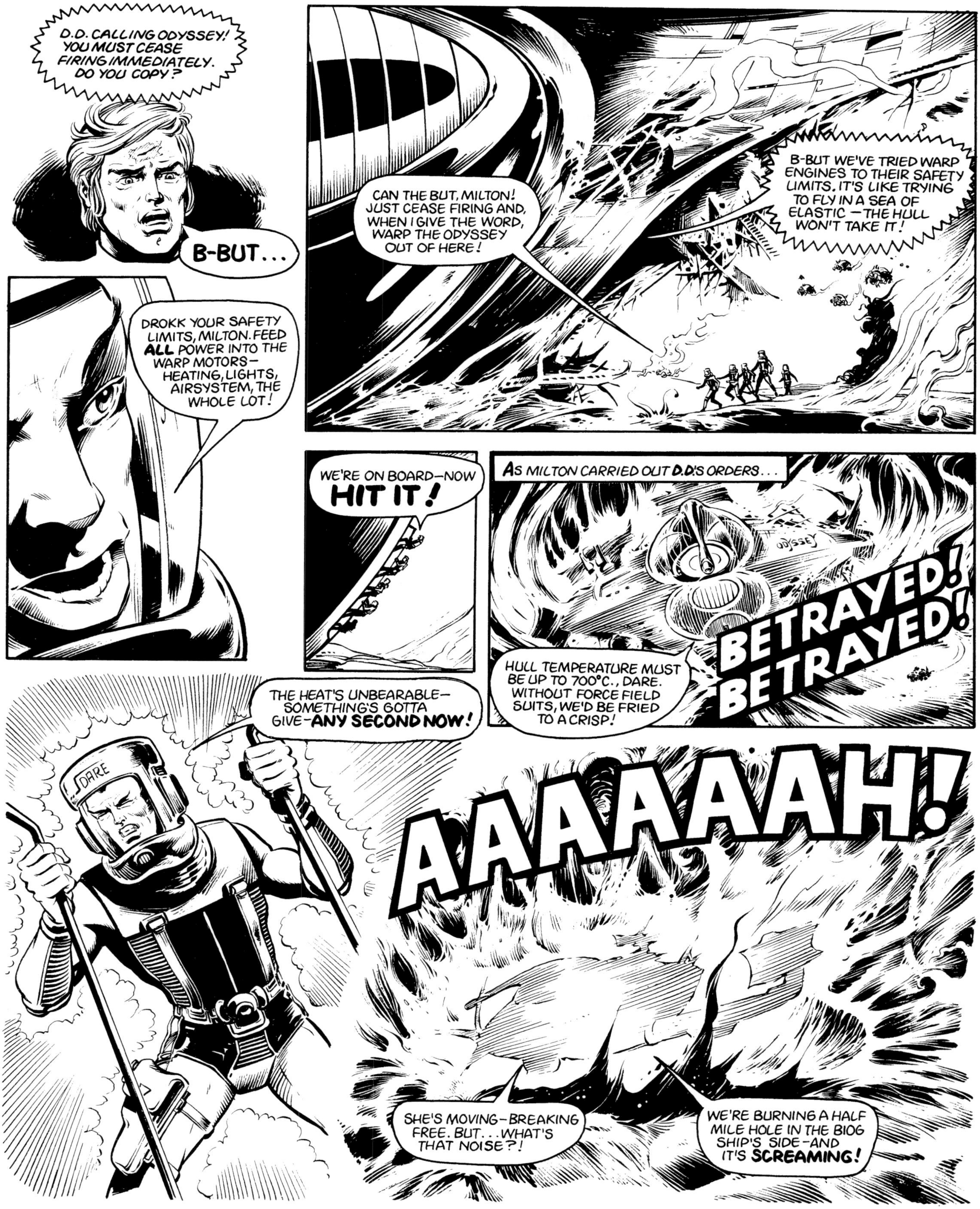
D.D. CALLING ODYSSEY! YOU MUST CEASE FIRING IMMEDIATELY. DO YOU COPY?
B-BUT...
CAN THE BUT, MILTON! JUST CEASE FIRING AND, WHEN I GIVE THE WORD, WARP THE ODYSSEY OUT OF HERE!
B-BUT WE'VE TRIED WARP ENGINES TO THEIR SAFETY LIMITS. IT'S LIKE TRYING TO FLY IN A SEA OF ELASTIC — THE HULL WON'T TAKE IT!
DROKK YOUR SAFETY LIMITS, MILTON. FEED ALL POWER INTO THE WARP MOTORS— HEATING, LIGHTS, AIRSYSTEM, THE WHOLE LOT!
WE'RE ON BOARD—NOW HIT IT!
AS MILTON CARRIED OUT D.D.'S ORDERS...
ODYSSEY
BETRAYED! BETRAYED!
HULL TEMPERATURE MUST BE UP TO 700°C., DARE. WITHOUT FORCE FIELD SUITS, WE'D BE FRIED TO A CRISP!
THE HEAT'S UNBEARABLE— SOMETHING'S GOTTA GIVE—ANY SECOND NOW!
DARE
AAAAAAAH!
SHE'S MOVING—BREAKING FREE. BUT... WHAT'S THAT NOISE?!
WE'RE BURNING A HALF MILE HOLE IN THE BIOG SHIP'S SIDE—AND IT'S SCREAMING!

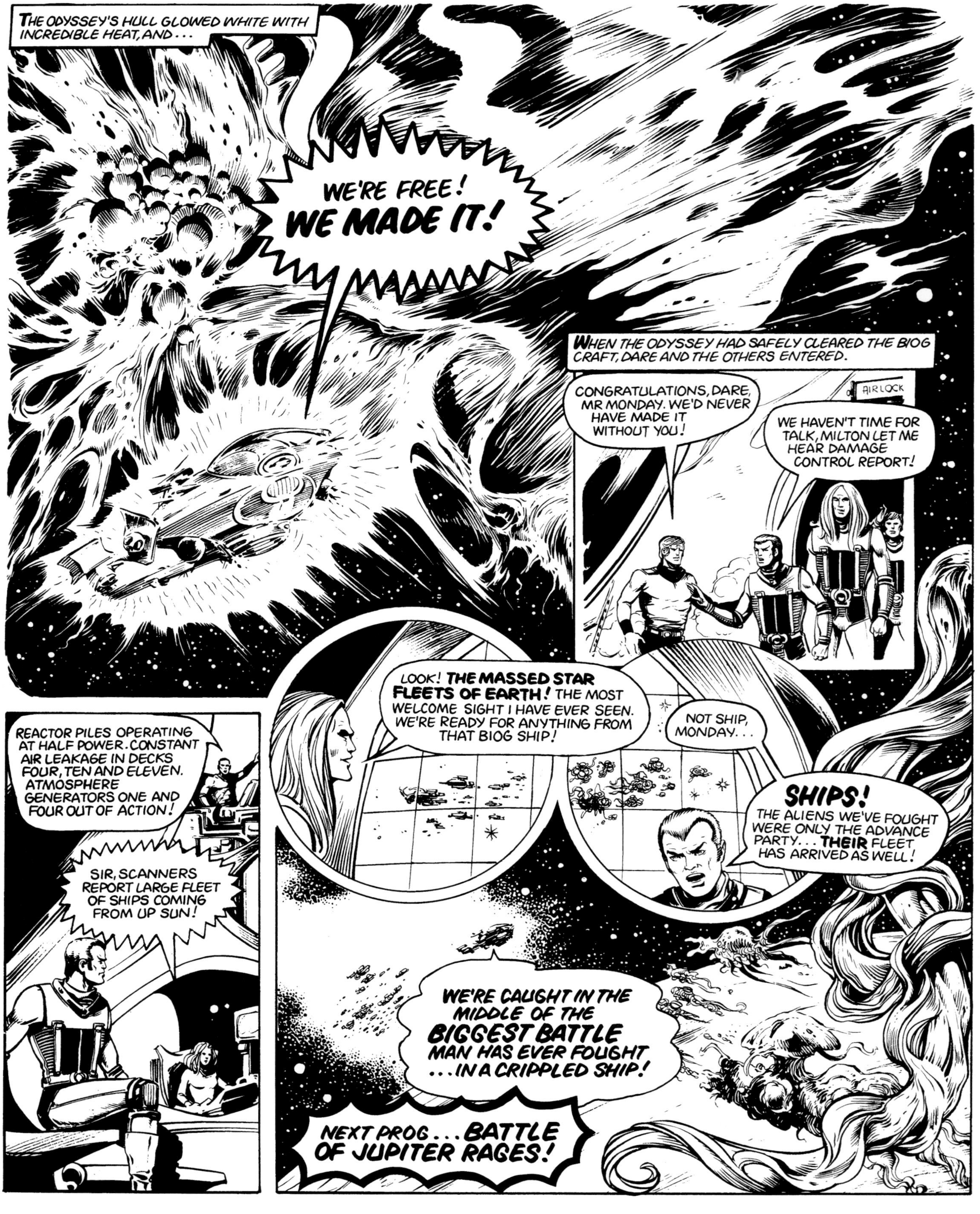
THE ODYSSEY'S HULL GLOWED WHITE WITH INCREDIBLE HEAT, AND...
WE'RE FREE! WE MADE IT!
WHEN THE ODYSSEY HAD SAFELY CLEARED THE BIOG CRAFT, DARE AND THE OTHERS ENTERED.
AIR LOCK
CONGRATULATIONS, DARE, MR MONDAY. WE'D NEVER HAVE MADE IT WITHOUT YOU!
WE HAVEN'T TIME FOR TALK, MILTON LET ME HEAR DAMAGE CONTROL REPORT!
REACTOR PILES OPERATING AT HALF POWER. CONSTANT AIR LEAKAGE IN DECKS FOUR, TEN AND ELEVEN. ATMOSPHERE GENERATORS ONE AND FOUR OUT OF ACTION!
SIR, SCANNERS REPORT LARGE FLEET OF SHIPS COMING FROM UP SUN!
LOOK! THE MASSED STAR FLEETS OF EARTH! THE MOST WELCOME SIGHT I HAVE EVER SEEN. WE'RE READY FOR ANYTHING FROM THAT BIOG SHIP!
NOT SHIP, MONDAY...
SHIPS! THE ALIENS WE'VE FOUGHT WERE ONLY THE ADVANCE PARTY... THEIR FLEET HAS ARRIVED AS WELL!
WE'RE CAUGHT IN THE MIDDLE OF THE BIGGEST BATTLE MAN HAS EVER FOUGHT ...IN A CRIPPLED SHIP!
NEXT PROG... BATTLE OF JUPITER RAGES!

DAN DARE

MY PART IN HIS REVIVAL
PART NINE

The first **Dan Dare** story concludes some 10 or 12 weeks later. By now, I've realized that the readers appreciate really wild SF which – most importantly - compensates for our poor quality paper. So I want the second story (*Hollow World*) to be even visually wilder and this was written by Steve Moore. There was a great vertical opening spread showing **Dan Dare** arriving at a London teleport station.

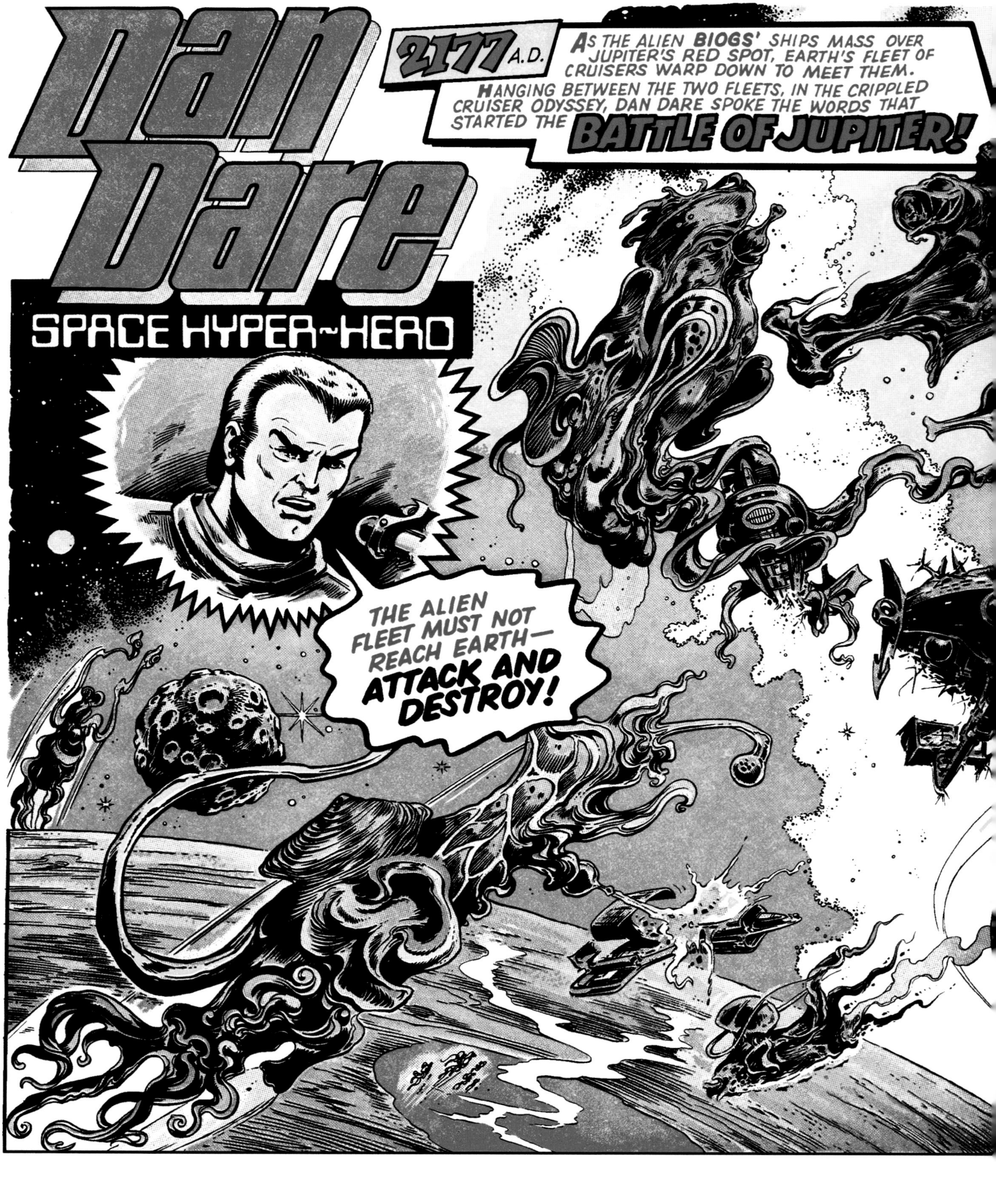
Dan Dare
SPACE HYPER~HERO
2177 A.D.
AS THE ALIEN BIOGS' SHIPS MASS OVER JUPITER'S RED SPOT, EARTH'S FLEET OF CRUISERS WARP DOWN TO MEET THEM.
HANGING BETWEEN THE TWO FLEETS, IN THE CRIPPLED CRUISER ODYSSEY, DAN DARE SPOKE THE WORDS THAT STARTED THE BATTLE OF JUPITER!
THE ALIEN FLEET MUST NOT REACH EARTH— ATTACK AND DESTROY!

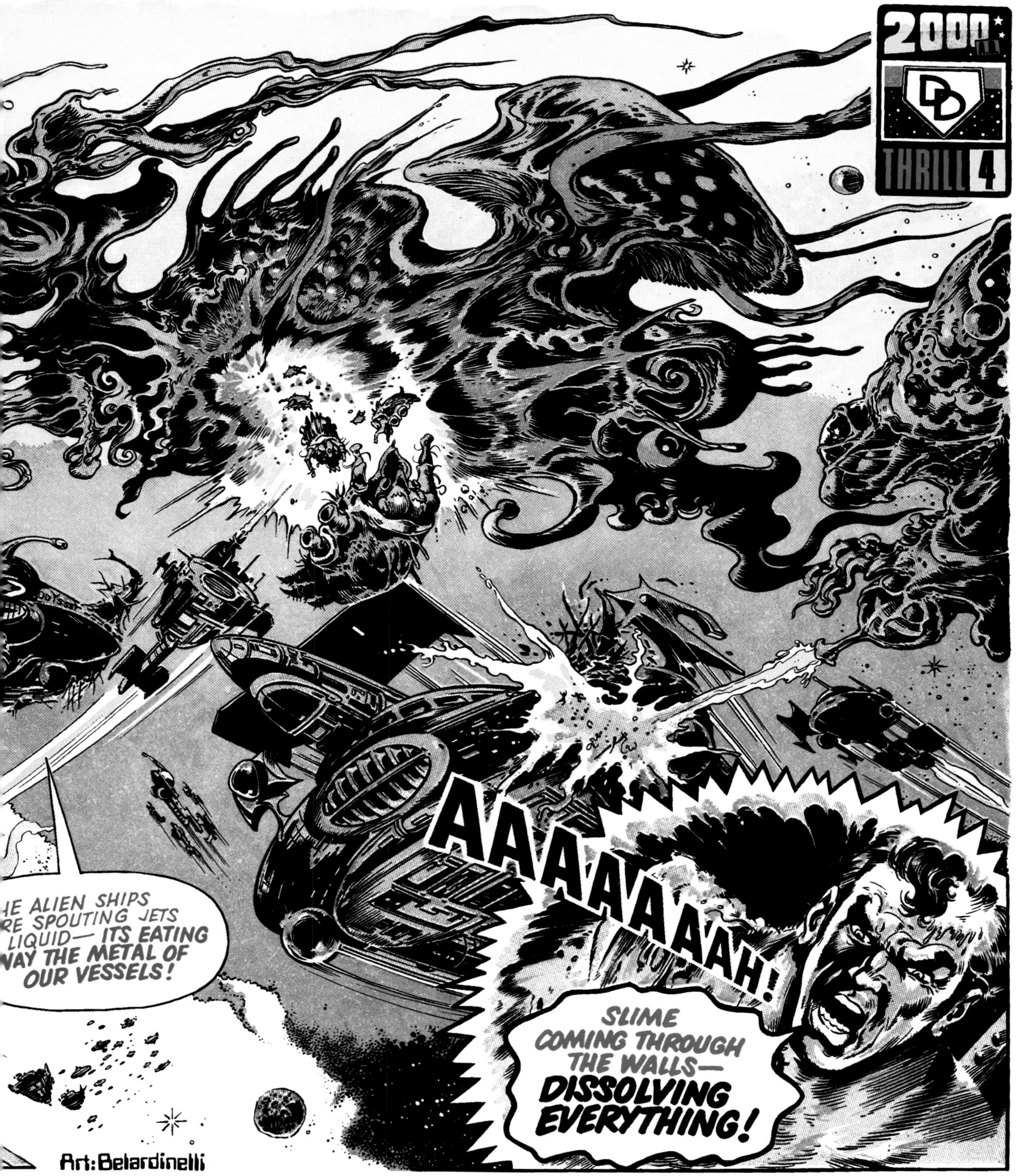
2000 A.D.
THRILL 4
HE ALIEN SHIPS
RE SPOUTING JETS
LIQUID— ITS EATING
WAY THE METAL OF
OUR VESSELS!
AAAAAAAAAH!
SLIME COMING THROUGH THE WALLS— DISSOLVING EVERYTHING!
Art: Belardinelli

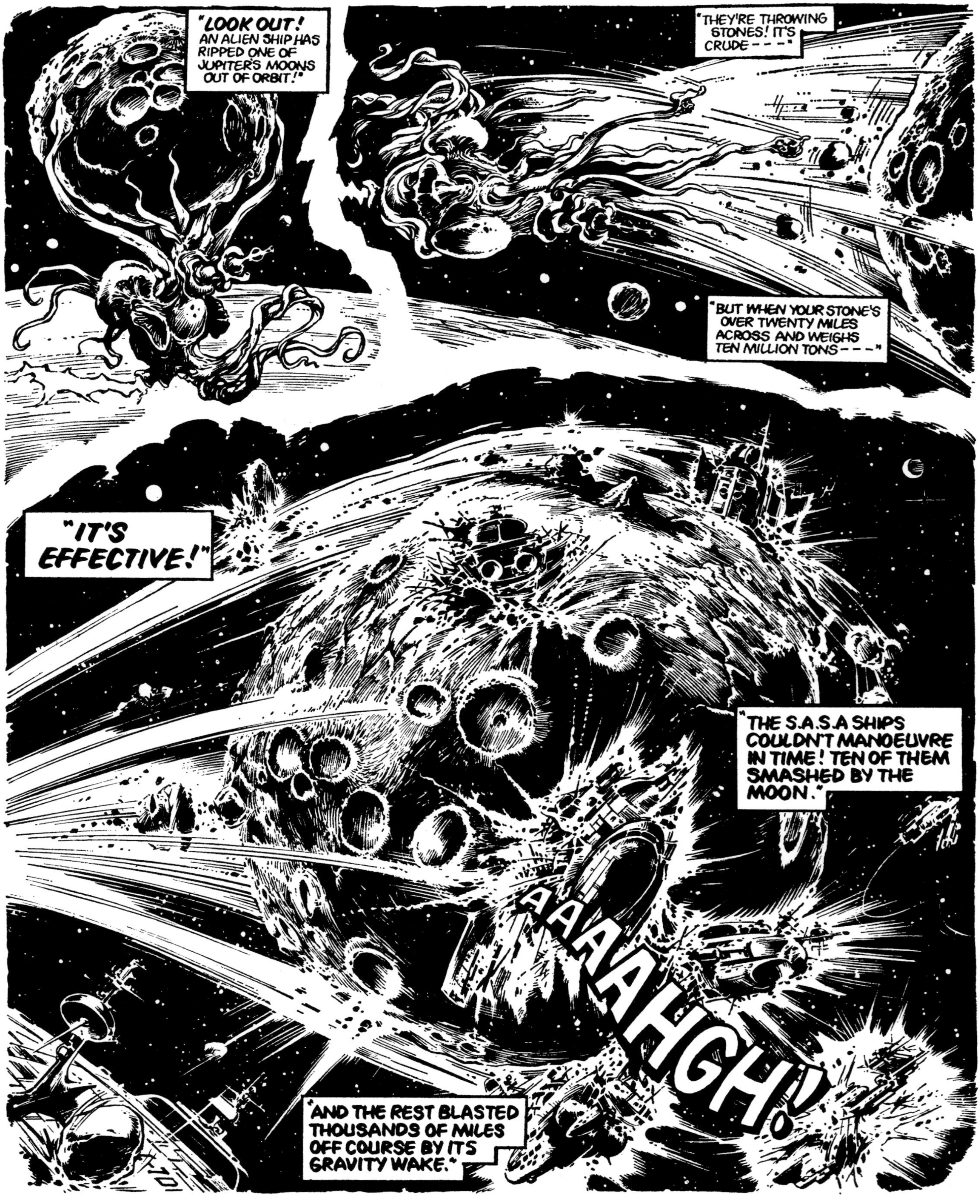
"LOOK OUT! AN ALIEN SHIP HAS RIPPED ONE OF JUPITER'S MOONS OUT OF ORBIT!"
"THEY'RE THROWING STONES! IT'S CRUDE---"
"BUT WHEN YOUR STONE'S OVER TWENTY MILES ACROSS AND WEIGHS TEN MILLION TONS---"
"IT'S EFFECTIVE!"
"THE S.A.S.A SHIPS COULDN'T MANOEUVRE IN TIME! TEN OF THEM SMASHED BY THE MOON."
AAAAAHGH!
"AND THE REST BLASTED THOUSANDS OF MILES OFF COURSE BY ITS GRAVITY WAKE."

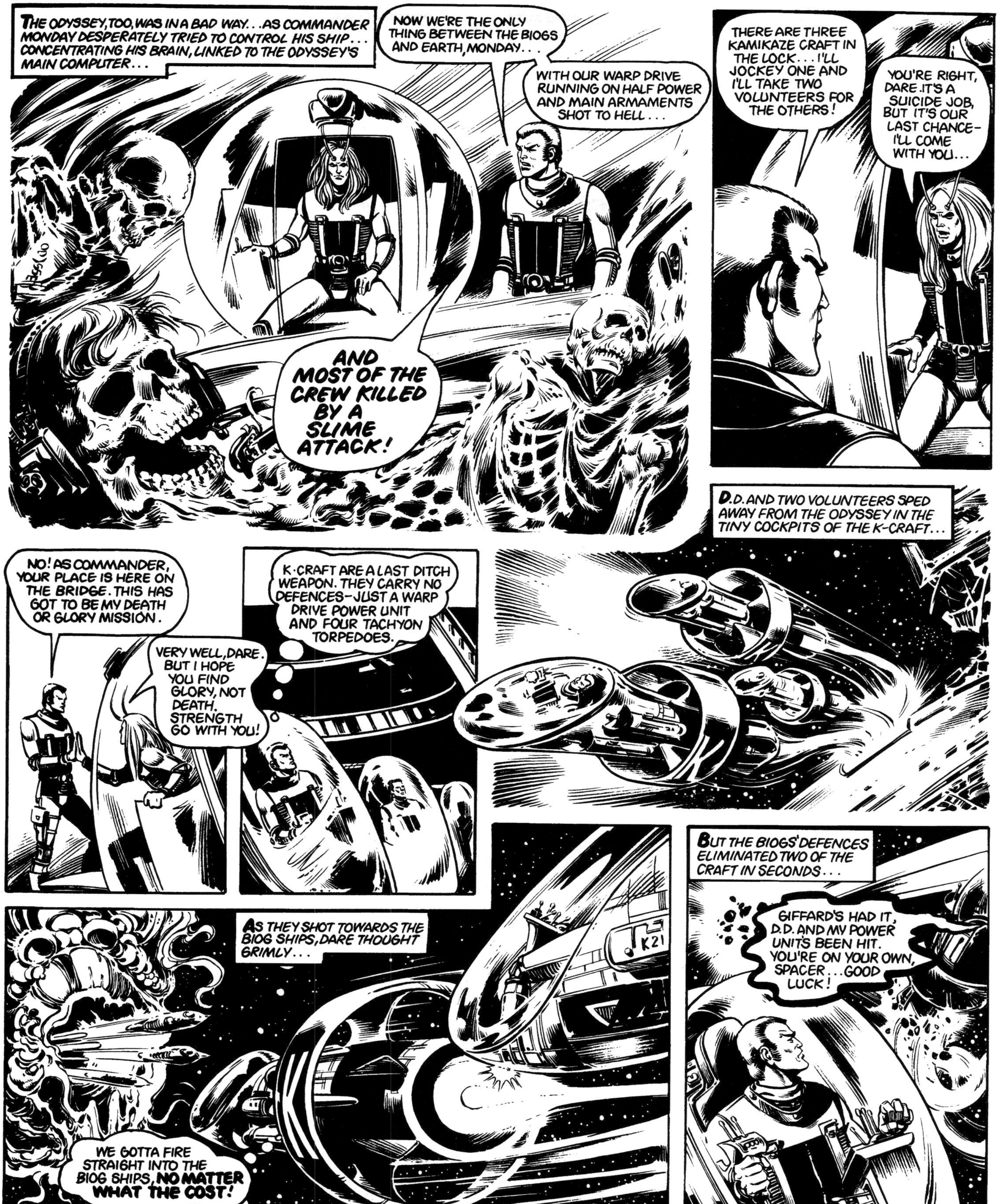

THE ODYSSEY, TOO, WAS IN A BAD WAY... AS COMMANDER MONDAY DESPERATELY TRIED TO CONTROL HIS SHIP... CONCENTRATING HIS BRAIN, LINKED TO THE ODYSSEY'S MAIN COMPUTER...
NOW WE'RE THE ONLY THING BETWEEN THE BIOGS AND EARTH, MONDAY...
WITH OUR WARP DRIVE RUNNING ON HALF POWER AND MAIN ARMAMENTS SHOT TO HELL...
AND MOST OF THE CREW KILLED BY A SLIME ATTACK!
THERE ARE THREE KAMIKAZE CRAFT IN THE LOCK... I'LL JOCKEY ONE AND I'LL TAKE TWO VOLUNTEERS FOR THE OTHERS!
YOU'RE RIGHT, DARE. IT'S A SUICIDE JOB, BUT IT'S OUR LAST CHANCE-I'LL COME WITH YOU...
NO! AS COMMANDER, YOUR PLACE IS HERE ON THE BRIDGE. THIS HAS GOT TO BE MY DEATH OR GLORY MISSION.
VERY WELL, DARE. BUT I HOPE YOU FIND GLORY, NOT DEATH. STRENGTH GO WITH YOU!
K-CRAFT ARE A LAST DITCH WEAPON. THEY CARRY NO DEFENCES-JUST A WARP DRIVE POWER UNIT AND FOUR TACHYON TORPEDOES.
D.D. AND TWO VOLUNTEERS SPED AWAY FROM THE ODYSSEY IN THE TINY COCKPITS OF THE K-CRAFT...
AS THEY SHOT TOWARDS THE BIOG SHIPS, DARE THOUGHT GRIMLY...
WE GOTTA FIRE STRAIGHT INTO THE BIOG SHIPS, NO MATTER WHAT THE COST!
K21
BUT THE BIOGS' DEFENCES ELIMINATED TWO OF THE CRAFT IN SECONDS...
GIFFARD'S HAD IT, D.D. AND MY POWER UNIT'S BEEN HIT. YOU'RE ON YOUR OWN, SPACER... GOOD LUCK!

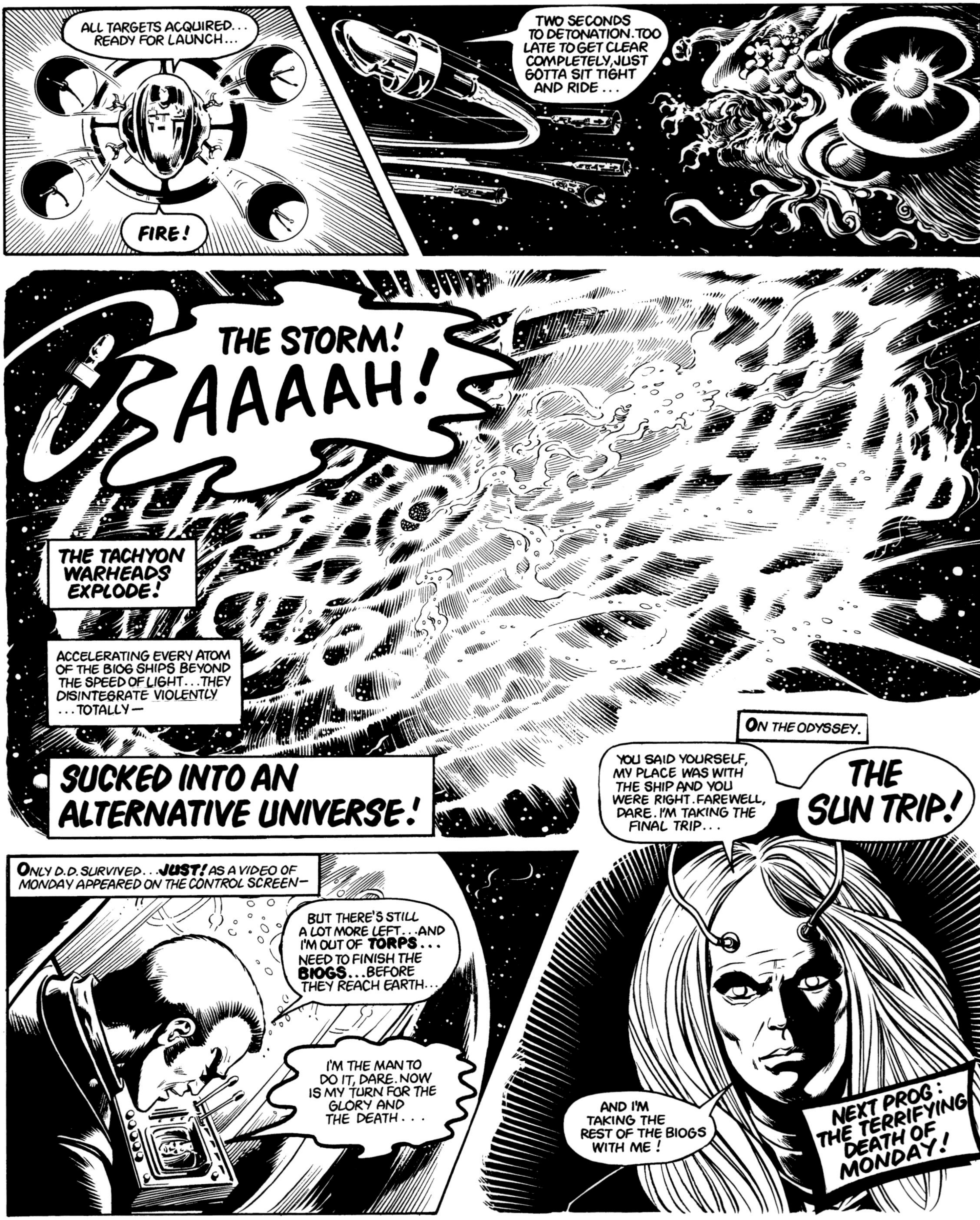

ALL TARGETS ACQUIRED... READY FOR LAUNCH...
FIRE!
TWO SECONDS TO DETONATION. TOO LATE TO GET CLEAR COMPLETELY, JUST GOTTA SIT TIGHT AND RIDE...
THE STORM!
AAAAH!
THE TACHYON WARHEADS EXPLODE!
ACCELERATING EVERY ATOM OF THE BIOG SHIPS BEYOND THE SPEED OF LIGHT... THEY DISINTEGRATE VIOLENTLY ... TOTALLY—
SUCKED INTO AN ALTERNATIVE UNIVERSE!
ONLY D.D. SURVIVED... JUST! AS A VIDEO OF MONDAY APPEARED ON THE CONTROL SCREEN—
BUT THERE'S STILL A LOT MORE LEFT... AND I'M OUT OF TORPS... NEED TO FINISH THE BIOGS... BEFORE THEY REACH EARTH...
I'M THE MAN TO DO IT, DARE. NOW IS MY TURN FOR THE GLORY AND THE DEATH...
ON THE ODYSSEY.
YOU SAID YOURSELF, MY PLACE WAS WITH THE SHIP AND YOU WERE RIGHT. FAREWELL, DARE. I'M TAKING THE FINAL TRIP...
THE SUN TRIP!
AND I'M TAKING THE REST OF THE BIOGS WITH ME!
NEXT PROG: THE TERRIFYING DEATH OF MONDAY!

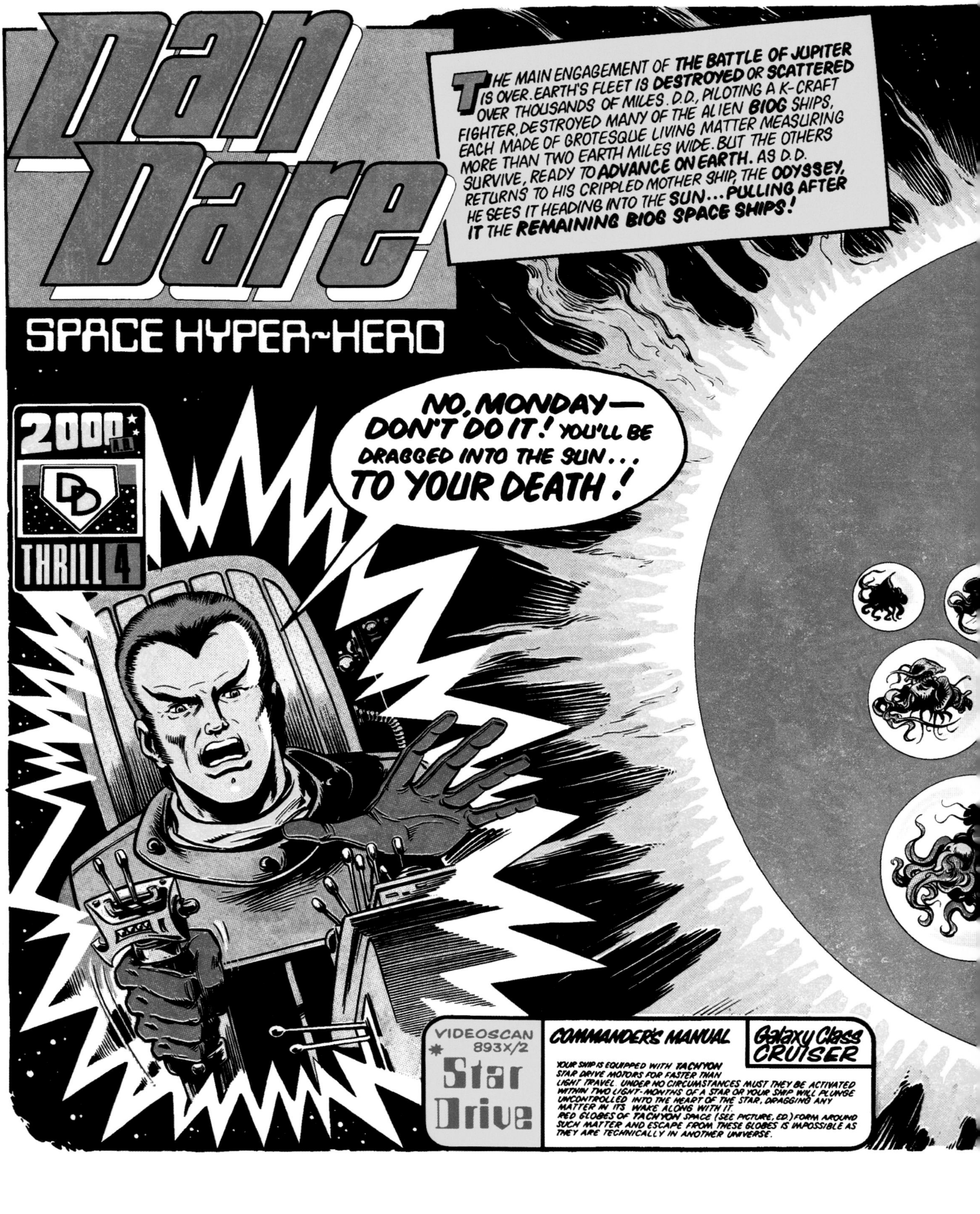
Dan Dare
SPACE HYPER~HERO
THE MAIN ENGAGEMENT OF THE BATTLE OF JUPITER IS OVER. EARTH'S FLEET IS DESTROYED OR SCATTERED OVER THOUSANDS OF MILES. D.D., PILOTING A K-CRAFT FIGHTER, DESTROYED MANY OF THE ALIEN BIOG SHIPS, EACH MADE OF GROTESQUE LIVING MATTER MEASURING MORE THAN TWO EARTH MILES WIDE. BUT THE OTHERS SURVIVE, READY TO ADVANCE ON EARTH. AS D.D. RETURNS TO HIS CRIPPLED MOTHER SHIP, THE ODYSSEY, HE SEES IT HEADING INTO THE SUN... PULLING AFTER IT THE REMAINING BIOG SPACE SHIPS!
2000 A.D.
DD
THRILL 4
NO, MONDAY— DON'T DO IT! YOU'LL BE DRAGGED INTO THE SUN... TO YOUR DEATH!
VIDEOSCAN 893X/2
Star Drive
COMMANDER'S MANUAL
Galaxy Class CRUISER
YOUR SHIP IS EQUIPPED WITH TACHYON STAR DRIVE MOTORS FOR FASTER THAN LIGHT TRAVEL. UNDER NO CIRCUMSTANCES MUST THEY BE ACTIVATED WITHIN TWO LIGHT-MONTHS OF A STAR OR YOUR SHIP WILL PLUNGE UNCONTROLLED INTO THE HEART OF THE STAR, DRAGGING ANY MATTER IN ITS WAKE ALONG WITH IT.
RED GLOBES OF TACHYON SPACE (SEE PICTURE, ED.) FORM AROUND SUCH MATTER AND ESCAPE FROM THESE GLOBES IS IMPOSSIBLE AS THEY ARE TECHNICALLY IN ANOTHER UNIVERSE.

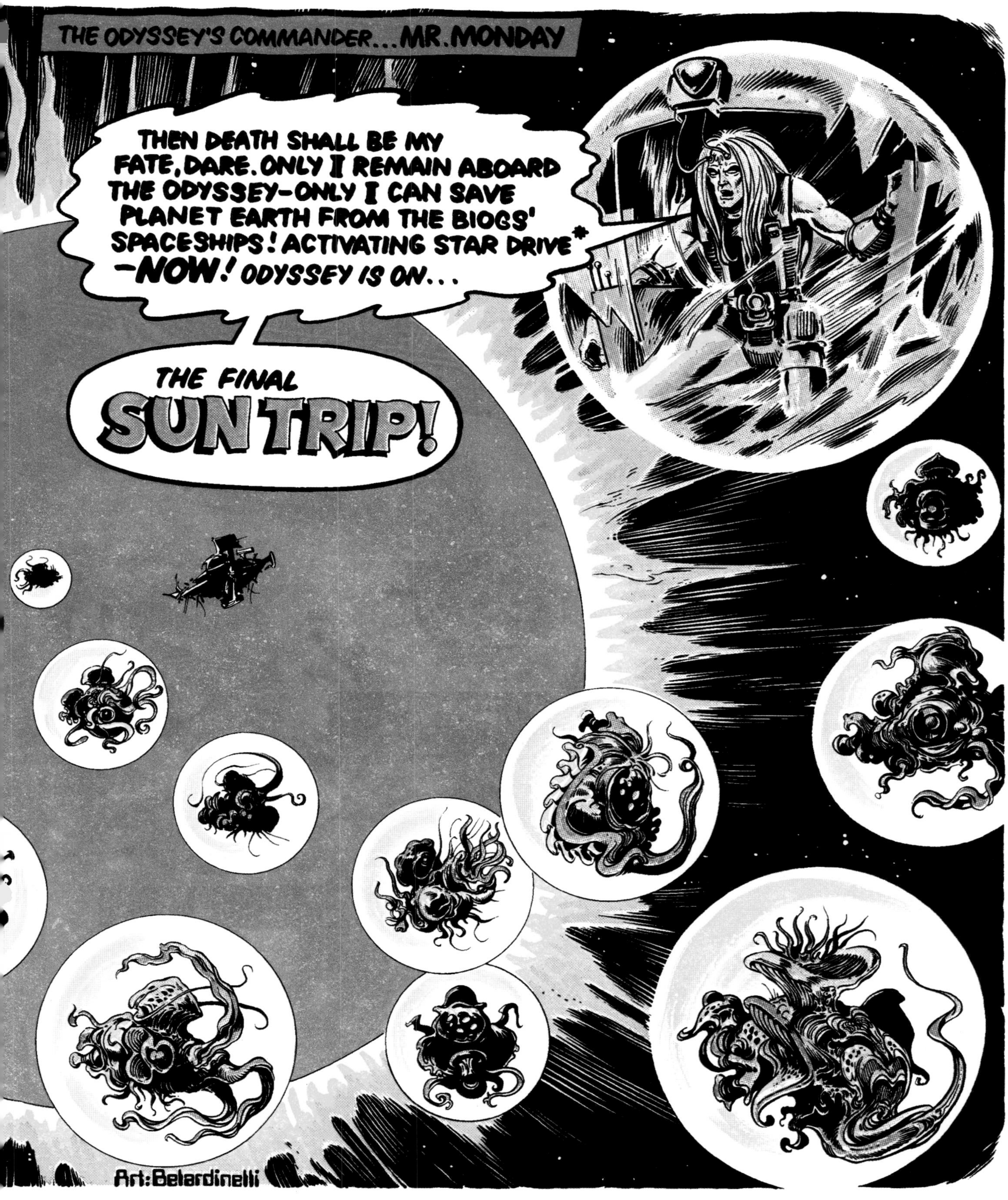
THE ODYSSEY'S COMMANDER... MR. MONDAY
THEN DEATH SHALL BE MY FATE, DARE. ONLY I REMAIN ABOARD THE ODYSSEY–ONLY I CAN SAVE PLANET EARTH FROM THE BIOGS' SPACESHIPS! ACTIVATING STAR DRIVE* –NOW! ODYSSEY IS ON...
THE FINAL SUN TRIP!
Art: Belardinelli

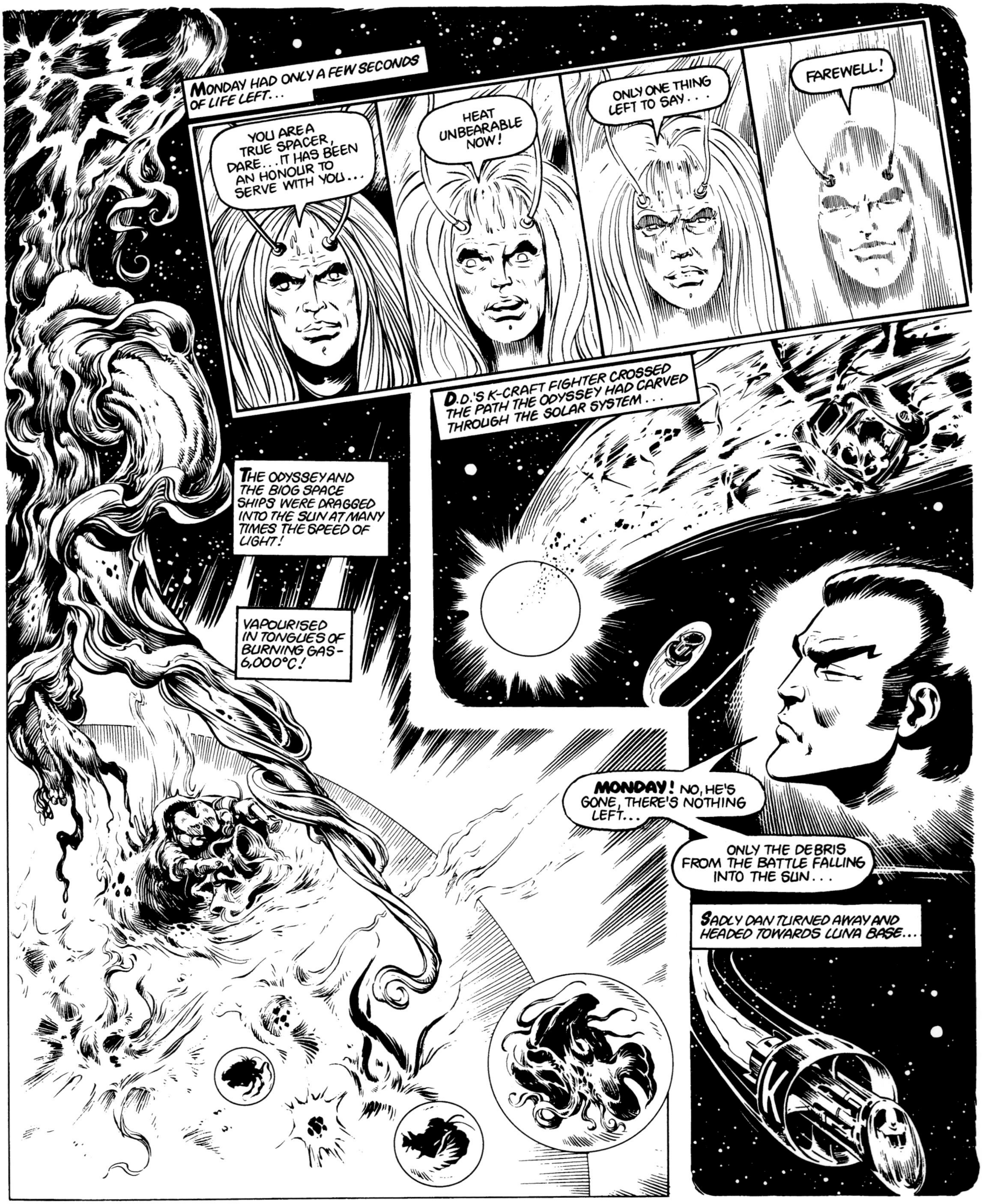
MONDAY HAD ONLY A FEW SECONDS OF LIFE LEFT...
YOU ARE A TRUE SPACER, DARE... IT HAS BEEN AN HONOUR TO SERVE WITH YOU...
HEAT UNBEARABLE NOW!
ONLY ONE THING LEFT TO SAY...
FAREWELL!
D.D.'S K-CRAFT FIGHTER CROSSED THE PATH THE ODYSSEY HAD CARVED THROUGH THE SOLAR SYSTEM...
THE ODYSSEY AND THE BIOG SPACE SHIPS WERE DRAGGED INTO THE SUN AT MANY TIMES THE SPEED OF LIGHT!
VAPOURISED IN TONGUES OF BURNING GAS - 6,000°C!
MONDAY! NO, HE'S GONE, THERE'S NOTHING LEFT...
ONLY THE DEBRIS FROM THE BATTLE FALLING INTO THE SUN...
SADLY DAN TURNED AWAY AND HEADED TOWARDS LUNA BASE...

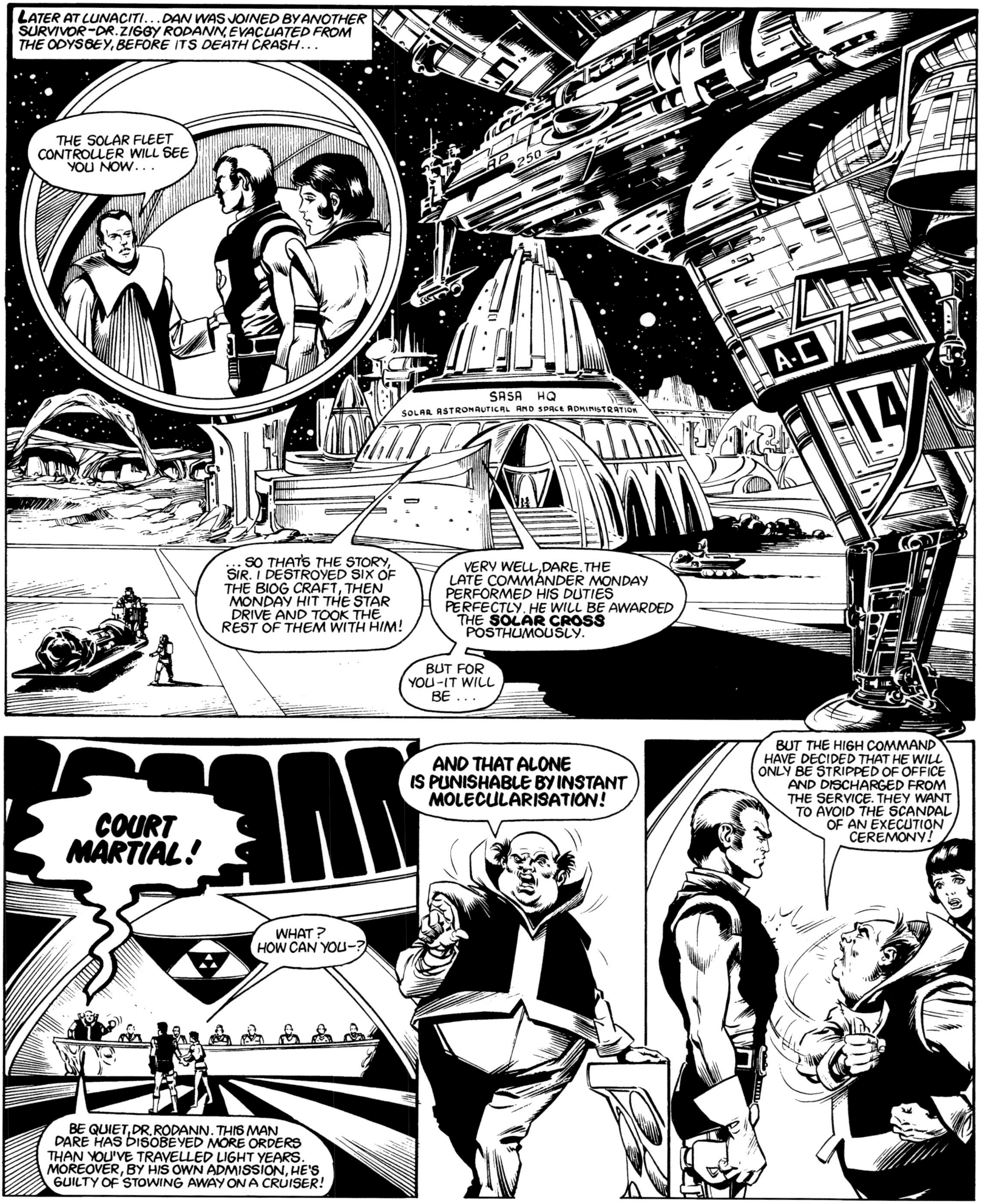
LATER AT LUNACITI... DAN WAS JOINED BY ANOTHER SURVIVOR-DR. ZIGGY RODANN, EVACUATED FROM THE ODYSSEY, BEFORE ITS DEATH CRASH...
THE SOLAR FLEET CONTROLLER WILL SEE YOU NOW...
AP 250
SASA HQ
SOLAR ASTRONAUTICAL AND SPACE ADMINISTRATION
A-C
14
...SO THAT'S THE STORY, SIR. I DESTROYED SIX OF THE BIOG CRAFT, THEN MONDAY HIT THE STAR DRIVE AND TOOK THE REST OF THEM WITH HIM!
VERY WELL, DARE. THE LATE COMMANDER MONDAY PERFORMED HIS DUTIES PERFECTLY. HE WILL BE AWARDED THE SOLAR CROSS POSTHUMOUSLY.
BUT FOR YOU-IT WILL BE...
COURT MARTIAL!
WHAT? HOW CAN YOU-?
BE QUIET, DR. RODANN. THIS MAN DARE HAS DISOBEYED MORE ORDERS THAN YOU'VE TRAVELLED LIGHT YEARS. MOREOVER, BY HIS OWN ADMISSION, HE'S GUILTY OF STOWING AWAY ON A CRUISER!
AND THAT ALONE IS PUNISHABLE BY INSTANT MOLECULARISATION!
BUT THE HIGH COMMAND HAVE DECIDED THAT HE WILL ONLY BE STRIPPED OF OFFICE AND DISCHARGED FROM THE SERVICE. THEY WANT TO AVOID THE SCANDAL OF AN EXECUTION CEREMONY!

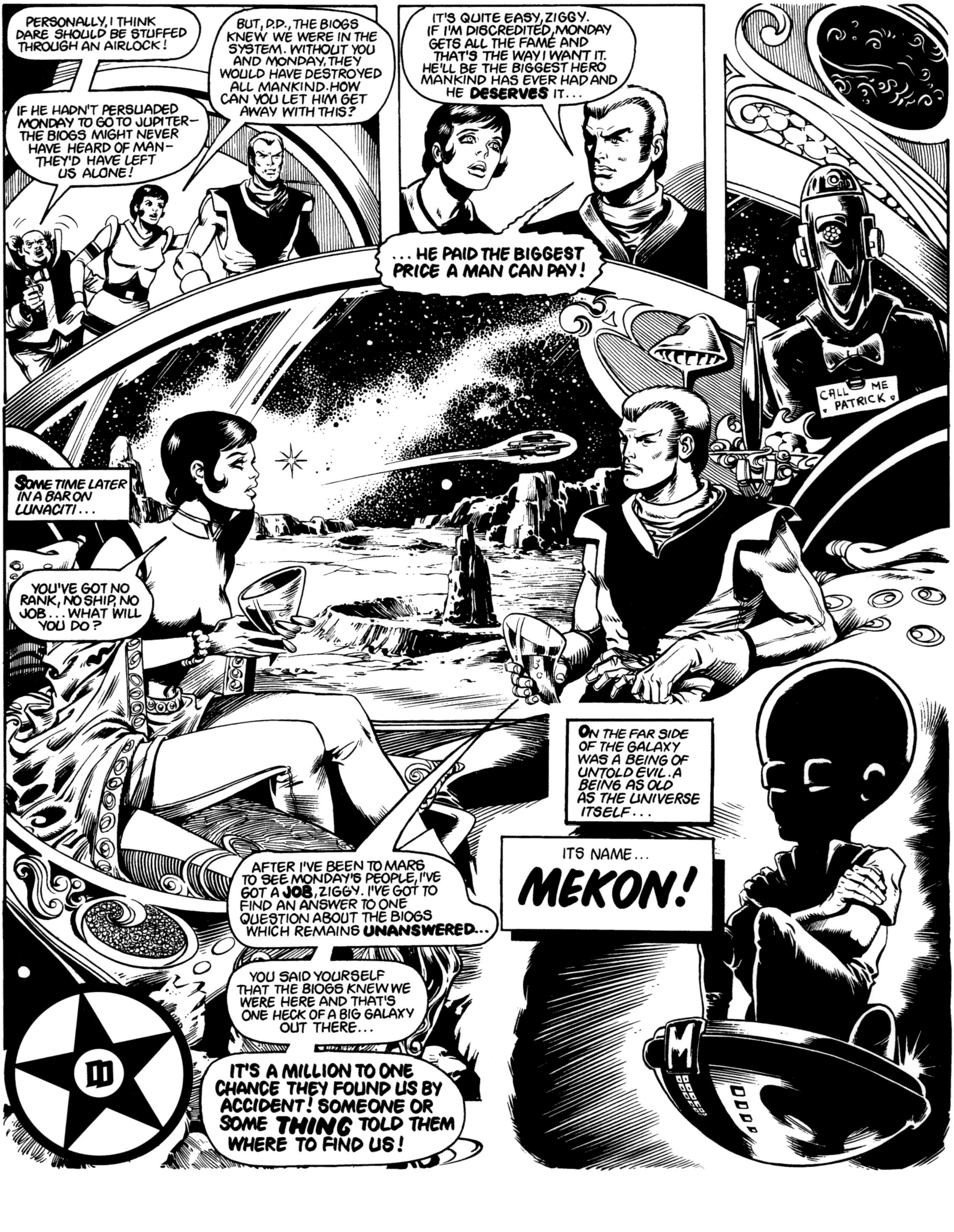
PERSONALLY, I THINK DARE SHOULD BE STUFFED THROUGH AN AIRLOCK!
IF HE HADN'T PERSUADED MONDAY TO GO TO JUPITER–THE BIOGS MIGHT NEVER HAVE HEARD OF MAN–THEY'D HAVE LEFT US ALONE!
BUT, D.D., THE BIOGS KNEW WE WERE IN THE SYSTEM. WITHOUT YOU AND MONDAY, THEY WOULD HAVE DESTROYED ALL MANKIND. HOW CAN YOU LET HIM GET AWAY WITH THIS?
IT'S QUITE EASY, ZIGGY. IF I'M DISCREDITED, MONDAY GETS ALL THE FAME AND THAT'S THE WAY I WANT IT. HE'LL BE THE BIGGEST HERO MANKIND HAS EVER HAD AND HE DESERVES IT...
... HE PAID THE BIGGEST PRICE A MAN CAN PAY!
SOME TIME LATER IN A BAR ON LUNACITI...
CALL ME PATRICK
YOU'VE GOT NO RANK, NO SHIP, NO JOB... WHAT WILL YOU DO?
AFTER I'VE BEEN TO MARS TO SEE MONDAY'S PEOPLE, I'VE GOT A JOB, ZIGGY. I'VE GOT TO FIND AN ANSWER TO ONE QUESTION ABOUT THE BIOGS WHICH REMAINS UNANSWERED...
YOU SAID YOURSELF THAT THE BIOGS KNEW WE WERE HERE AND THAT'S ONE HECK OF A BIG GALAXY OUT THERE...
IT'S A MILLION TO ONE CHANCE THEY FOUND US BY ACCIDENT! SOMEONE OR SOME THING TOLD THEM WHERE TO FIND US!
ON THE FAR SIDE OF THE GALAXY WAS A BEING OF UNTOLD EVIL. A BEING AS OLD AS THE UNIVERSE ITSELF...
ITS NAME...
MEKON!

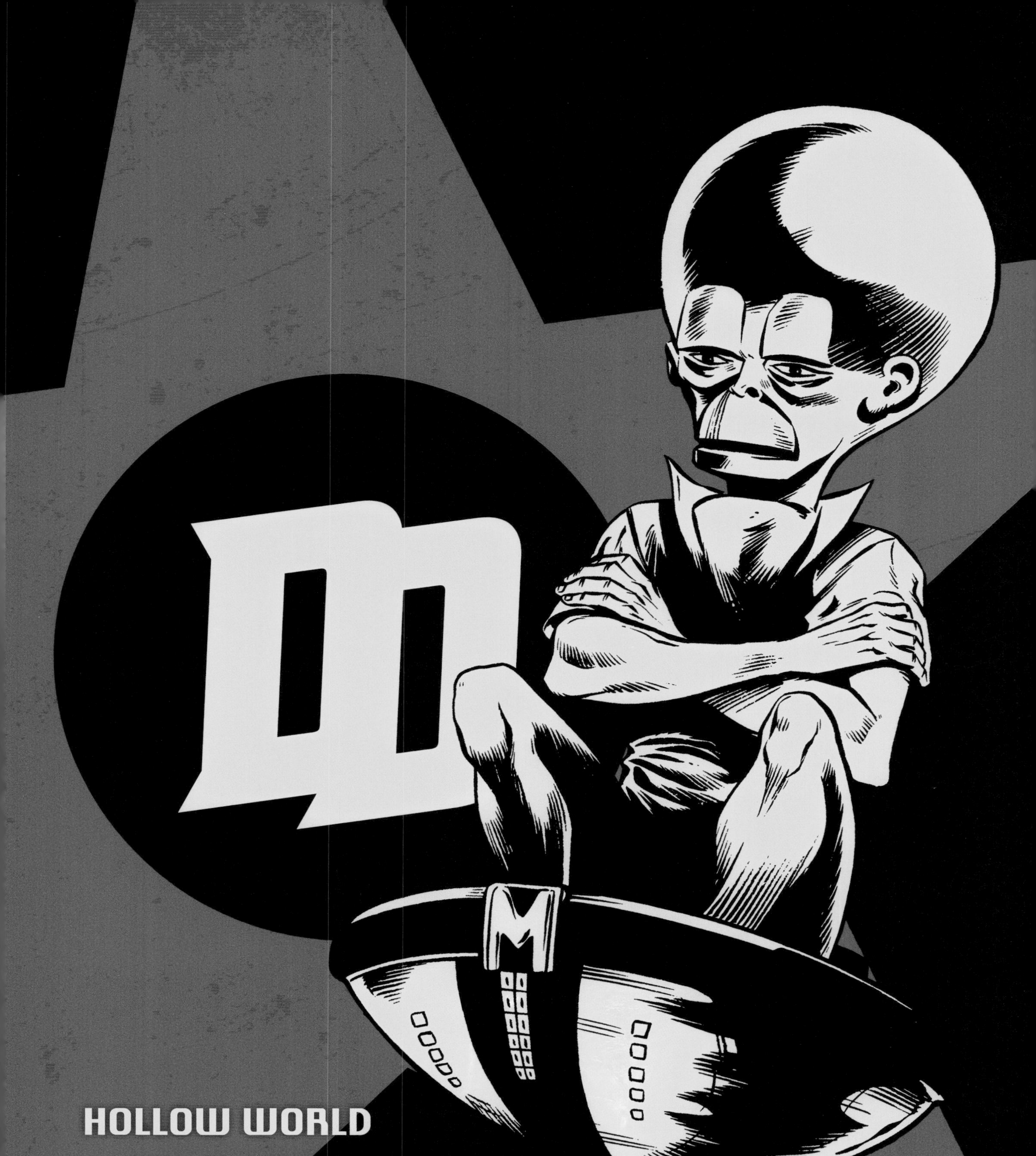

HOLLOW WORLD

Script: Steve Moore
Art: Massimo Belardinelli
Letters: Peter Knight, John Aldrich, Bill Nuttall, J Swain, Tony Jacob, Jack Potter, Tom Frame

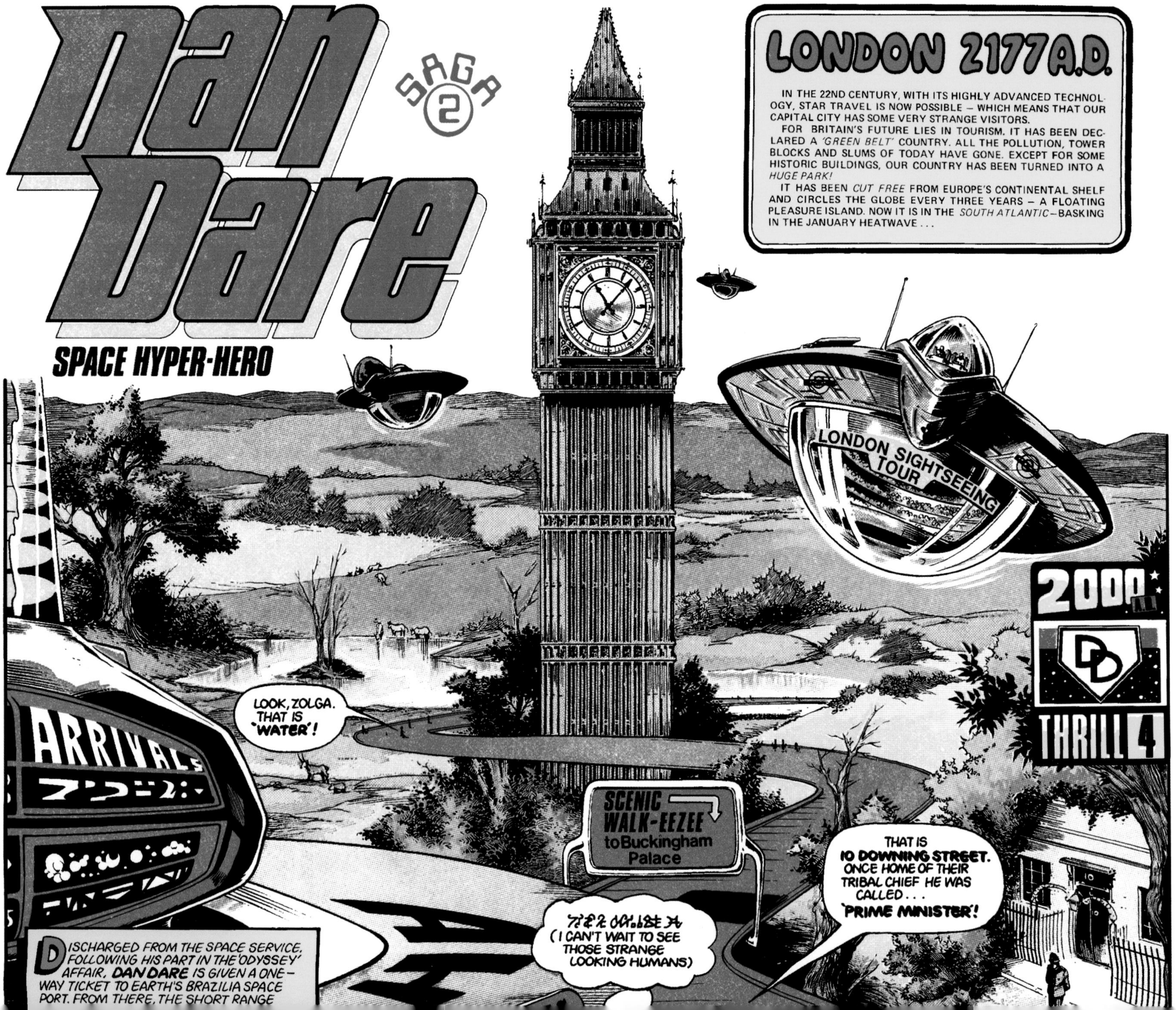
DAN DARE
SAGA 2
SPACE HYPER-HERO
LONDON 2177 A.D.
IN THE 22ND CENTURY, WITH ITS HIGHLY ADVANCED TECHNOLOGY, STAR TRAVEL IS NOW POSSIBLE – WHICH MEANS THAT OUR CAPITAL CITY HAS SOME VERY STRANGE VISITORS.
FOR BRITAIN'S FUTURE LIES IN TOURISM. IT HAS BEEN DECLARED A *'GREEN BELT'* COUNTRY. ALL THE POLLUTION, TOWER BLOCKS AND SLUMS OF TODAY HAVE GONE. EXCEPT FOR SOME HISTORIC BUILDINGS, OUR COUNTRY HAS BEEN TURNED INTO A *HUGE PARK!*
IT HAS BEEN *CUT FREE* FROM EUROPE'S CONTINENTAL SHELF AND CIRCLES THE GLOBE EVERY THREE YEARS – A FLOATING PLEASURE ISLAND. NOW IT IS IN THE *SOUTH ATLANTIC* – BASKING IN THE JANUARY HEATWAVE . . .
LONDON SIGHTSEEING TOUR
2000 A.D.
THRILL 4
ARRIVALS
LOOK, ZOLGA. THAT IS 'WATER'!
SCENIC WALK-EEZEE to Buckingham Palace
(I CAN'T WAIT TO SEE THOSE STRANGE LOOKING HUMANS)
THAT IS 10 DOWNING STREET. ONCE HOME OF THEIR TRIBAL CHIEF HE WAS CALLED . . . 'PRIME MINISTER'!
DISCHARGED FROM THE SPACE SERVICE, FOLLOWING HIS PART IN THE 'ODYSSEY' AFFAIR, DAN DARE IS GIVEN A ONE-WAY TICKET TO EARTH'S BRAZILIA SPACE PORT. FROM THERE, THE SHORT RANGE

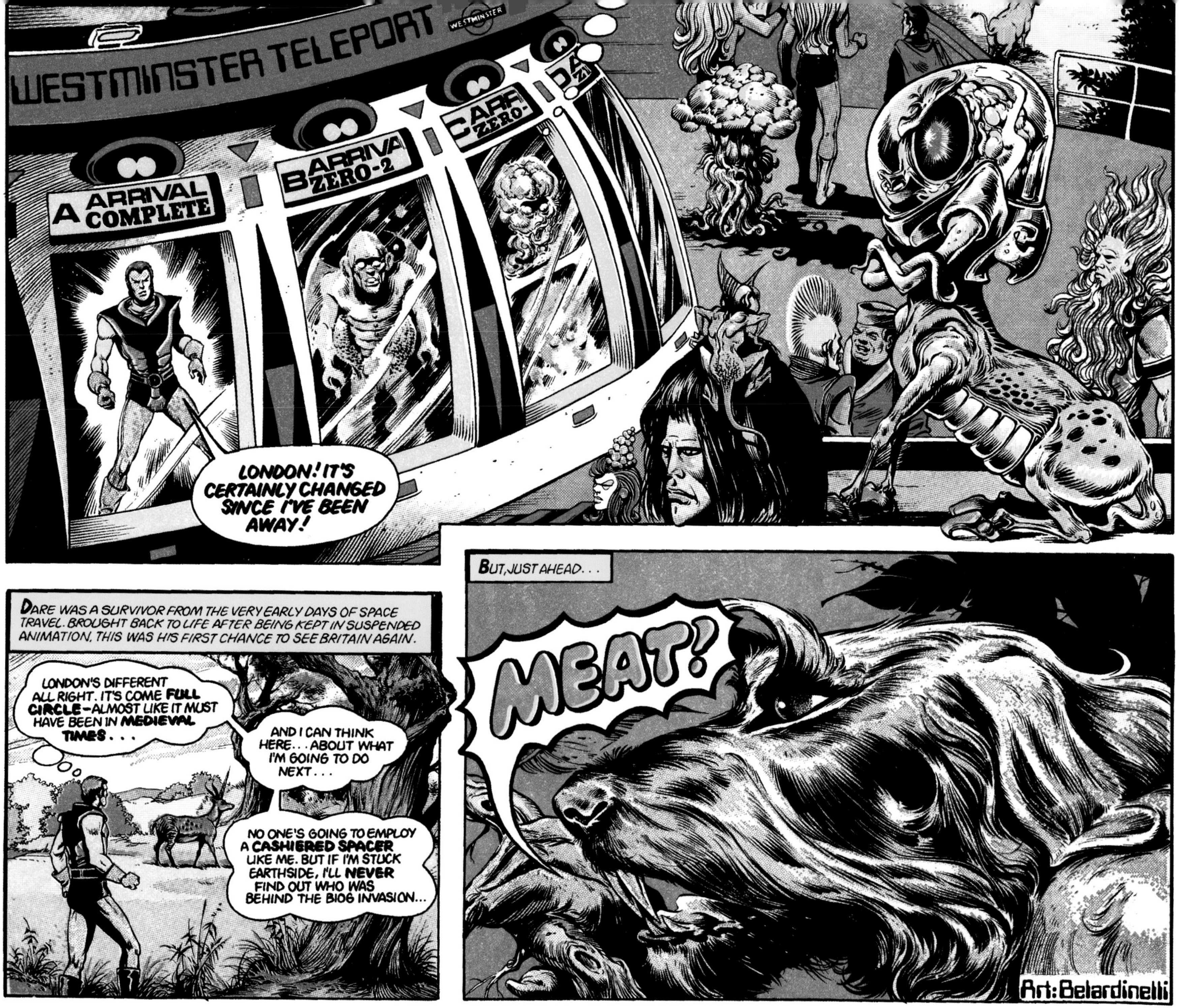
WESTMINSTER TELEPORT
WESTMINSTER
A ARRIVAL COMPLETE
B ARRIVA ZERO-2
C ARR ZERO-
LONDON! IT'S CERTAINLY CHANGED SINCE I'VE BEEN AWAY!
DARE WAS A SURVIVOR FROM THE VERY EARLY DAYS OF SPACE TRAVEL. BROUGHT BACK TO LIFE AFTER BEING KEPT IN SUSPENDED ANIMATION, THIS WAS HIS FIRST CHANCE TO SEE BRITAIN AGAIN.
LONDON'S DIFFERENT ALL RIGHT. IT'S COME FULL CIRCLE—ALMOST LIKE IT MUST HAVE BEEN IN MEDIEVAL TIMES . . .
AND I CAN THINK HERE. . . ABOUT WHAT I'M GOING TO DO NEXT . . .
NO ONE'S GOING TO EMPLOY A CASHIERED SPACER LIKE ME. BUT IF I'M STUCK EARTHSIDE, I'LL NEVER FIND OUT WHO WAS BEHIND THE BIOG INVASION...
BUT, JUST AHEAD . . .
MEAT!
Art: Belardinelli

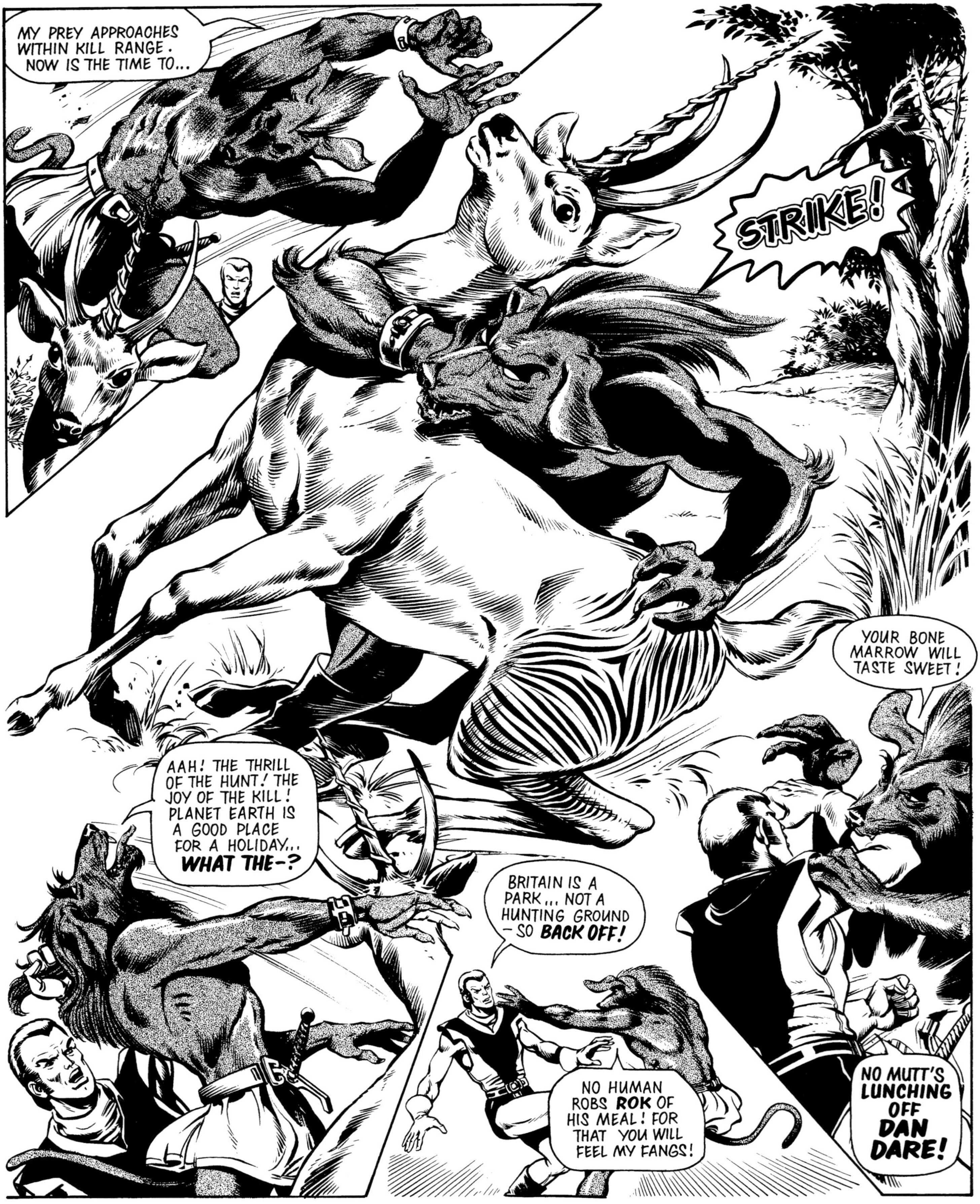

MY PREY APPROACHES WITHIN KILL RANGE. NOW IS THE TIME TO...
STRIKE!
YOUR BONE MARROW WILL TASTE SWEET!
AAH! THE THRILL OF THE HUNT! THE JOY OF THE KILL! PLANET EARTH IS A GOOD PLACE FOR A HOLIDAY... WHAT THE-?
BRITAIN IS A PARK... NOT A HUNTING GROUND - SO BACK OFF!
NO HUMAN ROBS ROK OF HIS MEAL! FOR THAT YOU WILL FEEL MY FANGS!
NO MUTT'S LUNCHING OFF DAN DARE!

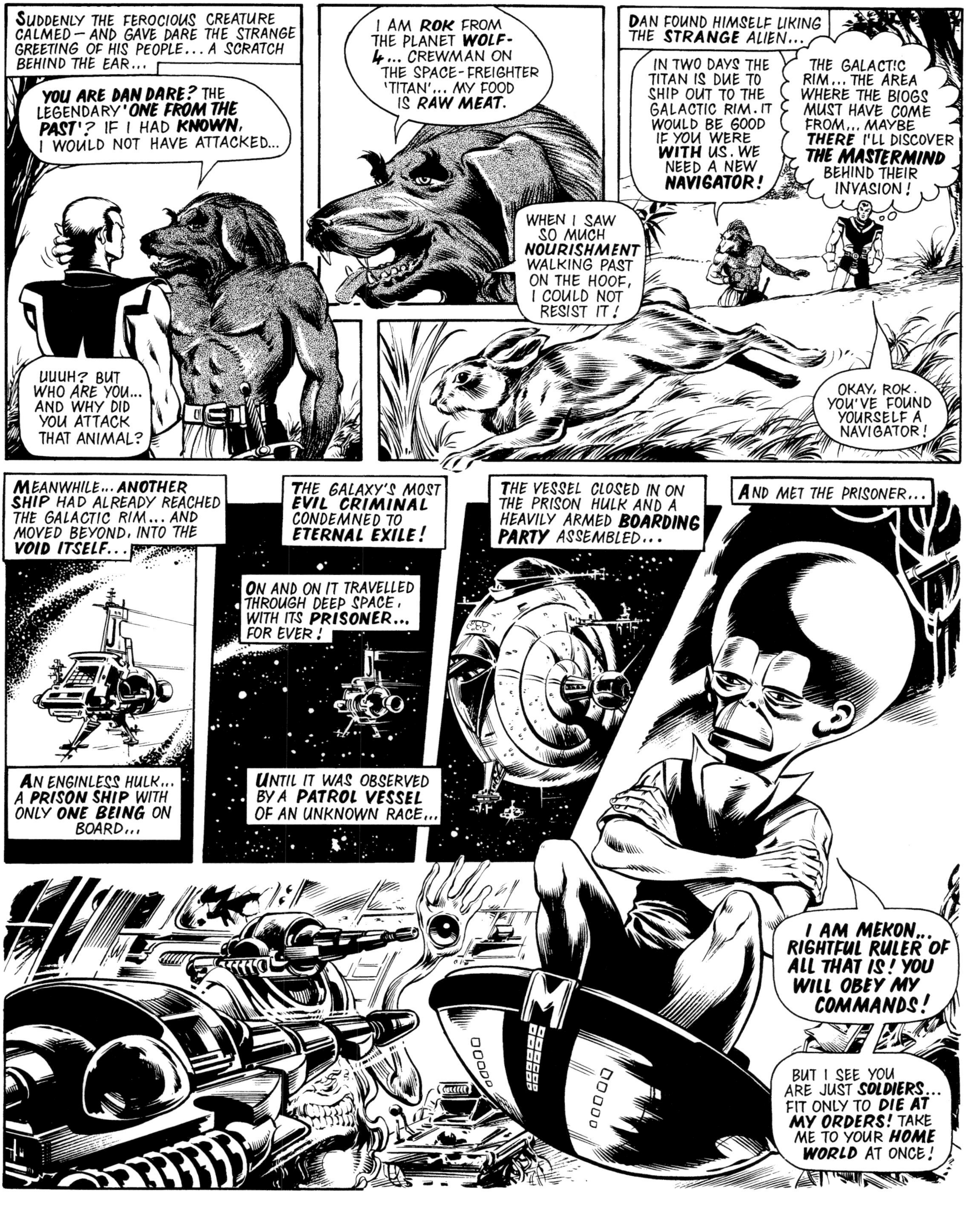
SUDDENLY THE FEROCIOUS CREATURE CALMED — AND GAVE DARE THE STRANGE GREETING OF HIS PEOPLE... A SCRATCH BEHIND THE EAR...
YOU ARE DAN DARE? THE LEGENDARY 'ONE FROM THE PAST'? IF I HAD KNOWN, I WOULD NOT HAVE ATTACKED...
UUUH? BUT WHO ARE YOU... AND WHY DID YOU ATTACK THAT ANIMAL?
I AM ROK FROM THE PLANET WOLF-4... CREWMAN ON THE SPACE-FREIGHTER 'TITAN'... MY FOOD IS RAW MEAT.
WHEN I SAW SO MUCH NOURISHMENT WALKING PAST ON THE HOOF, I COULD NOT RESIST IT!
DAN FOUND HIMSELF LIKING THE STRANGE ALIEN...
IN TWO DAYS THE TITAN IS DUE TO SHIP OUT TO THE GALACTIC RIM. IT WOULD BE GOOD IF YOU WERE WITH US. WE NEED A NEW NAVIGATOR!
THE GALACTIC RIM... THE AREA WHERE THE BIOGS MUST HAVE COME FROM... MAYBE THERE I'LL DISCOVER THE MASTERMIND BEHIND THEIR INVASION!
OKAY, ROK. YOU'VE FOUND YOURSELF A NAVIGATOR!
MEANWHILE... ANOTHER SHIP HAD ALREADY REACHED THE GALACTIC RIM... AND MOVED BEYOND, INTO THE VOID ITSELF...
AN ENGINLESS HULK... A PRISON SHIP WITH ONLY ONE BEING ON BOARD...
THE GALAXY'S MOST EVIL CRIMINAL CONDEMNED TO ETERNAL EXILE!
ON AND ON IT TRAVELLED THROUGH DEEP SPACE, WITH ITS PRISONER... FOR EVER!
UNTIL IT WAS OBSERVED BY A PATROL VESSEL OF AN UNKNOWN RACE...
THE VESSEL CLOSED IN ON THE PRISON HULK AND A HEAVILY ARMED BOARDING PARTY ASSEMBLED...
AND MET THE PRISONER...
I AM MEKON... RIGHTFUL RULER OF ALL THAT IS! YOU WILL OBEY MY COMMANDS!
BUT I SEE YOU ARE JUST SOLDIERS... FIT ONLY TO DIE AT MY ORDERS! TAKE ME TO YOUR HOME WORLD AT ONCE!

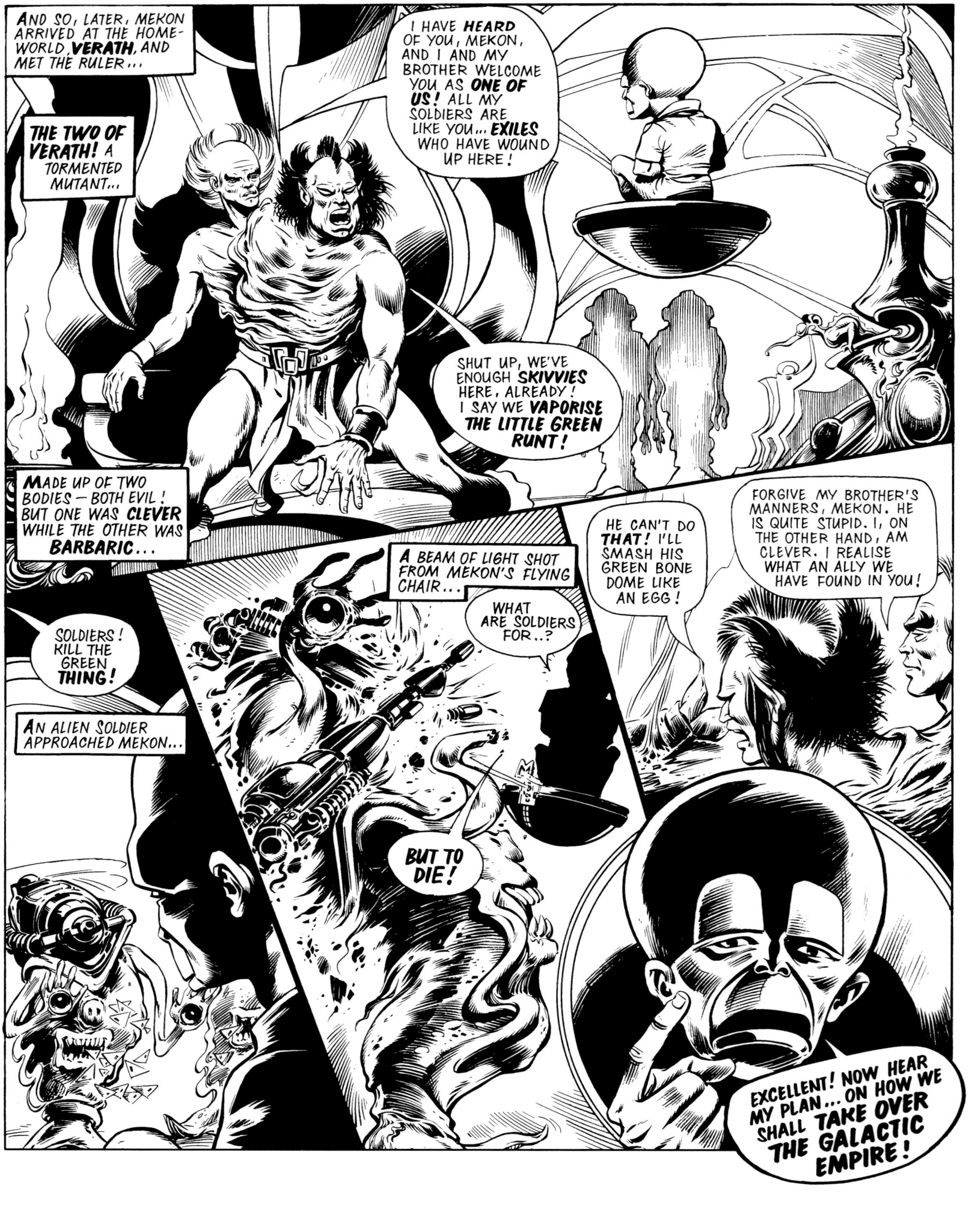

AND SO, LATER, MEKON ARRIVED AT THE HOME-WORLD, VERATH, AND MET THE RULER...
I HAVE HEARD OF YOU, MEKON, AND I AND MY BROTHER WELCOME YOU AS ONE OF US! ALL MY SOLDIERS ARE LIKE YOU... EXILES WHO HAVE WOUND UP HERE!
THE TWO OF VERATH! A TORMENTED MUTANT...
SHUT UP, WE'VE ENOUGH SKIVVIES HERE, ALREADY! I SAY WE VAPORISE THE LITTLE GREEN RUNT!
MADE UP OF TWO BODIES — BOTH EVIL! BUT ONE WAS CLEVER WHILE THE OTHER WAS BARBARIC...
SOLDIERS! KILL THE GREEN THING!
AN ALIEN SOLDIER APPROACHED MEKON...
A BEAM OF LIGHT SHOT FROM MEKON'S FLYING CHAIR...
WHAT ARE SOLDIERS FOR..?
BUT TO DIE!
HE CAN'T DO THAT! I'LL SMASH HIS GREEN BONE DOME LIKE AN EGG!
FORGIVE MY BROTHER'S MANNERS, MEKON. HE IS QUITE STUPID. I, ON THE OTHER HAND, AM CLEVER. I REALISE WHAT AN ALLY WE HAVE FOUND IN YOU!
EXCELLENT! NOW HEAR MY PLAN... ON HOW WE SHALL TAKE OVER THE GALACTIC EMPIRE!

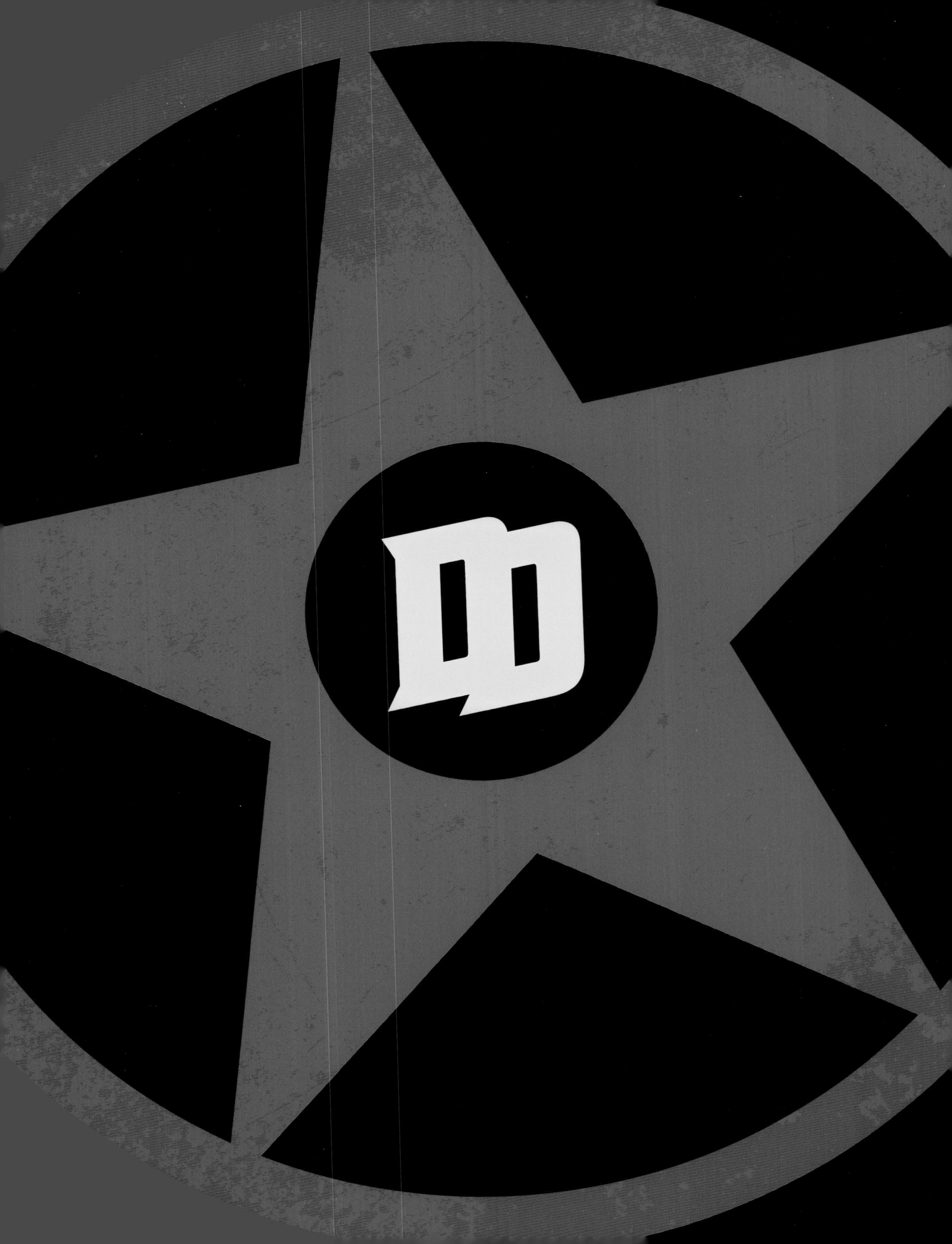

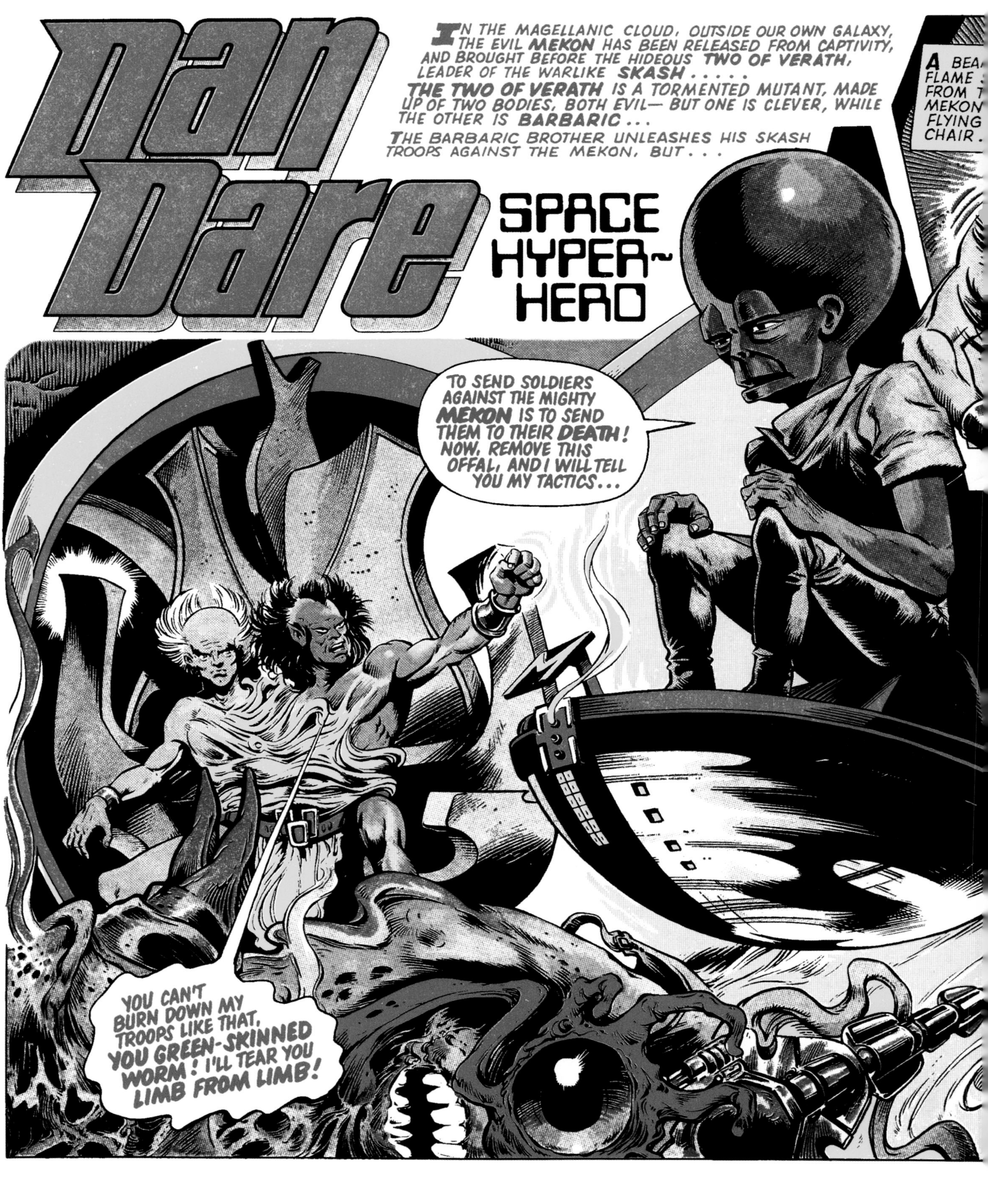

Dan Dare
SPACE HYPER~HERO
IN THE MAGELLANIC CLOUD, OUTSIDE OUR OWN GALAXY, THE EVIL MEKON HAS BEEN RELEASED FROM CAPTIVITY, AND BROUGHT BEFORE THE HIDEOUS TWO OF VERATH, LEADER OF THE WARLIKE SKASH . . . . .
THE TWO OF VERATH IS A TORMENTED MUTANT, MADE UP OF TWO BODIES, BOTH EVIL— BUT ONE IS CLEVER, WHILE THE OTHER IS BARBARIC . . .
THE BARBARIC BROTHER UNLEASHES HIS SKASH TROOPS AGAINST THE MEKON, BUT . . .
TO SEND SOLDIERS AGAINST THE MIGHTY MEKON IS TO SEND THEM TO THEIR DEATH! NOW, REMOVE THIS OFFAL, AND I WILL TELL YOU MY TACTICS...
YOU CAN'T BURN DOWN MY TROOPS LIKE THAT, YOU GREEN-SKINNED WORM! I'LL TEAR YOU LIMB FROM LIMB!

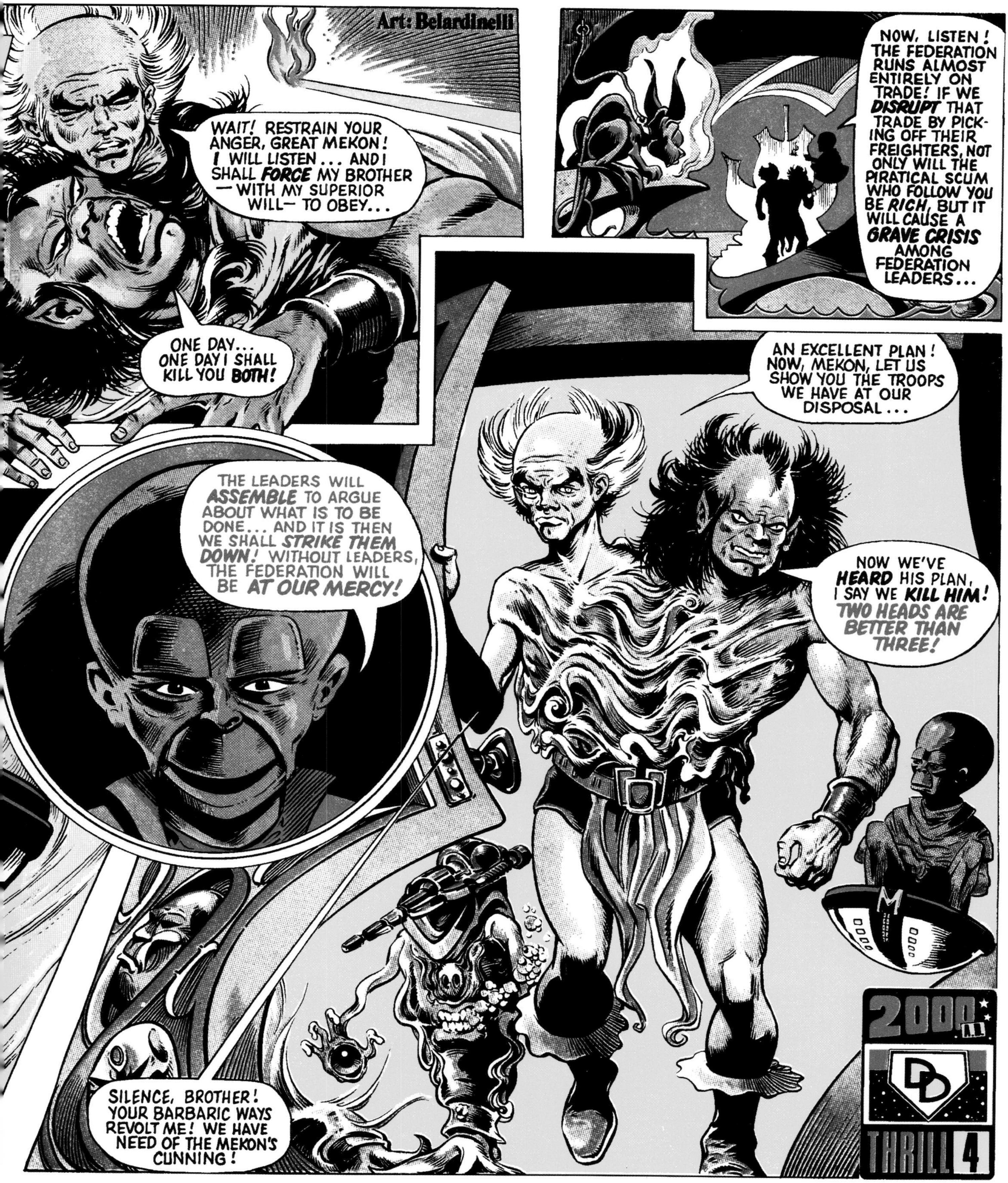
Art: Belardinelli
WAIT! RESTRAIN YOUR ANGER, GREAT MEKON! I WILL LISTEN... AND I SHALL FORCE MY BROTHER — WITH MY SUPERIOR WILL— TO OBEY...
ONE DAY... ONE DAY I SHALL KILL YOU BOTH!
NOW, LISTEN! THE FEDERATION RUNS ALMOST ENTIRELY ON TRADE! IF WE DISRUPT THAT TRADE BY PICKING OFF THEIR FREIGHTERS, NOT ONLY WILL THE PIRATICAL SCUM WHO FOLLOW YOU BE RICH, BUT IT WILL CAUSE A GRAVE CRISIS AMONG FEDERATION LEADERS...
AN EXCELLENT PLAN! NOW, MEKON, LET US SHOW YOU THE TROOPS WE HAVE AT OUR DISPOSAL...
THE LEADERS WILL ASSEMBLE TO ARGUE ABOUT WHAT IS TO BE DONE... AND IT IS THEN WE SHALL STRIKE THEM DOWN! WITHOUT LEADERS, THE FEDERATION WILL BE AT OUR MERCY!
NOW WE'VE HEARD HIS PLAN, I SAY WE KILL HIM! TWO HEADS ARE BETTER THAN THREE!
SILENCE, BROTHER! YOUR BARBARIC WAYS REVOLT ME! WE HAVE NEED OF THE MEKON'S CUNNING!
2000 A.D.
THRILL 4

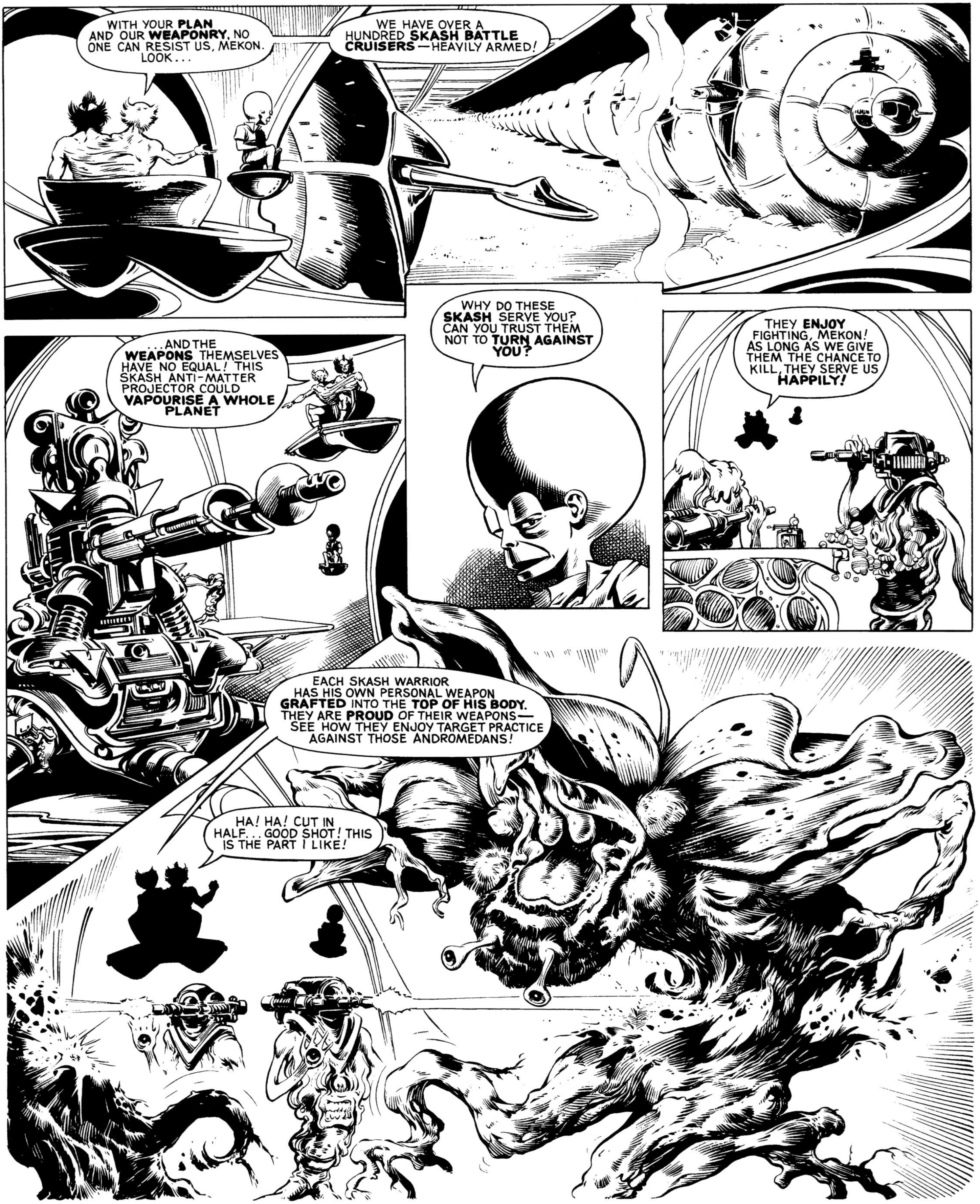

WITH YOUR PLAN AND OUR WEAPONRY, NO ONE CAN RESIST US, MEKON. LOOK...
WE HAVE OVER A HUNDRED SKASH BATTLE CRUISERS—HEAVILY ARMED!
...AND THE WEAPONS THEMSELVES HAVE NO EQUAL! THIS SKASH ANTI-MATTER PROJECTOR COULD VAPOURISE A WHOLE PLANET
WHY DO THESE SKASH SERVE YOU? CAN YOU TRUST THEM NOT TO TURN AGAINST YOU?
THEY ENJOY FIGHTING, MEKON! AS LONG AS WE GIVE THEM THE CHANCE TO KILL, THEY SERVE US HAPPILY!
EACH SKASH WARRIOR HAS HIS OWN PERSONAL WEAPON GRAFTED INTO THE TOP OF HIS BODY. THEY ARE PROUD OF THEIR WEAPONS— SEE HOW THEY ENJOY TARGET PRACTICE AGAINST THOSE ANDROMEDANS!
HA! HA! CUT IN HALF... GOOD SHOT! THIS IS THE PART I LIKE!

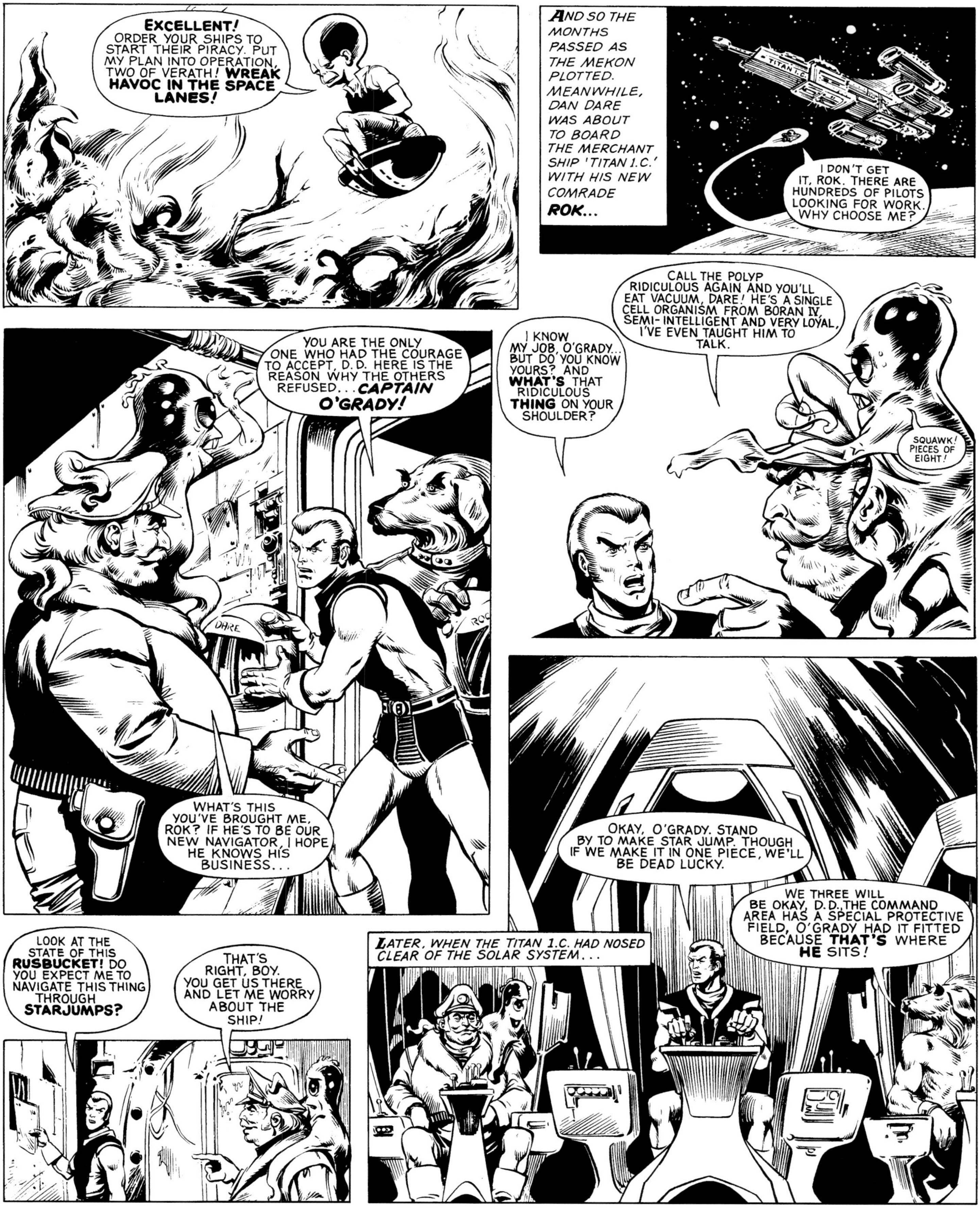
EXCELLENT! ORDER YOUR SHIPS TO START THEIR PIRACY. PUT MY PLAN INTO OPERATION, TWO OF VERATH! WREAK HAVOC IN THE SPACE LANES!
AND SO THE MONTHS PASSED AS THE MEKON PLOTTED. MEANWHILE, DAN DARE WAS ABOUT TO BOARD THE MERCHANT SHIP 'TITAN 1.C.' WITH HIS NEW COMRADE ROK...
I DON'T GET IT, ROK. THERE ARE HUNDREDS OF PILOTS LOOKING FOR WORK. WHY CHOOSE ME?
YOU ARE THE ONLY ONE WHO HAD THE COURAGE TO ACCEPT, D.D. HERE IS THE REASON WHY THE OTHERS REFUSED... CAPTAIN O'GRADY!
WHAT'S THIS YOU'VE BROUGHT ME, ROK? IF HE'S TO BE OUR NEW NAVIGATOR, I HOPE HE KNOWS HIS BUSINESS...
I KNOW MY JOB, O'GRADY... BUT DO YOU KNOW YOURS? AND WHAT'S THAT RIDICULOUS THING ON YOUR SHOULDER?
CALL THE POLYP RIDICULOUS AGAIN AND YOU'LL EAT VACUUM, DARE! HE'S A SINGLE CELL ORGANISM FROM BORAN IV, SEMI-INTELLIGENT AND VERY LOYAL, I'VE EVEN TAUGHT HIM TO TALK.
SQUAWK! PIECES OF EIGHT!
LOOK AT THE STATE OF THIS RUSBUCKET! DO YOU EXPECT ME TO NAVIGATE THIS THING THROUGH STARJUMPS?
THAT'S RIGHT, BOY. YOU GET US THERE AND LET ME WORRY ABOUT THE SHIP!
LATER, WHEN THE TITAN 1.C. HAD NOSED CLEAR OF THE SOLAR SYSTEM...
OKAY, O'GRADY. STAND BY TO MAKE STAR JUMP. THOUGH IF WE MAKE IT IN ONE PIECE, WE'LL BE DEAD LUCKY.
WE THREE WILL BE OKAY, D.D. THE COMMAND AREA HAS A SPECIAL PROTECTIVE FIELD, O'GRADY HAD IT FITTED BECAUSE THAT'S WHERE HE SITS!

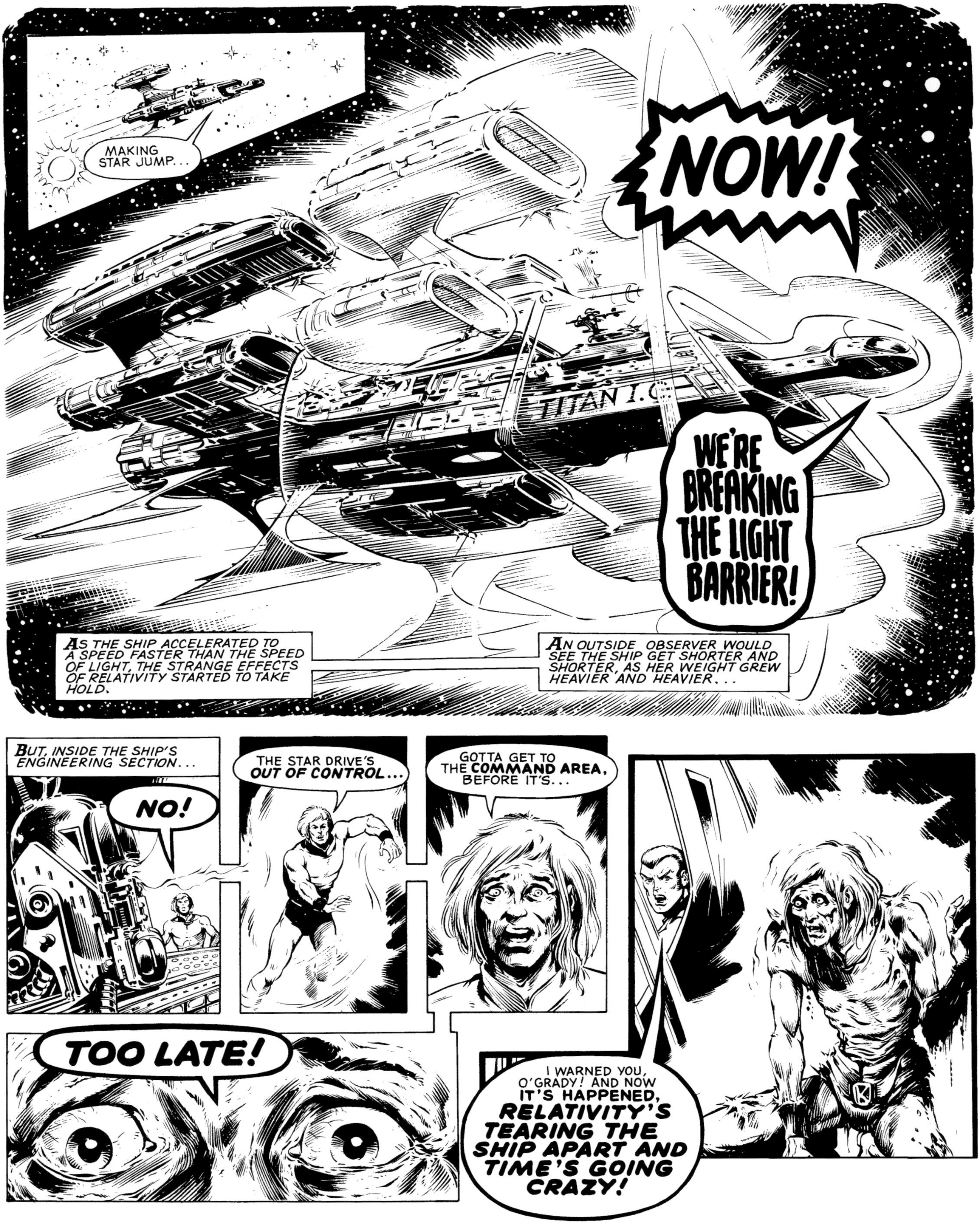
MAKING STAR JUMP...
NOW!
TITAN I.C.
WE'RE BREAKING THE LIGHT BARRIER!
AS THE SHIP ACCELERATED TO A SPEED FASTER THAN THE SPEED OF LIGHT, THE STRANGE EFFECTS OF RELATIVITY STARTED TO TAKE HOLD.
AN OUTSIDE OBSERVER WOULD SEE THE SHIP GET SHORTER AND SHORTER, AS HER WEIGHT GREW HEAVIER AND HEAVIER...
BUT, INSIDE THE SHIP'S ENGINEERING SECTION...
NO!
THE STAR DRIVE'S OUT OF CONTROL...
GOTTA GET TO THE COMMAND AREA, BEFORE IT'S...
TOO LATE!
I WARNED YOU, O'GRADY! AND NOW IT'S HAPPENED, RELATIVITY'S TEARING THE SHIP APART AND TIME'S GOING CRAZY!

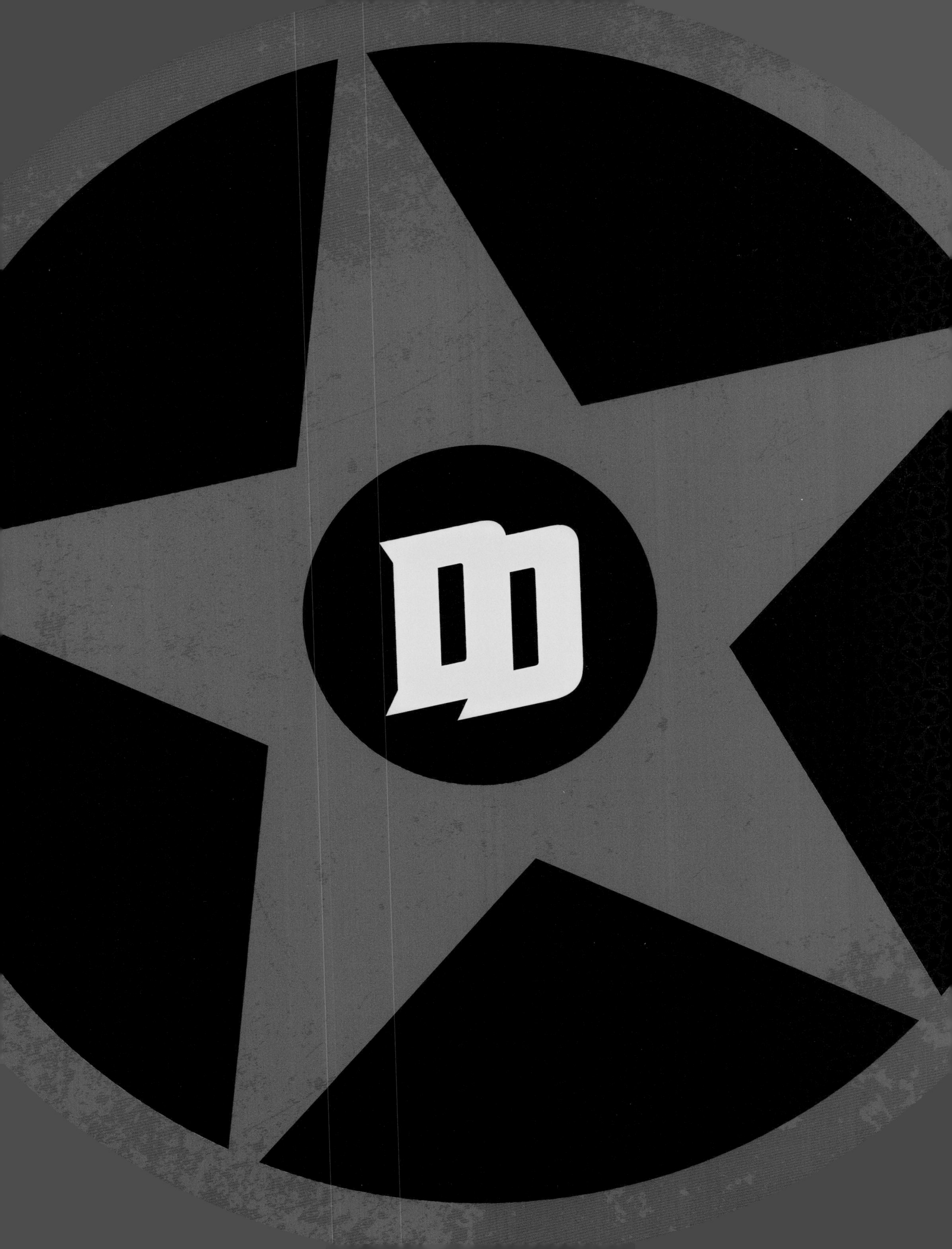

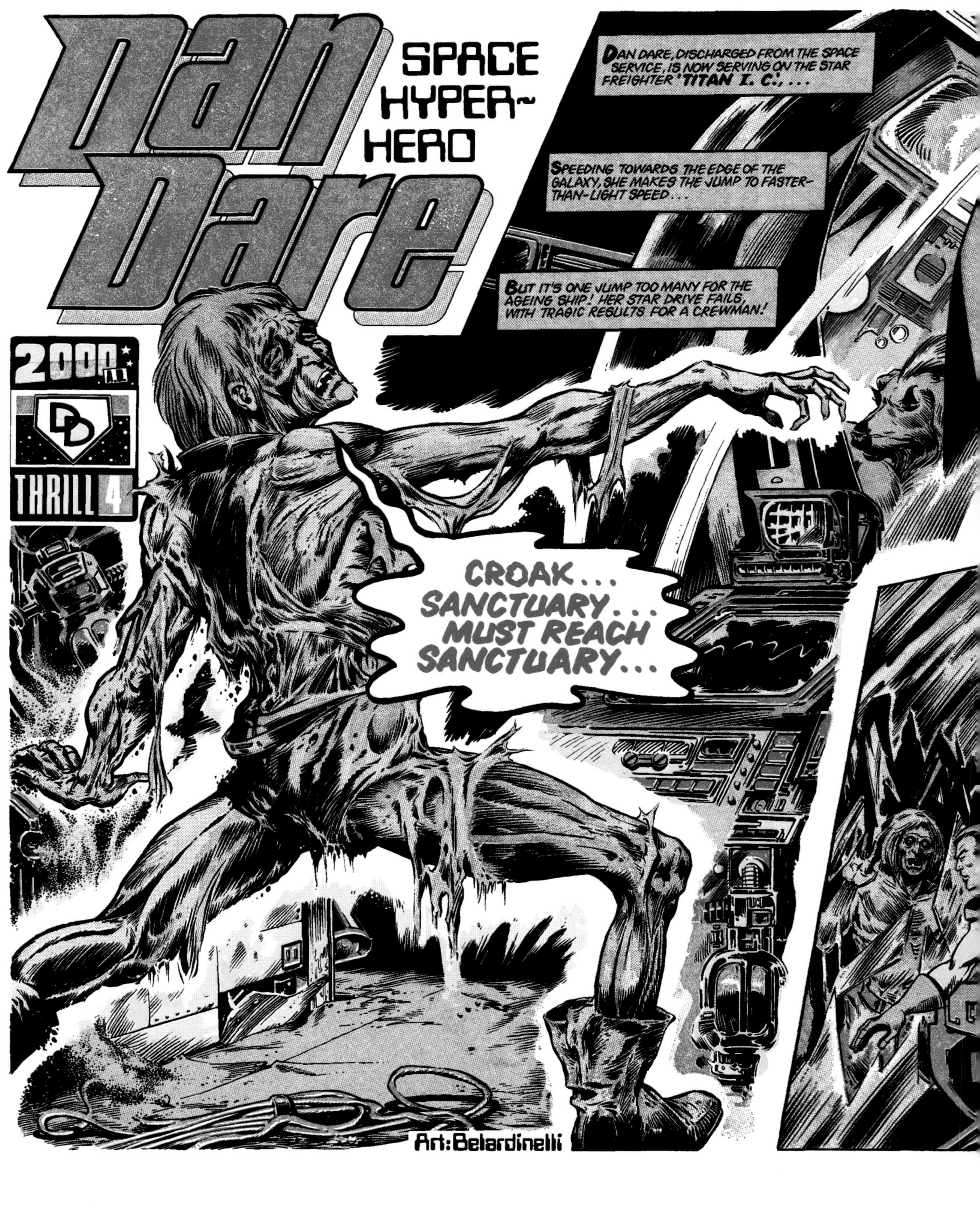
Dan Dare
SPACE HYPER~HERO
2000 A.D.
THRILL 4
DAN DARE, DISCHARGED FROM THE SPACE SERVICE, IS NOW SERVING ON THE STAR FREIGHTER 'TITAN I. C.', ...
SPEEDING TOWARDS THE EDGE OF THE GALAXY, SHE MAKES THE JUMP TO FASTER-THAN-LIGHT SPEED...
BUT IT'S ONE JUMP TOO MANY FOR THE AGEING SHIP! HER STAR DRIVE FAILS, WITH TRAGIC RESULTS FOR A CREWMAN!
CROAK... SANCTUARY... MUST REACH SANCTUARY...
Art: Belardinelli

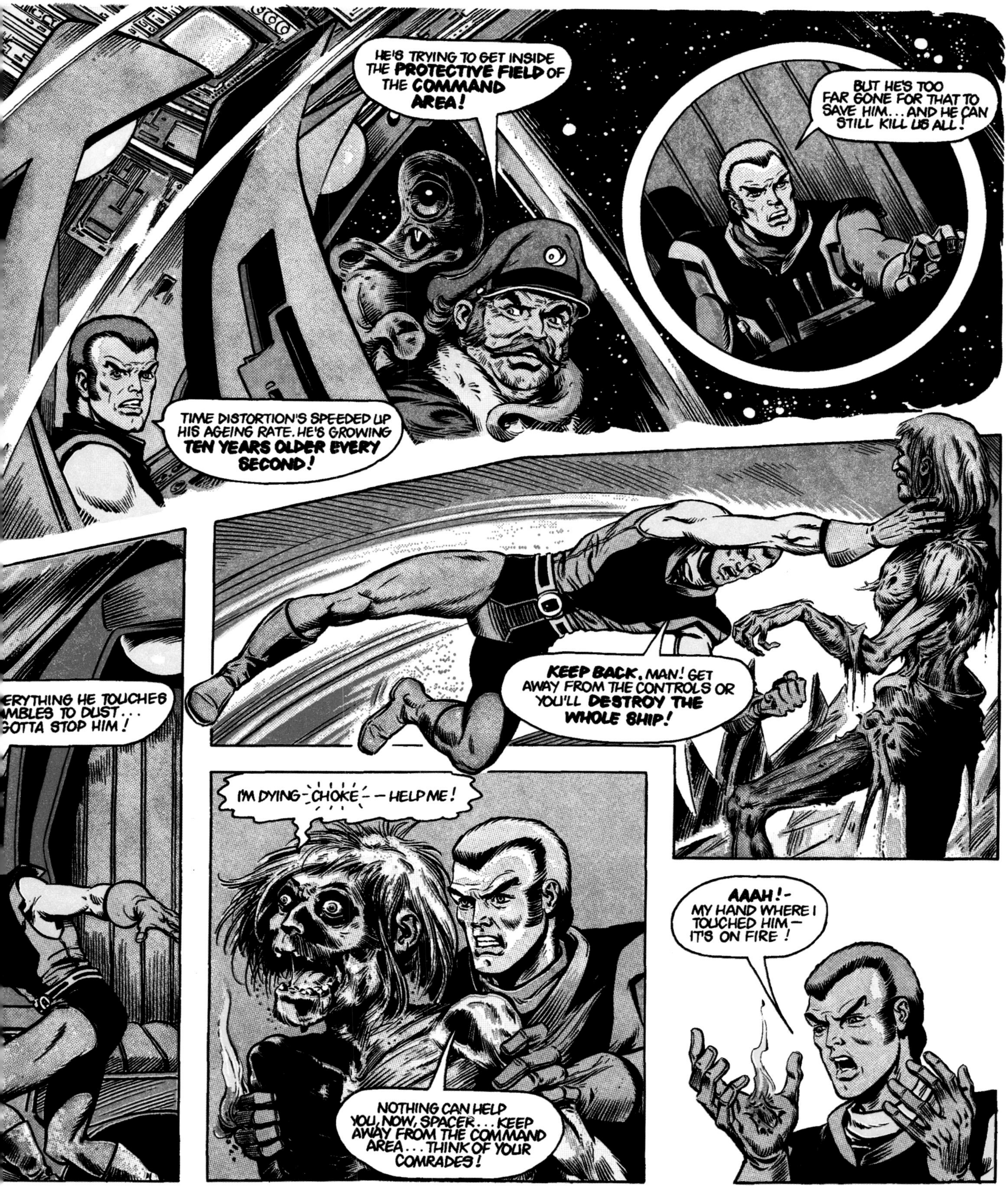

HE'S TRYING TO GET INSIDE THE **PROTECTIVE FIELD** OF THE **COMMAND AREA!**
BUT HE'S TOO FAR GONE FOR THAT TO SAVE HIM... AND HE CAN STILL KILL US ALL!
TIME DISTORTION'S SPEEDED UP HIS AGEING RATE. HE'S GROWING **TEN YEARS OLDER EVERY SECOND!**
ERYTHING HE TOUCHES MBLES TO DUST... GOTTA STOP HIM!
KEEP BACK, MAN! GET AWAY FROM THE CONTROLS OR YOU'LL **DESTROY THE WHOLE SHIP!**
I'M DYING - CHOKE - - HELP ME!
NOTHING CAN HELP YOU, NOW, SPACER... KEEP AWAY FROM THE COMMAND AREA... THINK OF YOUR COMRADES!
AAAH! - MY HAND WHERE I TOUCHED HIM - IT'S ON FIRE!

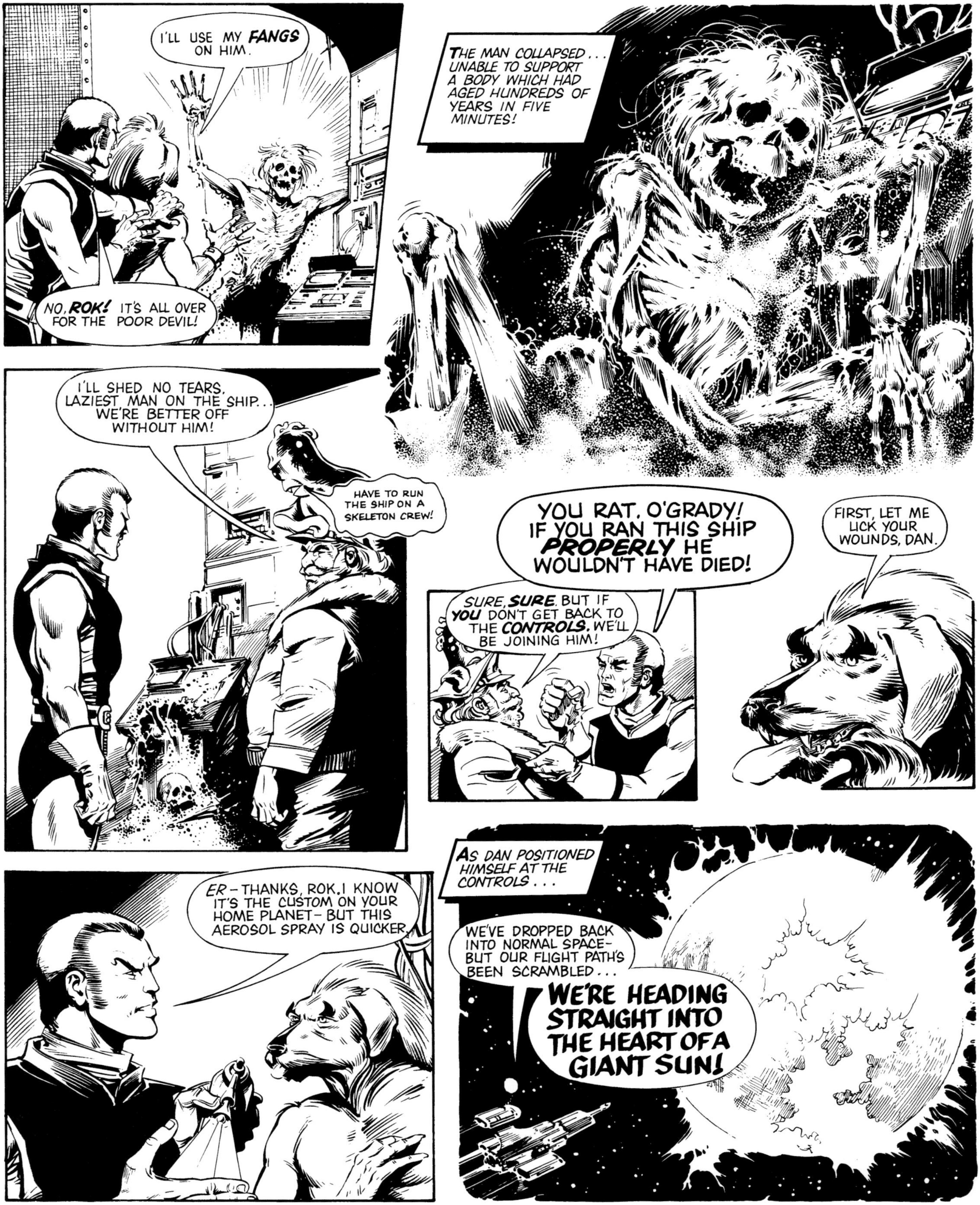
I'LL USE MY FANGS ON HIM.
NO, ROK! IT'S ALL OVER FOR THE POOR DEVIL!
THE MAN COLLAPSED... UNABLE TO SUPPORT A BODY WHICH HAD AGED HUNDREDS OF YEARS IN FIVE MINUTES!
I'LL SHED NO TEARS. LAZIEST MAN ON THE SHIP... WE'RE BETTER OFF WITHOUT HIM!
HAVE TO RUN THE SHIP ON A SKELETON CREW!
YOU RAT, O'GRADY! IF YOU RAN THIS SHIP PROPERLY HE WOULDN'T HAVE DIED!
SURE, SURE, BUT IF YOU DON'T GET BACK TO THE CONTROLS, WE'LL BE JOINING HIM!
FIRST, LET ME LICK YOUR WOUNDS, DAN.
ER - THANKS, ROK. I KNOW IT'S THE CUSTOM ON YOUR HOME PLANET - BUT THIS AEROSOL SPRAY IS QUICKER.
AS DAN POSITIONED HIMSELF AT THE CONTROLS...
WE'VE DROPPED BACK INTO NORMAL SPACE - BUT OUR FLIGHT PATH'S BEEN SCRAMBLED...
WE'RE HEADING STRAIGHT INTO THE HEART OF A GIANT SUN!

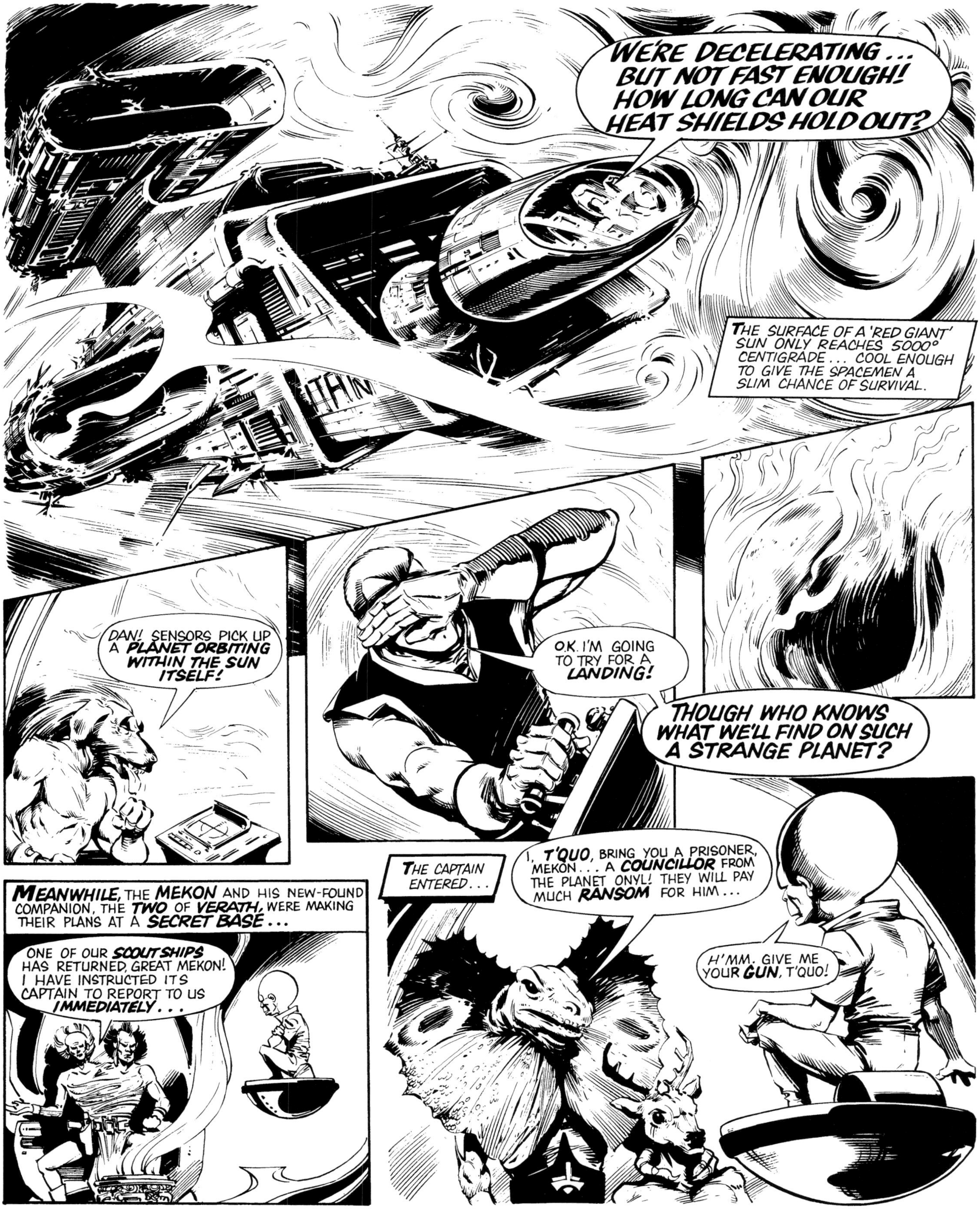
WE'RE DECELERATING... BUT NOT FAST ENOUGH! HOW LONG CAN OUR HEAT SHIELDS HOLD OUT?
THE SURFACE OF A 'RED GIANT' SUN ONLY REACHES 5000° CENTIGRADE... COOL ENOUGH TO GIVE THE SPACEMEN A SLIM CHANCE OF SURVIVAL.
DAN! SENSORS PICK UP A PLANET ORBITING WITHIN THE SUN ITSELF!
O.K. I'M GOING TO TRY FOR A LANDING!
THOUGH WHO KNOWS WHAT WE'LL FIND ON SUCH A STRANGE PLANET?
MEANWHILE, THE MEKON AND HIS NEW-FOUND COMPANION, THE TWO OF VERATH, WERE MAKING THEIR PLANS AT A SECRET BASE...
ONE OF OUR SCOUT SHIPS HAS RETURNED, GREAT MEKON! I HAVE INSTRUCTED ITS CAPTAIN TO REPORT TO US IMMEDIATELY...
THE CAPTAIN ENTERED...
I, T'QUO, BRING YOU A PRISONER, MEKON... A COUNCILLOR FROM THE PLANET ONYL! THEY WILL PAY MUCH RANSOM FOR HIM...
H'MM. GIVE ME YOUR GUN, T'QUO!

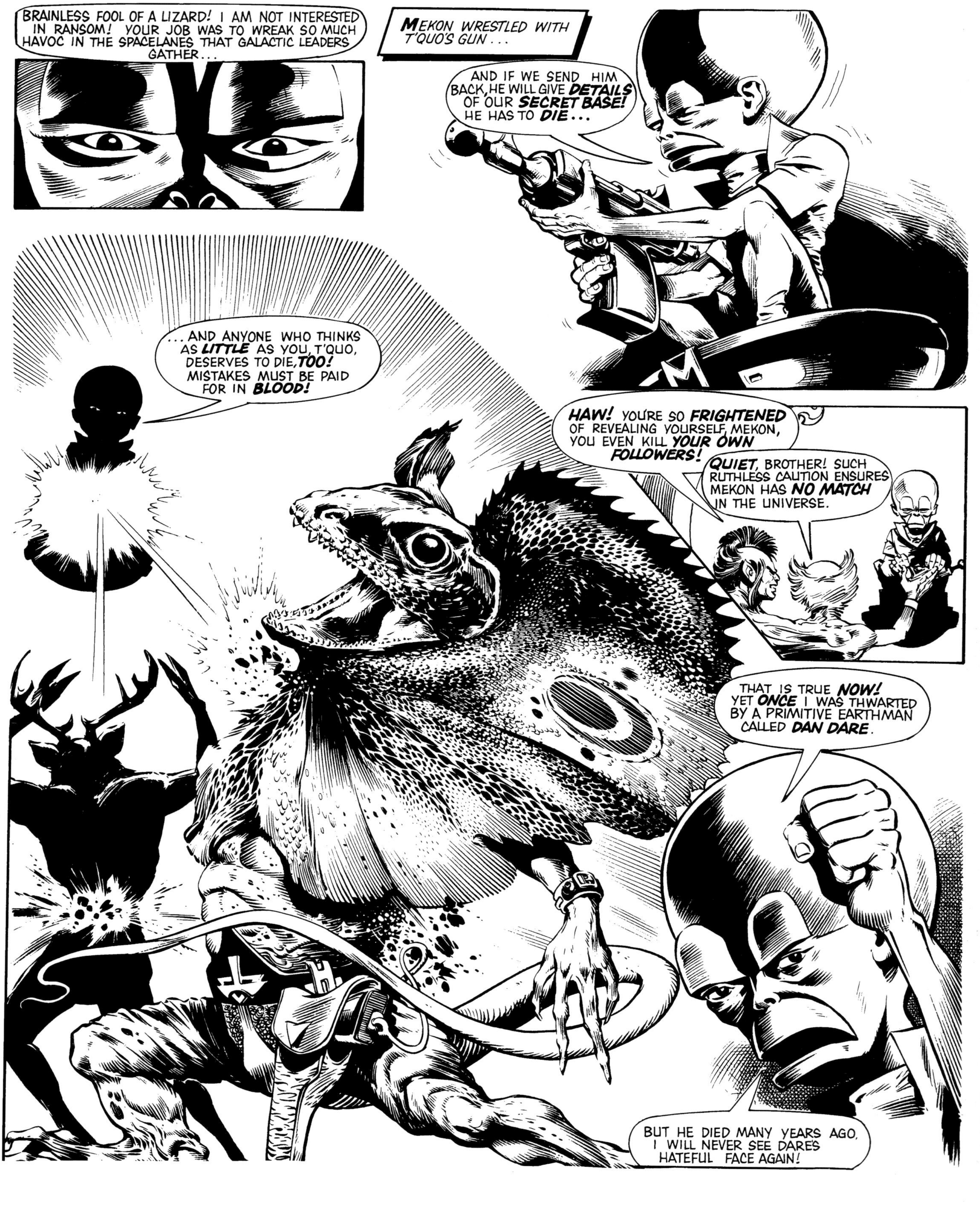

BRAINLESS FOOL OF A LIZARD! I AM NOT INTERESTED IN RANSOM! YOUR JOB WAS TO WREAK SO MUCH HAVOC IN THE SPACELANES THAT GALACTIC LEADERS GATHER...
MEKON WRESTLED WITH T'QUO'S GUN...
AND IF WE SEND HIM BACK, HE WILL GIVE DETAILS OF OUR SECRET BASE! HE HAS TO DIE...
...AND ANYONE WHO THINKS AS LITTLE AS YOU, T'QUO, DESERVES TO DIE, TOO! MISTAKES MUST BE PAID FOR IN BLOOD!
HAW! YOU'RE SO FRIGHTENED OF REVEALING YOURSELF, MEKON, YOU EVEN KILL YOUR OWN FOLLOWERS!
QUIET, BROTHER! SUCH RUTHLESS CAUTION ENSURES MEKON HAS NO MATCH IN THE UNIVERSE.
THAT IS TRUE NOW! YET ONCE I WAS THWARTED BY A PRIMITIVE EARTHMAN CALLED DAN DARE.
BUT HE DIED MANY YEARS AGO. I WILL NEVER SEE DARE'S HATEFUL FACE AGAIN!

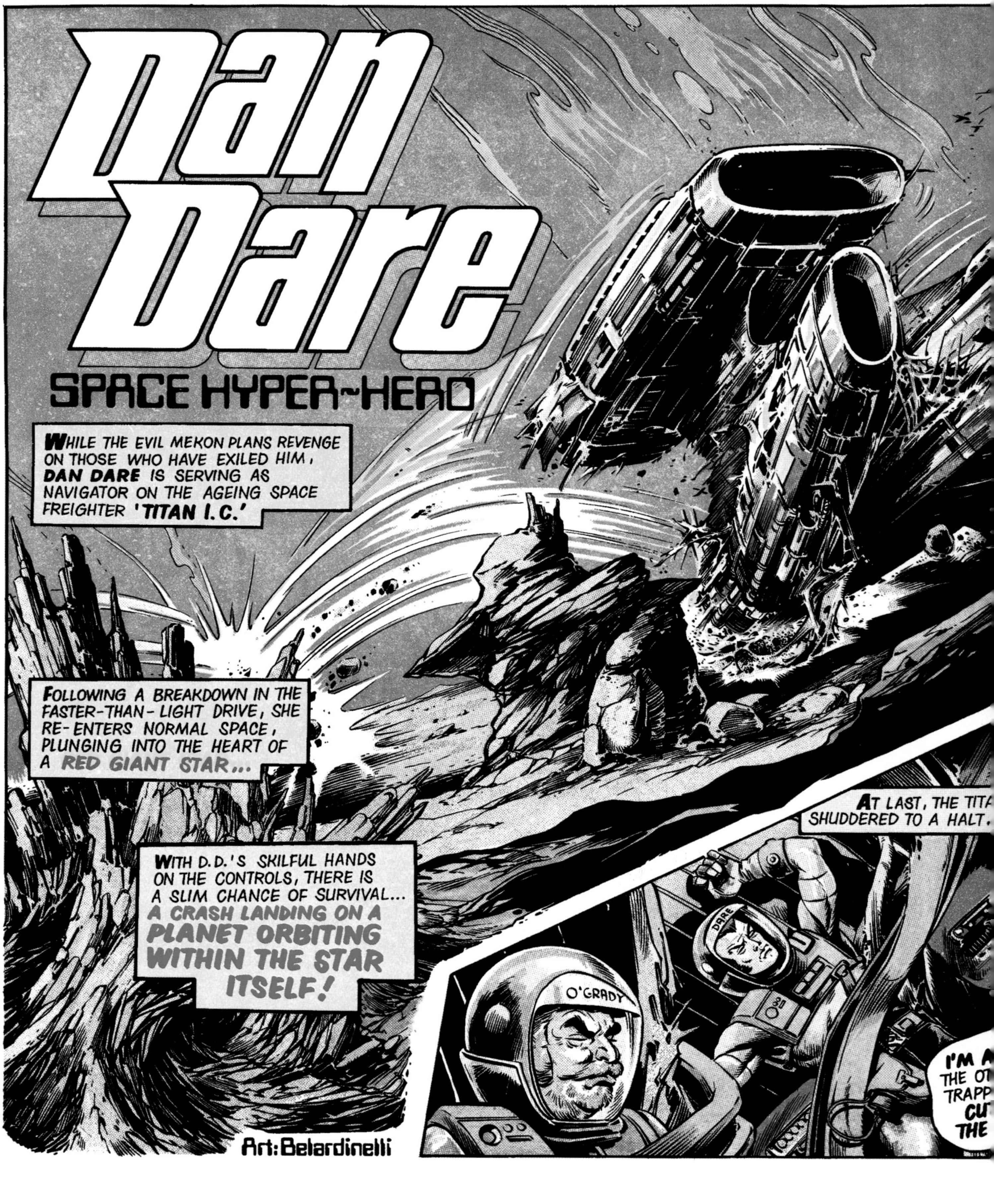
DAN DARE
SPACE HYPER~HERO
WHILE THE EVIL MEKON PLANS REVENGE ON THOSE WHO HAVE EXILED HIM, DAN DARE IS SERVING AS NAVIGATOR ON THE AGEING SPACE FREIGHTER 'TITAN I.C.'
FOLLOWING A BREAKDOWN IN THE FASTER-THAN-LIGHT DRIVE, SHE RE-ENTERS NORMAL SPACE, PLUNGING INTO THE HEART OF A RED GIANT STAR...
WITH D.D.'S SKILFUL HANDS ON THE CONTROLS, THERE IS A SLIM CHANCE OF SURVIVAL... A CRASH LANDING ON A PLANET ORBITING WITHIN THE STAR ITSELF!
AT LAST, THE TITA
SHUDDERED TO A HALT.
O'GRADY
DARE
I'M A
THE OT
TRAPP
CU
THE
Art: Belardinelli

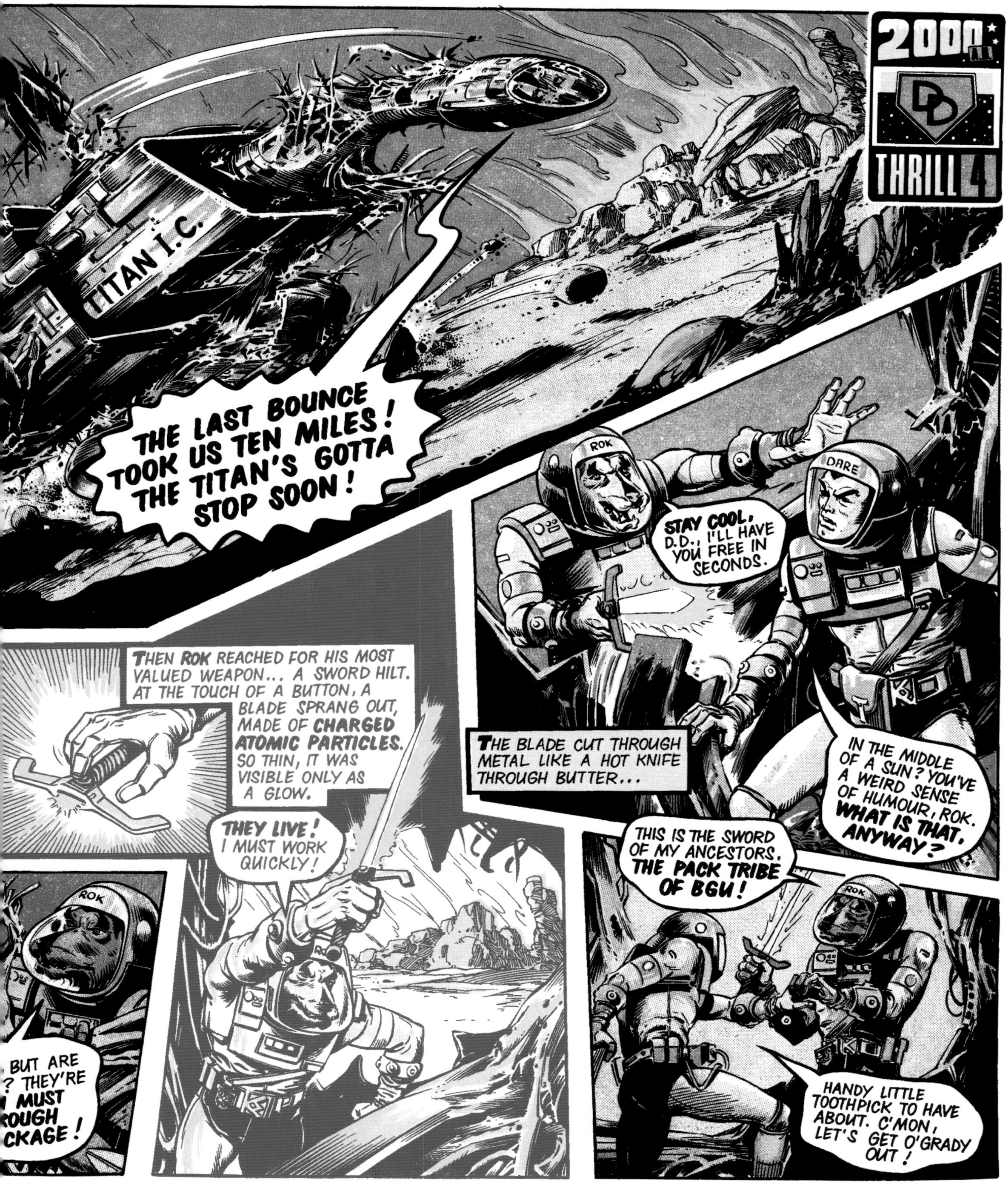

2000 AD
DD
THRILL 4
TITAN I.C.
THE LAST BOUNCE TOOK US TEN MILES! THE TITAN'S GOTTA STOP SOON!
ROK
DARE
STAY COOL, D.D., I'LL HAVE YOU FREE IN SECONDS.
THE BLADE CUT THROUGH METAL LIKE A HOT KNIFE THROUGH BUTTER...
IN THE MIDDLE OF A SUN? YOU'VE A WEIRD SENSE OF HUMOUR, ROK. WHAT IS THAT, ANYWAY?
THEN ROK REACHED FOR HIS MOST VALUED WEAPON... A SWORD HILT. AT THE TOUCH OF A BUTTON, A BLADE SPRANG OUT, MADE OF CHARGED ATOMIC PARTICLES. SO THIN, IT WAS VISIBLE ONLY AS A GLOW.
THEY LIVE! I MUST WORK QUICKLY!
BUT ARE ? THEY'RE MUST ROUGH CKAGE!
THIS IS THE SWORD OF MY ANCESTORS, THE PACK TRIBE OF BGU!
HANDY LITTLE TOOTHPICK TO HAVE ABOUT. C'MON, LET'S GET O'GRADY OUT!

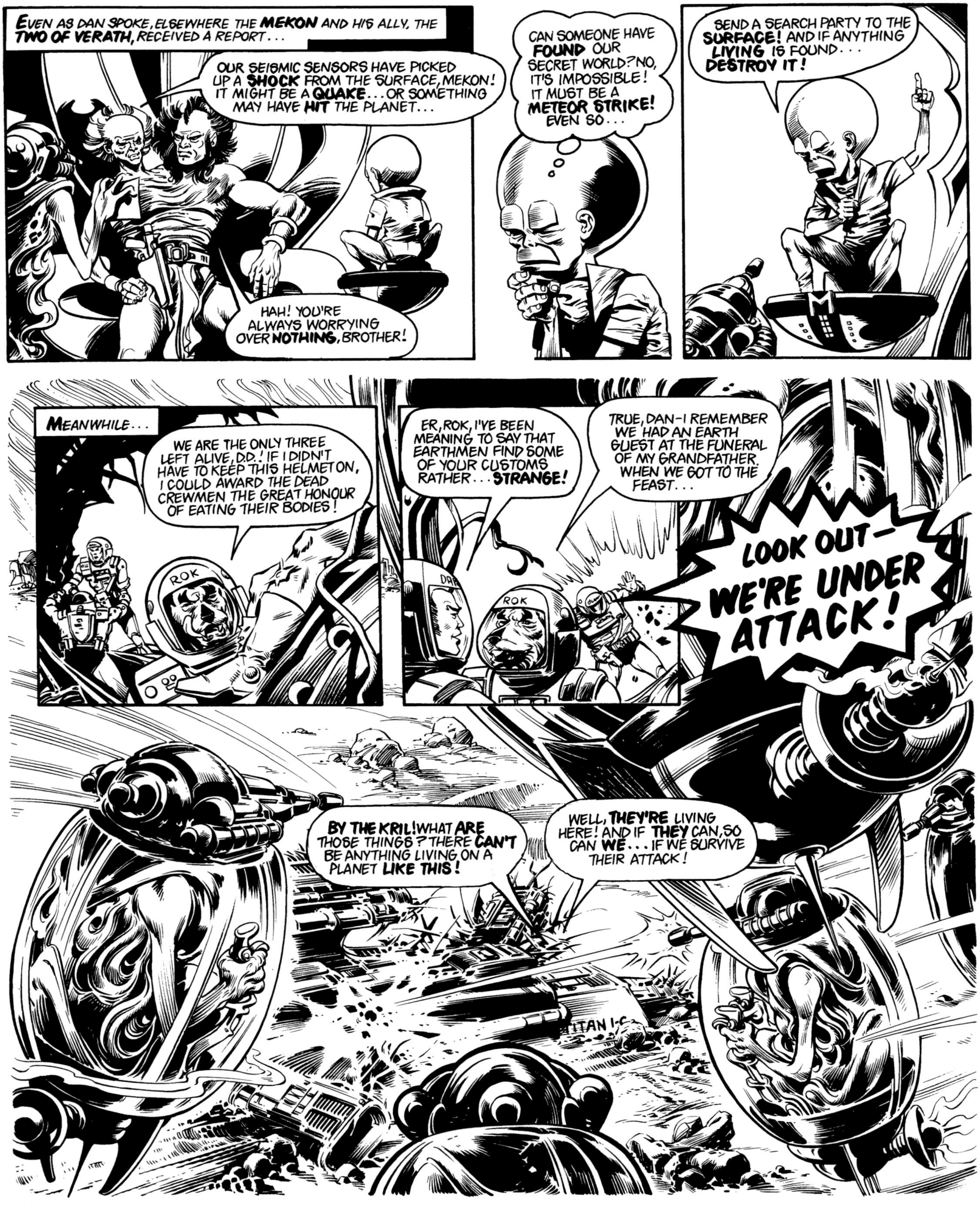
EVEN AS DAN SPOKE, ELSEWHERE THE MEKON AND HIS ALLY, THE TWO OF VERATH, RECEIVED A REPORT...
OUR SEISMIC SENSORS HAVE PICKED UP A SHOCK FROM THE SURFACE, MEKON! IT MIGHT BE A QUAKE... OR SOMETHING MAY HAVE HIT THE PLANET...
HAH! YOU'RE ALWAYS WORRYING OVER NOTHING, BROTHER!
CAN SOMEONE HAVE FOUND OUR SECRET WORLD? NO, IT'S IMPOSSIBLE! IT MUST BE A METEOR STRIKE! EVEN SO...
SEND A SEARCH PARTY TO THE SURFACE! AND IF ANYTHING LIVING IS FOUND... DESTROY IT!
MEANWHILE...
WE ARE THE ONLY THREE LEFT ALIVE, D.D.! IF I DIDN'T HAVE TO KEEP THIS HELMET ON, I COULD AWARD THE DEAD CREWMEN THE GREAT HONOUR OF EATING THEIR BODIES!
ROK
ER, ROK, I'VE BEEN MEANING TO SAY THAT EARTHMEN FIND SOME OF YOUR CUSTOMS RATHER... STRANGE!
TRUE, DAN-I REMEMBER WE HAD AN EARTH GUEST AT THE FUNERAL OF MY GRANDFATHER. WHEN WE GOT TO THE FEAST...
LOOK OUT- WE'RE UNDER ATTACK!
BY THE KRIL! WHAT ARE THOSE THINGS? THERE CAN'T BE ANYTHING LIVING ON A PLANET LIKE THIS!
WELL, THEY'RE LIVING HERE! AND IF THEY CAN, SO CAN WE... IF WE SURVIVE THEIR ATTACK!

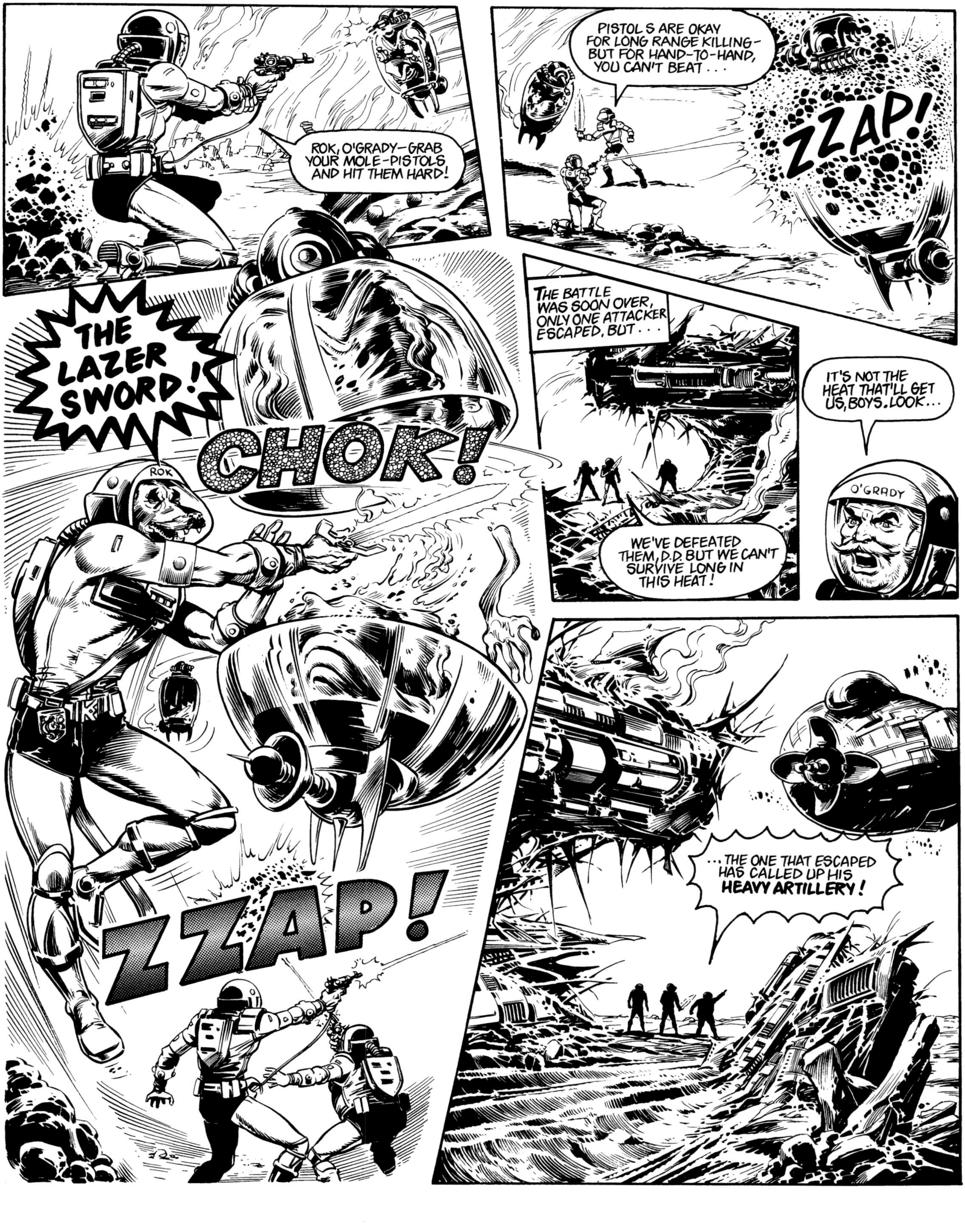
ROK, O'GRADY–GRAB YOUR MOLE-PISTOLS AND HIT THEM HARD!
PISTOLS ARE OKAY FOR LONG RANGE KILLING– BUT FOR HAND-TO-HAND, YOU CAN'T BEAT . . .
ZZAP!
THE LAZER SWORD!
ROK
CHOK!
ZZAP!
THE BATTLE WAS SOON OVER, ONLY ONE ATTACKER ESCAPED, BUT . . .
WE'VE DEFEATED THEM, D.D. BUT WE CAN'T SURVIVE LONG IN THIS HEAT!
IT'S NOT THE HEAT THAT'LL GET US, BOYS. LOOK...
O'GRADY
... THE ONE THAT ESCAPED HAS CALLED UP HIS **HEAVY ARTILLERY**!

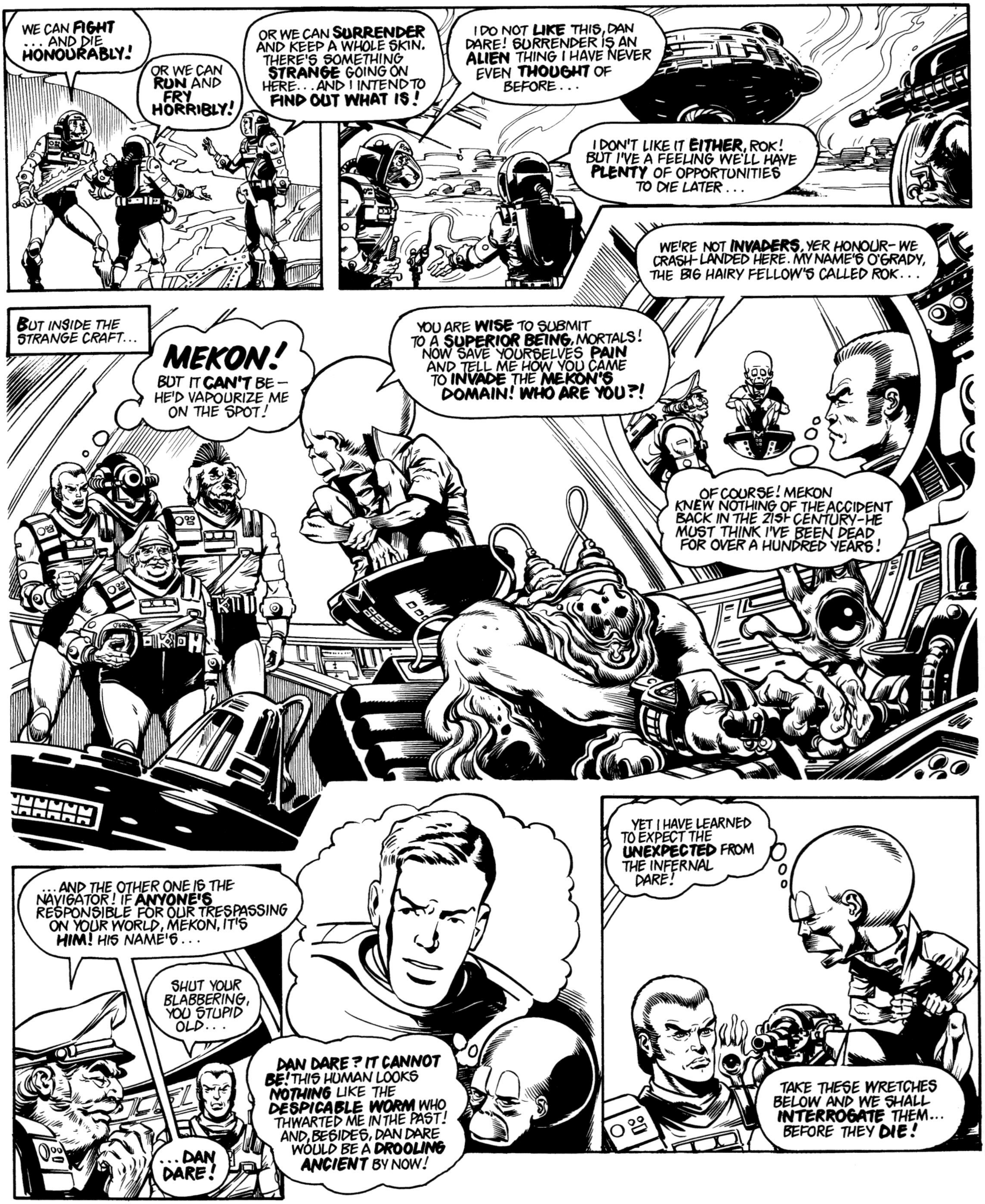

WE CAN FIGHT ... AND DIE HONOURABLY!
OR WE CAN RUN AND FRY HORRIBLY!
OR WE CAN SURRENDER AND KEEP A WHOLE SKIN. THERE'S SOMETHING STRANGE GOING ON HERE... AND I INTEND TO FIND OUT WHAT IS!
I DO NOT LIKE THIS, DAN DARE! SURRENDER IS AN ALIEN THING I HAVE NEVER EVEN THOUGHT OF BEFORE...
I DON'T LIKE IT EITHER, ROK! BUT I'VE A FEELING WE'LL HAVE PLENTY OF OPPORTUNITIES TO DIE LATER...
BUT INSIDE THE STRANGE CRAFT...
MEKON! BUT IT CAN'T BE — HE'D VAPOURIZE ME ON THE SPOT!
YOU ARE WISE TO SUBMIT TO A SUPERIOR BEING, MORTALS! NOW SAVE YOURSELVES PAIN AND TELL ME HOW YOU CAME TO INVADE THE MEKON'S DOMAIN! WHO ARE YOU?!
WE'RE NOT INVADERS, YER HONOUR- WE CRASH-LANDED HERE. MY NAME'S O'GRADY, THE BIG HAIRY FELLOW'S CALLED ROK...
OF COURSE! MEKON KNEW NOTHING OF THE ACCIDENT BACK IN THE 21st CENTURY-HE MUST THINK I'VE BEEN DEAD FOR OVER A HUNDRED YEARS!
...AND THE OTHER ONE IS THE NAVIGATOR! IF ANYONE'S RESPONSIBLE FOR OUR TRESPASSING ON YOUR WORLD, MEKON, IT'S HIM! HIS NAME'S...
SHUT YOUR BLABBERING, YOU STUPID OLD...
...DAN DARE!
DAN DARE? IT CANNOT BE! THIS HUMAN LOOKS NOTHING LIKE THE DESPICABLE WORM WHO THWARTED ME IN THE PAST! AND, BESIDES, DAN DARE WOULD BE A DROOLING ANCIENT BY NOW!
YET I HAVE LEARNED TO EXPECT THE UNEXPECTED FROM THE INFERNAL DARE!
TAKE THESE WRETCHES BELOW AND WE SHALL INTERROGATE THEM... BEFORE THEY DIE!

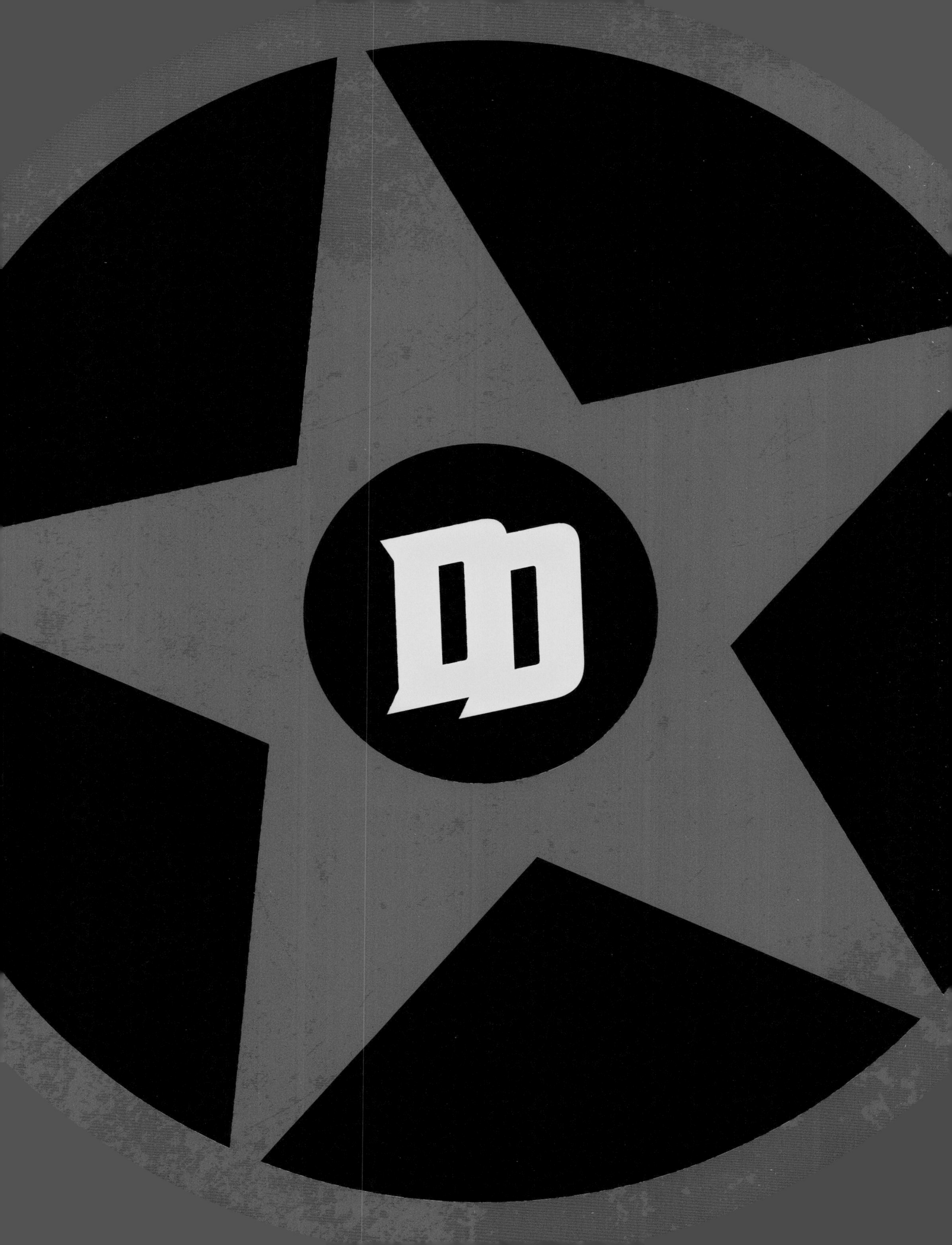

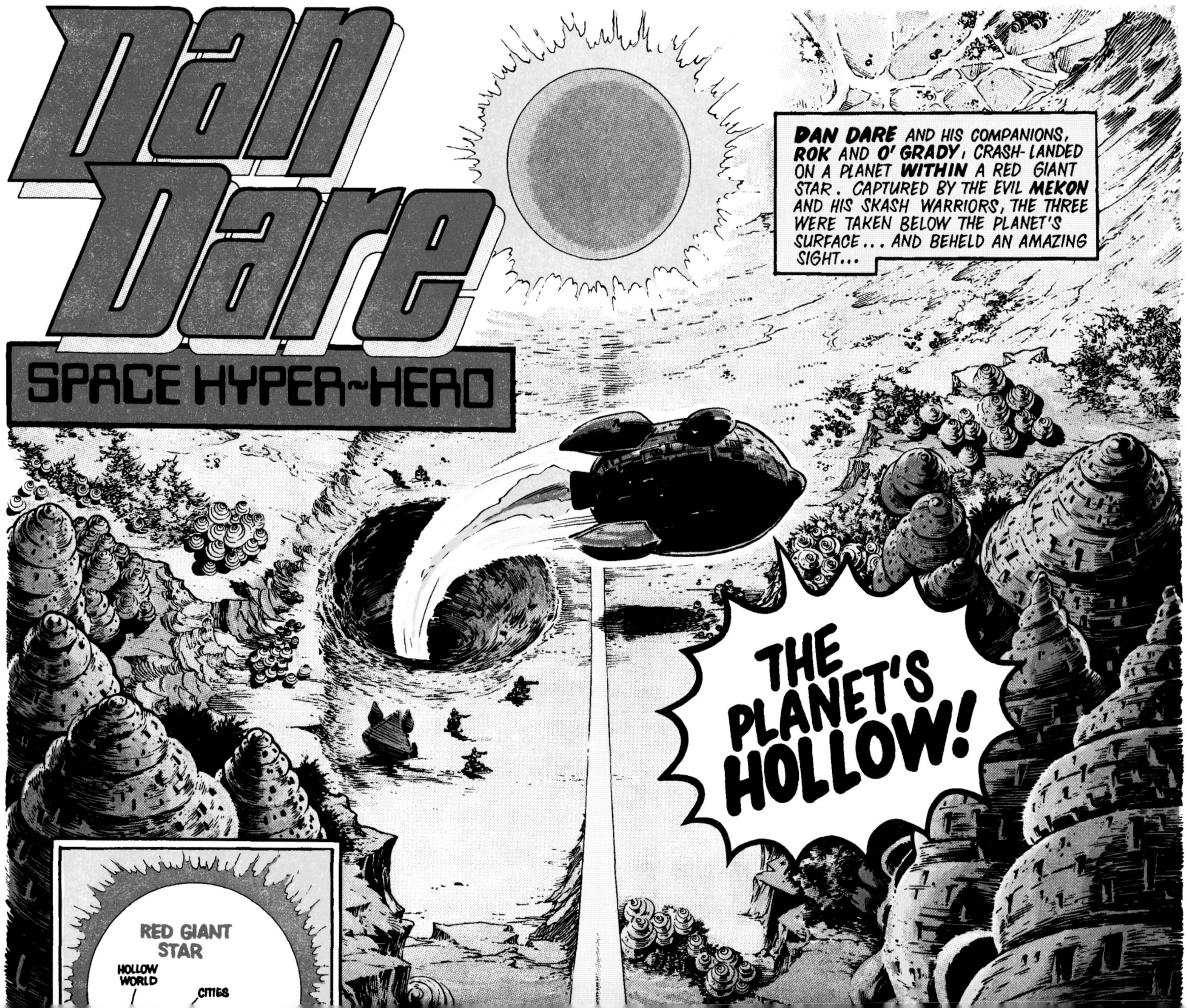
Dan Dare
SPACE HYPER~HERO
DAN DARE AND HIS COMPANIONS, ROK AND O' GRADY, CRASH-LANDED ON A PLANET WITHIN A RED GIANT STAR. CAPTURED BY THE EVIL MEKON AND HIS SKASH WARRIORS, THE THREE WERE TAKEN BELOW THE PLANET'S SURFACE... AND BEHELD AN AMAZING SIGHT...
THE PLANET'S HOLLOW!
RED GIANT STAR
HOLLOW WORLD
CITIES

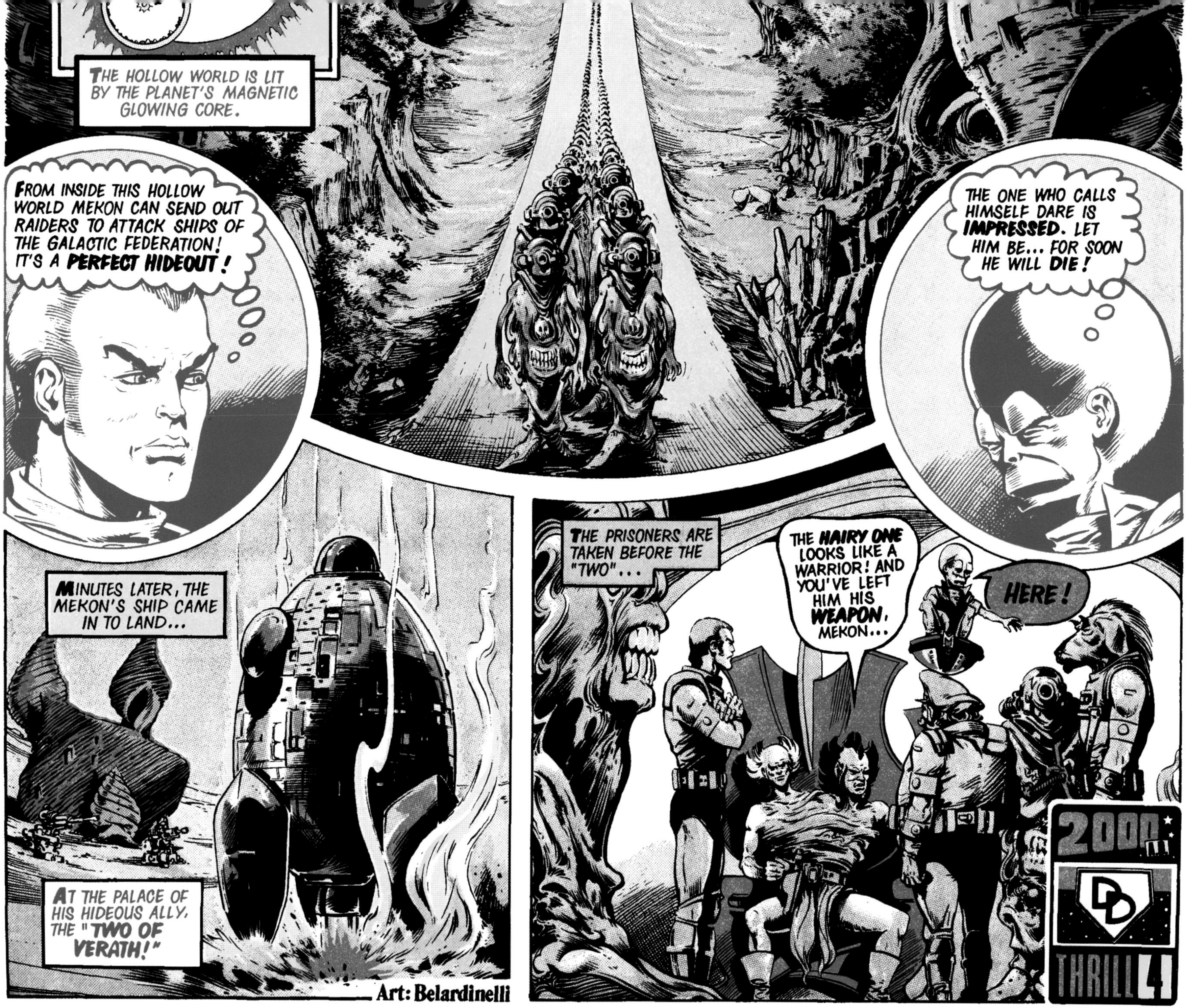
THE HOLLOW WORLD IS LIT BY THE PLANET'S MAGNETIC GLOWING CORE.
FROM INSIDE THIS HOLLOW WORLD MEKON CAN SEND OUT RAIDERS TO ATTACK SHIPS OF THE GALACTIC FEDERATION! IT'S A PERFECT HIDEOUT!
THE ONE WHO CALLS HIMSELF DARE IS IMPRESSED. LET HIM BE... FOR SOON HE WILL DIE!
MINUTES LATER, THE MEKON'S SHIP CAME IN TO LAND...
AT THE PALACE OF HIS HIDEOUS ALLY, THE "TWO OF VERATH!"
THE PRISONERS ARE TAKEN BEFORE THE "TWO"...
THE HAIRY ONE LOOKS LIKE A WARRIOR! AND YOU'VE LEFT HIM HIS WEAPON, MEKON...
HERE!
2000 AD
THRILL 4

Art: Belardinelli

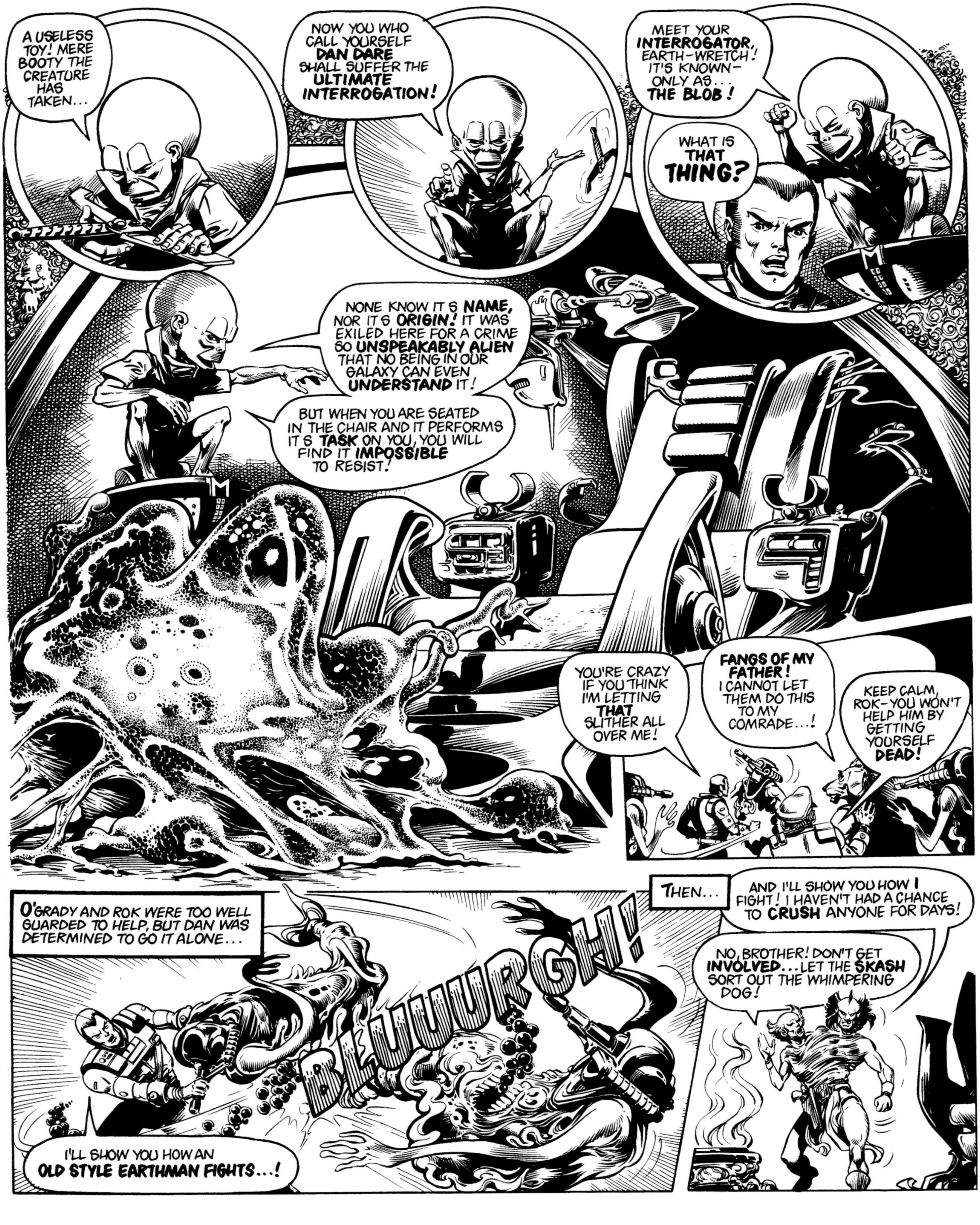
A USELESS TOY! MERE BOOTY THE CREATURE HAS TAKEN...
NOW YOU WHO CALL YOURSELF DAN DARE SHALL SUFFER THE ULTIMATE INTERROGATION!
MEET YOUR INTERROGATOR, EARTH-WRETCH! IT'S KNOWN-ONLY AS... THE BLOB!
WHAT IS THAT THING?
NONE KNOW IT'S NAME, NOR IT'S ORIGIN! IT WAS EXILED HERE FOR A CRIME SO UNSPEAKABLY ALIEN THAT NO BEING IN OUR GALAXY CAN EVEN UNDERSTAND IT!
BUT WHEN YOU ARE SEATED IN THE CHAIR AND IT PERFORMS IT'S TASK ON YOU, YOU WILL FIND IT IMPOSSIBLE TO RESIST!
YOU'RE CRAZY IF YOU THINK I'M LETTING THAT SLITHER ALL OVER ME!
FANGS OF MY FATHER! I CANNOT LET THEM DO THIS TO MY COMRADE...!
KEEP CALM, ROK-YOU WON'T HELP HIM BY GETTING YOURSELF DEAD!
O'GRADY AND ROK WERE TOO WELL GUARDED TO HELP, BUT DAN WAS DETERMINED TO GO IT ALONE...
BLUUUURGH!
I'LL SHOW YOU HOW AN OLD STYLE EARTHMAN FIGHTS...!
THEN...
AND I'LL SHOW YOU HOW I FIGHT! I HAVEN'T HAD A CHANCE TO CRUSH ANYONE FOR DAYS!
NO, BROTHER! DON'T GET INVOLVED... LET THE SKASH SORT OUT THE WHIMPERING DOG!

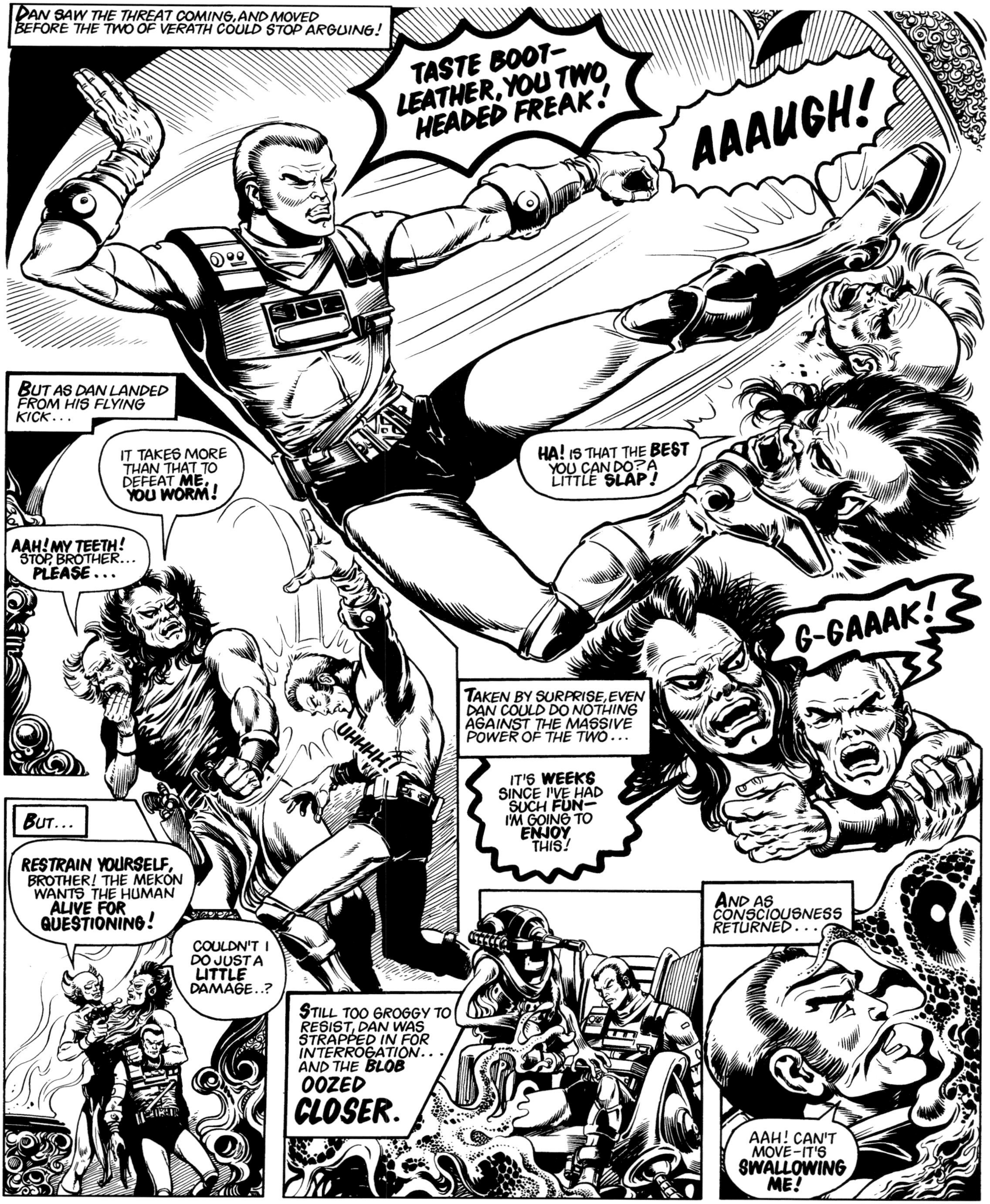
DAN SAW THE THREAT COMING, AND MOVED BEFORE THE TWO OF VERATH COULD STOP ARGUING!
TASTE BOOT-LEATHER, YOU TWO HEADED FREAK!
AAAUGH!
HA! IS THAT THE BEST YOU CAN DO? A LITTLE SLAP!
BUT AS DAN LANDED FROM HIS FLYING KICK...
IT TAKES MORE THAN THAT TO DEFEAT ME, YOU WORM!
AAH! MY TEETH! STOP, BROTHER... PLEASE...
UHHHH!
G-GAAAK!
TAKEN BY SURPRISE, EVEN DAN COULD DO NOTHING AGAINST THE MASSIVE POWER OF THE TWO...
IT'S WEEKS SINCE I'VE HAD SUCH FUN- I'M GOING TO ENJOY THIS!
BUT...
RESTRAIN YOURSELF, BROTHER! THE MEKON WANTS THE HUMAN ALIVE FOR QUESTIONING!
COULDN'T I DO JUST A LITTLE DAMAGE..?
STILL TOO GROGGY TO RESIST, DAN WAS STRAPPED IN FOR INTERROGATION... AND THE BLOB OOZED CLOSER.
AND AS CONSCIOUSNESS RETURNED...
AAH! CAN'T MOVE-IT'S SWALLOWING ME!

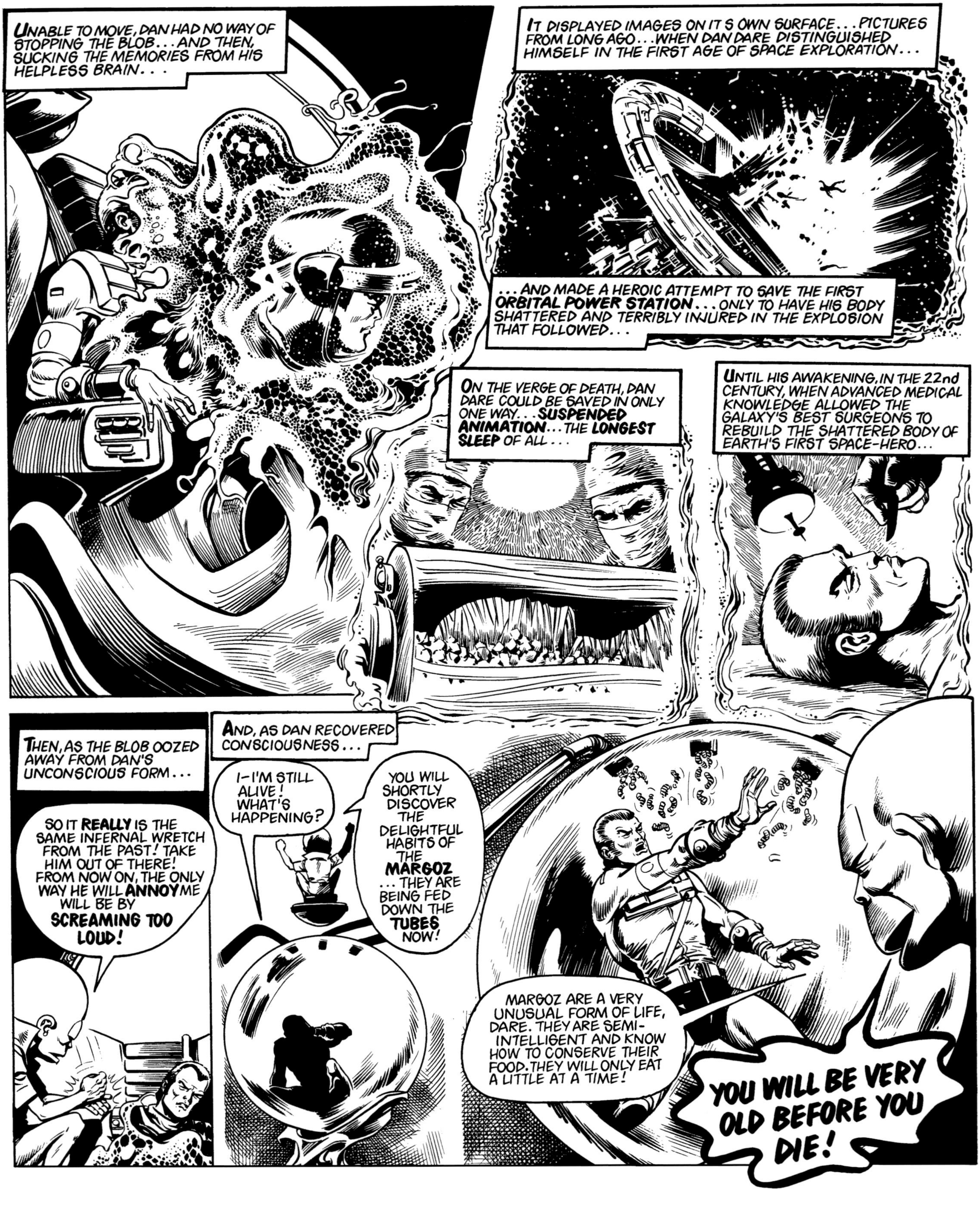

UNABLE TO MOVE, DAN HAD NO WAY OF STOPPING THE BLOB... AND THEN, SUCKING THE MEMORIES FROM HIS HELPLESS BRAIN...
IT DISPLAYED IMAGES ON IT'S OWN SURFACE... PICTURES FROM LONG AGO... WHEN DAN DARE DISTINGUISHED HIMSELF IN THE FIRST AGE OF SPACE EXPLORATION...
...AND MADE A HEROIC ATTEMPT TO SAVE THE FIRST ORBITAL POWER STATION... ONLY TO HAVE HIS BODY SHATTERED AND TERRIBLY INJURED IN THE EXPLOSION THAT FOLLOWED...
ON THE VERGE OF DEATH, DAN DARE COULD BE SAVED IN ONLY ONE WAY... SUSPENDED ANIMATION... THE LONGEST SLEEP OF ALL...
UNTIL HIS AWAKENING, IN THE 22nd CENTURY, WHEN ADVANCED MEDICAL KNOWLEDGE ALLOWED THE GALAXY'S BEST SURGEONS TO REBUILD THE SHATTERED BODY OF EARTH'S FIRST SPACE-HERO...
THEN, AS THE BLOB OOZED AWAY FROM DAN'S UNCONSCIOUS FORM...
SO IT REALLY IS THE SAME INFERNAL WRETCH FROM THE PAST! TAKE HIM OUT OF THERE! FROM NOW ON, THE ONLY WAY HE WILL ANNOY ME WILL BE BY SCREAMING TOO LOUD!
AND, AS DAN RECOVERED CONSCIOUSNESS...
I-I'M STILL ALIVE! WHAT'S HAPPENING?
YOU WILL SHORTLY DISCOVER THE DELIGHTFUL HABITS OF THE MARGOZ ... THEY ARE BEING FED DOWN THE TUBES NOW!
MARGOZ ARE A VERY UNUSUAL FORM OF LIFE, DARE. THEY ARE SEMI-INTELLIGENT AND KNOW HOW TO CONSERVE THEIR FOOD. THEY WILL ONLY EAT A LITTLE AT A TIME!
YOU WILL BE VERY OLD BEFORE YOU DIE!

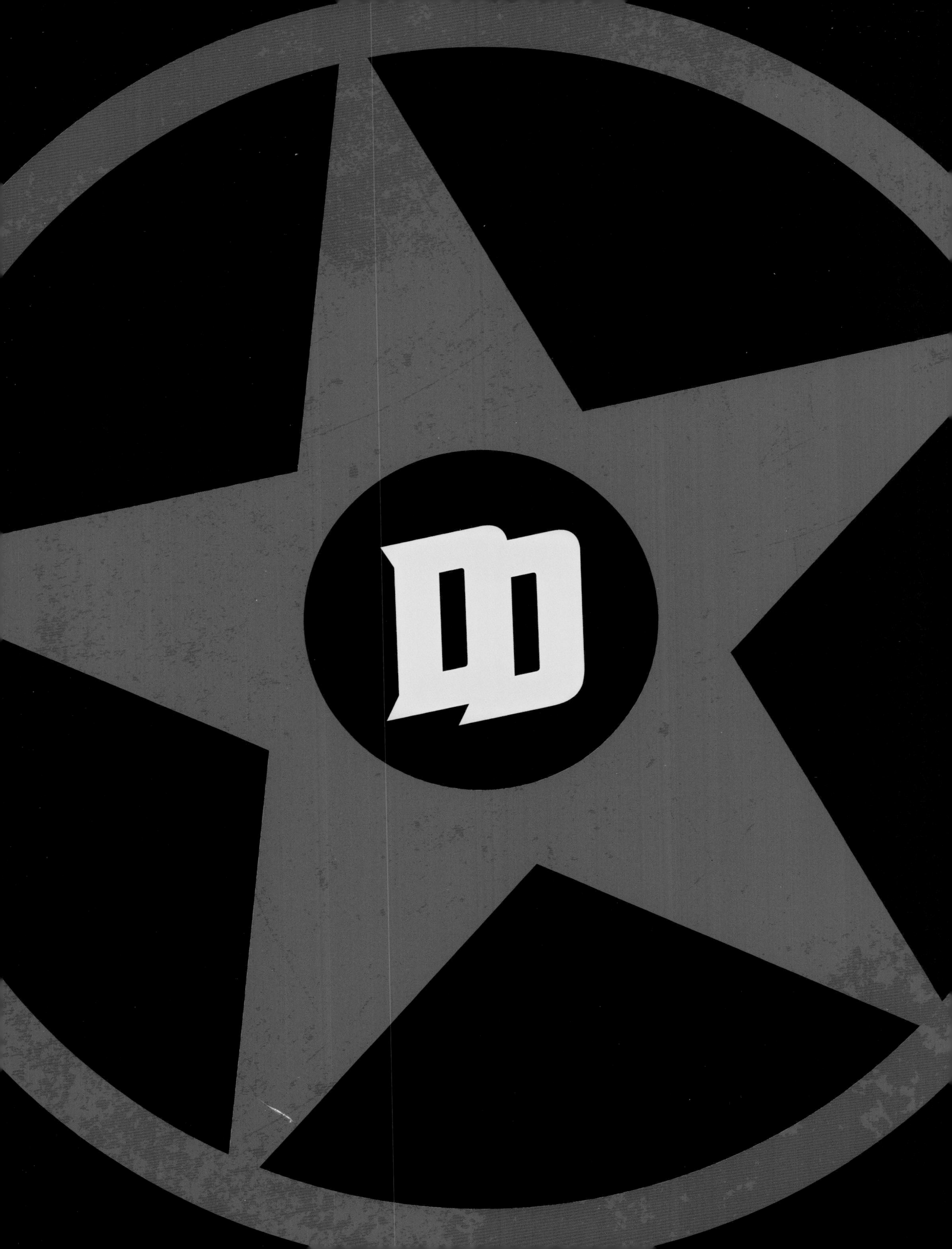

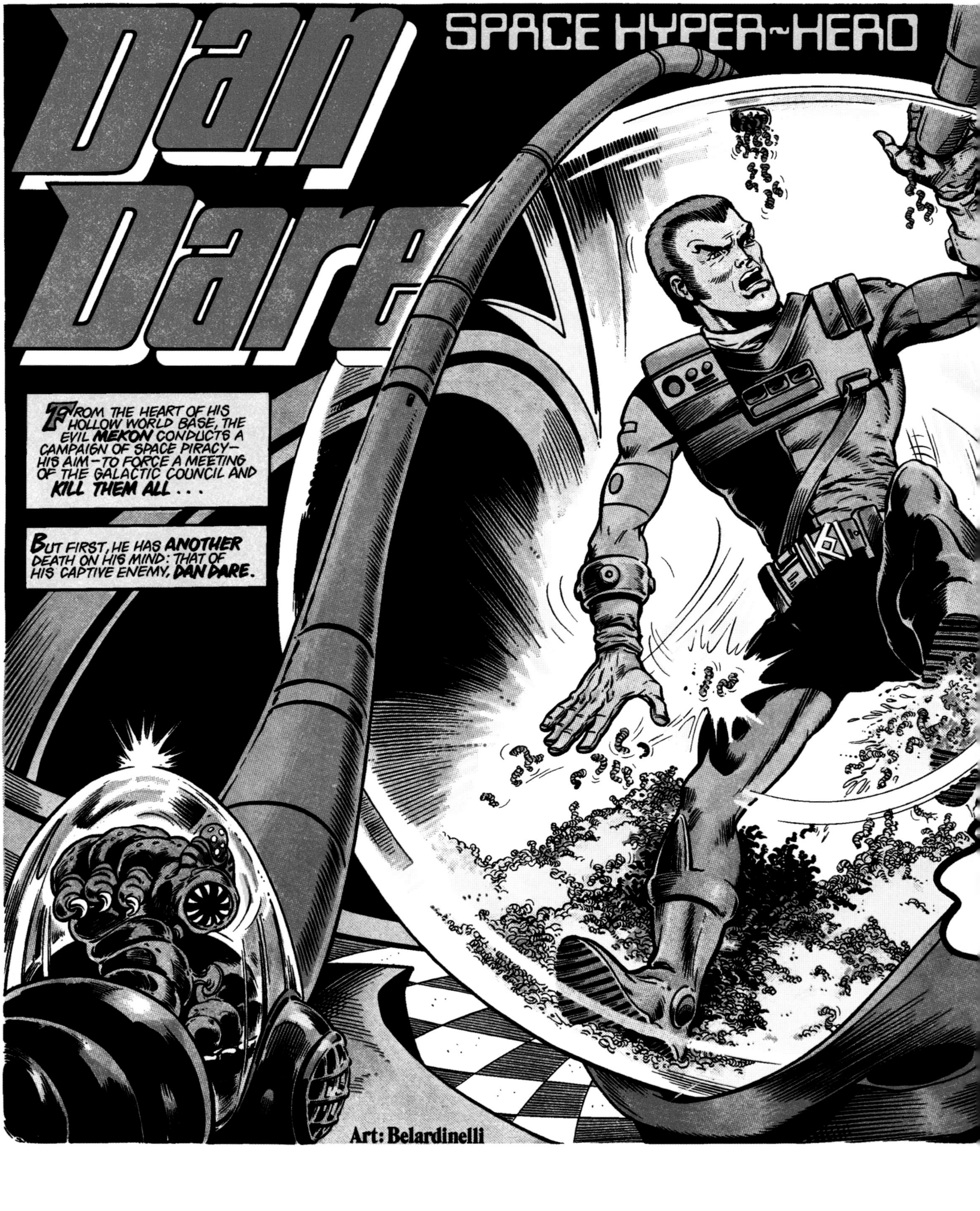

Dan Dare
SPACE HYPER~HERO
FROM THE HEART OF HIS HOLLOW WORLD BASE, THE EVIL MEKON CONDUCTS A CAMPAIGN OF SPACE PIRACY— HIS AIM—TO FORCE A MEETING OF THE GALACTIC COUNCIL AND KILL THEM ALL . . .
BUT FIRST, HE HAS ANOTHER DEATH ON HIS MIND: THAT OF HIS CAPTIVE ENEMY, DAN DARE.
Art: Belardinelli

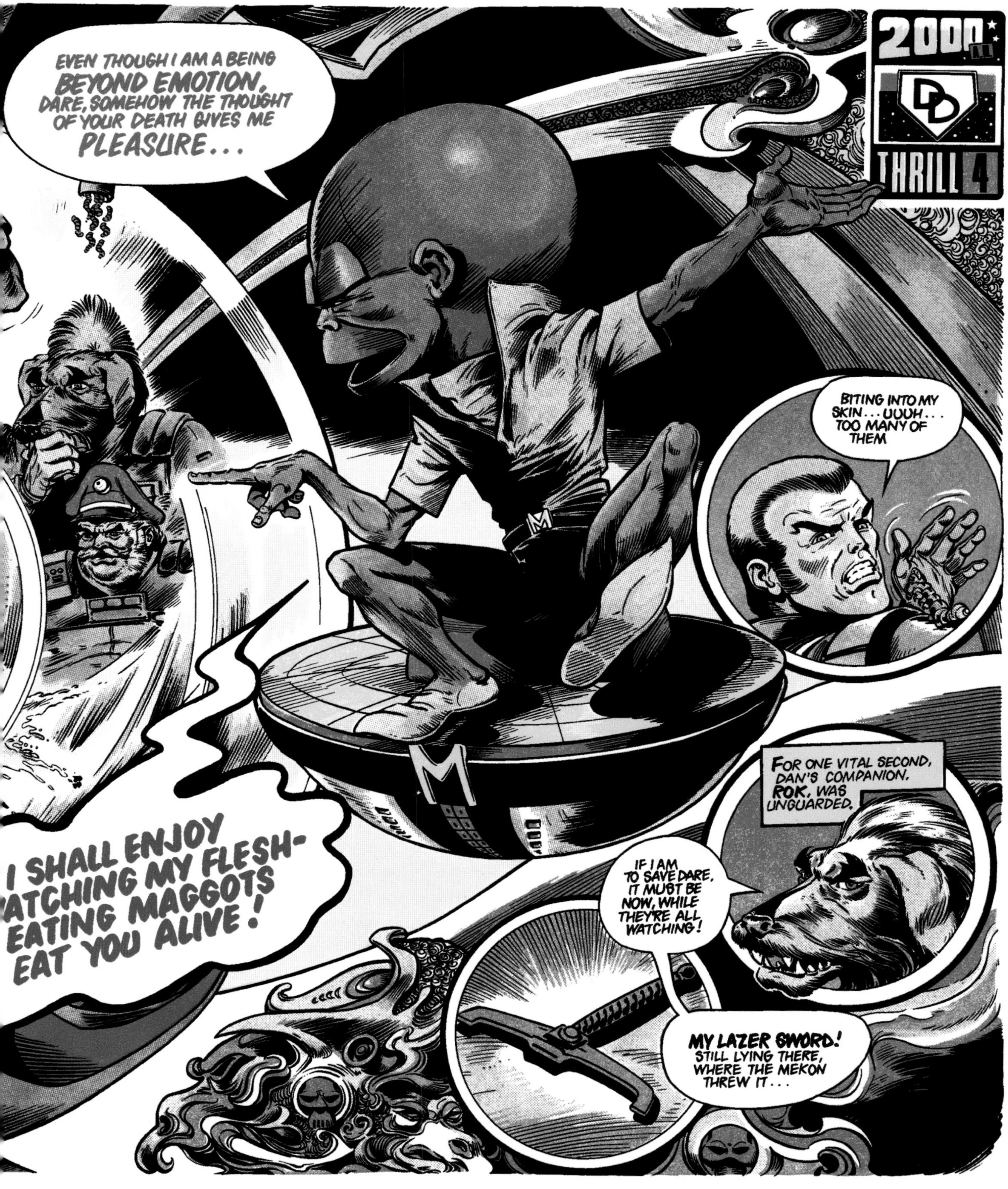
2000 AD
THRILL 4
EVEN THOUGH I AM A BEING BEYOND EMOTION, DARE, SOMEHOW THE THOUGHT OF YOUR DEATH GIVES ME PLEASURE...
BITING INTO MY SKIN... UUUH... TOO MANY OF THEM
I SHALL ENJOY WATCHING MY FLESH-EATING MAGGOTS EAT YOU ALIVE!
FOR ONE VITAL SECOND, DAN'S COMPANION, ROK, WAS UNGUARDED.
IF I AM TO SAVE DARE, IT MUST BE NOW, WHILE THEY'RE ALL WATCHING!
MY LAZER SWORD! STILL LYING THERE, WHERE THE MEKON THREW IT...

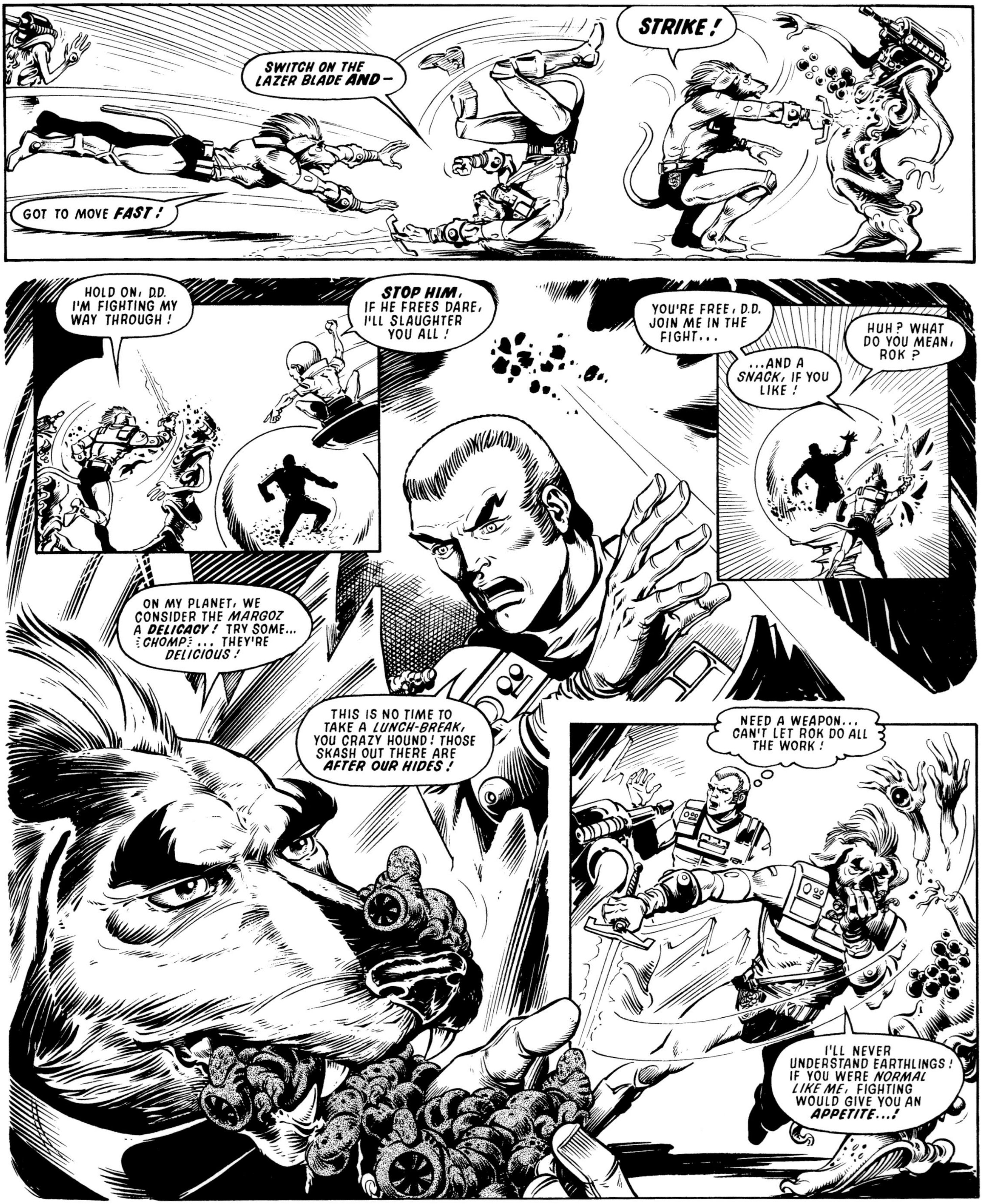
SWITCH ON THE LAZER BLADE AND—
GOT TO MOVE FAST!
STRIKE!
HOLD ON, D.D. I'M FIGHTING MY WAY THROUGH!
STOP HIM, IF HE FREES DARE, I'LL SLAUGHTER YOU ALL!
YOU'RE FREE, D.D. JOIN ME IN THE FIGHT...
...AND A SNACK, IF YOU LIKE!
HUH? WHAT DO YOU MEAN, ROK?
ON MY PLANET, WE CONSIDER THE MARGOZ A DELICACY! TRY SOME... CHOMP... THEY'RE DELICIOUS!
THIS IS NO TIME TO TAKE A LUNCH-BREAK, YOU CRAZY HOUND! THOSE SKASH OUT THERE ARE AFTER OUR HIDES!
NEED A WEAPON... CAN'T LET ROK DO ALL THE WORK!
I'LL NEVER UNDERSTAND EARTHLINGS! IF YOU WERE NORMAL LIKE ME, FIGHTING WOULD GIVE YOU AN APPETITE...!

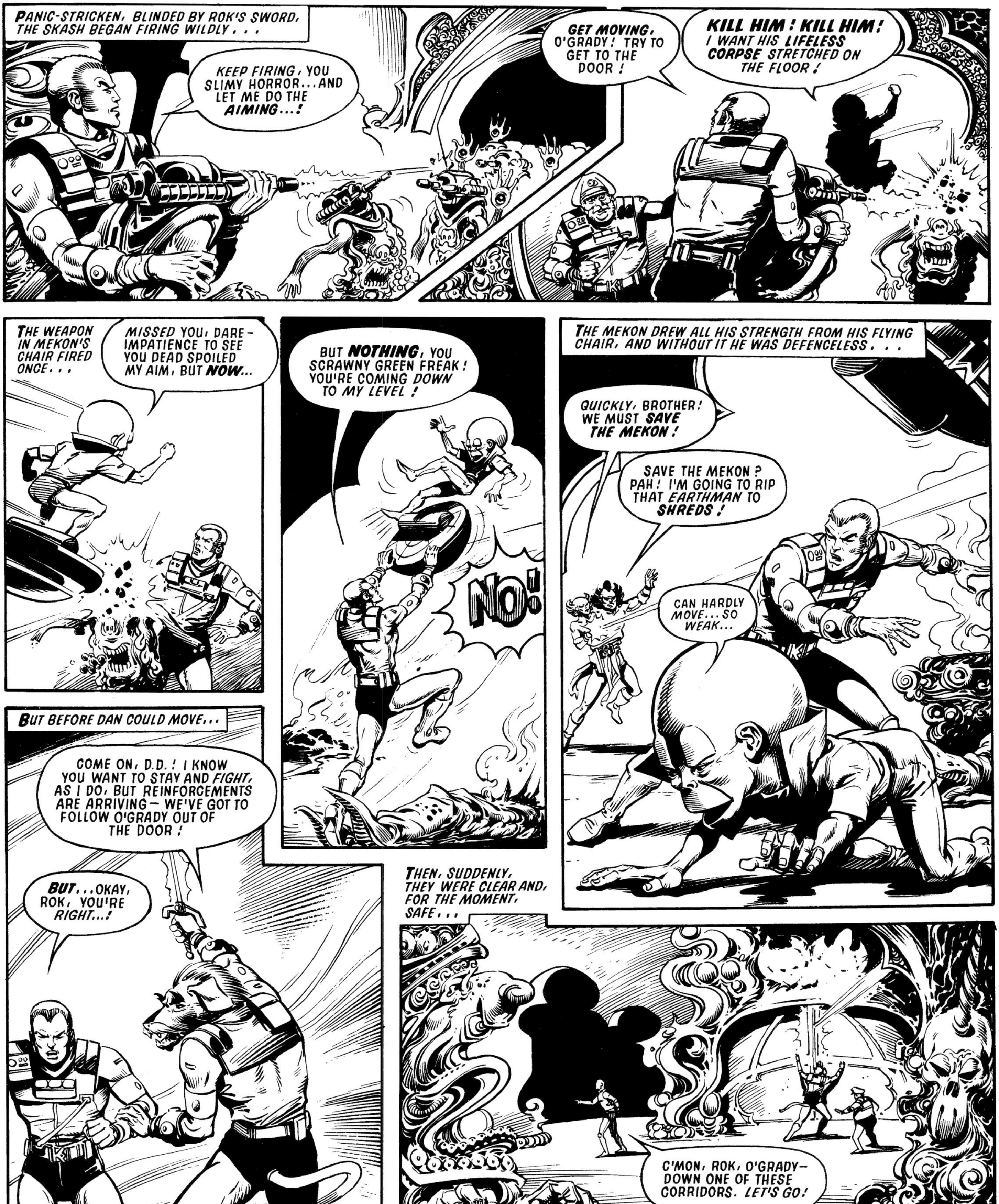

PANIC-STRICKEN, BLINDED BY ROK'S SWORD, THE SKASH BEGAN FIRING WILDLY . . .
KEEP FIRING, YOU SLIMY HORROR...AND LET ME DO THE AIMING...!
GET MOVING, O'GRADY! TRY TO GET TO THE DOOR!
KILL HIM! KILL HIM! I WANT HIS LIFELESS CORPSE STRETCHED ON THE FLOOR!
THE WEAPON IN MEKON'S CHAIR FIRED ONCE . . .
MISSED YOU, DARE-IMPATIENCE TO SEE YOU DEAD SPOILED MY AIM, BUT NOW...
BUT NOTHING, YOU SCRAWNY GREEN FREAK! YOU'RE COMING DOWN TO MY LEVEL!
NO!
THE MEKON DREW ALL HIS STRENGTH FROM HIS FLYING CHAIR, AND WITHOUT IT HE WAS DEFENCELESS . . .
QUICKLY, BROTHER! WE MUST SAVE THE MEKON!
SAVE THE MEKON? PAH! I'M GOING TO RIP THAT EARTHMAN TO SHREDS!
CAN HARDLY MOVE...SO WEAK...
BUT BEFORE DAN COULD MOVE...
COME ON, D.D.! I KNOW YOU WANT TO STAY AND FIGHT, AS I DO, BUT REINFORCEMENTS ARE ARRIVING— WE'VE GOT TO FOLLOW O'GRADY OUT OF THE DOOR!
BUT...OKAY, ROK, YOU'RE RIGHT...!
THEN, SUDDENLY, THEY WERE CLEAR AND, FOR THE MOMENT, SAFE . . .
C'MON, ROK, O'GRADY— DOWN ONE OF THESE CORRIDORS. LET'S GO!

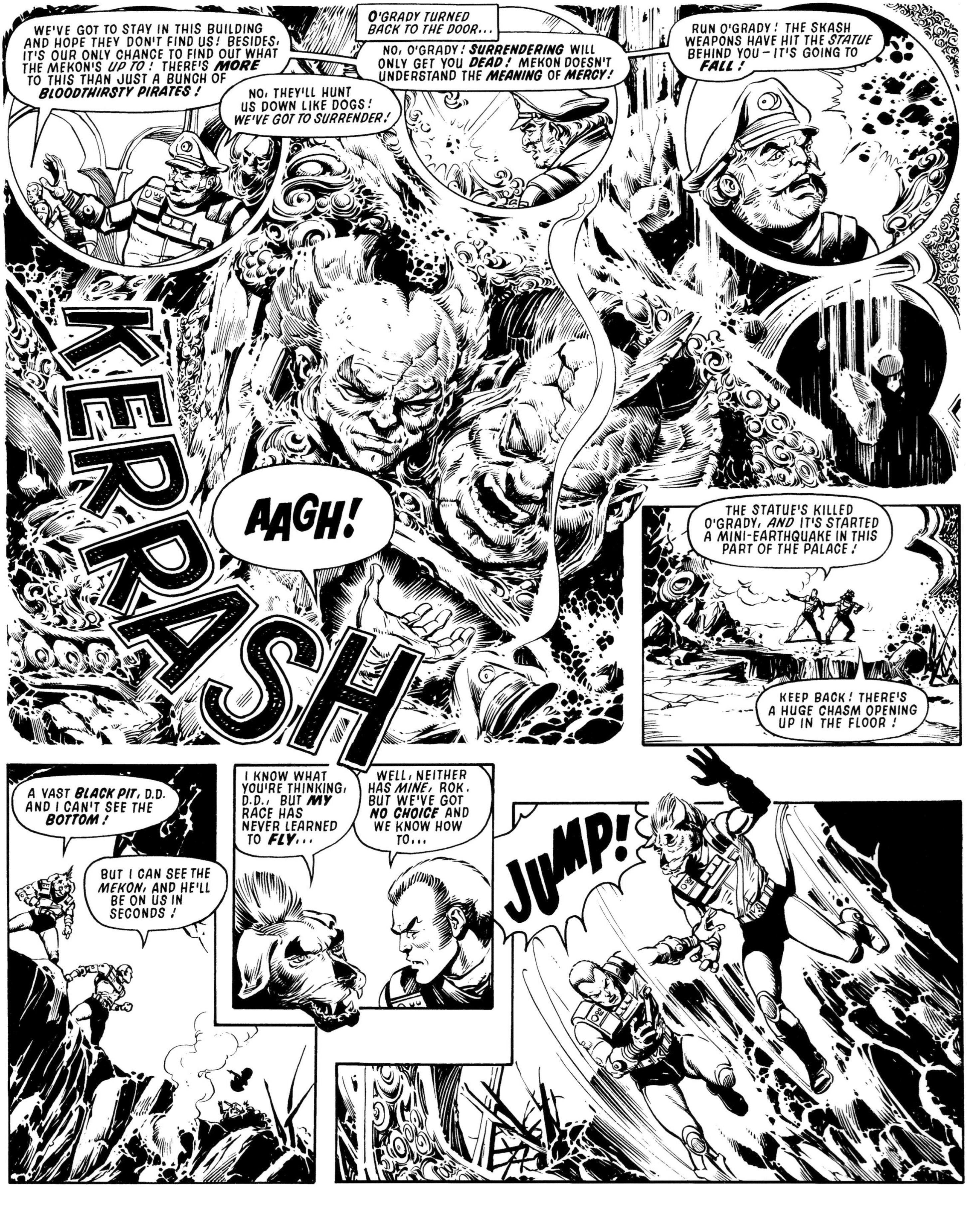

WE'VE GOT TO STAY IN THIS BUILDING AND HOPE THEY DON'T FIND US! BESIDES, IT'S OUR ONLY CHANCE TO FIND OUT WHAT THE MEKON'S UP TO! THERE'S MORE TO THIS THAN JUST A BUNCH OF BLOODTHIRSTY PIRATES!
NO, THEY'LL HUNT US DOWN LIKE DOGS! WE'VE GOT TO SURRENDER!
O'GRADY TURNED BACK TO THE DOOR...
NO, O'GRADY! SURRENDERING WILL ONLY GET YOU DEAD! MEKON DOESN'T UNDERSTAND THE MEANING OF MERCY!
RUN O'GRADY! THE SKASH WEAPONS HAVE HIT THE STATUE BEHIND YOU – IT'S GOING TO FALL!
KERRASH
AAGH!
THE STATUE'S KILLED O'GRADY, AND IT'S STARTED A MINI-EARTHQUAKE IN THIS PART OF THE PALACE!
KEEP BACK! THERE'S A HUGE CHASM OPENING UP IN THE FLOOR!
A VAST BLACK PIT, D.D. AND I CAN'T SEE THE BOTTOM!
BUT I CAN SEE THE MEKON, AND HE'LL BE ON US IN SECONDS!
I KNOW WHAT YOU'RE THINKING, D.D., BUT MY RACE HAS NEVER LEARNED TO FLY...
WELL, NEITHER HAS MINE, ROK. BUT WE'VE GOT NO CHOICE AND WE KNOW HOW TO...
JUMP!

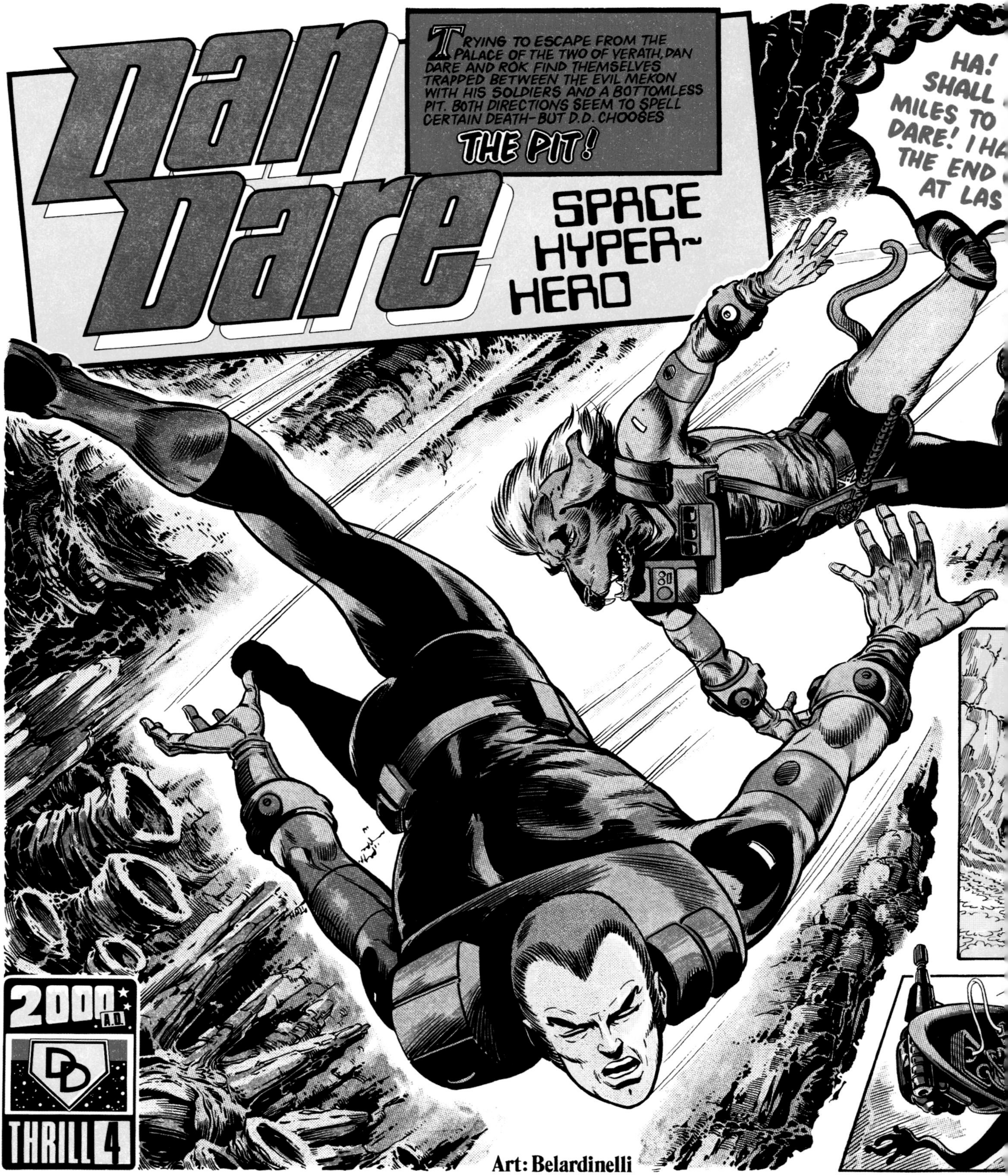

DAN DARE
TRYING TO ESCAPE FROM THE PALACE OF THE TWO OF YERATH, DAN DARE AND ROK FIND THEMSELVES TRAPPED BETWEEN THE EVIL MEKON WITH HIS SOLDIERS AND A BOTTOMLESS PIT. BOTH DIRECTIONS SEEM TO SPELL CERTAIN DEATH–BUT D.D. CHOOSES
THE PIT!
SPACE HYPER~HERO
HA! SHALL
MILES TO
DARE! I HA
THE END
AT LAS
2000 A.D.
DD
THRILL 4

Art: Belardinelli

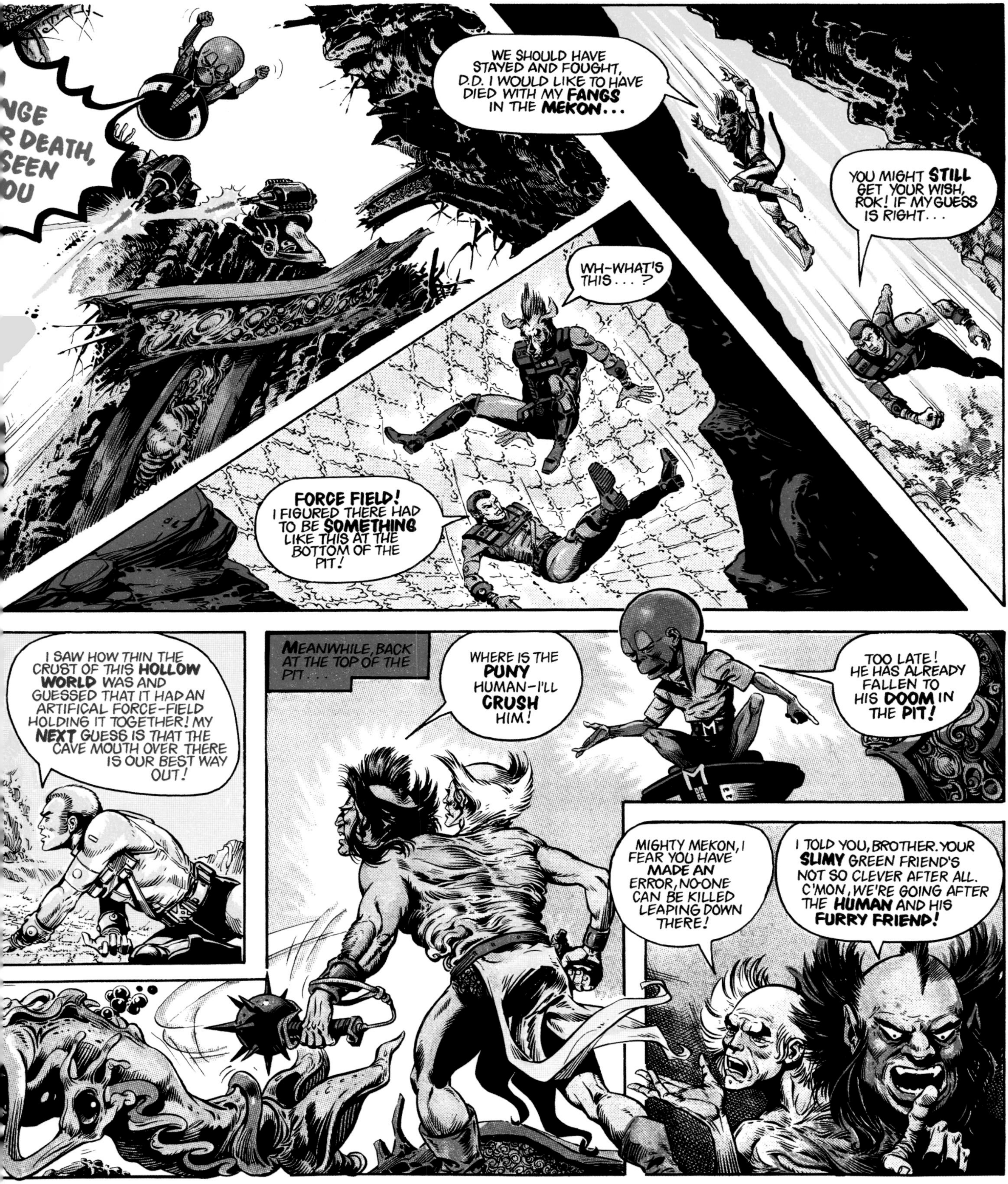

NGE
R DEATH,
SEEN
OU
WE SHOULD HAVE STAYED AND FOUGHT, D.D. I WOULD LIKE TO HAVE DIED WITH MY FANGS IN THE MEKON...
YOU MIGHT STILL GET YOUR WISH, ROK! IF MY GUESS IS RIGHT...
WH-WHAT'S THIS...?
FORCE FIELD! I FIGURED THERE HAD TO BE SOMETHING LIKE THIS AT THE BOTTOM OF THE PIT!
I SAW HOW THIN THE CRUST OF THIS HOLLOW WORLD WAS AND GUESSED THAT IT HAD AN ARTIFICAL FORCE-FIELD HOLDING IT TOGETHER! MY NEXT GUESS IS THAT THE CAVE MOUTH OVER THERE IS OUR BEST WAY OUT!
MEANWHILE, BACK AT THE TOP OF THE PIT...
WHERE IS THE PUNY HUMAN—I'LL CRUSH HIM!
TOO LATE! HE HAS ALREADY FALLEN TO HIS DOOM IN THE PIT!
MIGHTY MEKON, I FEAR YOU HAVE MADE AN ERROR, NO-ONE CAN BE KILLED LEAPING DOWN THERE!
I TOLD YOU, BROTHER. YOUR SLIMY GREEN FRIEND'S NOT SO CLEVER AFTER ALL. C'MON, WE'RE GOING AFTER THE HUMAN AND HIS FURRY FRIEND!

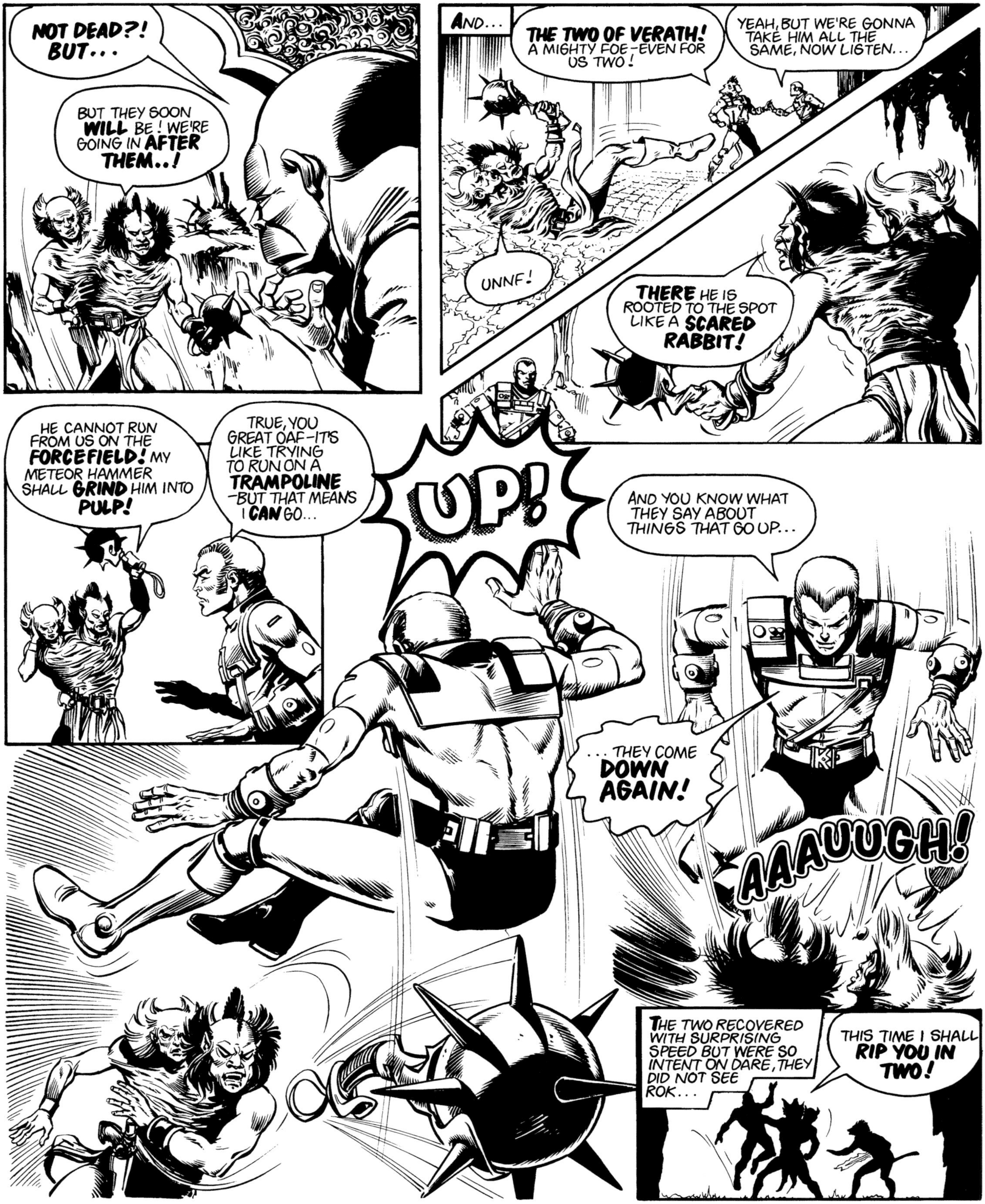

NOT DEAD?! BUT...
BUT THEY SOON WILL BE! WE'RE GOING IN AFTER THEM..!
AND...
THE TWO OF VERATH! A MIGHTY FOE–EVEN FOR US TWO!
YEAH, BUT WE'RE GONNA TAKE HIM ALL THE SAME, NOW LISTEN...
UNNF!
THERE HE IS ROOTED TO THE SPOT LIKE A SCARED RABBIT!
HE CANNOT RUN FROM US ON THE FORCEFIELD! MY METEOR HAMMER SHALL GRIND HIM INTO PULP!
TRUE, YOU GREAT OAF–IT'S LIKE TRYING TO RUN ON A TRAMPOLINE –BUT THAT MEANS I CAN GO...
UP!
AND YOU KNOW WHAT THEY SAY ABOUT THINGS THAT GO UP...
...THEY COME DOWN AGAIN!
AAAUUGH!
THE TWO RECOVERED WITH SURPRISING SPEED BUT WERE SO INTENT ON DARE, THEY DID NOT SEE ROK...
THIS TIME I SHALL RIP YOU IN TWO!

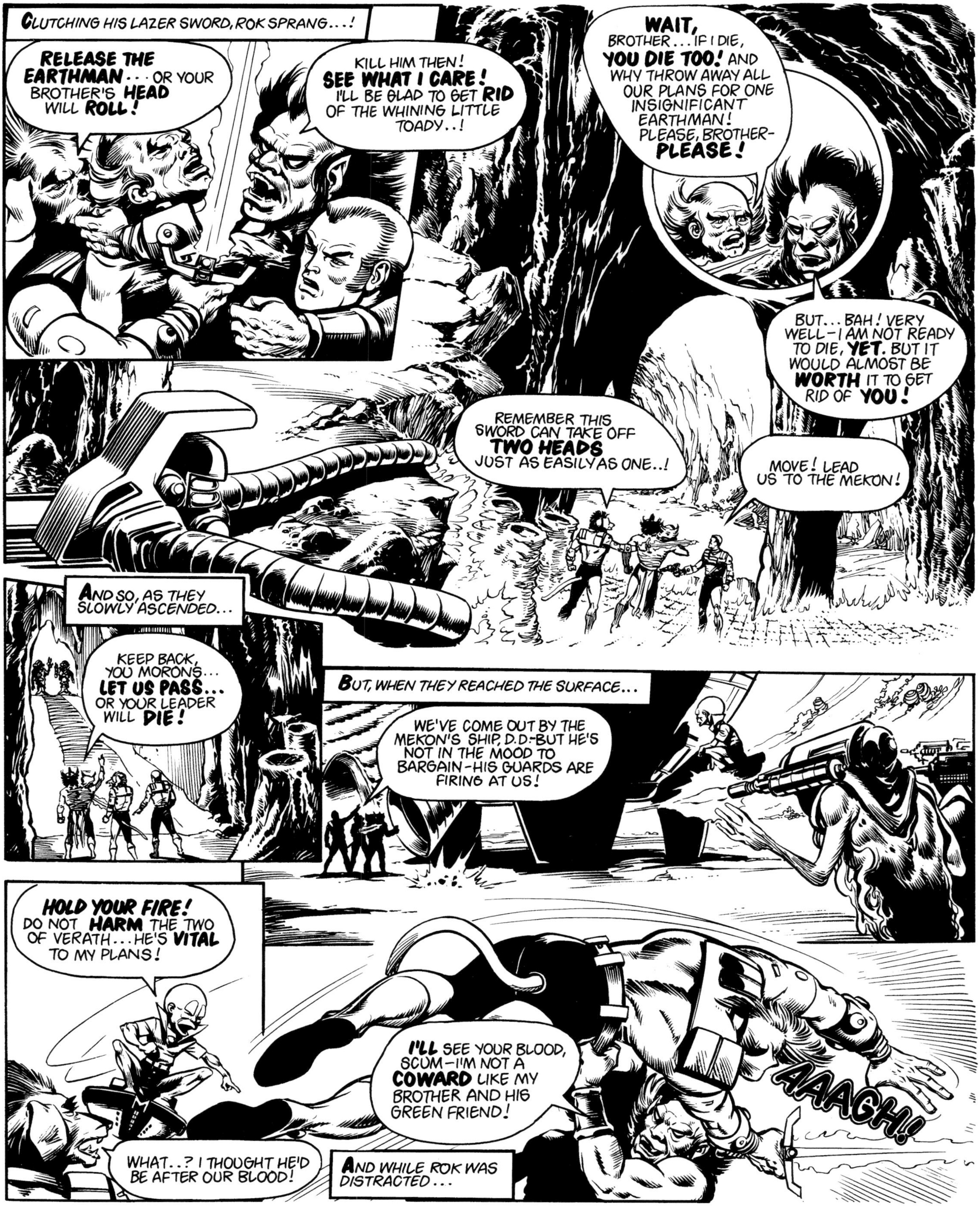

CLUTCHING HIS LAZER SWORD, ROK SPRANG...!
RELEASE THE EARTHMAN... OR YOUR BROTHER'S HEAD WILL ROLL!
KILL HIM THEN! SEE WHAT I CARE! I'LL BE GLAD TO GET RID OF THE WHINING LITTLE TOADY..!
WAIT, BROTHER... IF I DIE, YOU DIE TOO! AND WHY THROW AWAY ALL OUR PLANS FOR ONE INSIGNIFICANT EARTHMAN! PLEASE, BROTHER- PLEASE!
BUT... BAH! VERY WELL-I AM NOT READY TO DIE, YET. BUT IT WOULD ALMOST BE WORTH IT TO GET RID OF YOU!
REMEMBER THIS SWORD CAN TAKE OFF TWO HEADS JUST AS EASILY AS ONE..!
MOVE! LEAD US TO THE MEKON!
AND SO, AS THEY SLOWLY ASCENDED...
KEEP BACK, YOU MORONS... LET US PASS... OR YOUR LEADER WILL DIE!
BUT, WHEN THEY REACHED THE SURFACE...
WE'VE COME OUT BY THE MEKON'S SHIP, D.D.-BUT HE'S NOT IN THE MOOD TO BARGAIN-HIS GUARDS ARE FIRING AT US!
HOLD YOUR FIRE! DO NOT HARM THE TWO OF VERATH... HE'S VITAL TO MY PLANS!
I'LL SEE YOUR BLOOD, SCUM-I'M NOT A COWARD LIKE MY BROTHER AND HIS GREEN FRIEND!
AAAGH!
WHAT..? I THOUGHT HE'D BE AFTER OUR BLOOD!
AND WHILE ROK WAS DISTRACTED...

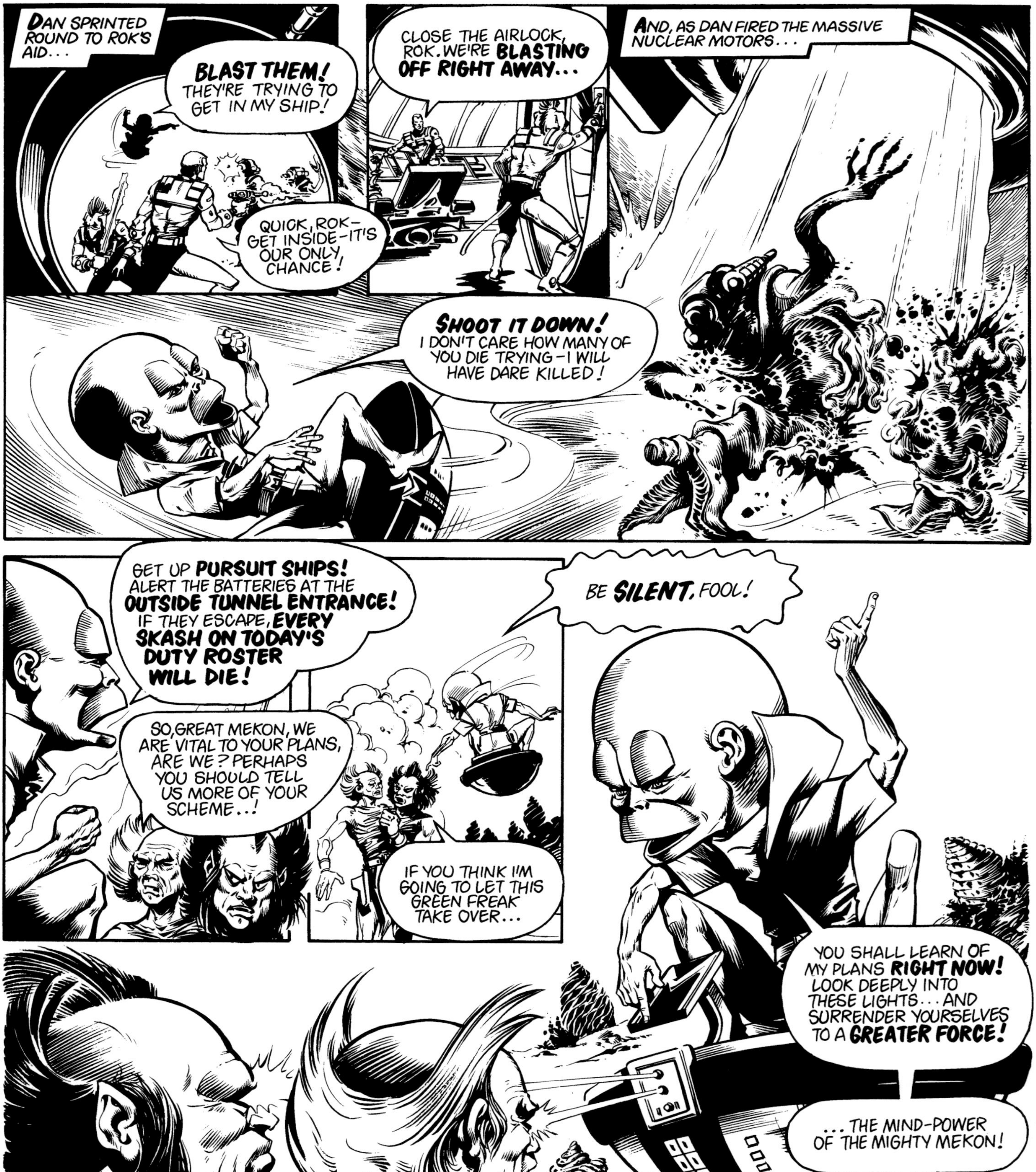

DAN SPRINTED ROUND TO ROK'S AID...
BLAST THEM! THEY'RE TRYING TO GET IN MY SHIP!
QUICK, ROK– GET INSIDE–IT'S OUR ONLY CHANCE!
CLOSE THE AIRLOCK, ROK. WE'RE BLASTING OFF RIGHT AWAY...
AND, AS DAN FIRED THE MASSIVE NUCLEAR MOTORS...
SHOOT IT DOWN! I DON'T CARE HOW MANY OF YOU DIE TRYING–I WILL HAVE DARE KILLED!
GET UP PURSUIT SHIPS! ALERT THE BATTERIES AT THE OUTSIDE TUNNEL ENTRANCE! IF THEY ESCAPE, EVERY SKASH ON TODAY'S DUTY ROSTER WILL DIE!
SO, GREAT MEKON, WE ARE VITAL TO YOUR PLANS, ARE WE? PERHAPS YOU SHOULD TELL US MORE OF YOUR SCHEME..!
IF YOU THINK I'M GOING TO LET THIS GREEN FREAK TAKE OVER...
BE SILENT, FOOL!
YOU SHALL LEARN OF MY PLANS RIGHT NOW! LOOK DEEPLY INTO THESE LIGHTS... AND SURRENDER YOURSELVES TO A GREATER FORCE!
... THE MIND-POWER OF THE MIGHTY MEKON!

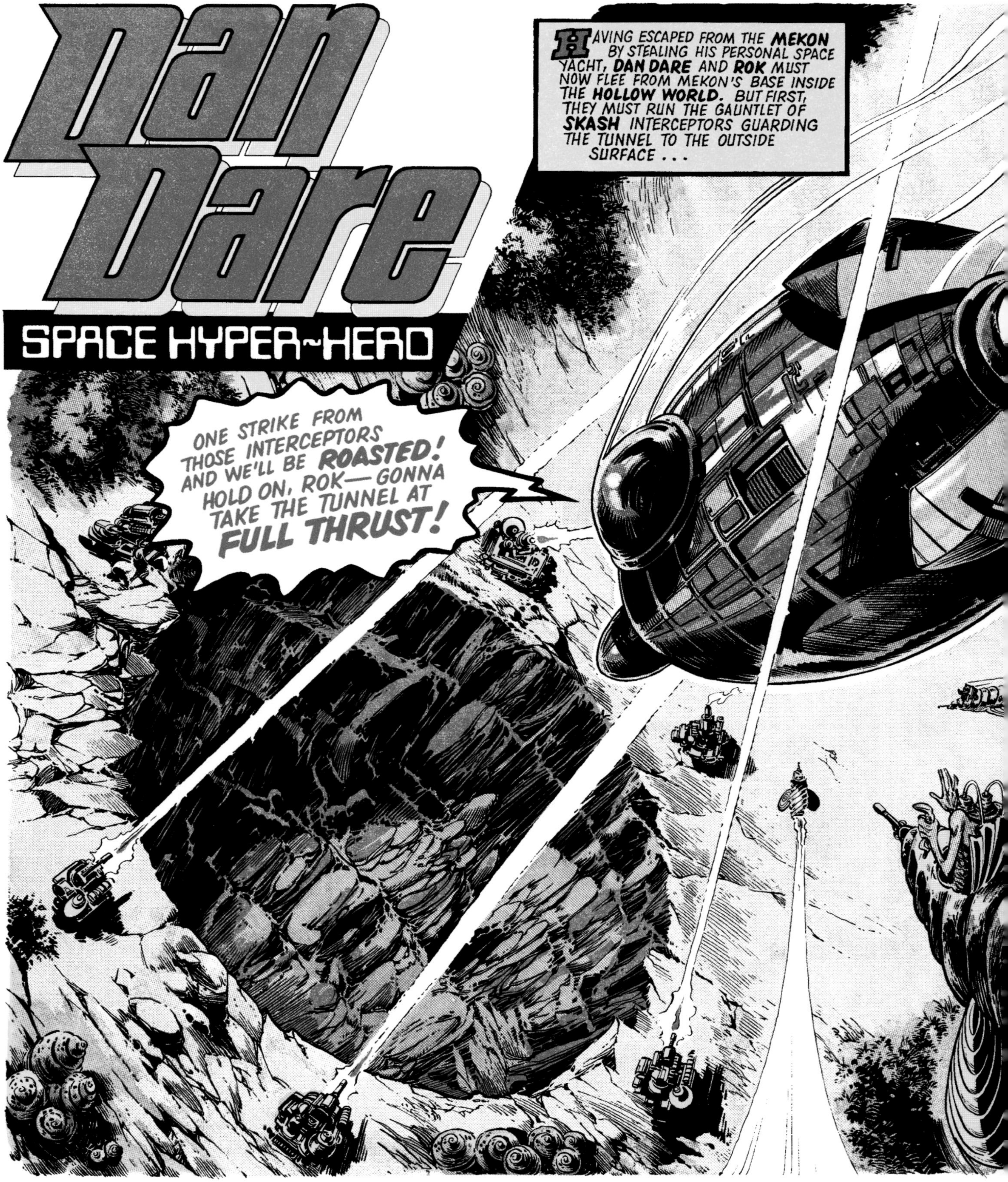
Dan Dare
SPACE HYPER~HERO
HAVING ESCAPED FROM THE MEKON BY STEALING HIS PERSONAL SPACE YACHT, DAN DARE AND ROK MUST NOW FLEE FROM MEKON'S BASE INSIDE THE HOLLOW WORLD. BUT FIRST, THEY MUST RUN THE GAUNTLET OF SKASH INTERCEPTORS GUARDING THE TUNNEL TO THE OUTSIDE SURFACE ...
ONE STRIKE FROM THOSE INTERCEPTORS AND WE'LL BE ROASTED! HOLD ON, ROK— GONNA TAKE THE TUNNEL AT FULL THRUST!

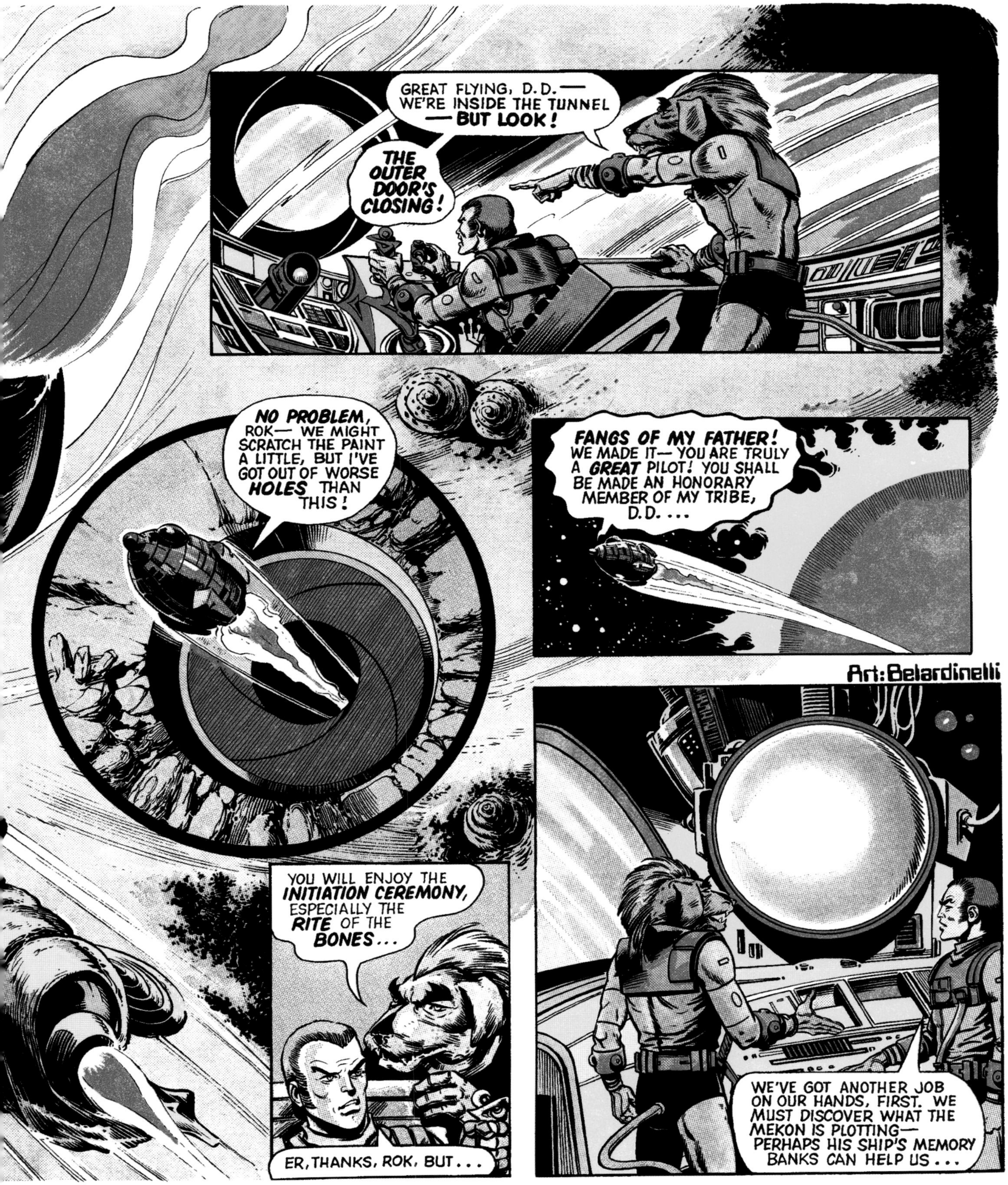
GREAT FLYING, D.D.— WE'RE INSIDE THE TUNNEL —BUT LOOK!
THE OUTER DOOR'S CLOSING!
NO PROBLEM, ROK— WE MIGHT SCRATCH THE PAINT A LITTLE, BUT I'VE GOT OUT OF WORSE HOLES THAN THIS!
FANGS OF MY FATHER! WE MADE IT— YOU ARE TRULY A GREAT PILOT! YOU SHALL BE MADE AN HONORARY MEMBER OF MY TRIBE, D.D. ...
Art: Belardinelli
YOU WILL ENJOY THE INITIATION CEREMONY, ESPECIALLY THE RITE OF THE BONES...
ER, THANKS, ROK, BUT...
WE'VE GOT ANOTHER JOB ON OUR HANDS, FIRST. WE MUST DISCOVER WHAT THE MEKON IS PLOTTING— PERHAPS HIS SHIP'S MEMORY BANKS CAN HELP US...

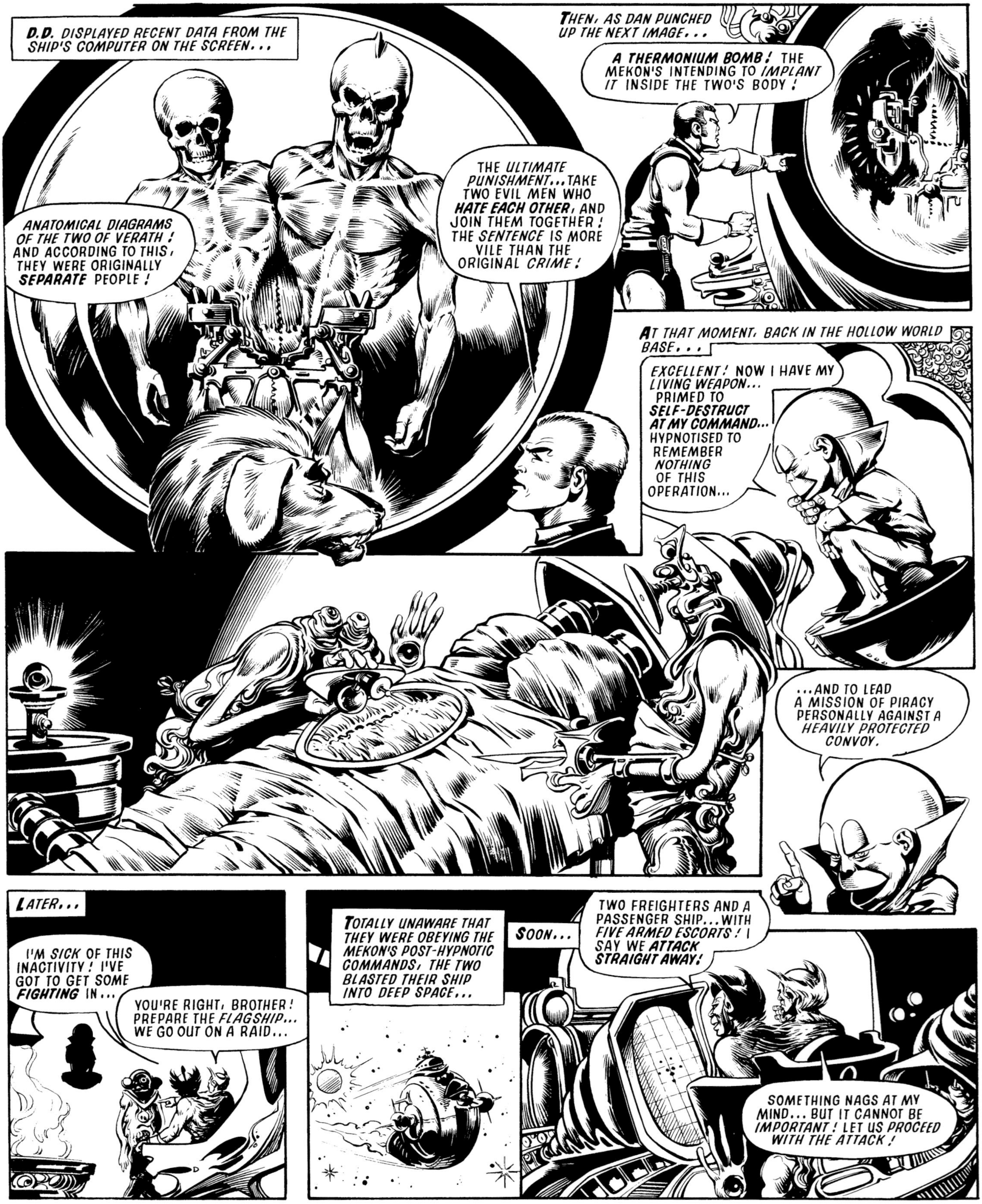

D.D. DISPLAYED RECENT DATA FROM THE SHIP'S COMPUTER ON THE SCREEN...
ANATOMICAL DIAGRAMS OF THE TWO OF VERATH! AND ACCORDING TO THIS, THEY WERE ORIGINALLY SEPARATE PEOPLE!
THE ULTIMATE PUNISHMENT... TAKE TWO EVIL MEN WHO HATE EACH OTHER, AND JOIN THEM TOGETHER! THE SENTENCE IS MORE VILE THAN THE ORIGINAL CRIME!
THEN, AS DAN PUNCHED UP THE NEXT IMAGE...
A THERMONIUM BOMB! THE MEKON'S INTENDING TO IMPLANT IT INSIDE THE TWO'S BODY!
AT THAT MOMENT, BACK IN THE HOLLOW WORLD BASE...
EXCELLENT! NOW I HAVE MY LIVING WEAPON... PRIMED TO SELF-DESTRUCT AT MY COMMAND... HYPNOTISED TO REMEMBER NOTHING OF THIS OPERATION...
...AND TO LEAD A MISSION OF PIRACY PERSONALLY AGAINST A HEAVILY PROTECTED CONVOY.
LATER...
I'M SICK OF THIS INACTIVITY! I'VE GOT TO GET SOME FIGHTING IN...
YOU'RE RIGHT, BROTHER! PREPARE THE FLAGSHIP... WE GO OUT ON A RAID...
TOTALLY UNAWARE THAT THEY WERE OBEYING THE MEKON'S POST-HYPNOTIC COMMANDS, THE TWO BLASTED THEIR SHIP INTO DEEP SPACE...
SOON...
TWO FREIGHTERS AND A PASSENGER SHIP... WITH FIVE ARMED ESCORTS! I SAY WE ATTACK STRAIGHT AWAY!
SOMETHING NAGS AT MY MIND... BUT IT CANNOT BE IMPORTANT! LET US PROCEED WITH THE ATTACK!

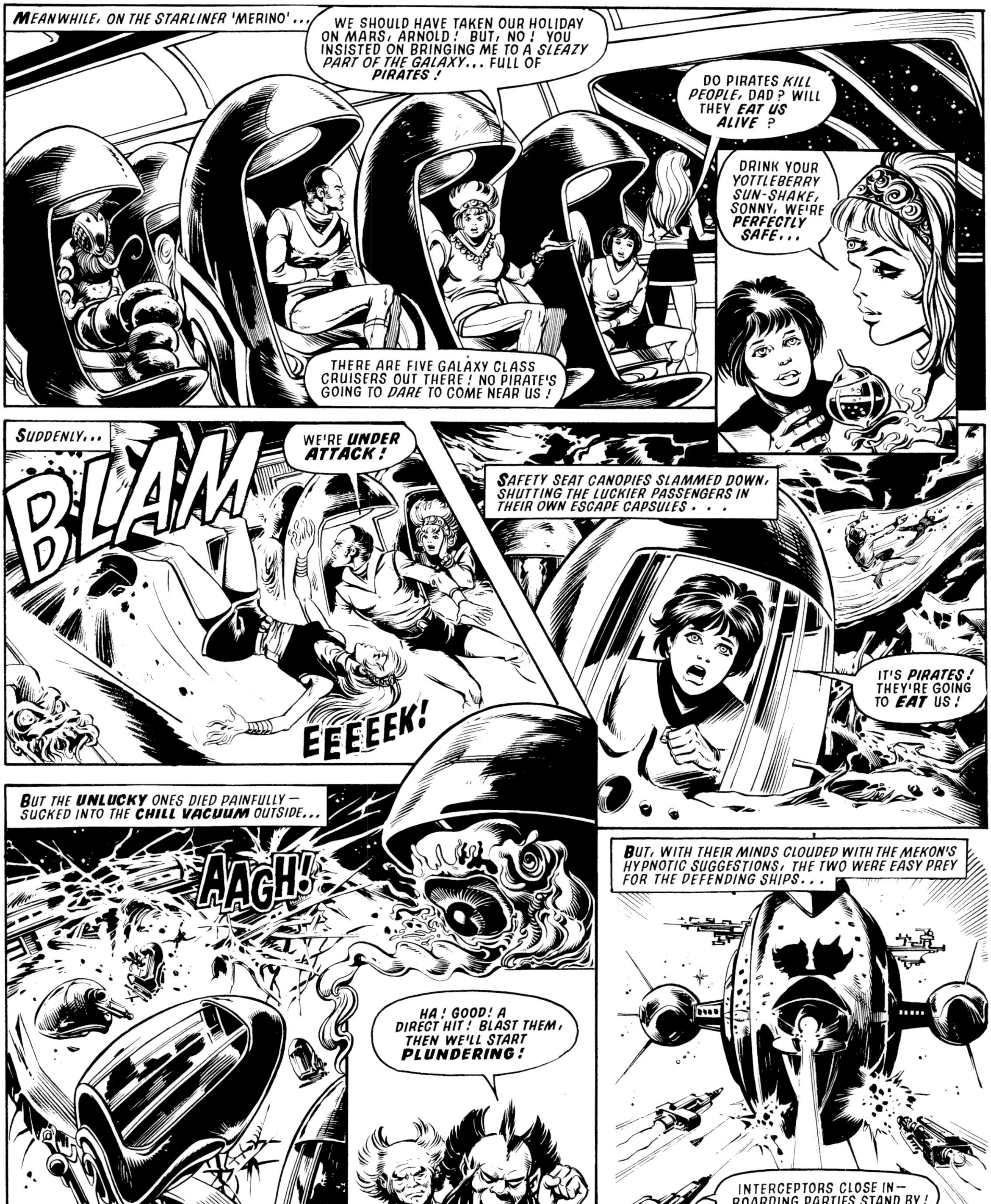
MEANWHILE, ON THE STARLINER 'MERINO'...
WE SHOULD HAVE TAKEN OUR HOLIDAY ON MARS, ARNOLD! BUT, NO! YOU INSISTED ON BRINGING ME TO A SLEAZY PART OF THE GALAXY... FULL OF PIRATES!
DO PIRATES KILL PEOPLE, DAD? WILL THEY EAT US ALIVE?
DRINK YOUR YOTTLEBERRY SUN-SHAKE, SONNY, WE'RE PERFECTLY SAFE...
THERE ARE FIVE GALAXY CLASS CRUISERS OUT THERE! NO PIRATE'S GOING TO DARE TO COME NEAR US!
SUDDENLY...
BLAM
WE'RE UNDER ATTACK!
EEEEEK!
SAFETY SEAT CANOPIES SLAMMED DOWN, SHUTTING THE LUCKIER PASSENGERS IN THEIR OWN ESCAPE CAPSULES . . .
IT'S PIRATES! THEY'RE GOING TO EAT US!
BUT THE UNLUCKY ONES DIED PAINFULLY — SUCKED INTO THE CHILL VACUUM OUTSIDE...
AAGH!
HA! GOOD! A DIRECT HIT! BLAST THEM, THEN WE'LL START PLUNDERING!
BUT, WITH THEIR MINDS CLOUDED WITH THE MEKON'S HYPNOTIC SUGGESTIONS, THE TWO WERE EASY PREY FOR THE DEFENDING SHIPS...
INTERCEPTORS CLOSE IN — BOARDING PARTIES STAND BY!

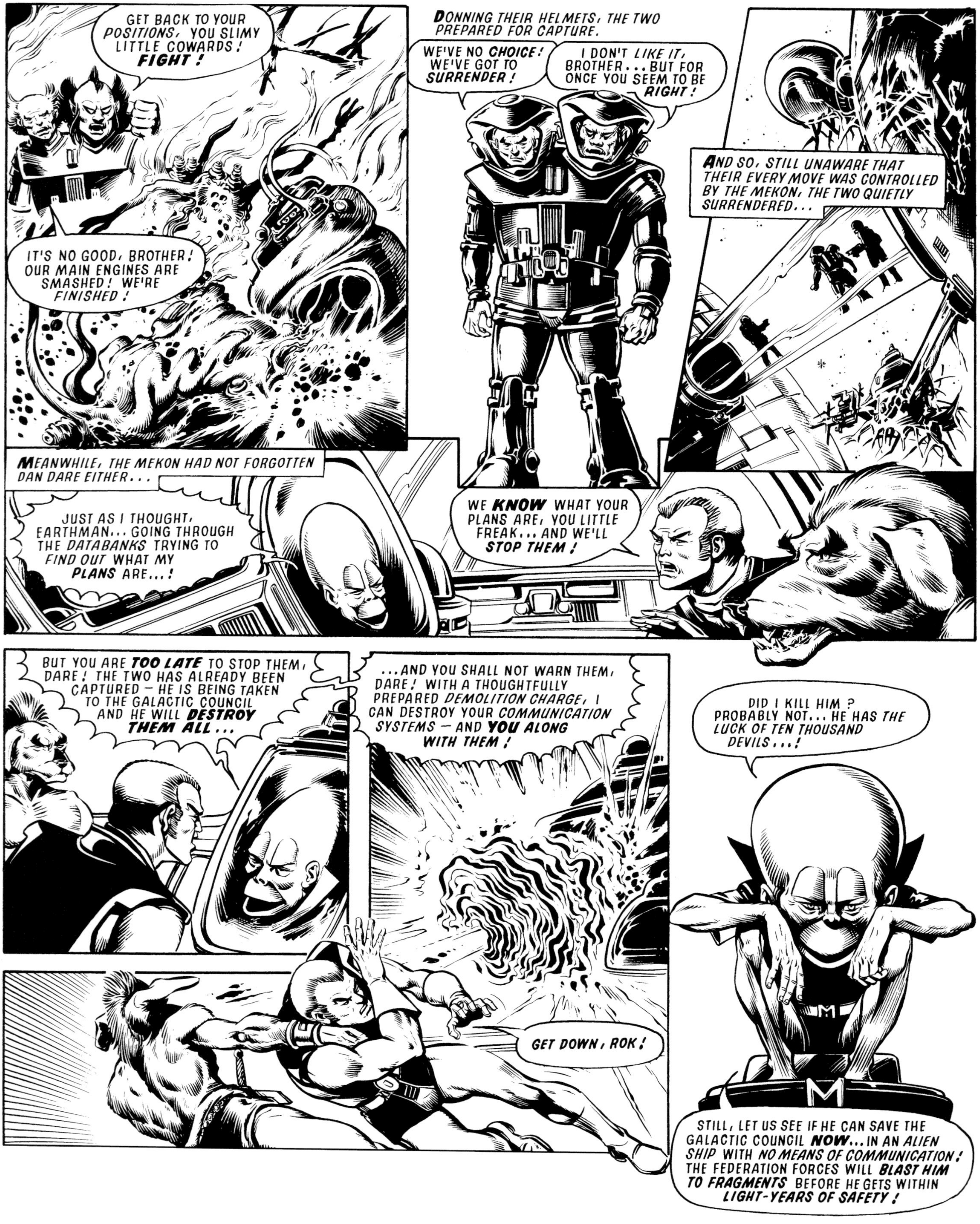
GET BACK TO YOUR POSITIONS, YOU SLIMY LITTLE COWARDS! FIGHT!
IT'S NO GOOD, BROTHER! OUR MAIN ENGINES ARE SMASHED! WE'RE FINISHED!
DONNING THEIR HELMETS, THE TWO PREPARED FOR CAPTURE.
WE'VE NO CHOICE! WE'VE GOT TO SURRENDER!
I DON'T LIKE IT, BROTHER... BUT FOR ONCE YOU SEEM TO BE RIGHT!
AND SO, STILL UNAWARE THAT THEIR EVERY MOVE WAS CONTROLLED BY THE MEKON, THE TWO QUIETLY SURRENDERED...
MEANWHILE, THE MEKON HAD NOT FORGOTTEN DAN DARE EITHER...
JUST AS I THOUGHT, EARTHMAN... GOING THROUGH THE DATABANKS TRYING TO FIND OUT WHAT MY PLANS ARE...!
WE KNOW WHAT YOUR PLANS ARE, YOU LITTLE FREAK... AND WE'LL STOP THEM!
BUT YOU ARE TOO LATE TO STOP THEM, DARE! THE TWO HAS ALREADY BEEN CAPTURED — HE IS BEING TAKEN TO THE GALACTIC COUNCIL AND HE WILL DESTROY THEM ALL...
...AND YOU SHALL NOT WARN THEM, DARE! WITH A THOUGHTFULLY PREPARED DEMOLITION CHARGE, I CAN DESTROY YOUR COMMUNICATION SYSTEMS — AND YOU ALONG WITH THEM!
GET DOWN, ROK!
DID I KILL HIM? PROBABLY NOT... HE HAS THE LUCK OF TEN THOUSAND DEVILS...!
STILL, LET US SEE IF HE CAN SAVE THE GALACTIC COUNCIL NOW... IN AN ALIEN SHIP WITH NO MEANS OF COMMUNICATION! THE FEDERATION FORCES WILL BLAST HIM TO FRAGMENTS BEFORE HE GETS WITHIN LIGHT-YEARS OF SAFETY!

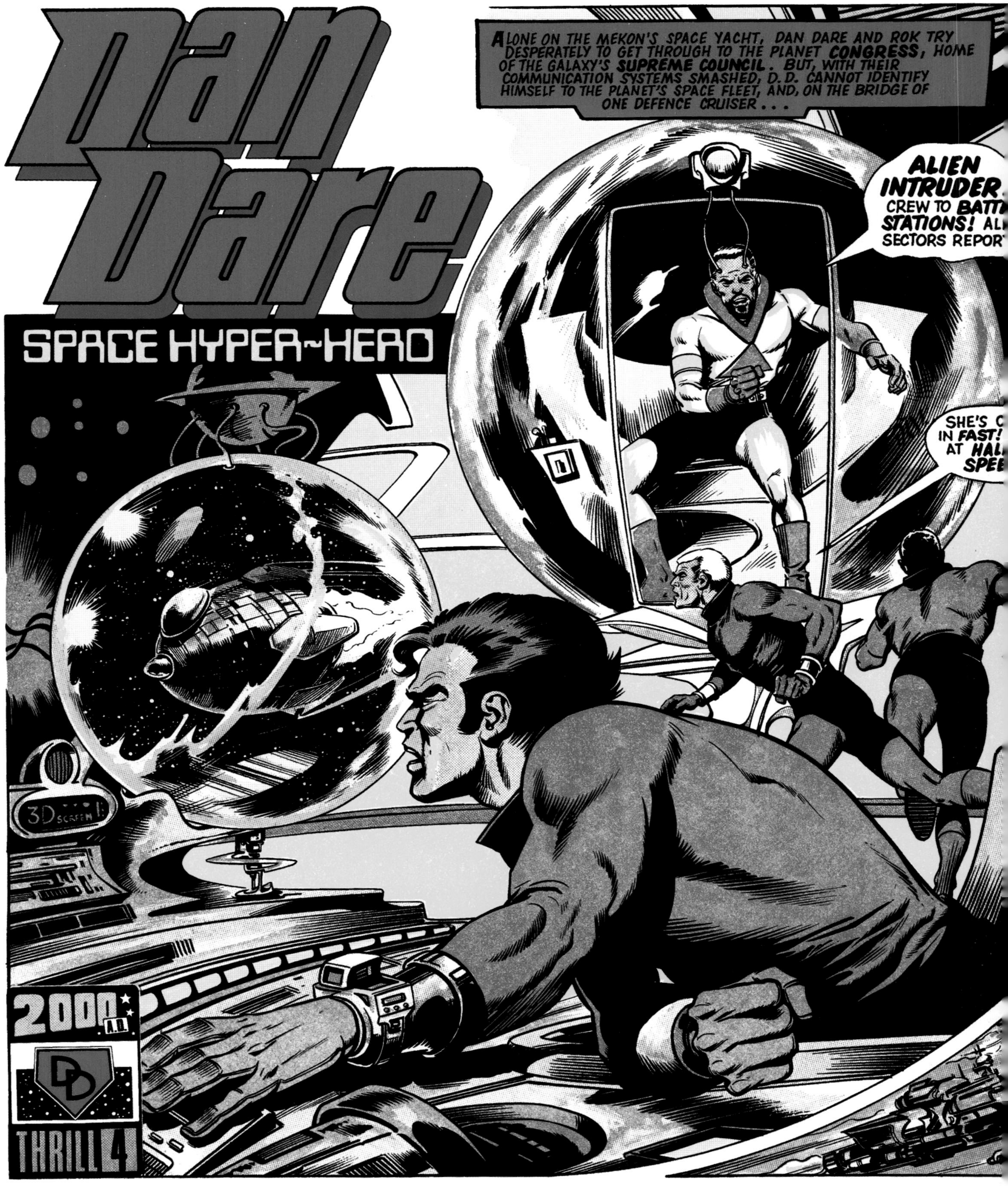

DAN DARE
SPACE HYPER~HERO
ALONE ON THE MEKON'S SPACE YACHT, DAN DARE AND ROK TRY DESPERATELY TO GET THROUGH TO THE PLANET CONGRESS, HOME OF THE GALAXY'S SUPREME COUNCIL. BUT, WITH THEIR COMMUNICATION SYSTEMS SMASHED, D.D. CANNOT IDENTIFY HIMSELF TO THE PLANET'S SPACE FLEET, AND, ON THE BRIDGE OF ONE DEFENCE CRUISER . . .
ALIEN INTRUDER. CREW TO BATT STATIONS! AL SECTORS REPOR
SHE'S IN FAST! AT HAL SPEE
3D SCREEN
2000 A.D.
THRILL 4

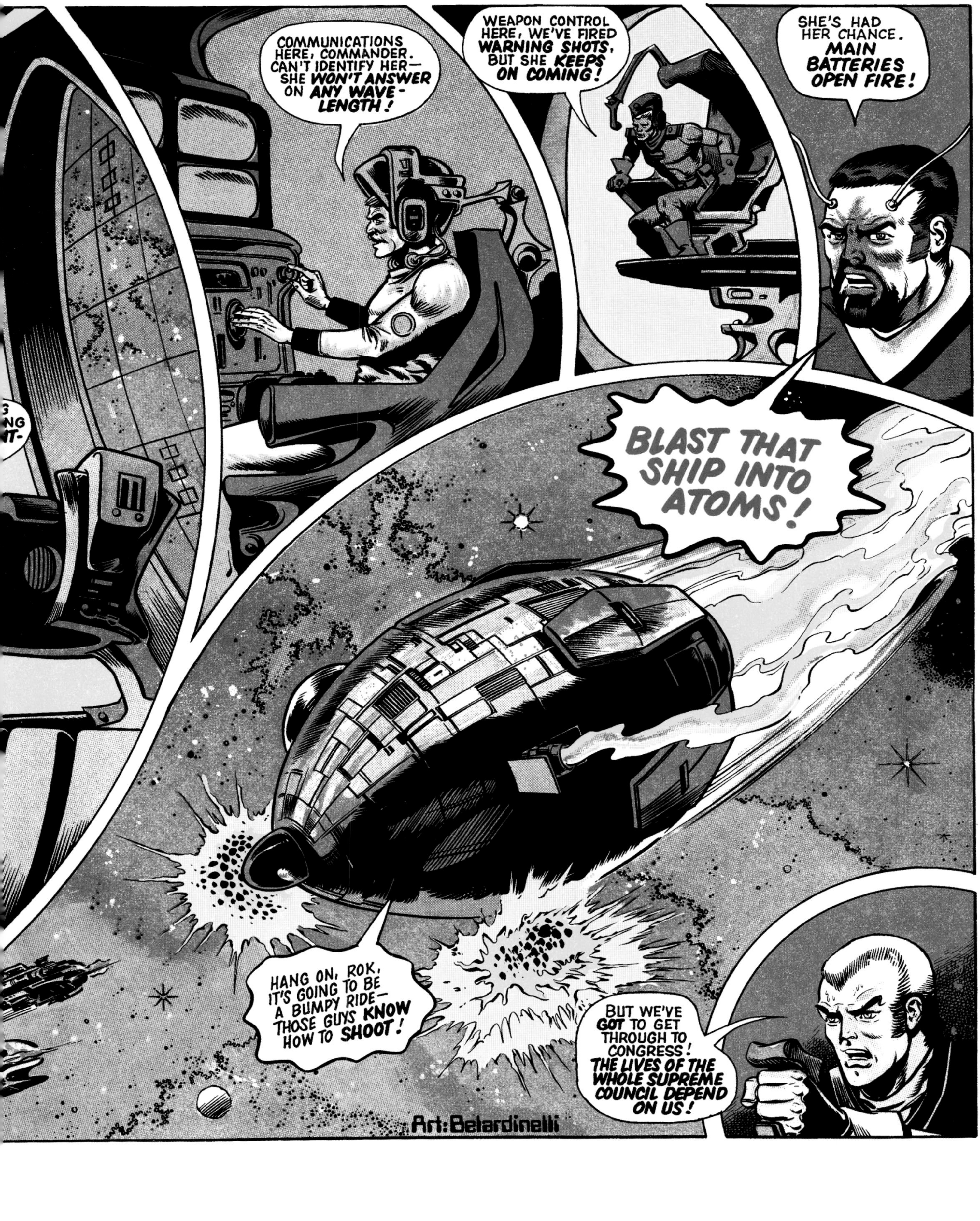
COMMUNICATIONS HERE, COMMANDER. CAN'T IDENTIFY HER— SHE WON'T ANSWER ON ANY WAVE-LENGTH!
WEAPON CONTROL HERE, WE'VE FIRED WARNING SHOTS, BUT SHE KEEPS ON COMING!
SHE'S HAD HER CHANCE. MAIN BATTERIES OPEN FIRE!
BLAST THAT SHIP INTO ATOMS!
HANG ON, ROK, IT'S GOING TO BE A BUMPY RIDE— THOSE GUYS KNOW HOW TO SHOOT!
BUT WE'VE GOT TO GET THROUGH TO CONGRESS! THE LIVES OF THE WHOLE SUPREME COUNCIL DEPEND ON US!
Art: Belardinelli

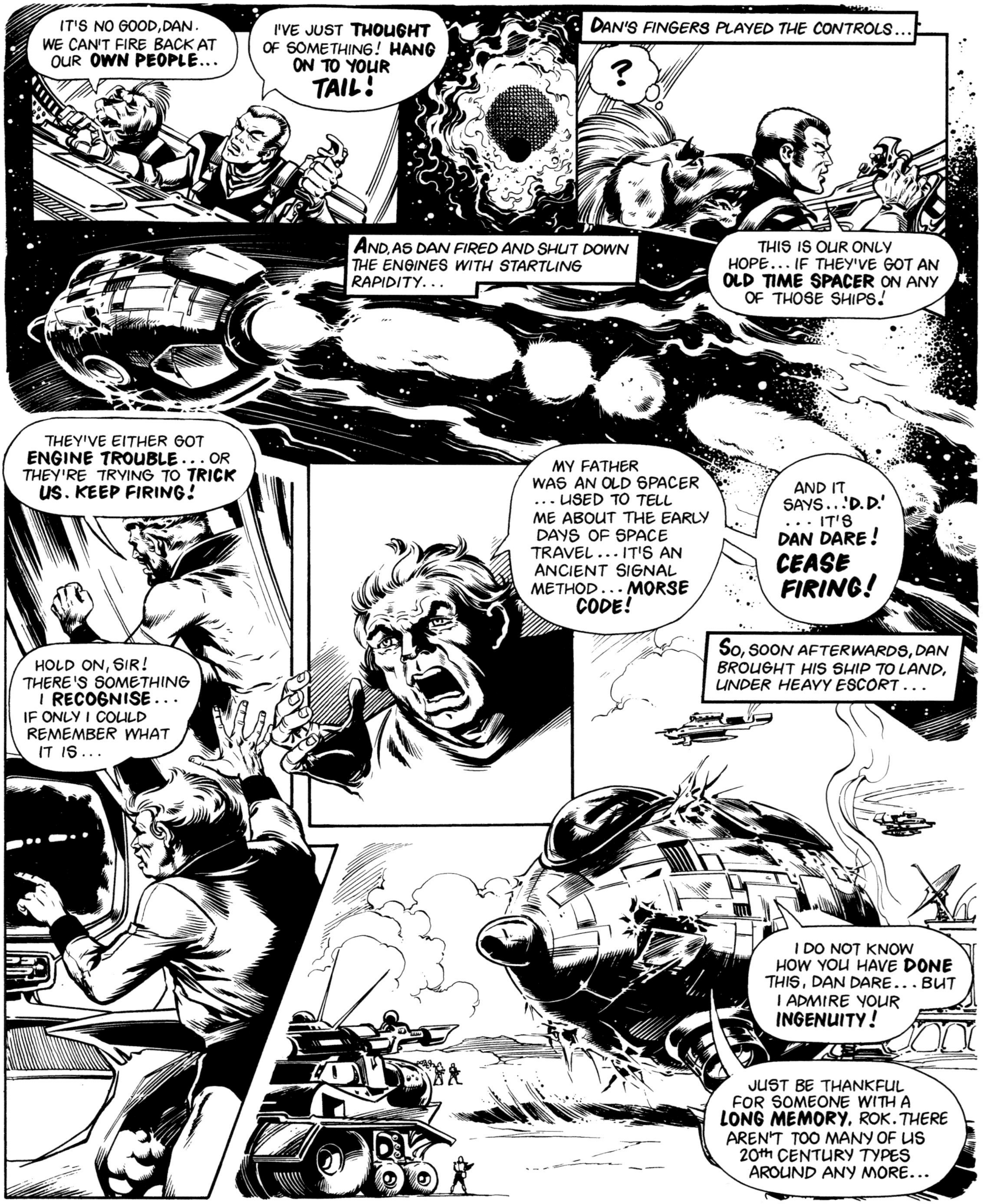

IT'S NO GOOD, DAN. WE CAN'T FIRE BACK AT OUR OWN PEOPLE...
I'VE JUST THOUGHT OF SOMETHING! HANG ON TO YOUR TAIL!
DAN'S FINGERS PLAYED THE CONTROLS...
?
AND, AS DAN FIRED AND SHUT DOWN THE ENGINES WITH STARTLING RAPIDITY...
THIS IS OUR ONLY HOPE... IF THEY'VE GOT AN OLD TIME SPACER ON ANY OF THOSE SHIPS!
THEY'VE EITHER GOT ENGINE TROUBLE... OR THEY'RE TRYING TO TRICK US. KEEP FIRING!
HOLD ON, SIR! THERE'S SOMETHING I RECOGNISE... IF ONLY I COULD REMEMBER WHAT IT IS...
MY FATHER WAS AN OLD SPACER ... USED TO TELL ME ABOUT THE EARLY DAYS OF SPACE TRAVEL... IT'S AN ANCIENT SIGNAL METHOD... MORSE CODE!
AND IT SAYS...'D.D.' ... IT'S DAN DARE! CEASE FIRING!
SO, SOON AFTERWARDS, DAN BROUGHT HIS SHIP TO LAND, UNDER HEAVY ESCORT...
I DO NOT KNOW HOW YOU HAVE DONE THIS, DAN DARE... BUT I ADMIRE YOUR INGENUITY!
JUST BE THANKFUL FOR SOMEONE WITH A LONG MEMORY, ROK. THERE AREN'T TOO MANY OF US 20th CENTURY TYPES AROUND ANY MORE...

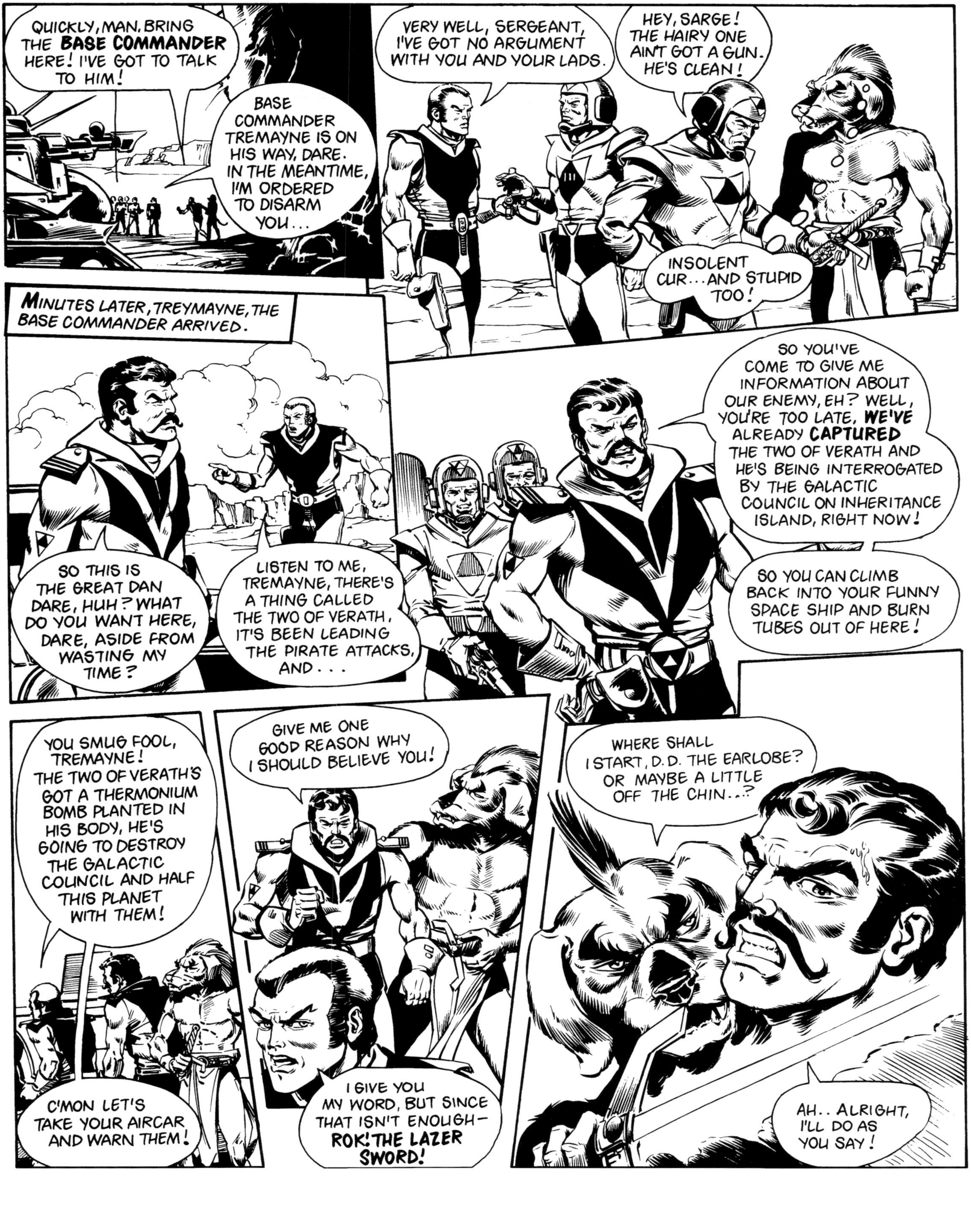
QUICKLY, MAN, BRING THE BASE COMMANDER HERE! I'VE GOT TO TALK TO HIM!
BASE COMMANDER TREMAYNE IS ON HIS WAY, DARE. IN THE MEANTIME, I'M ORDERED TO DISARM YOU...
VERY WELL, SERGEANT, I'VE GOT NO ARGUMENT WITH YOU AND YOUR LADS.
HEY, SARGE! THE HAIRY ONE AIN'T GOT A GUN. HE'S CLEAN!
INSOLENT CUR... AND STUPID TOO!
MINUTES LATER, TREYMAYNE, THE BASE COMMANDER ARRIVED.
SO THIS IS THE GREAT DAN DARE, HUH? WHAT DO YOU WANT HERE, DARE, ASIDE FROM WASTING MY TIME?
LISTEN TO ME, TREMAYNE, THERE'S A THING CALLED THE TWO OF VERATH, IT'S BEEN LEADING THE PIRATE ATTACKS, AND...
SO YOU'VE COME TO GIVE ME INFORMATION ABOUT OUR ENEMY, EH? WELL, YOU'RE TOO LATE, WE'VE ALREADY CAPTURED THE TWO OF VERATH AND HE'S BEING INTERROGATED BY THE GALACTIC COUNCIL ON INHERITANCE ISLAND, RIGHT NOW!
SO YOU CAN CLIMB BACK INTO YOUR FUNNY SPACE SHIP AND BURN TUBES OUT OF HERE!
YOU SMUG FOOL, TREMAYNE! THE TWO OF VERATH'S GOT A THERMONIUM BOMB PLANTED IN HIS BODY, HE'S GOING TO DESTROY THE GALACTIC COUNCIL AND HALF THIS PLANET WITH THEM!
C'MON LET'S TAKE YOUR AIRCAR AND WARN THEM!
GIVE ME ONE GOOD REASON WHY I SHOULD BELIEVE YOU!
I GIVE YOU MY WORD, BUT SINCE THAT ISN'T ENOUGH– ROK! THE LAZER SWORD!
WHERE SHALL I START, D.D. THE EARLOBE? OR MAYBE A LITTLE OFF THE CHIN..?
AH.. ALRIGHT, I'LL DO AS YOU SAY!

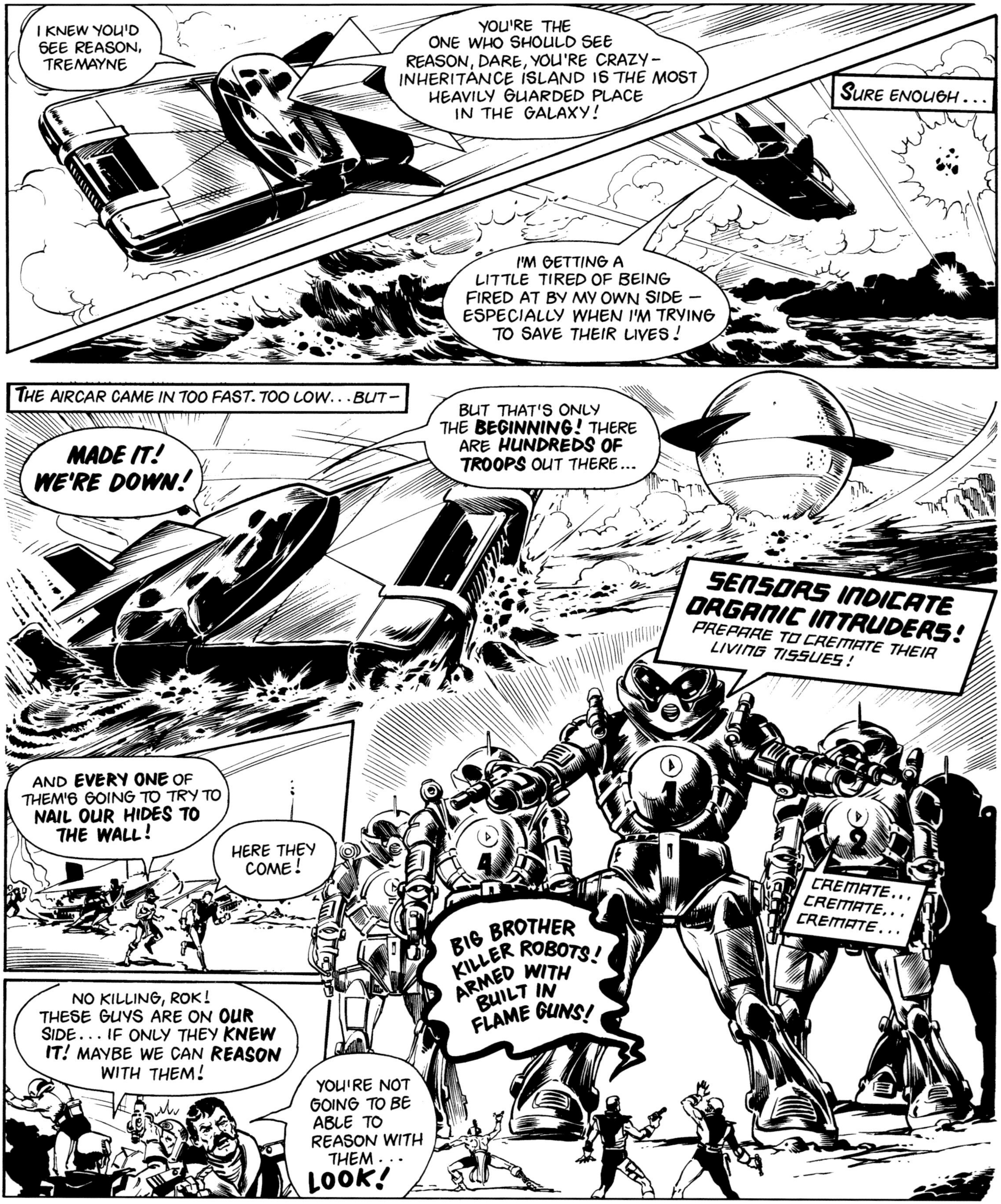

I KNEW YOU'D SEE REASON, TREMAYNE
YOU'RE THE ONE WHO SHOULD SEE REASON, DARE, YOU'RE CRAZY – INHERITANCE ISLAND IS THE MOST HEAVILY GUARDED PLACE IN THE GALAXY!
SURE ENOUGH...
I'M GETTING A LITTLE TIRED OF BEING FIRED AT BY MY OWN SIDE – ESPECIALLY WHEN I'M TRYING TO SAVE THEIR LIVES!
THE AIRCAR CAME IN TOO FAST. TOO LOW... BUT –
MADE IT! WE'RE DOWN!
BUT THAT'S ONLY THE BEGINNING! THERE ARE HUNDREDS OF TROOPS OUT THERE...
SENSORS INDICATE ORGANIC INTRUDERS! PREPARE TO CREMATE THEIR LIVING TISSUES!
AND EVERY ONE OF THEM'S GOING TO TRY TO NAIL OUR HIDES TO THE WALL!
HERE THEY COME!
CREMATE... CREMATE... CREMATE...
BIG BROTHER KILLER ROBOTS! ARMED WITH BUILT IN FLAME GUNS!
NO KILLING, ROK! THESE GUYS ARE ON OUR SIDE... IF ONLY THEY KNEW IT! MAYBE WE CAN REASON WITH THEM!
YOU'RE NOT GOING TO BE ABLE TO REASON WITH THEM... LOOK!

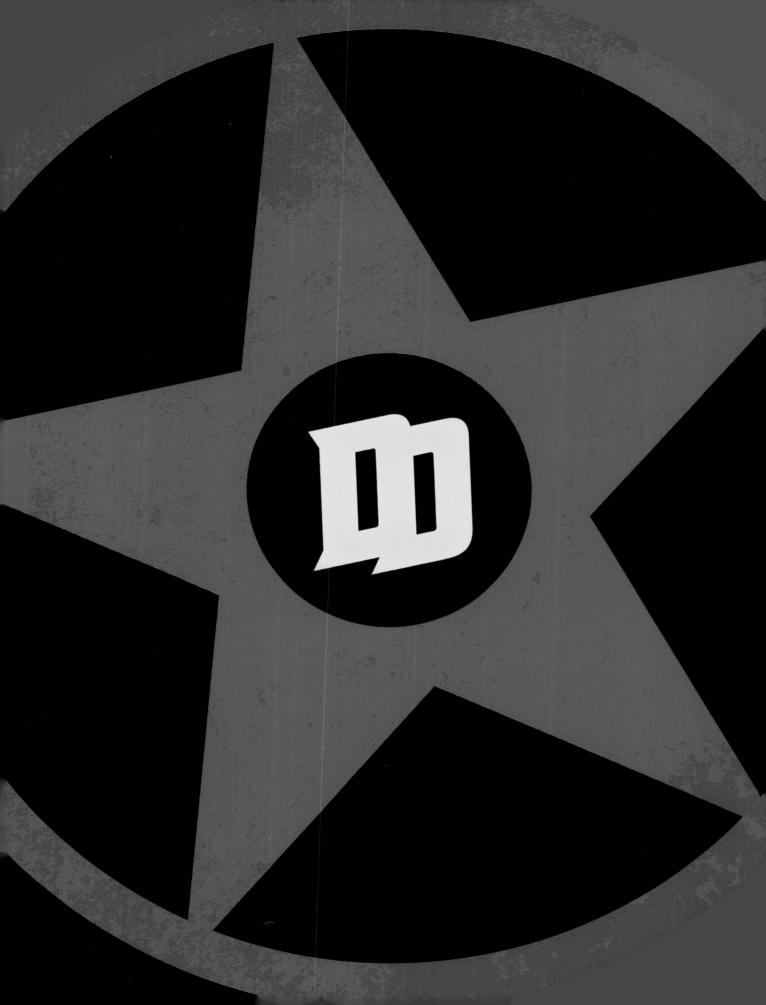

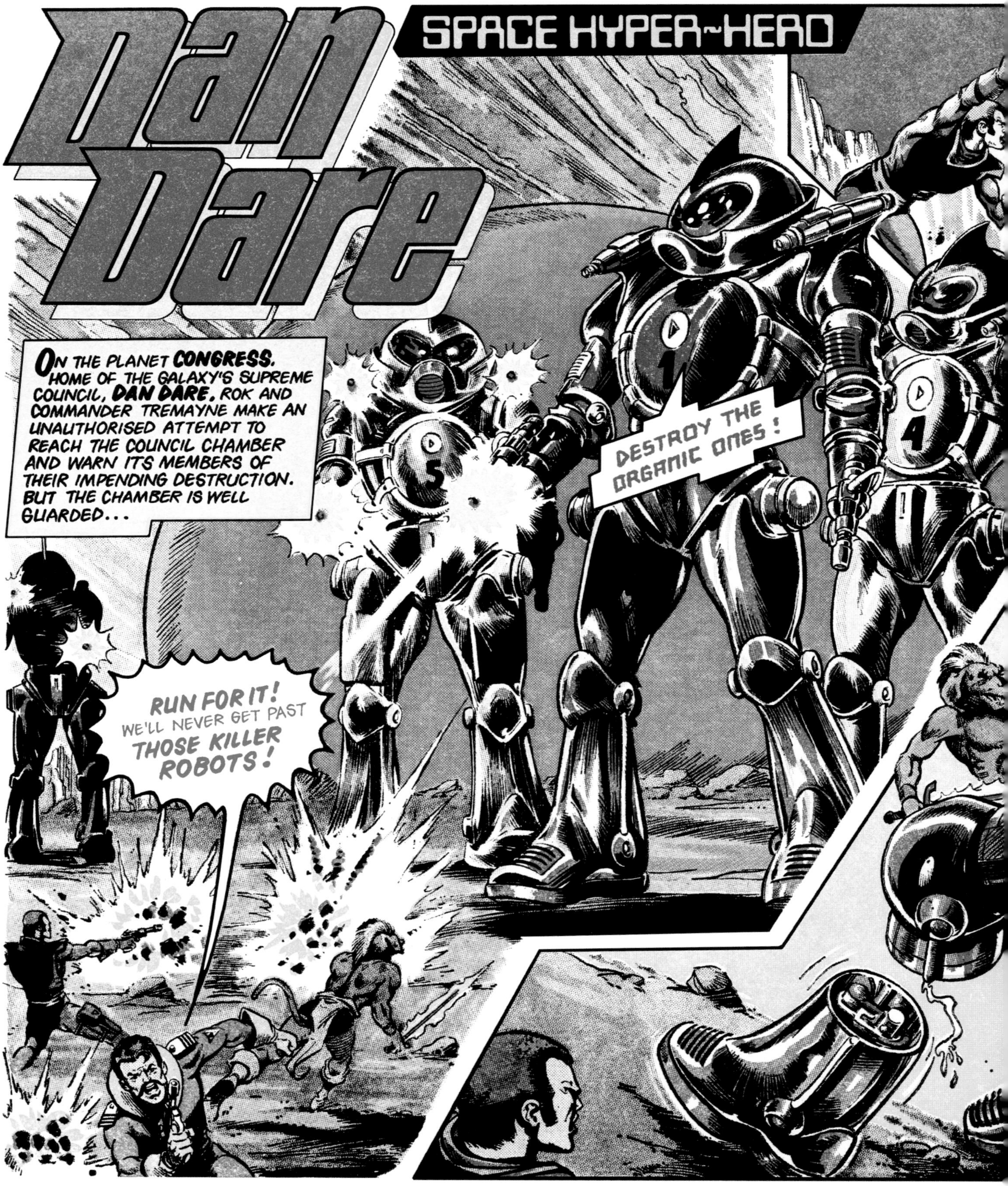

DAN DARE
SPACE HYPER~HERO
ON THE PLANET CONGRESS. HOME OF THE GALAXY'S SUPREME COUNCIL, DAN DARE, ROK AND COMMANDER TREMAYNE MAKE AN UNAUTHORISED ATTEMPT TO REACH THE COUNCIL CHAMBER AND WARN ITS MEMBERS OF THEIR IMPENDING DESTRUCTION. BUT THE CHAMBER IS WELL GUARDED...
DESTROY THE ORGANIC ONES!
RUN FOR IT! WE'LL NEVER GET PAST THOSE KILLER ROBOTS!

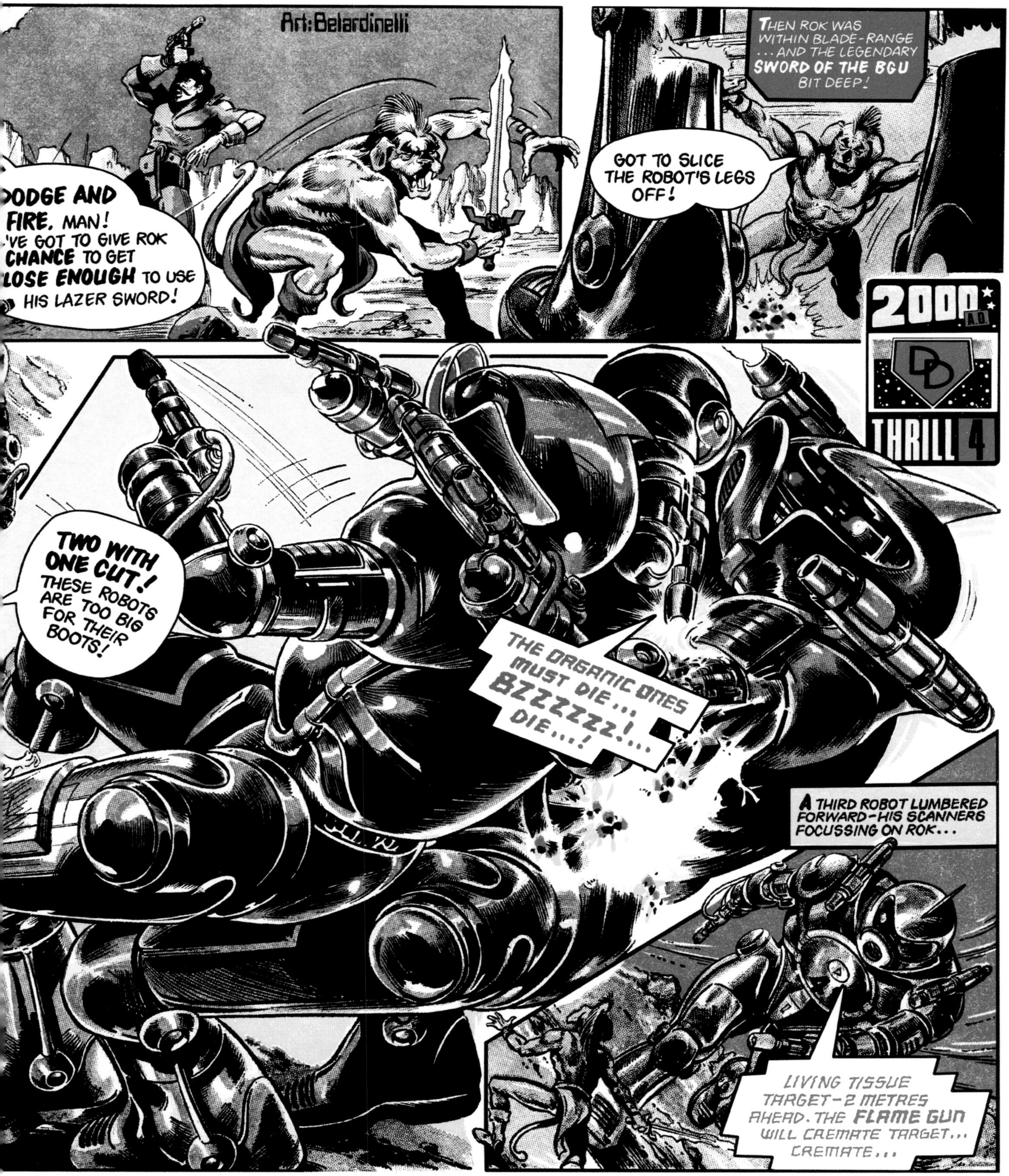

Art: Belardinelli
DODGE AND FIRE, MAN! I'VE GOT TO GIVE ROK A CHANCE TO GET CLOSE ENOUGH TO USE HIS LAZER SWORD!
THEN ROK WAS WITHIN BLADE-RANGE ... AND THE LEGENDARY SWORD OF THE BGU BIT DEEP!
GOT TO SLICE THE ROBOT'S LEGS OFF!
2000 A.D.
THRILL 4
TWO WITH ONE CUT! THESE ROBOTS ARE TOO BIG FOR THEIR BOOTS!
THE ORGANIC ONES MUST DIE... BZZZZZZ!... DIE...!
A THIRD ROBOT LUMBERED FORWARD-HIS SCANNERS FOCUSSING ON ROK...
LIVING TISSUE TARGET-2 METRES AHEAD. THE FLAME GUN WILL CREMATE TARGET... CREMATE...

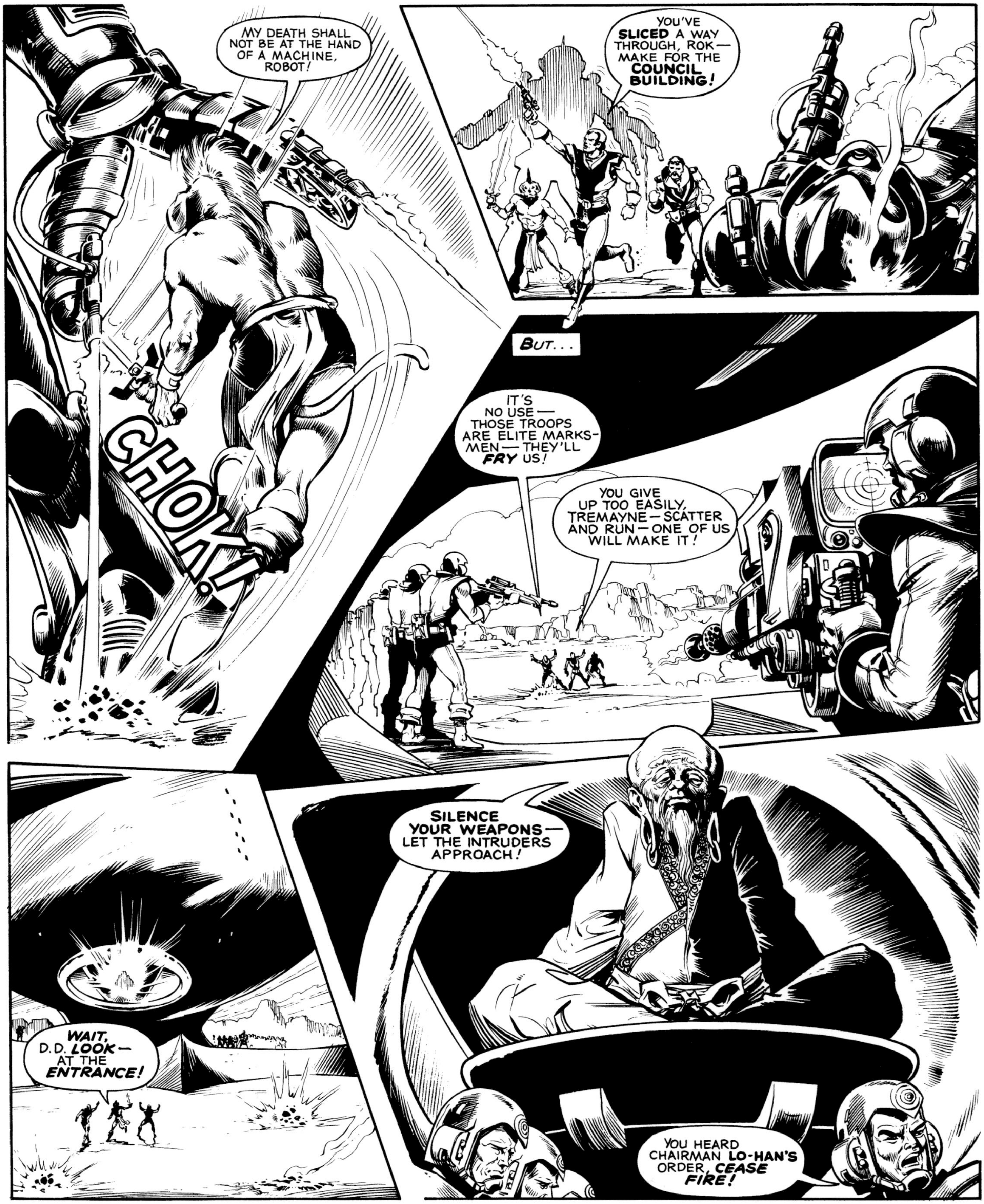
MY DEATH SHALL NOT BE AT THE HAND OF A MACHINE, ROBOT!
CHOK!
YOU'VE SLICED A WAY THROUGH, ROK— MAKE FOR THE COUNCIL BUILDING!
BUT...
IT'S NO USE— THOSE TROOPS ARE ELITE MARKS-MEN— THEY'LL FRY US!
YOU GIVE UP TOO EASILY, TREMAYNE— SCATTER AND RUN— ONE OF US WILL MAKE IT!
WAIT, D.D. LOOK— AT THE ENTRANCE!
SILENCE YOUR WEAPONS— LET THE INTRUDERS APPROACH!
YOU HEARD CHAIRMAN LO-HAN'S ORDER. CEASE FIRE!

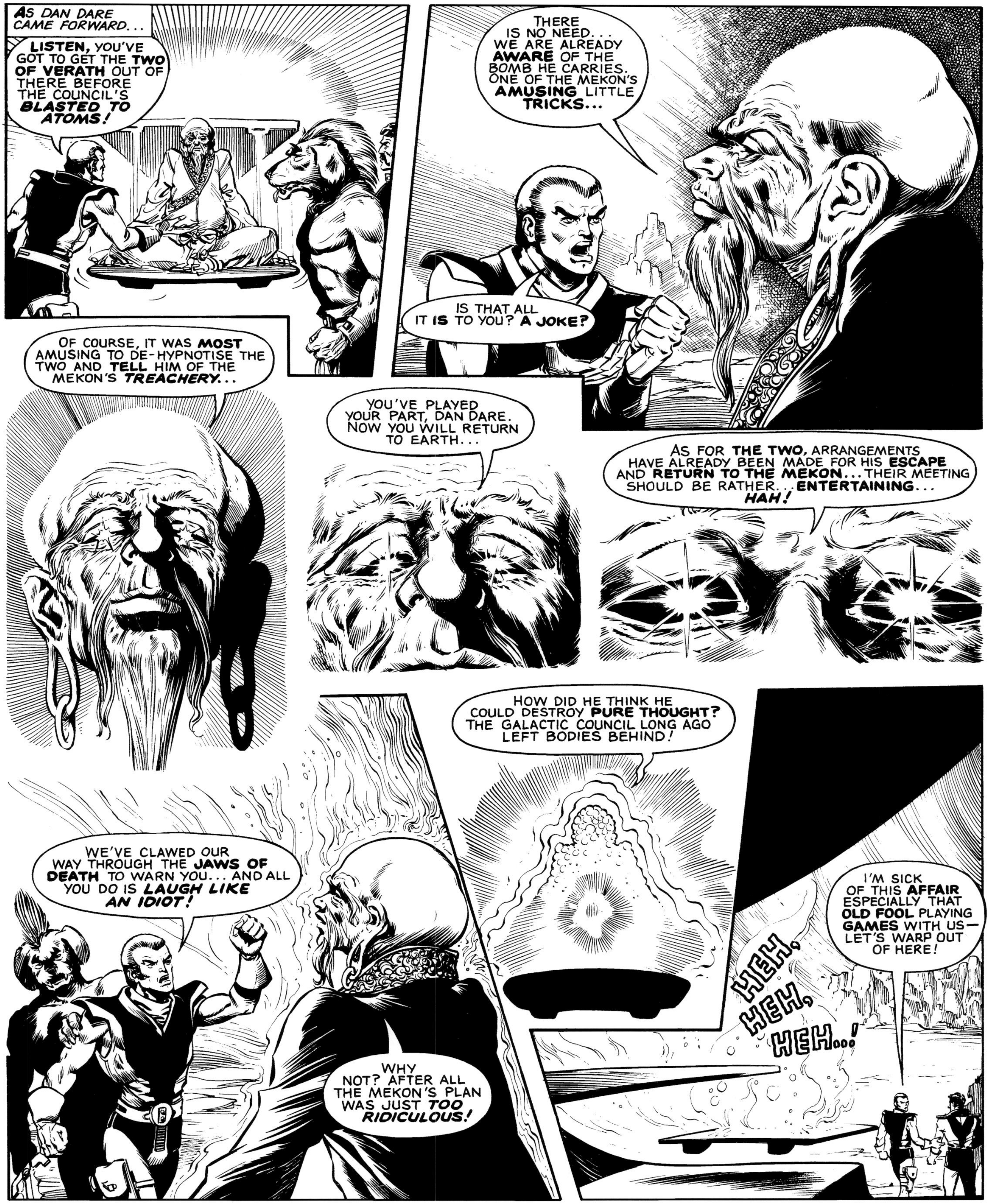
AS DAN DARE CAME FORWARD...
LISTEN, YOU'VE GOT TO GET THE TWO OF VERATH OUT OF THERE BEFORE THE COUNCIL'S BLASTED TO ATOMS!
THERE IS NO NEED... WE ARE ALREADY AWARE OF THE BOMB HE CARRIES. ONE OF THE MEKON'S AMUSING LITTLE TRICKS...
IS THAT ALL IT IS TO YOU? A JOKE?
OF COURSE, IT WAS MOST AMUSING TO DE-HYPNOTISE THE TWO AND TELL HIM OF THE MEKON'S TREACHERY...
YOU'VE PLAYED YOUR PART, DAN DARE. NOW YOU WILL RETURN TO EARTH...
AS FOR THE TWO, ARRANGEMENTS HAVE ALREADY BEEN MADE FOR HIS ESCAPE AND RETURN TO THE MEKON... THEIR MEETING SHOULD BE RATHER... ENTERTAINING... HAH!
WE'VE CLAWED OUR WAY THROUGH THE JAWS OF DEATH TO WARN YOU... AND ALL YOU DO IS LAUGH LIKE AN IDIOT!
WHY NOT? AFTER ALL THE MEKON'S PLAN WAS JUST TOO RIDICULOUS!
HOW DID HE THINK HE COULD DESTROY PURE THOUGHT? THE GALACTIC COUNCIL LONG AGO LEFT BODIES BEHIND!
HEH, HEH, HEH...!
I'M SICK OF THIS AFFAIR ESPECIALLY THAT OLD FOOL PLAYING GAMES WITH US— LET'S WARP OUT OF HERE!

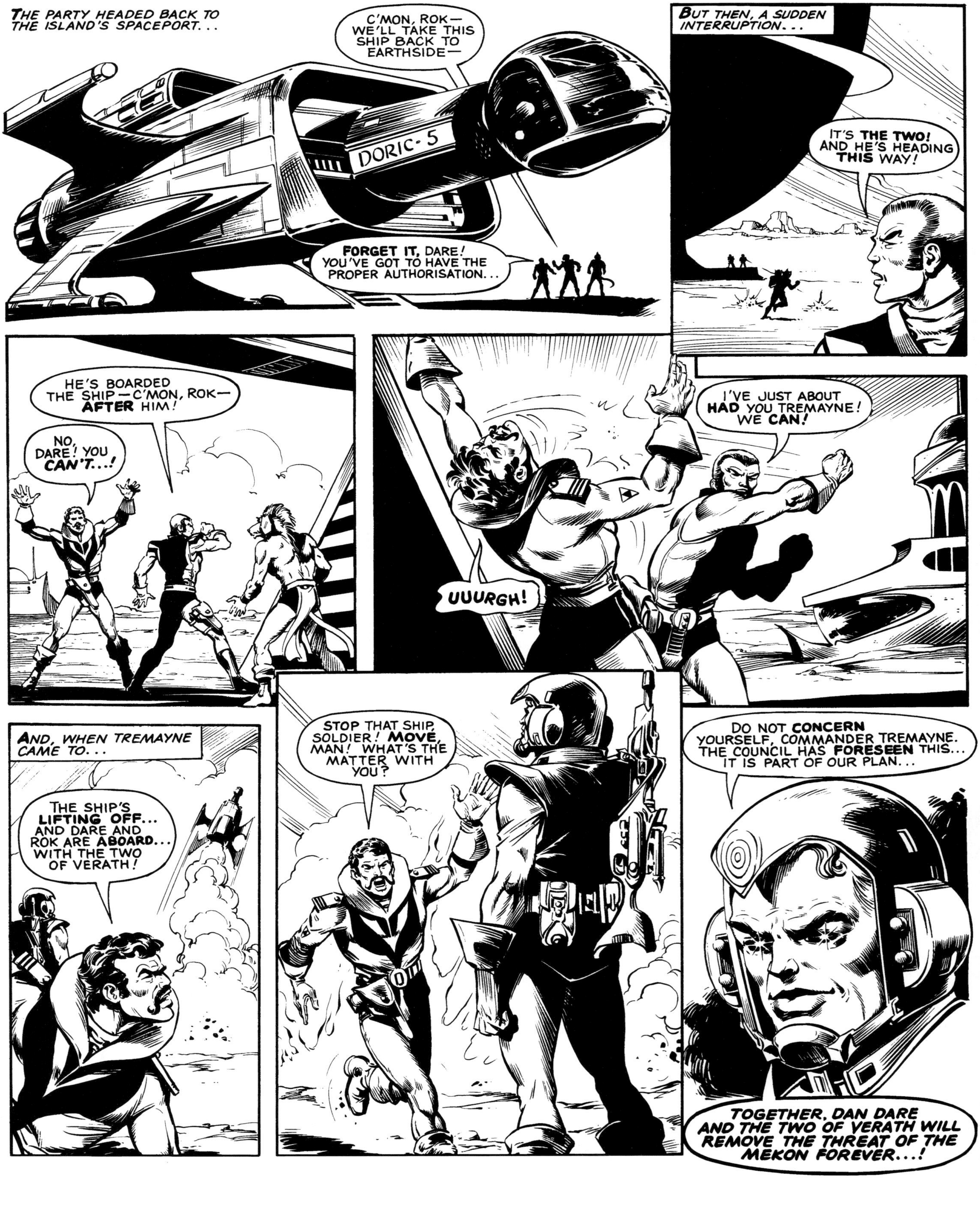

THE PARTY HEADED BACK TO THE ISLAND'S SPACEPORT...
C'MON, ROK— WE'LL TAKE THIS SHIP BACK TO EARTHSIDE—
DORIC-5
FORGET IT, DARE! YOU'VE GOT TO HAVE THE PROPER AUTHORISATION...
BUT THEN, A SUDDEN INTERRUPTION...
IT'S THE TWO! AND HE'S HEADING THIS WAY!
HE'S BOARDED THE SHIP—C'MON, ROK— AFTER HIM!
NO, DARE! YOU CAN'T...!
I'VE JUST ABOUT HAD YOU TREMAYNE! WE CAN!
UUURGH!
AND, WHEN TREMAYNE CAME TO...
THE SHIP'S LIFTING OFF... AND DARE AND ROK ARE ABOARD... WITH THE TWO OF VERATH!
STOP THAT SHIP, SOLDIER! MOVE, MAN! WHAT'S THE MATTER WITH YOU?
DO NOT CONCERN YOURSELF, COMMANDER TREMAYNE. THE COUNCIL HAS FORESEEN THIS... IT IS PART OF OUR PLAN...
TOGETHER, DAN DARE AND THE TWO OF VERATH WILL REMOVE THE THREAT OF THE MEKON FOREVER...!

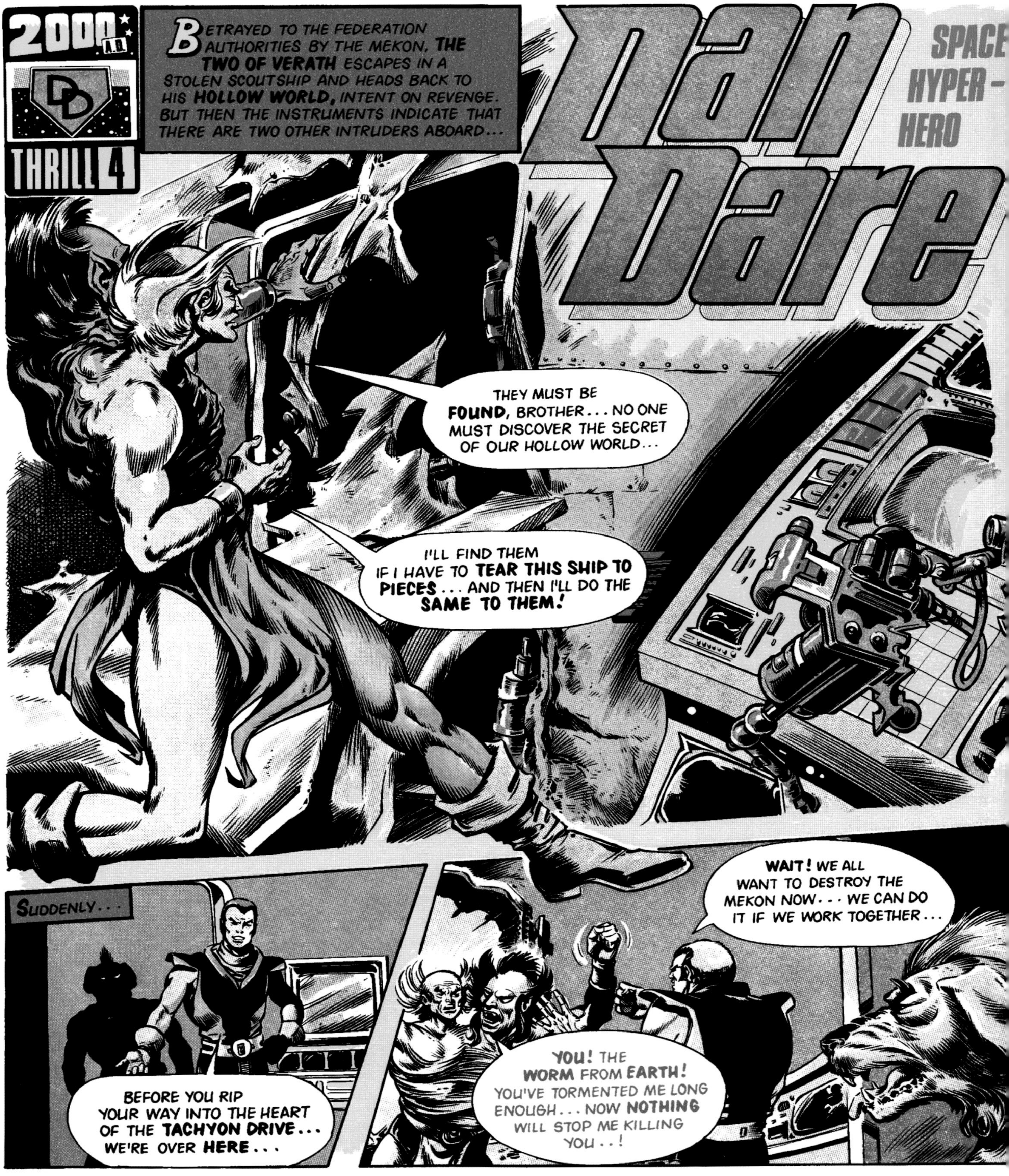
2000 A.D.
THRILL 4
Dan Dare
SPACE HYPER-HERO
BETRAYED TO THE FEDERATION AUTHORITIES BY THE MEKON, THE TWO OF VERATH ESCAPES IN A STOLEN SCOUTSHIP AND HEADS BACK TO HIS HOLLOW WORLD, INTENT ON REVENGE. BUT THEN THE INSTRUMENTS INDICATE THAT THERE ARE TWO OTHER INTRUDERS ABOARD...
THEY MUST BE FOUND, BROTHER... NO ONE MUST DISCOVER THE SECRET OF OUR HOLLOW WORLD...
I'LL FIND THEM IF I HAVE TO TEAR THIS SHIP TO PIECES... AND THEN I'LL DO THE SAME TO THEM!
SUDDENLY...
BEFORE YOU RIP YOUR WAY INTO THE HEART OF THE TACHYON DRIVE... WE'RE OVER HERE...
YOU! THE WORM FROM EARTH! YOU'VE TORMENTED ME LONG ENOUGH... NOW NOTHING WILL STOP ME KILLING YOU..!
WAIT! WE ALL WANT TO DESTROY THE MEKON NOW... WE CAN DO IT IF WE WORK TOGETHER...

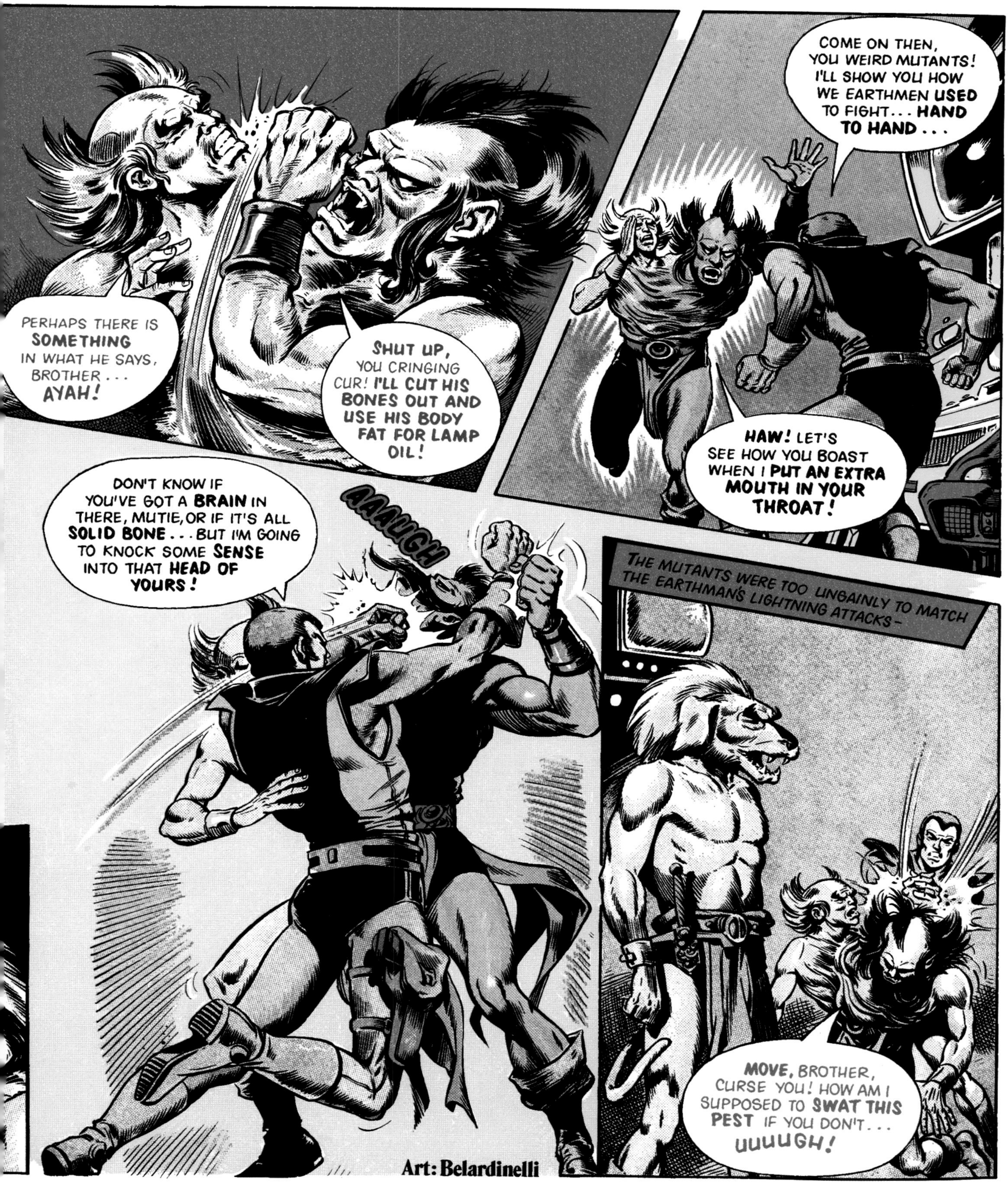
PERHAPS THERE IS SOMETHING IN WHAT HE SAYS, BROTHER . . . AYAH!
SHUT UP, YOU CRINGING CUR! I'LL CUT HIS BONES OUT AND USE HIS BODY FAT FOR LAMP OIL!
COME ON THEN, YOU WEIRD MUTANTS! I'LL SHOW YOU HOW WE EARTHMEN USED TO FIGHT... HAND TO HAND . . .
HAW! LET'S SEE HOW YOU BOAST WHEN I PUT AN EXTRA MOUTH IN YOUR THROAT!
DON'T KNOW IF YOU'VE GOT A BRAIN IN THERE, MUTIE, OR IF IT'S ALL SOLID BONE . . . BUT I'M GOING TO KNOCK SOME SENSE INTO THAT HEAD OF YOURS!
AAAUGH
THE MUTANTS WERE TOO UNGAINLY TO MATCH THE EARTHMAN'S LIGHTNING ATTACKS–
MOVE, BROTHER, CURSE YOU! HOW AM I SUPPOSED TO SWAT THIS PEST IF YOU DON'T . . . UUUUGH!
Art: Belardinelli

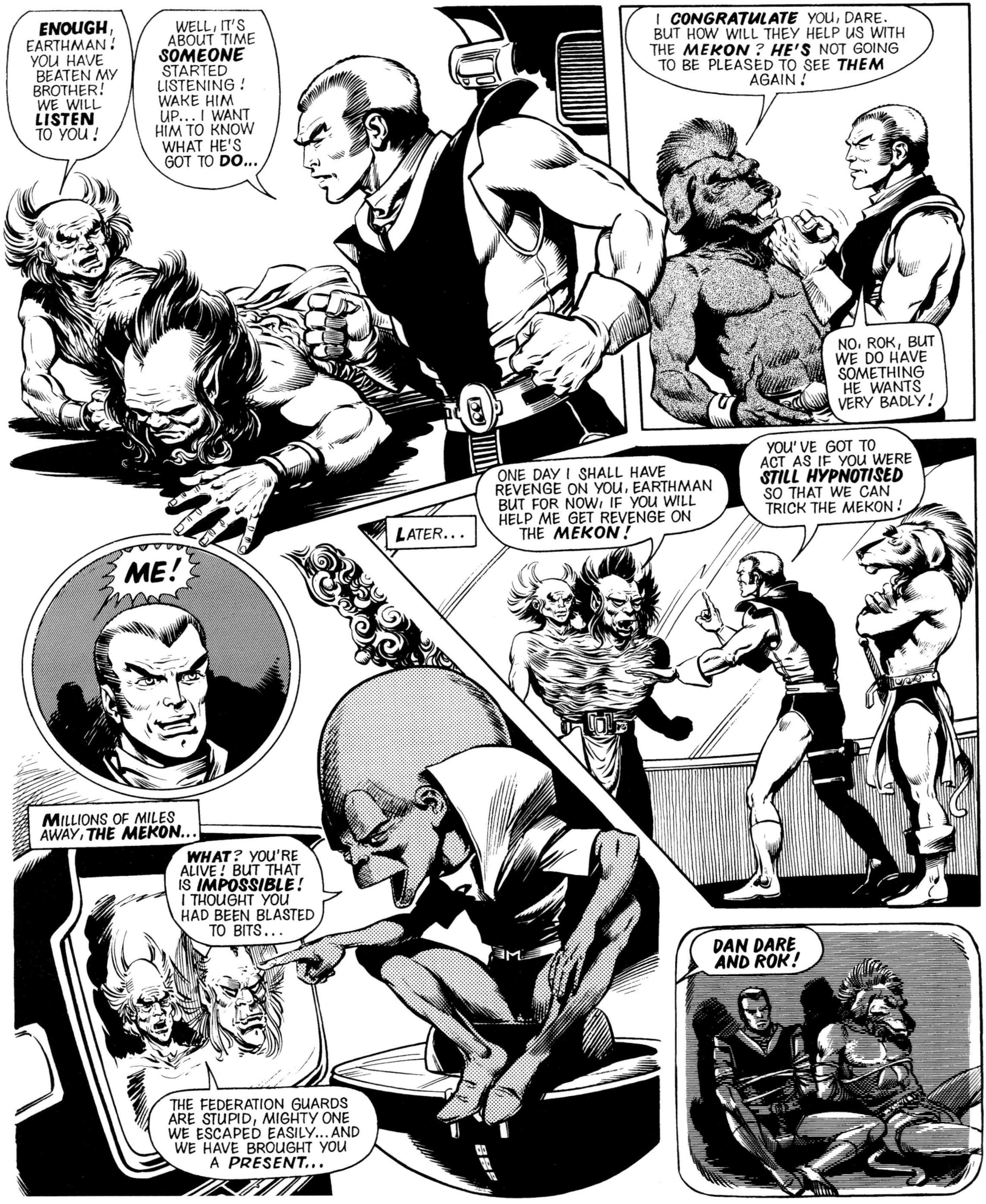

ENOUGH, EARTHMAN! YOU HAVE BEATEN MY BROTHER! WE WILL LISTEN TO YOU!
WELL, IT'S ABOUT TIME SOMEONE STARTED LISTENING! WAKE HIM UP... I WANT HIM TO KNOW WHAT HE'S GOT TO DO...
I CONGRATULATE YOU, DARE. BUT HOW WILL THEY HELP US WITH THE MEKON? HE'S NOT GOING TO BE PLEASED TO SEE THEM AGAIN!
NO, ROK, BUT WE DO HAVE SOMETHING HE WANTS VERY BADLY!
ME!
LATER...
ONE DAY I SHALL HAVE REVENGE ON YOU, EARTHMAN BUT FOR NOW, IF YOU WILL HELP ME GET REVENGE ON THE MEKON!
YOU'VE GOT TO ACT AS IF YOU WERE STILL HYPNOTISED SO THAT WE CAN TRICK THE MEKON!
MILLIONS OF MILES AWAY, THE MEKON...
WHAT? YOU'RE ALIVE! BUT THAT IS IMPOSSIBLE! I THOUGHT YOU HAD BEEN BLASTED TO BITS...
THE FEDERATION GUARDS ARE STUPID, MIGHTY ONE WE ESCAPED EASILY... AND WE HAVE BROUGHT YOU A PRESENT...
DAN DARE AND ROK!

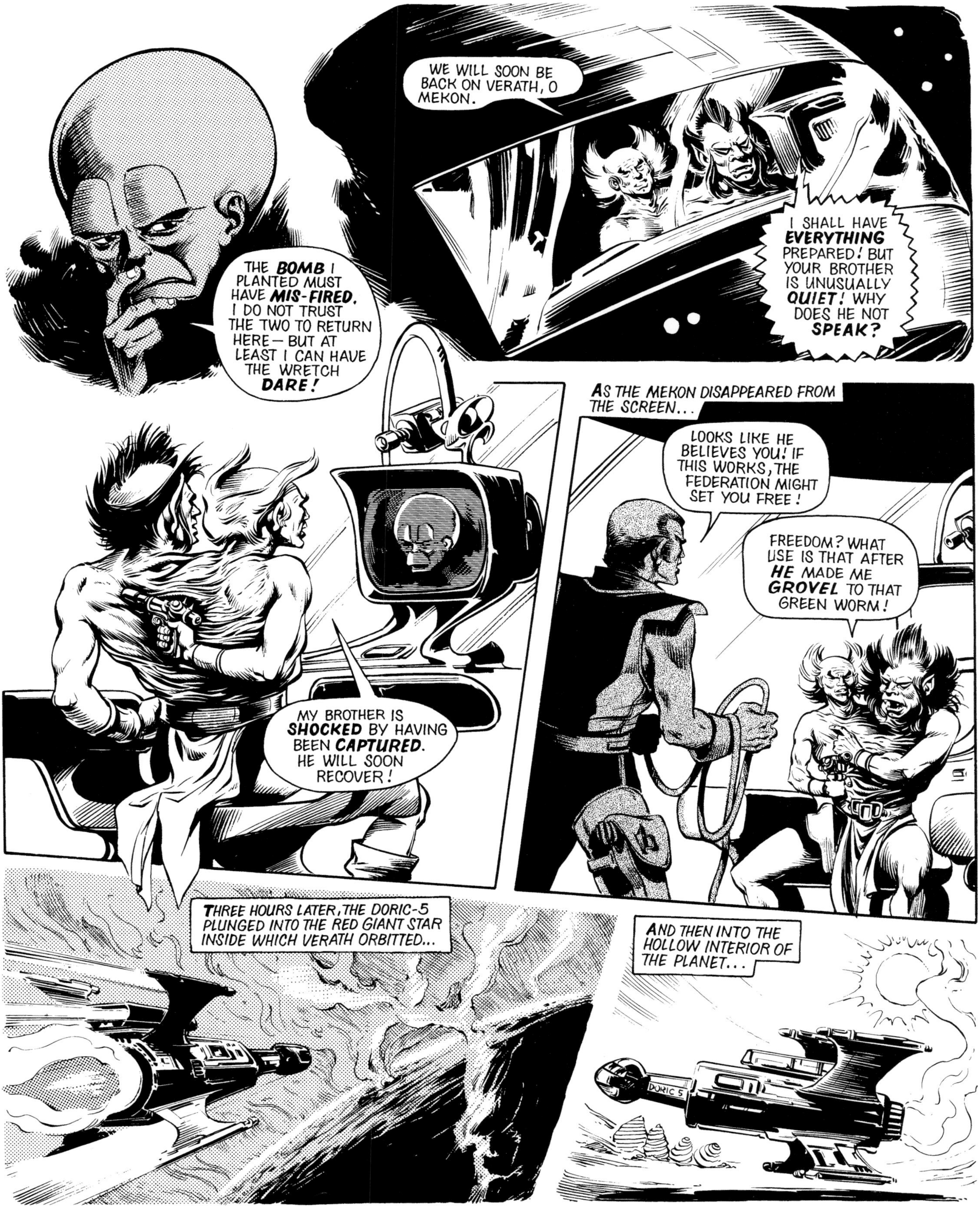
WE WILL SOON BE BACK ON VERATH, O MEKON.
I SHALL HAVE EVERYTHING PREPARED! BUT YOUR BROTHER IS UNUSUALLY QUIET! WHY DOES HE NOT SPEAK?
THE BOMB I PLANTED MUST HAVE MIS-FIRED. I DO NOT TRUST THE TWO TO RETURN HERE— BUT AT LEAST I CAN HAVE THE WRETCH DARE!
MY BROTHER IS SHOCKED BY HAVING BEEN CAPTURED. HE WILL SOON RECOVER!
AS THE MEKON DISAPPEARED FROM THE SCREEN...
LOOKS LIKE HE BELIEVES YOU! IF THIS WORKS, THE FEDERATION MIGHT SET YOU FREE!
FREEDOM? WHAT USE IS THAT AFTER HE MADE ME GROVEL TO THAT GREEN WORM!
THREE HOURS LATER, THE DORIC-5 PLUNGED INTO THE RED GIANT STAR INSIDE WHICH VERATH ORBITTED...
AND THEN INTO THE HOLLOW INTERIOR OF THE PLANET...
DORIC 5

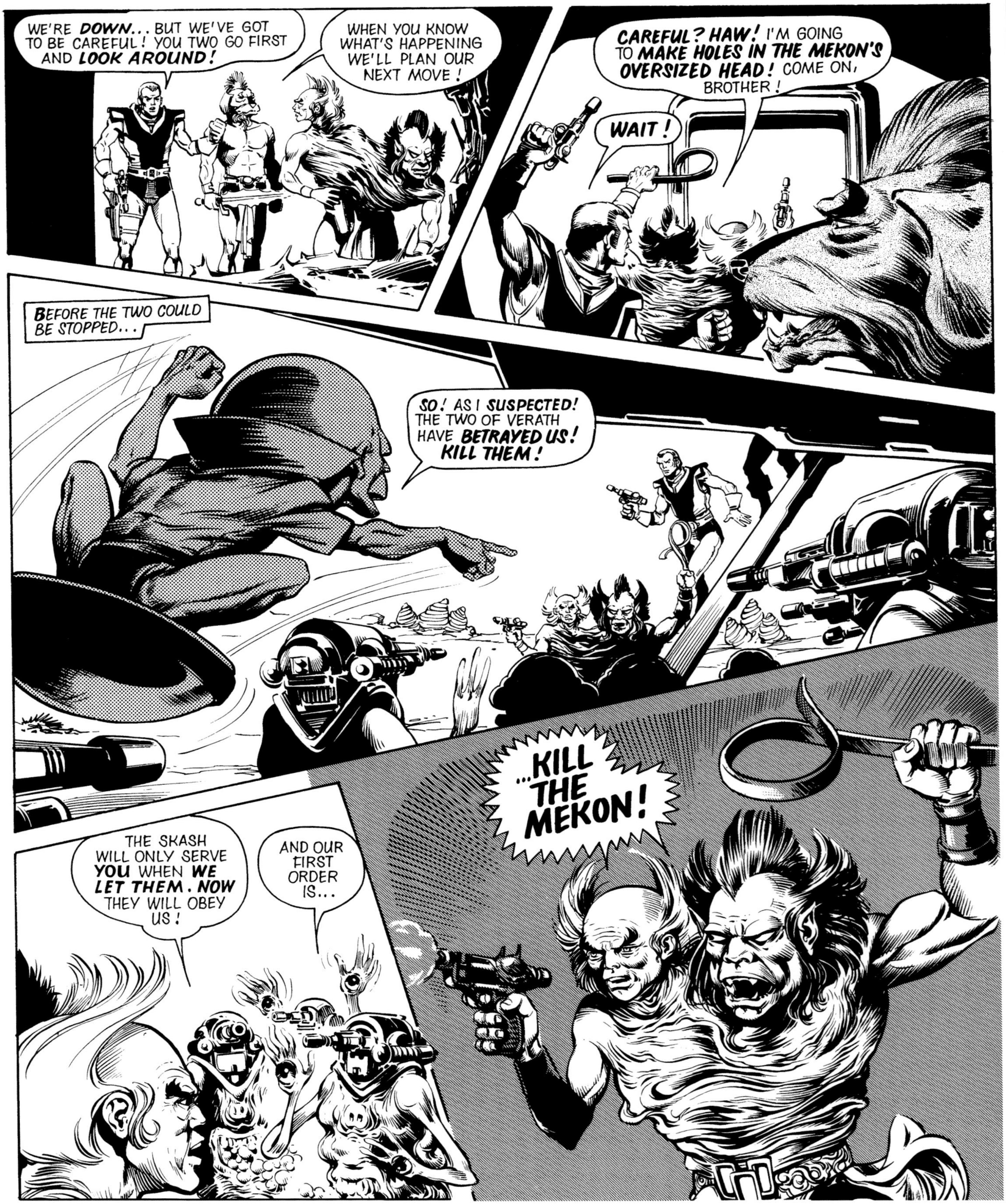

WE'RE DOWN... BUT WE'VE GOT TO BE CAREFUL! YOU TWO GO FIRST AND LOOK AROUND!
WHEN YOU KNOW WHAT'S HAPPENING WE'LL PLAN OUR NEXT MOVE!
CAREFUL? HAW! I'M GOING TO MAKE HOLES IN THE MEKON'S OVERSIZED HEAD! COME ON, BROTHER!
WAIT!
BEFORE THE TWO COULD BE STOPPED...
SO! AS I SUSPECTED! THE TWO OF VERATH HAVE BETRAYED US! KILL THEM!
THE SKASH WILL ONLY SERVE YOU WHEN WE LET THEM. NOW THEY WILL OBEY US!
AND OUR FIRST ORDER IS...
...KILL THE MEKON!

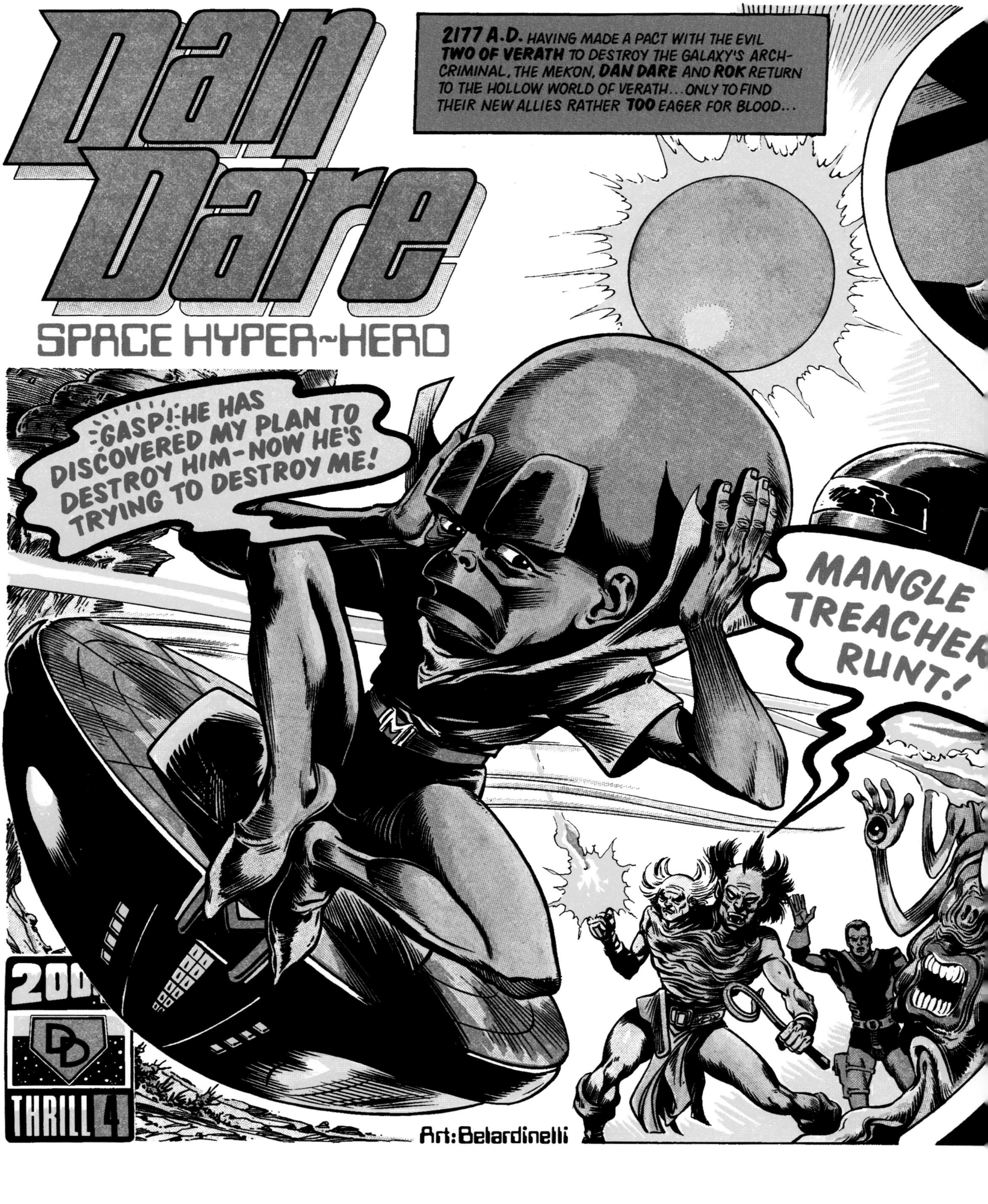
DAN DARE
SPACE HYPER~HERO
2177 A.D. HAVING MADE A PACT WITH THE EVIL TWO OF VERATH TO DESTROY THE GALAXY'S ARCH-CRIMINAL, THE MEKON, DAN DARE AND ROK RETURN TO THE HOLLOW WORLD OF VERATH... ONLY TO FIND THEIR NEW ALLIES RATHER TOO EAGER FOR BLOOD...
GASP! HE HAS DISCOVERED MY PLAN TO DESTROY HIM-NOW HE'S TRYING TO DESTROY ME!
MANGLE TREACHER RUNT!
THRILL 4
Art: Belardinelli

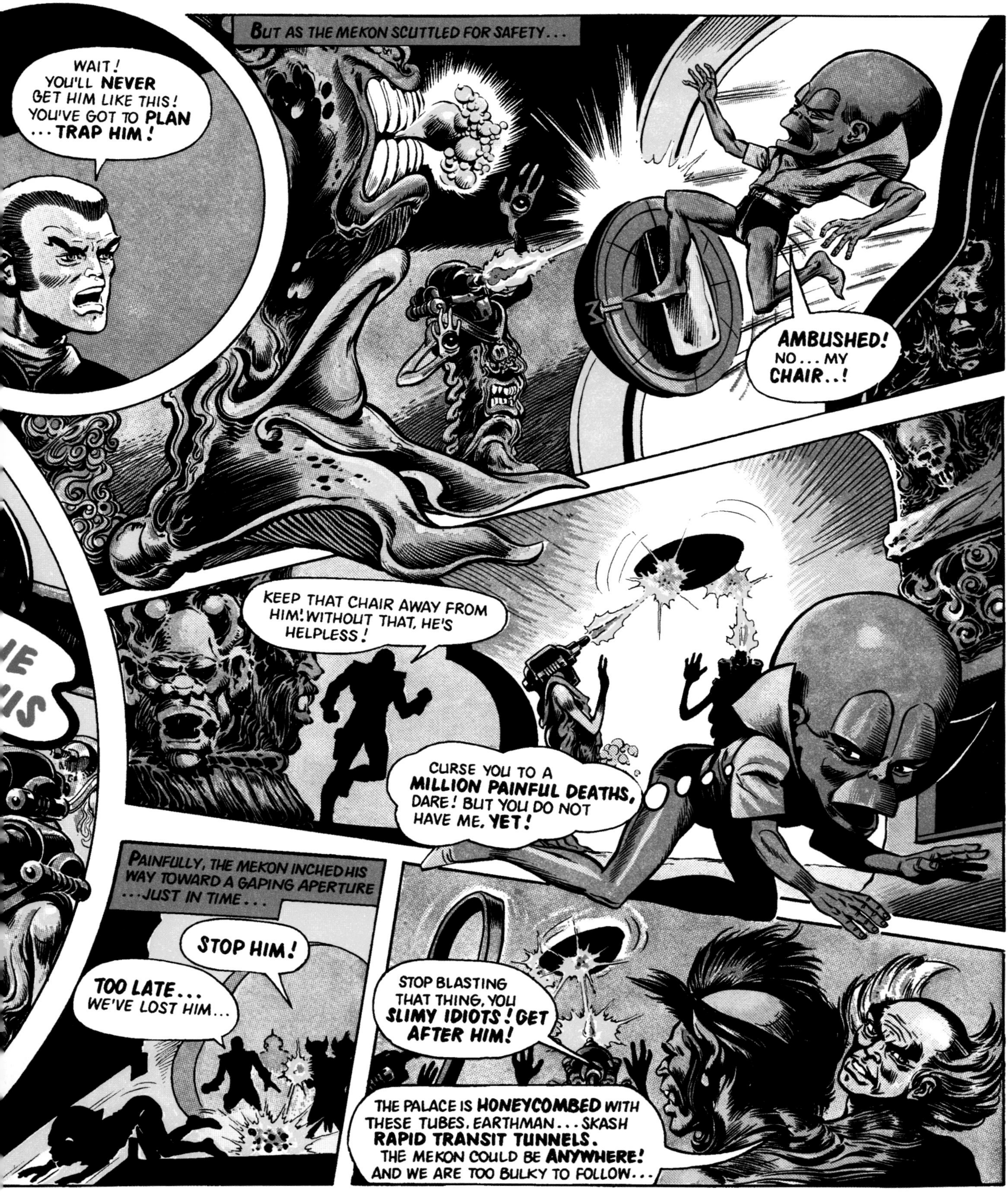

WAIT! YOU'LL NEVER GET HIM LIKE THIS! YOU'VE GOT TO PLAN ... TRAP HIM!
BUT AS THE MEKON SCUTTLED FOR SAFETY...
AMBUSHED! NO... MY CHAIR..!
KEEP THAT CHAIR AWAY FROM HIM! WITHOUT THAT, HE'S HELPLESS!
CURSE YOU TO A MILLION PAINFUL DEATHS, DARE! BUT YOU DO NOT HAVE ME, YET!
PAINFULLY, THE MEKON INCHED HIS WAY TOWARD A GAPING APERTURE ...JUST IN TIME...
STOP HIM!
TOO LATE... WE'VE LOST HIM...
STOP BLASTING THAT THING, YOU SLIMY IDIOTS! GET AFTER HIM!
THE PALACE IS HONEYCOMBED WITH THESE TUBES, EARTHMAN... SKASH RAPID TRANSIT TUNNELS. THE MEKON COULD BE ANYWHERE! AND WE ARE TOO BULKY TO FOLLOW...

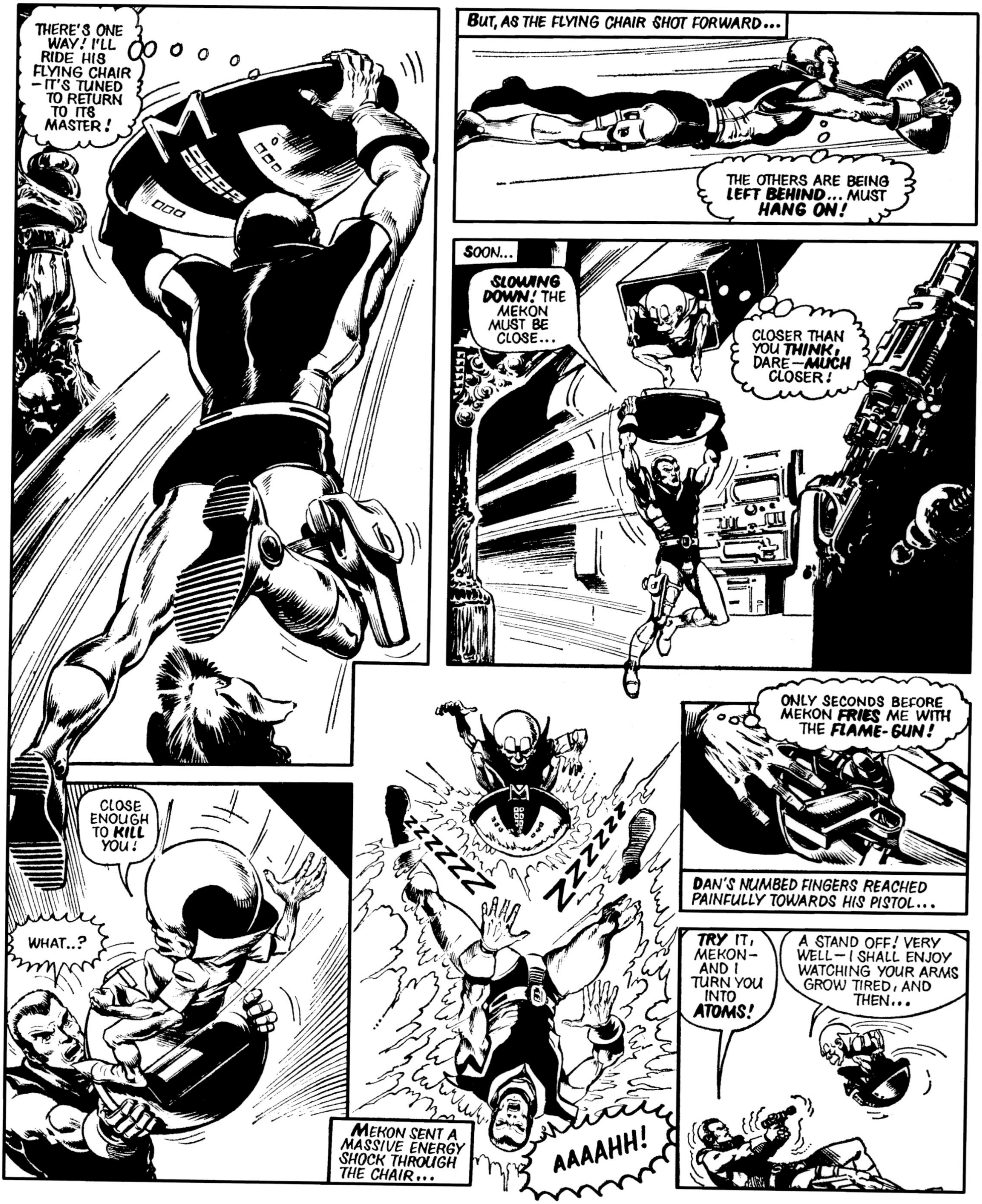

THERE'S ONE WAY! I'LL RIDE HIS FLYING CHAIR – IT'S TUNED TO RETURN TO ITS MASTER!
BUT, AS THE FLYING CHAIR SHOT FORWARD...
THE OTHERS ARE BEING LEFT BEHIND... MUST HANG ON!
SOON...
SLOWING DOWN! THE MEKON MUST BE CLOSE...
CLOSER THAN YOU THINK, DARE – MUCH CLOSER!
CLOSE ENOUGH TO KILL YOU!
WHAT..?
ZZZZZZ
ZZZZZZ
MEKON SENT A MASSIVE ENERGY SHOCK THROUGH THE CHAIR...
AAAAHH!
ONLY SECONDS BEFORE MEKON FRIES ME WITH THE FLAME-GUN!
DAN'S NUMBED FINGERS REACHED PAINFULLY TOWARDS HIS PISTOL...
TRY IT, MEKON – AND I TURN YOU INTO ATOMS!
A STAND OFF! VERY WELL – I SHALL ENJOY WATCHING YOUR ARMS GROW TIRED, AND THEN...

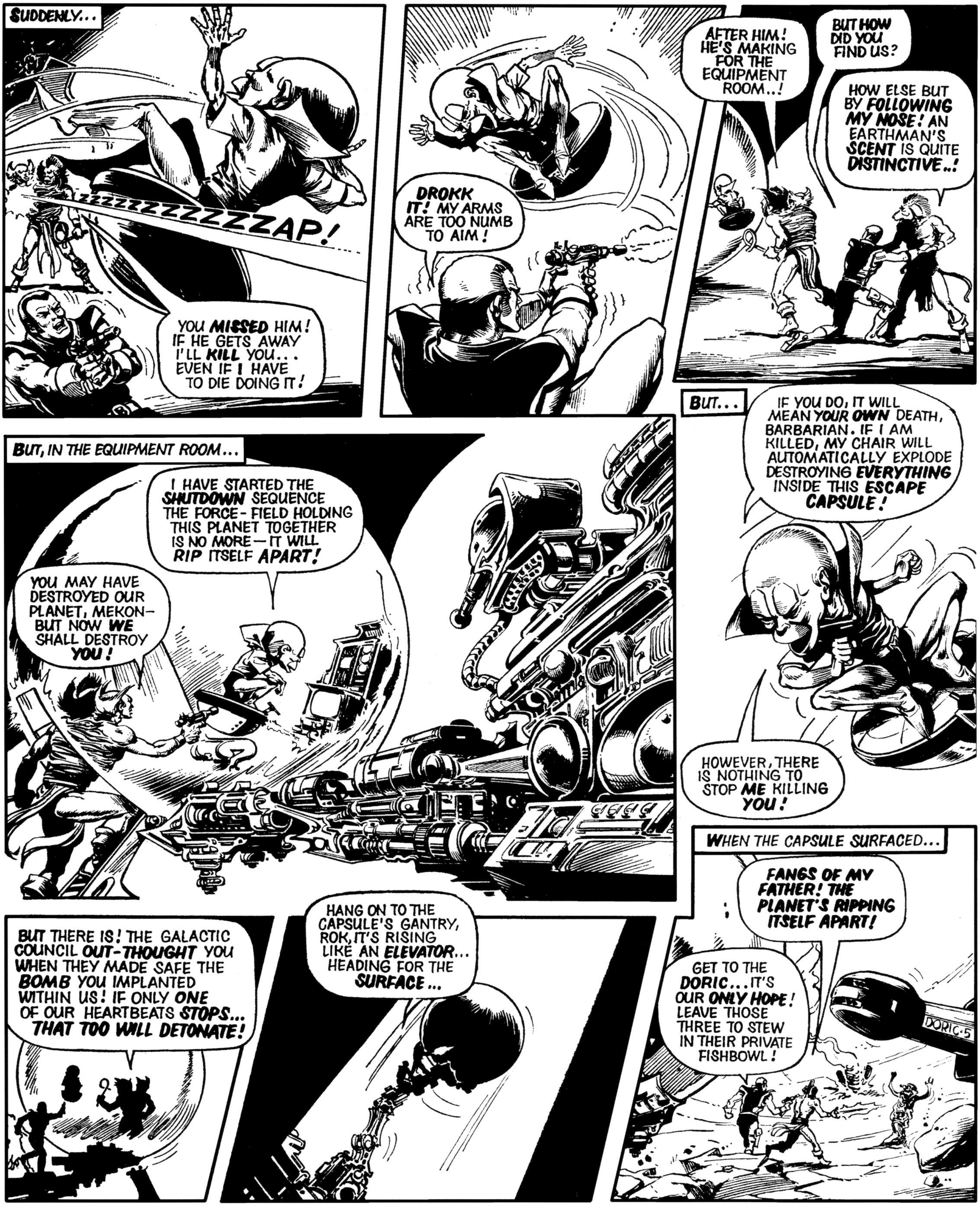
SUDDENLY...
ZZZZZZZZZZZZZZZZZAP!
YOU MISSED HIM! IF HE GETS AWAY I'LL KILL YOU... EVEN IF I HAVE TO DIE DOING IT!
DROKK IT! MY ARMS ARE TOO NUMB TO AIM!
AFTER HIM! HE'S MAKING FOR THE EQUIPMENT ROOM..!
BUT HOW DID YOU FIND US?
HOW ELSE BUT BY FOLLOWING MY NOSE! AN EARTHMAN'S SCENT IS QUITE DISTINCTIVE..!
BUT, IN THE EQUIPMENT ROOM...
I HAVE STARTED THE SHUTDOWN SEQUENCE THE FORCE-FIELD HOLDING THIS PLANET TOGETHER IS NO MORE — IT WILL RIP ITSELF APART!
YOU MAY HAVE DESTROYED OUR PLANET, MEKON- BUT NOW WE SHALL DESTROY YOU!
BUT...
IF YOU DO, IT WILL MEAN YOUR OWN DEATH, BARBARIAN. IF I AM KILLED, MY CHAIR WILL AUTOMATICALLY EXPLODE DESTROYING EVERYTHING INSIDE THIS ESCAPE CAPSULE!
HOWEVER, THERE IS NOTHING TO STOP ME KILLING YOU!
BUT THERE IS! THE GALACTIC COUNCIL OUT-THOUGHT YOU WHEN THEY MADE SAFE THE BOMB YOU IMPLANTED WITHIN US! IF ONLY ONE OF OUR HEARTBEATS STOPS... THAT TOO WILL DETONATE!
HANG ON TO THE CAPSULE'S GANTRY, ROK, IT'S RISING LIKE AN ELEVATOR... HEADING FOR THE SURFACE...
WHEN THE CAPSULE SURFACED...
FANGS OF MY FATHER! THE PLANET'S RIPPING ITSELF APART!
GET TO THE DORIC... IT'S OUR ONLY HOPE! LEAVE THOSE THREE TO STEW IN THEIR PRIVATE FISHBOWL!
DORIC·5

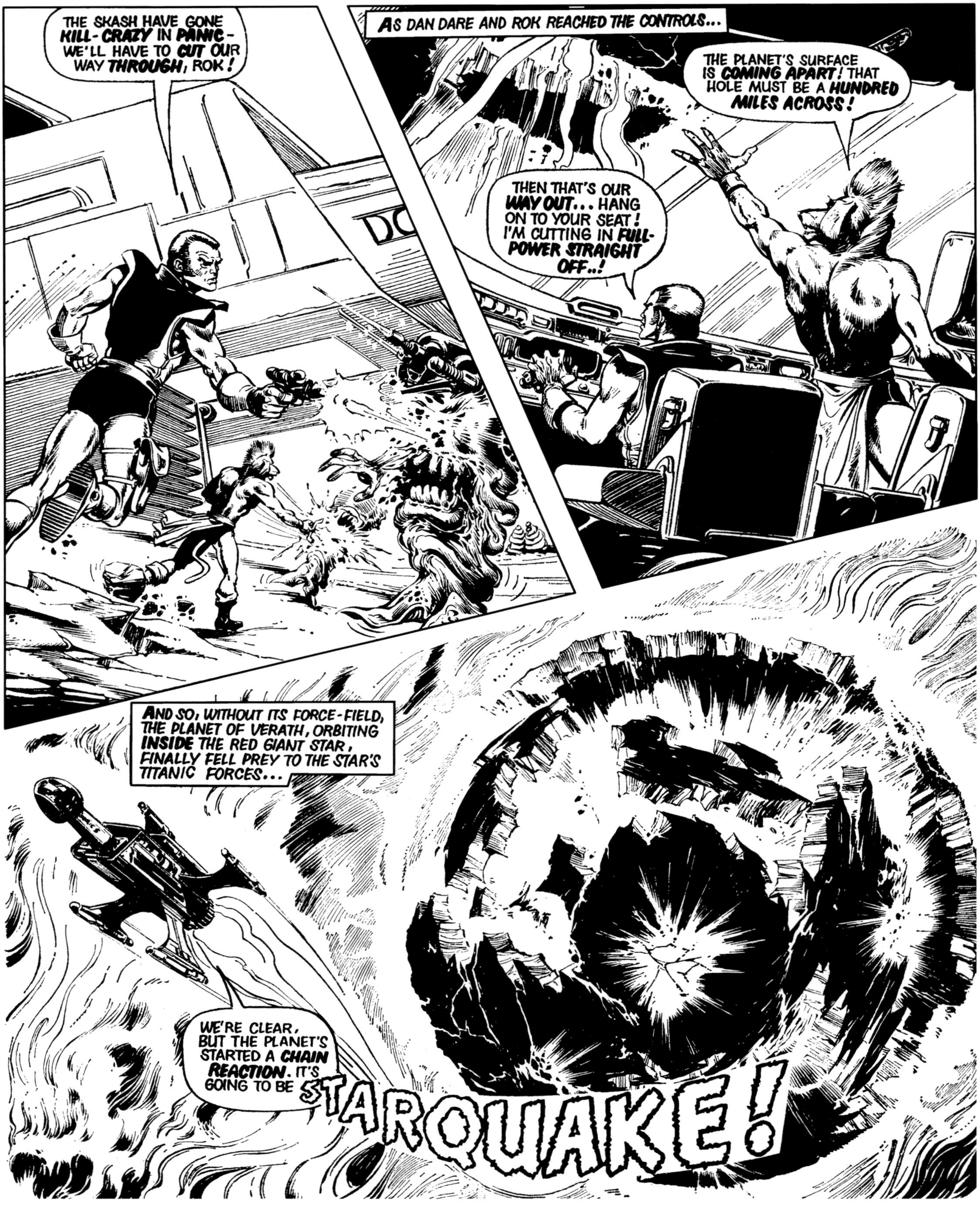
THE SKASH HAVE GONE KILL-CRAZY IN PANIC - WE'LL HAVE TO CUT OUR WAY THROUGH, ROK!
AS DAN DARE AND ROK REACHED THE CONTROLS...
THE PLANET'S SURFACE IS COMING APART! THAT HOLE MUST BE A HUNDRED MILES ACROSS!
THEN THAT'S OUR WAY OUT... HANG ON TO YOUR SEAT! I'M CUTTING IN FULL-POWER STRAIGHT OFF..!
AND SO, WITHOUT ITS FORCE-FIELD, THE PLANET OF VERATH, ORBITING INSIDE THE RED GIANT STAR, FINALLY FELL PREY TO THE STAR'S TITANIC FORCES...
WE'RE CLEAR, BUT THE PLANET'S STARTED A CHAIN REACTION. IT'S GOING TO BE STARQUAKE!

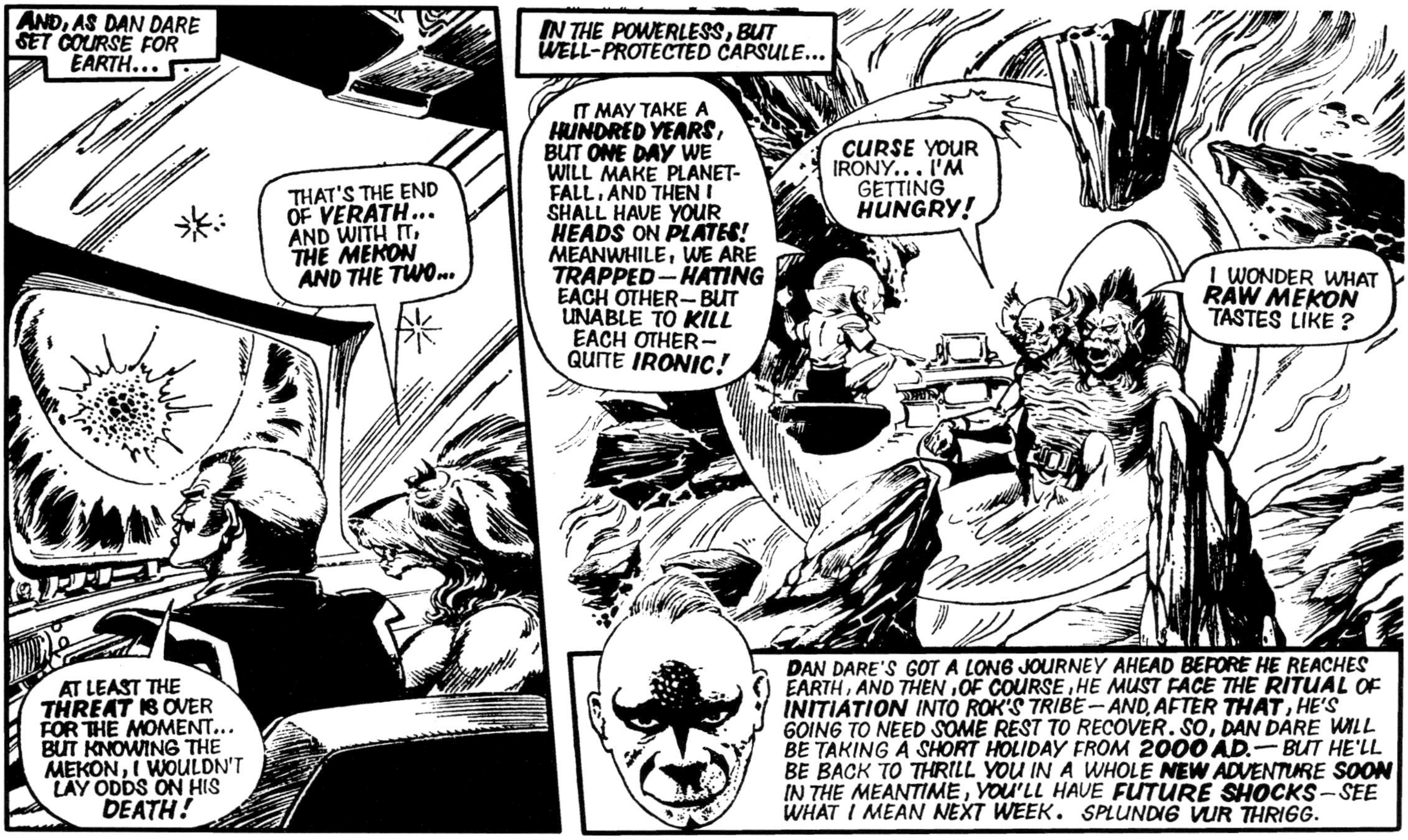

AND, AS DAN DARE SET COURSE FOR EARTH...
THAT'S THE END OF VERATH... AND WITH IT, THE MEKON AND THE TWO...
AT LEAST THE THREAT IS OVER FOR THE MOMENT... BUT KNOWING THE MEKON, I WOULDN'T LAY ODDS ON HIS DEATH!
IN THE POWERLESS, BUT WELL-PROTECTED CAPSULE...
IT MAY TAKE A HUNDRED YEARS, BUT ONE DAY WE WILL MAKE PLANET-FALL, AND THEN I SHALL HAVE YOUR HEADS ON PLATES! MEANWHILE, WE ARE TRAPPED—HATING EACH OTHER—BUT UNABLE TO KILL EACH OTHER—QUITE IRONIC!
CURSE YOUR IRONY... I'M GETTING HUNGRY!
I WONDER WHAT RAW MEKON TASTES LIKE?
DAN DARE'S GOT A LONG JOURNEY AHEAD BEFORE HE REACHES EARTH, AND THEN, OF COURSE, HE MUST FACE THE RITUAL OF INITIATION INTO ROK'S TRIBE—AND, AFTER THAT, HE'S GOING TO NEED SOME REST TO RECOVER. SO, DAN DARE WILL BE TAKING A SHORT HOLIDAY FROM 2000 A.D.—BUT HE'LL BE BACK TO THRILL YOU IN A WHOLE NEW ADVENTURE SOON IN THE MEANTIME, YOU'LL HAVE FUTURE SHOCKS—SEE WHAT I MEAN NEXT WEEK. SPLUNDIG VUR THRIGG.

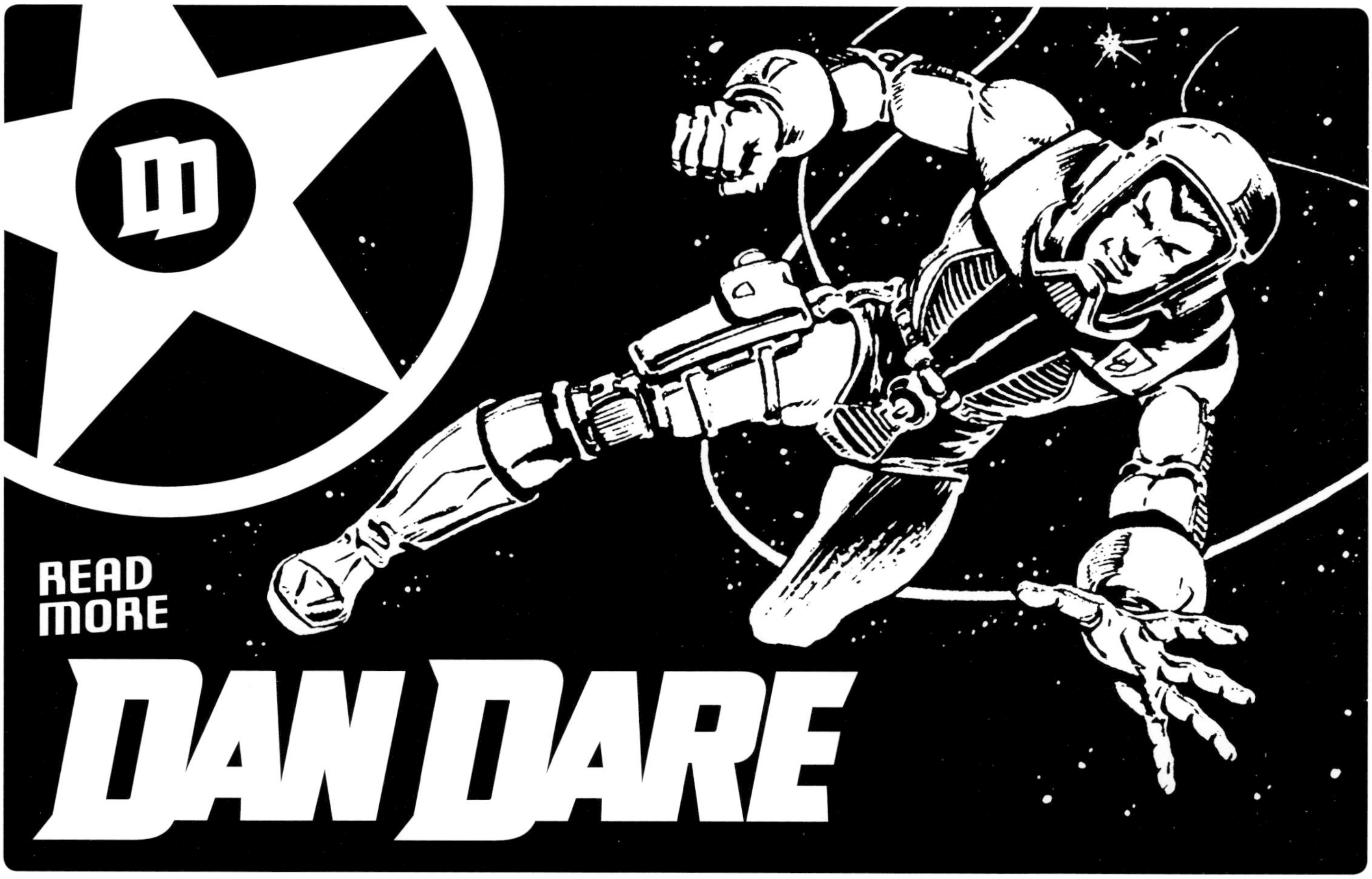

DD
READ MORE
DAN DARE

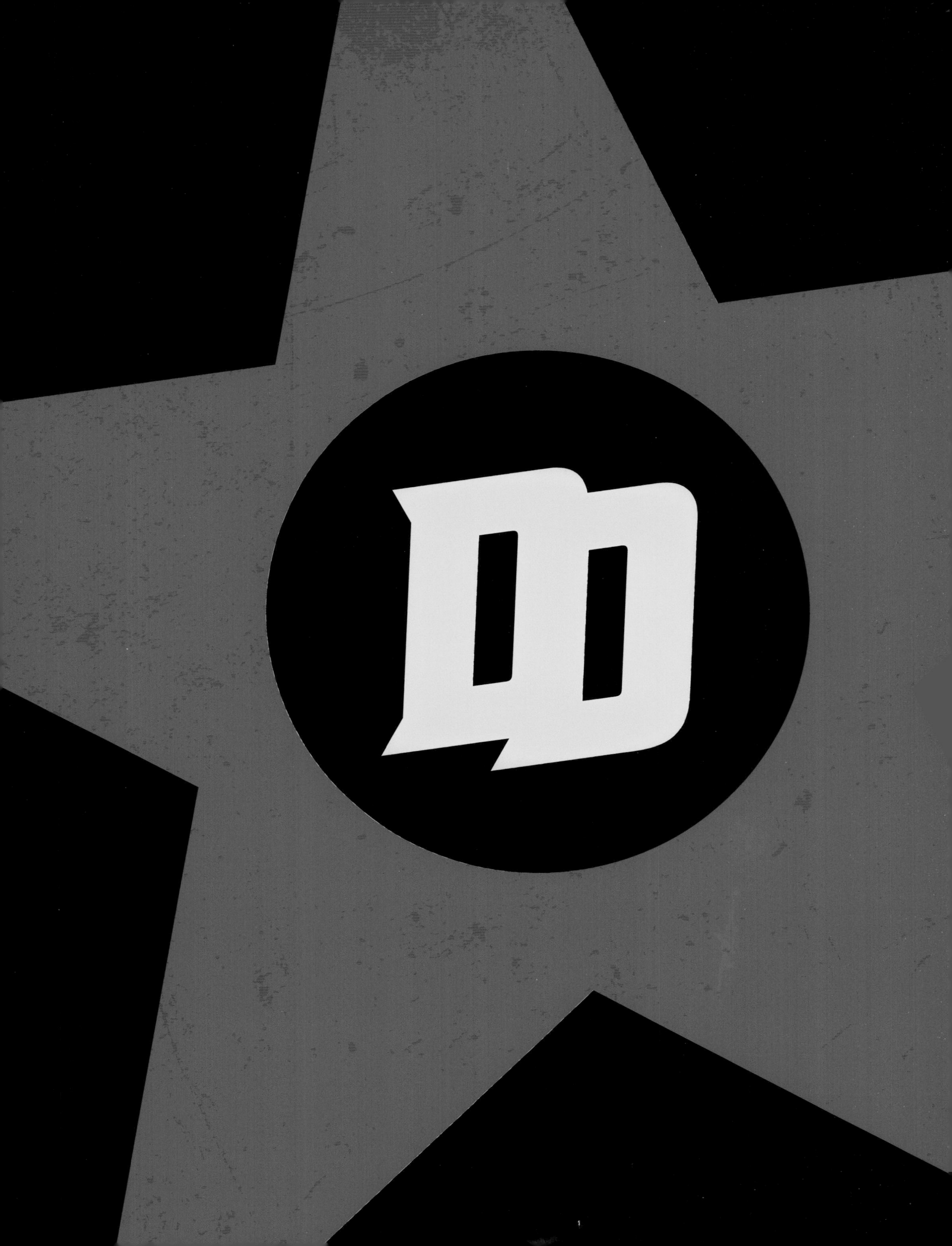

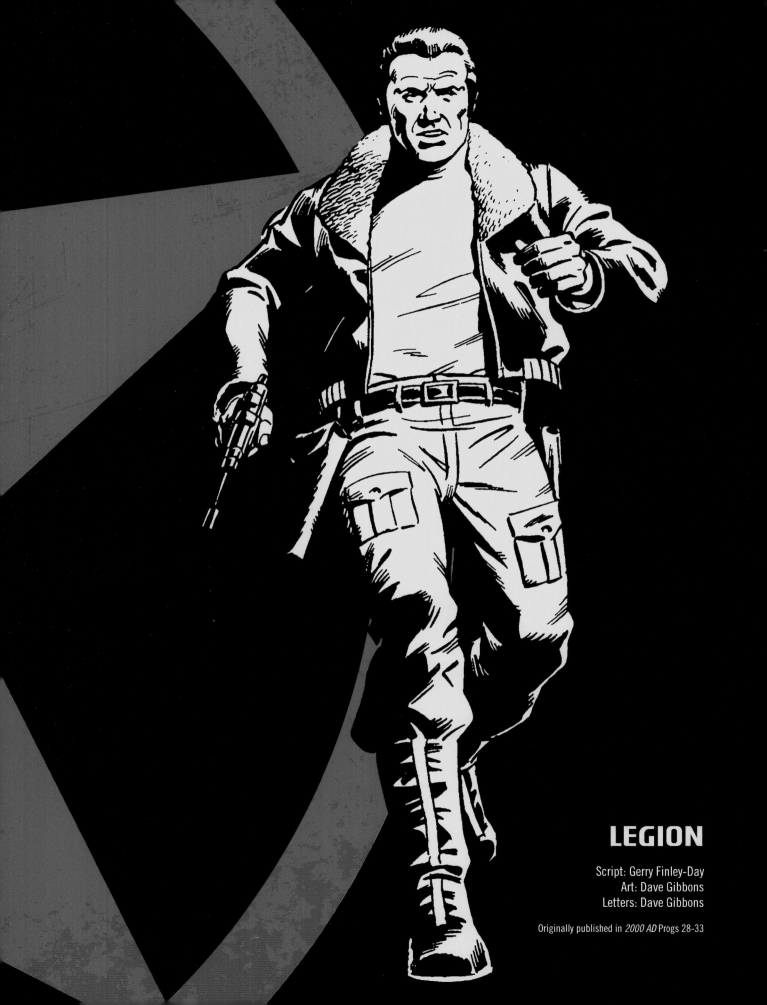

LEGION

Script: Gerry Finley-Day
Art: Dave Gibbons
Letters: Dave Gibbons

Originally published in *2000 AD* Progs 28-33

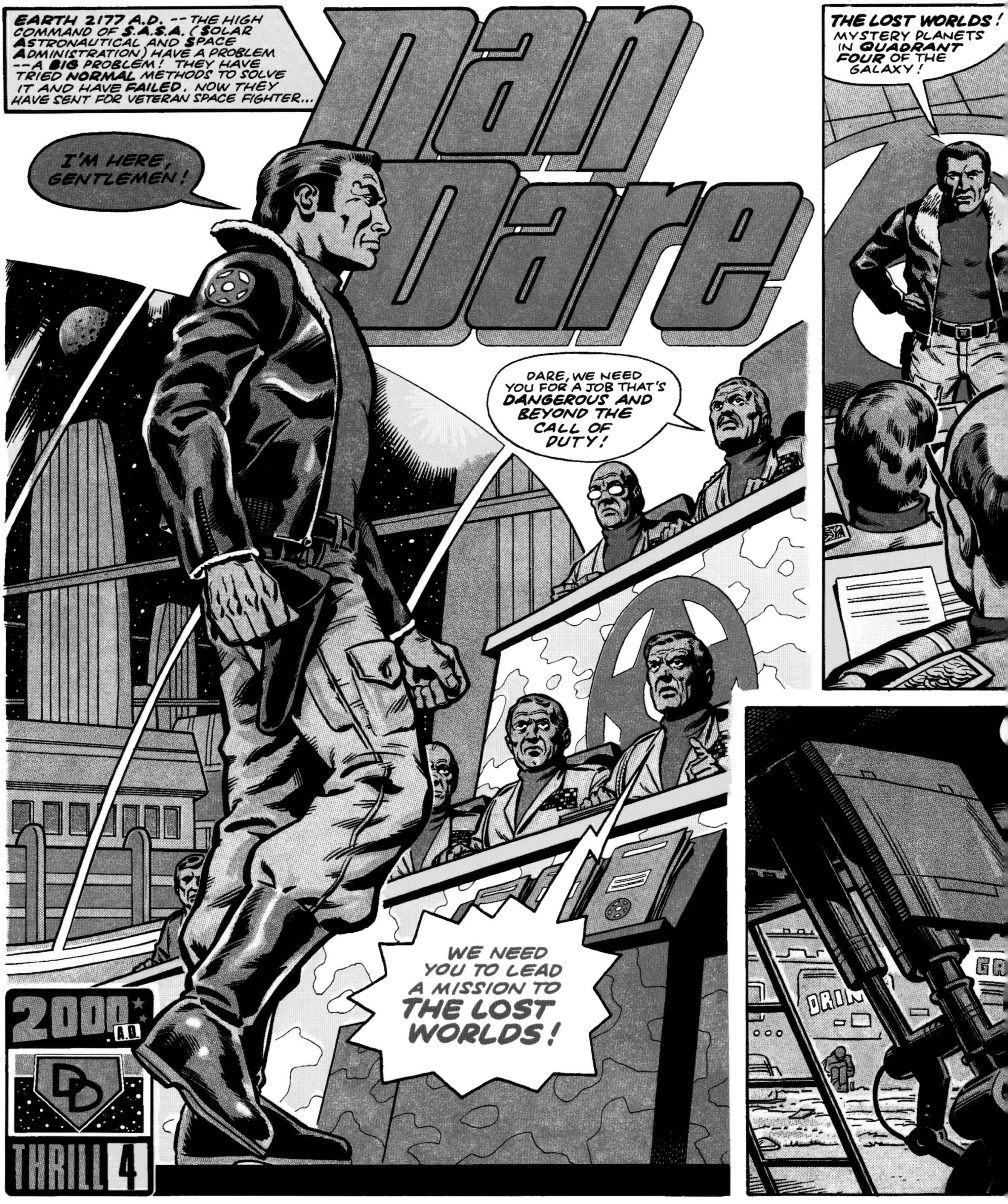

EARTH 2177 A.D. -- THE HIGH COMMAND OF S.A.S.A. (SOLAR ASTRONAUTICAL AND SPACE ADMINISTRATION) HAVE A PROBLEM --A BIG PROBLEM! THEY HAVE TRIED NORMAL METHODS TO SOLVE IT AND HAVE FAILED. NOW THEY HAVE SENT FOR VETERAN SPACE FIGHTER...
DAN DARE
I'M HERE, GENTLEMEN!
DARE, WE NEED YOU FOR A JOB THAT'S DANGEROUS AND BEYOND THE CALL OF DUTY!
WE NEED YOU TO LEAD A MISSION TO THE LOST WORLDS!
2000 A.D.
THRILL 4
THE LOST WORLDS! MYSTERY PLANETS IN QUADRANT FOUR OF THE GALAXY!

Art: Gibbons

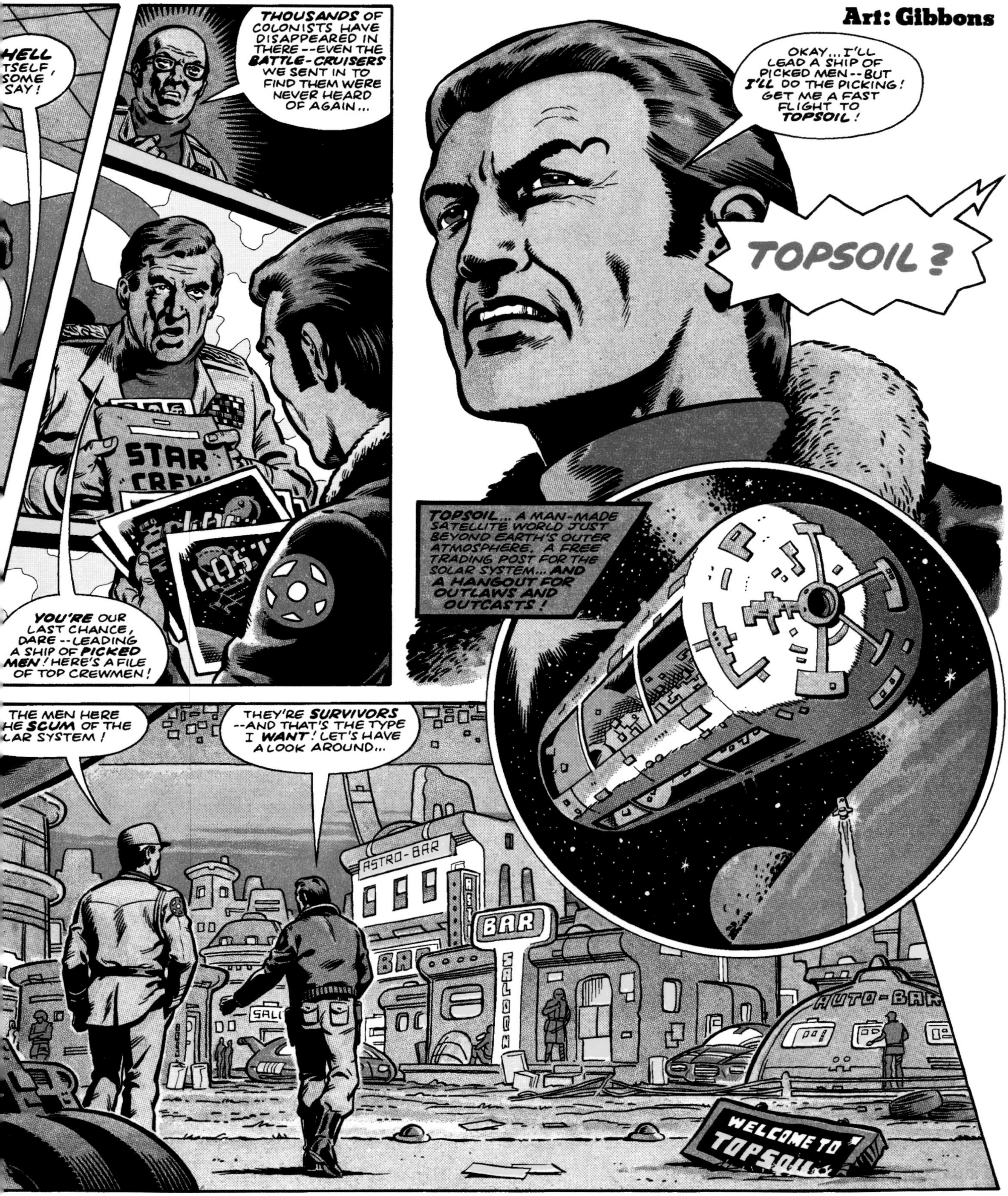

HELL
TSELF, SOME SAY!
THOUSANDS OF COLONISTS HAVE DISAPPEARED IN THERE -- EVEN THE BATTLE-CRUISERS WE SENT IN TO FIND THEM WERE NEVER HEARD OF AGAIN...
STAR CREW
YOU'RE OUR LAST CHANCE, DARE -- LEADING A SHIP OF PICKED MEN! HERE'S A FILE OF TOP CREWMEN!
OKAY... I'LL LEAD A SHIP OF PICKED MEN -- BUT I'LL DO THE PICKING! GET ME A FAST FLIGHT TO TOPSOIL!
TOPSOIL?
TOPSOIL... A MAN-MADE SATELLITE WORLD JUST BEYOND EARTH'S OUTER ATMOSPHERE. A FREE TRADING POST FOR THE SOLAR SYSTEM... AND A HANGOUT FOR OUTLAWS AND OUTCASTS!
THE MEN HERE HE SCUM OF THE LAR SYSTEM!
THEY'RE SURVIVORS -- AND THAT'S THE TYPE I WANT! LET'S HAVE A LOOK AROUND...
ASTRO-BAR
BAR
SALOON
AUTO-BAR
WELCOME TO TOPSOIL

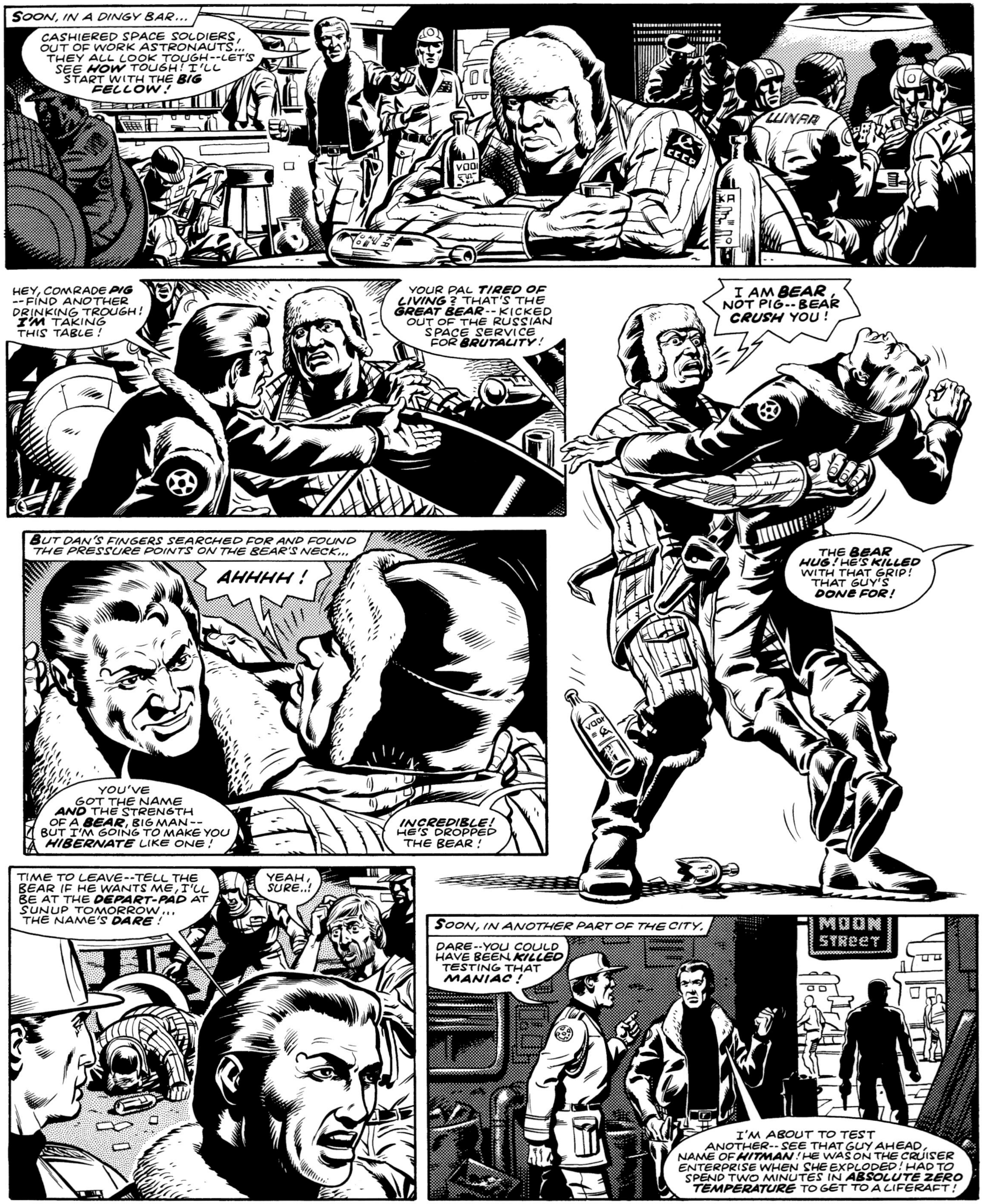
SOON, IN A DINGY BAR...
CASHIERED SPACE SOLDIERS, OUT OF WORK ASTRONAUTS... THEY ALL LOOK TOUGH--LET'S SEE HOW TOUGH! I'LL START WITH THE BIG FELLOW!
HEY, COMRADE PIG--FIND ANOTHER DRINKING TROUGH! I'M TAKING THIS TABLE!
YOUR PAL TIRED OF LIVING? THAT'S THE GREAT BEAR--KICKED OUT OF THE RUSSIAN SPACE SERVICE FOR BRUTALITY!
I AM BEAR, NOT PIG--BEAR CRUSH YOU!
THE BEAR HUG! HE'S KILLED WITH THAT GRIP! THAT GUY'S DONE FOR!
BUT DAN'S FINGERS SEARCHED FOR AND FOUND THE PRESSURE POINTS ON THE BEAR'S NECK...
AHHHH!
YOU'VE GOT THE NAME AND THE STRENGTH OF A BEAR, BIG MAN--BUT I'M GOING TO MAKE YOU HIBERNATE LIKE ONE!
INCREDIBLE! HE'S DROPPED THE BEAR!
TIME TO LEAVE--TELL THE BEAR IF HE WANTS ME, I'LL BE AT THE DEPART-PAD AT SUNUP TOMORROW... THE NAME'S DARE!
YEAH, SURE..!
SOON, IN ANOTHER PART OF THE CITY.
MOON STREET
DARE--YOU COULD HAVE BEEN KILLED TESTING THAT MANIAC!
I'M ABOUT TO TEST ANOTHER--SEE THAT GUY AHEAD, NAME OF HITMAN! HE WAS ON THE CRUISER ENTERPRISE WHEN SHE EXPLODED! HAD TO SPEND TWO MINUTES IN ABSOLUTE ZERO TEMPERATURE TO GET TO A LIFERAFT!

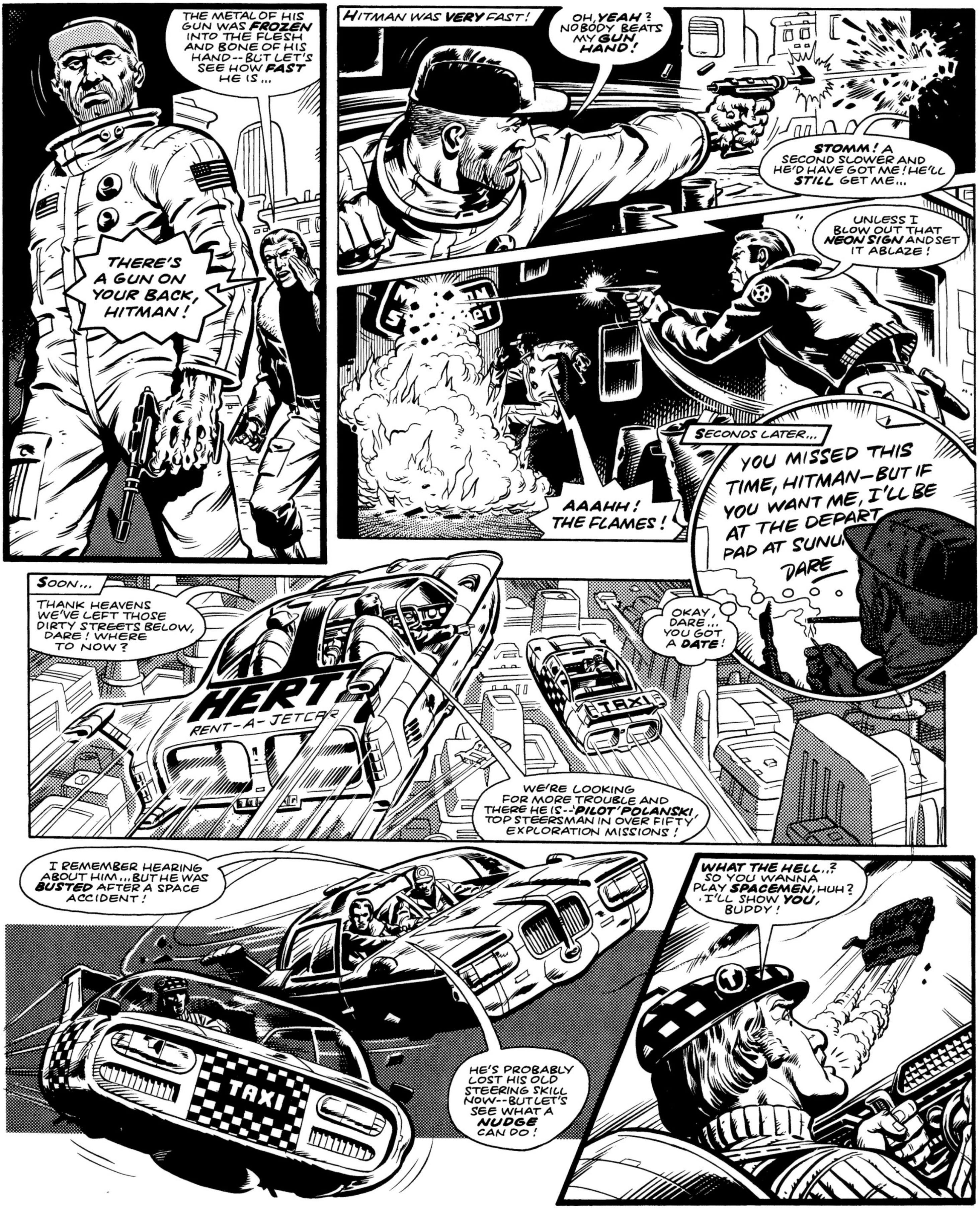

THE METAL OF HIS GUN WAS FROZEN INTO THE FLESH AND BONE OF HIS HAND--BUT LET'S SEE HOW FAST HE IS...
THERE'S A GUN ON YOUR BACK, HITMAN!
HITMAN WAS VERY FAST!
OH, YEAH? NOBODY BEATS MY GUN HAND!
STOMM! A SECOND SLOWER AND HE'D HAVE GOT ME! HE'LL STILL GET ME...
UNLESS I BLOW OUT THAT NEON SIGN AND SET IT ABLAZE!
AAAHH! THE FLAMES!
SECONDS LATER...
YOU MISSED THIS TIME, HITMAN—BUT IF YOU WANT ME, I'LL BE AT THE DEPART PAD AT SUNU
DARE
SOON...
THANK HEAVENS WE'VE LEFT THOSE DIRTY STREETS BELOW, DARE! WHERE TO NOW?
OKAY, DARE... YOU GOT A DATE!
HERT
RENT-A-JETCAR
TAXI
WE'RE LOOKING FOR MORE TROUBLE AND THERE HE IS--'PILOT' POLANSKI, TOP STEERSMAN IN OVER FIFTY EXPLORATION MISSIONS!
I REMEMBER HEARING ABOUT HIM... BUT HE WAS BUSTED AFTER A SPACE ACCIDENT!
TAXI
HE'S PROBABLY LOST HIS OLD STEERING SKILL NOW--BUT LET'S SEE WHAT A NUDGE CAN DO!
WHAT THE HELL..? SO YOU WANNA PLAY SPACEMEN, HUH? I'LL SHOW YOU, BUDDY!

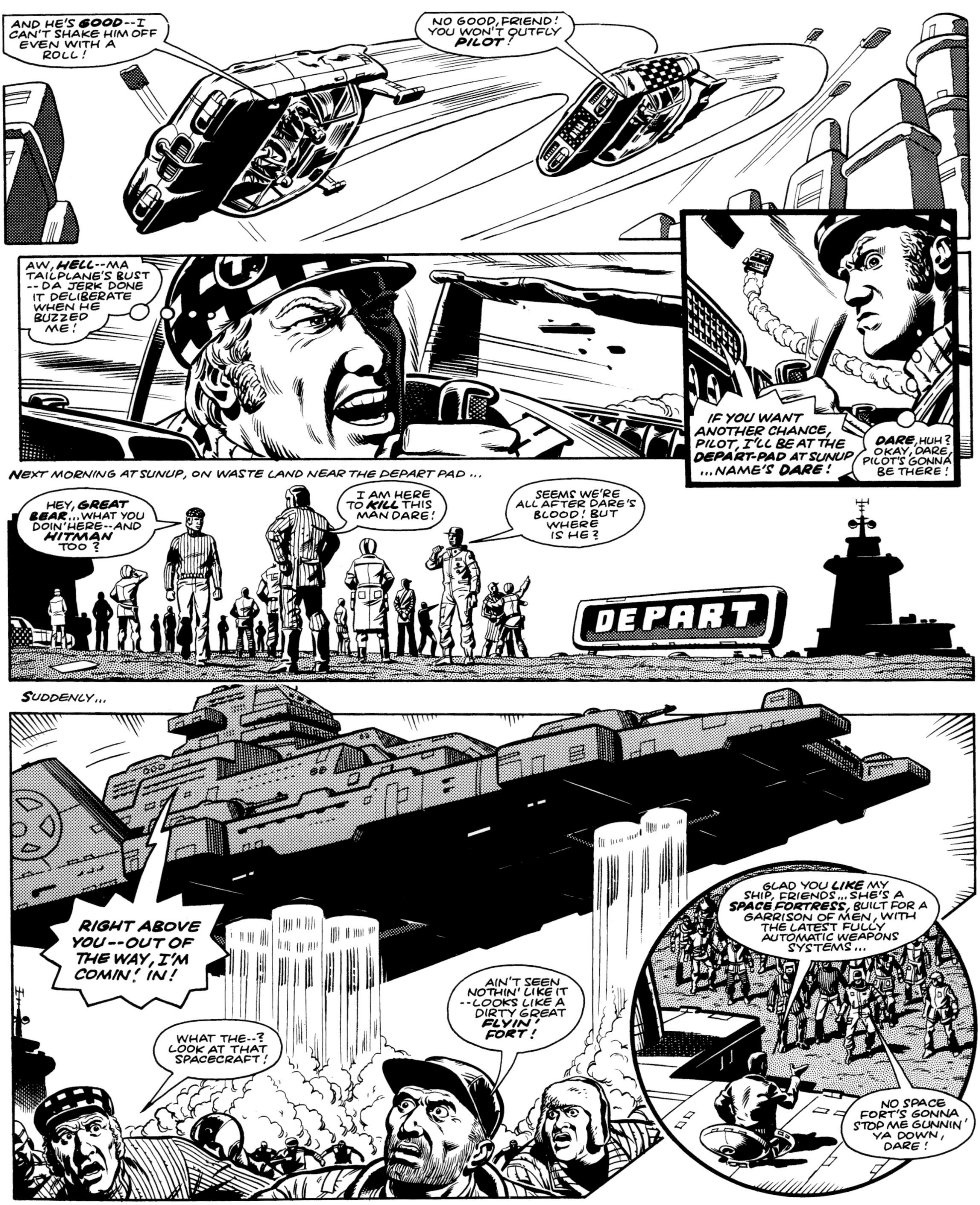
AND HE'S GOOD--I CAN'T SHAKE HIM OFF EVEN WITH A ROLL!
NO GOOD, FRIEND! YOU WON'T OUTFLY PILOT!
AW, HELL--MA TAILPLANE'S BUST--DA JERK DONE IT DELIBERATE WHEN HE BUZZED ME!
IF YOU WANT ANOTHER CHANCE, PILOT, I'LL BE AT THE DEPART-PAD AT SUNUP ...NAME'S DARE!
DARE, HUH? OKAY, DARE, PILOT'S GONNA BE THERE!
NEXT MORNING AT SUNUP, ON WASTE LAND NEAR THE DEPART PAD ...
HEY, GREAT BEAR...WHAT YOU DOIN' HERE--AND HITMAN TOO?
I AM HERE TO KILL THIS MAN DARE!
SEEMS WE'RE ALL AFTER DARE'S BLOOD! BUT WHERE IS HE?
DEPART
SUDDENLY...
RIGHT ABOVE YOU--OUT OF THE WAY, I'M COMIN' IN!
WHAT THE--? LOOK AT THAT SPACECRAFT!
AIN'T SEEN NOTHIN' LIKE IT--LOOKS LIKE A DIRTY GREAT FLYIN' FORT!
GLAD YOU LIKE MY SHIP, FRIENDS... SHE'S A SPACE FORTRESS, BUILT FOR A GARRISON OF MEN, WITH THE LATEST FULLY AUTOMATIC WEAPONS SYSTEMS...
NO SPACE FORT'S GONNA STOP ME GUNNIN' YA DOWN, DARE!

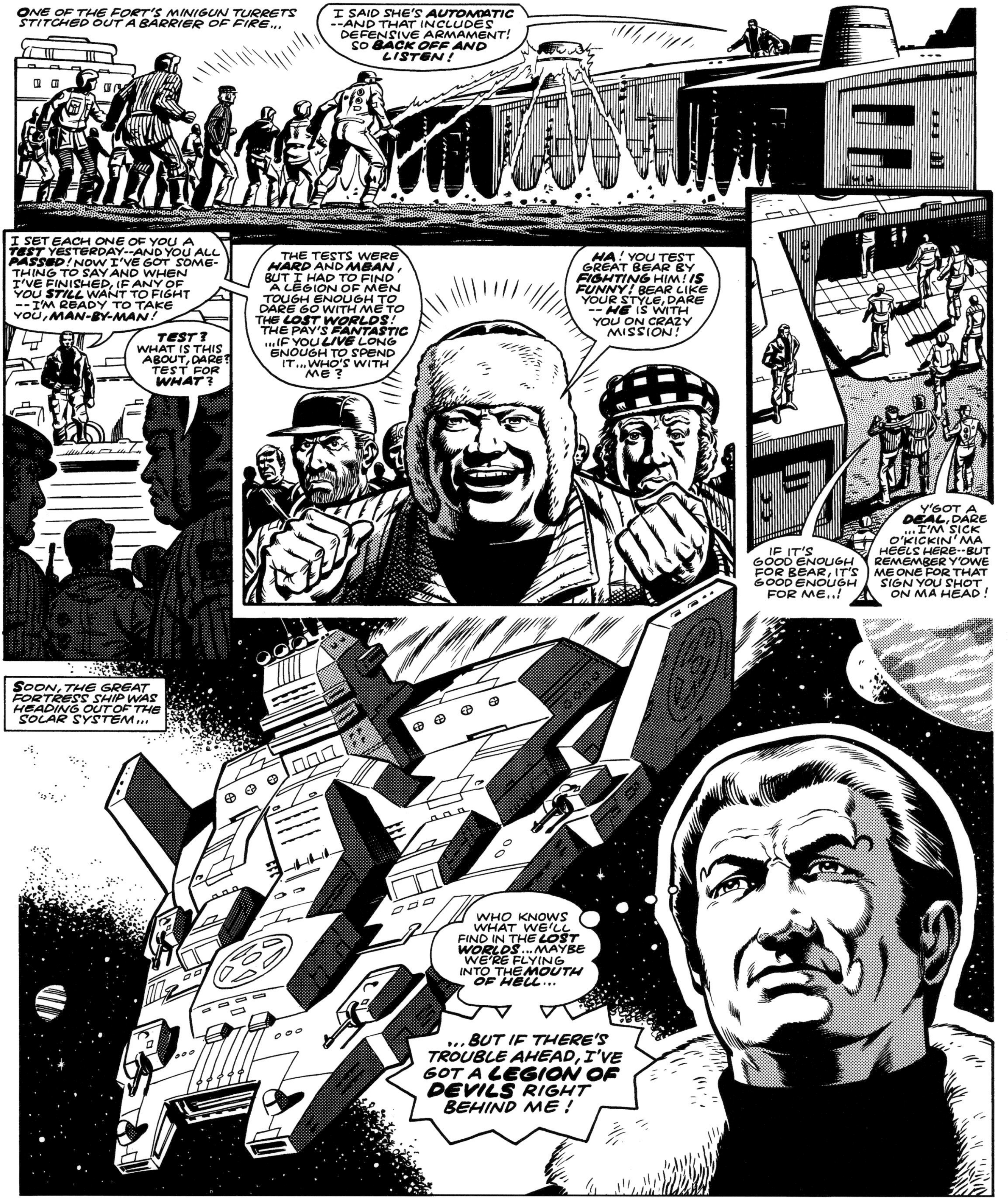
ONE OF THE FORT'S MINIGUN TURRETS STITCHED OUT A BARRIER OF FIRE...
I SAID SHE'S AUTOMATIC --AND THAT INCLUDES DEFENSIVE ARMAMENT! SO BACK OFF AND LISTEN!
I SET EACH ONE OF YOU A TEST YESTERDAY--AND YOU ALL PASSED! NOW I'VE GOT SOMETHING TO SAY AND WHEN I'VE FINISHED, IF ANY OF YOU STILL WANT TO FIGHT --I'M READY TO TAKE YOU, MAN-BY-MAN!
TEST? WHAT IS THIS ABOUT, DARE? TEST FOR WHAT?
THE TESTS WERE HARD AND MEAN, BUT I HAD TO FIND A LEGION OF MEN TOUGH ENOUGH TO DARE GO WITH ME TO THE LOST WORLDS! THE PAY'S FANTASTIC ...IF YOU LIVE LONG ENOUGH TO SPEND IT... WHO'S WITH ME?
HA! YOU TEST GREAT BEAR BY FIGHTING HIM! IS FUNNY! BEAR LIKE YOUR STYLE, DARE --HE IS WITH YOU ON CRAZY MISSION!
IF IT'S GOOD ENOUGH FOR BEAR, IT'S GOOD ENOUGH FOR ME..!
Y'GOT A DEAL, DARE ...I'M SICK O'KICKIN' MA HEELS HERE--BUT REMEMBER Y'OWE ME ONE FOR THAT SIGN YOU SHOT ON MA HEAD!
SOON, THE GREAT FORTRESS SHIP WAS HEADING OUT OF THE SOLAR SYSTEM...
WHO KNOWS WHAT WE'LL FIND IN THE LOST WORLDS... MAYBE WE'RE FLYING INTO THE MOUTH OF HELL...
...BUT IF THERE'S TROUBLE AHEAD, I'VE GOT A LEGION OF DEVILS RIGHT BEHIND ME!

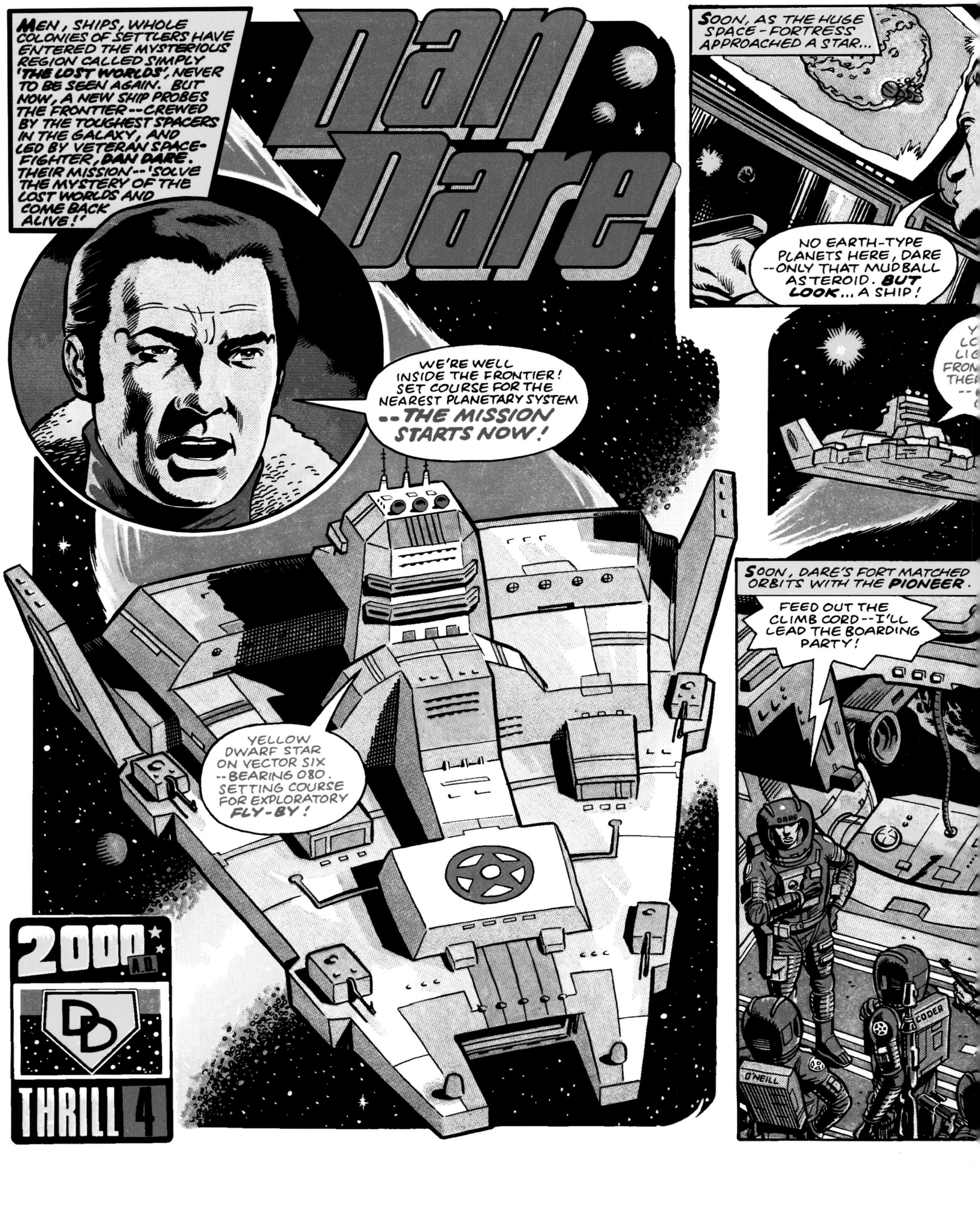
MEN, SHIPS, WHOLE COLONIES OF SETTLERS HAVE ENTERED THE MYSTERIOUS REGION CALLED SIMPLY 'THE LOST WORLDS', NEVER TO BE SEEN AGAIN. BUT NOW, A NEW SHIP PROBES THE FRONTIER--CREWED BY THE TOUGHEST SPACERS IN THE GALAXY, AND LED BY VETERAN SPACE-FIGHTER, DAN DARE. THEIR MISSION--'SOLVE THE MYSTERY OF THE LOST WORLDS AND COME BACK ALIVE!'
DAN DARE
WE'RE WELL INSIDE THE FRONTIER! SET COURSE FOR THE NEAREST PLANETARY SYSTEM --THE MISSION STARTS NOW!
YELLOW DWARF STAR ON VECTOR SIX --BEARING 080. SETTING COURSE FOR EXPLORATORY FLY-BY!
2000 A.D.
DD
THRILL 4
SOON, AS THE HUGE SPACE-FORTRESS APPROACHED A STAR...
NO EARTH-TYPE PLANETS HERE, DARE --ONLY THAT MUDBALL ASTEROID. BUT LOOK... A SHIP!
SOON, DARE'S FORT MATCHED ORBITS WITH THE PIONEER.
FEED OUT THE CLIMB CORD--I'LL LEAD THE BOARDING PARTY!
DARE
CODER
O'NEILL

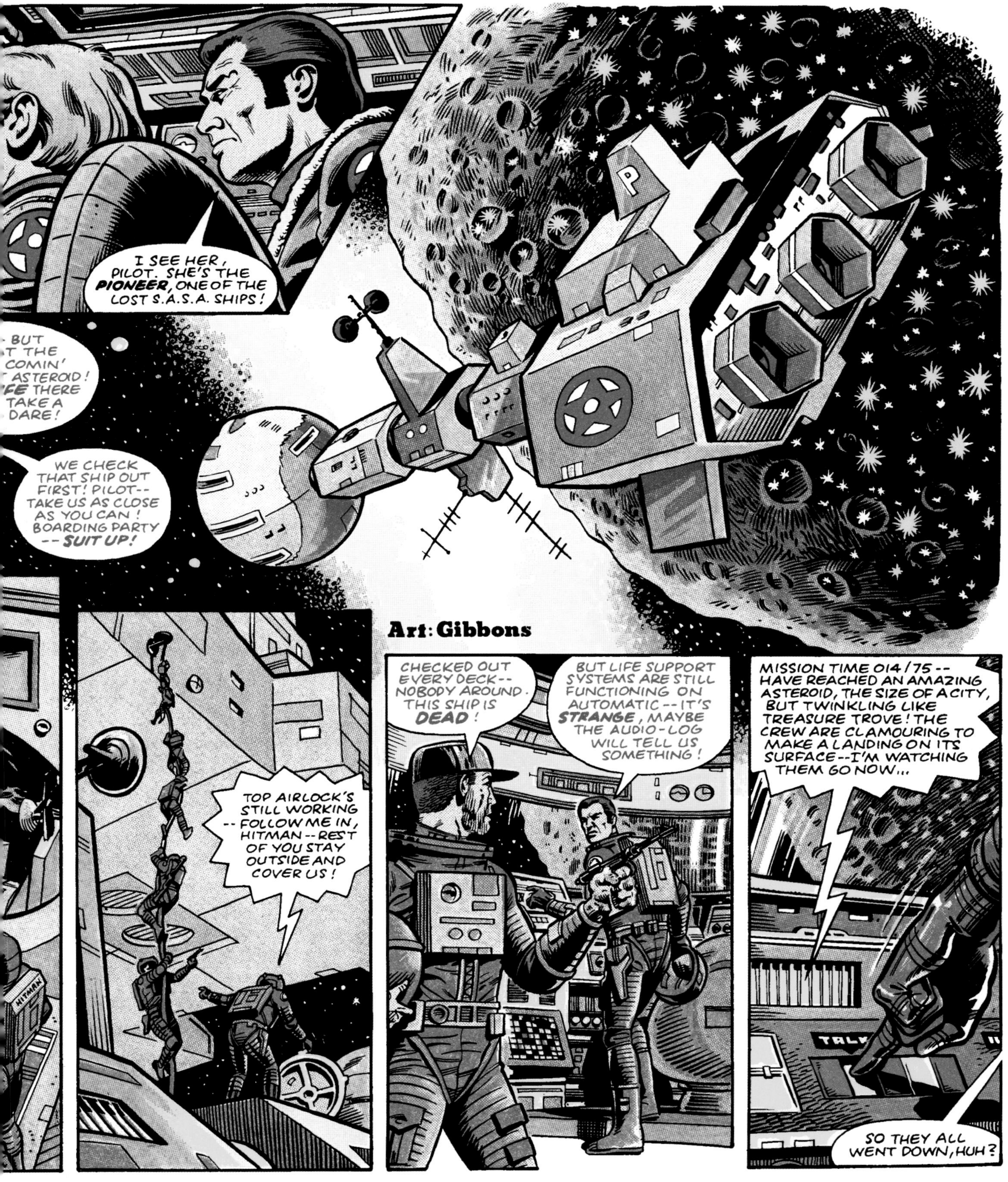
I SEE HER, PILOT. SHE'S THE PIONEER, ONE OF THE LOST S.A.S.A. SHIPS!
- BUT T THE COMIN' T ASTEROID! FE THERE TAKE A DARE!
WE CHECK THAT SHIP OUT FIRST! PILOT-- TAKE US AS CLOSE AS YOU CAN! BOARDING PARTY -- SUIT UP!
P
Art: Gibbons
TOP AIRLOCK'S STILL WORKING -- FOLLOW ME IN, HITMAN -- REST OF YOU STAY OUTSIDE AND COVER US!
HITMAN
CHECKED OUT EVERY DECK-- NOBODY AROUND. THIS SHIP IS DEAD!
BUT LIFE SUPPORT SYSTEMS ARE STILL FUNCTIONING ON AUTOMATIC -- IT'S STRANGE, MAYBE THE AUDIO-LOG WILL TELL US SOMETHING!
MISSION TIME 014/75 -- HAVE REACHED AN AMAZING ASTEROID, THE SIZE OF A CITY, BUT TWINKLING LIKE TREASURE TROVE! THE CREW ARE CLAMOURING TO MAKE A LANDING ON ITS SURFACE--I'M WATCHING THEM GO NOW...
SO THEY ALL WENT DOWN, HUH?

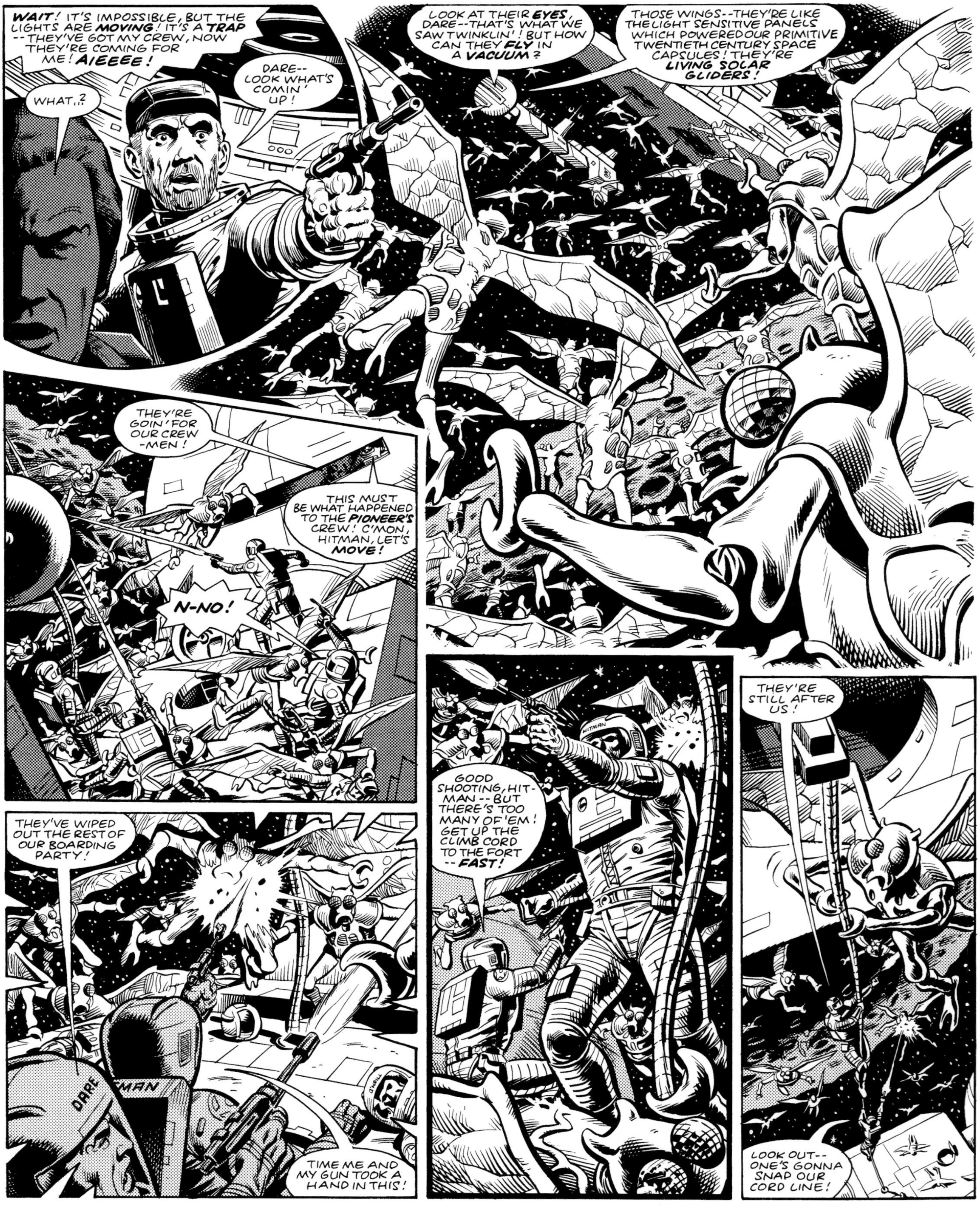
WAIT! IT'S IMPOSSIBLE, BUT THE LIGHTS ARE MOVING! IT'S A TRAP --THEY'VE GOT MY CREW, NOW THEY'RE COMING FOR ME! AIEEEE!
WHAT...?
DARE-- LOOK WHAT'S COMIN' UP!
LOOK AT THEIR EYES, DARE--THAT'S WHAT WE SAW TWINKLIN'! BUT HOW CAN THEY FLY IN A VACUUM?
THOSE WINGS--THEY'RE LIKE THE LIGHT SENSITIVE PANELS WHICH POWERED OUR PRIMITIVE TWENTIETH CENTURY SPACE CAPSULES! THEY'RE LIVING SOLAR GLIDERS!
THEY'RE GOIN' FOR OUR CREW -MEN!
THIS MUST BE WHAT HAPPENED TO THE PIONEER'S CREW! C'MON, HITMAN, LET'S MOVE!
N-NO!
THEY'VE WIPED OUT THE REST OF OUR BOARDING PARTY!
TIME ME AND MY GUN TOOK A HAND IN THIS!
GOOD SHOOTING, HIT-MAN -- BUT THERE'S TOO MANY OF 'EM! GET UP THE CLIMB CORD TO THE FORT --FAST!
THEY'RE STILL AFTER US!
LOOK OUT-- ONE'S GONNA SNAP OUR CORD LINE!

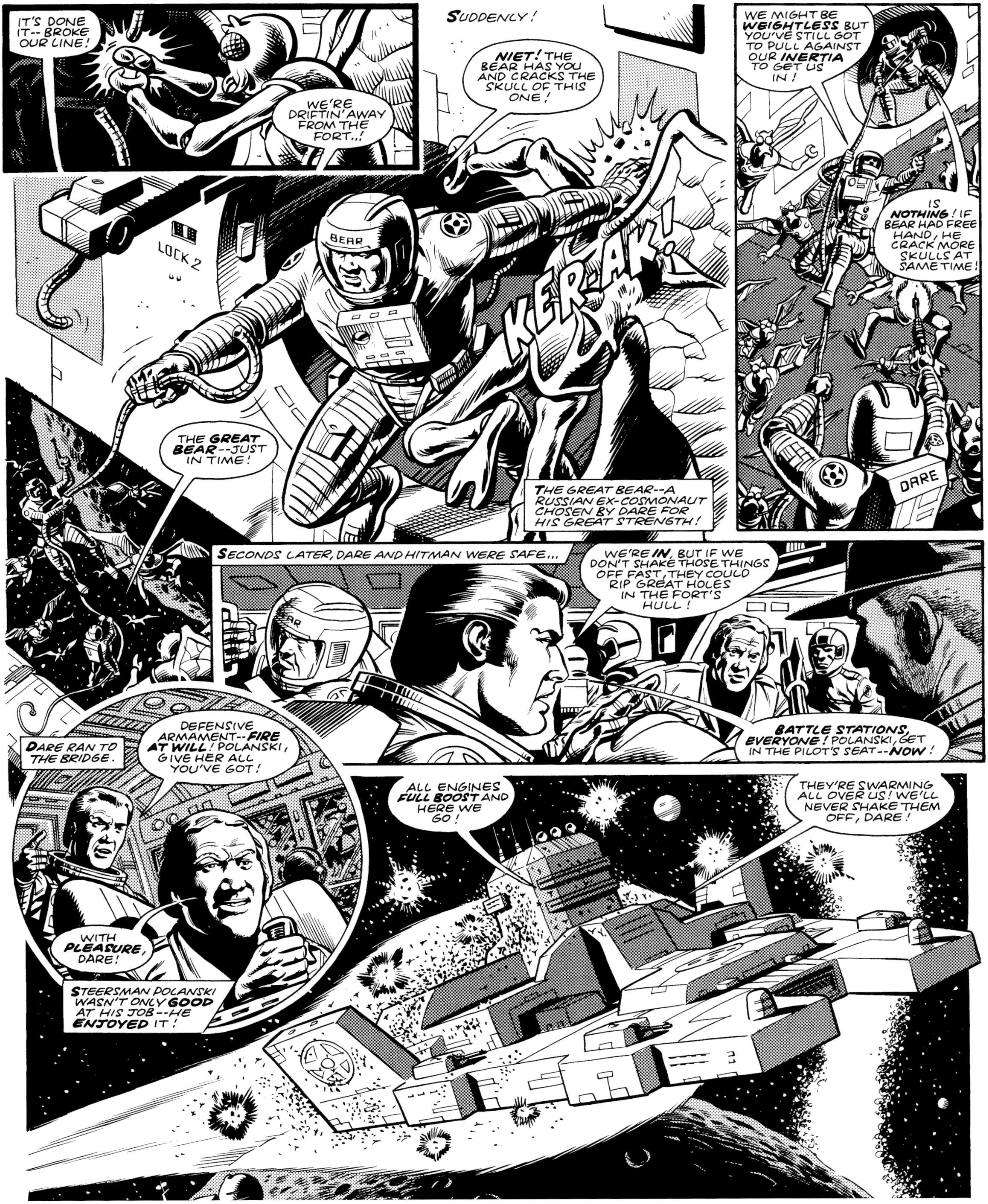
IT'S DONE IT-- BROKE OUR LINE!
WE'RE DRIFTIN' AWAY FROM THE FORT..!
SUDDENLY!
NIET! THE BEAR HAS YOU AND CRACKS THE SKULL OF THIS ONE!
KER-AK!
BEAR
LOCK 2
THE GREAT BEAR--JUST IN TIME!
THE GREAT BEAR--A RUSSIAN EX-COSMONAUT CHOSEN BY DARE FOR HIS GREAT STRENGTH!
WE MIGHT BE WEIGHTLESS BUT YOU'VE STILL GOT TO PULL AGAINST OUR INERTIA TO GET US IN!
IS NOTHING! IF BEAR HAD FREE HAND, HE CRACK MORE SKULLS AT SAME TIME!
DARE
SECONDS LATER, DARE AND HITMAN WERE SAFE...
WE'RE IN, BUT IF WE DON'T SHAKE THOSE THINGS OFF FAST, THEY COULD RIP GREAT HOLES IN THE FORT'S HULL!
BATTLE STATIONS, EVERYONE! POLANSKI, GET IN THE PILOT'S SEAT--NOW!
DARE RAN TO THE BRIDGE.
DEFENSIVE ARMAMENT--FIRE AT WILL! POLANSKI, GIVE HER ALL YOU'VE GOT!
WITH PLEASURE, DARE!
STEERSMAN POLANSKI WASN'T ONLY GOOD AT HIS JOB--HE ENJOYED IT!
ALL ENGINES FULL BOOST AND HERE WE GO!
THEY'RE SWARMING ALL OVER US! WE'LL NEVER SHAKE THEM OFF, DARE!

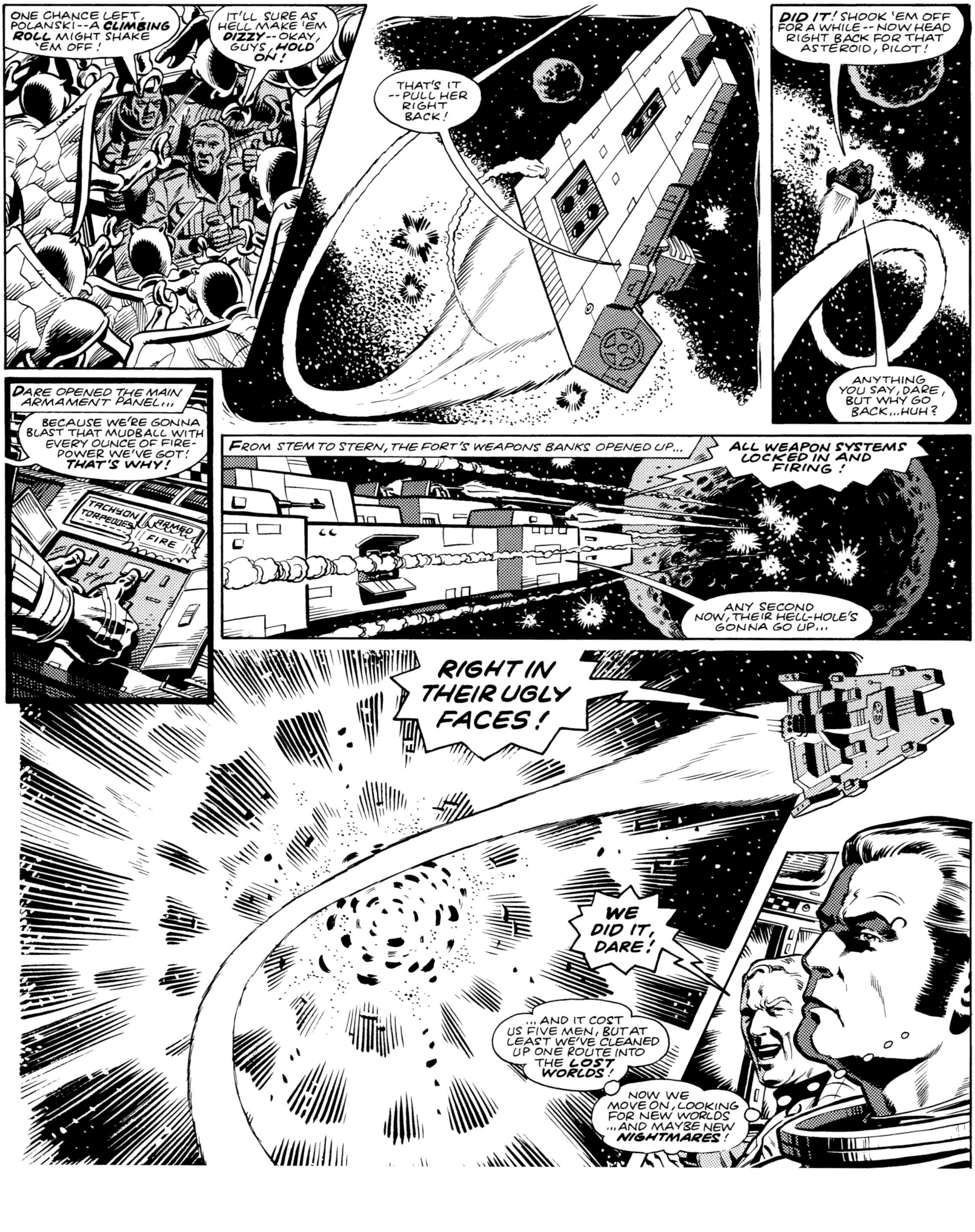
ONE CHANCE LEFT, POLANSKI--A CLIMBING ROLL MIGHT SHAKE 'EM OFF!
IT'LL SURE AS HELL MAKE 'EM DIZZY--OKAY, GUYS, HOLD ON!
THAT'S IT --PULL HER RIGHT BACK!
DID IT! SHOOK 'EM OFF FOR A WHILE--NOW HEAD RIGHT BACK FOR THAT ASTEROID, PILOT!
ANYTHING YOU SAY, DARE, BUT WHY GO BACK...HUH?
DARE OPENED THE MAIN ARMAMENT PANEL...
BECAUSE WE'RE GONNA BLAST THAT MUDBALL WITH EVERY OUNCE OF FIRE-POWER WE'VE GOT! THAT'S WHY!
TACHYON TORPEDOES
ARMED
FIRE
FROM STEM TO STERN, THE FORT'S WEAPONS BANKS OPENED UP...
ALL WEAPON SYSTEMS LOCKED IN AND FIRING!
ANY SECOND NOW, THEIR HELL-HOLE'S GONNA GO UP...
RIGHT IN THEIR UGLY FACES!
WE DID IT, DARE!
...AND IT COST US FIVE MEN, BUT AT LEAST WE'VE CLEANED UP ONE ROUTE INTO THE LOST WORLDS!
NOW WE MOVE ON, LOOKING FOR NEW WORLDS ...AND MAYBE NEW NIGHTMARES!

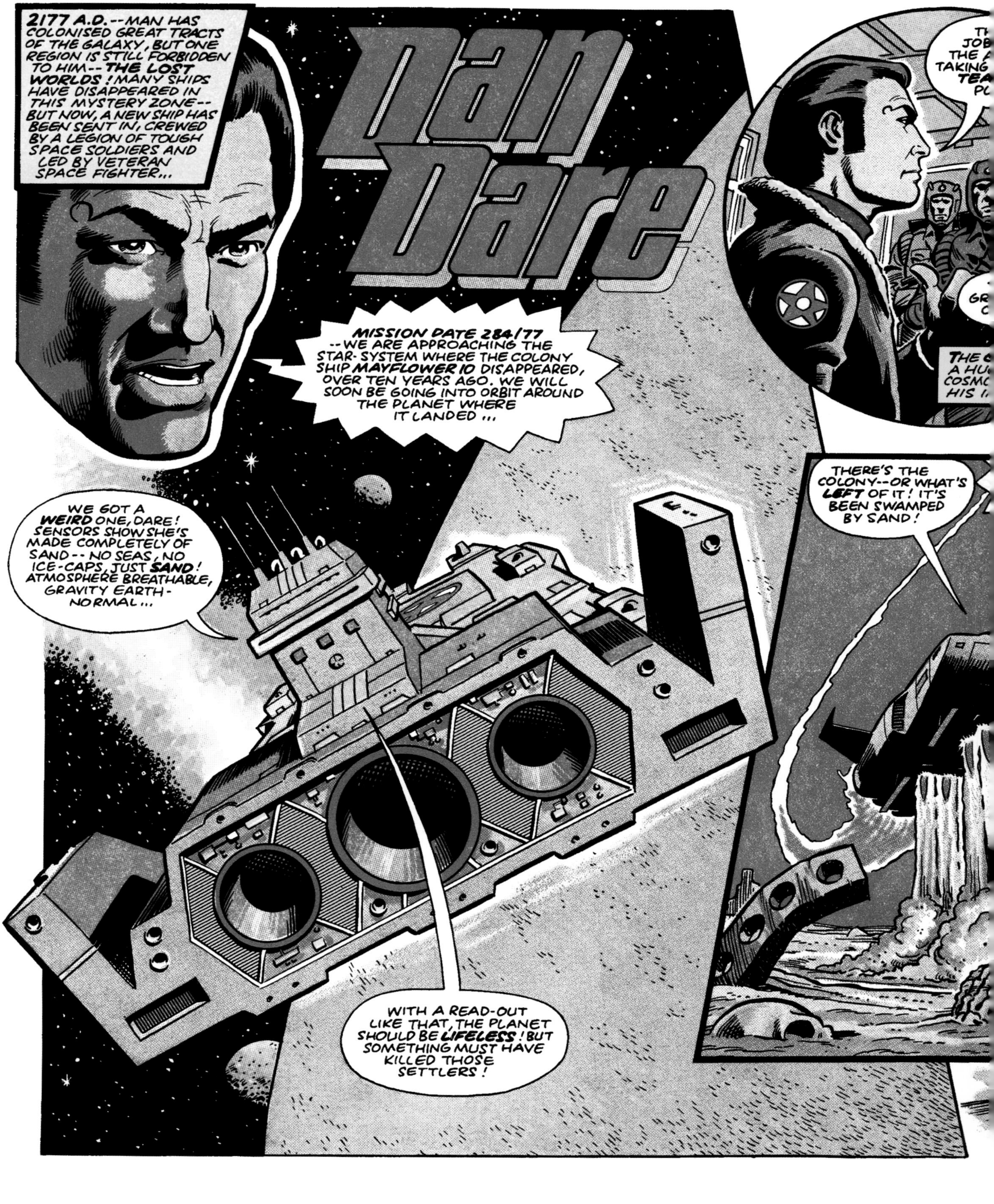

2177 A.D.--MAN HAS COLONISED GREAT TRACTS OF THE GALAXY, BUT ONE REGION IS STILL FORBIDDEN TO HIM--THE LOST WORLDS! MANY SHIPS HAVE DISAPPEARED IN THIS MYSTERY ZONE--BUT NOW, A NEW SHIP HAS BEEN SENT IN, CREWED BY A LEGION OF TOUGH SPACE SOLDIERS AND LED BY VETERAN SPACE FIGHTER...
Dan Dare
MISSION DATE 284/77--WE ARE APPROACHING THE STAR-SYSTEM WHERE THE COLONY SHIP MAYFLOWER 10 DISAPPEARED, OVER TEN YEARS AGO. WE WILL SOON BE GOING INTO ORBIT AROUND THE PLANET WHERE IT LANDED...
WE GOT A WEIRD ONE, DARE! SENSORS SHOW SHE'S MADE COMPLETELY OF SAND--NO SEAS, NO ICE-CAPS, JUST SAND! ATMOSPHERE BREATHABLE, GRAVITY EARTH-NORMAL...
WITH A READ-OUT LIKE THAT, THE PLANET SHOULD BE LIFELESS! BUT SOMETHING MUST HAVE KILLED THOSE SETTLERS!
THERE'S THE COLONY--OR WHAT'S LEFT OF IT! IT'S BEEN SWAMPED BY SAND!

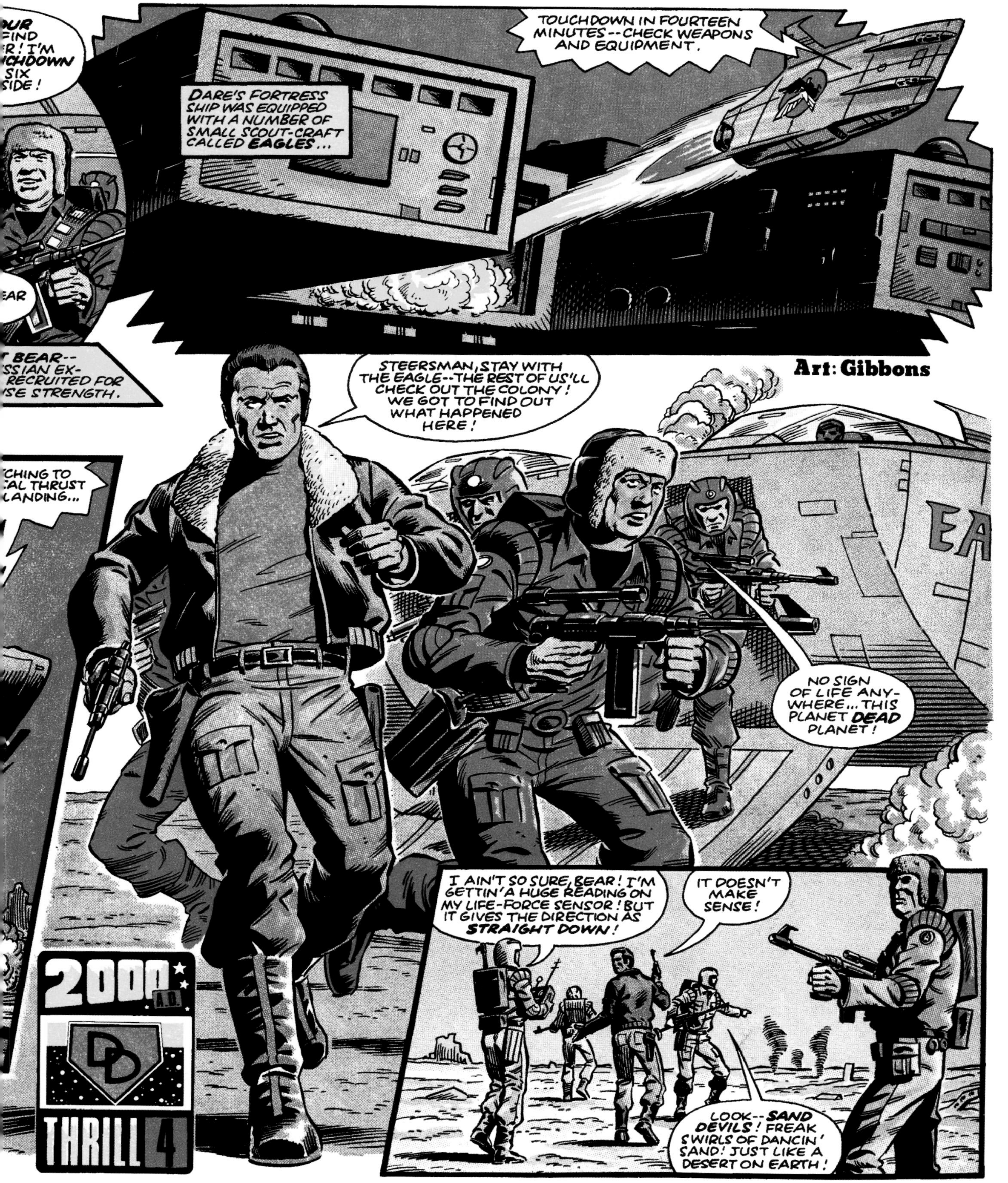

TOUCHDOWN IN FOURTEEN MINUTES--CHECK WEAPONS AND EQUIPMENT.
DARE'S FORTRESS SHIP WAS EQUIPPED WITH A NUMBER OF SMALL SCOUT-CRAFT CALLED EAGLES...
Art: Gibbons
STEERSMAN, STAY WITH THE EAGLE--THE REST OF US'LL CHECK OUT THE COLONY! WE GOT TO FIND OUT WHAT HAPPENED HERE!
NO SIGN OF LIFE ANYWHERE... THIS PLANET DEAD PLANET!
I AIN'T SO SURE, BEAR! I'M GETTIN' A HUGE READING ON MY LIFE-FORCE SENSOR! BUT IT GIVES THE DIRECTION AS STRAIGHT DOWN!
IT DOESN'T MAKE SENSE!
LOOK--SAND DEVILS! FREAK SWIRLS OF DANCIN' SAND! JUST LIKE A DESERT ON EARTH!
2000 A.D.
THRILL 4

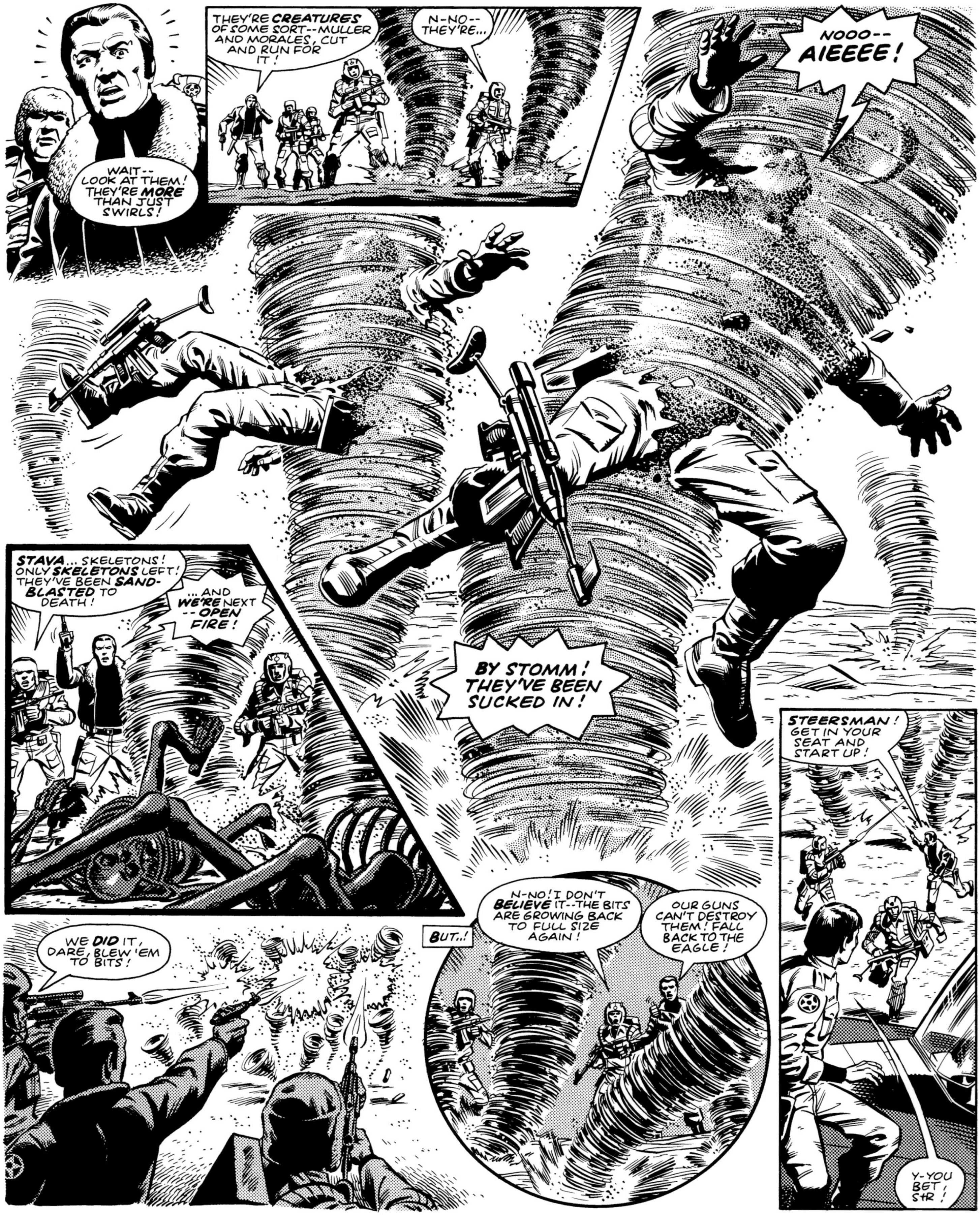
WAIT-- LOOK AT THEM! THEY'RE MORE THAN JUST SWIRLS!
THEY'RE CREATURES OF SOME SORT--MULLER AND MORALES, CUT AND RUN FOR IT!
N-NO-- THEY'RE...
NOOO-- AIEEEE!
STAVA... SKELETONS! ONLY SKELETONS LEFT! THEY'VE BEEN SAND-BLASTED TO DEATH!
...AND WE'RE NEXT --OPEN FIRE!
BY STOMM! THEY'VE BEEN SUCKED IN!
STEERSMAN! GET IN YOUR SEAT AND START UP!
WE DID IT, DARE, BLEW 'EM TO BITS!
BUT...!
N-NO! I DON'T BELIEVE IT--THE BITS ARE GROWING BACK TO FULL SIZE AGAIN!
OUR GUNS CAN'T DESTROY THEM! FALL BACK TO THE EAGLE!
Y-YOU BET, SIR!

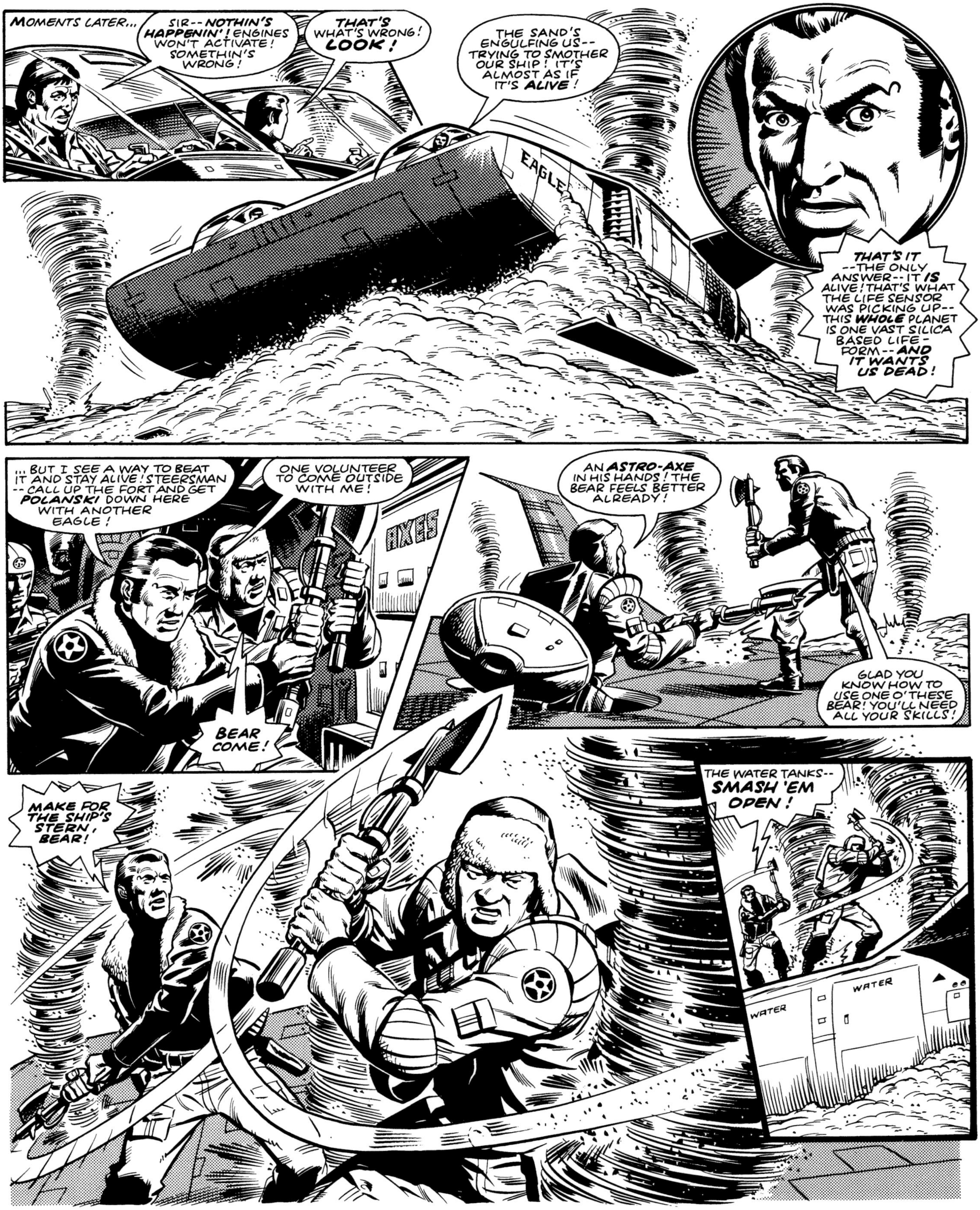
MOMENTS LATER...
SIR--NOTHIN'S HAPPENIN'! ENGINES WON'T ACTIVATE! SOMETHIN'S WRONG!
THAT'S WHAT'S WRONG! LOOK!
THE SAND'S ENGULFING US--TRYING TO SMOTHER OUR SHIP! IT'S ALMOST AS IF IT'S ALIVE!
EAGLE
THAT'S IT--THE ONLY ANSWER--IT IS ALIVE! THAT'S WHAT THE LIFE SENSOR WAS PICKING UP--THIS WHOLE PLANET IS ONE VAST SILICA BASED LIFE-FORM--AND IT WANTS US DEAD!
...BUT I SEE A WAY TO BEAT IT AND STAY ALIVE! STEERSMAN--CALL UP THE FORT AND GET POLANSKI DOWN HERE WITH ANOTHER EAGLE!
ONE VOLUNTEER TO COME OUTSIDE WITH ME!
AXES
BEAR COME!
AN ASTRO-AXE IN HIS HANDS! THE BEAR FEELS BETTER ALREADY!
GLAD YOU KNOW HOW TO USE ONE O' THESE BEAR! YOU'LL NEED ALL YOUR SKILLS!
MAKE FOR THE SHIP'S STERN, BEAR!
THE WATER TANKS--SMASH 'EM OPEN!
WATER
WATER

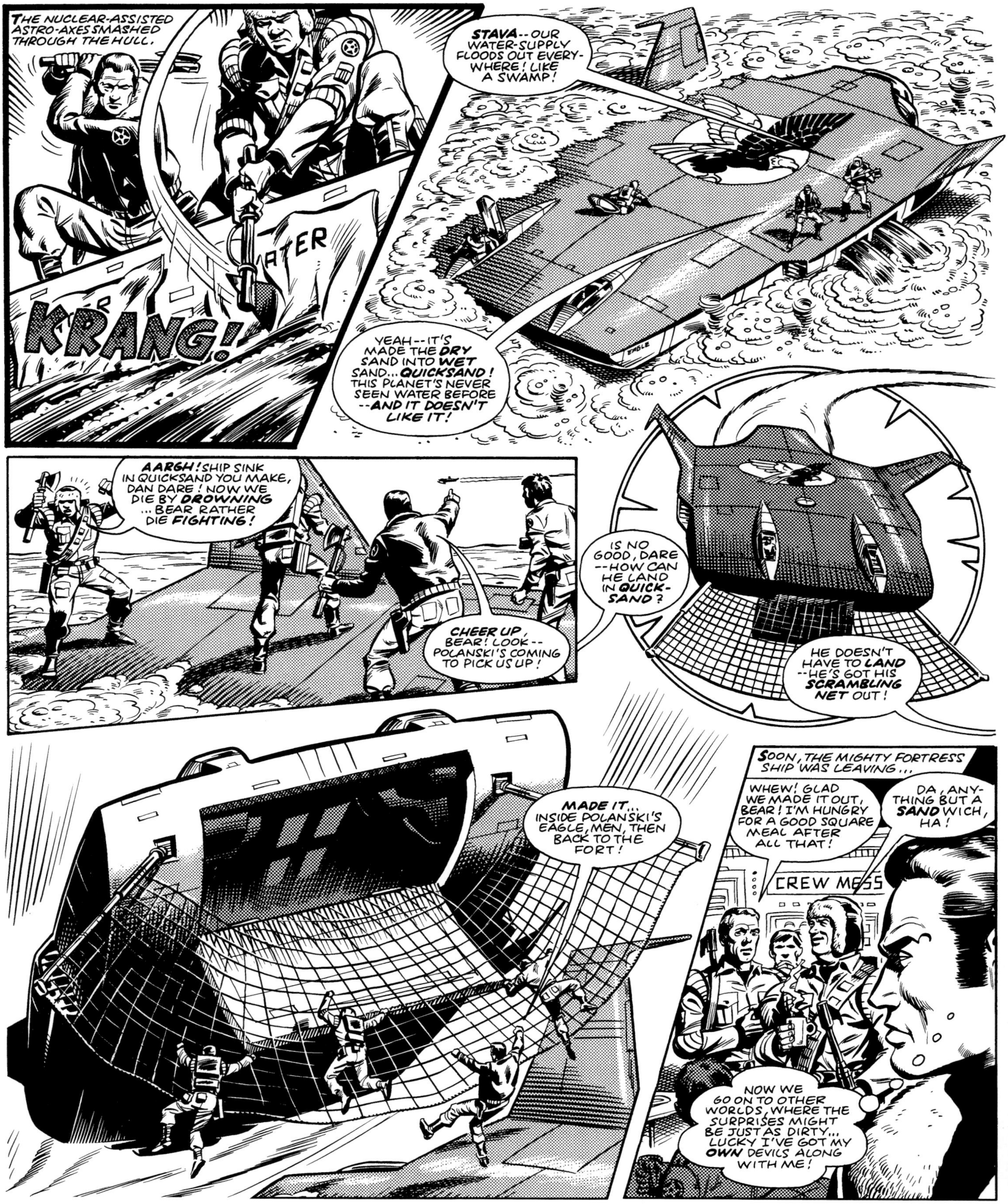
THE NUCLEAR-ASSISTED ASTRO-AXES SMASHED THROUGH THE HULL.
KRANG!
STAVA -- OUR WATER-SUPPLY FLOODS OUT EVERY-WHERE! LIKE A SWAMP!
YEAH -- IT'S MADE THE DRY SAND INTO WET SAND... QUICKSAND! THIS PLANET'S NEVER SEEN WATER BEFORE -- AND IT DOESN'T LIKE IT!
AARGH! SHIP SINK IN QUICKSAND YOU MAKE, DAN DARE! NOW WE DIE BY DROWNING ... BEAR RATHER DIE FIGHTING!
CHEER UP, BEAR! LOOK -- POLANSKI'S COMING TO PICK US UP!
IS NO GOOD, DARE -- HOW CAN HE LAND IN QUICK-SAND?
HE DOESN'T HAVE TO LAND -- HE'S GOT HIS SCRAMBLING NET OUT!
MADE IT... INSIDE POLANSKI'S EAGLE, MEN, THEN BACK TO THE FORT!
SOON, THE MIGHTY FORTRESS SHIP WAS LEAVING...
WHEW! GLAD WE MADE IT OUT, BEAR! I'M HUNGRY FOR A GOOD SQUARE MEAL AFTER ALL THAT!
DA, ANY-THING BUT A SAND WICH, HA!
CREW MESS
NOW WE GO ON TO OTHER WORLDS, WHERE THE SURPRISES MIGHT BE JUST AS DIRTY... LUCKY I'VE GOT MY OWN DEVILS ALONG WITH ME!

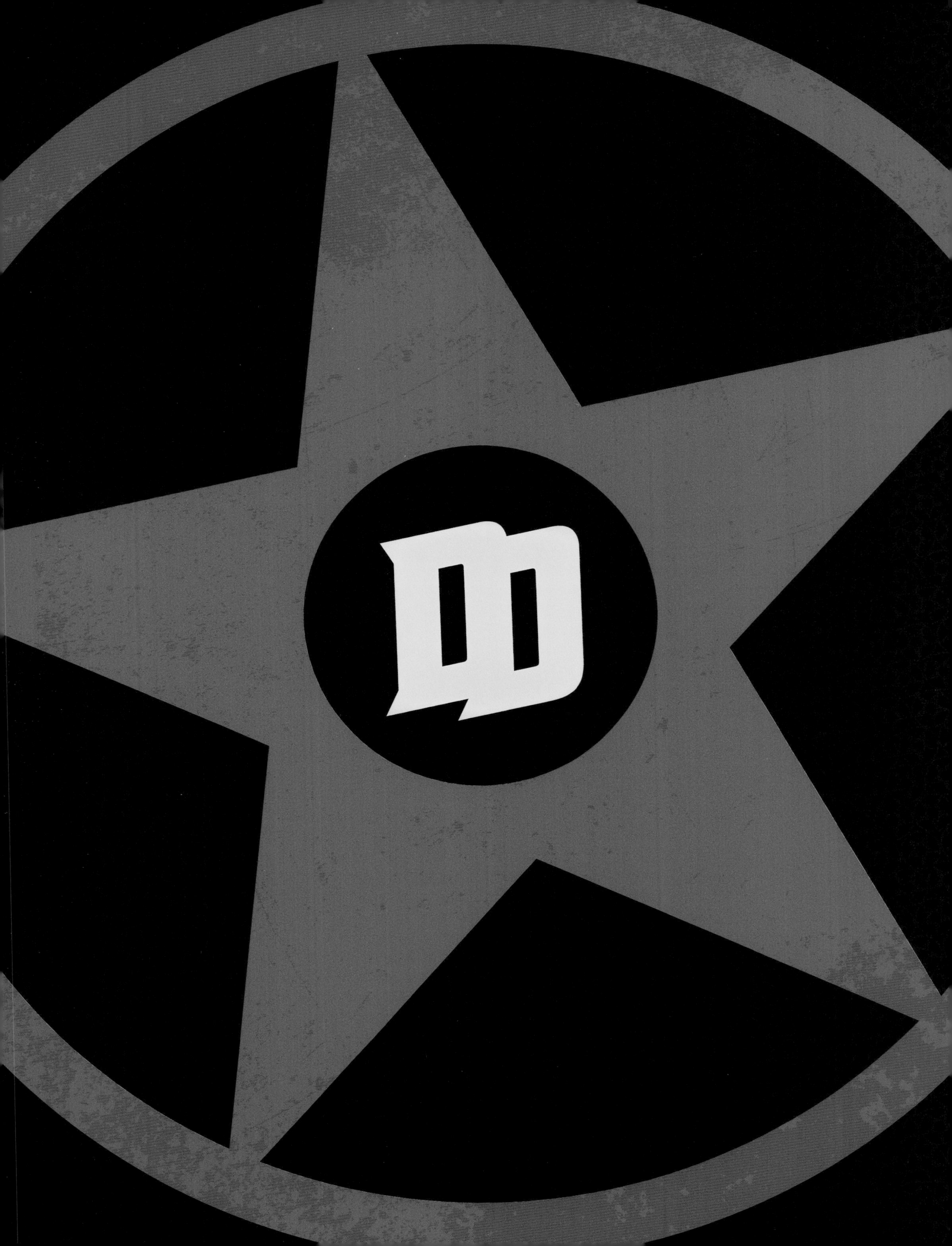

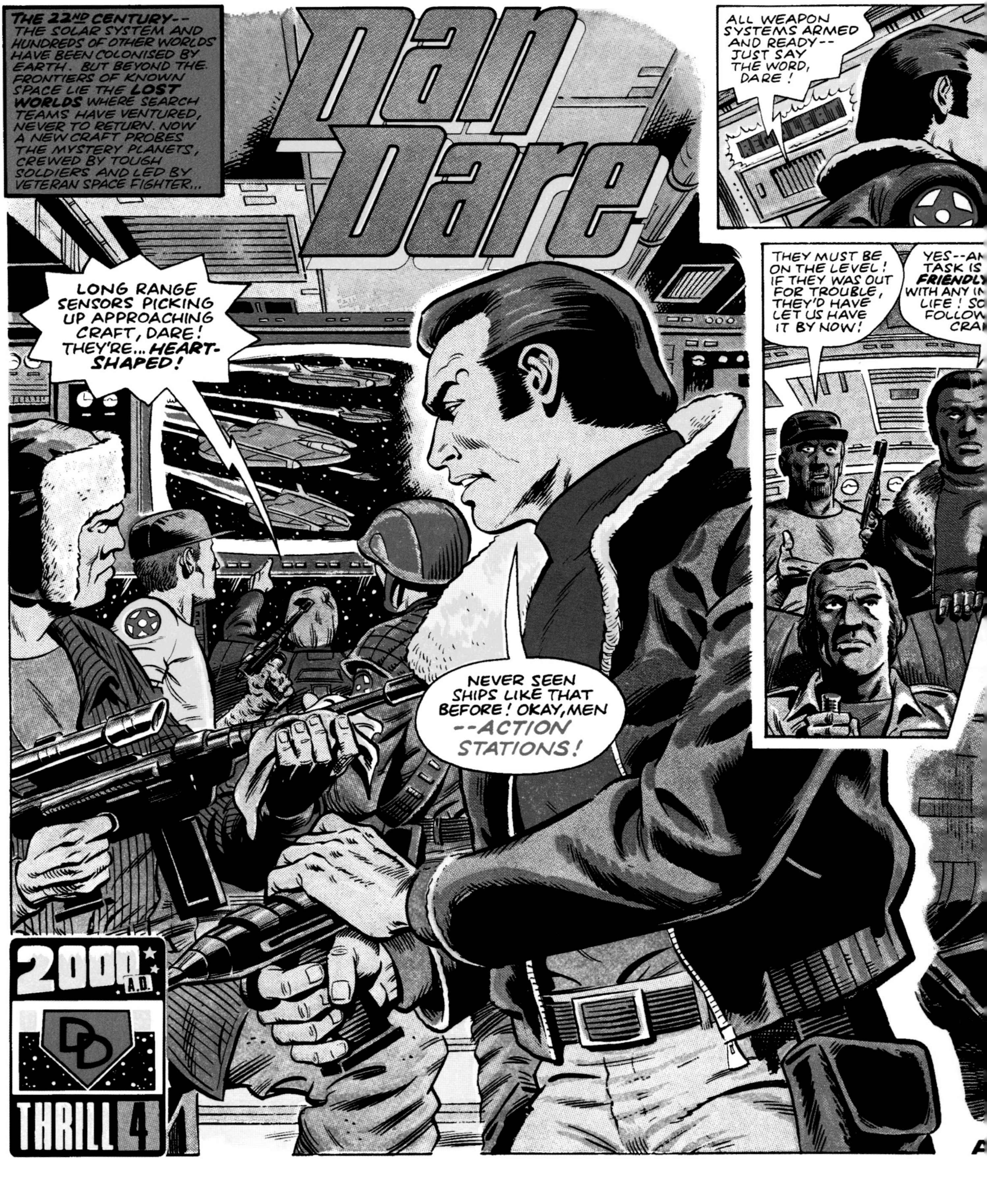
THE 22ND CENTURY-- THE SOLAR SYSTEM AND HUNDREDS OF OTHER WORLDS HAVE BEEN COLONISED BY EARTH. BUT BEYOND THE FRONTIERS OF KNOWN SPACE LIE THE LOST WORLDS WHERE SEARCH TEAMS HAVE VENTURED, NEVER TO RETURN. NOW A NEW CRAFT PROBES THE MYSTERY PLANETS, CREWED BY TOUGH SOLDIERS AND LED BY VETERAN SPACE FIGHTER...
DAN DARE
LONG RANGE SENSORS PICKING UP APPROACHING CRAFT, DARE! THEY'RE... HEART-SHAPED!
NEVER SEEN SHIPS LIKE THAT BEFORE! OKAY, MEN --ACTION STATIONS!
2000 A.D.
DD
THRILL 4
ALL WEAPON SYSTEMS ARMED AND READY-- JUST SAY THE WORD, DARE!
THEY MUST BE ON THE LEVEL! IF THEY WAS OUT FOR TROUBLE, THEY'D HAVE LET US HAVE IT BY NOW!

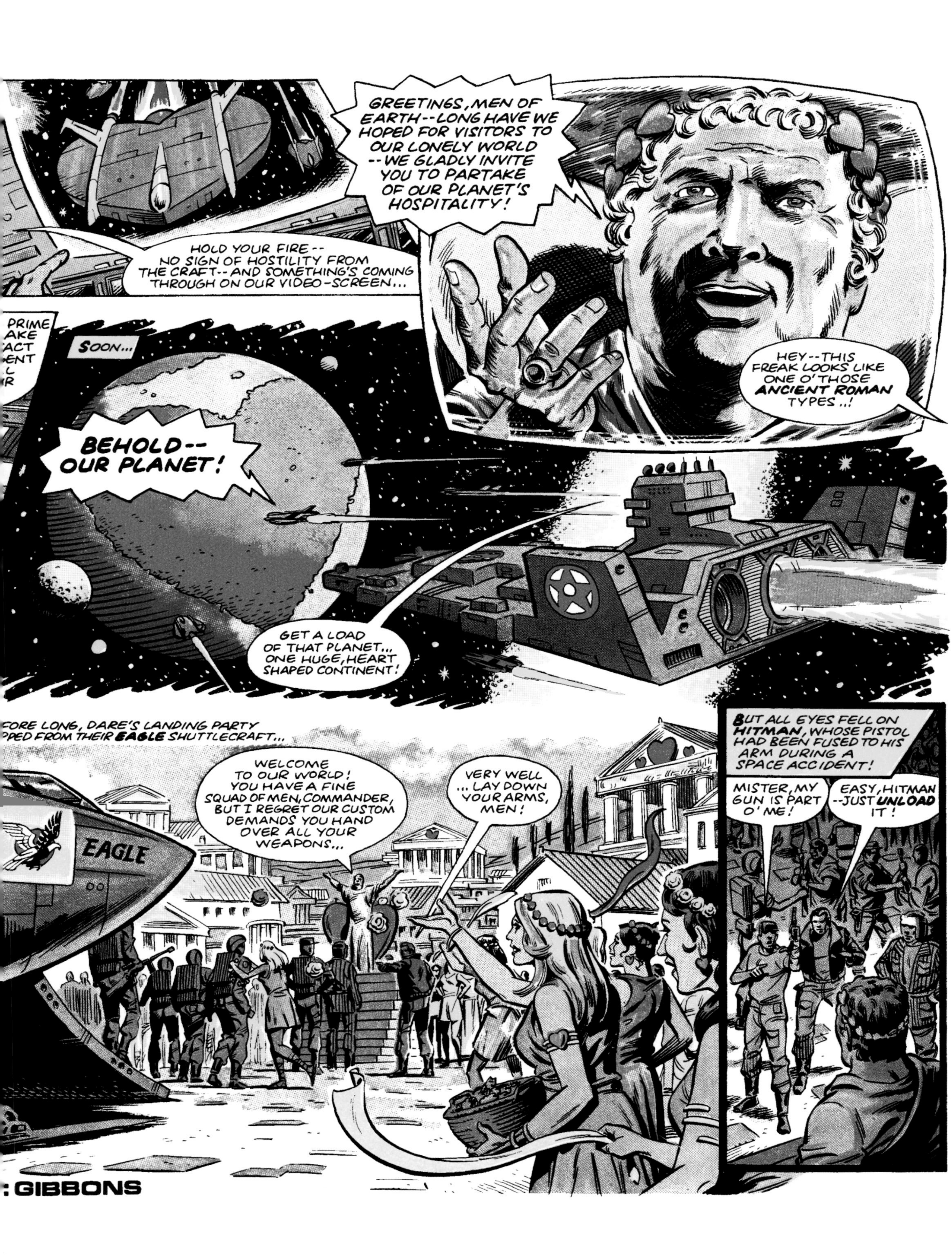

GREETINGS, MEN OF EARTH--LONG HAVE WE HOPED FOR VISITORS TO OUR LONELY WORLD --WE GLADLY INVITE YOU TO PARTAKE OF OUR PLANET'S HOSPITALITY!
HOLD YOUR FIRE-- NO SIGN OF HOSTILITY FROM THE CRAFT--AND SOMETHING'S COMING THROUGH ON OUR VIDEO-SCREEN...
HEY--THIS FREAK LOOKS LIKE ONE O' THOSE ANCIENT ROMAN TYPES..!
SOON...
BEHOLD-- OUR PLANET!
GET A LOAD OF THAT PLANET... ONE HUGE, HEART SHAPED CONTINENT!
...FORE LONG, DARE'S LANDING PARTY ...PPED FROM THEIR EAGLE SHUTTLECRAFT...
EAGLE
WELCOME TO OUR WORLD! YOU HAVE A FINE SQUAD OF MEN, COMMANDER, BUT I REGRET OUR CUSTOM DEMANDS YOU HAND OVER ALL YOUR WEAPONS...
VERY WELL ...LAY DOWN YOUR ARMS, MEN!
BUT ALL EYES FELL ON HITMAN, WHOSE PISTOL HAD BEEN FUSED TO HIS ARM DURING A SPACE ACCIDENT!
MISTER, MY GUN IS PART O' ME!
EASY, HITMAN --JUST UNLOAD IT!
: GIBBONS

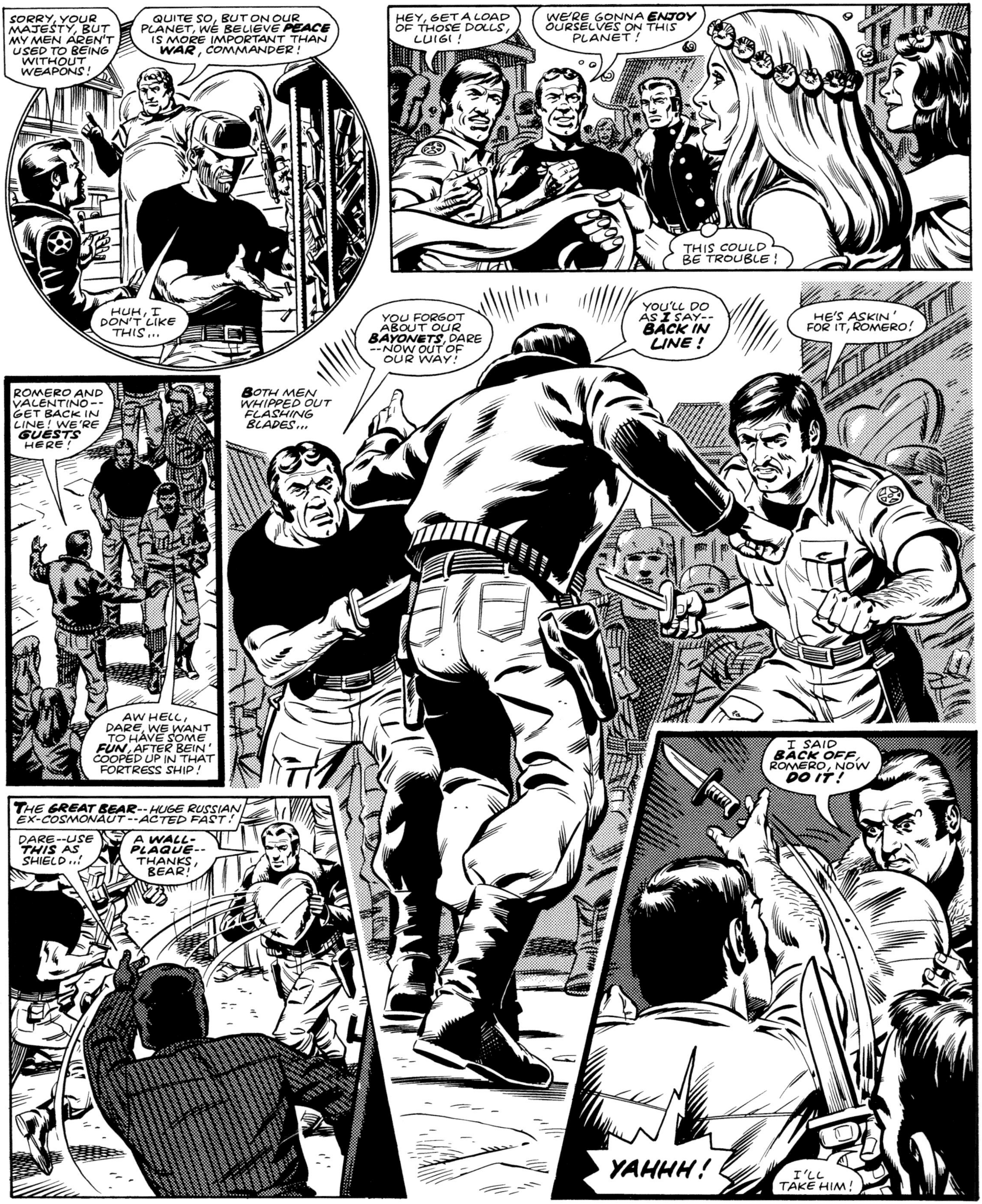
SORRY, YOUR MAJESTY, BUT MY MEN AREN'T USED TO BEING WITHOUT WEAPONS!
QUITE SO, BUT ON OUR PLANET, WE BELIEVE PEACE IS MORE IMPORTANT THAN WAR, COMMANDER!
HUH, I DON'T LIKE THIS...
HEY, GET A LOAD OF THOSE DOLLS, LUIGI!
WE'RE GONNA ENJOY OURSELVES ON THIS PLANET!
THIS COULD BE TROUBLE!
ROMERO AND VALENTINO--GET BACK IN LINE! WE'RE GUESTS HERE!
AW HELL, DARE, WE WANT TO HAVE SOME FUN, AFTER BEIN' COOPED UP IN THAT FORTRESS SHIP!
BOTH MEN WHIPPED OUT FLASHING BLADES...
YOU FORGOT ABOUT OUR BAYONETS, DARE --NOW OUT OF OUR WAY!
YOU'LL DO AS I SAY-- BACK IN LINE!
HE'S ASKIN' FOR IT, ROMERO!
THE GREAT BEAR--HUGE RUSSIAN EX-COSMONAUT--ACTED FAST!
DARE--USE THIS AS SHIELD..!
A WALL-PLAQUE--THANKS, BEAR!
I SAID BACK OFF, ROMERO, NOW DO IT!
YAHHH!
I'LL TAKE HIM!

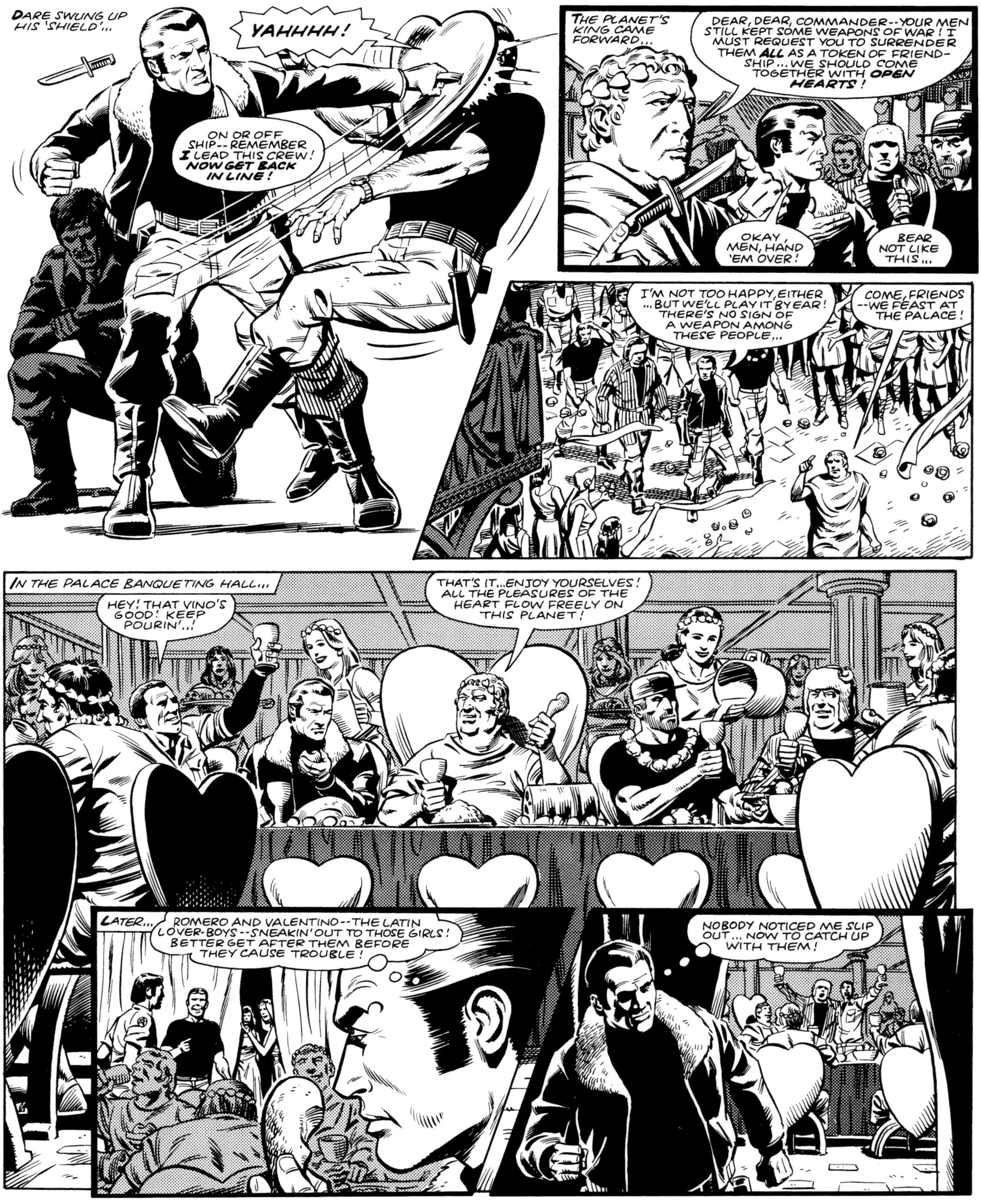

DARE SWUNG UP HIS 'SHIELD'...
YAHHHH!
ON OR OFF SHIP--REMEMBER I LEAD THIS CREW! NOW GET BACK IN LINE!
THE PLANET'S KING CAME FORWARD...
DEAR, DEAR, COMMANDER--YOUR MEN STILL KEPT SOME WEAPONS OF WAR! I MUST REQUEST YOU TO SURRENDER THEM ALL AS A TOKEN OF FRIENDSHIP... WE SHOULD COME TOGETHER WITH OPEN HEARTS!
OKAY, MEN, HAND 'EM OVER!
BEAR NOT LIKE THIS...
I'M NOT TOO HAPPY, EITHER ...BUT WE'LL PLAY IT BY EAR! THERE'S NO SIGN OF A WEAPON AMONG THESE PEOPLE...
COME, FRIENDS --WE FEAST AT THE PALACE!
IN THE PALACE BANQUETING HALL...
HEY! THAT VINO'S GOOD! KEEP POURIN'..!
THAT'S IT...ENJOY YOURSELVES! ALL THE PLEASURES OF THE HEART FLOW FREELY ON THIS PLANET!
LATER...
ROMERO AND VALENTINO--THE LATIN LOVER-BOYS--SNEAKIN' OUT TO THOSE GIRLS! BETTER GET AFTER THEM BEFORE THEY CAUSE TROUBLE!
NOBODY NOTICED ME SLIP OUT... NOW TO CATCH UP WITH THEM!

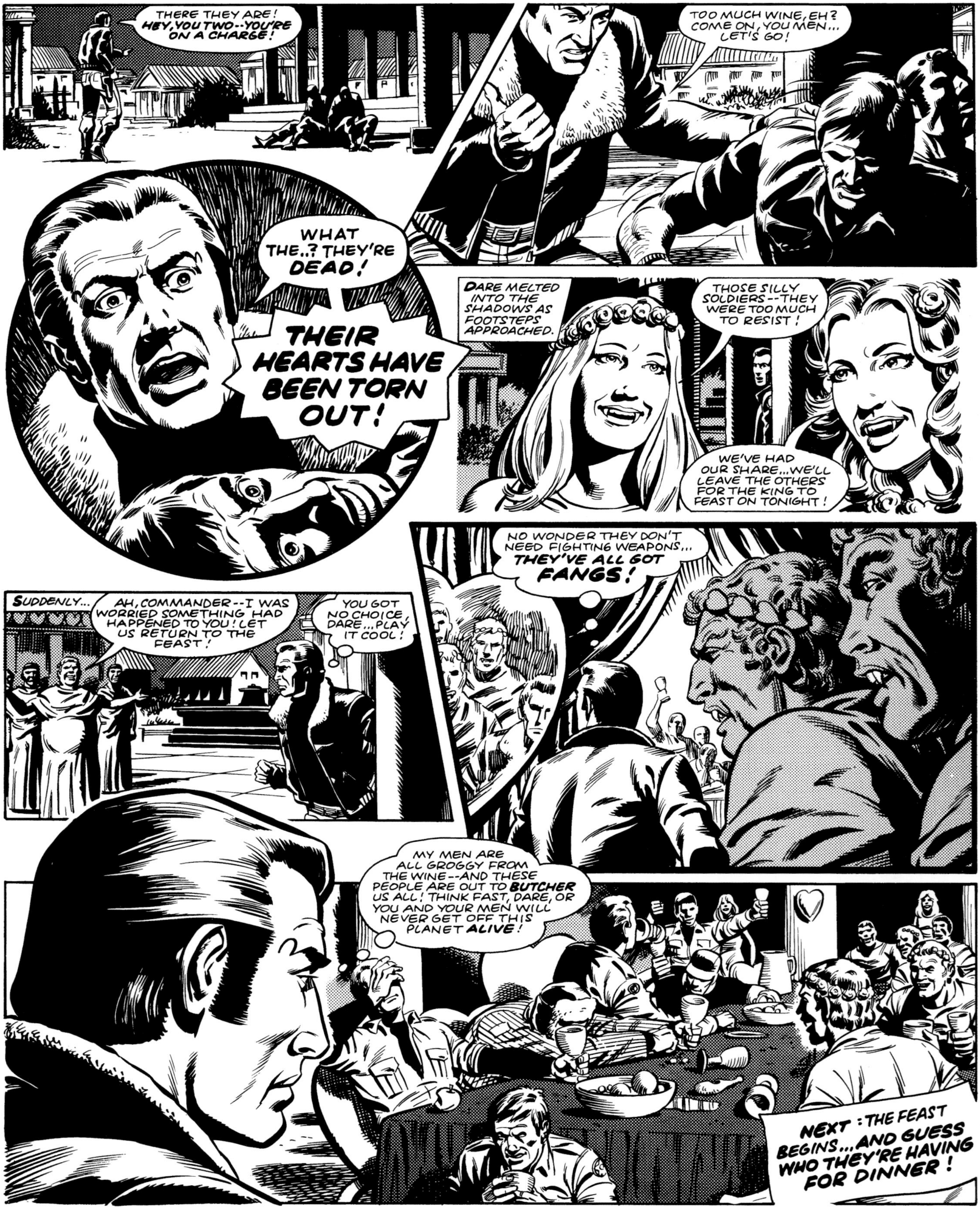
THERE THEY ARE! HEY, YOU TWO--YOU'RE ON A CHARGE!
TOO MUCH WINE, EH? COME ON, YOU MEN... LET'S GO!
WHAT THE..? THEY'RE DEAD!
THEIR HEARTS HAVE BEEN TORN OUT!
DARE MELTED INTO THE SHADOWS AS FOOTSTEPS APPROACHED.
THOSE SILLY SOLDIERS--THEY WERE TOO MUCH TO RESIST!
WE'VE HAD OUR SHARE... WE'LL LEAVE THE OTHERS FOR THE KING TO FEAST ON TONIGHT!
SUDDENLY...
AH, COMMANDER--I WAS WORRIED SOMETHING HAD HAPPENED TO YOU! LET US RETURN TO THE FEAST!
YOU GOT NO CHOICE, DARE... PLAY IT COOL!
NO WONDER THEY DON'T NEED FIGHTING WEAPONS... THEY'VE ALL GOT FANGS!
MY MEN ARE ALL GROGGY FROM THE WINE--AND THESE PEOPLE ARE OUT TO BUTCHER US ALL! THINK FAST, DARE, OR YOU AND YOUR MEN WILL NEVER GET OFF THIS PLANET ALIVE!
NEXT: THE FEAST BEGINS... AND GUESS WHO THEY'RE HAVING FOR DINNER!

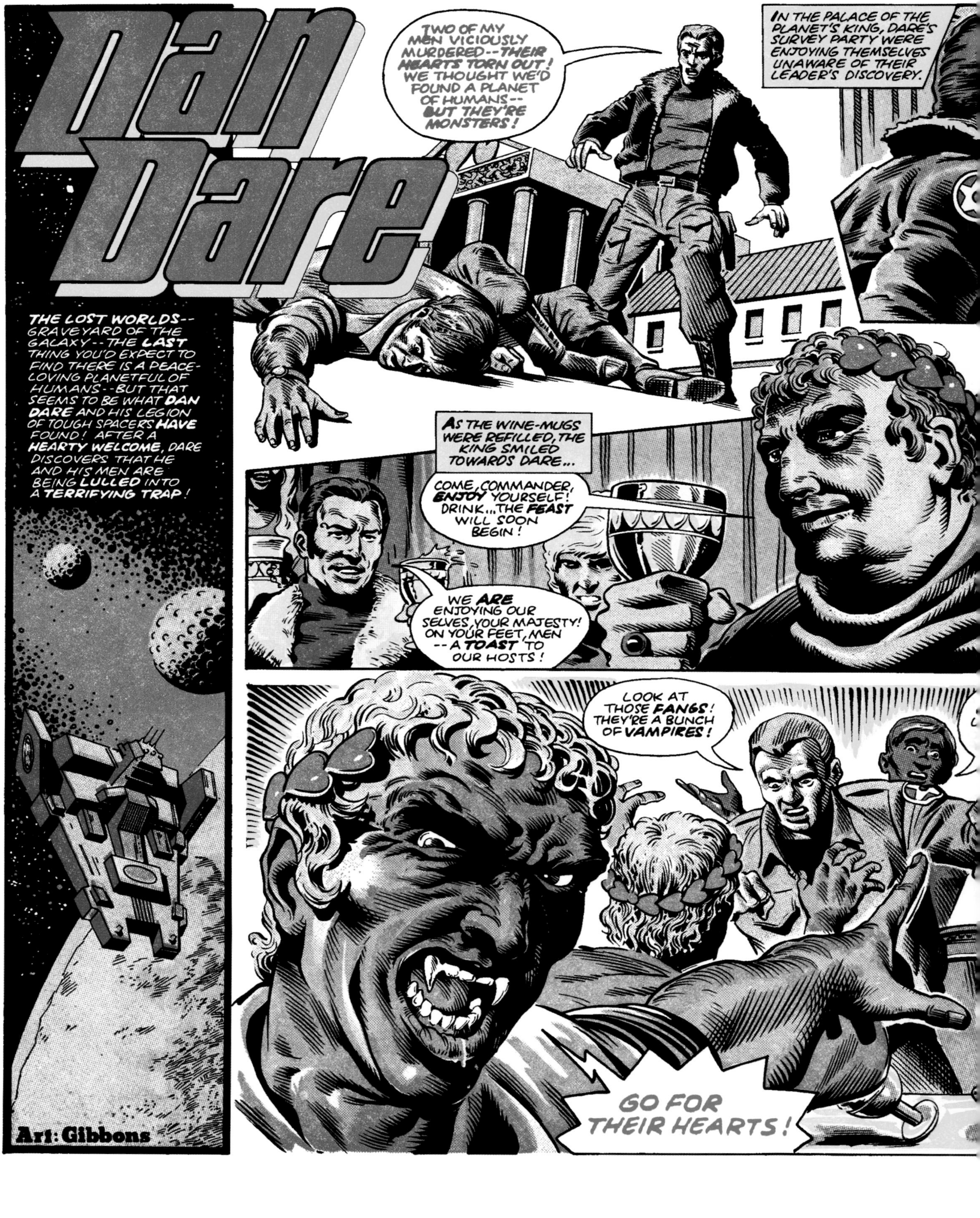
Dan Dare
THE LOST WORLDS--GRAVEYARD OF THE GALAXY--THE LAST THING YOU'D EXPECT TO FIND THERE IS A PEACE-LOVING PLANETFUL OF HUMANS--BUT THAT SEEMS TO BE WHAT DAN DARE AND HIS LEGION OF TOUGH SPACERS HAVE FOUND! AFTER A HEARTY WELCOME, DARE DISCOVERS THAT HE AND HIS MEN ARE BEING LULLED INTO A TERRIFYING TRAP!
Art: Gibbons
TWO OF MY MEN VICIOUSLY MURDERED--THEIR HEARTS TORN OUT! WE THOUGHT WE'D FOUND A PLANET OF HUMANS--BUT THEY'RE MONSTERS!
IN THE PALACE OF THE PLANET'S KING, DARE'S SURVEY PARTY WERE ENJOYING THEMSELVES UNAWARE OF THEIR LEADER'S DISCOVERY.
AS THE WINE-MUGS WERE REFILLED, THE KING SMILED TOWARDS DARE...
COME, COMMANDER, ENJOY YOURSELF! DRINK...THE FEAST WILL SOON BEGIN!
WE ARE ENJOYING OUR SELVES, YOUR MAJESTY! ON YOUR FEET, MEN--A TOAST TO OUR HOSTS!
LOOK AT THOSE FANGS! THEY'RE A BUNCH OF VAMPIRES!
GO FOR THEIR HEARTS!

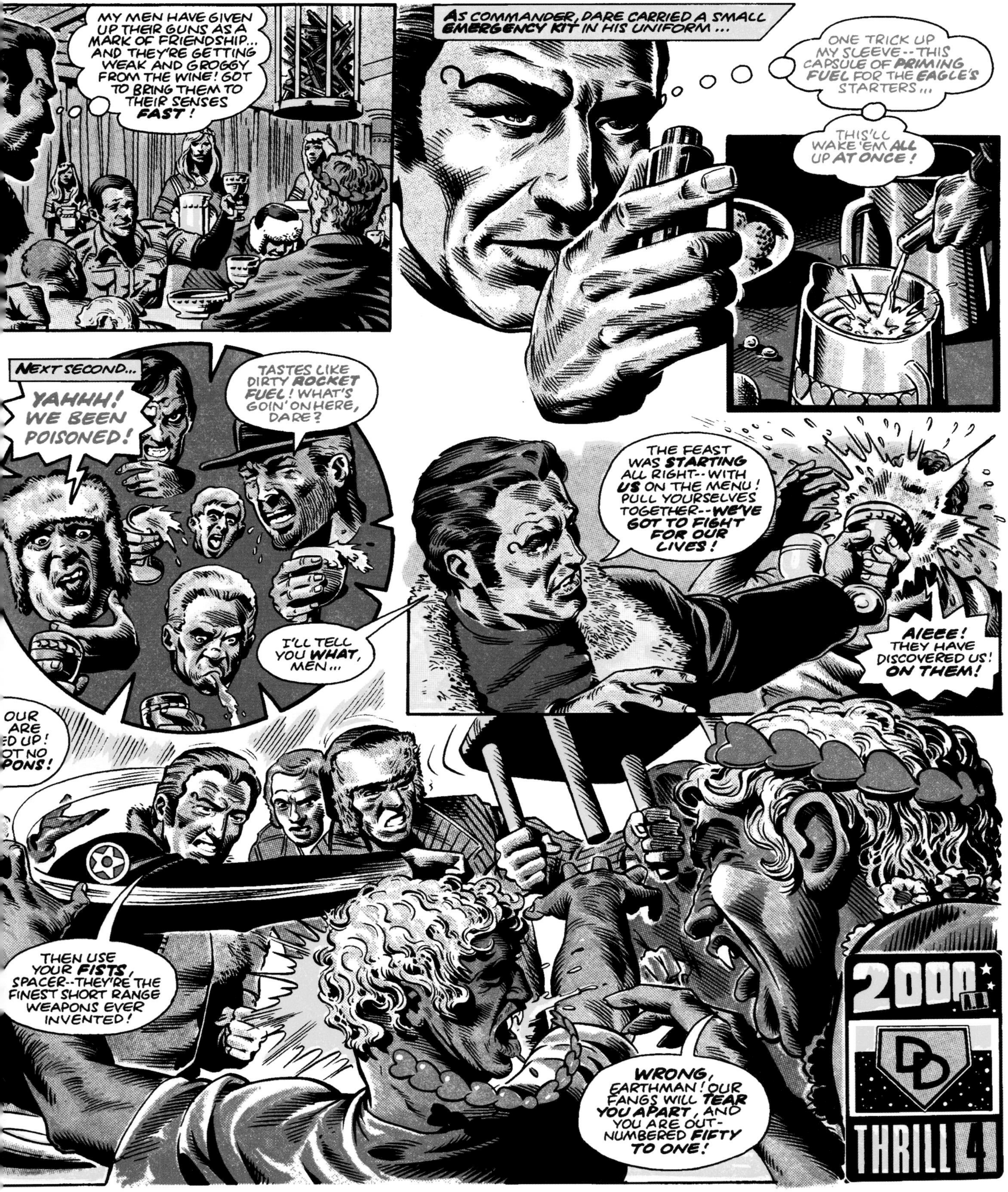
MY MEN HAVE GIVEN UP THEIR GUNS AS A MARK OF FRIENDSHIP... AND THEY'RE GETTING WEAK AND GROGGY FROM THE WINE! GOT TO BRING THEM TO THEIR SENSES FAST!
AS COMMANDER, DARE CARRIED A SMALL EMERGENCY KIT IN HIS UNIFORM...
ONE TRICK UP MY SLEEVE--THIS CAPSULE OF PRIMING FUEL FOR THE EAGLE'S STARTERS...
THIS'LL WAKE 'EM ALL UP AT ONCE!
NEXT SECOND...
YAHHH! WE BEEN POISONED!
TASTES LIKE DIRTY ROCKET FUEL! WHAT'S GOIN' ON HERE, DARE?
I'LL TELL YOU WHAT, MEN...
THE FEAST WAS STARTING ALL RIGHT--WITH US ON THE MENU! PULL YOURSELVES TOGETHER--WE'VE GOT TO FIGHT FOR OUR LIVES!
AIEEE! THEY HAVE DISCOVERED US! ON THEM!
THEN USE YOUR FISTS, SPACER--THEY'RE THE FINEST SHORT RANGE WEAPONS EVER INVENTED!
WRONG, EARTHMAN! OUR FANGS WILL TEAR YOU APART, AND YOU ARE OUT-NUMBERED FIFTY TO ONE!
2000 A.D.
THRILL 4

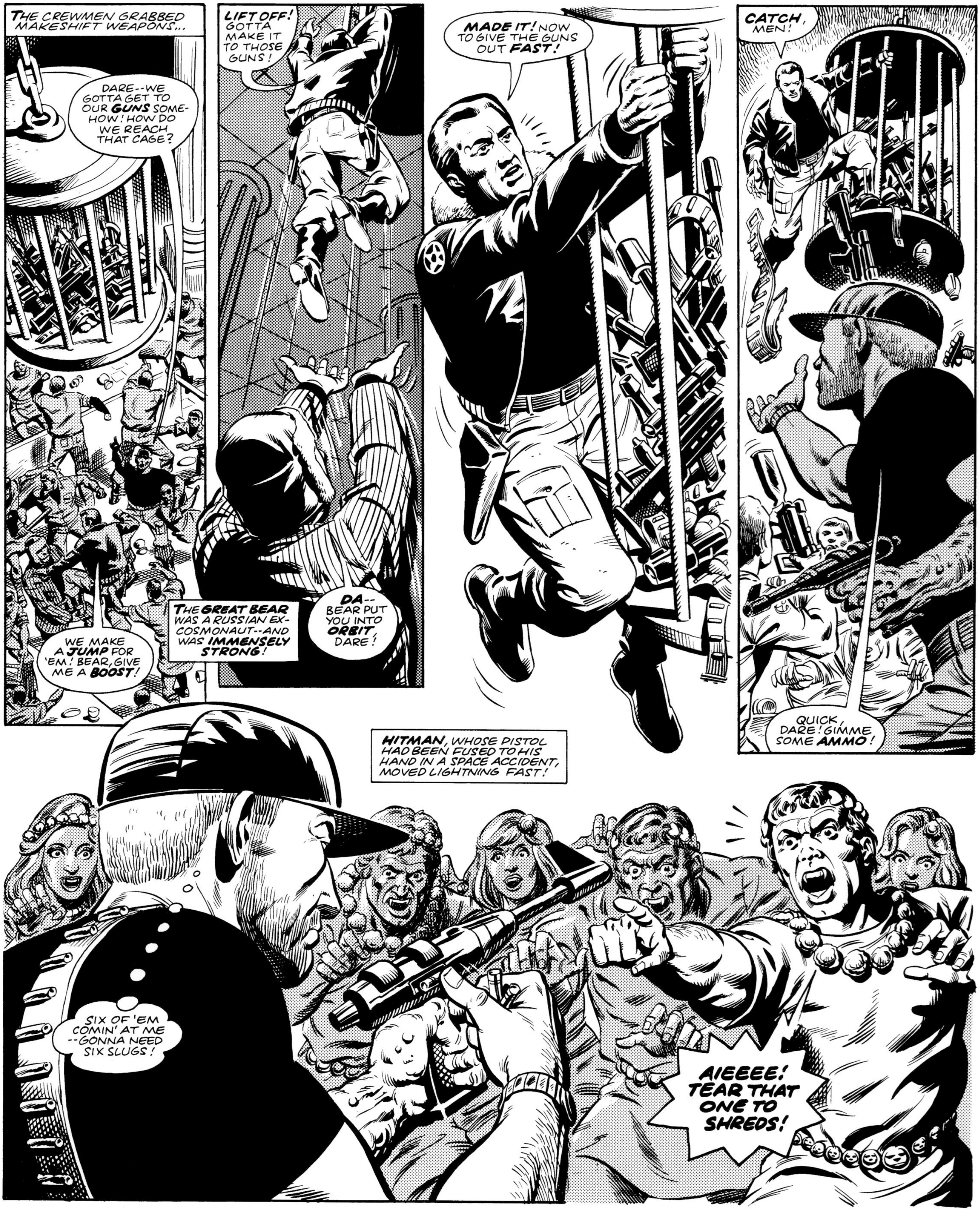
THE CREWMEN GRABBED MAKESHIFT WEAPONS...
DARE--WE GOTTA GET TO OUR GUNS SOME-HOW! HOW DO WE REACH THAT CAGE?
WE MAKE A JUMP FOR 'EM! BEAR, GIVE ME A BOOST!
LIFT OFF! GOTTA MAKE IT TO THOSE GUNS!
THE GREAT BEAR WAS A RUSSIAN EX-COSMONAUT--AND WAS IMMENSELY STRONG!
DA-- BEAR PUT YOU INTO ORBIT, DARE!
MADE IT! NOW TO GIVE THE GUNS OUT FAST!
CATCH, MEN!
QUICK, DARE! GIMME SOME AMMO!
HITMAN, WHOSE PISTOL HAD BEEN FUSED TO HIS HAND IN A SPACE ACCIDENT, MOVED LIGHTNING FAST!
SIX OF 'EM COMIN' AT ME --GONNA NEED SIX SLUGS!
AIEEEE! TEAR THAT ONE TO SHREDS!

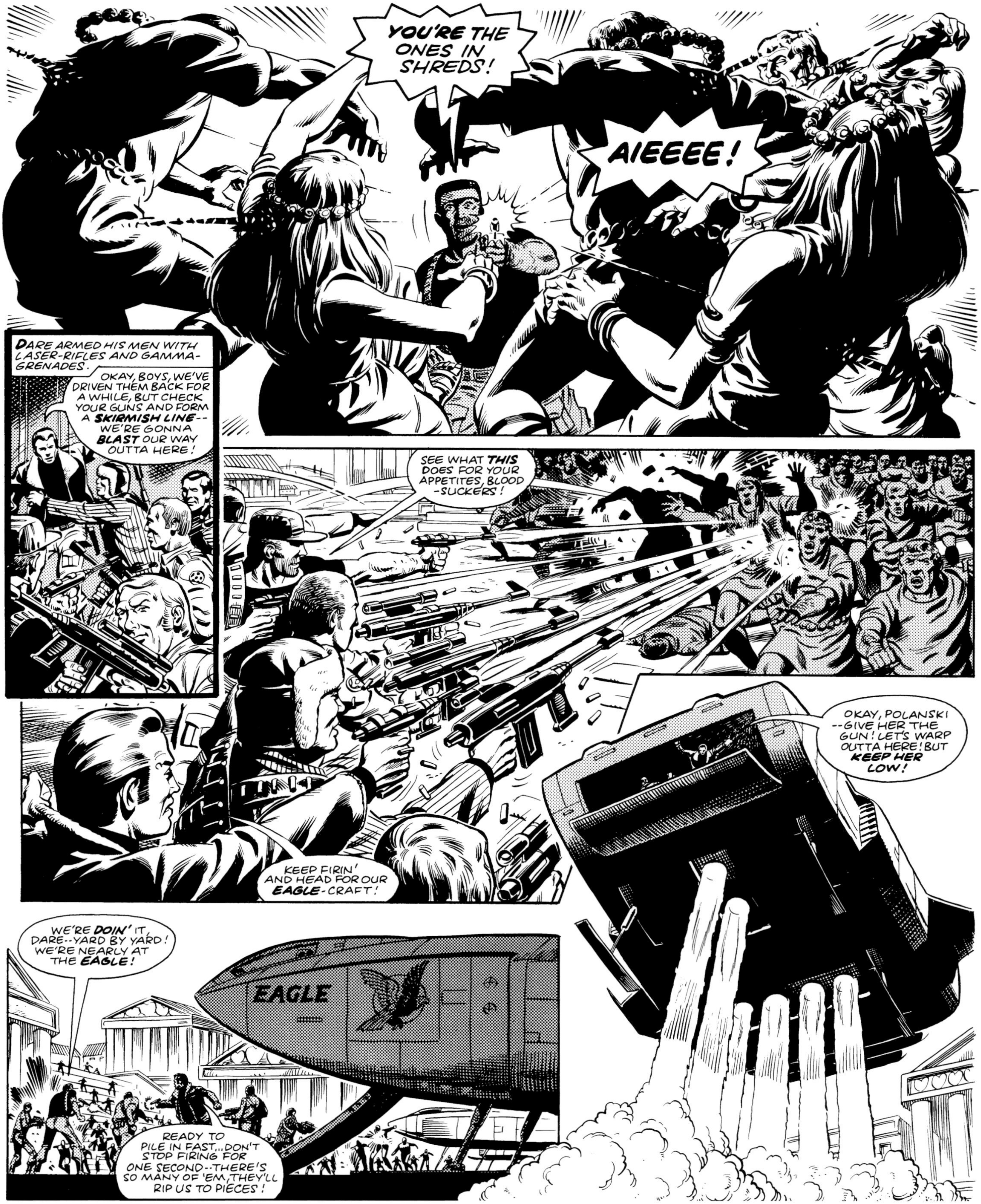

YOU'RE THE ONES IN SHREDS!
AIEEEE!
DARE ARMED HIS MEN WITH LASER-RIFLES AND GAMMA-GRENADES.
OKAY, BOYS, WE'VE DRIVEN THEM BACK FOR A WHILE, BUT CHECK YOUR GUNS AND FORM A SKIRMISH LINE-- WE'RE GONNA BLAST OUR WAY OUTTA HERE!
SEE WHAT THIS DOES FOR YOUR APPETITES, BLOOD-SUCKERS!
KEEP FIRIN' AND HEAD FOR OUR EAGLE-CRAFT!
OKAY, POLANSKI --GIVE HER THE GUN! LET'S WARP OUTTA HERE! BUT KEEP HER LOW!
WE'RE DOIN' IT, DARE--YARD BY YARD! WE'RE NEARLY AT THE EAGLE!
EAGLE
READY TO PILE IN FAST... DON'T STOP FIRING FOR ONE SECOND--THERE'S SO MANY OF 'EM, THEY'LL RIP US TO PIECES!

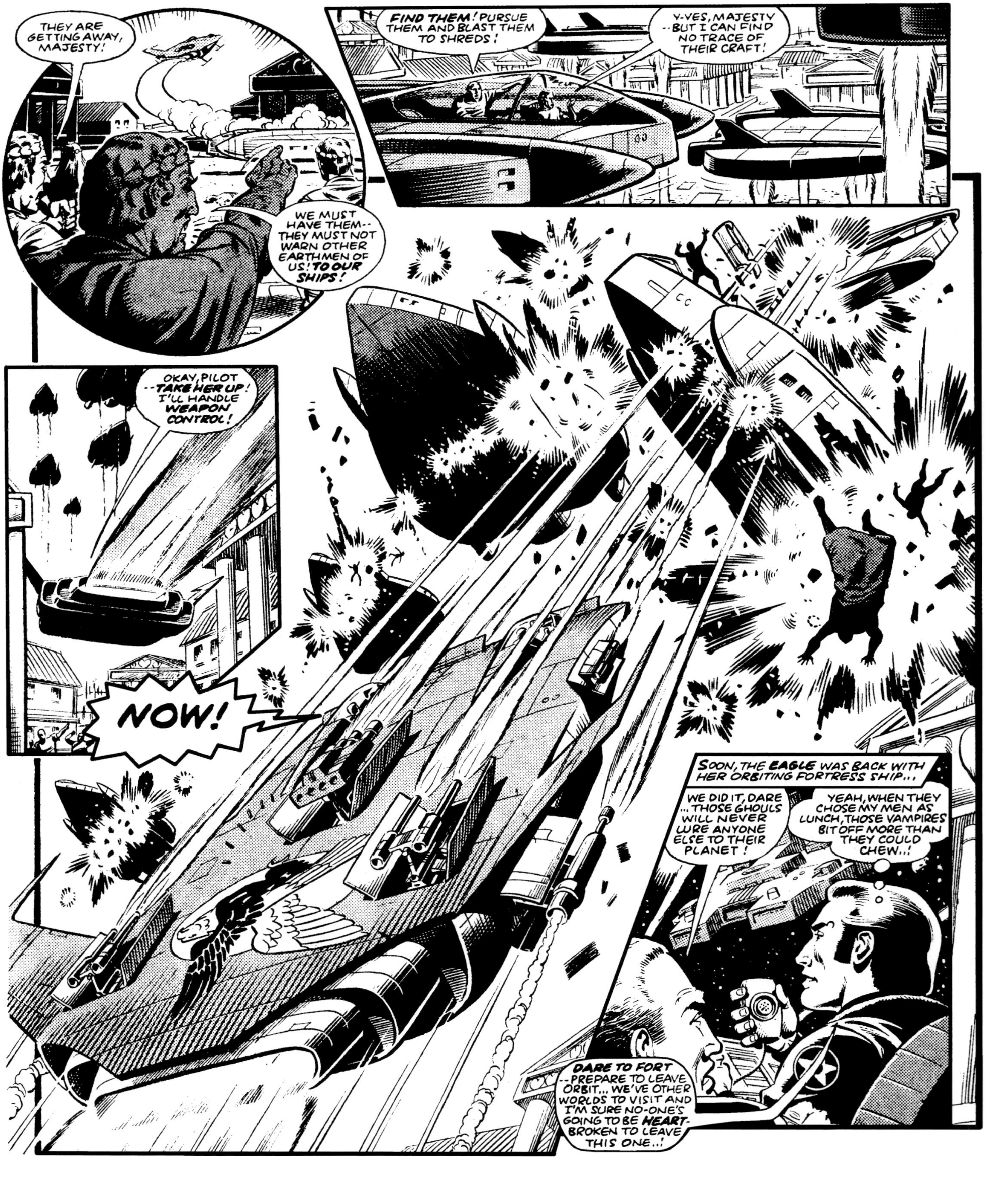
THEY ARE GETTING AWAY, MAJESTY!
WE MUST HAVE THEM-- THEY MUST NOT WARN OTHER EARTHMEN OF US! TO OUR SHIPS!
FIND THEM! PURSUE THEM AND BLAST THEM TO SHREDS!
Y-YES, MAJESTY --BUT I CAN FIND NO TRACE OF THEIR CRAFT!
OKAY, PILOT --TAKE HER UP! I'LL HANDLE WEAPON CONTROL!
NOW!
SOON, THE EAGLE WAS BACK WITH HER ORBITING FORTRESS SHIP...
WE DID IT, DARE ...THOSE GHOULS WILL NEVER LURE ANYONE ELSE TO THEIR PLANET!
YEAH, WHEN THEY CHOSE MY MEN AS LUNCH, THOSE VAMPIRES BIT OFF MORE THAN THEY COULD CHEW...!
DARE TO FORT --PREPARE TO LEAVE ORBIT... WE'VE OTHER WORLDS TO VISIT AND I'M SURE NO-ONE'S GOING TO BE HEART-BROKEN TO LEAVE THIS ONE...!

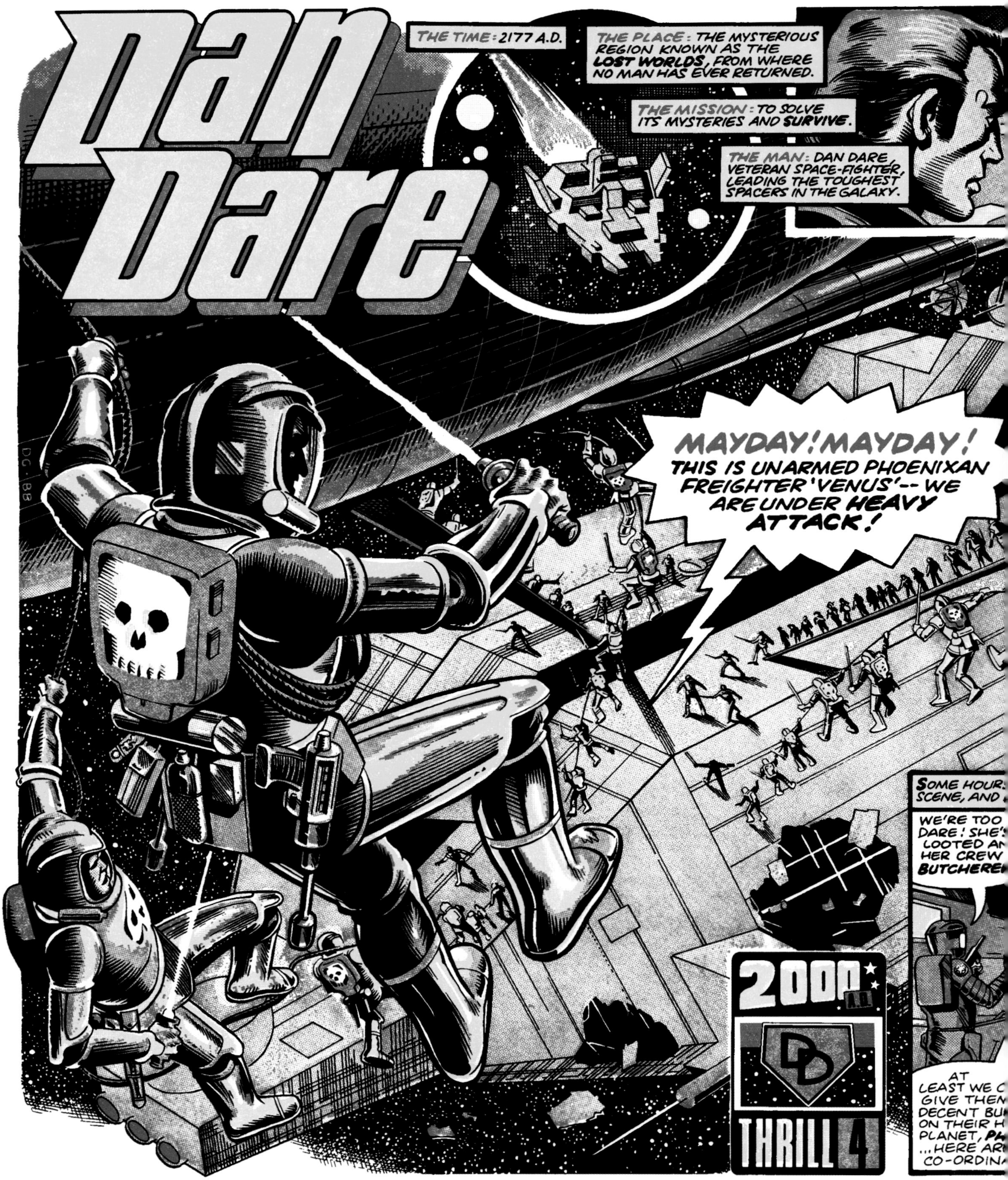
DAN DARE
THE TIME: 2177 A.D.
THE PLACE: THE MYSTERIOUS REGION KNOWN AS THE LOST WORLDS, FROM WHERE NO MAN HAS EVER RETURNED.
THE MISSION: TO SOLVE ITS MYSTERIES AND SURVIVE.
THE MAN: DAN DARE, VETERAN SPACE-FIGHTER, LEADING THE TOUGHEST SPACERS IN THE GALAXY.
MAYDAY! MAYDAY! THIS IS UNARMED PHOENIXAN FREIGHTER 'VENUS'-- WE ARE UNDER HEAVY ATTACK!
2000 A.D.
THRILL 4
DG. 88

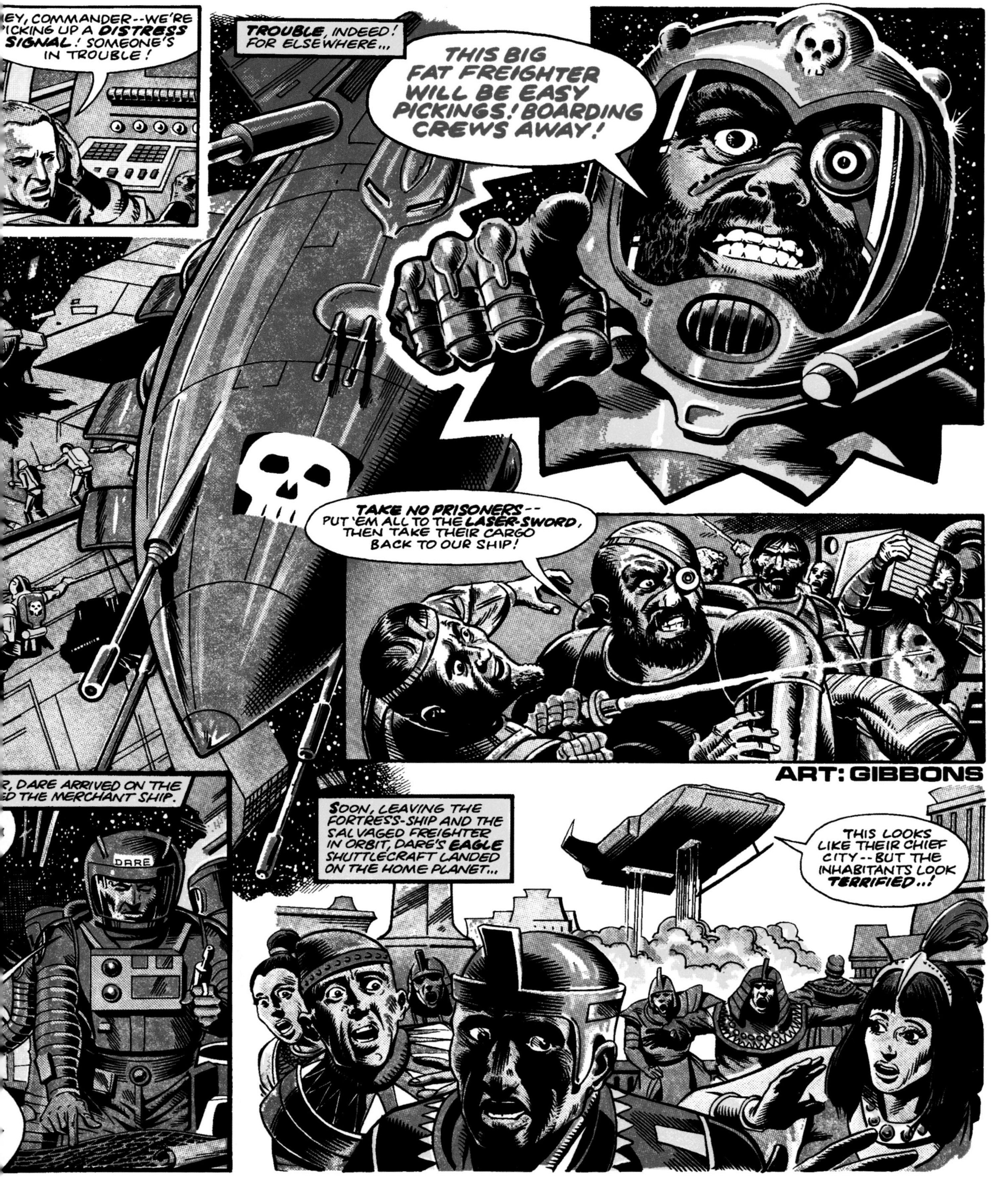

EY, COMMANDER--WE'RE PICKING UP A DISTRESS SIGNAL! SOMEONE'S IN TROUBLE!
TROUBLE, INDEED! FOR ELSEWHERE...
THIS BIG FAT FREIGHTER WILL BE EASY PICKINGS! BOARDING CREWS AWAY!
TAKE NO PRISONERS--PUT 'EM ALL TO THE LASER-SWORD, THEN TAKE THEIR CARGO BACK TO OUR SHIP!
ART: GIBBONS
R, DARE ARRIVED ON THE
D THE MERCHANT SHIP.
DARE
SOON, LEAVING THE FORTRESS-SHIP AND THE SALVAGED FREIGHTER IN ORBIT, DARE'S EAGLE SHUTTLECRAFT LANDED ON THE HOME PLANET...
THIS LOOKS LIKE THEIR CHIEF CITY--BUT THE INHABITANTS LOOK TERRIFIED..!

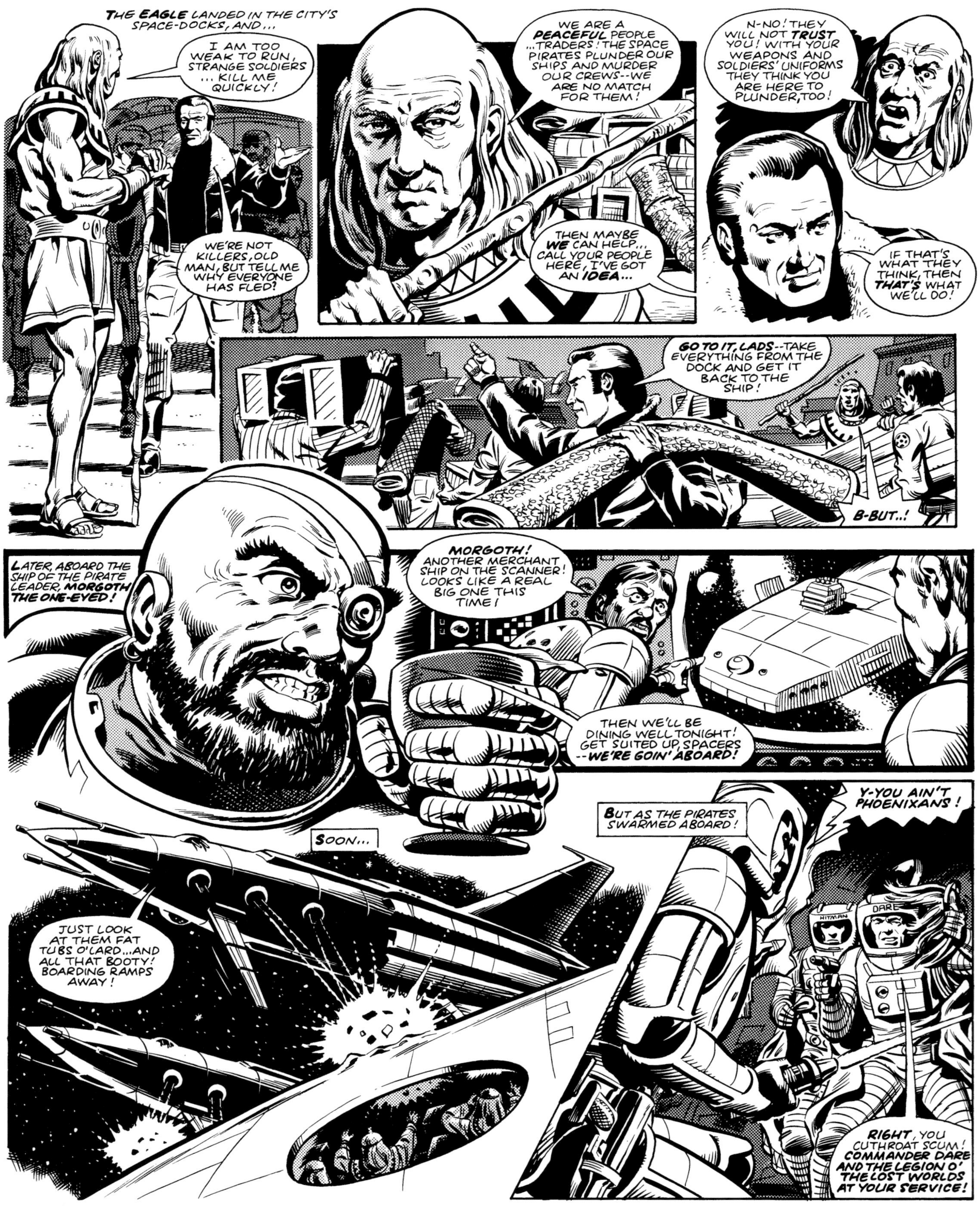

THE EAGLE LANDED IN THE CITY'S SPACE-DOCKS, AND...
I AM TOO WEAK TO RUN, STRANGE SOLDIERS ... KILL ME QUICKLY!
WE'RE NOT KILLERS, OLD MAN, BUT TELL ME WHY EVERYONE HAS FLED?
WE ARE A PEACEFUL PEOPLE ...TRADERS! THE SPACE PIRATES PLUNDER OUR SHIPS AND MURDER OUR CREWS--WE ARE NO MATCH FOR THEM!
THEN MAYBE WE CAN HELP... CALL YOUR PEOPLE HERE, I'VE GOT AN IDEA...
N-NO! THEY WILL NOT TRUST YOU! WITH YOUR WEAPONS AND SOLDIERS' UNIFORMS THEY THINK YOU ARE HERE TO PLUNDER, TOO!
IF THAT'S WHAT THEY THINK, THEN THAT'S WHAT WE'LL DO!
GO TO IT, LADS--TAKE EVERYTHING FROM THE DOCK AND GET IT BACK TO THE SHIP!
B-BUT..!
LATER, ABOARD THE SHIP OF THE PIRATE LEADER, MORGOTH THE ONE-EYED!
MORGOTH! ANOTHER MERCHANT SHIP ON THE SCANNER! LOOKS LIKE A REAL BIG ONE THIS TIME!
THEN WE'LL BE DINING WELL TONIGHT! GET SUITED UP, SPACERS --WE'RE GOIN' ABOARD!
SOON...
JUST LOOK AT THEM FAT TUBS O'LARD...AND ALL THAT BOOTY! BOARDING RAMPS AWAY!
BUT AS THE PIRATES SWARMED ABOARD!
Y-YOU AIN'T PHOENIXANS!
HITMAN
DARE
RIGHT, YOU CUTHROAT SCUM! COMMANDER DARE AND THE LEGION O' THE LOST WORLDS AT YOUR SERVICE!

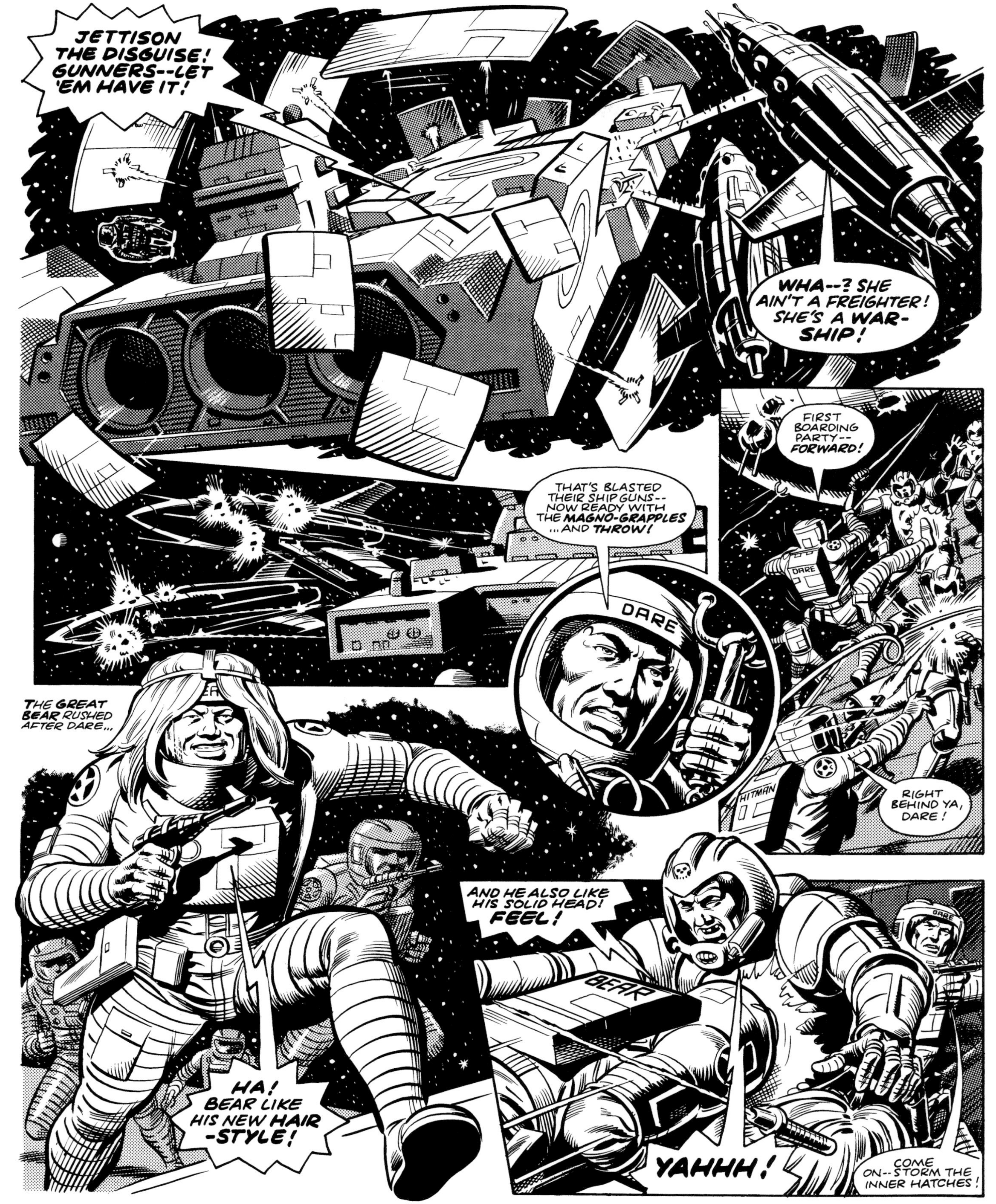

JETTISON THE DISGUISE! GUNNERS--LET 'EM HAVE IT!
WHA--? SHE AIN'T A FREIGHTER! SHE'S A WAR-SHIP!
THAT'S BLASTED THEIR SHIP GUNS--NOW READY WITH THE MAGNO-GRAPPLES ...AND THROW!
DARE
FIRST BOARDING PARTY--FORWARD!
DARE
HITMAN
RIGHT BEHIND YA, DARE!
THE GREAT BEAR RUSHED AFTER DARE...
HA! BEAR LIKE HIS NEW HAIR-STYLE!
AND HE ALSO LIKE HIS SOLID HEAD! FEEL!
BEAR
DARE
YAHHH!
COME ON--STORM THE INNER HATCHES!

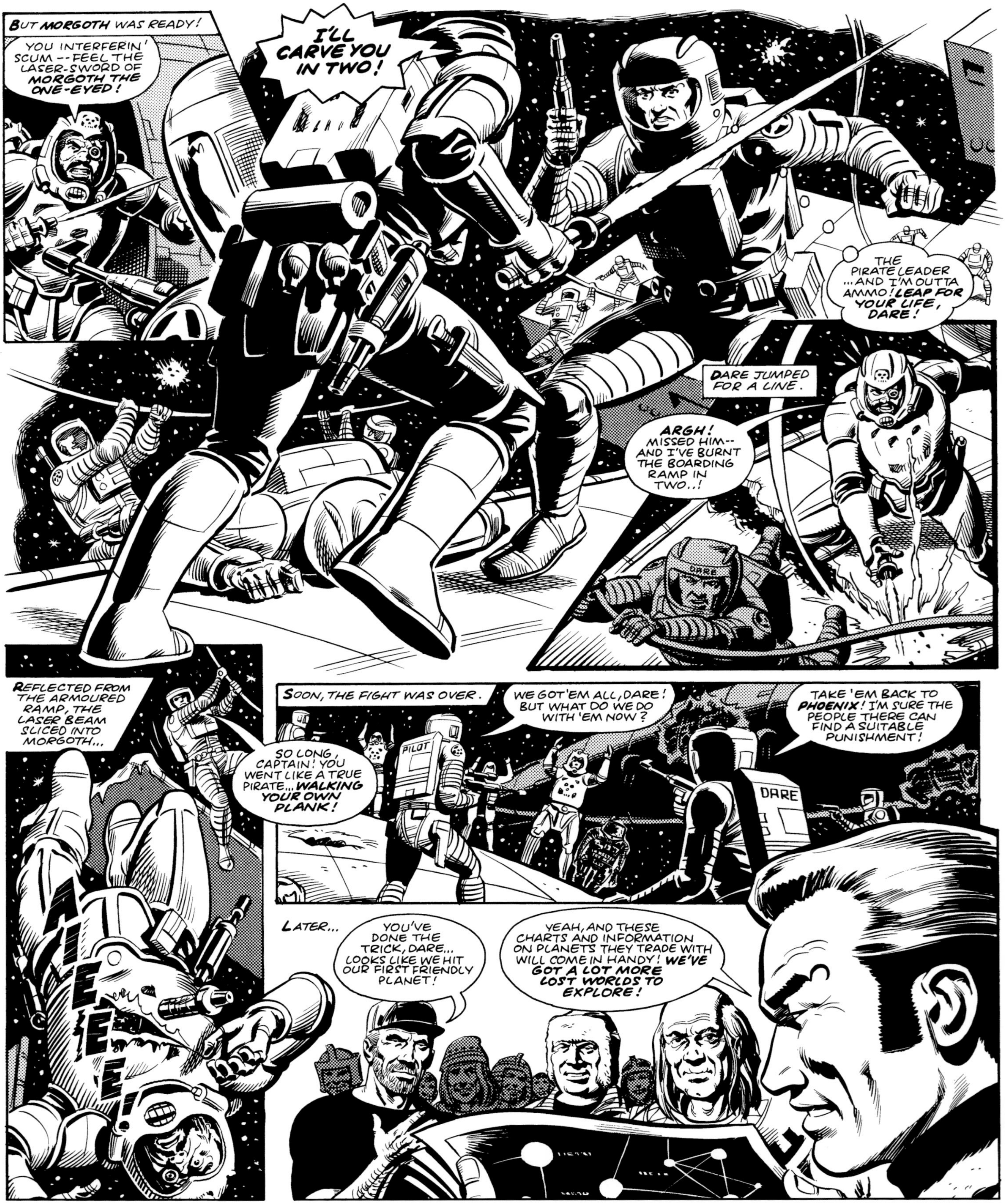

BUT MORGOTH WAS READY!
YOU INTERFERIN' SCUM -- FEEL THE LASER-SWORD OF MORGOTH THE ONE-EYED!
I'LL CARVE YOU IN TWO!
THE PIRATE LEADER ...AND I'M OUTTA AMMO! LEAP FOR YOUR LIFE, DARE!
DARE JUMPED FOR A LINE.
ARGH! MISSED HIM-- AND I'VE BURNT THE BOARDING RAMP IN TWO..!
DARE
REFLECTED FROM THE ARMOURED RAMP, THE LASER BEAM SLICED INTO MORGOTH...
SO LONG, CAPTAIN! YOU WENT LIKE A TRUE PIRATE... WALKING YOUR OWN PLANK!
AIEEEEE!
SOON, THE FIGHT WAS OVER.
PILOT
WE GOT 'EM ALL, DARE! BUT WHAT DO WE DO WITH 'EM NOW?
TAKE 'EM BACK TO PHOENIX! I'M SURE THE PEOPLE THERE CAN FIND A SUITABLE PUNISHMENT!
DARE
LATER...
YOU'VE DONE THE TRICK, DARE... LOOKS LIKE WE HIT OUR FIRST FRIENDLY PLANET!
YEAH, AND THESE CHARTS AND INFORMATION ON PLANETS THEY TRADE WITH WILL COME IN HANDY! WE'VE GOT A LOT MORE LOST WORLDS TO EXPLORE!

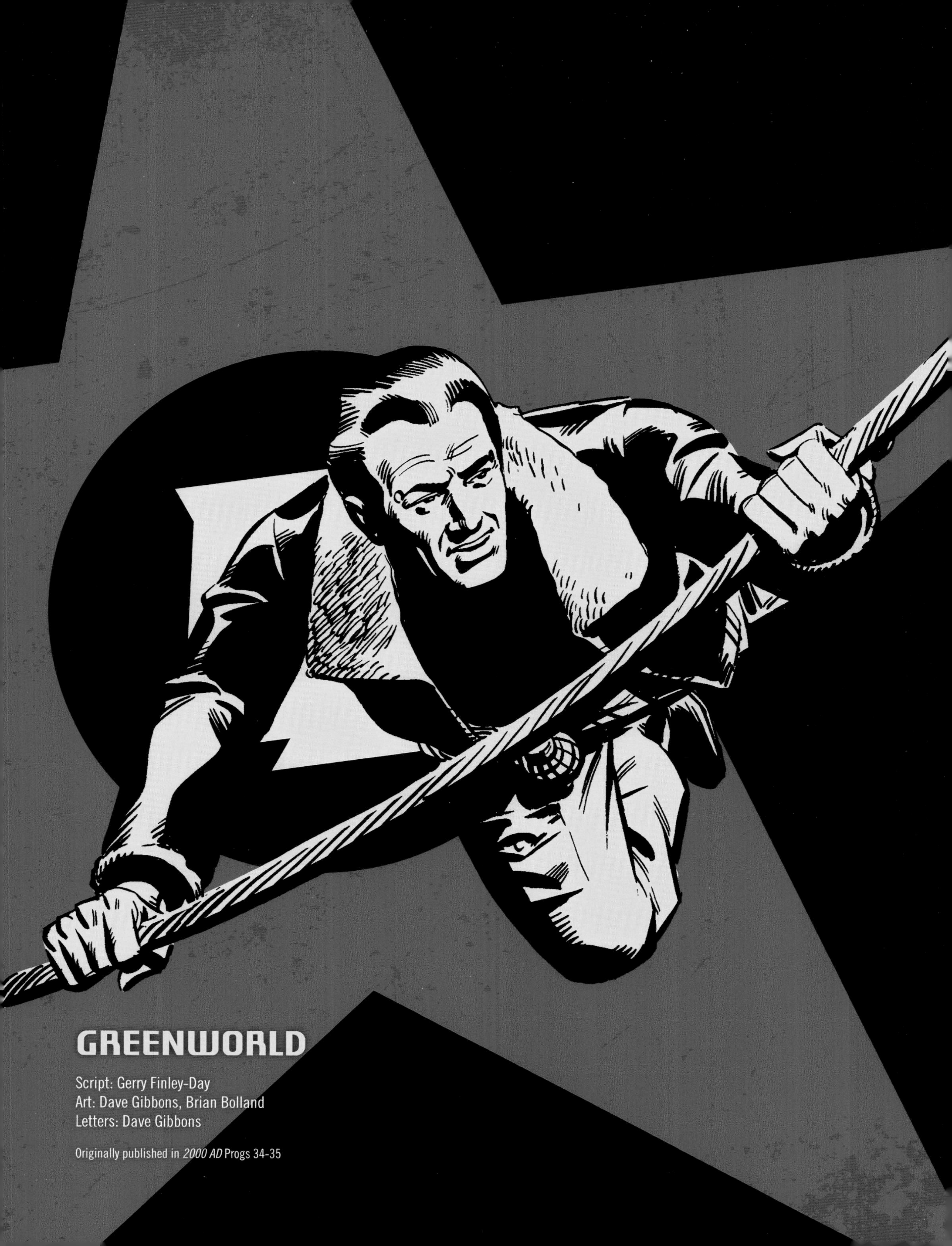

GREENWORLD

Script: Gerry Finley-Day
Art: Dave Gibbons, Brian Bolland
Letters: Dave Gibbons

Originally published in *2000 AD* Progs 34-35

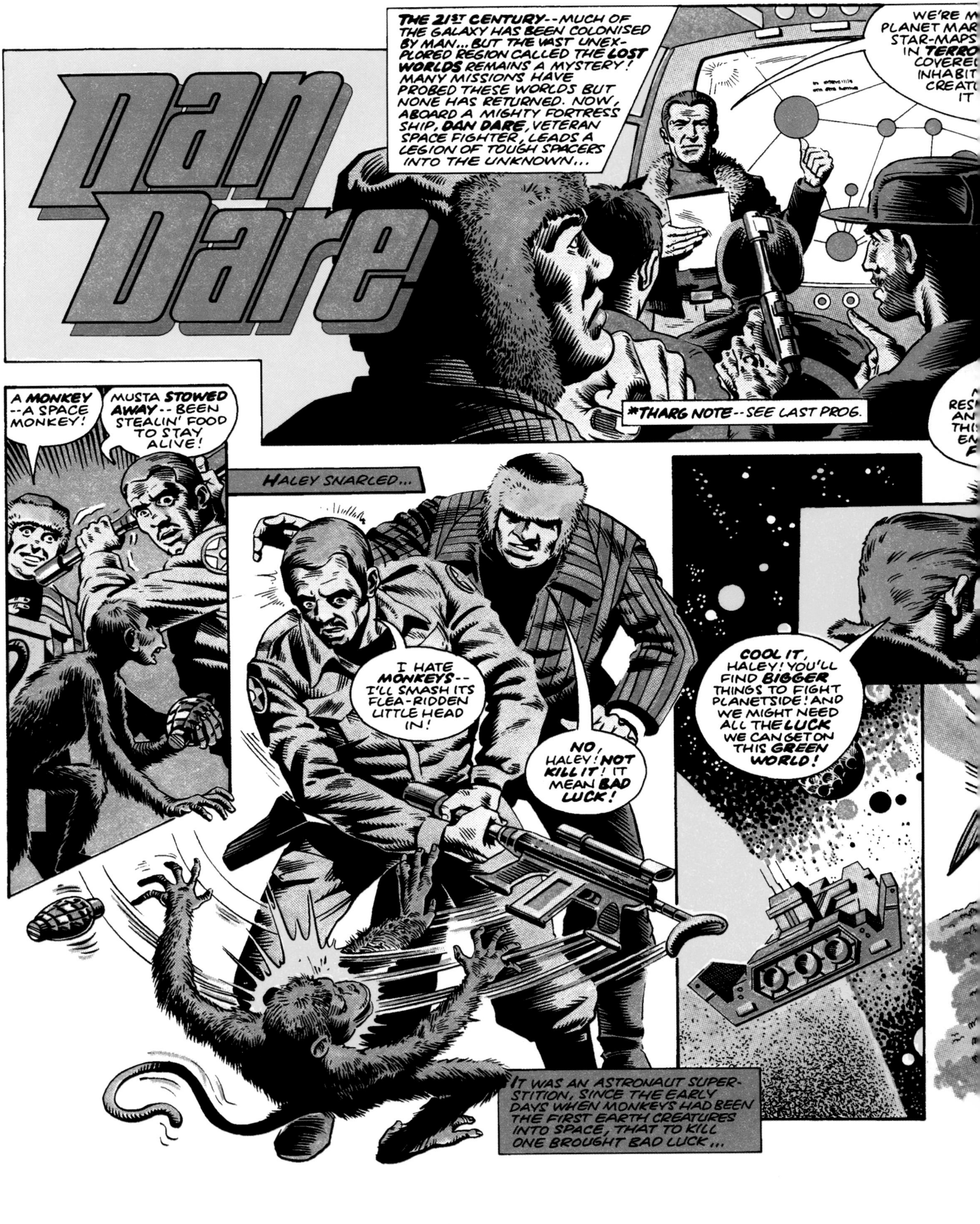
Dan Dare
THE 21ST CENTURY--MUCH OF THE GALAXY HAS BEEN COLONISED BY MAN... BUT THE VAST UNEXPLORED REGION CALLED THE LOST WORLDS REMAINS A MYSTERY! MANY MISSIONS HAVE PROBED THESE WORLDS BUT NONE HAS RETURNED. NOW, ABOARD A MIGHTY FORTRESS SHIP, DAN DARE, VETERAN SPACE FIGHTER, LEADS A LEGION OF TOUGH SPACERS INTO THE UNKNOWN...
*THARG NOTE--SEE LAST PROG.
A MONKEY --A SPACE MONKEY!
MUSTA STOWED AWAY--BEEN STEALIN' FOOD TO STAY ALIVE!
HALEY SNARLED...
I HATE MONKEYS-- I'LL SMASH ITS FLEA-RIDDEN LITTLE HEAD IN!
NO, HALEY! NOT KILL IT! IT MEAN BAD LUCK!
COOL IT, HALEY! YOU'LL FIND BIGGER THINGS TO FIGHT PLANETSIDE! AND WE MIGHT NEED ALL THE LUCK WE CAN GET ON THIS GREEN WORLD!
IT WAS AN ASTRONAUT SUPERSTITION, SINCE THE EARLY DAYS WHEN MONKEYS HAD BEEN THE FIRST EARTH CREATURES INTO SPACE, THAT TO KILL ONE BROUGHT BAD LUCK...

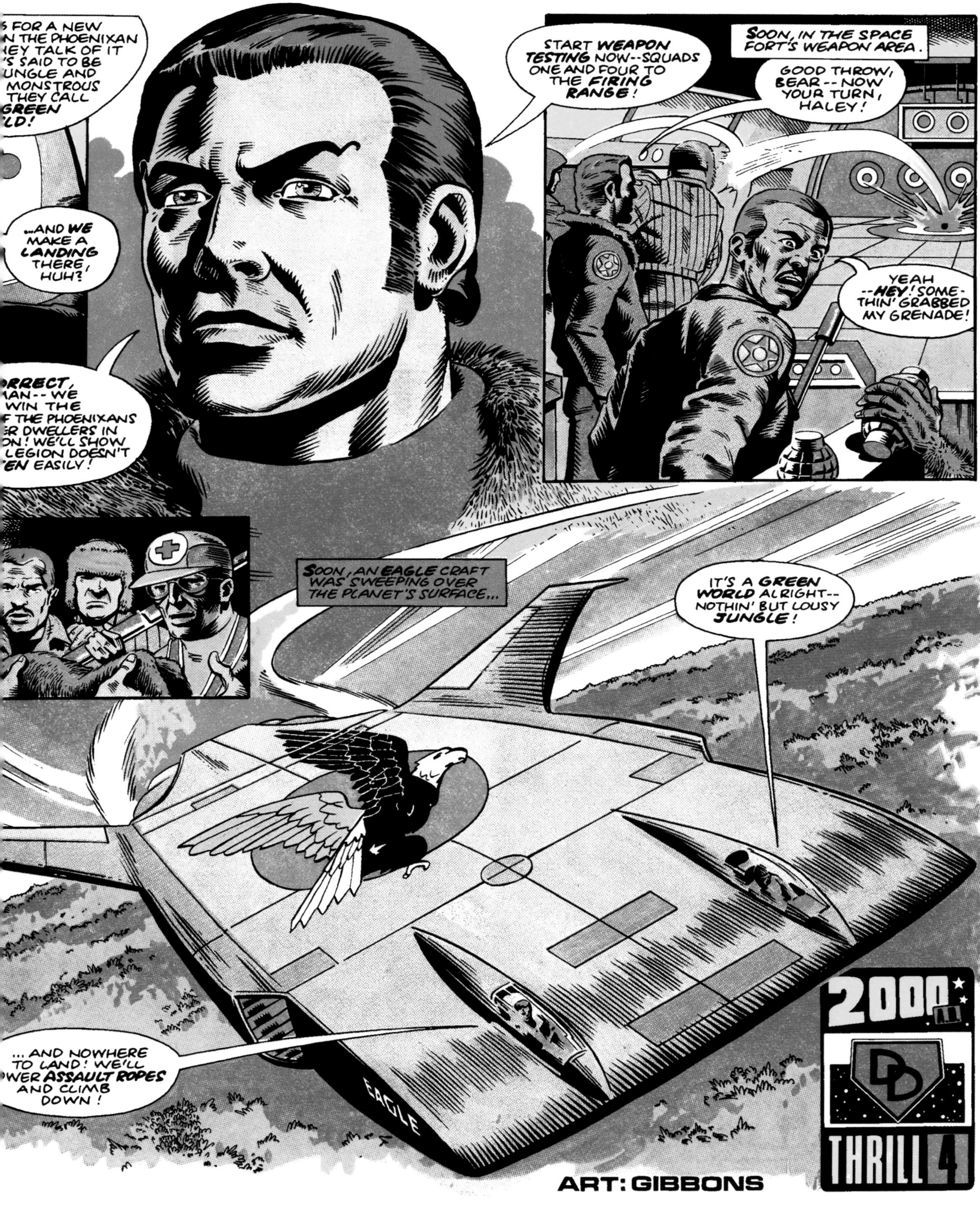

S FOR A NEW
N THE PHOENIXAN
HEY TALK OF IT
'S SAID TO BE
UNGLE AND
MONSTROUS
THEY CALL
GREEN
LD!
...AND WE MAKE A LANDING THERE, HUH?
ORRECT, MAN-- WE WIN THE F THE PHOENIXANS ER DWELLERS IN ON! WE'LL SHOW LEGION DOESN'T EN EASILY!
START WEAPON TESTING NOW--SQUADS ONE AND FOUR TO THE FIRING RANGE!
SOON, IN THE SPACE FORT'S WEAPON AREA.
GOOD THROW, BEAR--NOW YOUR TURN, HALEY!
YEAH --HEY! SOME-THIN' GRABBED MY GRENADE!
SOON, AN EAGLE CRAFT WAS SWEEPING OVER THE PLANET'S SURFACE...
IT'S A GREEN WORLD ALRIGHT-- NOTHIN' BUT LOUSY JUNGLE!
... AND NOWHERE TO LAND! WE'LL WER ASSAULT ROPES AND CLIMB DOWN!
EAGLE
2000 A.D.
THRILL 4

ART: GIBBONS

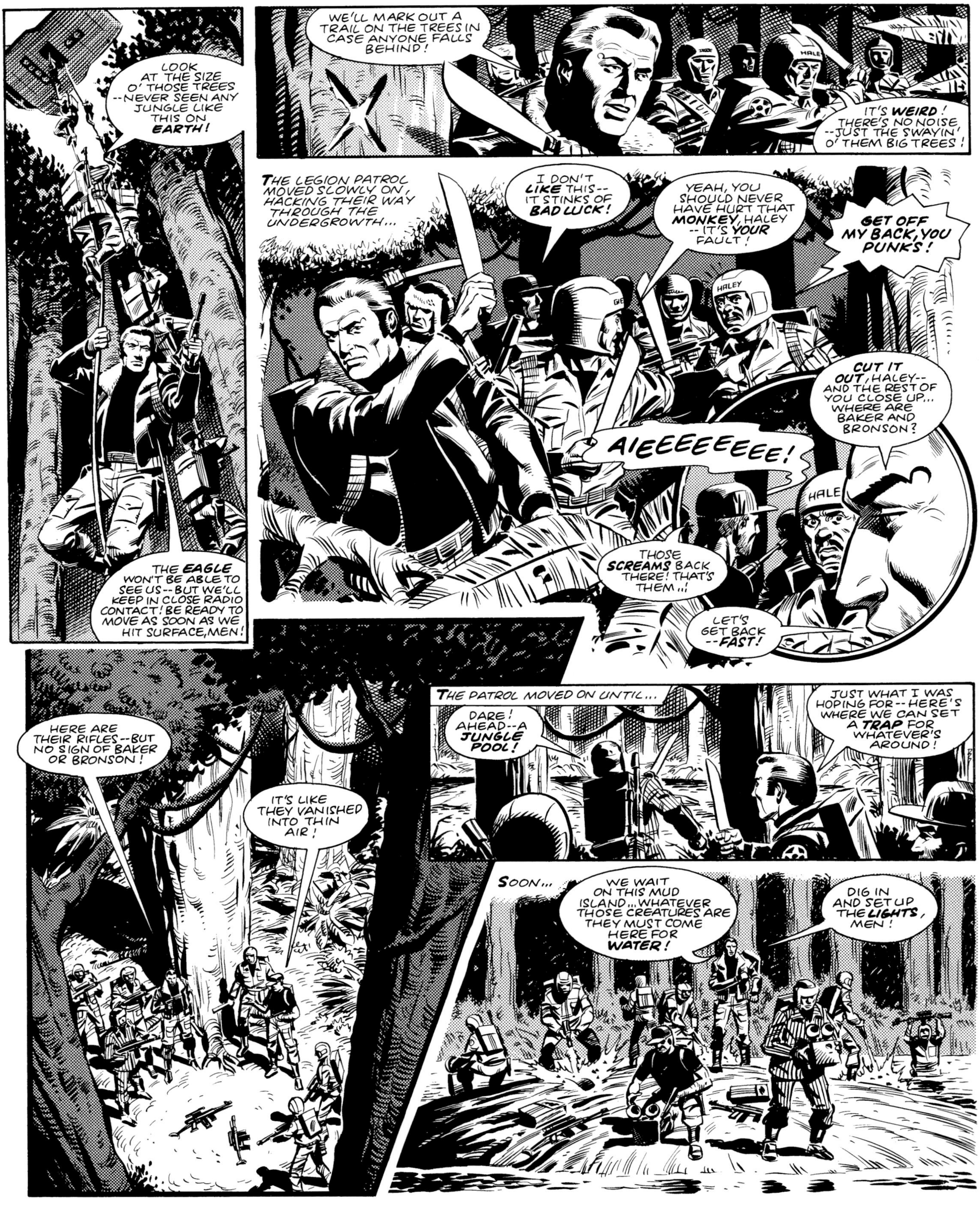
LOOK AT THE SIZE O' THOSE TREES --NEVER SEEN ANY JUNGLE LIKE THIS ON EARTH!
THE EAGLE WON'T BE ABLE TO SEE US--BUT WE'LL KEEP IN CLOSE RADIO CONTACT! BE READY TO MOVE AS SOON AS WE HIT SURFACE, MEN!
WE'LL MARK OUT A TRAIL ON THE TREES IN CASE ANYONE FALLS BEHIND!
IT'S WEIRD! THERE'S NO NOISE, --JUST THE SWAYIN' O' THEM BIG TREES!
THE LEGION PATROL MOVED SLOWLY ON, HACKING THEIR WAY THROUGH THE UNDERGROWTH...
I DON'T LIKE THIS-- IT STINKS OF BAD LUCK!
YEAH, YOU SHOULD NEVER HAVE HURT THAT MONKEY, HALEY --IT'S YOUR FAULT!
GET OFF MY BACK, YOU PUNKS!
HALEY
AIEEEEEEEEE!
CUT IT OUT, HALEY-- AND THE REST OF YOU CLOSE UP... WHERE ARE BAKER AND BRONSON?
THOSE SCREAMS BACK THERE! THAT'S THEM...!
LET'S GET BACK --FAST!
HERE ARE THEIR RIFLES--BUT NO SIGN OF BAKER OR BRONSON!
IT'S LIKE THEY VANISHED INTO THIN AIR!
THE PATROL MOVED ON UNTIL...
DARE! AHEAD--A JUNGLE POOL!
JUST WHAT I WAS HOPING FOR--HERE'S WHERE WE CAN SET A TRAP FOR WHATEVER'S AROUND!
SOON...
WE WAIT ON THIS MUD ISLAND... WHATEVER THOSE CREATURES ARE THEY MUST COME HERE FOR WATER!
DIG IN AND SET UP THE LIGHTS, MEN!

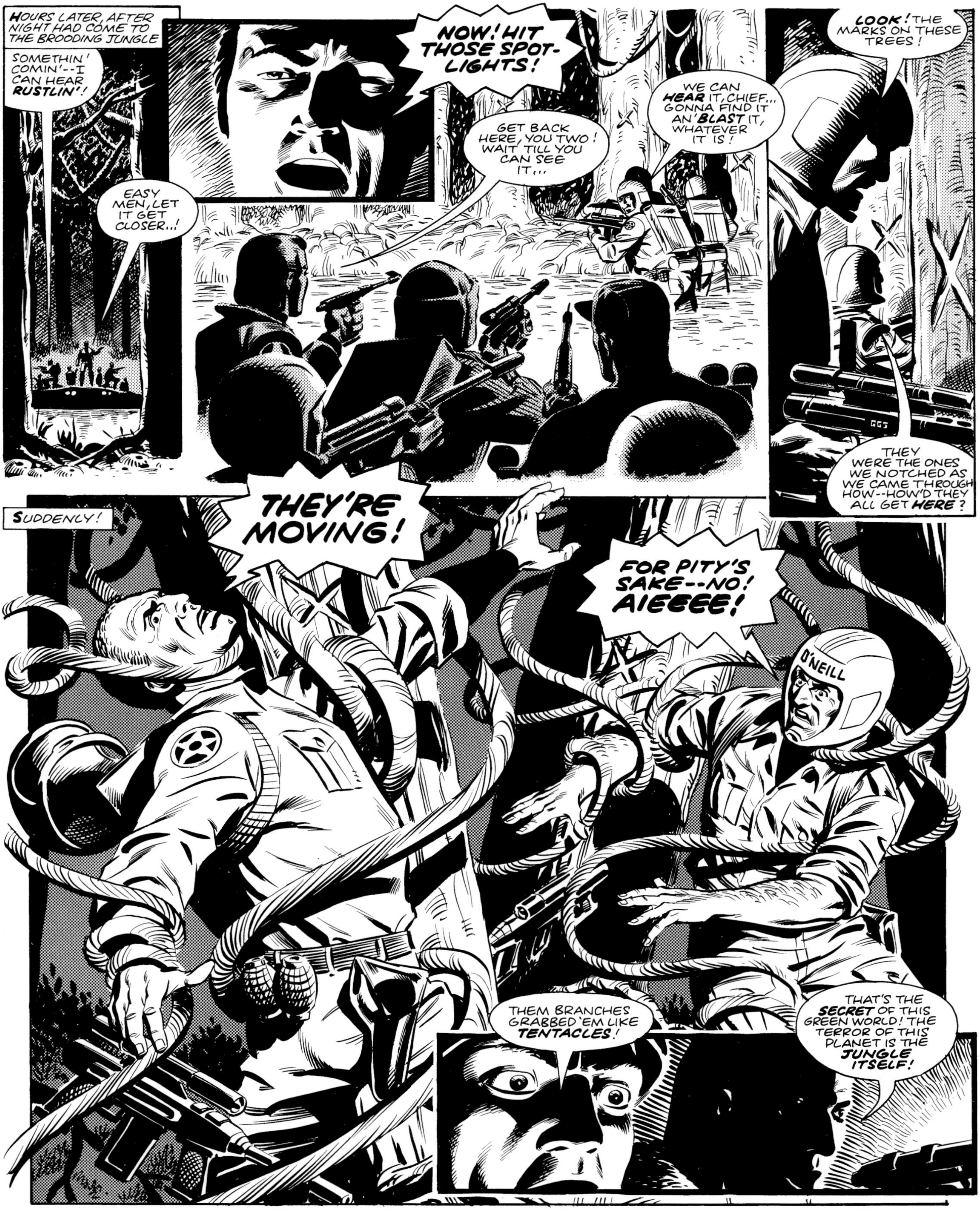

HOURS LATER, AFTER NIGHT HAD COME TO THE BROODING JUNGLE
SOMETHIN' COMIN'--I CAN HEAR RUSTLIN'!
EASY MEN, LET IT GET CLOSER...!
NOW! HIT THOSE SPOT-LIGHTS!
GET BACK HERE, YOU TWO! WAIT TILL YOU CAN SEE IT...
WE CAN HEAR IT, CHIEF... GONNA FIND IT AN' BLAST IT, WHATEVER IT IS!
LOOK! THE MARKS ON THESE TREES!
THEY WERE THE ONES WE NOTCHED AS WE CAME THROUGH HOW--HOW'D THEY ALL GET HERE?
SUDDENLY!
THEY'RE MOVING!
FOR PITY'S SAKE--NO! AIEEEE!
O'NEILL
THEM BRANCHES GRABBED 'EM LIKE TENTACLES!
THAT'S THE SECRET OF THIS GREEN WORLD! THE TERROR OF THIS PLANET IS THE JUNGLE ITSELF!

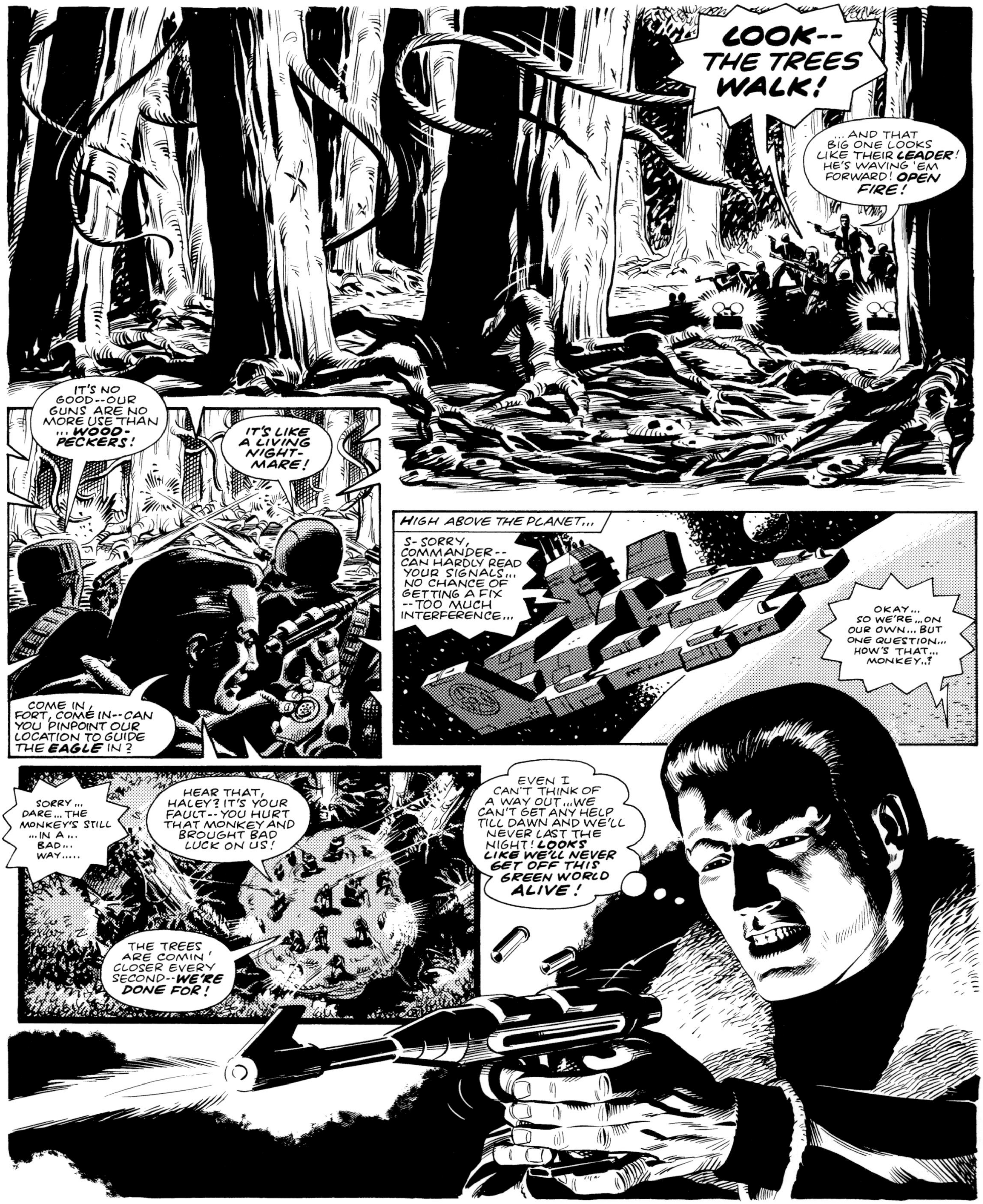
LOOK-- THE TREES WALK!
... AND THAT BIG ONE LOOKS LIKE THEIR LEADER! HE'S WAVING 'EM FORWARD! OPEN FIRE!
IT'S NO GOOD--OUR GUNS ARE NO MORE USE THAN ... WOOD-PECKERS!
IT'S LIKE A LIVING NIGHT-MARE!
COME IN, FORT, COME IN--CAN YOU PINPOINT OUR LOCATION TO GUIDE THE EAGLE IN?
HIGH ABOVE THE PLANET...
S-SORRY, COMMANDER--CAN HARDLY READ YOUR SIGNALS... NO CHANCE OF GETTING A FIX --TOO MUCH INTERFERENCE...
OKAY... SO WE'RE... ON OUR OWN... BUT ONE QUESTION... HOW'S THAT... MONKEY..?
SORRY... DARE... THE MONKEY'S STILL ...IN A... BAD... WAY.....
HEAR THAT, HALEY? IT'S YOUR FAULT--YOU HURT THAT MONKEY AND BROUGHT BAD LUCK ON US!
THE TREES ARE COMIN' CLOSER EVERY SECOND--WE'RE DONE FOR!
EVEN I CAN'T THINK OF A WAY OUT... WE CAN'T GET ANY HELP TILL DAWN AND WE'LL NEVER LAST THE NIGHT! LOOKS LIKE WE'LL NEVER GET OFF THIS GREEN WORLD ALIVE!

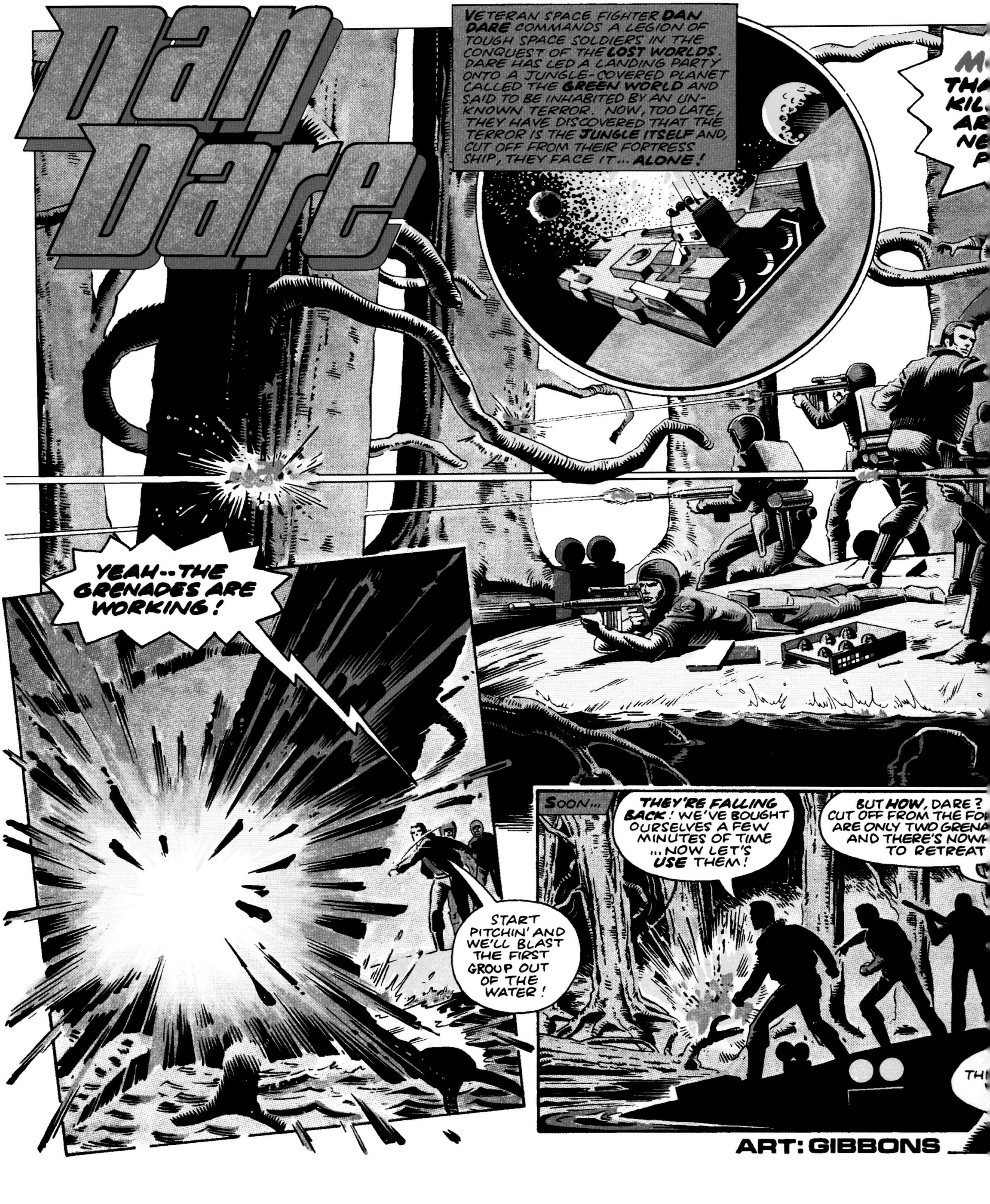

DAN DARE
VETERAN SPACE FIGHTER DAN DARE COMMANDS A LEGION OF TOUGH SPACE SOLDIERS IN THE CONQUEST OF THE LOST WORLDS. DARE HAS LED A LANDING PARTY ONTO A JUNGLE-COVERED PLANET CALLED THE GREEN WORLD AND SAID TO BE INHABITED BY AN UNKNOWN TERROR. NOW, TOO LATE, THEY HAVE DISCOVERED THAT THE TERROR IS THE JUNGLE ITSELF AND, CUT OFF FROM THEIR FORTRESS SHIP, THEY FACE IT... ALONE!
YEAH--THE GRENADES ARE WORKING!
START PITCHIN' AND WE'LL BLAST THE FIRST GROUP OUT OF THE WATER!
SOON...
THEY'RE FALLING BACK! WE'VE BOUGHT OURSELVES A FEW MINUTES OF TIME ...NOW LET'S USE THEM!
BUT HOW, DARE? CUT OFF FROM THE FO ARE ONLY TWO GRENA AND THERE'S NOWH TO RETREAT
ART: GIBBONS

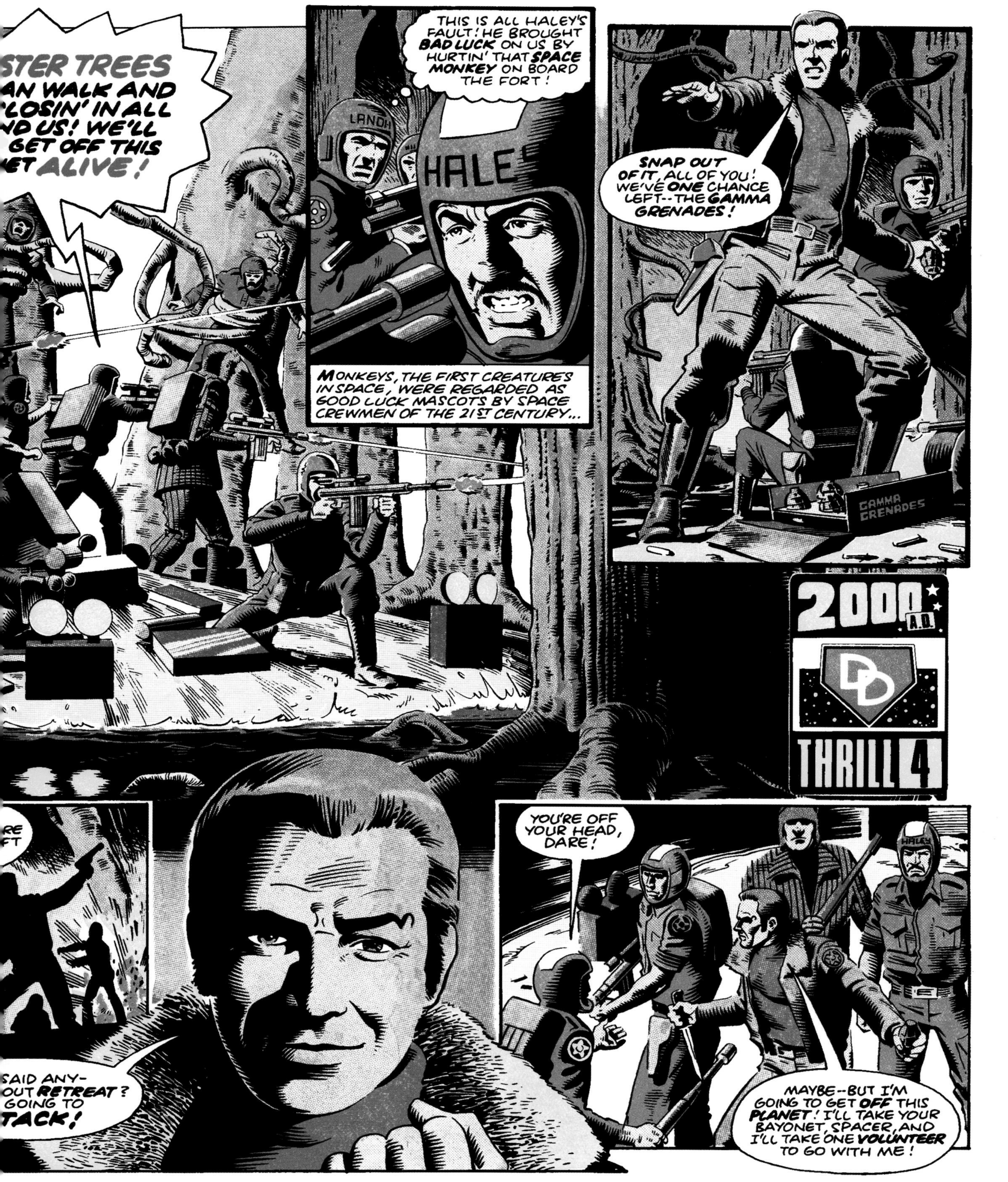

STER TREES
AN WALK AND
'CLOSIN' IN ALL
ND US! WE'LL
GET OFF THIS
ET ALIVE!
THIS IS ALL HALEY'S FAULT! HE BROUGHT BAD LUCK ON US BY HURTIN' THAT SPACE MONKEY ON BOARD THE FORT!
MONKEYS, THE FIRST CREATURES IN SPACE, WERE REGARDED AS GOOD LUCK MASCOTS BY SPACE CREWMEN OF THE 21ST CENTURY...
SNAP OUT OF IT, ALL OF YOU! WE'VE ONE CHANCE LEFT--THE GAMMA GRENADES!
GAMMA GRENADES
2000 A.D.
THRILL 4
SAID ANY-
OUT RETREAT?
GOING TO
TACK!
YOU'RE OFF YOUR HEAD, DARE!
MAYBE--BUT I'M GOING TO GET OFF THIS PLANET! I'LL TAKE YOUR BAYONET, SPACER, AND I'LL TAKE ONE VOLUNTEER TO GO WITH ME!

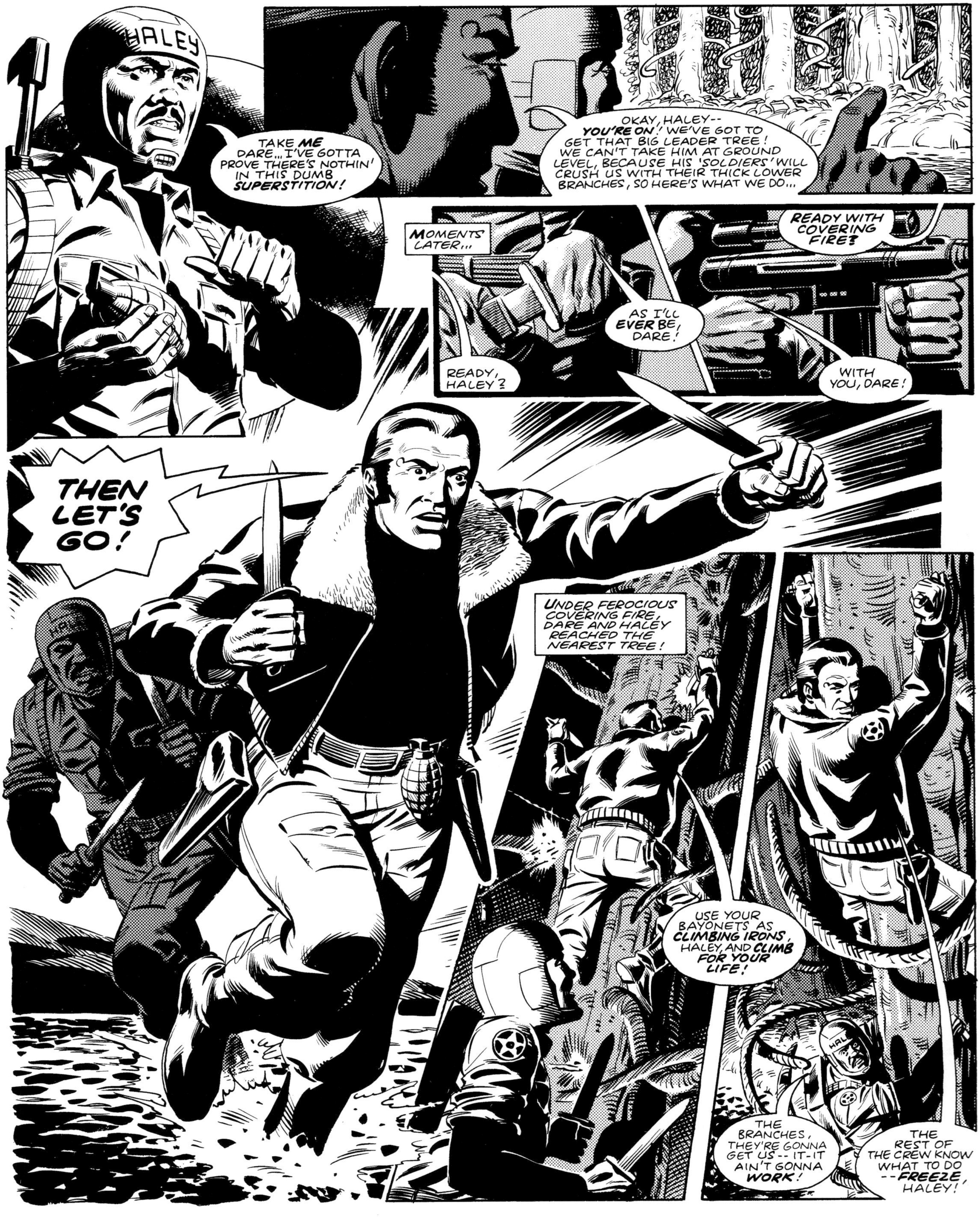

TAKE ME DARE... I'VE GOTTA PROVE THERE'S NOTHIN' IN THIS DUMB SUPERSTITION!
OKAY, HALEY-- YOU'RE ON! WE'VE GOT TO GET THAT BIG LEADER TREE! WE CAN'T TAKE HIM AT GROUND LEVEL, BECAUSE HIS 'SOLDIERS' WILL CRUSH US WITH THEIR THICK LOWER BRANCHES, SO HERE'S WHAT WE DO...
MOMENTS LATER...
READY, HALEY?
AS I'LL EVER BE, DARE!
READY WITH COVERING FIRE?
WITH YOU, DARE!
THEN LET'S GO!
UNDER FEROCIOUS COVERING FIRE, DARE AND HALEY REACHED THE NEAREST TREE!
USE YOUR BAYONETS AS CLIMBING IRONS, HALEY, AND CLIMB FOR YOUR LIFE!
THE BRANCHES, THEY'RE GONNA GET US -- IT-IT AIN'T GONNA WORK!
THE REST OF THE CREW KNOW WHAT TO DO --FREEZE, HALEY!

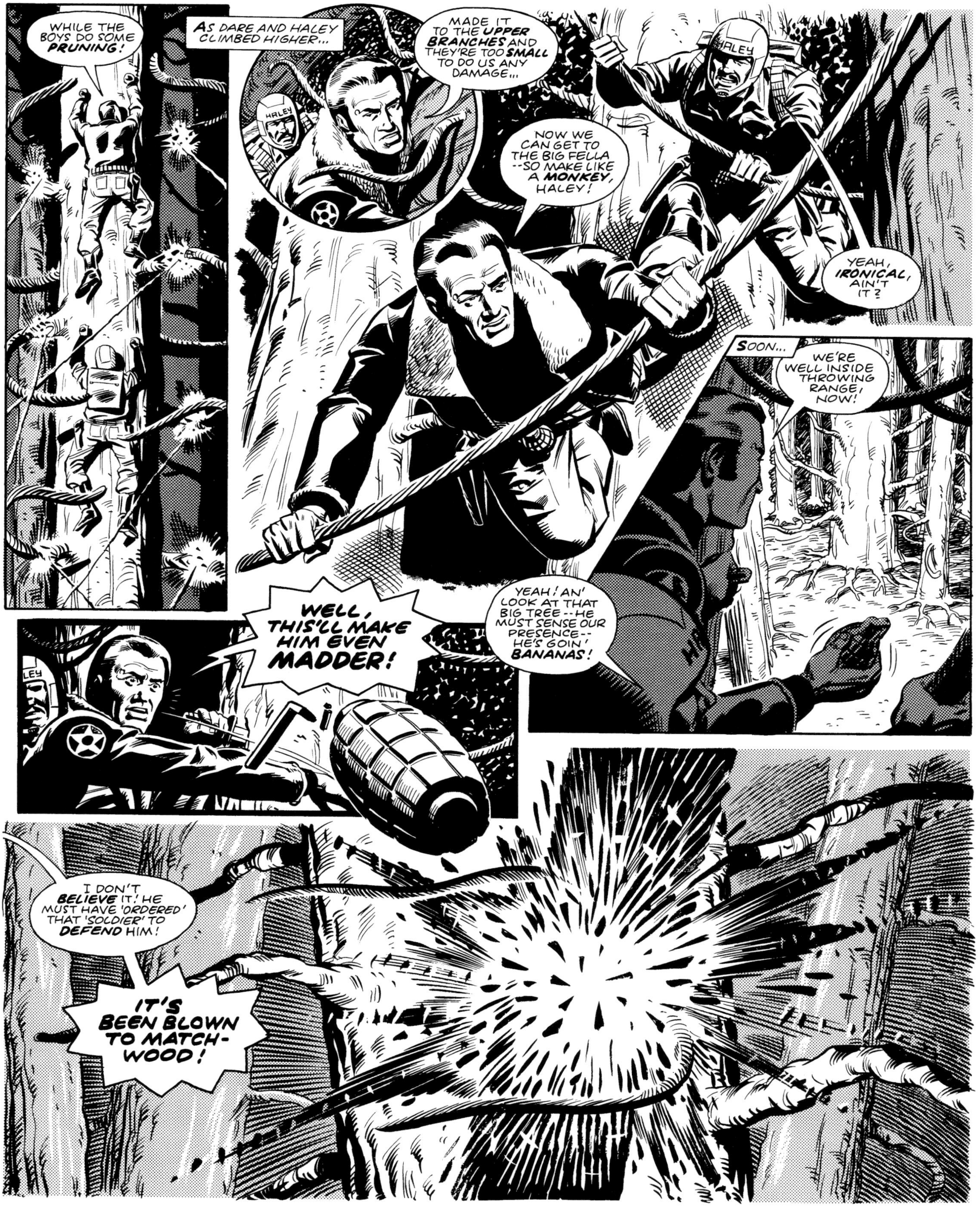

WHILE THE BOYS DO SOME PRUNING!
AS DARE AND HALEY CLIMBED HIGHER...
MADE IT TO THE UPPER BRANCHES AND THEY'RE TOO SMALL TO DO US ANY DAMAGE...
HALEY
NOW WE CAN GET TO THE BIG FELLA --SO MAKE LIKE A MONKEY, HALEY!
HALEY
YEAH, IRONICAL, AIN'T IT?
SOON...
WE'RE WELL INSIDE THROWING RANGE, NOW!
YEAH! AN' LOOK AT THAT BIG TREE --HE MUST SENSE OUR PRESENCE-- HE'S GOIN' BANANAS!
WELL, THIS'LL MAKE HIM EVEN MADDER!
I DON'T BELIEVE IT! HE MUST HAVE 'ORDERED' THAT 'SOLDIER' TO DEFEND HIM!
IT'S BEEN BLOWN TO MATCH-WOOD!

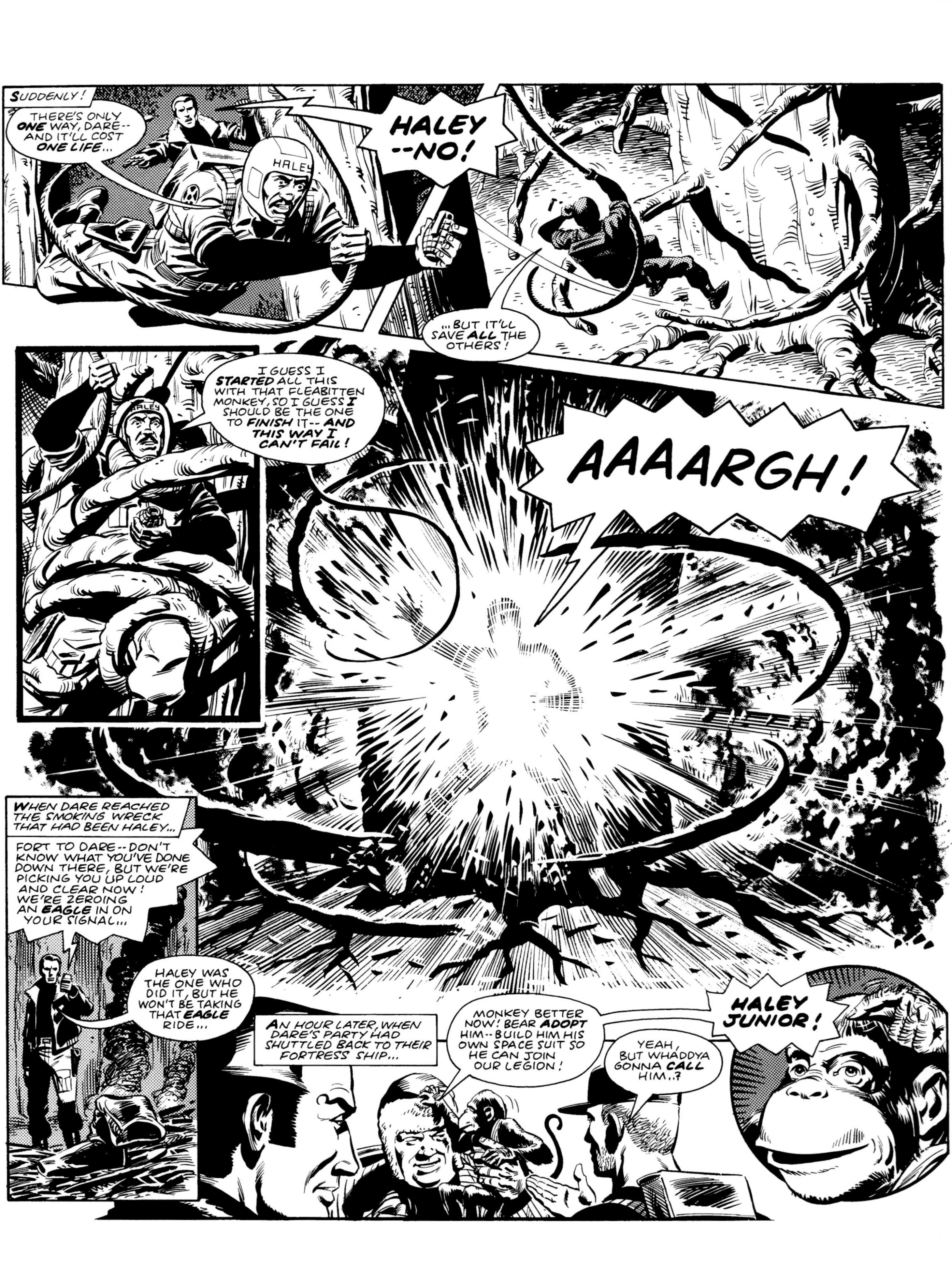
SUDDENLY!
THERE'S ONLY ONE WAY, DARE-- AND IT'LL COST ONE LIFE...
HALEY --NO!
...BUT IT'LL SAVE ALL THE OTHERS!
I GUESS I STARTED ALL THIS WITH THAT FLEABITTEN MONKEY, SO I GUESS I SHOULD BE THE ONE TO FINISH IT-- AND THIS WAY I CAN'T FAIL!
AAAARGH!
WHEN DARE REACHED THE SMOKING WRECK THAT HAD BEEN HALEY...
FORT TO DARE-- DON'T KNOW WHAT YOU'VE DONE DOWN THERE, BUT WE'RE PICKING YOU UP LOUD AND CLEAR NOW! WE'RE ZEROING AN EAGLE IN ON YOUR SIGNAL...
HALEY WAS THE ONE WHO DID IT, BUT HE WON'T BE TAKING THAT EAGLE RIDE...
AN HOUR LATER, WHEN DARE'S PARTY HAD SHUTTLED BACK TO THEIR FORTRESS SHIP...
MONKEY BETTER NOW! BEAR ADOPT HIM-- BUILD HIM HIS OWN SPACE SUIT SO HE CAN JOIN OUR LEGION!
YEAH, BUT WHADDYA GONNA CALL HIM..?
HALEY JUNIOR!

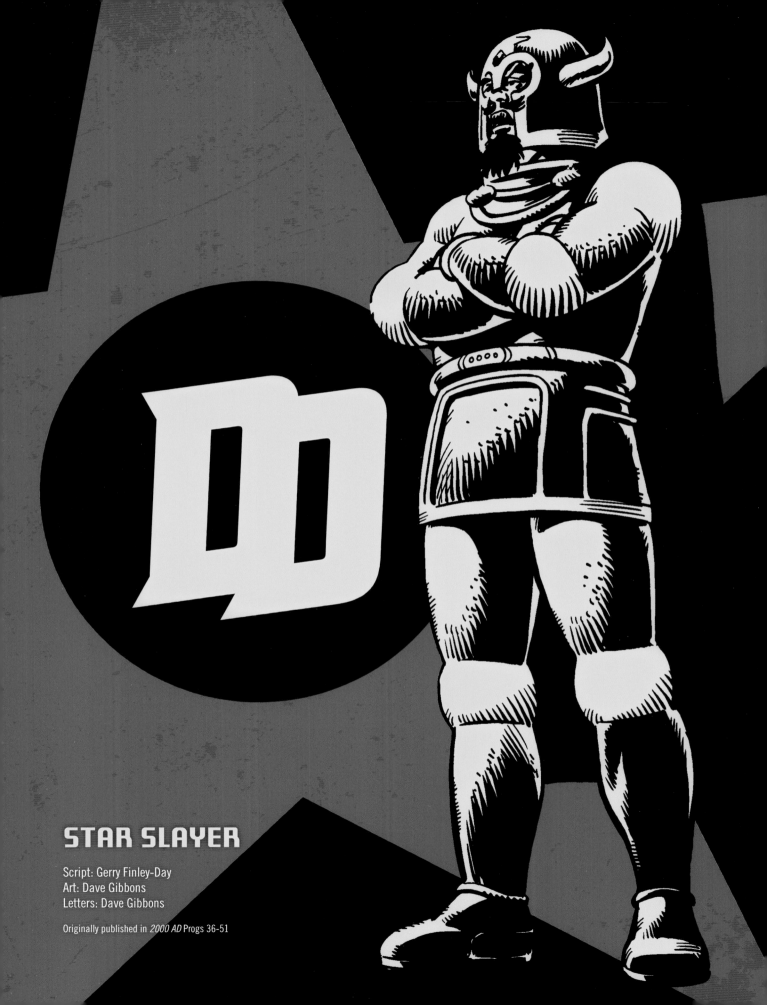

STAR SLAYER

Script: Gerry Finley-Day
Art: Dave Gibbons
Letters: Dave Gibbons

Originally published in *2000 AD* Progs 36-51

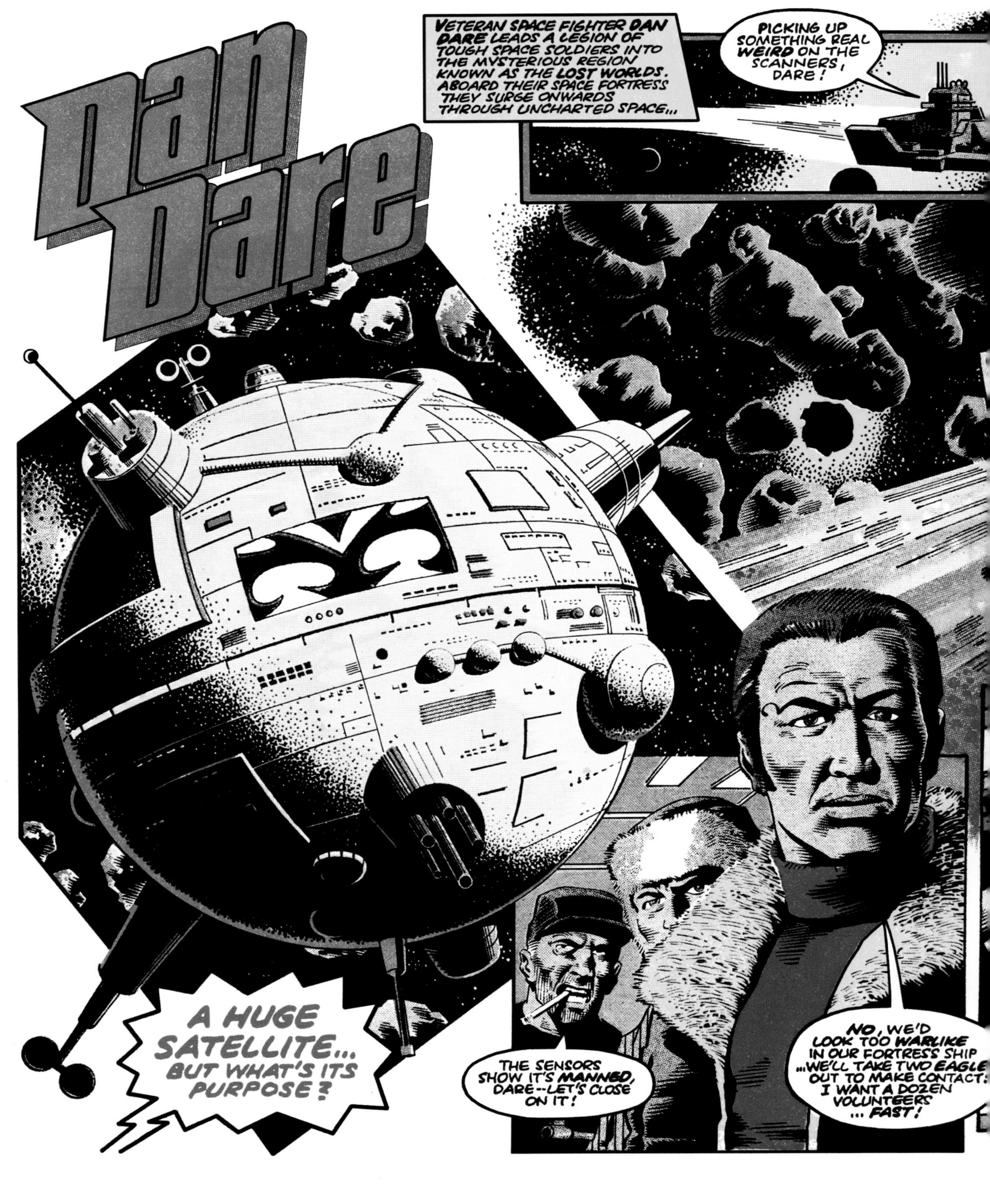

DAN DARE
VETERAN SPACE FIGHTER DAN DARE LEADS A LEGION OF TOUGH SPACE SOLDIERS INTO THE MYSTERIOUS REGION KNOWN AS THE LOST WORLDS. ABOARD THEIR SPACE FORTRESS THEY SURGE ONWARDS THROUGH UNCHARTED SPACE...
PICKING UP SOMETHING REAL WEIRD ON THE SCANNERS, DARE!
A HUGE SATELLITE... BUT WHAT'S ITS PURPOSE?
THE SENSORS SHOW IT'S MANNED, DARE--LET'S CLOSE ON IT!
NO, WE'D LOOK TOO WARLIKE IN OUR FORTRESS SHIP ...WE'LL TAKE TWO EAGLES OUT TO MAKE CONTACT! I WANT A DOZEN VOLUNTEERS ... FAST!

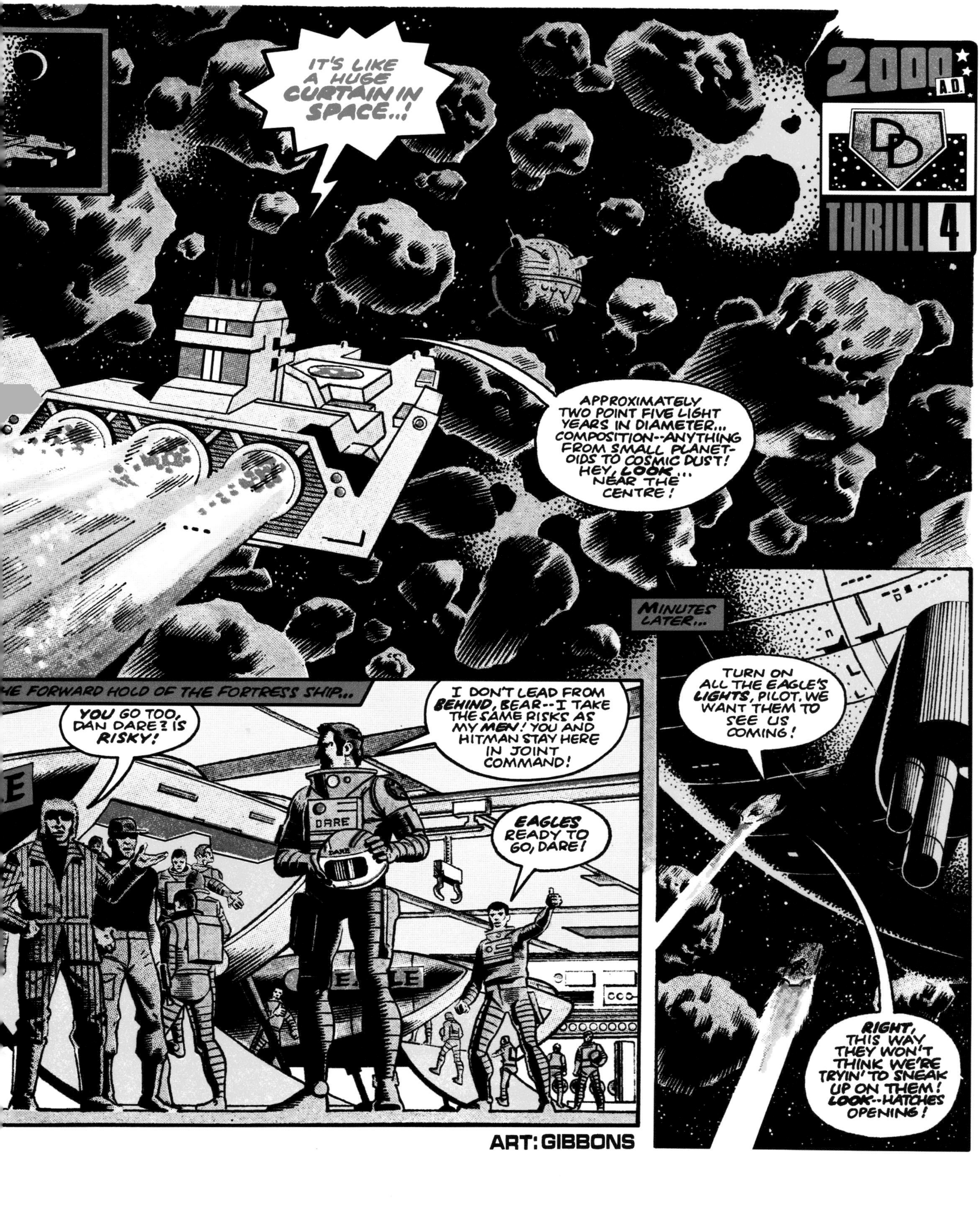
2000 A.D.
THRILL 4
IT'S LIKE A HUGE CURTAIN IN SPACE..!
APPROXIMATELY TWO POINT FIVE LIGHT YEARS IN DIAMETER... COMPOSITION--ANYTHING FROM SMALL PLANET-OIDS TO COSMIC DUST! HEY, LOOK... NEAR THE CENTRE!
HE FORWARD HOLD OF THE FORTRESS SHIP...
YOU GO TOO, DAN DARE? IS RISKY!
I DON'T LEAD FROM BEHIND, BEAR--I TAKE THE SAME RISKS AS MY MEN! YOU AND HITMAN STAY HERE IN JOINT COMMAND!
DARE
EAGLES READY TO GO, DARE!
MINUTES LATER...
TURN ON ALL THE EAGLE'S LIGHTS, PILOT. WE WANT THEM TO SEE US COMING!
RIGHT, THIS WAY THEY WON'T THINK WE'RE TRYIN' TO SNEAK UP ON THEM! LOOK--HATCHES OPENING!

ART: GIBBONS

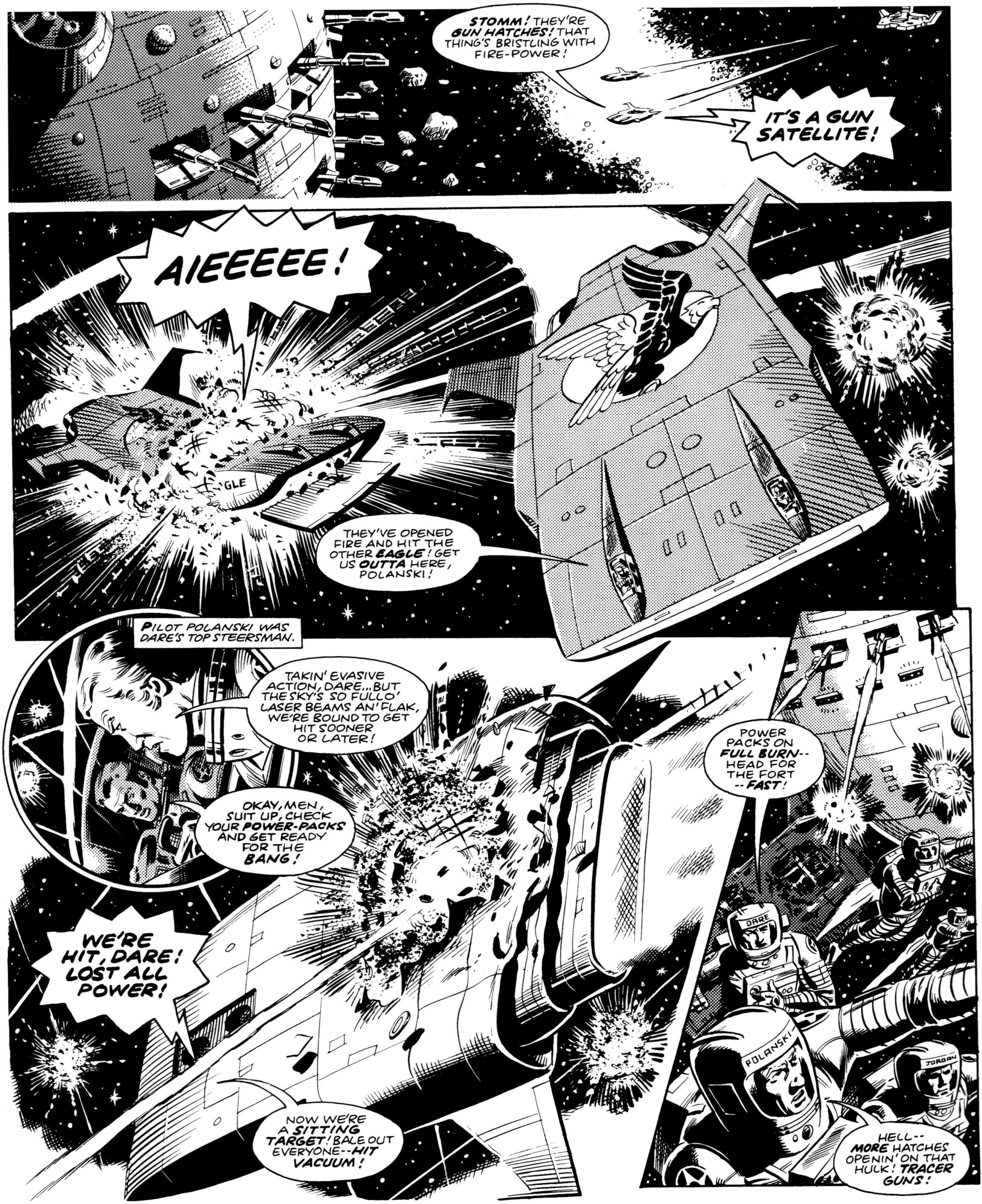
STOMM! THEY'RE GUN HATCHES! THAT THING'S BRISTLING WITH FIRE-POWER!
IT'S A GUN SATELLITE!
AIEEEEE!
GLE
THEY'VE OPENED FIRE AND HIT THE OTHER EAGLE! GET US OUTTA HERE, POLANSKI!
PILOT POLANSKI WAS DARE'S TOP STEERSMAN.
TAKIN' EVASIVE ACTION, DARE... BUT, THE SKY'S SO FULL O' LASER BEAMS AN' FLAK, WE'RE BOUND TO GET HIT SOONER OR LATER!
OKAY, MEN, SUIT UP, CHECK YOUR POWER-PACKS AND GET READY FOR THE BANG!
WE'RE HIT, DARE! LOST ALL POWER!
NOW WE'RE A SITTING TARGET! BALE OUT EVERYONE--HIT VACUUM!
POWER PACKS ON FULL BURN-- HEAD FOR THE FORT --FAST!
DARE
POLANSKI
JORDAN
HELL-- MORE HATCHES OPENIN' ON THAT HULK! TRACER GUNS!

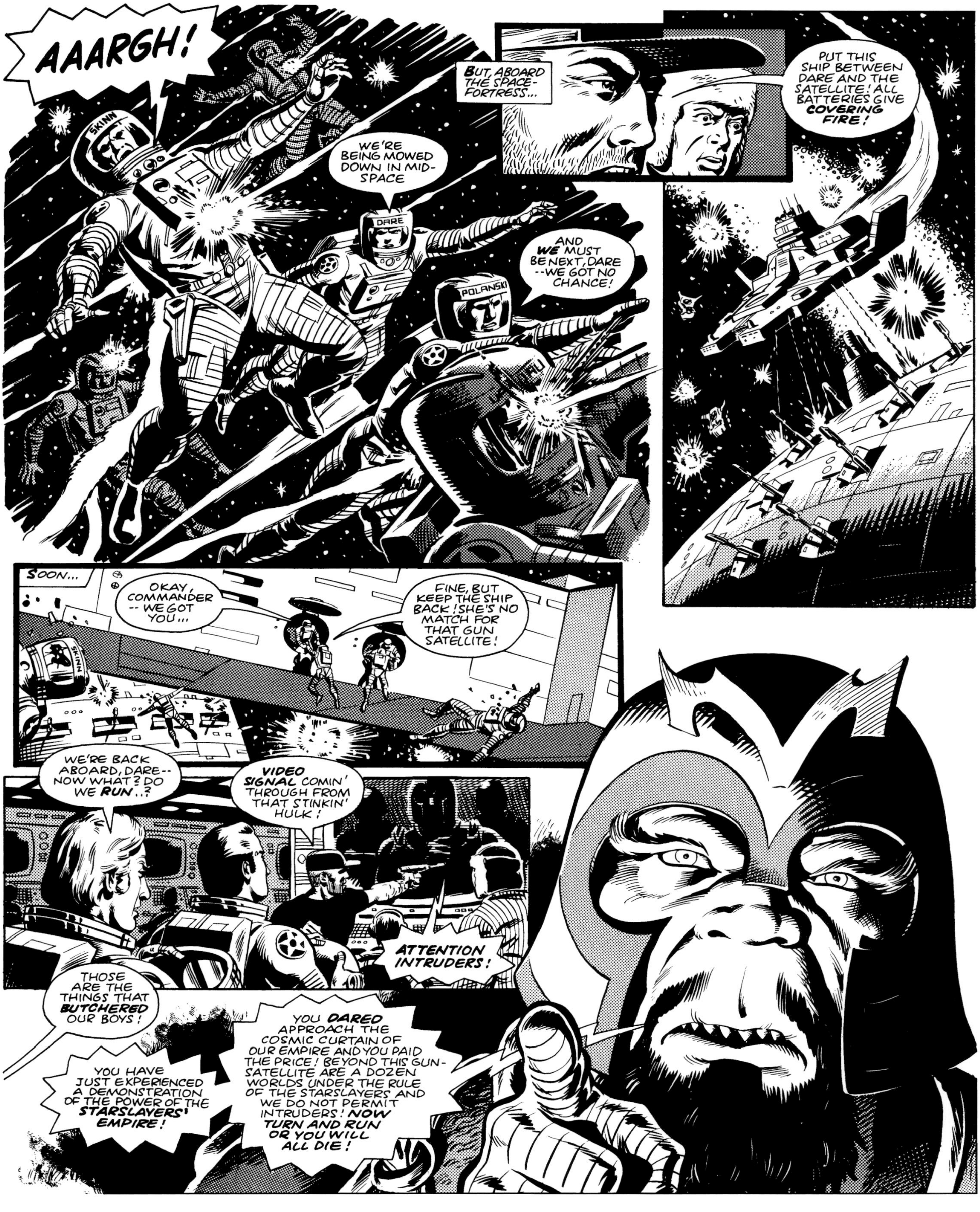
AAARGH!
WE'RE BEING MOWED DOWN IN MID-SPACE
AND WE MUST BE NEXT, DARE --WE GOT NO CHANCE!
BUT, ABOARD THE SPACE-FORTRESS...
PUT THIS SHIP BETWEEN DARE AND THE SATELLITE! ALL BATTERIES GIVE COVERING FIRE!
SOON...
OKAY, COMMANDER -- WE GOT YOU...
FINE, BUT KEEP THE SHIP BACK! SHE'S NO MATCH FOR THAT GUN SATELLITE!
WE'RE BACK ABOARD, DARE-- NOW WHAT? DO WE RUN..?
VIDEO SIGNAL COMIN' THROUGH FROM THAT STINKIN' HULK!
ATTENTION INTRUDERS!
THOSE ARE THE THINGS THAT BUTCHERED OUR BOYS!
YOU HAVE JUST EXPERIENCED A DEMONSTRATION OF THE POWER OF THE STARSLAYERS' EMPIRE!
YOU DARED APPROACH THE COSMIC CURTAIN OF OUR EMPIRE AND YOU PAID THE PRICE! BEYOND THIS GUN-SATELLITE ARE A DOZEN WORLDS UNDER THE RULE OF THE STARSLAYERS AND WE DO NOT PERMIT INTRUDERS! NOW TURN AND RUN OR YOU WILL ALL DIE!

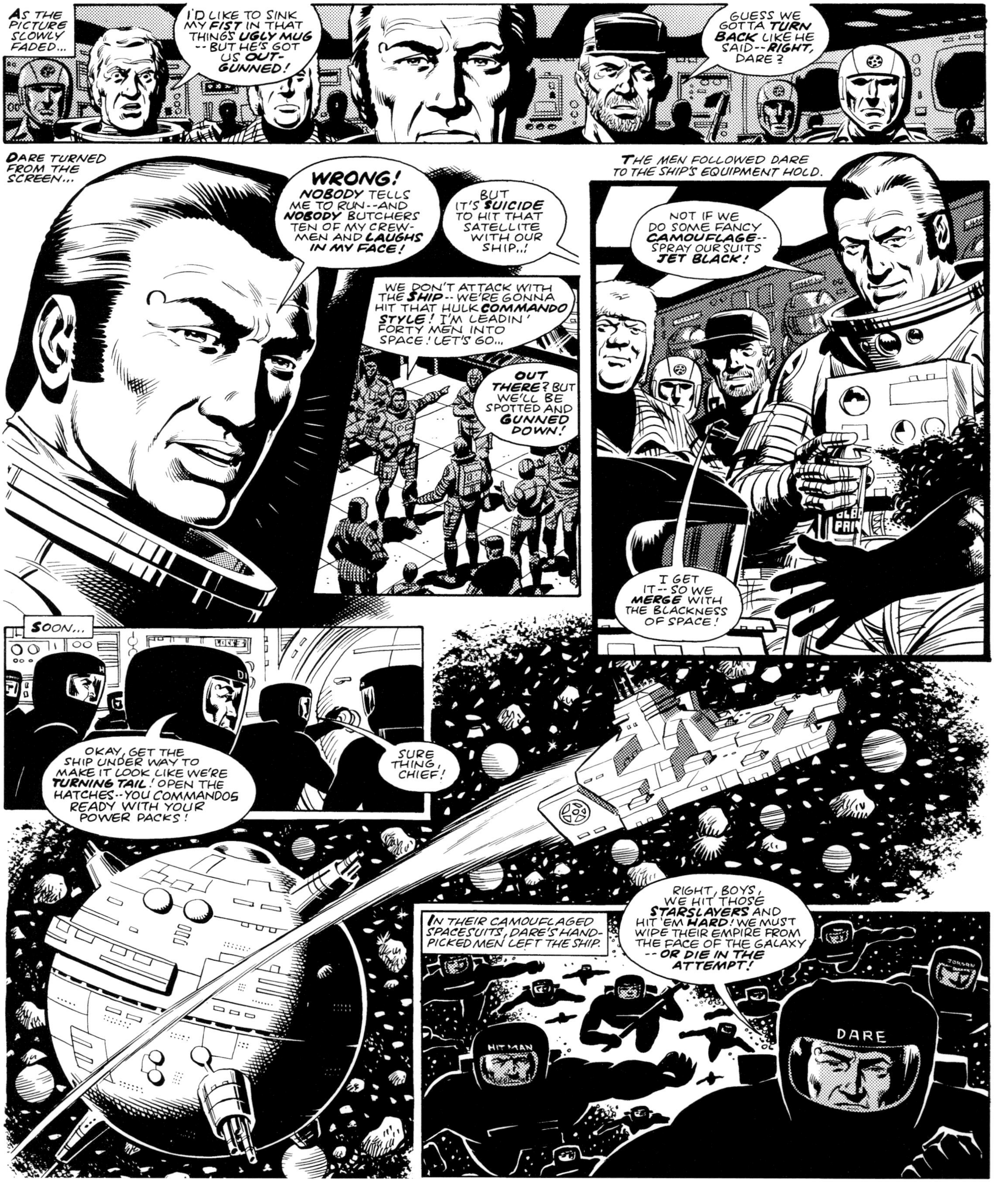
AS THE PICTURE SLOWLY FADED...
I'D LIKE TO SINK MY FIST IN THAT THINGS UGLY MUG -- BUT HE'S GOT US OUT-GUNNED!
GUESS WE GOTTA TURN BACK LIKE HE SAID -- RIGHT, DARE?
DARE TURNED FROM THE SCREEN...
WRONG! NOBODY TELLS ME TO RUN -- AND NOBODY BUTCHERS TEN OF MY CREW-MEN AND LAUGHS IN MY FACE!
BUT IT'S SUICIDE TO HIT THAT SATELLITE WITH OUR SHIP..!
WE DON'T ATTACK WITH THE SHIP -- WE'RE GONNA HIT THAT HULK COMMANDO STYLE! I'M LEADIN' FORTY MEN INTO SPACE! LET'S GO...
OUT THERE? BUT WE'LL BE SPOTTED AND GUNNED DOWN!
THE MEN FOLLOWED DARE TO THE SHIP'S EQUIPMENT HOLD.
NOT IF WE DO SOME FANCY CAMOUFLAGE -- SPRAY OUR SUITS JET BLACK!
I GET IT -- SO WE MERGE WITH THE BLACKNESS OF SPACE!
SOON...
LOCK 3
OKAY, GET THE SHIP UNDER WAY TO MAKE IT LOOK LIKE WE'RE TURNING TAIL! OPEN THE HATCHES -- YOU COMMANDOS READY WITH YOUR POWER PACKS!
SURE THING, CHIEF!
IN THEIR CAMOUFLAGED SPACESUITS, DARE'S HAND-PICKED MEN LEFT THE SHIP.
RIGHT, BOYS, WE HIT THOSE STARSLAYERS AND HIT 'EM HARD! WE MUST WIPE THEIR EMPIRE FROM THE FACE OF THE GALAXY -- OR DIE IN THE ATTEMPT!
HITMAN
DARE

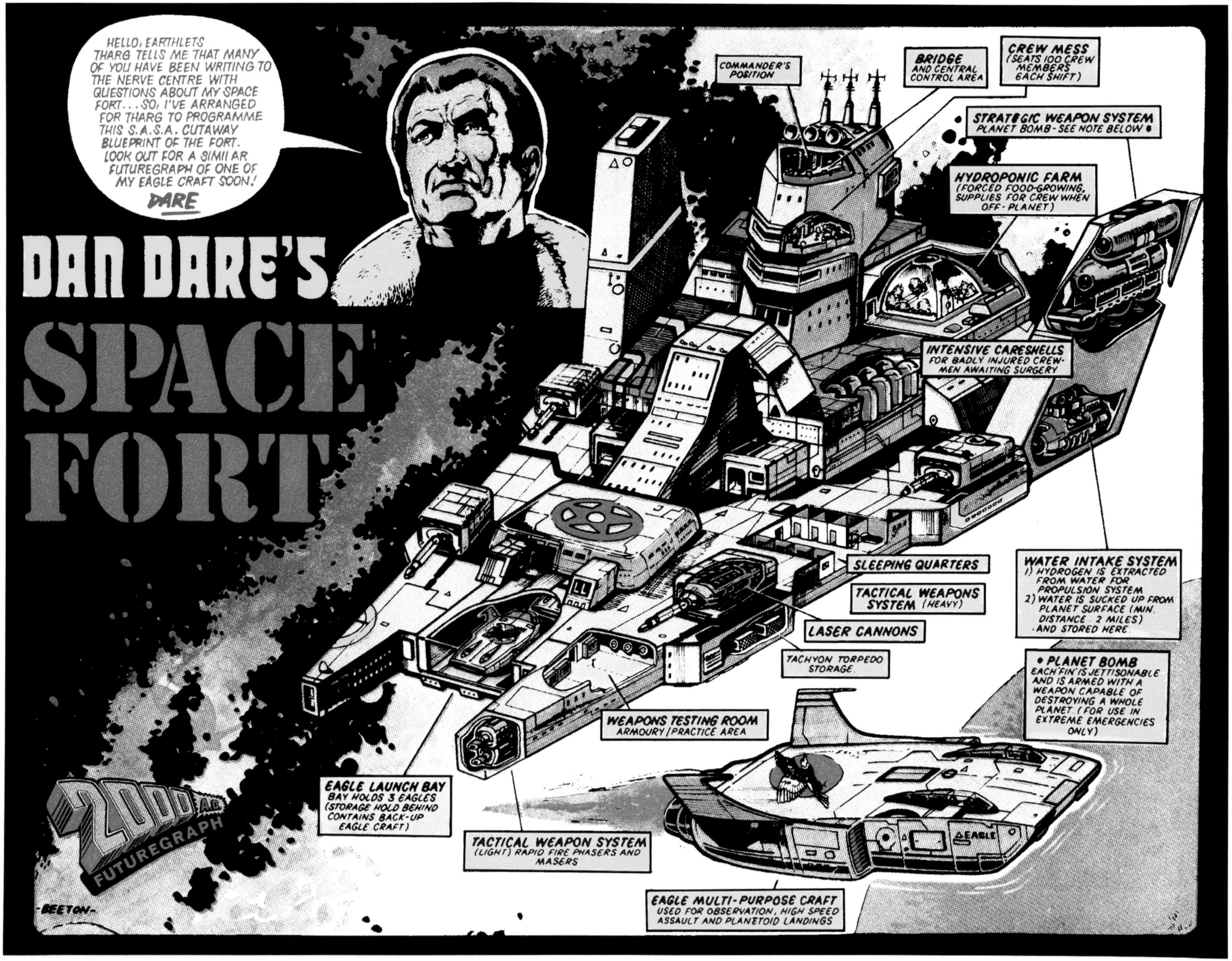
HELLO, EARTHLETS THARG TELLS ME THAT MANY OF YOU HAVE BEEN WRITING TO THE NERVE CENTRE WITH QUESTIONS ABOUT MY SPACE FORT... SO, I'VE ARRANGED FOR THARG TO PROGRAMME THIS S.A.S.A. CUTAWAY BLUEPRINT OF THE FORT. LOOK OUT FOR A SIMILAR FUTUREGRAPH OF ONE OF MY EAGLE CRAFT SOON! DARE
DAN DARE'S
SPACE FORT
COMMANDER'S POSITION
BRIDGE AND CENTRAL CONTROL AREA
CREW MESS (SEATS 100 CREW MEMBERS EACH SHIFT)
STRATEGIC WEAPON SYSTEM PLANET BOMB - SEE NOTE BELOW *
HYDROPONIC FARM (FORCED FOOD-GROWING, SUPPLIES FOR CREW WHEN OFF-PLANET)
INTENSIVE CARESHELLS FOR BADLY INJURED CREW-MEN AWAITING SURGERY
SLEEPING QUARTERS
TACTICAL WEAPONS SYSTEM (HEAVY)
LASER CANNONS
TACHYON TORPEDO STORAGE.
WATER INTAKE SYSTEM 1) HYDROGEN IS EXTRACTED FROM WATER FOR PROPULSION SYSTEM 2) WATER IS SUCKED UP FROM PLANET SURFACE (MIN. DISTANCE. 2 MILES) AND STORED HERE.
* PLANET BOMB EACH FIN IS JETTISONABLE AND IS ARMED WITH A WEAPON CAPABLE OF DESTROYING A WHOLE PLANET. (FOR USE IN EXTREME EMERGENCIES ONLY)
WEAPONS TESTING ROOM ARMOURY/PRACTICE AREA
EAGLE LAUNCH BAY BAY HOLDS 3 EAGLES (STORAGE HOLD BEHIND CONTAINS BACK-UP EAGLE CRAFT)
TACTICAL WEAPON SYSTEM (LIGHT) RAPID FIRE PHASERS AND MASERS
EAGLE MULTI-PURPOSE CRAFT USED FOR OBSERVATION, HIGH SPEED ASSAULT AND PLANETOID LANDINGS
EAGLE
2000 A.D. FUTUREGRAPH
-BEETON-

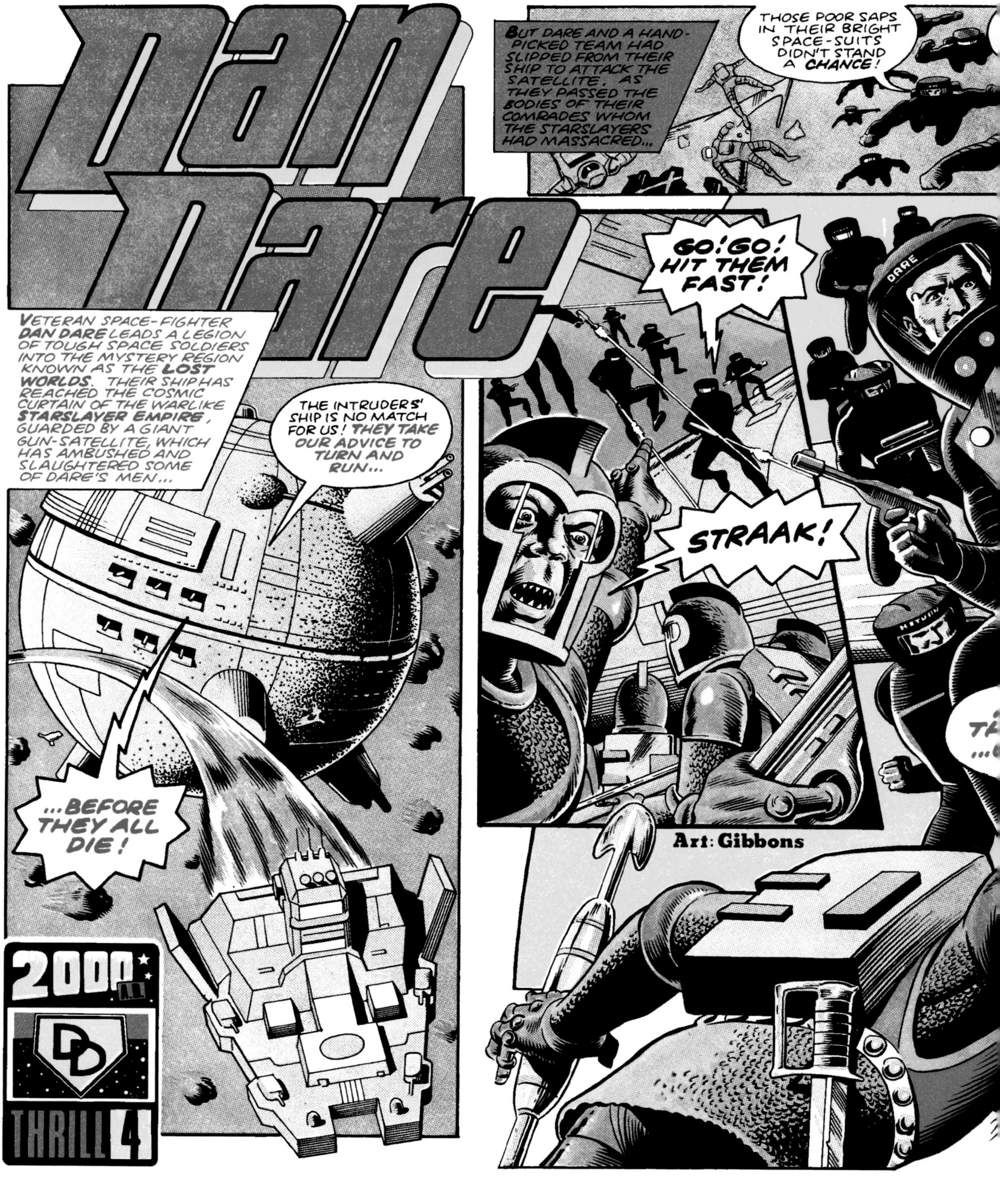
Dan Dare
VETERAN SPACE-FIGHTER DAN DARE LEADS A LEGION OF TOUGH SPACE SOLDIERS INTO THE MYSTERY REGION KNOWN AS THE LOST WORLDS. THEIR SHIP HAS REACHED THE COSMIC CURTAIN OF THE WARLIKE STARSLAYER EMPIRE, GUARDED BY A GIANT GUN-SATELLITE, WHICH HAS AMBUSHED AND SLAUGHTERED SOME OF DARE'S MEN...
THE INTRUDERS' SHIP IS NO MATCH FOR US! THEY TAKE OUR ADVICE TO TURN AND RUN...
...BEFORE THEY ALL DIE!
2000 A.D.
DD
THRILL 4
BUT DARE AND A HAND-PICKED TEAM HAD SLIPPED FROM THEIR SHIP TO ATTACK THE SATELLITE. AS THEY PASSED THE BODIES OF THEIR COMRADES WHOM THE STARSLAYERS HAD MASSACRED...
THOSE POOR SAPS IN THEIR BRIGHT SPACE-SUITS DIDN'T STAND A CHANCE!
GO! GO! HIT THEM FAST!
DARE
STRAAK!
Art: Gibbons

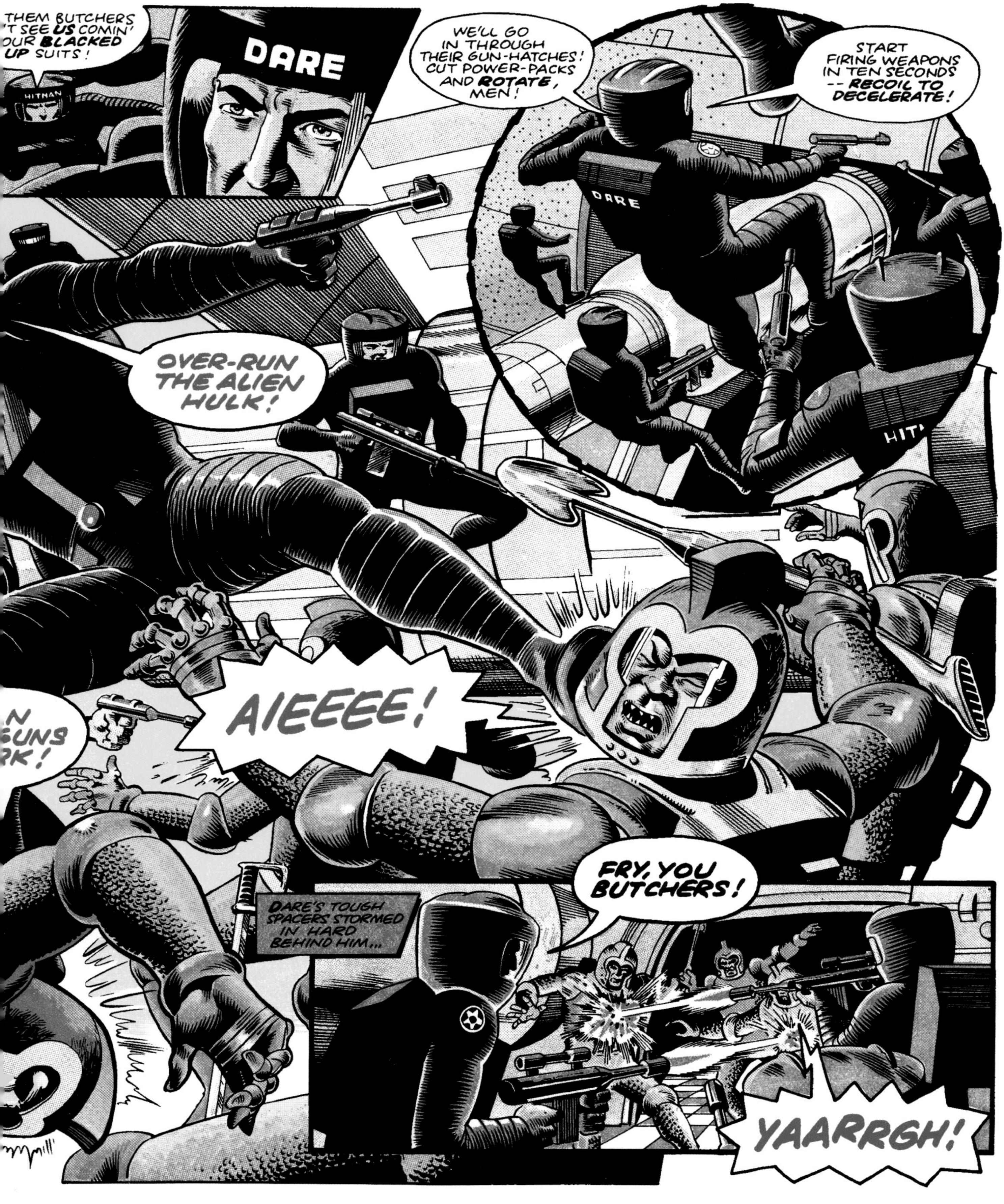
THEM BUTCHERS 'T SEE US COMIN' OUR BLACKED UP SUITS!
DARE
HITMAN
WE'LL GO IN THROUGH THEIR GUN-HATCHES! CUT POWER-PACKS AND ROTATE, MEN!
START FIRING WEAPONS IN TEN SECONDS -- RECOIL TO DECELERATE!
DARE
OVER-RUN THE ALIEN HULK!
AIEEEE!
DARE'S TOUGH SPACERS STORMED IN HARD BEHIND HIM...
FRY, YOU BUTCHERS!
YAARRGH!

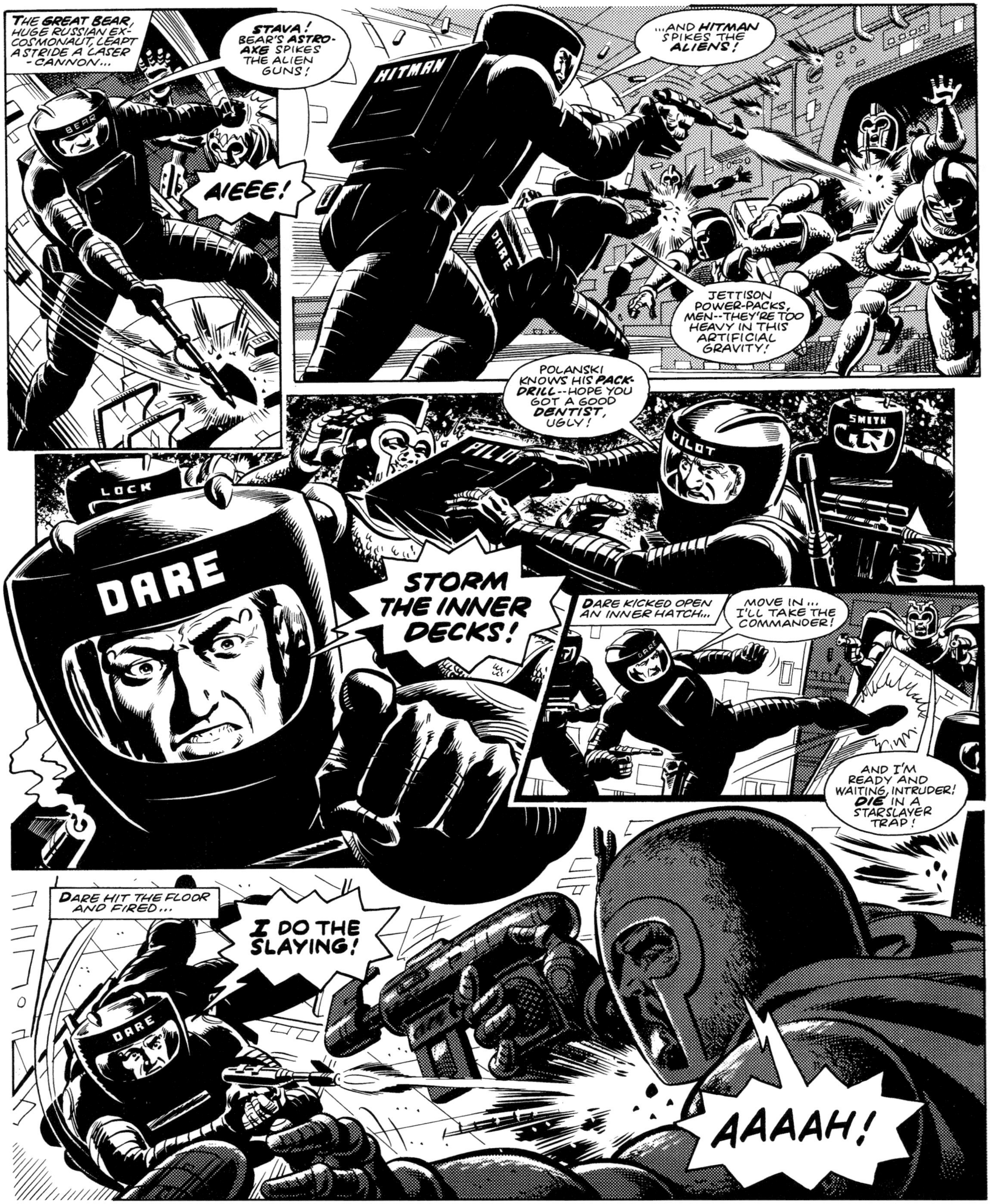

THE GREAT BEAR, HUGE RUSSIAN EX-COSMONAUT, LEAPT ASTRIDE A LASER-CANNON...
STAVA! BEAR'S ASTRO-AXE SPIKES THE ALIEN GUNS!
AIEEE!
...AND HITMAN SPIKES THE ALIENS!
JETTISON POWER-PACKS, MEN--THEY'RE TOO HEAVY IN THIS ARTIFICIAL GRAVITY!
POLANSKI KNOWS HIS PACK-DRILL--HOPE YOU GOT A GOOD DENTIST, UGLY!
STORM THE INNER DECKS!
DARE KICKED OPEN AN INNER HATCH...
MOVE IN... I'LL TAKE THE COMMANDER!
AND I'M READY AND WAITING, INTRUDER! DIE IN A STARSLAYER TRAP!
DARE HIT THE FLOOR AND FIRED...
I DO THE SLAYING!
AAAAH!

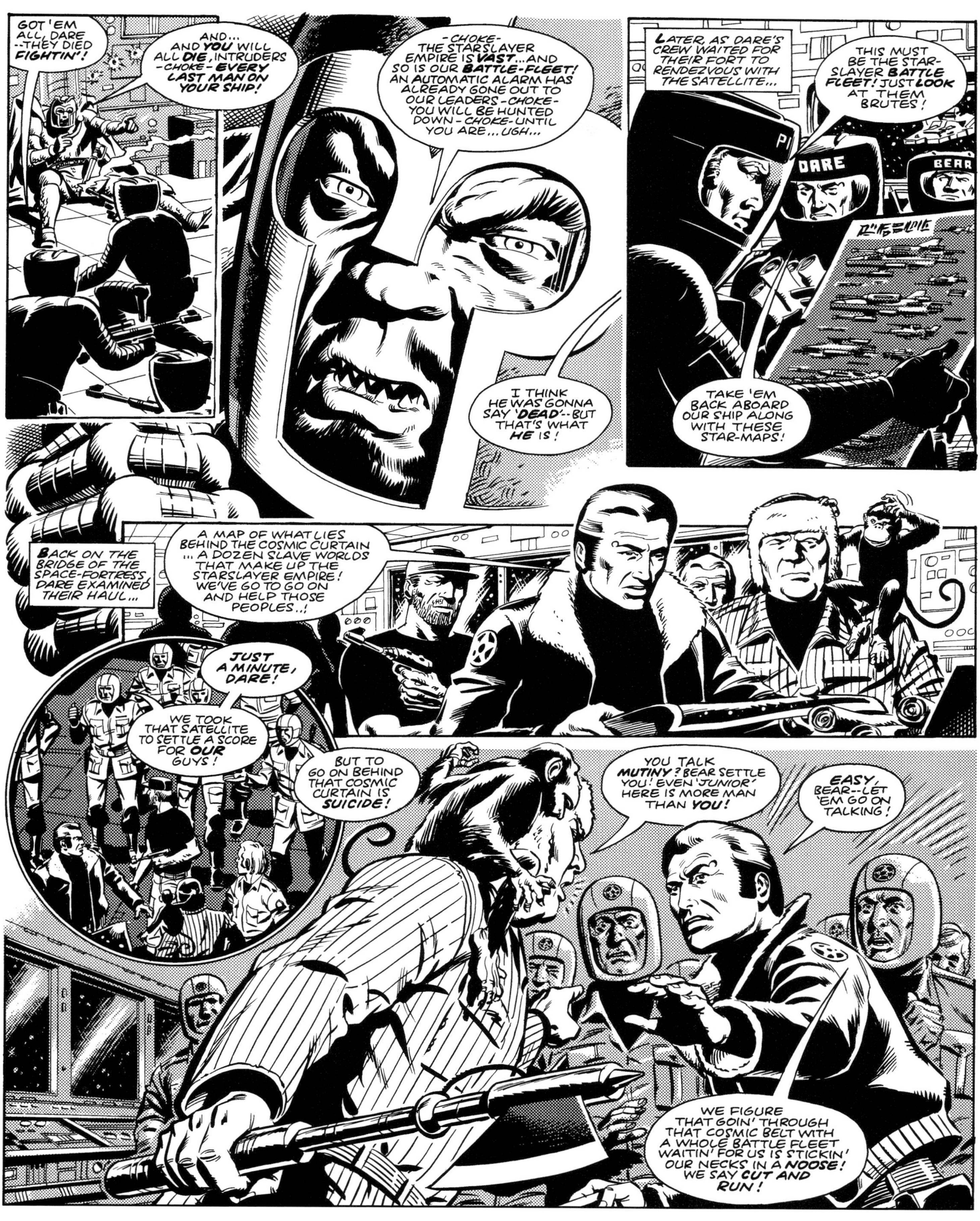

GOT 'EM ALL, DARE --THEY DIED FIGHTIN'!
AND... AND YOU WILL ALL DIE, INTRUDERS -CHOKE- EVERY LAST MAN ON YOUR SHIP!
-CHOKE- THE STARSLAYER EMPIRE IS VAST...AND SO IS OUR BATTLE-FLEET! AN AUTOMATIC ALARM HAS ALREADY GONE OUT TO OUR LEADERS -CHOKE- YOU WILL BE HUNTED DOWN -CHOKE- UNTIL YOU ARE... UGH...
I THINK HE WAS GONNA SAY 'DEAD'--BUT THAT'S WHAT HE IS!
LATER, AS DARE'S CREW WAITED FOR THEIR FORT TO RENDEZVOUS WITH THE SATELLITE...
THIS MUST BE THE STAR-SLAYER BATTLE FLEET! JUST LOOK AT THEM BRUTES!
DARE
BEAR
TAKE 'EM BACK ABOARD OUR SHIP ALONG WITH THESE STAR-MAPS!
BACK ON THE BRIDGE OF THE SPACE-FORTRESS, DARE EXAMINED THEIR HAUL...
A MAP OF WHAT LIES BEHIND THE COSMIC CURTAIN ... A DOZEN SLAVE WORLDS THAT MAKE UP THE STARSLAYER EMPIRE! WE'VE GOT TO GO ON AND HELP THOSE PEOPLES..!
JUST A MINUTE, DARE!
WE TOOK THAT SATELLITE TO SETTLE A SCORE FOR OUR GUYS!
BUT TO GO ON BEHIND THAT COSMIC CURTAIN IS SUICIDE!
YOU TALK MUTINY? BEAR SETTLE YOU! EVEN 'JUNIOR' HERE IS MORE MAN THAN YOU!
EASY, BEAR--LET 'EM GO ON TALKING!
WE FIGURE THAT GOIN' THROUGH THAT COSMIC BELT WITH A WHOLE BATTLE FLEET WAITIN' FOR US IS STICKIN' OUR NECKS IN A NOOSE! WE SAY CUT AND RUN!

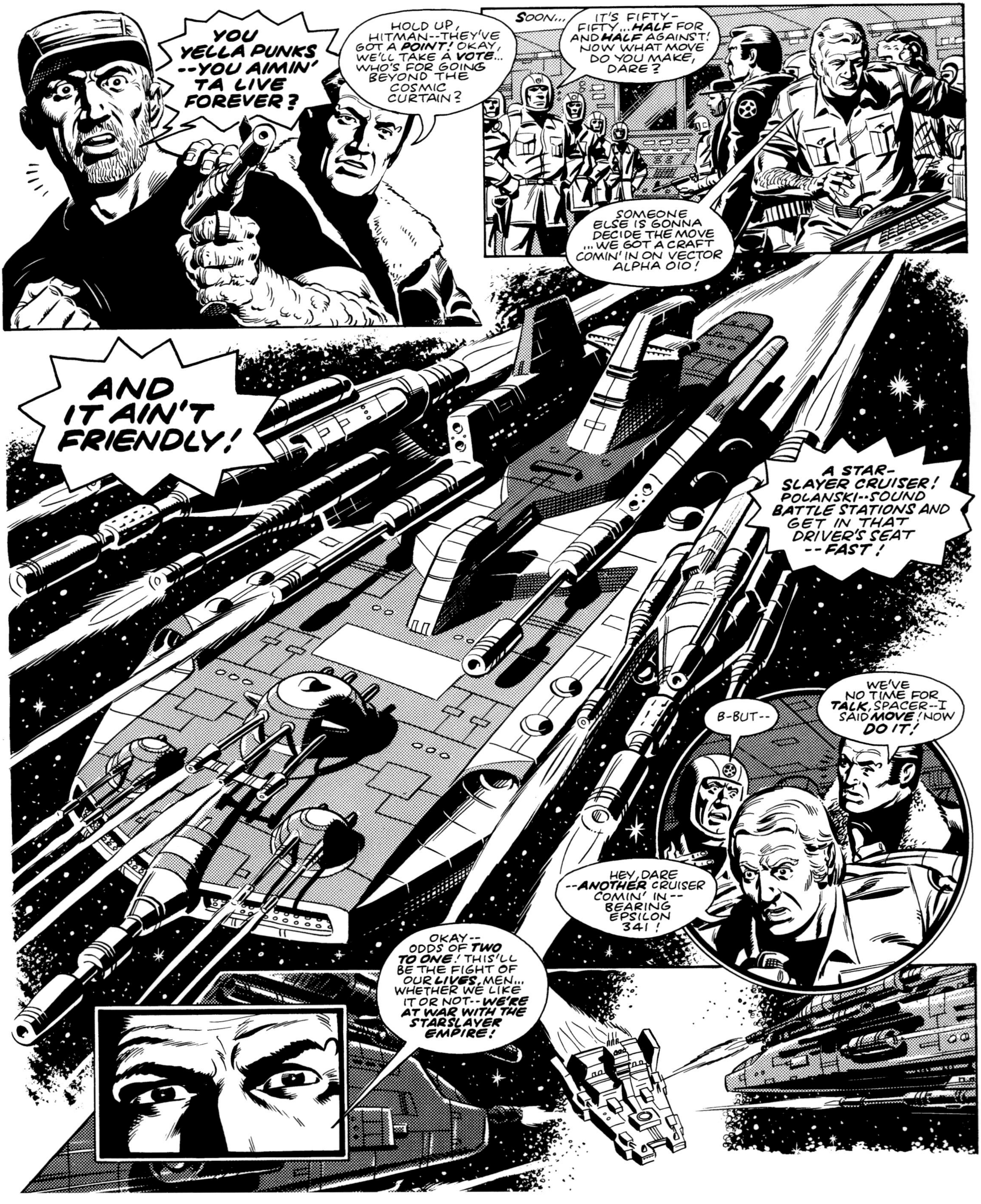

YOU YELLA PUNKS --YOU AIMIN' TA LIVE FOREVER?
HOLD UP, HITMAN--THEY'VE GOT A POINT! OKAY, WE'LL TAKE A VOTE... WHO'S FOR GOING BEYOND THE COSMIC CURTAIN?
SOON...
IT'S FIFTY-FIFTY... HALF FOR AND HALF AGAINST! NOW WHAT MOVE DO YOU MAKE, DARE?
SOMEONE ELSE IS GONNA DECIDE THE MOVE ...WE GOT A CRAFT COMIN' IN ON VECTOR ALPHA 010!
AND IT AIN'T FRIENDLY!
A STAR-SLAYER CRUISER! POLANSKI--SOUND BATTLE STATIONS AND GET IN THAT DRIVER'S SEAT --FAST!
B-BUT--
WE'VE NO TIME FOR TALK, SPACER--I SAID MOVE! NOW DO IT!
HEY, DARE --ANOTHER CRUISER COMIN' IN-- BEARING EPSILON 341!
OKAY-- ODDS OF TWO TO ONE! THIS'LL BE THE FIGHT OF OUR LIVES, MEN... WHETHER WE LIKE IT OR NOT--WE'RE AT WAR WITH THE STARSLAYER EMPIRE!

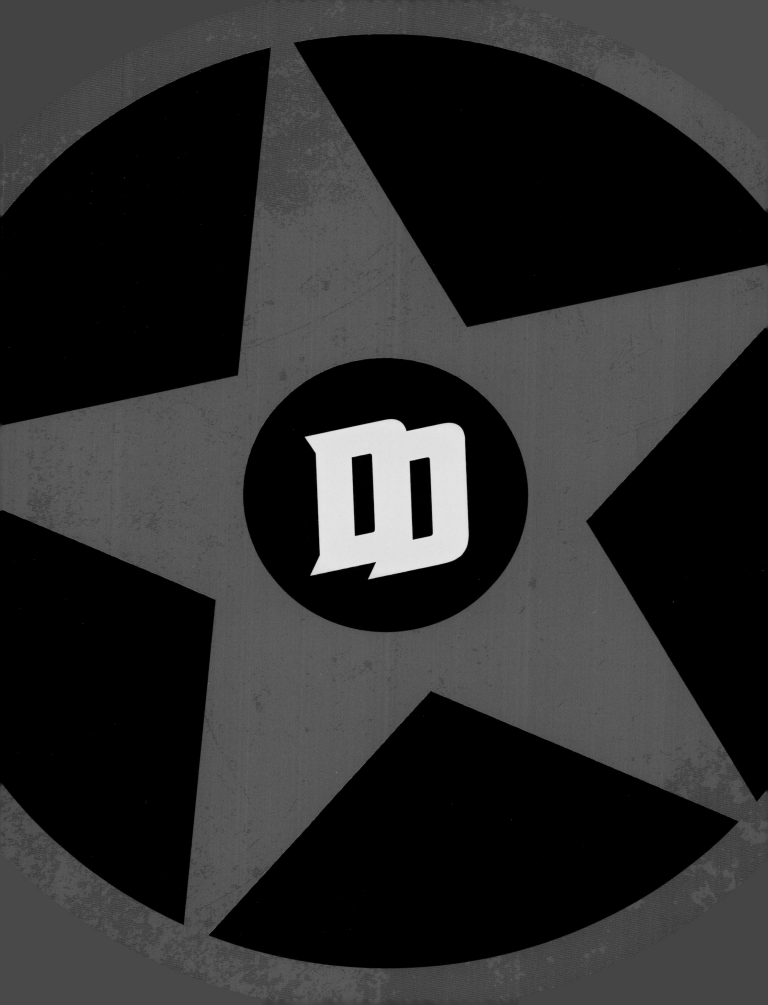

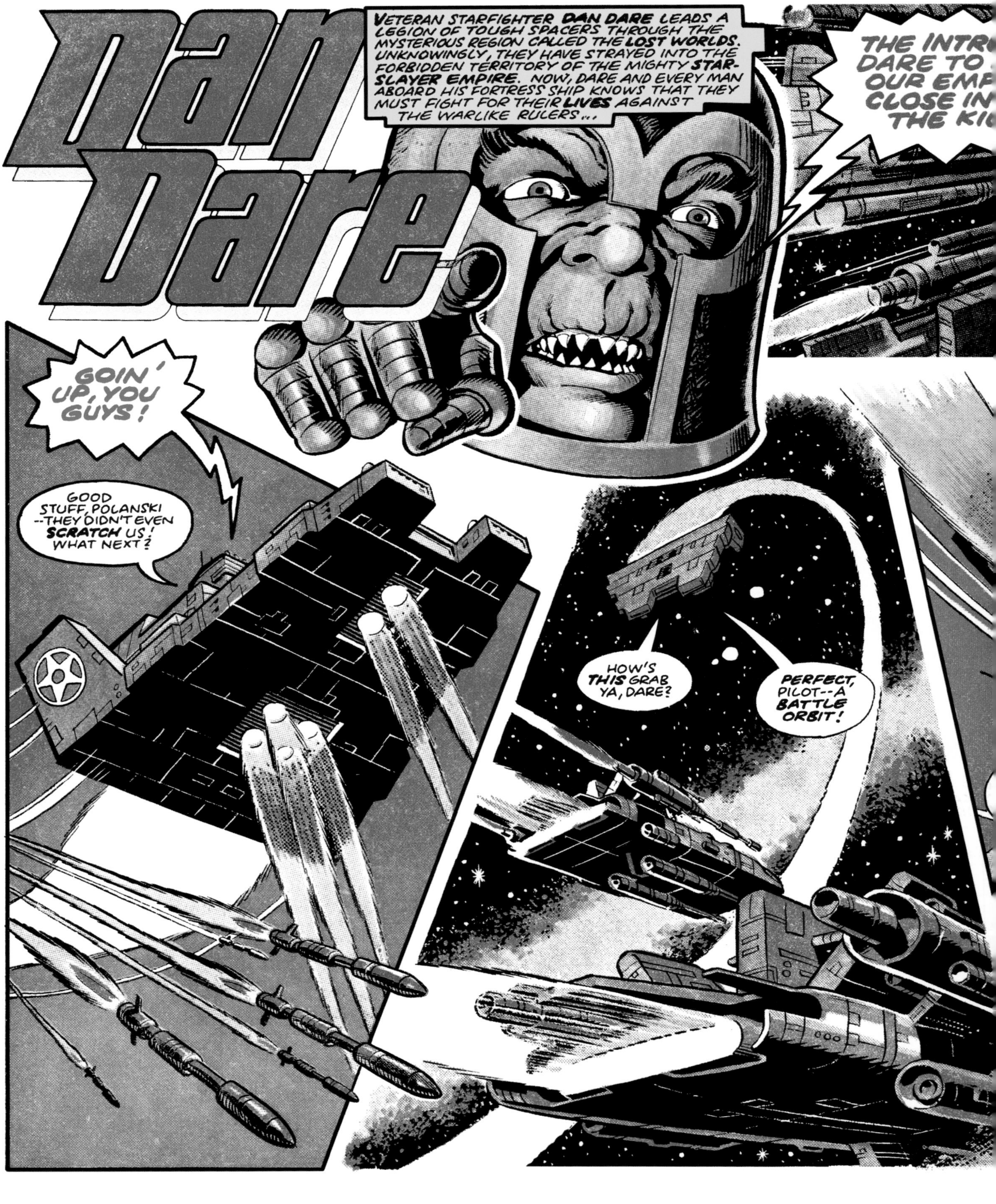
DAN DARE
VETERAN STARFIGHTER DAN DARE LEADS A LEGION OF TOUGH SPACERS THROUGH THE MYSTERIOUS REGION CALLED THE LOST WORLDS. UNKNOWINGLY, THEY HAVE STRAYED INTO THE FORBIDDEN TERRITORY OF THE MIGHTY STAR-SLAYER EMPIRE. NOW, DARE AND EVERY MAN ABOARD HIS FORTRESS SHIP KNOWS THAT THEY MUST FIGHT FOR THEIR LIVES AGAINST THE WARLIKE RULERS...
THE INTR DARE TO OUR EMP CLOSE IN THE KI
GOIN' UP, YOU GUYS!
GOOD STUFF, POLANSKI --THEY DIDN'T EVEN SCRATCH US! WHAT NEXT?
HOW'S THIS GRAB YA, DARE?
PERFECT, PILOT--A BATTLE ORBIT!

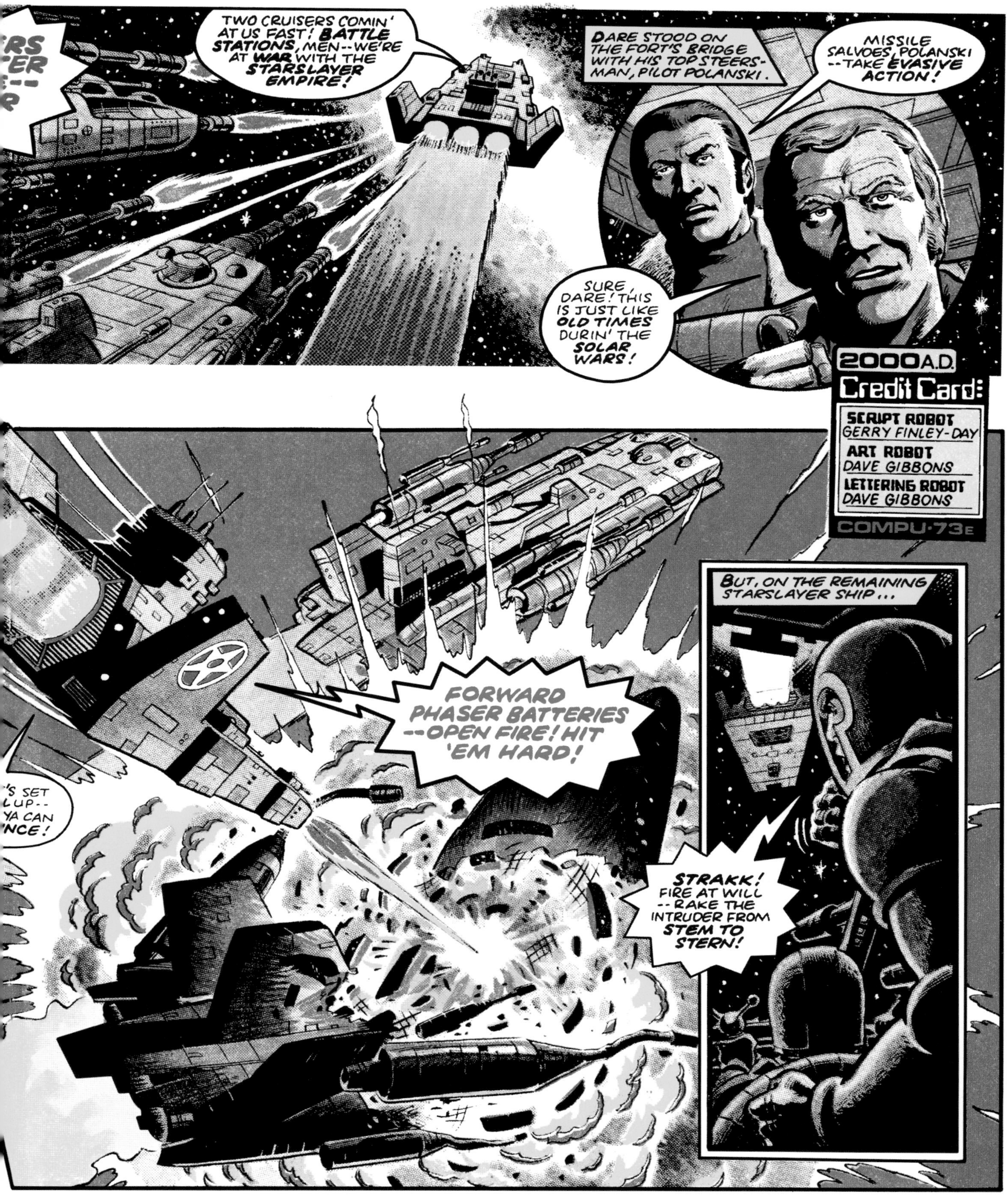

TWO CRUISERS COMIN' AT US FAST! BATTLE STATIONS, MEN--WE'RE AT WAR WITH THE STARSLAYER EMPIRE!
DARE STOOD ON THE FORT'S BRIDGE WITH HIS TOP STEERSMAN, PILOT POLANSKI.
MISSILE SALVOES, POLANSKI --TAKE EVASIVE ACTION!
SURE, DARE! THIS IS JUST LIKE OLD TIMES DURIN' THE SOLAR WARS!
2000 A.D. Credit Card:
SCRIPT ROBOT GERRY FINLEY-DAY
ART ROBOT DAVE GIBBONS
LETTERING ROBOT DAVE GIBBONS
COMPU-73E
FORWARD PHASER BATTERIES --OPEN FIRE! HIT 'EM HARD!
BUT, ON THE REMAINING STARSLAYER SHIP...
STRAKK! FIRE AT WILL --RAKE THE INTRUDER FROM STEM TO STERN!

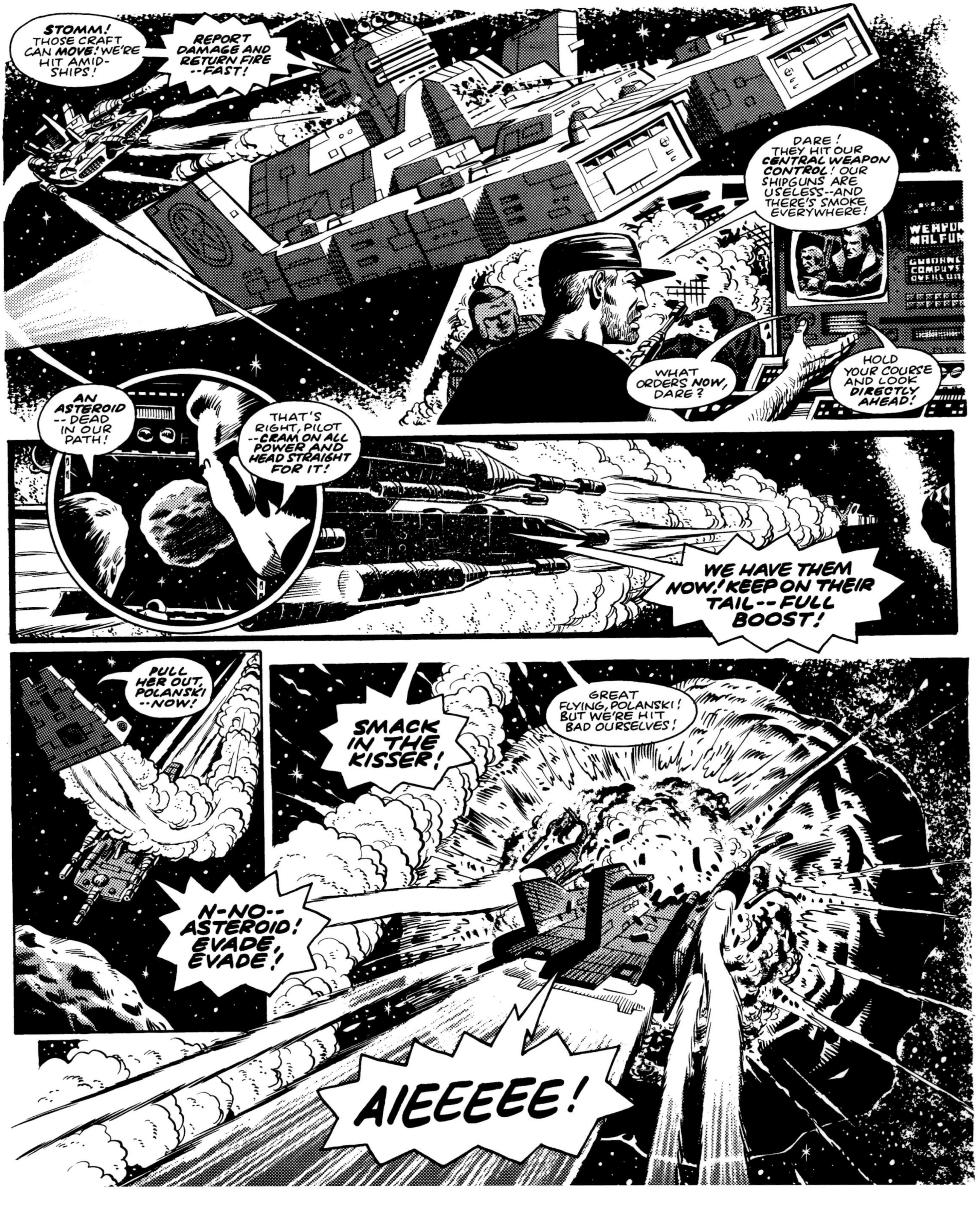

STOMM! THOSE CRAFT CAN MOVE! WE'RE HIT AMID-SHIPS!
REPORT DAMAGE AND RETURN FIRE --FAST!
DARE! THEY HIT OUR CENTRAL WEAPON CONTROL! OUR SHIPGUNS ARE USELESS--AND THERE'S SMOKE EVERYWHERE!
WHAT ORDERS NOW, DARE?
HOLD YOUR COURSE AND LOOK DIRECTLY AHEAD!
AN ASTEROID --DEAD IN OUR PATH!
THAT'S RIGHT, PILOT --CRAM ON ALL POWER AND HEAD STRAIGHT FOR IT!
WE HAVE THEM NOW! KEEP ON THEIR TAIL--FULL BOOST!
PULL HER OUT, POLANSKI --NOW!
N-NO-- ASTEROID! EVADE, EVADE!
SMACK IN THE KISSER!
GREAT FLYING, POLANSKI! BUT WE'RE HIT BAD OURSELVES!
AIEEEEE!

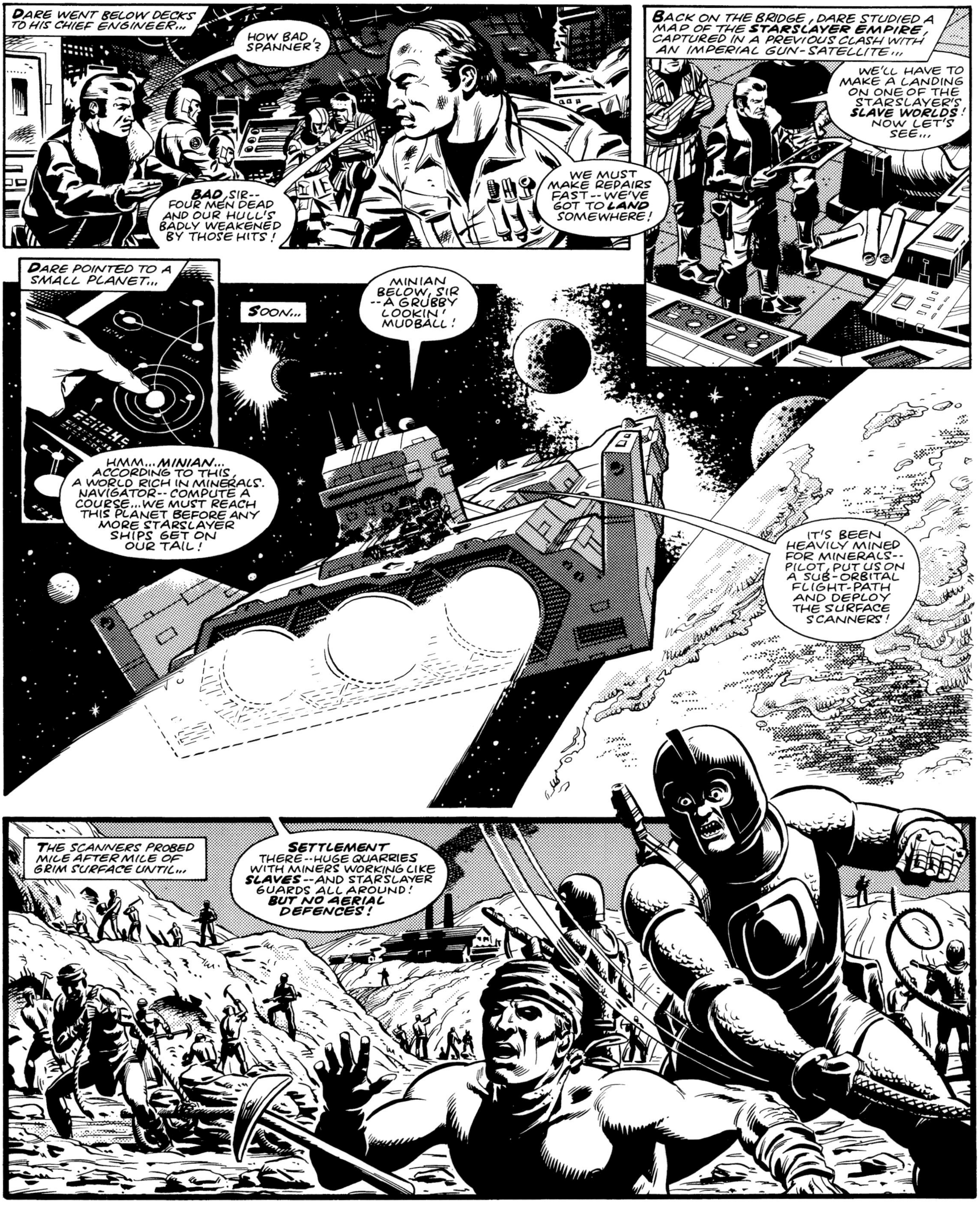
DARE WENT BELOW DECKS TO HIS CHIEF ENGINEER...
HOW BAD, SPANNER?
BAD, SIR-- FOUR MEN DEAD AND OUR HULL'S BADLY WEAKENED BY THOSE HITS!
WE MUST MAKE REPAIRS FAST--WE'VE GOT TO LAND SOMEWHERE!
BACK ON THE BRIDGE, DARE STUDIED A MAP OF THE STARSLAYER EMPIRE, CAPTURED IN A PREVIOUS CLASH WITH AN IMPERIAL GUN-SATELLITE...
WE'LL HAVE TO MAKE A LANDING ON ONE OF THE STARSLAYER'S SLAVE WORLDS! NOW LET'S SEE...
DARE POINTED TO A SMALL PLANET...
HMM... MINIAN... ACCORDING TO THIS, A WORLD RICH IN MINERALS. NAVIGATOR--COMPUTE A COURSE... WE MUST REACH THIS PLANET BEFORE ANY MORE STARSLAYER SHIPS GET ON OUR TAIL!
SOON...
MINIAN BELOW, SIR --A GRUBBY LOOKIN' MUDBALL!
IT'S BEEN HEAVILY MINED FOR MINERALS-- PILOT, PUT US ON A SUB-ORBITAL FLIGHT-PATH AND DEPLOY THE SURFACE SCANNERS!
THE SCANNERS PROBED MILE AFTER MILE OF GRIM SURFACE UNTIL...
SETTLEMENT THERE--HUGE QUARRIES WITH MINERS WORKING LIKE SLAVES--AND STARSLAYER GUARDS ALL AROUND! BUT NO AERIAL DEFENCES!

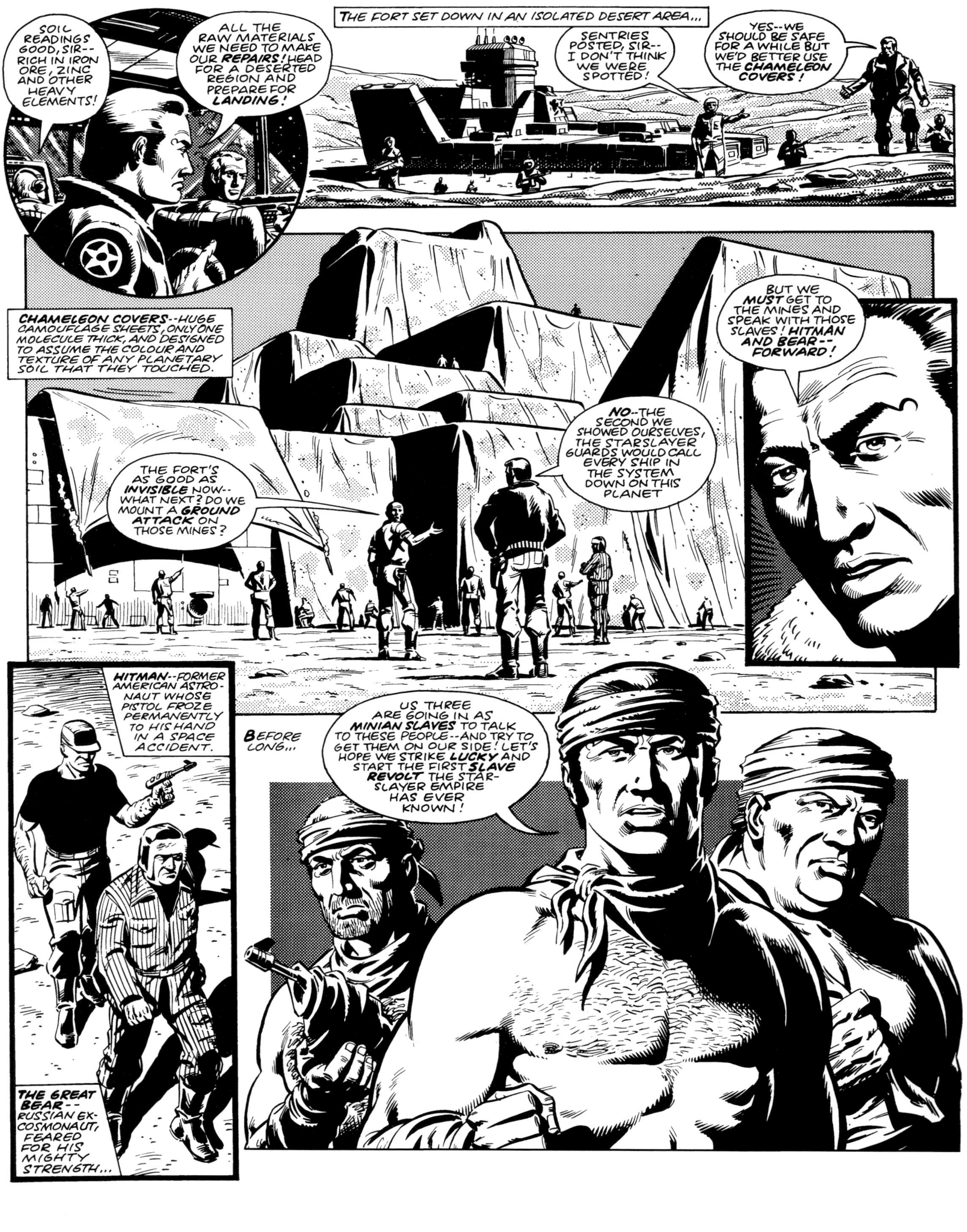

SOIL READINGS GOOD, SIR-- RICH IN IRON ORE, ZINC AND OTHER HEAVY ELEMENTS!
ALL THE RAW MATERIALS WE NEED TO MAKE OUR REPAIRS! HEAD FOR A DESERTED REGION AND PREPARE FOR LANDING!
THE FORT SET DOWN IN AN ISOLATED DESERT AREA...
SENTRIES POSTED, SIR-- I DON'T THINK WE WERE SPOTTED!
YES--WE SHOULD BE SAFE FOR A WHILE BUT WE'D BETTER USE THE CHAMELEON COVERS!
CHAMELEON COVERS--HUGE CAMOUFLAGE SHEETS, ONLY ONE MOLECULE THICK, AND DESIGNED TO ASSUME THE COLOUR AND TEXTURE OF ANY PLANETARY SOIL THAT THEY TOUCHED.
THE FORT'S AS GOOD AS INVISIBLE NOW-- WHAT NEXT? DO WE MOUNT A GROUND ATTACK ON THOSE MINES?
NO--THE SECOND WE SHOWED OURSELVES, THE STARSLAYER GUARDS WOULD CALL EVERY SHIP IN THE SYSTEM DOWN ON THIS PLANET
BUT WE MUST GET TO THE MINES AND SPEAK WITH THOSE SLAVES! HITMAN AND BEAR-- FORWARD!
HITMAN--FORMER AMERICAN ASTRONAUT WHOSE PISTOL FROZE PERMANENTLY TO HIS HAND IN A SPACE ACCIDENT.
THE GREAT BEAR-- RUSSIAN EX-COSMONAUT, FEARED FOR HIS MIGHTY STRENGTH...
BEFORE LONG...
US THREE ARE GOING IN AS MINIAN SLAVES TO TALK TO THESE PEOPLE--AND TRY TO GET THEM ON OUR SIDE! LET'S HOPE WE STRIKE LUCKY AND START THE FIRST SLAVE REVOLT THE STAR-SLAYER EMPIRE HAS EVER KNOWN!

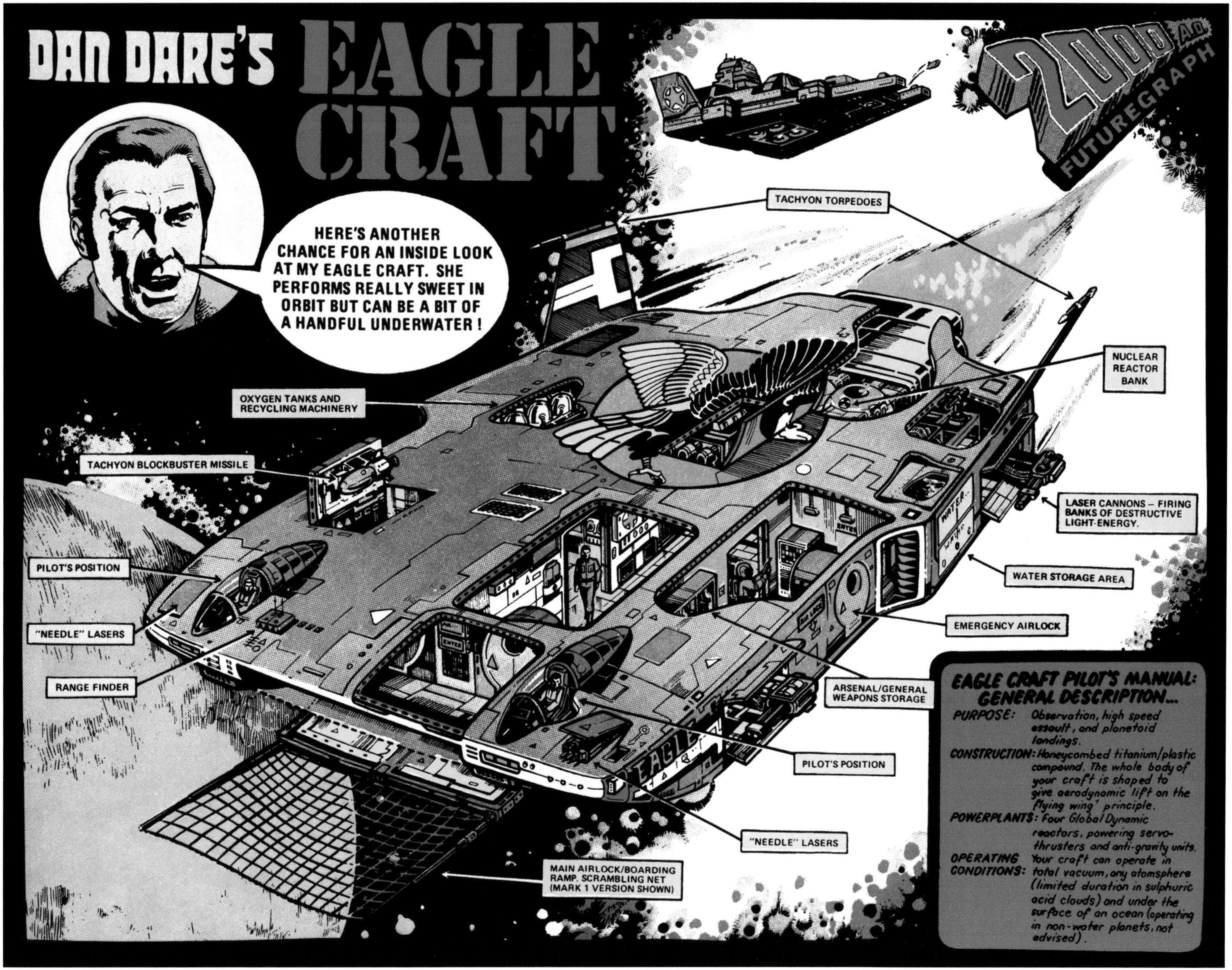

DAN DARE'S EAGLE CRAFT
2000 A.D. FUTUREGRAPH
HERE'S ANOTHER CHANCE FOR AN INSIDE LOOK AT MY EAGLE CRAFT. SHE PERFORMS REALLY SWEET IN ORBIT BUT CAN BE A BIT OF A HANDFUL UNDERWATER !
TACHYON TORPEDOES
NUCLEAR REACTOR BANK
OXYGEN TANKS AND RECYCLING MACHINERY
TACHYON BLOCKBUSTER MISSILE
LASER CANNONS – FIRING BANKS OF DESTRUCTIVE LIGHT-ENERGY.
WATER STORAGE AREA
PILOT'S POSITION
"NEEDLE" LASERS
RANGE FINDER
EMERGENCY AIRLOCK
ARSENAL/GENERAL WEAPONS STORAGE
PILOT'S POSITION
"NEEDLE" LASERS
MAIN AIRLOCK/BOARDING RAMP. SCRAMBLING NET (MARK 1 VERSION SHOWN)
EAGLE CRAFT PILOT'S MANUAL: GENERAL DESCRIPTION...
PURPOSE: Observation, high speed assault, and planetoid landings.
CONSTRUCTION: Honeycombed titanium/plastic compound. The whole body of your craft is shaped to give aerodynamic lift on the 'flying wing' principle.
POWERPLANTS: Four Global Dynamic reactors, powering servo-thrusters and anti-gravity units.
OPERATING CONDITIONS: Your craft can operate in total vacuum, any atomsphere (limited duration in sulphuric acid clouds) and under the surface of an ocean (operating in non-water planets, not advised).

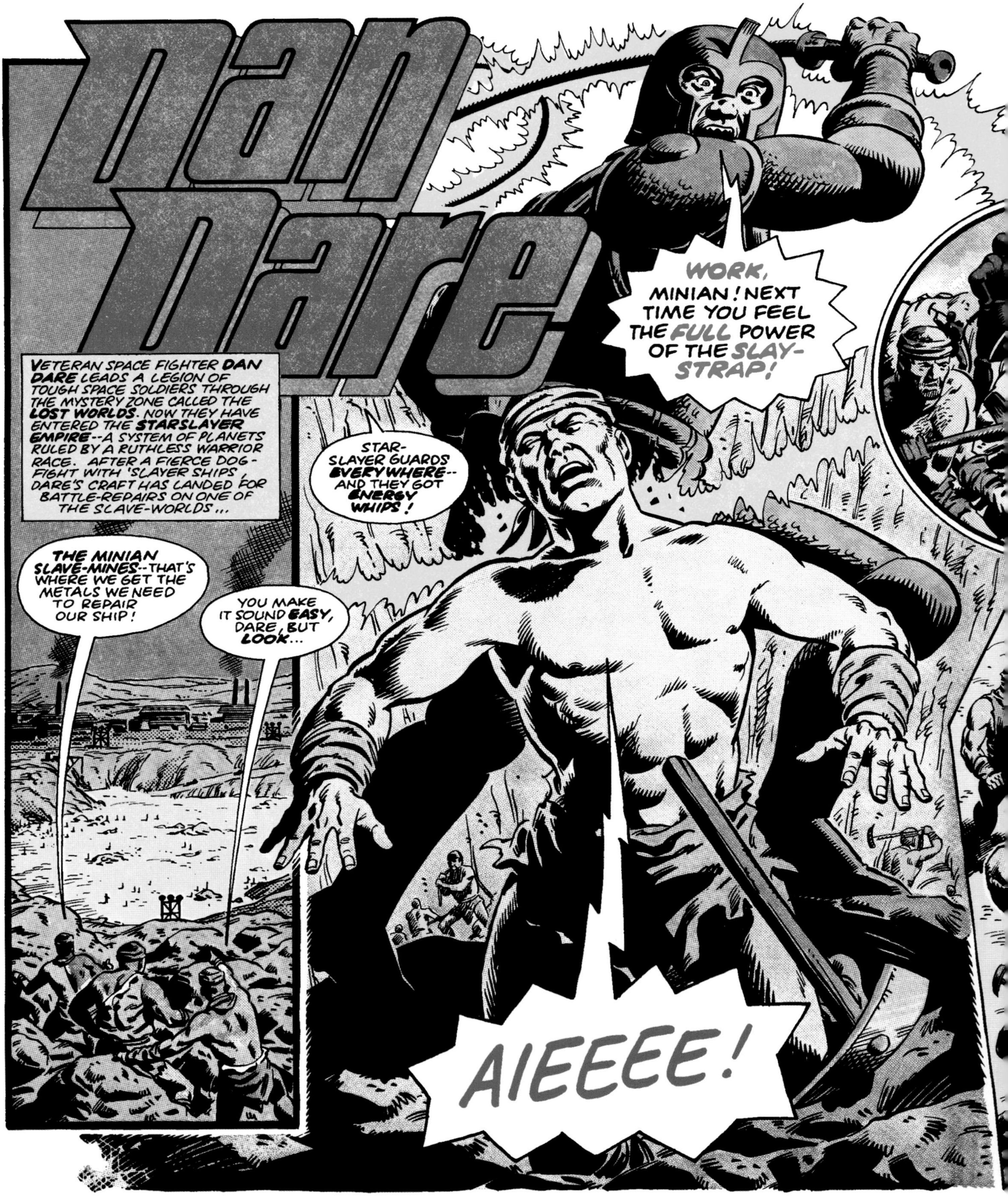
Dan Dare
VETERAN SPACE FIGHTER DAN DARE LEADS A LEGION OF TOUGH SPACE SOLDIERS THROUGH THE MYSTERY ZONE CALLED THE LOST WORLDS. NOW THEY HAVE ENTERED THE STARSLAYER EMPIRE--A SYSTEM OF PLANETS RULED BY A RUTHLESS WARRIOR RACE. AFTER A FIERCE DOG-FIGHT WITH 'SLAYER SHIPS, DARE'S CRAFT HAS LANDED FOR BATTLE-REPAIRS ON ONE OF THE SLAVE-WORLDS...
THE MINIAN SLAVE-MINES--THAT'S WHERE WE GET THE METALS WE NEED TO REPAIR OUR SHIP!
YOU MAKE IT SOUND EASY, DARE, BUT LOOK...
STAR-SLAYER GUARDS EVERYWHERE--AND THEY GOT ENERGY WHIPS!
WORK, MINIAN! NEXT TIME YOU FEEL THE FULL POWER OF THE SLAY-STRAP!
AIEEEE!

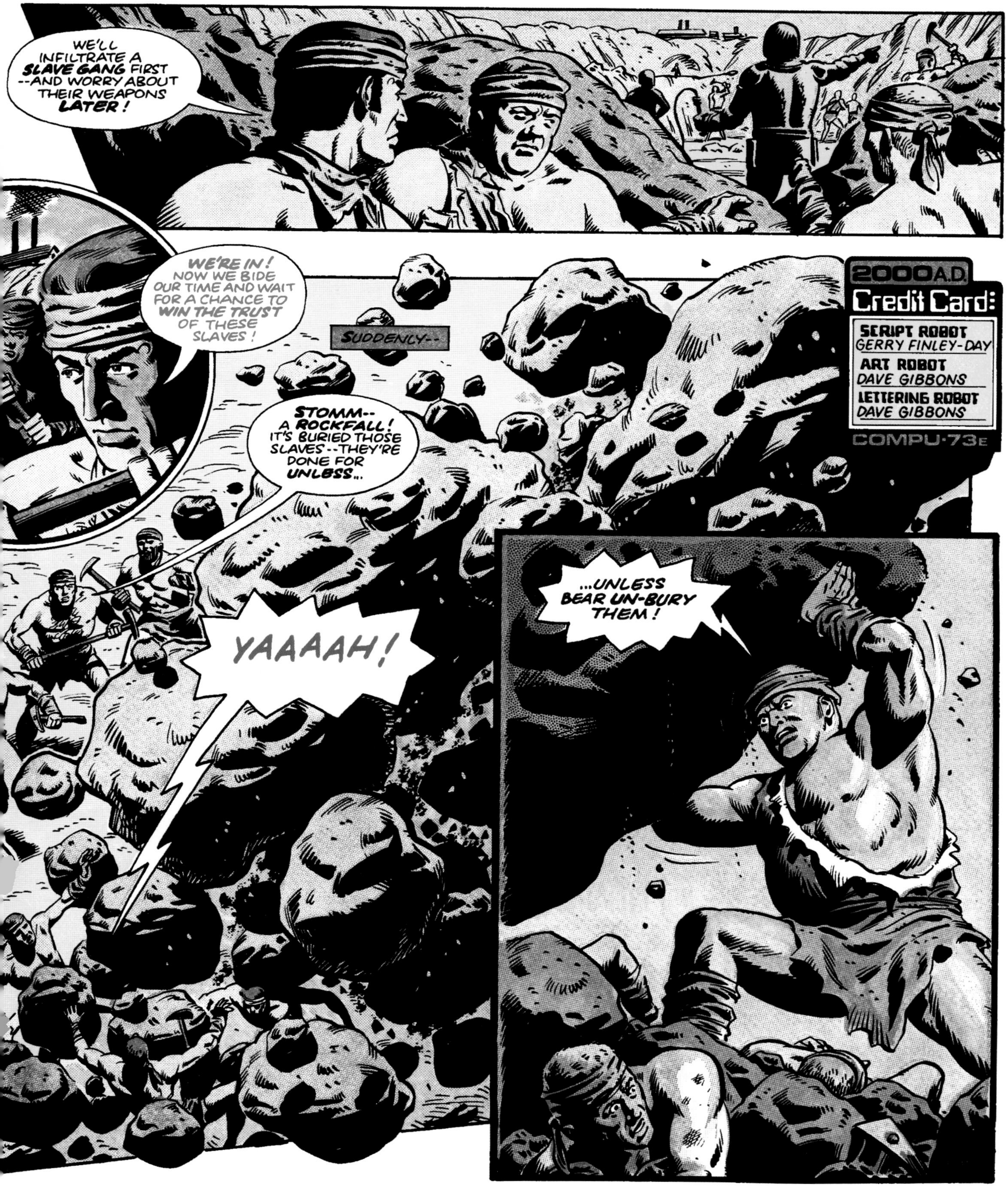

WE'LL INFILTRATE A SLAVE GANG FIRST --AND WORRY ABOUT THEIR WEAPONS LATER!
WE'RE IN! NOW WE BIDE OUR TIME AND WAIT FOR A CHANCE TO WIN THE TRUST OF THESE SLAVES!
SUDDENLY--
2000 A.D. Credit Card:
SCRIPT ROBOT GERRY FINLEY-DAY
ART ROBOT DAVE GIBBONS
LETTERING ROBOT DAVE GIBBONS
COMPU-73E
STOMM-- A ROCKFALL! IT'S BURIED THOSE SLAVES--THEY'RE DONE FOR UNLESS...
YAAAAH!
...UNLESS BEAR UN-BURY THEM!

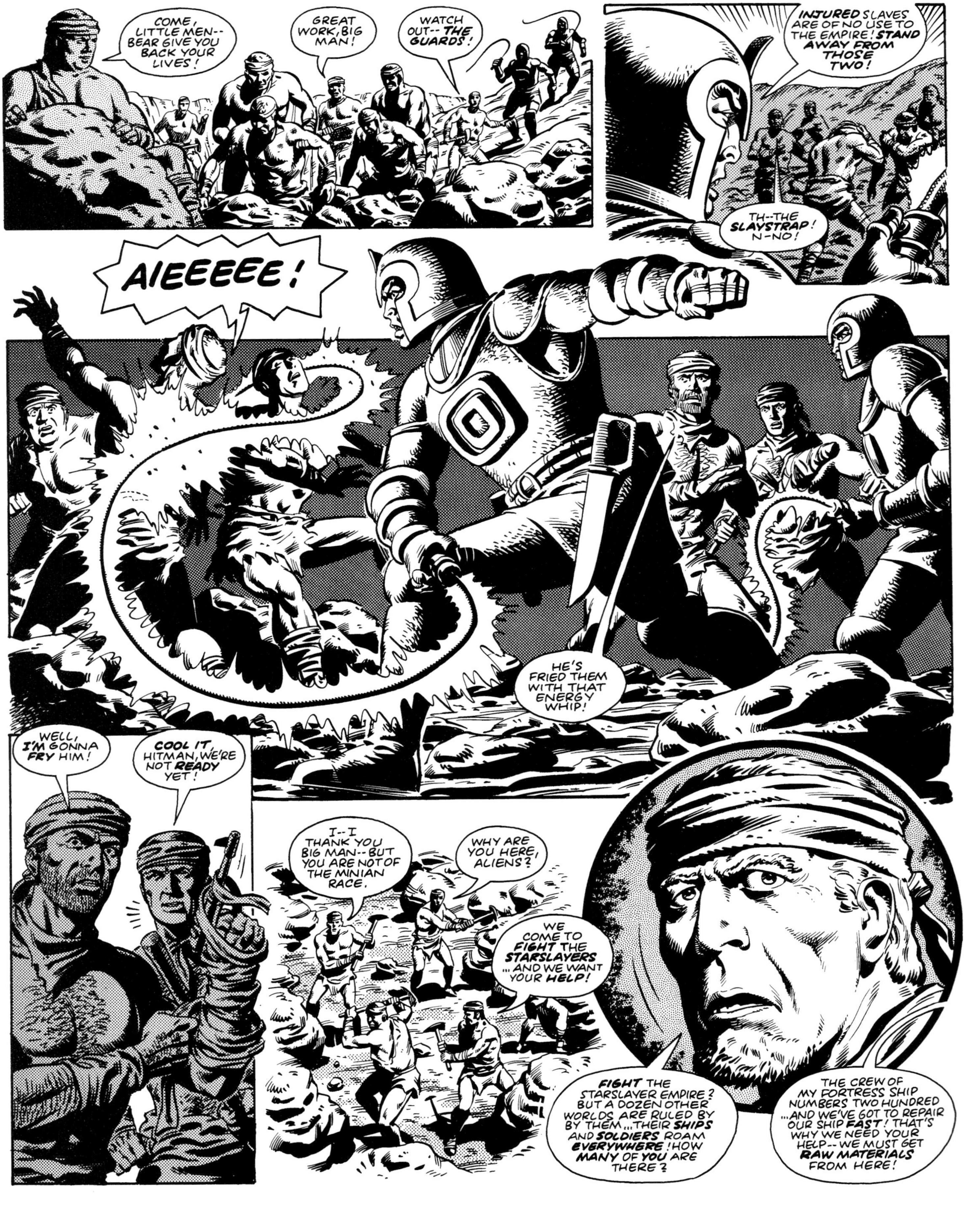

COME, LITTLE MEN-- BEAR GIVE YOU BACK YOUR LIVES!
GREAT WORK, BIG MAN!
WATCH OUT-- THE GUARDS!
INJURED SLAVES ARE OF NO USE TO THE EMPIRE! STAND AWAY FROM THOSE TWO!
TH--THE SLAYSTRAP! N-NO!
AIEEEEE!
HE'S FRIED THEM WITH THAT ENERGY WHIP!
WELL, I'M GONNA FRY HIM!
COOL IT, HITMAN, WE'RE NOT READY YET!
I--I THANK YOU BIG MAN--BUT YOU ARE NOT OF THE MINIAN RACE.
WHY ARE YOU HERE, ALIENS?
WE COME TO FIGHT THE STARSLAYERS ...AND WE WANT YOUR HELP!
FIGHT THE STARSLAYER EMPIRE? BUT A DOZEN OTHER WORLDS ARE RULED BY BY THEM... THEIR SHIPS AND SOLDIERS ROAM EVERYWHERE! HOW MANY OF YOU ARE THERE?
THE CREW OF MY FORTRESS SHIP NUMBERS TWO HUNDRED ...AND WE'VE GOT TO REPAIR OUR SHIP FAST! THAT'S WHY WE NEED YOUR HELP-- WE MUST GET RAW MATERIALS FROM HERE!

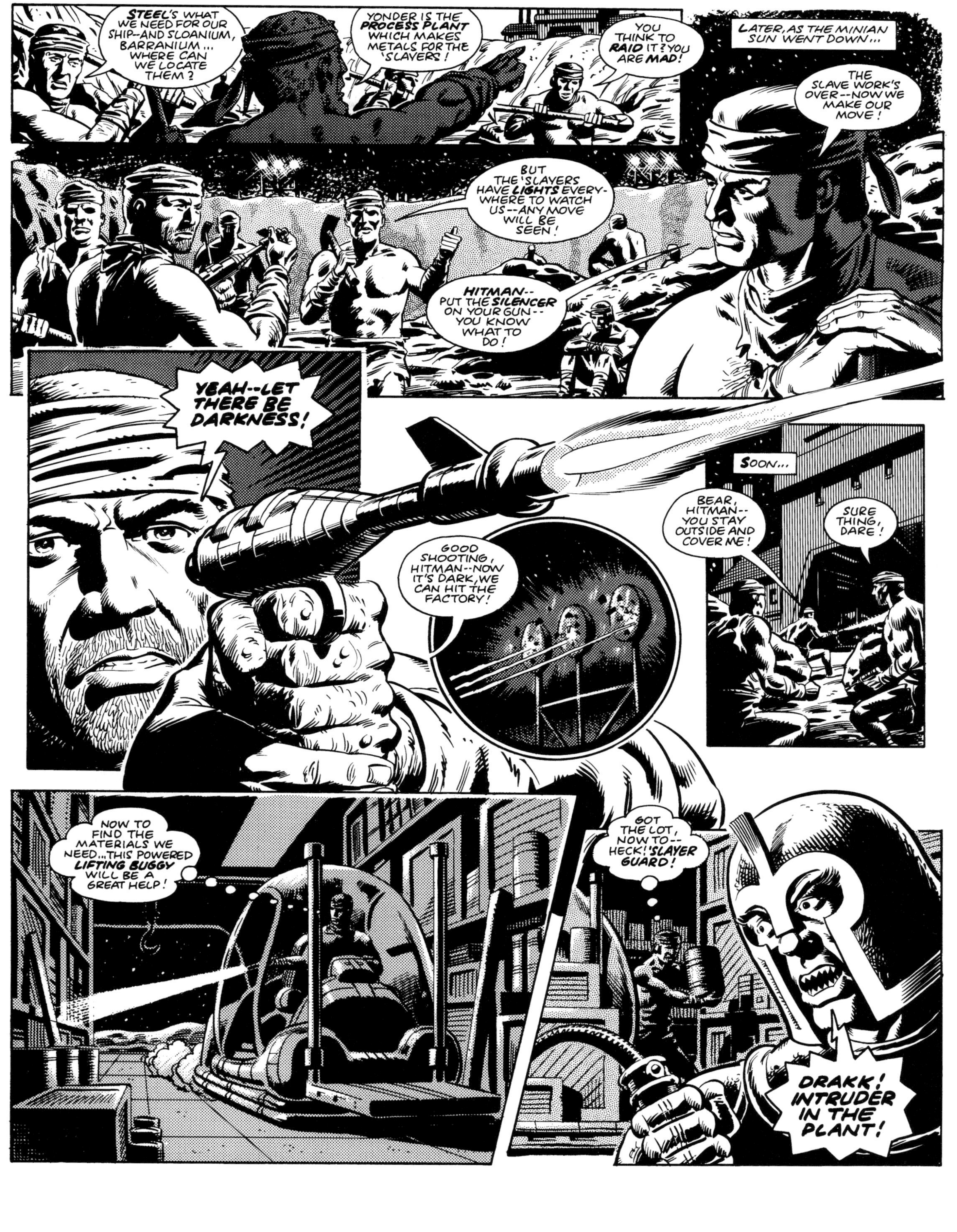
STEEL'S WHAT WE NEED FOR OUR SHIP--AND SLOANIUM, BARRANIUM ... WHERE CAN WE LOCATE THEM?
YONDER IS THE PROCESS PLANT WHICH MAKES METALS FOR THE 'SLAYERS!
YOU THINK TO RAID IT? YOU ARE MAD!
LATER, AS THE MINIAN SUN WENT DOWN...
THE SLAVE WORK'S OVER--NOW WE MAKE OUR MOVE!
BUT THE 'SLAYERS HAVE LIGHTS EVERY-WHERE TO WATCH US--ANY MOVE WILL BE SEEN!
HITMAN--PUT THE SILENCER ON YOUR GUN--YOU KNOW WHAT TO DO!
YEAH--LET THERE BE DARKNESS!
GOOD SHOOTING, HITMAN--NOW IT'S DARK, WE CAN HIT THE FACTORY!
SOON...
BEAR, HITMAN--YOU STAY OUTSIDE AND COVER ME!
SURE THING, DARE!
NOW TO FIND THE MATERIALS WE NEED...THIS POWERED LIFTING BUGGY WILL BE A GREAT HELP!
GOT THE LOT, NOW TO--HECK! 'SLAYER GUARD!
DRAKK! INTRUDER IN THE PLANT!

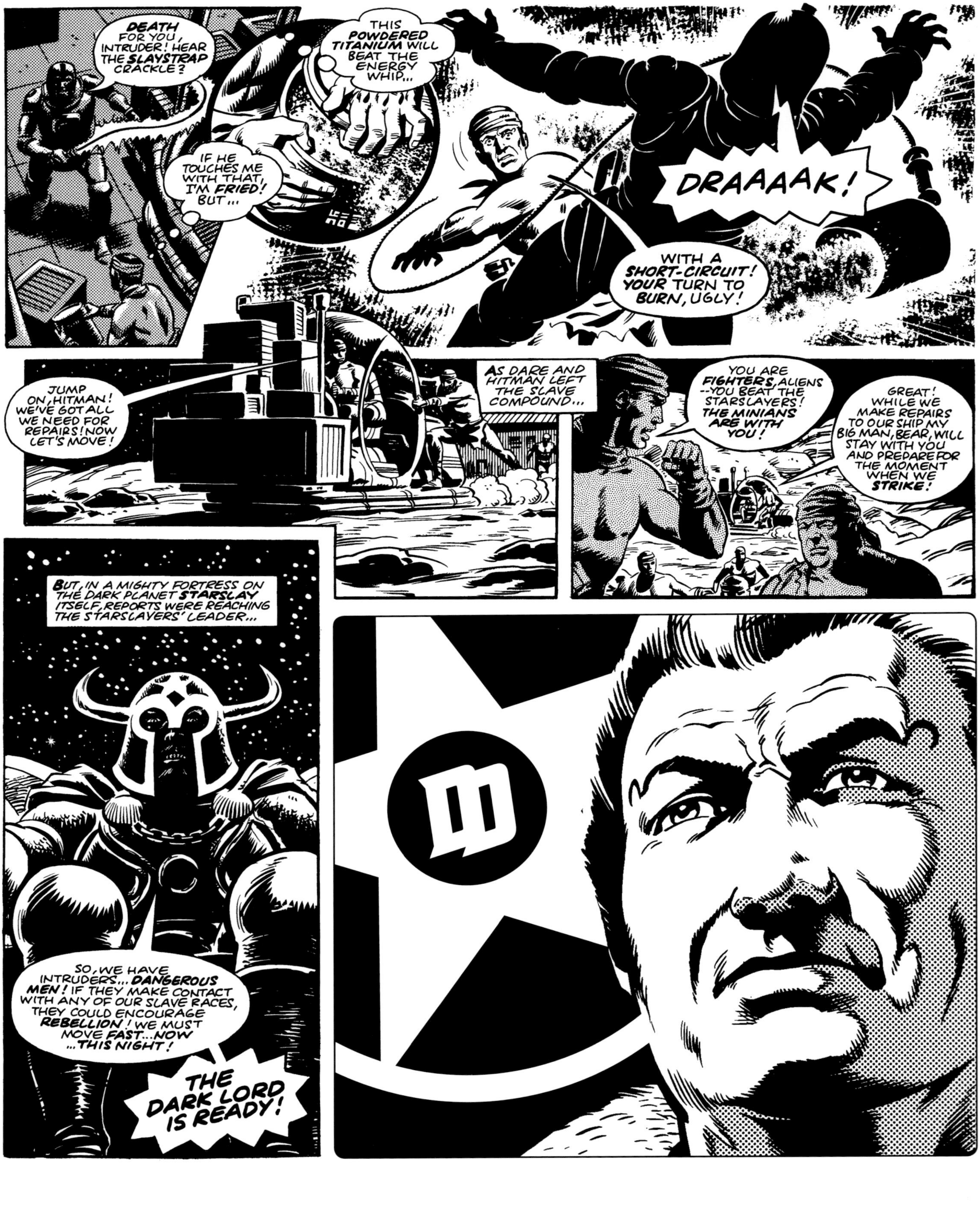

DEATH FOR YOU, INTRUDER! HEAR THE SLAYSTRAP CRACKLE?
THIS POWDERED TITANIUM WILL BEAT THE ENERGY WHIP...
IF HE TOUCHES ME WITH THAT, I'M FRIED! BUT...
DRAAAAK!
WITH A SHORT-CIRCUIT! YOUR TURN TO BURN, UGLY!
JUMP ON, HITMAN! WE'VE GOT ALL WE NEED FOR REPAIRS! NOW LET'S MOVE!
AS DARE AND HITMAN LEFT THE SLAVE COMPOUND...
YOU ARE FIGHTERS, ALIENS --YOU BEAT THE STARSLAYERS! THE MINIANS ARE WITH YOU!
GREAT! WHILE WE MAKE REPAIRS TO OUR SHIP MY BIG MAN, BEAR, WILL STAY WITH YOU AND PREPARE FOR THE MOMENT WHEN WE STRIKE!
BUT, IN A MIGHTY FORTRESS ON THE DARK PLANET STARSLAY ITSELF, REPORTS WERE REACHING THE STARSLAYERS' LEADER...
SO, WE HAVE INTRUDERS... DANGEROUS MEN! IF THEY MAKE CONTACT WITH ANY OF OUR SLAVE RACES, THEY COULD ENCOURAGE REBELLION! WE MUST MOVE FAST... NOW ...THIS NIGHT!
THE DARK LORD IS READY!

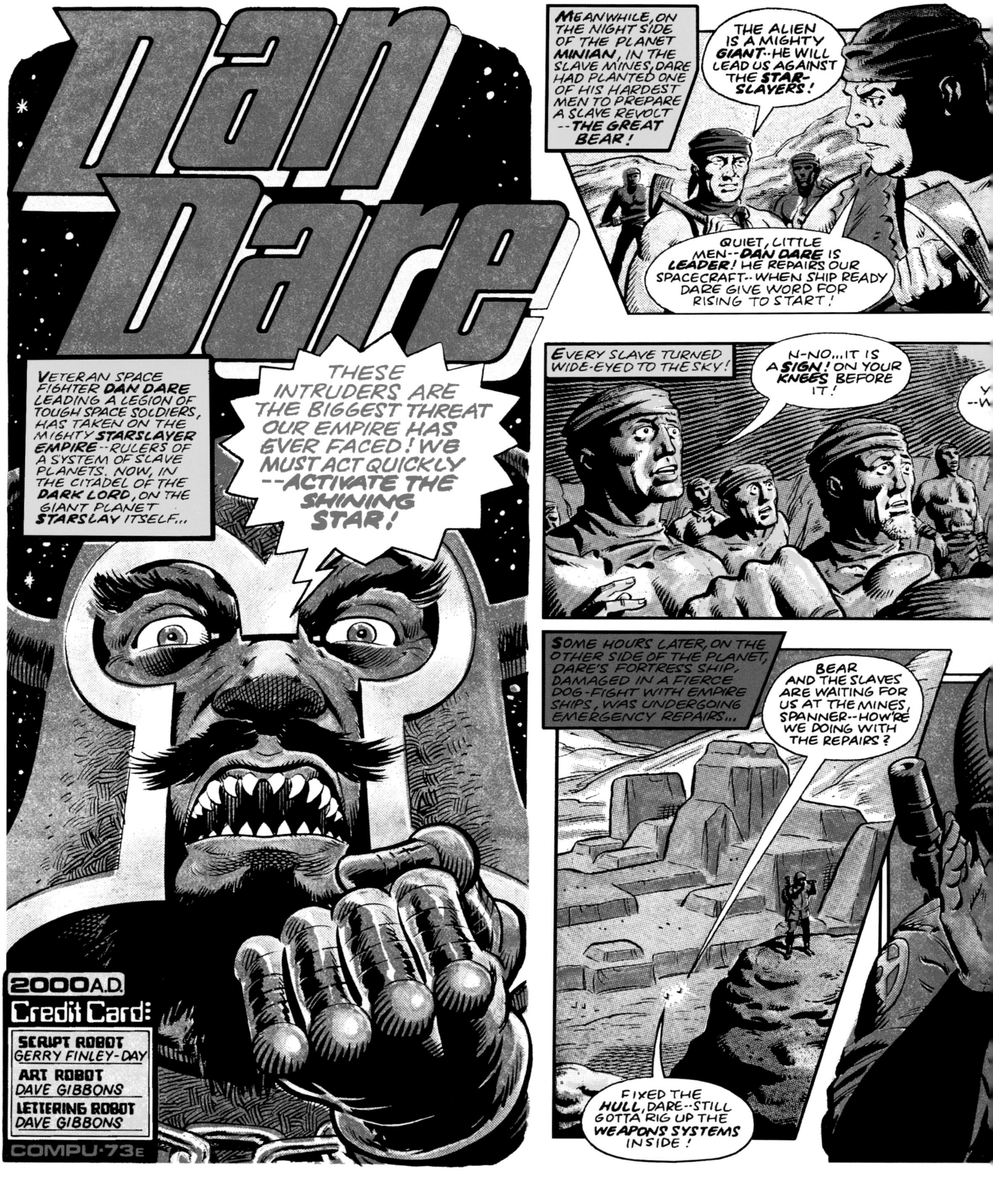
Dan Dare
VETERAN SPACE FIGHTER DAN DARE LEADING A LEGION OF TOUGH SPACE SOLDIERS, HAS TAKEN ON THE MIGHTY STARSLAYER EMPIRE --RULERS OF A SYSTEM OF SLAVE PLANETS. NOW, IN THE CITADEL OF THE DARK LORD, ON THE GIANT PLANET STARSLAY ITSELF...
THESE INTRUDERS ARE THE BIGGEST THREAT OUR EMPIRE HAS EVER FACED! WE MUST ACT QUICKLY --ACTIVATE THE SHINING STAR!
2000 A.D. Credit Card:
SCRIPT ROBOT GERRY FINLEY-DAY
ART ROBOT DAVE GIBBONS
LETTERING ROBOT DAVE GIBBONS
COMPU-73E
MEANWHILE, ON THE NIGHT SIDE OF THE PLANET MINIAN, IN THE SLAVE MINES, DARE HAD PLANTED ONE OF HIS HARDEST MEN TO PREPARE A SLAVE REVOLT --THE GREAT BEAR!
THE ALIEN IS A MIGHTY GIANT--HE WILL LEAD US AGAINST THE STAR-SLAYERS!
QUIET, LITTLE MEN--DAN DARE IS LEADER! HE REPAIRS OUR SPACECRAFT--WHEN SHIP READY DARE GIVE WORD FOR RISING TO START!
EVERY SLAVE TURNED WIDE-EYED TO THE SKY!
N-NO...IT IS A SIGN! ON YOUR KNEES BEFORE IT!
SOME HOURS LATER, ON THE OTHER SIDE OF THE PLANET, DARE'S FORTRESS SHIP, DAMAGED IN A FIERCE DOG-FIGHT WITH EMPIRE SHIPS, WAS UNDERGOING EMERGENCY REPAIRS...
BEAR AND THE SLAVES ARE WAITING FOR US AT THE MINES, SPANNER--HOW'RE WE DOING WITH THE REPAIRS?
FIXED THE HULL, DARE--STILL GOTTA RIG UP THE WEAPONS SYSTEMS INSIDE!

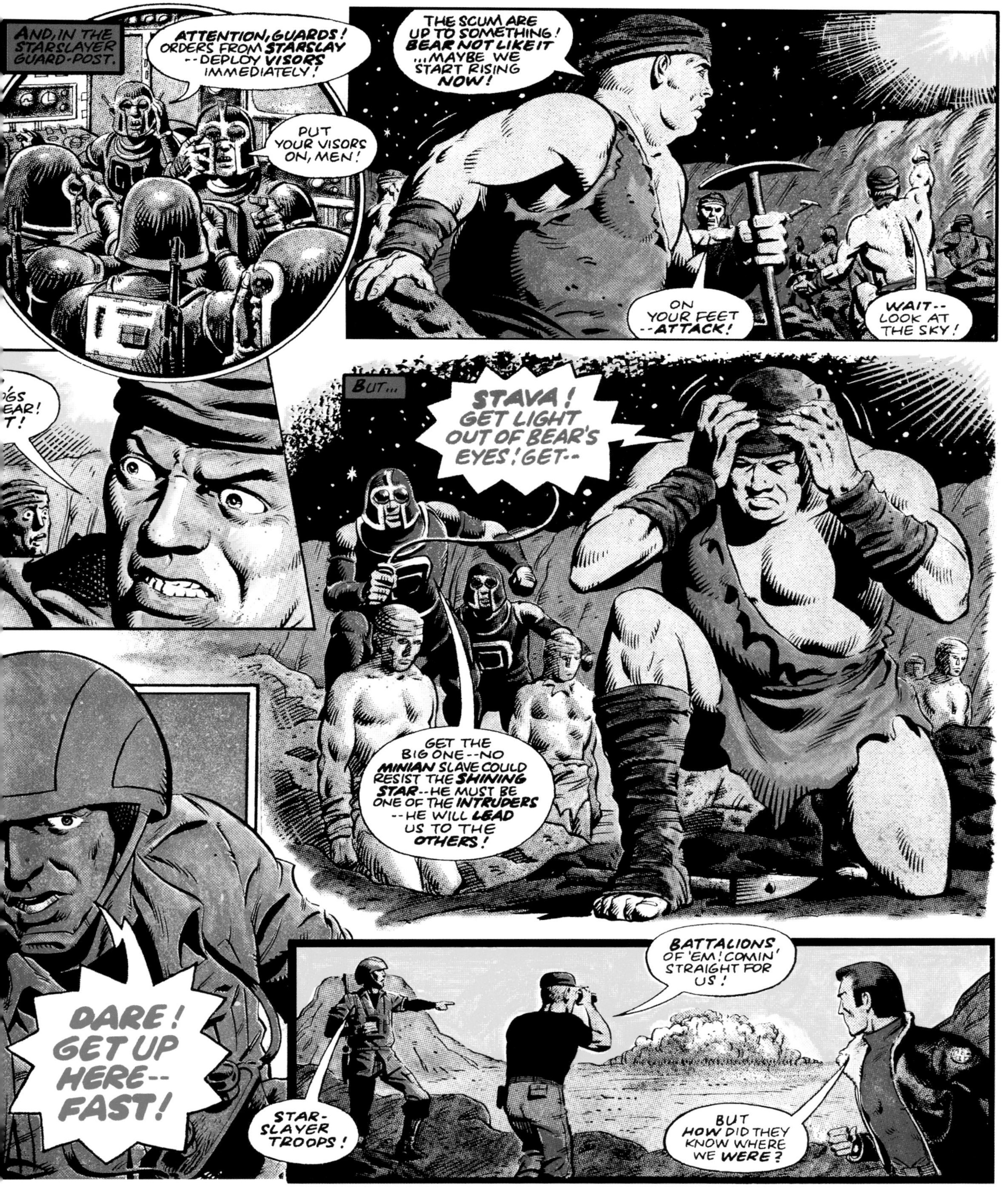
AND, IN THE STARSLAYER GUARD-POST.
ATTENTION, GUARDS! ORDERS FROM STARSLAY --DEPLOY VISORS IMMEDIATELY!
PUT YOUR VISORS ON, MEN!
THE SCUM ARE UP TO SOMETHING! BEAR NOT LIKE IT ...MAYBE WE START RISING NOW!
ON YOUR FEET --ATTACK!
WAIT-- LOOK AT THE SKY!
BUT...
STAVA! GET LIGHT OUT OF BEAR'S EYES! GET--
GET THE BIG ONE--NO MINIAN SLAVE COULD RESIST THE SHINING STAR--HE MUST BE ONE OF THE INTRUDERS --HE WILL LEAD US TO THE OTHERS!
DARE! GET UP HERE-- FAST!
BATTALIONS OF 'EM! COMIN' STRAIGHT FOR US!
STAR-SLAYER TROOPS!
BUT HOW DID THEY KNOW WHERE WE WERE?

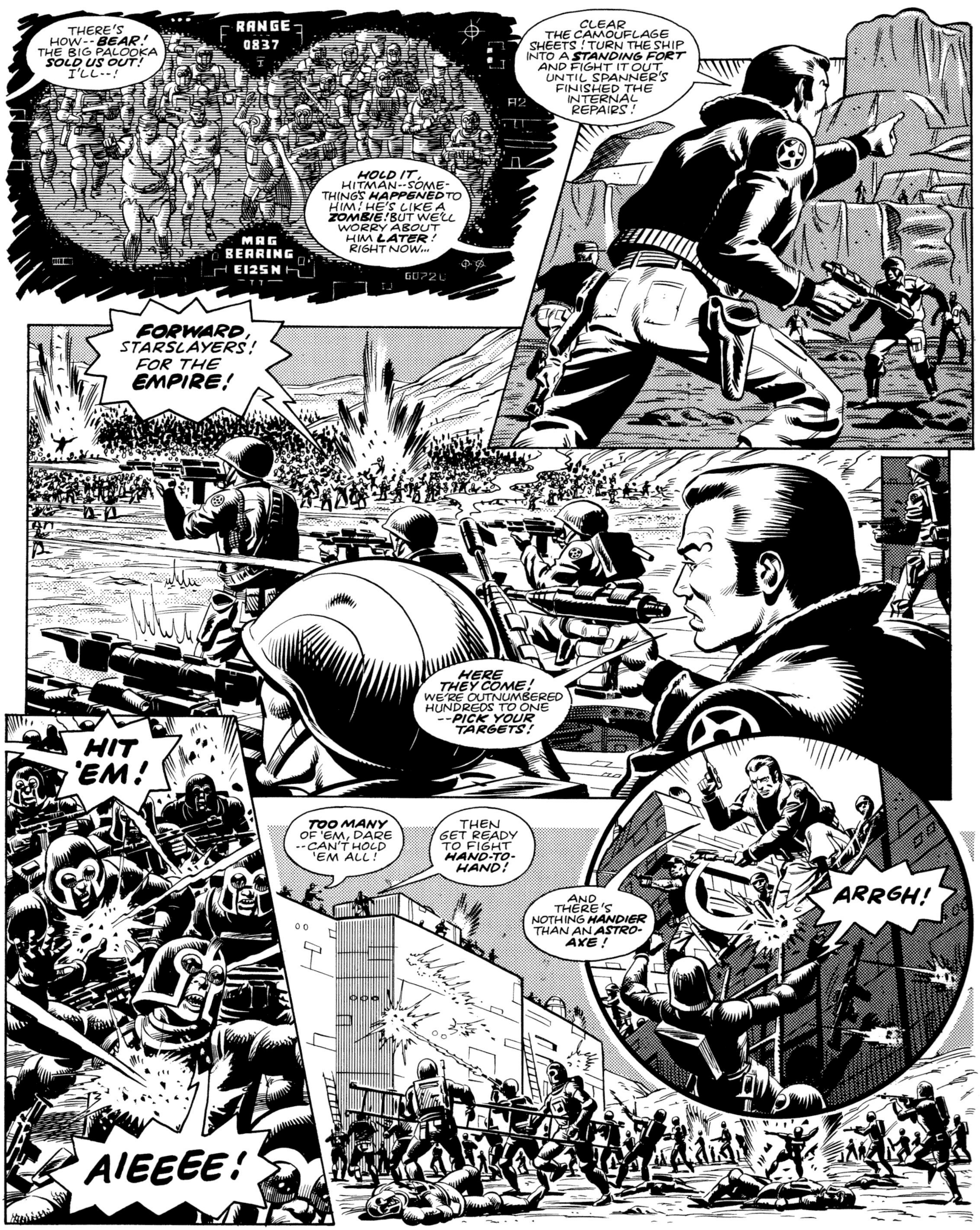
THERE'S HOW--BEAR! THE BIG PALOOKA SOLD US OUT! I'LL--!
RANGE 0837
HOLD IT, HITMAN--SOMETHING'S HAPPENED TO HIM! HE'S LIKE A ZOMBIE! BUT WE'LL WORRY ABOUT HIM LATER! RIGHT NOW...
MAG BEARING E125N
CLEAR THE CAMOUFLAGE SHEETS! TURN THE SHIP INTO A STANDING FORT AND FIGHT IT OUT UNTIL SPANNER'S FINISHED THE INTERNAL REPAIRS!
FORWARD, STARSLAYERS! FOR THE EMPIRE!
HERE THEY COME! WE'RE OUTNUMBERED HUNDREDS TO ONE --PICK YOUR TARGETS!
HIT 'EM!
AIEEEE!
TOO MANY OF 'EM, DARE --CAN'T HOLD 'EM ALL!
THEN GET READY TO FIGHT HAND-TO-HAND!
AND THERE'S NOTHING HANDIER THAN AN ASTRO-AXE!
ARRGH!

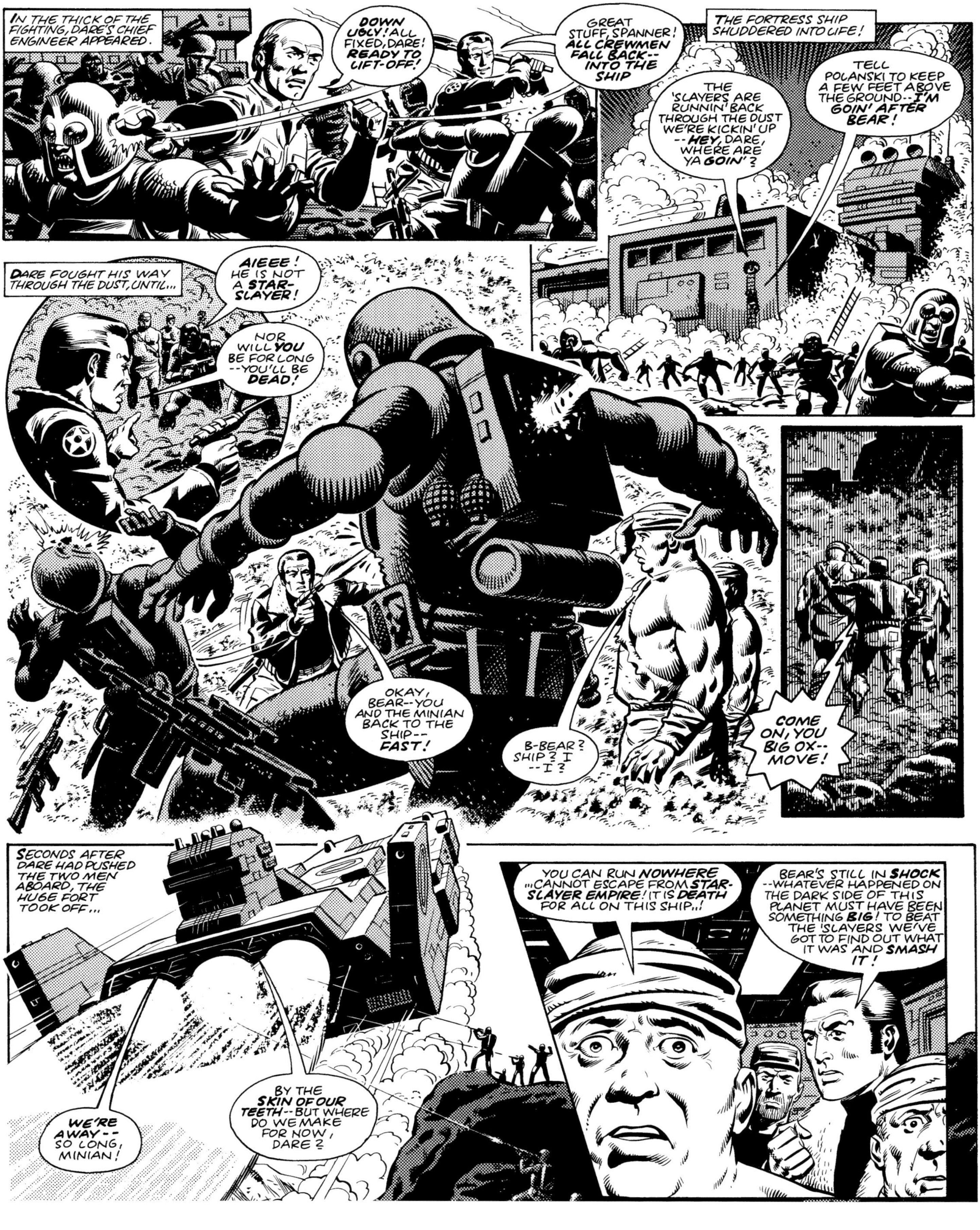
IN THE THICK OF THE FIGHTING, DARE'S CHIEF ENGINEER APPEARED.
DOWN UGLY! ALL FIXED, DARE! READY TO LIFT-OFF!
GREAT STUFF, SPANNER! ALL CREWMEN FALL BACK-- INTO THE SHIP
THE FORTRESS SHIP SHUDDERED INTO LIFE!
THE 'SLAYERS ARE RUNNIN' BACK THROUGH THE DUST WE'RE KICKIN' UP --HEY, DARE, WHERE ARE YA GOIN'?
TELL POLANSKI TO KEEP A FEW FEET ABOVE THE GROUND--I'M GOIN' AFTER BEAR!
DARE FOUGHT HIS WAY THROUGH THE DUST, UNTIL...
AIEEE! HE IS NOT A STAR-SLAYER!
NOR WILL YOU BE FOR LONG --YOU'LL BE DEAD!
OKAY, BEAR--YOU AND THE MINIAN BACK TO THE SHIP-- FAST!
B-BEAR? SHIP? I --I?
COME ON, YOU BIG OX-- MOVE!
SECONDS AFTER DARE HAD PUSHED THE TWO MEN ABOARD, THE HUGE FORT TOOK OFF...
WE'RE AWAY-- SO LONG, MINIAN!
BY THE SKIN OF OUR TEETH--BUT WHERE DO WE MAKE FOR NOW, DARE?
YOU CAN RUN NOWHERE ...CANNOT ESCAPE FROM STAR-SLAYER EMPIRE! IT IS DEATH FOR ALL ON THIS SHIP...!
BEAR'S STILL IN SHOCK --WHATEVER HAPPENED ON THE DARK SIDE OF THIS PLANET MUST HAVE BEEN SOMETHING BIG! TO BEAT THE 'SLAYERS WE'VE GOT TO FIND OUT WHAT IT WAS AND SMASH IT!

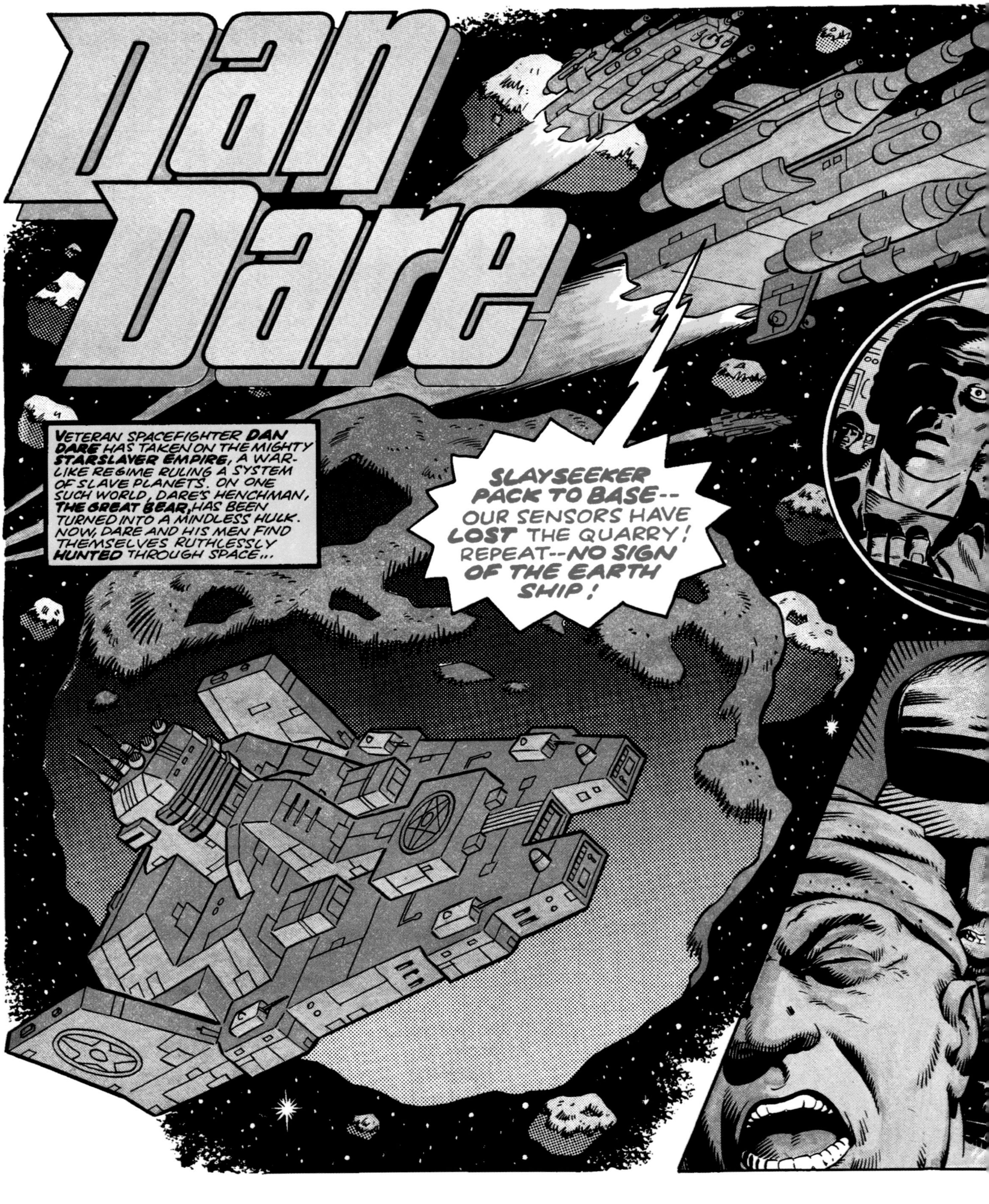
Dan Dare
VETERAN SPACEFIGHTER DAN DARE HAS TAKEN ON THE MIGHTY STARSLAYER EMPIRE, A WAR-LIKE REGIME RULING A SYSTEM OF SLAVE PLANETS. ON ONE SUCH WORLD, DARE'S HENCHMAN, THE GREAT BEAR, HAS BEEN TURNED INTO A MINDLESS HULK. NOW, DARE AND HIS MEN FIND THEMSELVES RUTHLESSLY HUNTED THROUGH SPACE...
SLAYSEEKER PACK TO BASE-- OUR SENSORS HAVE LOST THE QUARRY! REPEAT--NO SIGN OF THE EARTH SHIP!

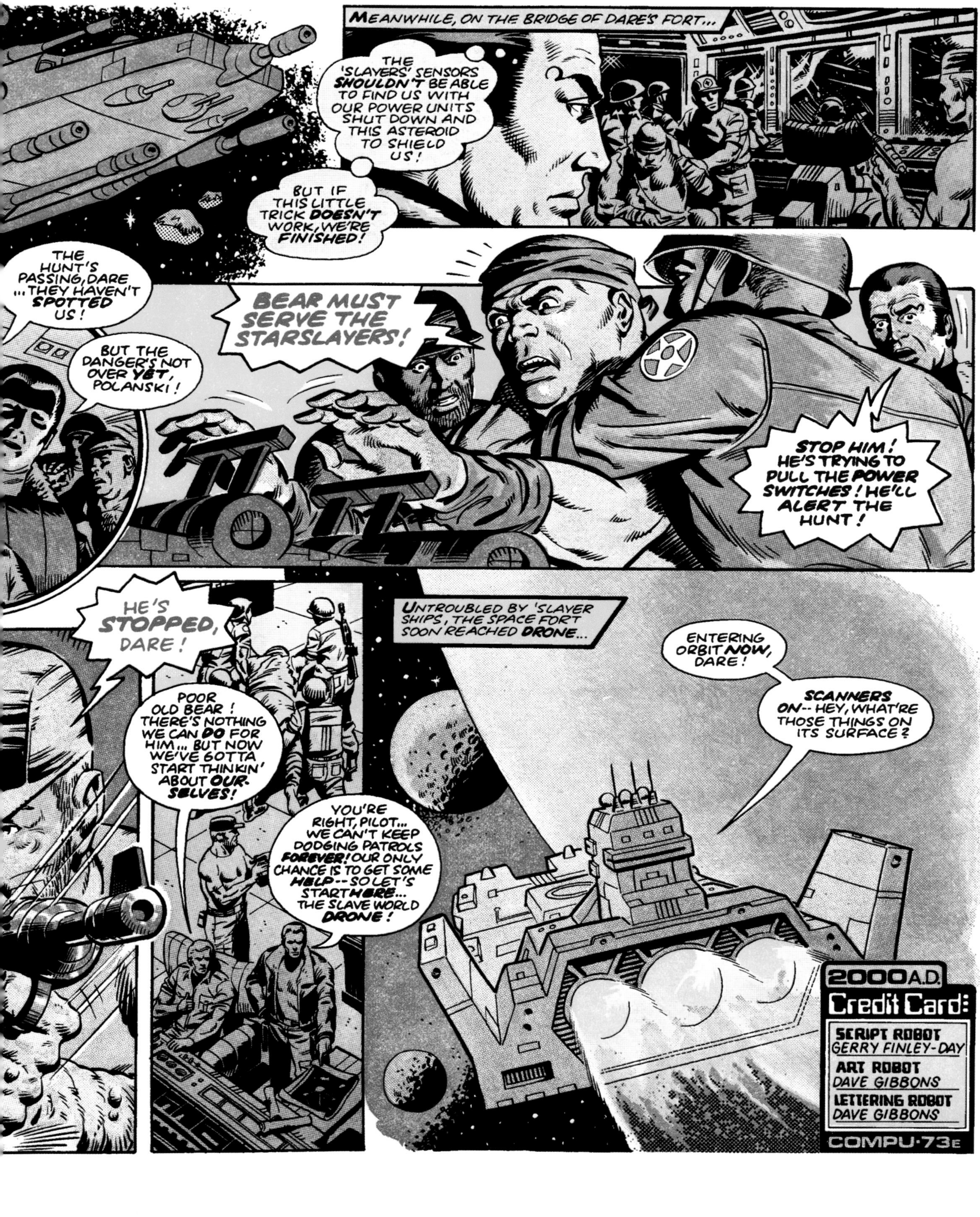

MEANWHILE, ON THE BRIDGE OF DARE'S FORT...
THE 'SLAYERS' SENSORS SHOULDN'T BE ABLE TO FIND US WITH OUR POWER UNITS SHUT DOWN AND THIS ASTEROID TO SHIELD US!
BUT IF THIS LITTLE TRICK DOESN'T WORK, WE'RE FINISHED!
THE HUNT'S PASSING, DARE ...THEY HAVEN'T SPOTTED US!
BUT THE DANGER'S NOT OVER YET, POLANSKI!
BEAR MUST SERVE THE STARSLAYERS!
STOP HIM! HE'S TRYING TO PULL THE POWER SWITCHES! HE'LL ALERT THE HUNT!
HE'S STOPPED, DARE!
POOR OLD BEAR! THERE'S NOTHING WE CAN DO FOR HIM... BUT NOW WE'VE GOTTA START THINKIN' ABOUT OURSELVES!
YOU'RE RIGHT, PILOT... WE CAN'T KEEP DODGING PATROLS FOREVER! OUR ONLY CHANCE IS TO GET SOME HELP-- SO LET'S START HERE... THE SLAVE WORLD DRONE!
UNTROUBLED BY 'SLAYER SHIPS, THE SPACE FORT SOON REACHED DRONE...
ENTERING ORBIT NOW, DARE!
SCANNERS ON-- HEY, WHAT'RE THOSE THINGS ON ITS SURFACE?
2000 A.D. Credit Card:
SCRIPT ROBOT GERRY FINLEY-DAY
ART ROBOT DAVE GIBBONS
LETTERING ROBOT DAVE GIBBONS
COMPU-73E

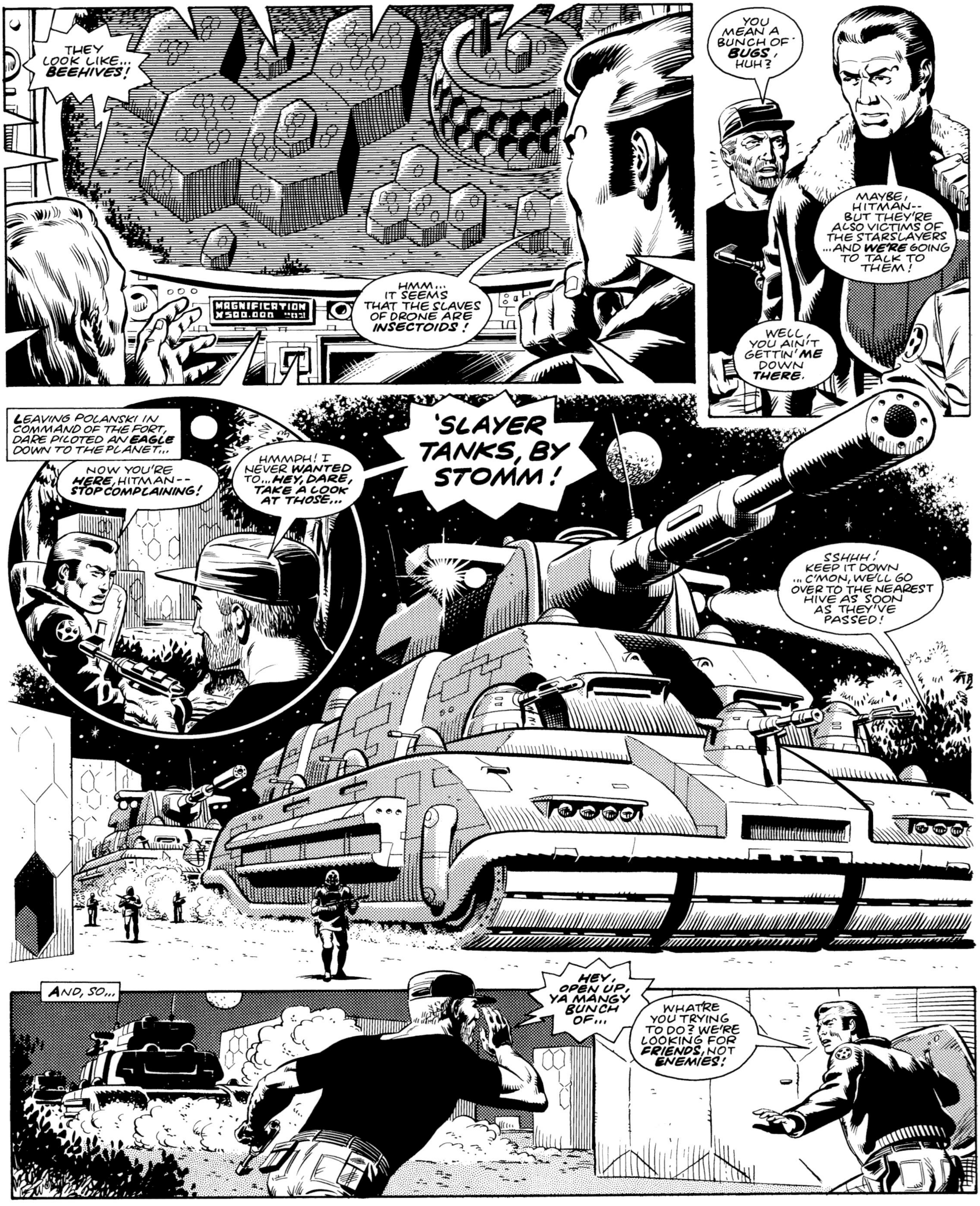
THEY LOOK LIKE... BEEHIVES!
HMM... IT SEEMS THAT THE SLAVES OF DRONE ARE INSECTOIDS!
MAGNIFICATION X500,000
YOU MEAN A BUNCH OF BUGS, HUH?
MAYBE, HITMAN-- BUT THEY'RE ALSO VICTIMS OF THE STARSLAYERS ...AND WE'RE GOING TO TALK TO THEM!
WELL, YOU AIN'T GETTIN' ME DOWN THERE.
LEAVING POLANSKI IN COMMAND OF THE FORT, DARE PILOTED AN EAGLE DOWN TO THE PLANET...
NOW YOU'RE HERE, HITMAN-- STOP COMPLAINING!
HMMPH! I NEVER WANTED TO... HEY, DARE, TAKE A LOOK AT THOSE...
'SLAYER TANKS, BY STOMM!
SSHHH! KEEP IT DOWN ...C'MON, WE'LL GO OVER TO THE NEAREST HIVE AS SOON AS THEY'VE PASSED!
AND, SO...
HEY, OPEN UP, YA MANGY BUNCH OF...
WHAT'RE YOU TRYING TO DO? WE'RE LOOKING FOR FRIENDS, NOT ENEMIES!

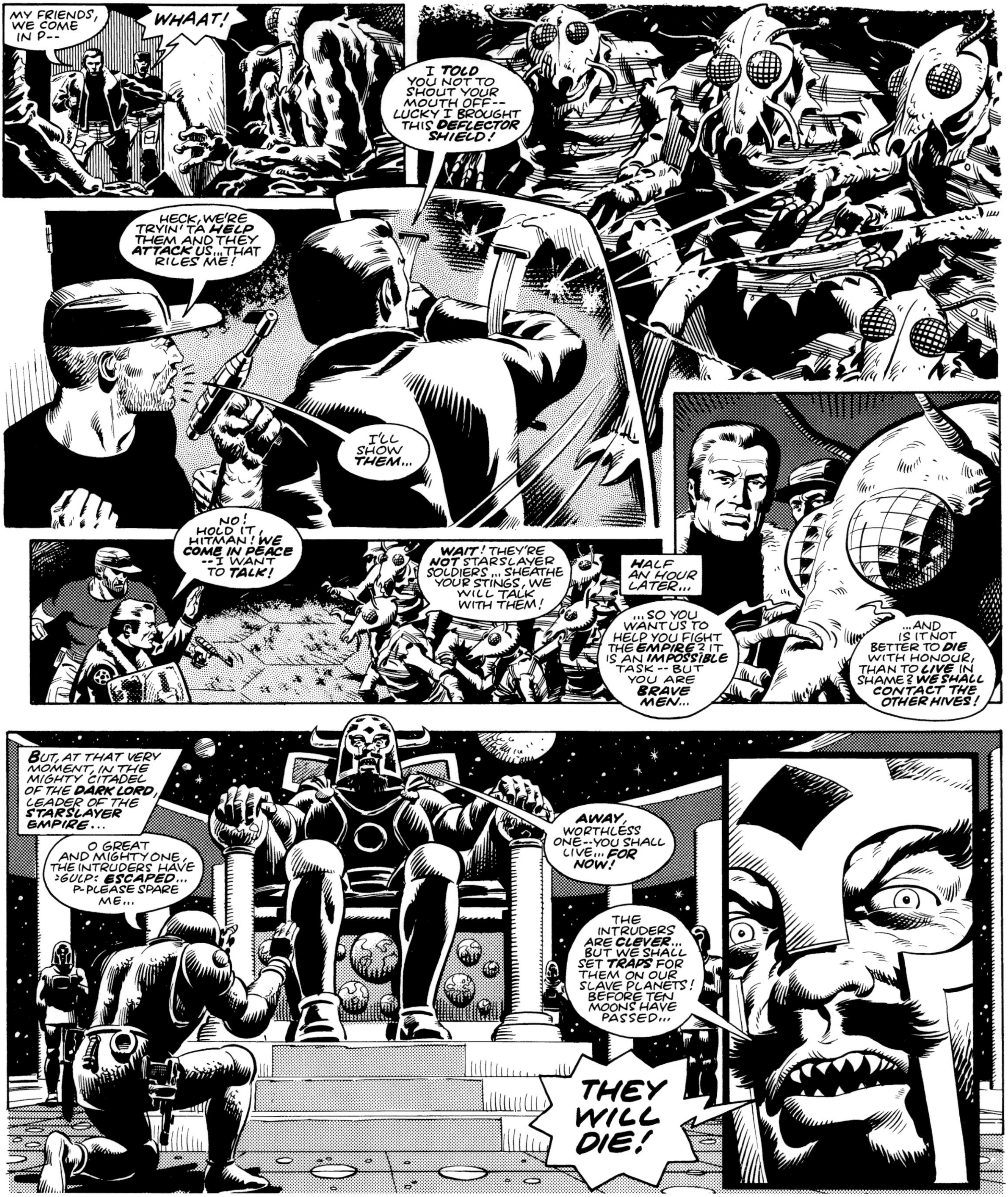

MY FRIENDS, WE COME IN P--
WHAAT!
I TOLD YOU NOT TO SHOUT YOUR MOUTH OFF-- LUCKY I BROUGHT THIS DEFLECTOR SHIELD!
HECK, WE'RE TRYIN' TA HELP THEM AND THEY ATTACK US... THAT RILES ME!
I'LL SHOW THEM...
NO! HOLD IT, HITMAN! WE COME IN PEACE -- I WANT TO TALK!
WAIT! THEY'RE NOT STARSLAYER SOLDIERS... SHEATHE YOUR STINGS, WE WILL TALK WITH THEM!
HALF AN HOUR LATER...
...SO YOU WANT US TO HELP YOU FIGHT THE EMPIRE? IT IS AN IMPOSSIBLE TASK -- BUT YOU ARE BRAVE MEN...
...AND IS IT NOT BETTER TO DIE WITH HONOUR, THAN TO LIVE IN SHAME? WE SHALL CONTACT THE OTHER HIVES!
BUT, AT THAT VERY MOMENT, IN THE MIGHTY CITADEL OF THE DARK LORD, LEADER OF THE STARSLAYER EMPIRE...
O GREAT AND MIGHTY ONE, THE INTRUDERS HAVE :GULP: ESCAPED... P-PLEASE SPARE ME...
AWAY, WORTHLESS ONE -- YOU SHALL LIVE... FOR NOW!
THE INTRUDERS ARE CLEVER... BUT WE SHALL SET TRAPS FOR THEM ON OUR SLAVE PLANETS! BEFORE TEN MOONS HAVE PASSED...
THEY WILL DIE!

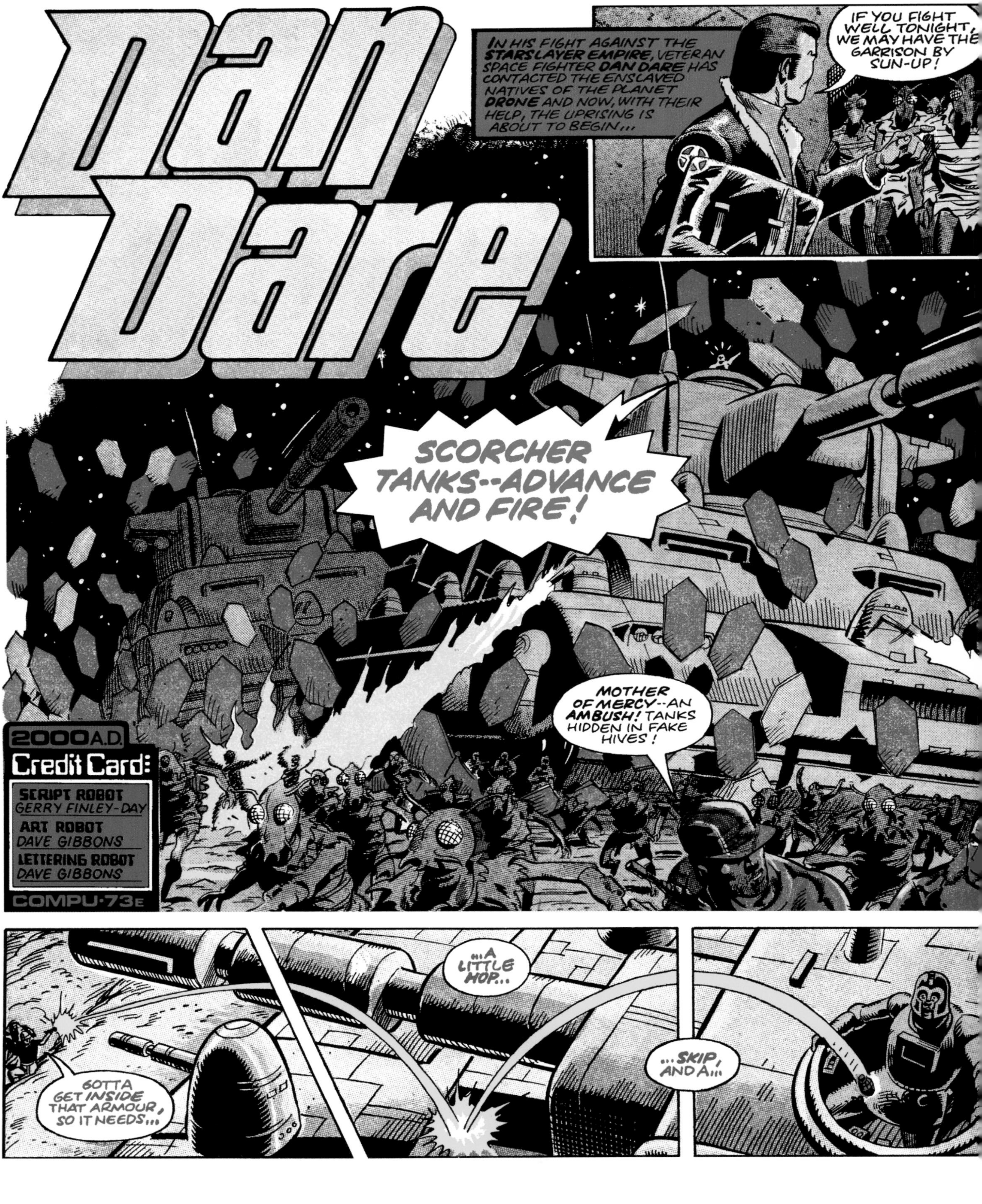
DAN DARE
IN HIS FIGHT AGAINST THE STARSLAYER EMPIRE, VETERAN SPACE FIGHTER DAN DARE HAS CONTACTED THE ENSLAVED NATIVES OF THE PLANET DRONE AND NOW, WITH THEIR HELP, THE UPRISING IS ABOUT TO BEGIN...
IF YOU FIGHT WELL TONIGHT, WE MAY HAVE THE GARRISON BY SUN-UP!
SCORCHER TANKS--ADVANCE AND FIRE!
MOTHER OF MERCY--AN AMBUSH! TANKS HIDDEN IN FAKE HIVES!
2000 A.D.
Credit Card:
SCRIPT ROBOT GERRY FINLEY-DAY
ART ROBOT DAVE GIBBONS
LETTERING ROBOT DAVE GIBBONS
COMPU-73E
GOTTA GET INSIDE THAT ARMOUR, SO IT NEEDS...
...A LITTLE HOP...
...SKIP, AND A...

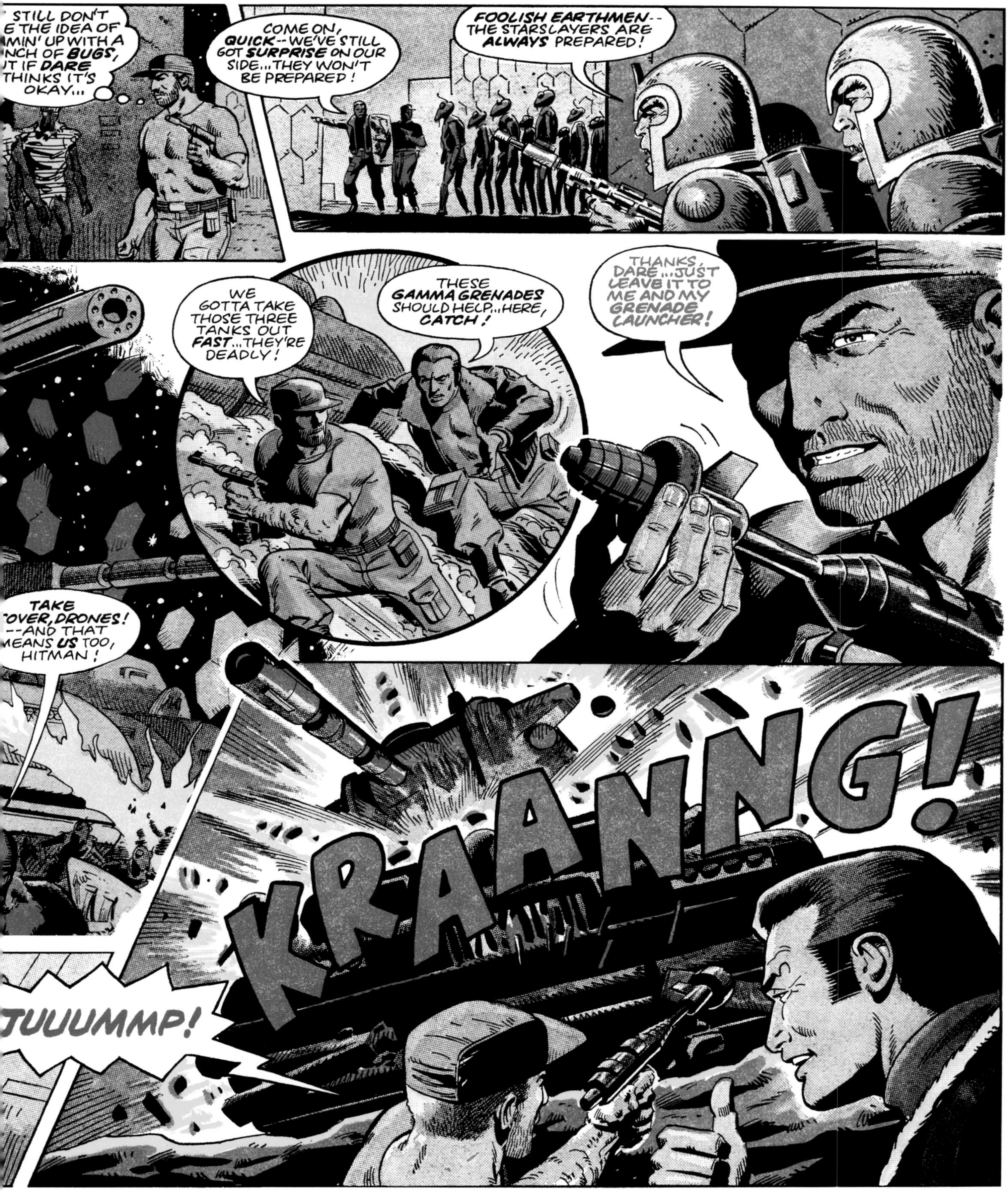

STILL DON'T
E THE IDEA OF
MIN' UP WITH A
NCH OF BUGS,
T IF DARE
THINKS IT'S
OKAY...
COME ON, QUICK-- WE'VE STILL GOT SURPRISE ON OUR SIDE... THEY WON'T BE PREPARED!
FOOLISH EARTHMEN-- THE STARSLAYERS ARE ALWAYS PREPARED!
WE GOTTA TAKE THOSE THREE TANKS OUT FAST... THEY'RE DEADLY!
THESE GAMMA GRENADES SHOULD HELP... HERE, CATCH!
THANKS, DARE... JUST LEAVE IT TO ME AND MY GRENADE LAUNCHER!
TAKE COVER, DRONES! --AND THAT MEANS US TOO, HITMAN!
KRAANNG!
JUUUMMP!

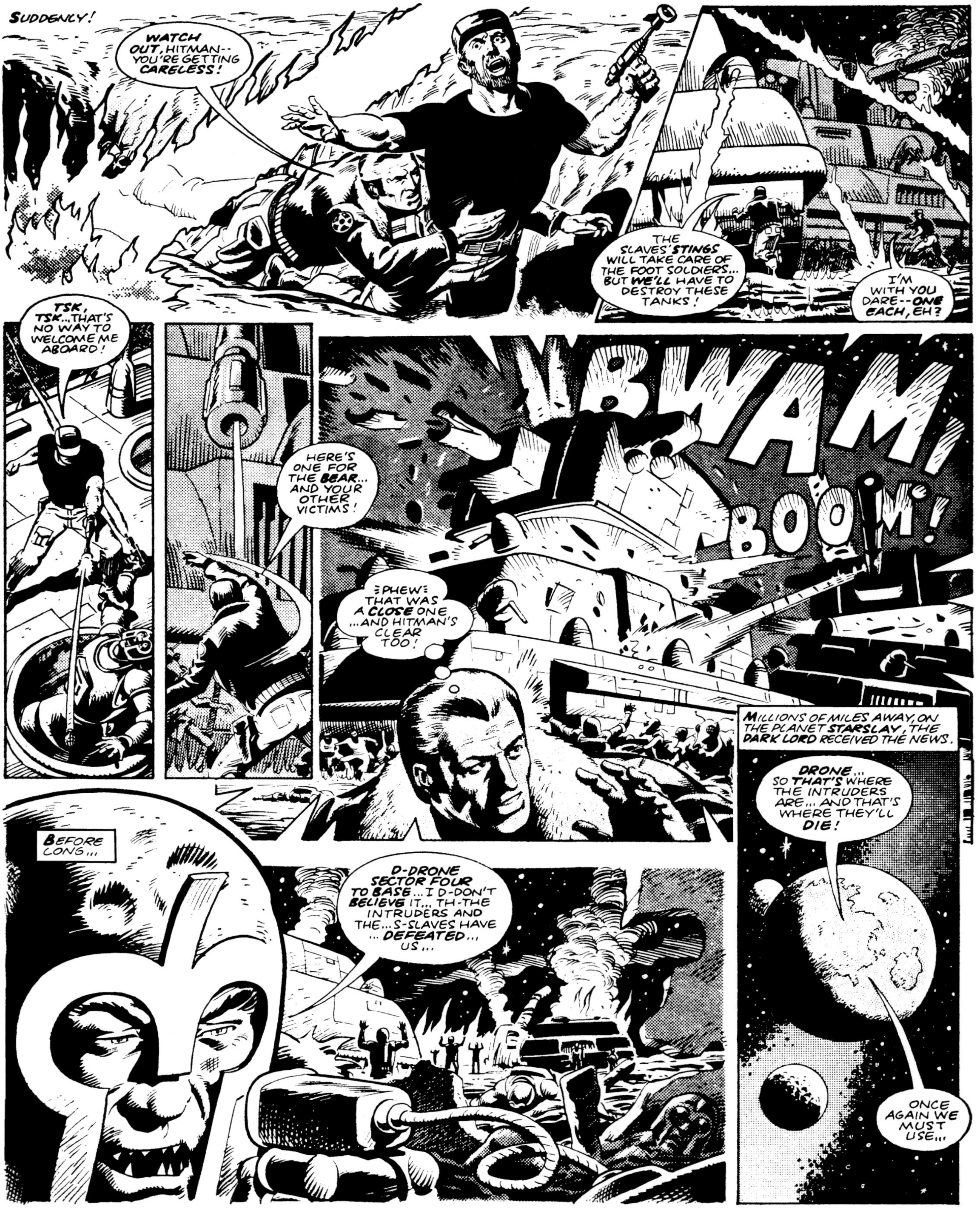
SUDDENLY!
WATCH OUT, HITMAN-- YOU'RE GETTING CARELESS!
THE SLAVES' STINGS WILL TAKE CARE OF THE FOOT SOLDIERS... BUT WE'LL HAVE TO DESTROY THESE TANKS!
I'M WITH YOU DARE--ONE EACH, EH?
TSK, TSK...THAT'S NO WAY TO WELCOME ME ABOARD!
HERE'S ONE FOR THE BEAR... AND YOUR OTHER VICTIMS!
BWAM!
BOOM!
PHEW THAT WAS A CLOSE ONE ...AND HITMAN'S CLEAR TOO!
MILLIONS OF MILES AWAY, ON THE PLANET STARSLAY, THE DARK LORD RECEIVED THE NEWS.
DRONE... SO THAT'S WHERE THE INTRUDERS ARE... AND THAT'S WHERE THEY'LL DIE!
ONCE AGAIN WE MUST USE...
BEFORE LONG...
D-DRONE SECTOR FOUR TO BASE... I D-DON'T BELIEVE IT... TH-THE INTRUDERS AND THE... S-SLAVES HAVE ... DEFEATED... US...

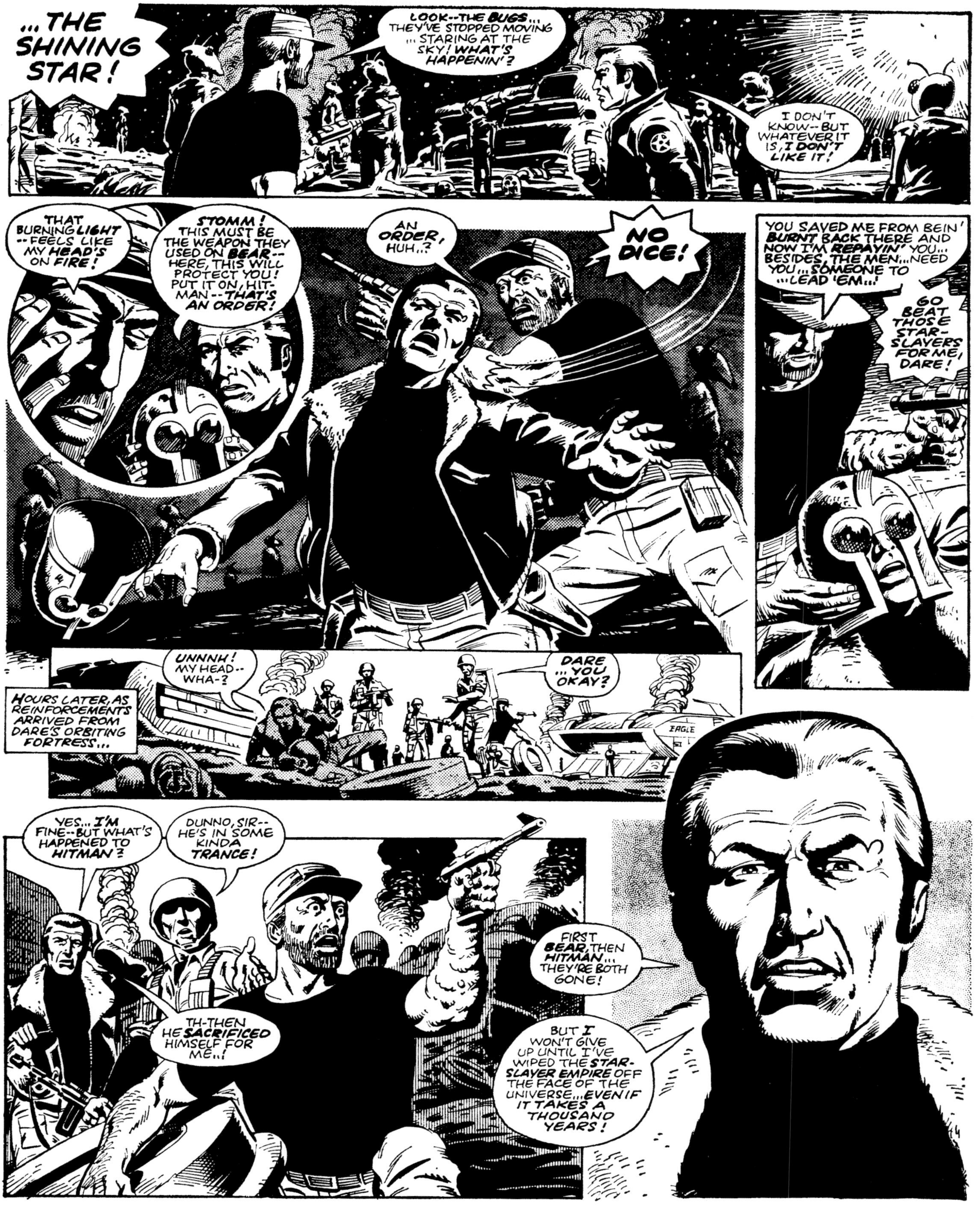

...THE SHINING STAR!
LOOK--THE BUGS... THEY'VE STOPPED MOVING ...STARING AT THE SKY! WHAT'S HAPPENIN'?
I DON'T KNOW--BUT WHATEVER IT IS, I DON'T LIKE IT!
THAT BURNING LIGHT --FEELS LIKE MY HEAD'S ON FIRE!
STOMM! THIS MUST BE THE WEAPON THEY USED ON BEAR-- HERE, THIS WILL PROTECT YOU! PUT IT ON, HIT-MAN --THAT'S AN ORDER!
AN ORDER, HUH..?
NO DICE!
YOU SAVED ME FROM BEIN' BURNT BACK THERE AND NOW I'M REPAYIN' YOU... BESIDES, THE MEN...NEED YOU...SOMEONE TO ...LEAD 'EM...!
GO BEAT THOSE STAR-SLAYERS FOR ME, DARE!
HOURS LATER, AS REINFORCEMENTS ARRIVED FROM DARE'S ORBITING FORTRESS...
UNNNH! MY HEAD-- WHA-?
DARE ...YOU OKAY?
EAGLE
YES... I'M FINE--BUT WHAT'S HAPPENED TO HITMAN?
DUNNO, SIR-- HE'S IN SOME KINDA TRANCE!
TH-THEN HE SACRIFICED HIMSELF FOR ME...!
FIRST BEAR, THEN HITMAN... THEY'RE BOTH GONE!
BUT I WON'T GIVE UP UNTIL I'VE WIPED THE STAR-SLAYER EMPIRE OFF THE FACE OF THE UNIVERSE... EVEN IF IT TAKES A THOUSAND YEARS!

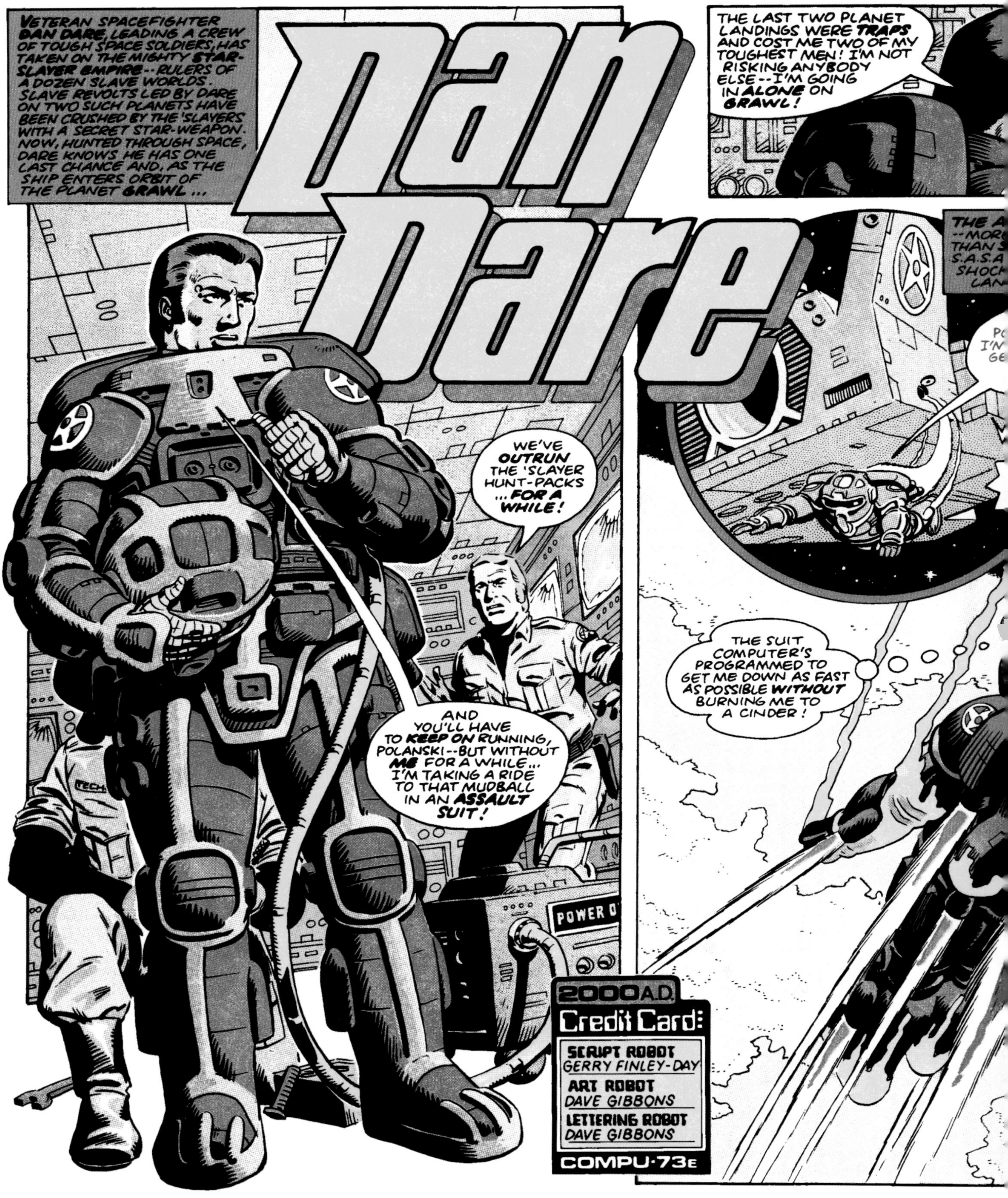
VETERAN SPACEFIGHTER DAN DARE, LEADING A CREW OF TOUGH SPACE SOLDIERS, HAS TAKEN ON THE MIGHTY STAR-SLAYER EMPIRE -- RULERS OF A DOZEN SLAVE WORLDS. SLAVE REVOLTS LED BY DARE ON TWO SUCH PLANETS HAVE BEEN CRUSHED BY THE 'SLAYERS WITH A SECRET STAR-WEAPON. NOW, HUNTED THROUGH SPACE, DARE KNOWS HE HAS ONE LAST CHANCE AND, AS THE SHIP ENTERS ORBIT OF THE PLANET GRAWL ...
DAN DARE
WE'VE OUTRUN THE 'SLAYER HUNT-PACKS ...FOR A WHILE!
AND YOU'LL HAVE TO KEEP ON RUNNING, POLANSKI--BUT WITHOUT ME FOR A WHILE... I'M TAKING A RIDE TO THAT MUDBALL IN AN ASSAULT SUIT!
TECH
POWER O
2000 A.D.
Credit Card:
SCRIPT ROBOT GERRY FINLEY-DAY
ART ROBOT DAVE GIBBONS
LETTERING ROBOT DAVE GIBBONS
COMPU-73E
THE LAST TWO PLANET LANDINGS WERE TRAPS AND COST ME TWO OF MY TOUGHEST MEN! I'M NOT RISKING ANYBODY ELSE--I'M GOING IN ALONE ON GRAWL!
THE SUIT COMPUTER'S PROGRAMMED TO GET ME DOWN AS FAST AS POSSIBLE WITHOUT BURNING ME TO A CINDER!

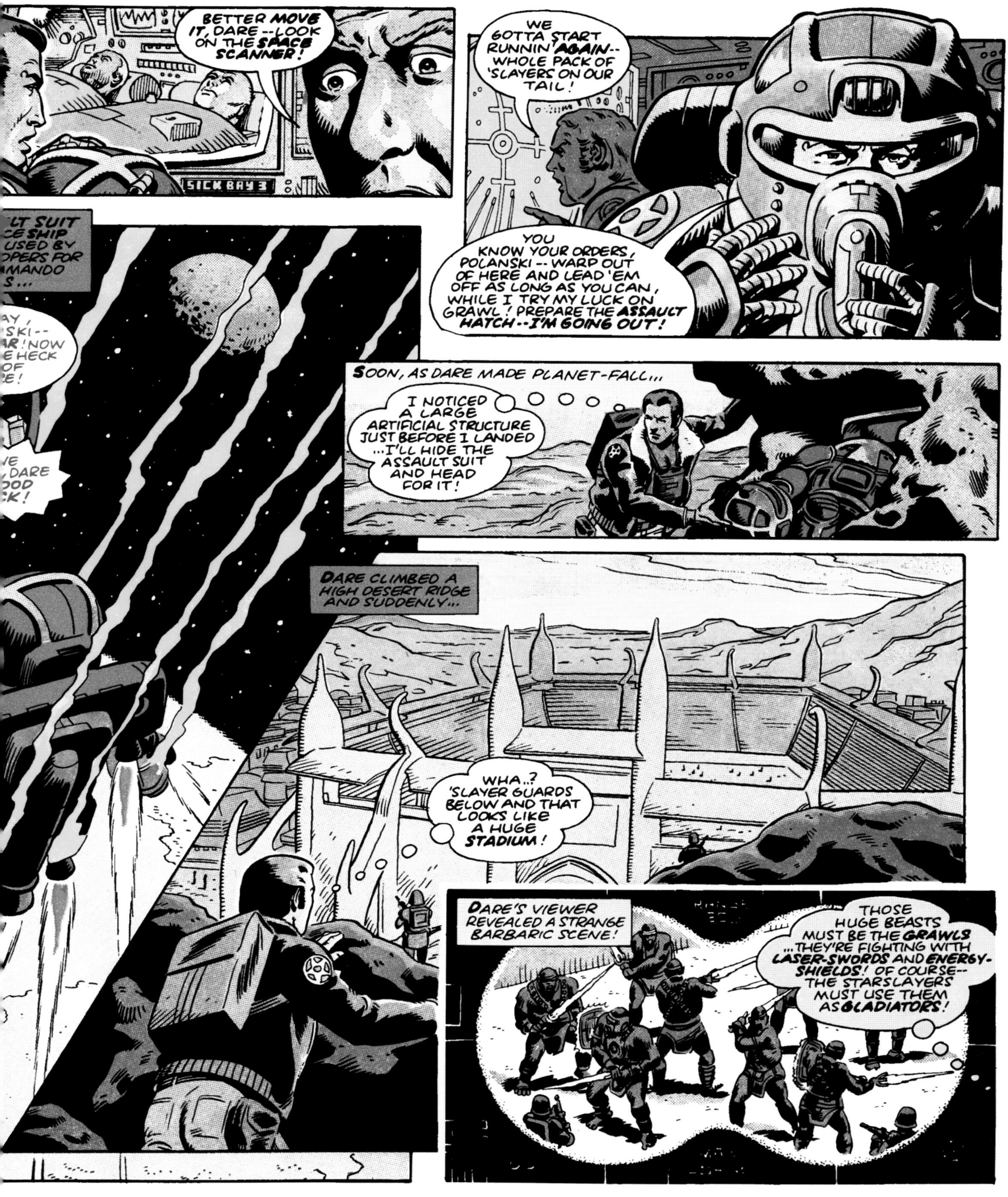
BETTER MOVE IT, DARE --LOOK ON THE SPACE SCANNER!
SICK BAY 3
WE GOTTA START RUNNIN' AGAIN-- WHOLE PACK OF 'SLAYERS ON OUR TAIL!
YOU KNOW YOUR ORDERS, POLANSKI -- WARP OUT OF HERE AND LEAD 'EM OFF AS LONG AS YOU CAN, WHILE I TRY MY LUCK ON GRAWL! PREPARE THE ASSAULT HATCH --I'M GOING OUT!
SOON, AS DARE MADE PLANET-FALL...
I NOTICED A LARGE ARTIFICIAL STRUCTURE JUST BEFORE I LANDED ...I'LL HIDE THE ASSAULT SUIT AND HEAD FOR IT!
DARE CLIMBED A HIGH DESERT RIDGE AND SUDDENLY...
WHA..? 'SLAYER GUARDS BELOW AND THAT LOOKS LIKE A HUGE STADIUM!
DARE'S VIEWER REVEALED A STRANGE BARBARIC SCENE!
THOSE HUGE BEASTS MUST BE THE GRAWLS ...THEY'RE FIGHTING WITH LASER-SWORDS AND ENERGY-SHIELDS! OF COURSE-- THE STARSLAYERS MUST USE THEM AS GLADIATORS!

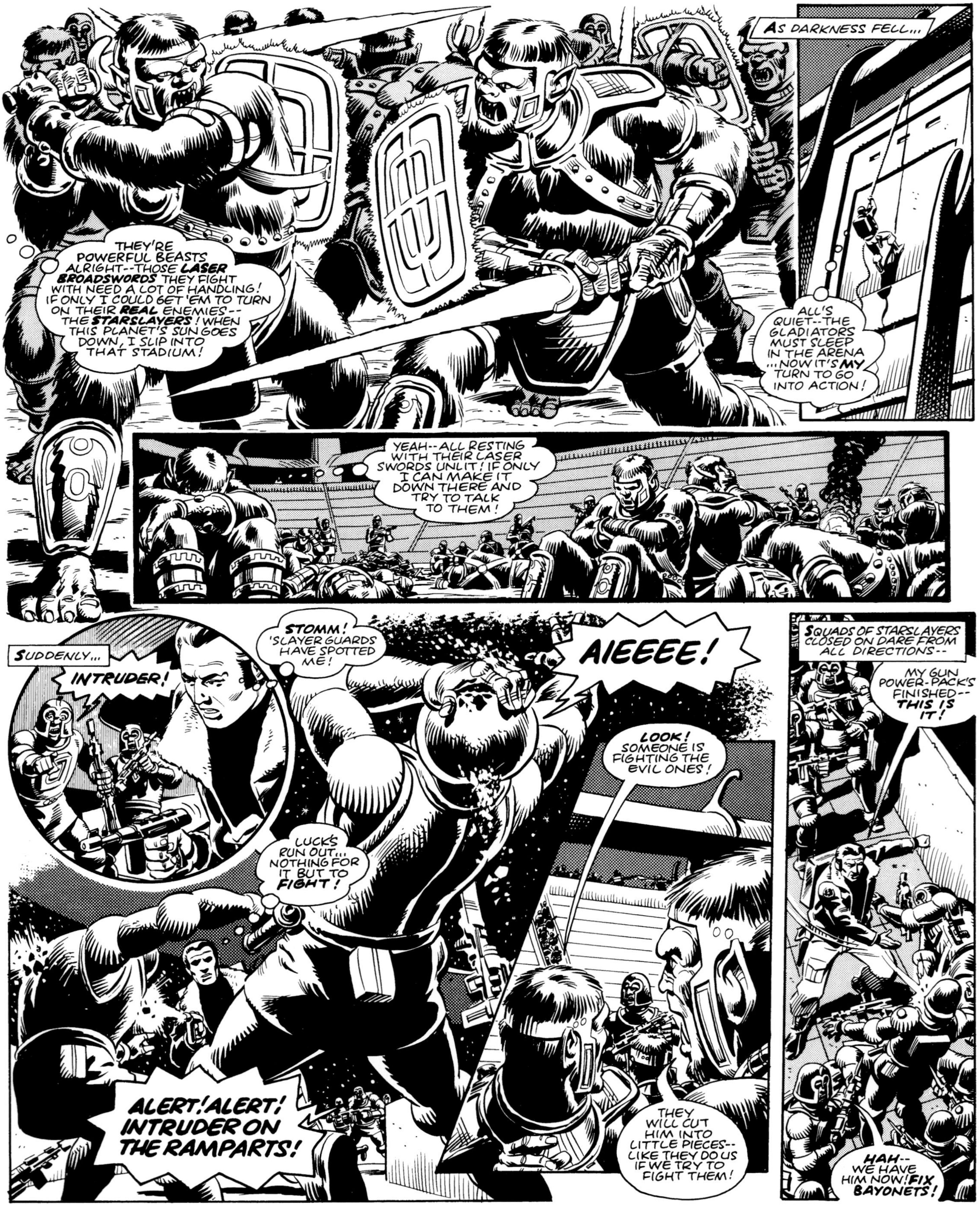
THEY'RE POWERFUL BEASTS ALRIGHT--THOSE LASER BROADSWORDS THEY FIGHT WITH NEED A LOT OF HANDLING! IF ONLY I COULD GET 'EM TO TURN ON THEIR REAL ENEMIES--THE STARSLAYERS! WHEN THIS PLANET'S SUN GOES DOWN, I SLIP INTO THAT STADIUM!
AS DARKNESS FELL...
ALL'S QUIET--THE GLADIATORS MUST SLEEP IN THE ARENA ...NOW IT'S MY TURN TO GO INTO ACTION!
YEAH--ALL RESTING WITH THEIR LASER SWORDS UNLIT! IF ONLY I CAN MAKE IT DOWN THERE AND TRY TO TALK TO THEM!
SUDDENLY...
INTRUDER!
STOMM! 'SLAYER GUARDS HAVE SPOTTED ME!
AIEEEE!
LUCK'S RUN OUT... NOTHING FOR IT BUT TO FIGHT!
ALERT! ALERT! INTRUDER ON THE RAMPARTS!
LOOK! SOMEONE IS FIGHTING THE EVIL ONES!
THEY WILL CUT HIM INTO LITTLE PIECES--LIKE THEY DO US IF WE TRY TO FIGHT THEM!
SQUADS OF STARSLAYERS CLOSED ON DARE FROM ALL DIRECTIONS--
MY GUN POWER-PACK'S FINISHED--THIS IS IT!
HAH--WE HAVE HIM NOW! FIX BAYONETS!

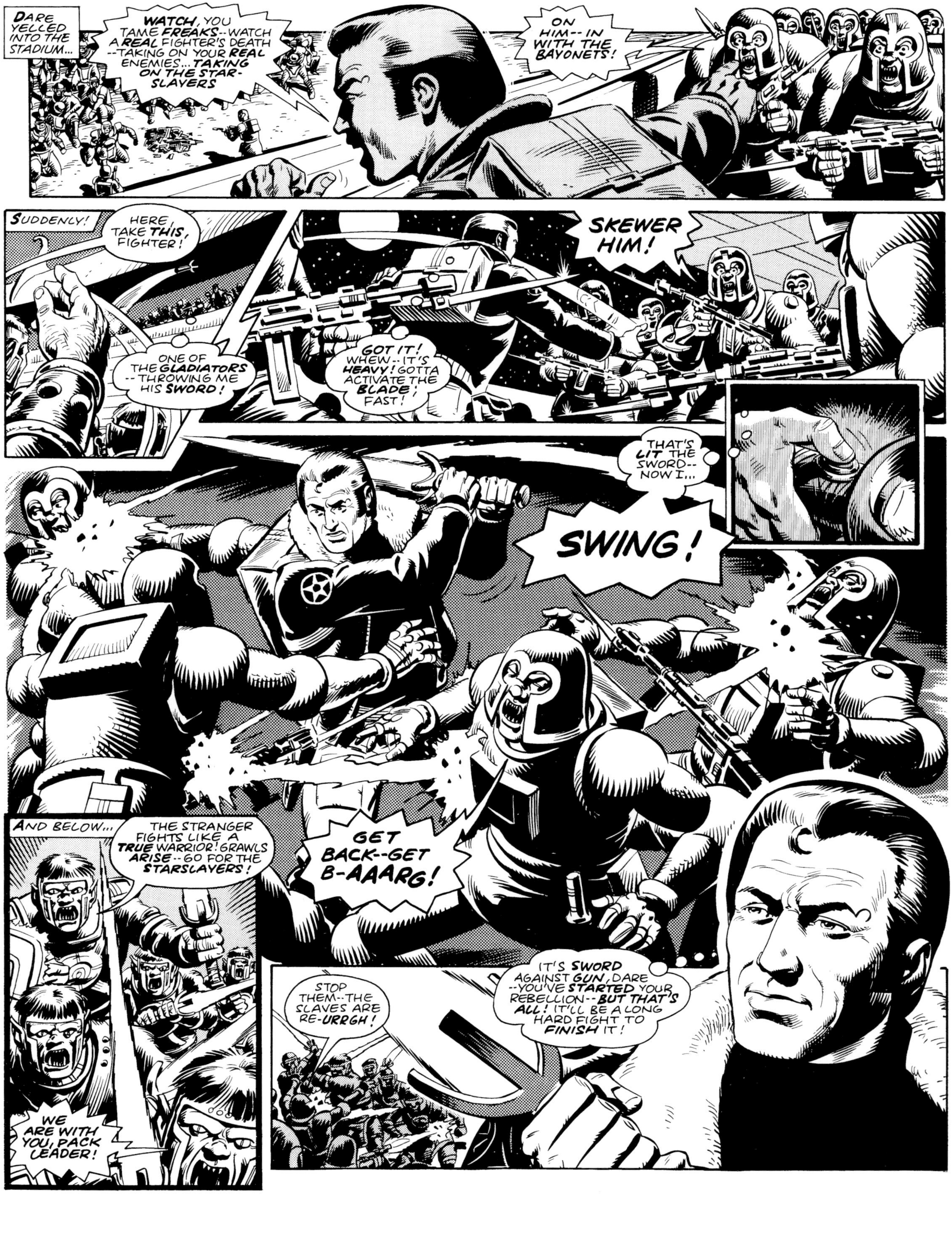
DARE YELLED INTO THE STADIUM...
WATCH, YOU TAME FREAKS--WATCH A REAL FIGHTER'S DEATH --TAKING ON YOUR REAL ENEMIES...TAKING ON THE STAR-SLAYERS
ON HIM--IN WITH THE BAYONETS!
SUDDENLY!
HERE, TAKE THIS, FIGHTER!
ONE OF THE GLADIATORS --THROWING ME HIS SWORD!
SKEWER HIM!
GOT IT! WHEW--IT'S HEAVY! GOTTA ACTIVATE THE BLADE; FAST!
THAT'S LIT THE SWORD--NOW I...
SWING!
AND BELOW...
THE STRANGER FIGHTS LIKE A TRUE WARRIOR! GRAWLS ARISE--GO FOR THE STARSLAYERS!
GET BACK--GET B-AAARG!
WE ARE WITH YOU, PACK LEADER!
STOP THEM--THE SLAVES ARE RE-URRGH!
IT'S SWORD AGAINST GUN, DARE --YOU'VE STARTED YOUR REBELLION--BUT THAT'S ALL! IT'LL BE A LONG HARD FIGHT TO FINISH IT!

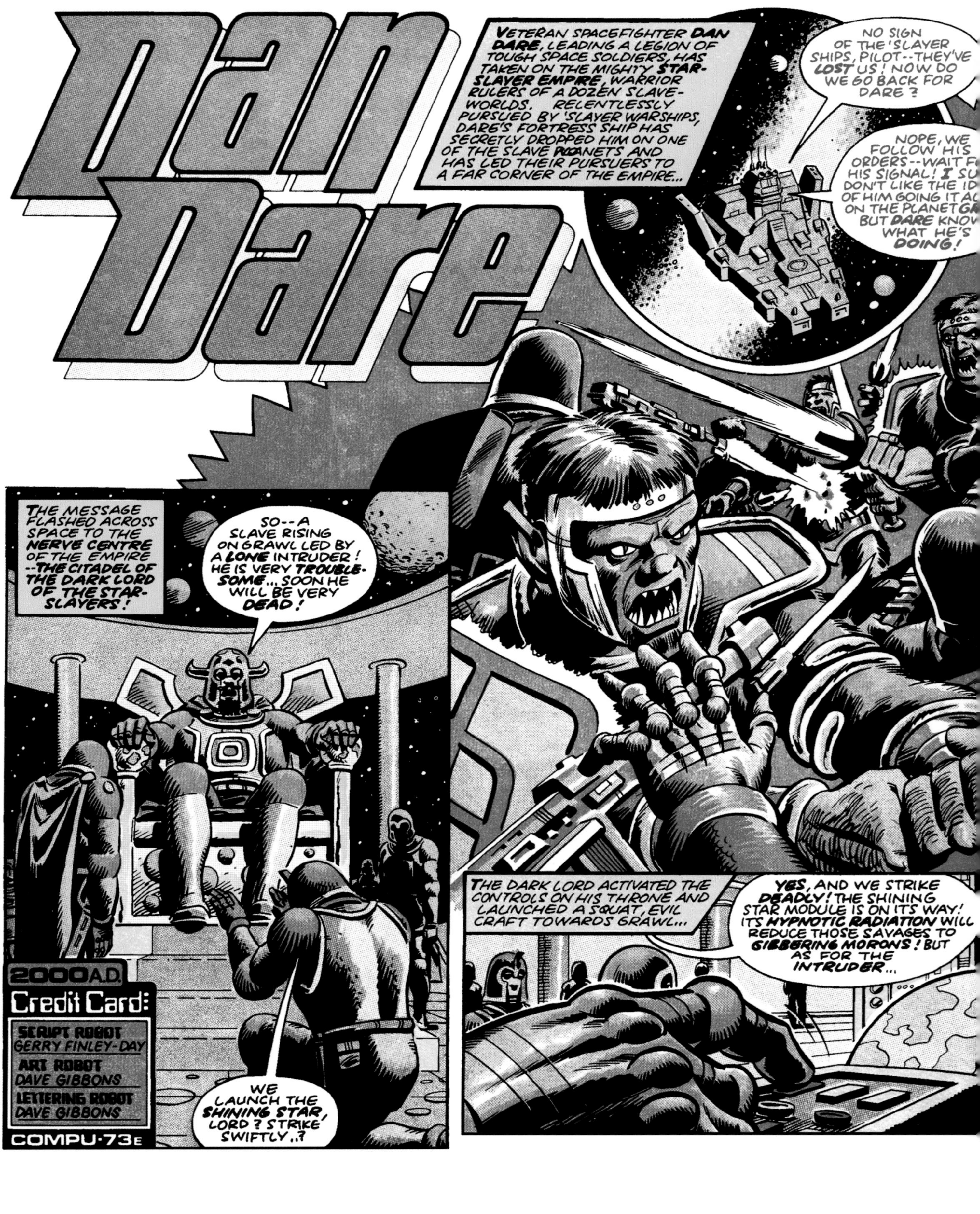

DAN DARE
VETERAN SPACEFIGHTER DAN DARE, LEADING A LEGION OF TOUGH SPACE SOLDIERS, HAS TAKEN ON THE MIGHTY STAR-SLAYER EMPIRE, WARRIOR RULERS OF A DOZEN SLAVE-WORLDS. RELENTLESSLY PURSUED BY 'SLAYER WARSHIPS, DARE'S FORTRESS SHIP HAS SECRETLY DROPPED HIM ON ONE OF THE SLAVE PLANETS AND HAS LED THEIR PURSUERS TO A FAR CORNER OF THE EMPIRE...
NO SIGN OF THE 'SLAYER SHIPS, PILOT--THEY'VE LOST US! NOW DO WE GO BACK FOR DARE?
NOPE, WE FOLLOW HIS ORDERS--WAIT F HIS SIGNAL! I SU DON'T LIKE THE ID OF HIM GOING IT AL ON THE PLANET GR BUT DARE KNOW WHAT HE'S DOING!
THE MESSAGE FLASHED ACROSS SPACE TO THE NERVE CENTRE OF THE EMPIRE --THE CITADEL OF THE DARK LORD OF THE STAR-SLAYERS!
SO--A SLAVE RISING ON GRAWL LED BY A LONE INTRUDER! HE IS VERY TROUBLESOME... SOON HE WILL BE VERY DEAD!
WE LAUNCH THE SHINING STAR, LORD? STRIKE SWIFTLY..?
2000 A.D. Credit Card:
SCRIPT ROBOT GERRY FINLEY-DAY
ART ROBOT DAVE GIBBONS
LETTERING ROBOT DAVE GIBBONS
COMPU-73E
THE DARK LORD ACTIVATED THE CONTROLS ON HIS THRONE AND LAUNCHED A SQUAT, EVIL CRAFT TOWARDS GRAWL...
YES, AND WE STRIKE DEADLY! THE SHINING STAR MODULE IS ON ITS WAY! ITS HYPNOTIC RADIATION WILL REDUCE THOSE SAVAGES TO GIBBERING MORONS! BUT AS FOR THE INTRUDER...

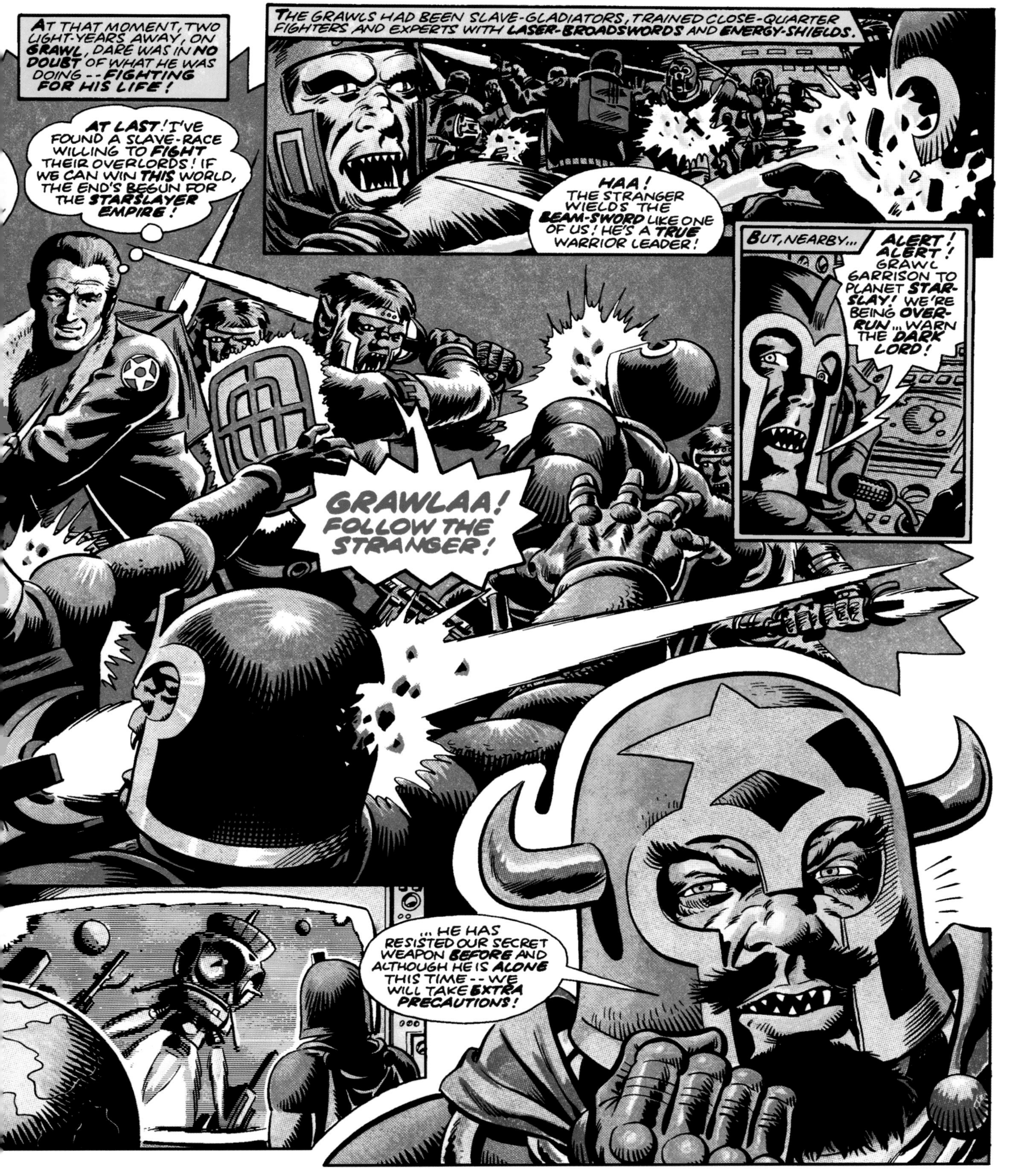
AT THAT MOMENT, TWO LIGHT-YEARS AWAY, ON GRAWL, DARE WAS IN NO DOUBT OF WHAT HE WAS DOING -- FIGHTING FOR HIS LIFE!
THE GRAWLS HAD BEEN SLAVE-GLADIATORS, TRAINED CLOSE-QUARTER FIGHTERS AND EXPERTS WITH LASER-BROADSWORDS AND ENERGY-SHIELDS.
HAA! THE STRANGER WIELDS THE BEAM-SWORD LIKE ONE OF US! HE'S A TRUE WARRIOR LEADER!
AT LAST! I'VE FOUND A SLAVE-RACE WILLING TO FIGHT THEIR OVERLORDS! IF WE CAN WIN THIS WORLD, THE END'S BEGUN FOR THE STARSLAYER EMPIRE!
BUT, NEARBY...
ALERT! ALERT! GRAWL GARRISON TO PLANET STAR-SLAY! WE'RE BEING OVER-RUN ... WARN THE DARK LORD!
GRAWLAA! FOLLOW THE STRANGER!
... HE HAS RESISTED OUR SECRET WEAPON BEFORE AND ALTHOUGH HE IS ALONE THIS TIME -- WE WILL TAKE EXTRA PRECAUTIONS!

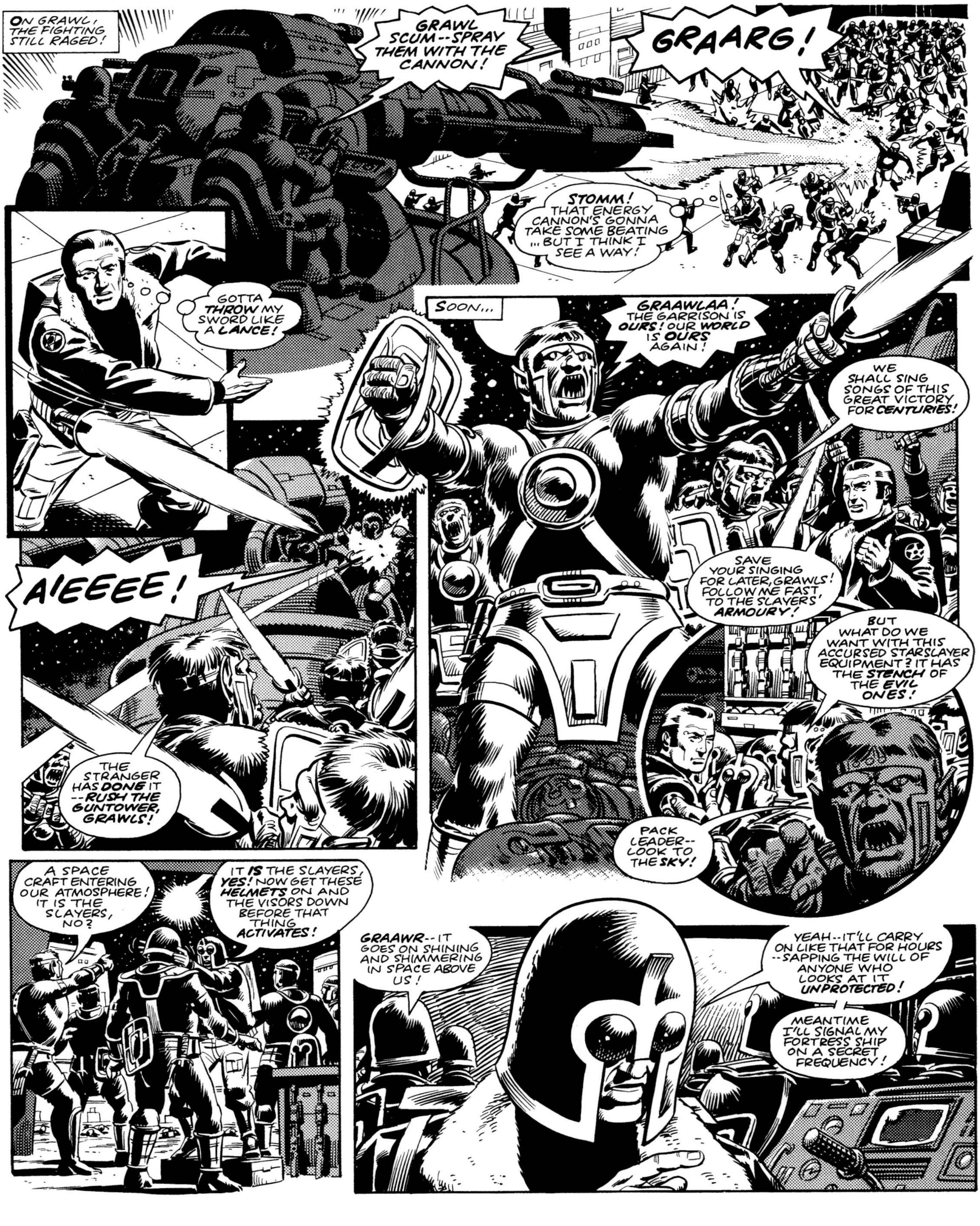

ON GRAWL, THE FIGHTING STILL RAGED!
GRAWL SCUM--SPRAY THEM WITH THE CANNON!
GRAARG!
STOMM! THAT ENERGY CANNON'S GONNA TAKE SOME BEATING ... BUT I THINK I SEE A WAY!
GOTTA THROW MY SWORD LIKE A LANCE!
AIEEEE!
THE STRANGER HAS DONE IT --RUSH THE GUNTOWER, GRAWLS!
SOON...
GRAAWLAA! THE GARRISON IS OURS! OUR WORLD IS OURS AGAIN!
WE SHALL SING SONGS OF THIS GREAT VICTORY FOR CENTURIES!
SAVE YOUR SINGING FOR LATER, GRAWLS! FOLLOW ME FAST TO THE SLAYERS' ARMOURY!
BUT WHAT DO WE WANT WITH THIS ACCURSED STARSLAYER EQUIPMENT? IT HAS THE STENCH OF THE EVIL ONES!
PACK LEADER-- LOOK TO THE SKY!
A SPACE CRAFT ENTERING OUR ATMOSPHERE! IT IS THE SLAYERS, NO?
IT IS THE SLAYERS, YES! NOW GET THESE HELMETS ON AND THE VISORS DOWN BEFORE THAT THING ACTIVATES!
GRAAWR--IT GOES ON SHINING AND SHIMMERING IN SPACE ABOVE US!
YEAH--IT'LL CARRY ON LIKE THAT FOR HOURS --SAPPING THE WILL OF ANYONE WHO LOOKS AT IT UNPROTECTED!
MEANTIME I'LL SIGNAL MY FORTRESS SHIP ON A SECRET FREQUENCY!

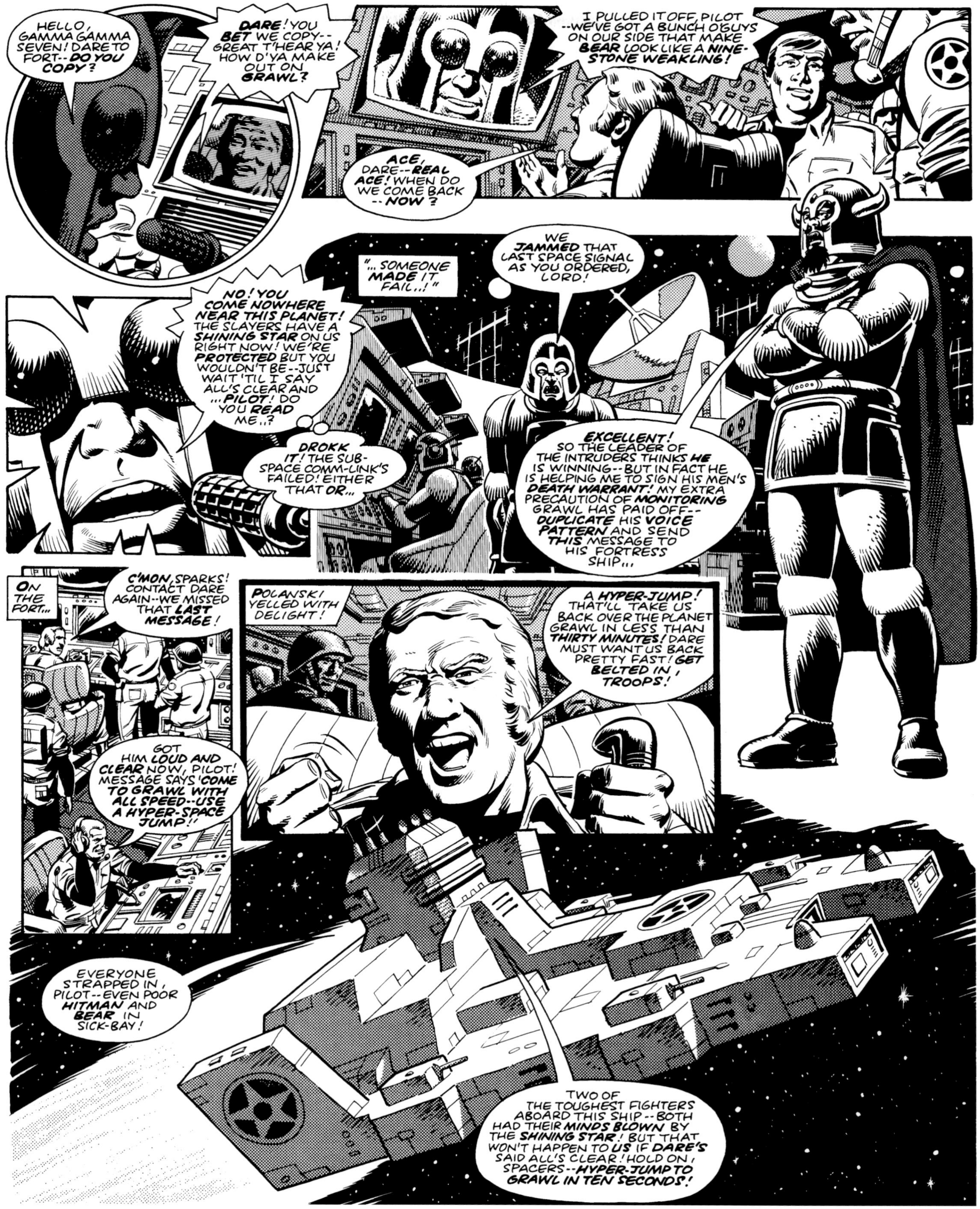

HELLO, GAMMA GAMMA SEVEN! DARE TO FORT-- DO YOU COPY?
DARE! YOU BET WE COPY-- GREAT T'HEAR YA! HOW D'YA MAKE OUT ON GRAWL?
I PULLED IT OFF, PILOT --WE'VE GOT A BUNCH O'GUYS ON OUR SIDE THAT MAKE BEAR LOOK LIKE A NINE-STONE WEAKLING!
ACE, DARE-- REAL ACE! WHEN DO WE COME BACK -- NOW?
NO! YOU COME NOWHERE NEAR THIS PLANET! THE SLAYERS HAVE A SHINING STAR ON US RIGHT NOW! WE'RE PROTECTED BUT YOU WOULDN'T BE--JUST WAIT 'TIL I SAY ALL'S CLEAR AND ...PILOT! DO YOU READ ME..?
DROKK IT! THE SUB-SPACE COMM-LINK'S FAILED! EITHER THAT OR...
"...SOMEONE MADE IT FAIL..!"
WE JAMMED THAT LAST SPACE SIGNAL AS YOU ORDERED, LORD!
EXCELLENT! SO THE LEADER OF THE INTRUDERS THINKS HE IS WINNING--BUT IN FACT HE IS HELPING ME TO SIGN HIS MEN'S DEATH WARRANT! MY EXTRA PRECAUTION OF MONITORING GRAWL HAS PAID OFF-- DUPLICATE HIS VOICE PATTERN AND SEND THIS MESSAGE TO HIS FORTRESS SHIP...
ON THE FORT...
C'MON, SPARKS! CONTACT DARE AGAIN--WE MISSED THAT LAST MESSAGE!
GOT HIM LOUD AND CLEAR NOW, PILOT! MESSAGE SAYS 'COME TO GRAWL WITH ALL SPEED--USE A HYPER-SPACE JUMP!'
POLANSKI YELLED WITH DELIGHT!
A HYPER-JUMP! THAT'LL TAKE US BACK OVER THE PLANET GRAWL IN LESS THAN THIRTY MINUTES! DARE MUST WANT US BACK PRETTY FAST! GET BELTED IN, TROOPS!
EVERYONE STRAPPED IN, PILOT--EVEN POOR HITMAN AND BEAR IN SICK-BAY!
TWO OF THE TOUGHEST FIGHTERS ABOARD THIS SHIP--BOTH HAD THEIR MINDS BLOWN BY THE SHINING STAR! BUT THAT WON'T HAPPEN TO US IF DARE'S SAID ALL'S CLEAR! HOLD ON, SPACERS--HYPER-JUMP TO GRAWL IN TEN SECONDS!

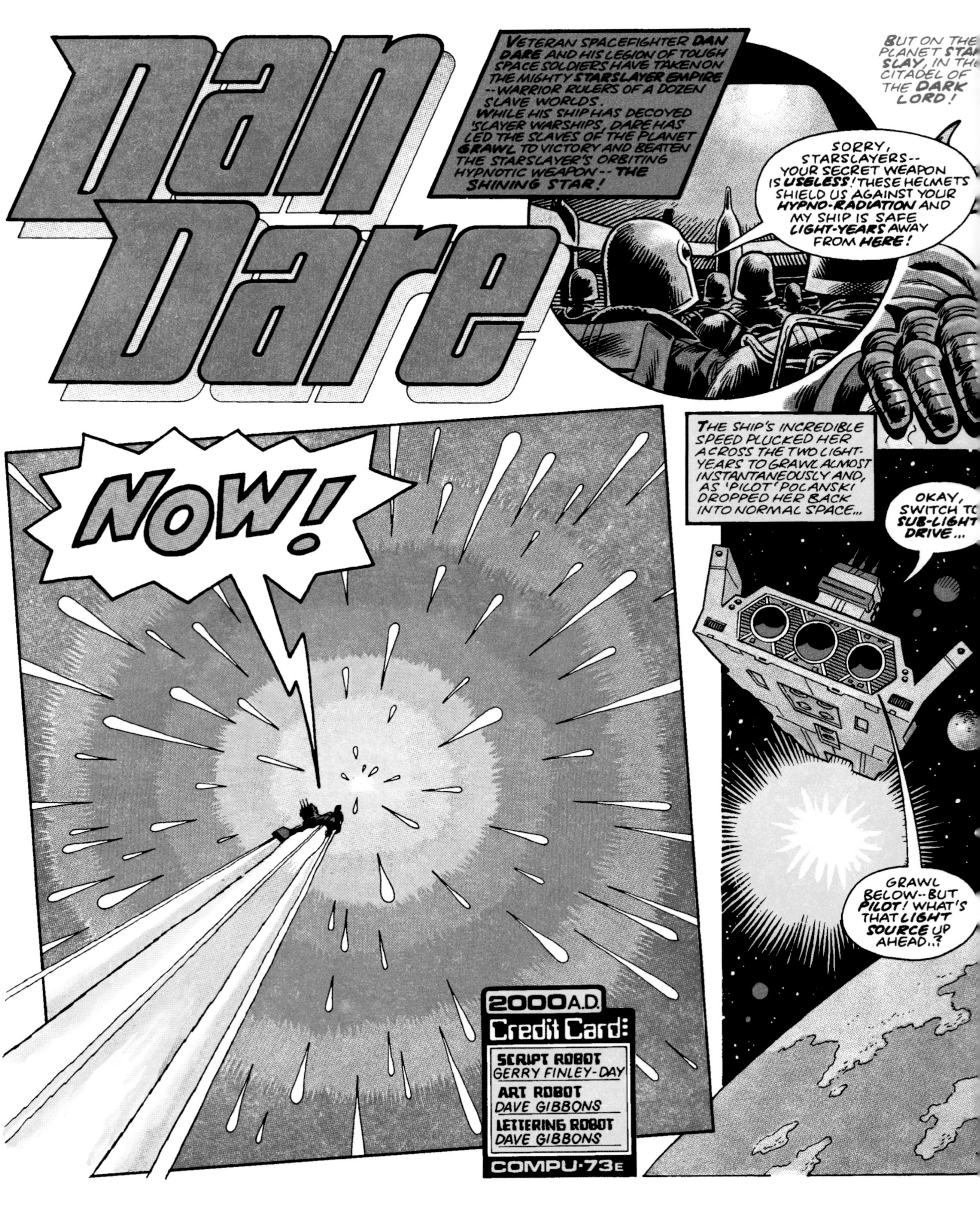
Dan Dare
VETERAN SPACEFIGHTER DAN DARE AND HIS LEGION OF TOUGH SPACE SOLDIERS HAVE TAKEN ON THE MIGHTY STARSLAYER EMPIRE --WARRIOR RULERS OF A DOZEN SLAVE WORLDS.
WHILE HIS SHIP HAS DECOYED 'SLAYER WARSHIPS, DARE HAS LED THE SLAVES OF THE PLANET GRAWL TO VICTORY AND BEATEN THE STARSLAYER'S ORBITING HYPNOTIC WEAPON -- THE SHINING STAR!
BUT ON THE PLANET STAR SLAY, IN THE CITADEL OF THE DARK LORD!
SORRY, STARSLAYERS-- YOUR SECRET WEAPON IS USELESS! THESE HELMETS SHIELD US AGAINST YOUR HYPNO-RADIATION AND MY SHIP IS SAFE LIGHT-YEARS AWAY FROM HERE!
NOW!
THE SHIP'S INCREDIBLE SPEED PLUCKED HER ACROSS THE TWO LIGHT-YEARS TO GRAWL ALMOST INSTANTANEOUSLY AND, AS 'PILOT' POLANSKI DROPPED HER BACK INTO NORMAL SPACE...
OKAY, SWITCH TO SUB-LIGHT DRIVE...
GRAWL BELOW--BUT PILOT! WHAT'S THAT LIGHT SOURCE UP AHEAD..?
2000 A.D. Credit Card:
SCRIPT ROBOT GERRY FINLEY-DAY
ART ROBOT DAVE GIBBONS
LETTERING ROBOT DAVE GIBBONS
COMPU-73E

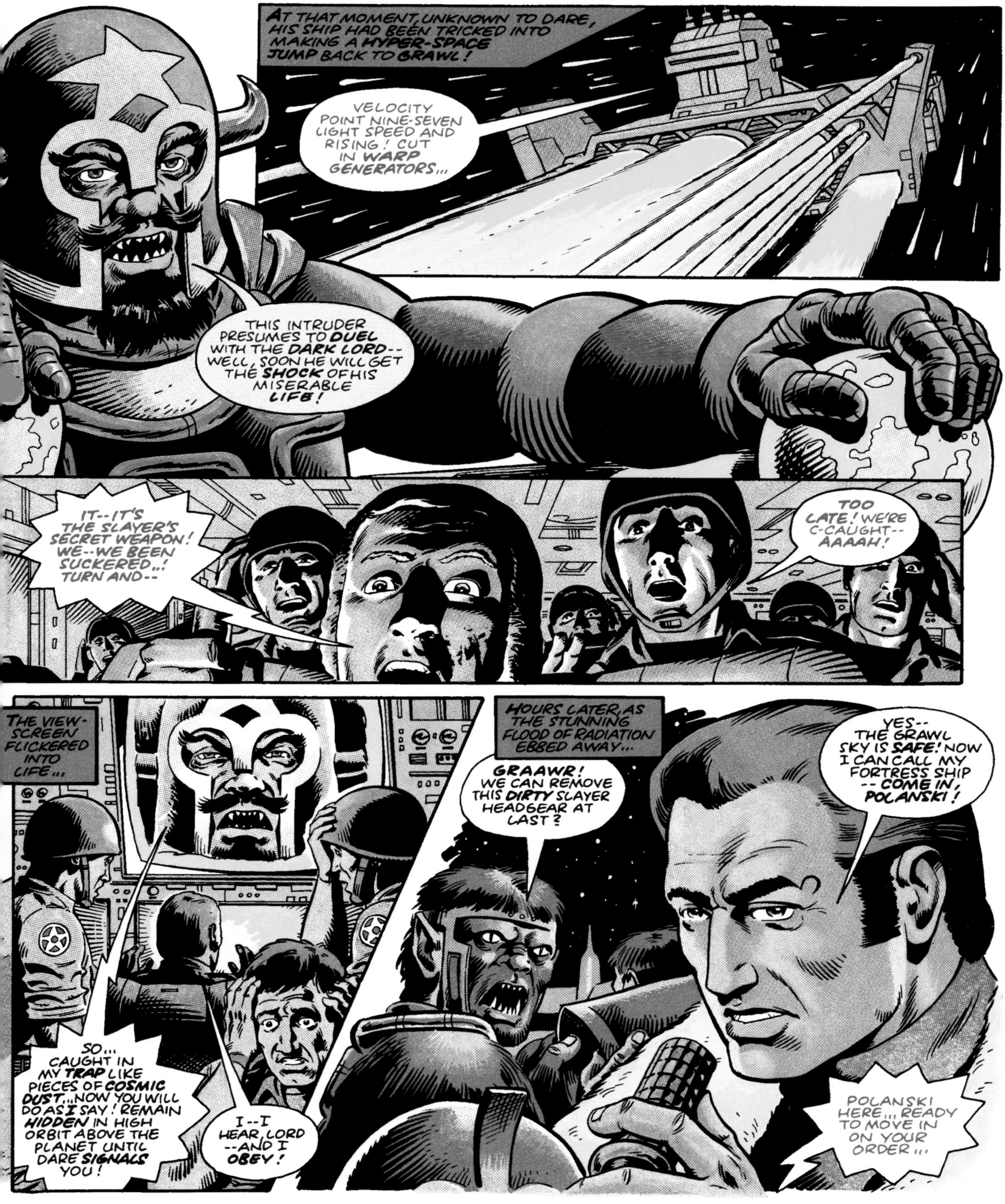

AT THAT MOMENT, UNKNOWN TO DARE, HIS SHIP HAD BEEN TRICKED INTO MAKING A HYPER-SPACE JUMP BACK TO GRAWL!
VELOCITY POINT NINE-SEVEN LIGHT SPEED AND RISING! CUT IN WARP GENERATORS...
THIS INTRUDER PRESUMES TO DUEL WITH THE DARK LORD-- WELL, SOON HE WILL GET THE SHOCK OF HIS MISERABLE LIFE!
IT--IT'S THE SLAYER'S SECRET WEAPON! WE--WE BEEN SUCKERED..! TURN AND--
TOO LATE! WE'RE C-CAUGHT-- AAAAH!
THE VIEW-SCREEN FLICKERED INTO LIFE...
SO... CAUGHT IN MY TRAP LIKE PIECES OF COSMIC DUST...NOW YOU WILL DO AS I SAY! REMAIN HIDDEN IN HIGH ORBIT ABOVE THE PLANET UNTIL DARE SIGNALS YOU!
I--I HEAR, LORD --AND I OBEY!
HOURS LATER, AS THE STUNNING FLOOD OF RADIATION EBBED AWAY...
GRAAWR! WE CAN REMOVE THIS DIRTY SLAYER HEADGEAR AT LAST?
YES-- THE GRAWL SKY IS SAFE! NOW I CAN CALL MY FORTRESS SHIP --COME IN, POLANSKI!
POLANSKI HERE... READY TO MOVE IN ON YOUR ORDER...

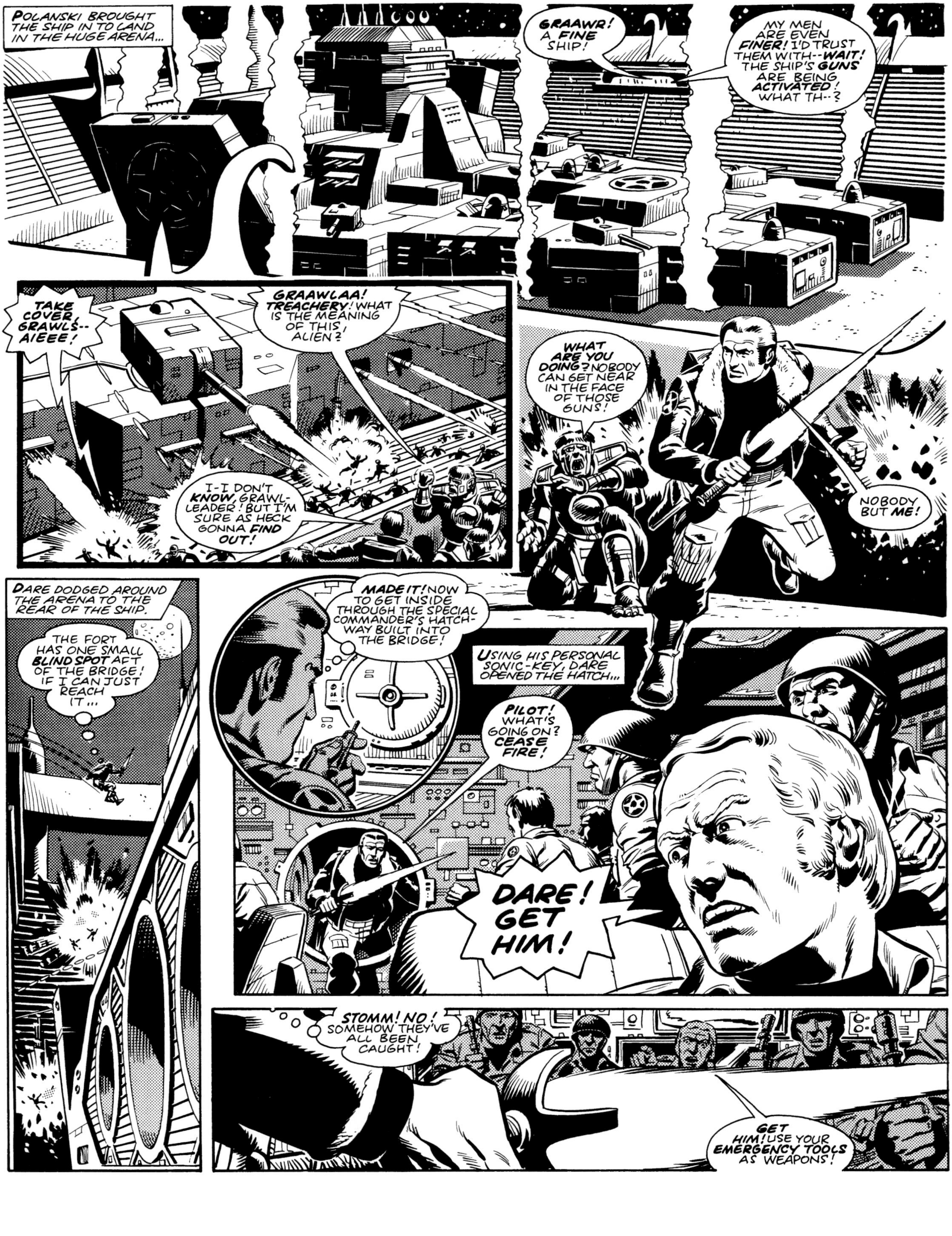

POLANSKI BROUGHT THE SHIP IN TO LAND IN THE HUGE ARENA...
GRAAWR! A FINE SHIP!
MY MEN ARE EVEN FINER! I'D TRUST THEM WITH--WAIT! THE SHIP'S GUNS ARE BEING ACTIVATED! WHAT TH--?
TAKE COVER, GRAWLS--AIEEE!
GRAAWLAA! TREACHERY! WHAT IS THE MEANING OF THIS, ALIEN?
I-I DON'T KNOW, GRAWL-LEADER! BUT I'M SURE AS HECK GONNA FIND OUT!
WHAT ARE YOU DOING? NOBODY CAN GET NEAR IN THE FACE OF THOSE GUNS!
NOBODY BUT ME!
DARE DODGED AROUND THE ARENA TO THE REAR OF THE SHIP.
THE FORT HAS ONE SMALL BLIND SPOT AFT OF THE BRIDGE! IF I CAN JUST REACH IT...
MADE IT! NOW TO GET INSIDE THROUGH THE SPECIAL COMMANDER'S HATCH-WAY BUILT INTO THE BRIDGE!
USING HIS PERSONAL SONIC-KEY, DARE OPENED THE HATCH...
PILOT! WHAT'S GOING ON? CEASE FIRE!
DARE! GET HIM!
STOMM! NO! SOMEHOW THEY'VE ALL BEEN CAUGHT!
GET HIM! USE YOUR EMERGENCY TOOLS AS WEAPONS!

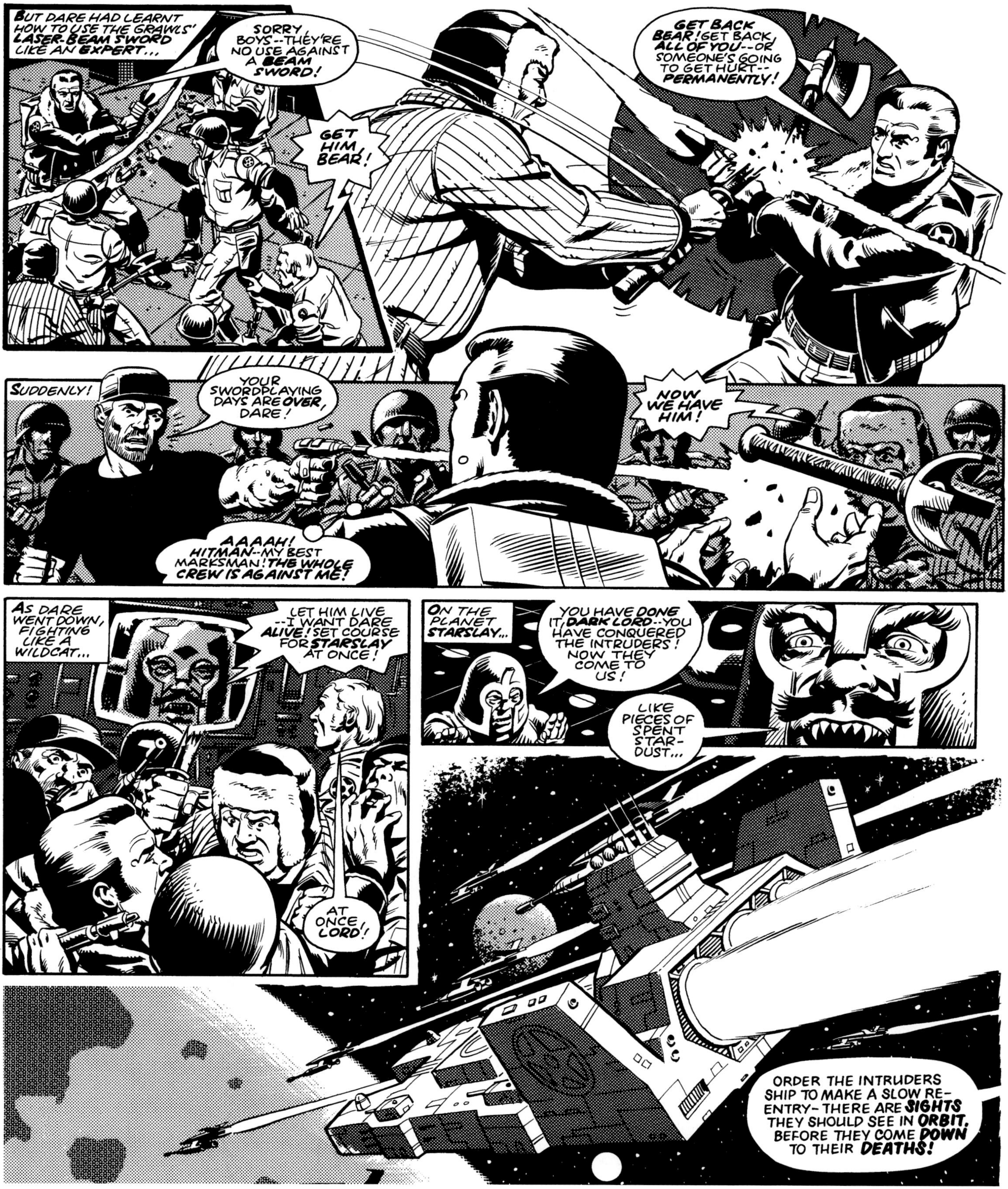
BUT DARE HAD LEARNT HOW TO USE THE GRAWLS' LASER-BEAM SWORD LIKE AN EXPERT...
SORRY, BOYS--THEY'RE NO USE AGAINST A BEAM SWORD!
GET HIM, BEAR!
GET BACK BEAR! GET BACK, ALL OF YOU--OR SOMEONE'S GOING TO GET HURT--PERMANENTLY!
SUDDENLY!
YOUR SWORDPLAYING DAYS ARE OVER, DARE!
NOW WE HAVE HIM!
AAAAH! HITMAN--MY BEST MARKSMAN! THE WHOLE CREW IS AGAINST ME!
AS DARE WENT DOWN, FIGHTING LIKE A WILDCAT...
LET HIM LIVE--I WANT DARE ALIVE! SET COURSE FOR STARSLAY AT ONCE!
AT ONCE, LORD!
ON THE PLANET STARSLAY...
YOU HAVE DONE IT, DARK LORD--YOU HAVE CONQUERED THE INTRUDERS! NOW THEY COME TO US!
LIKE PIECES OF SPENT STAR-DUST...
ORDER THE INTRUDERS SHIP TO MAKE A SLOW RE-ENTRY- THERE ARE SIGHTS THEY SHOULD SEE IN ORBIT, BEFORE THEY COME DOWN TO THEIR DEATHS!

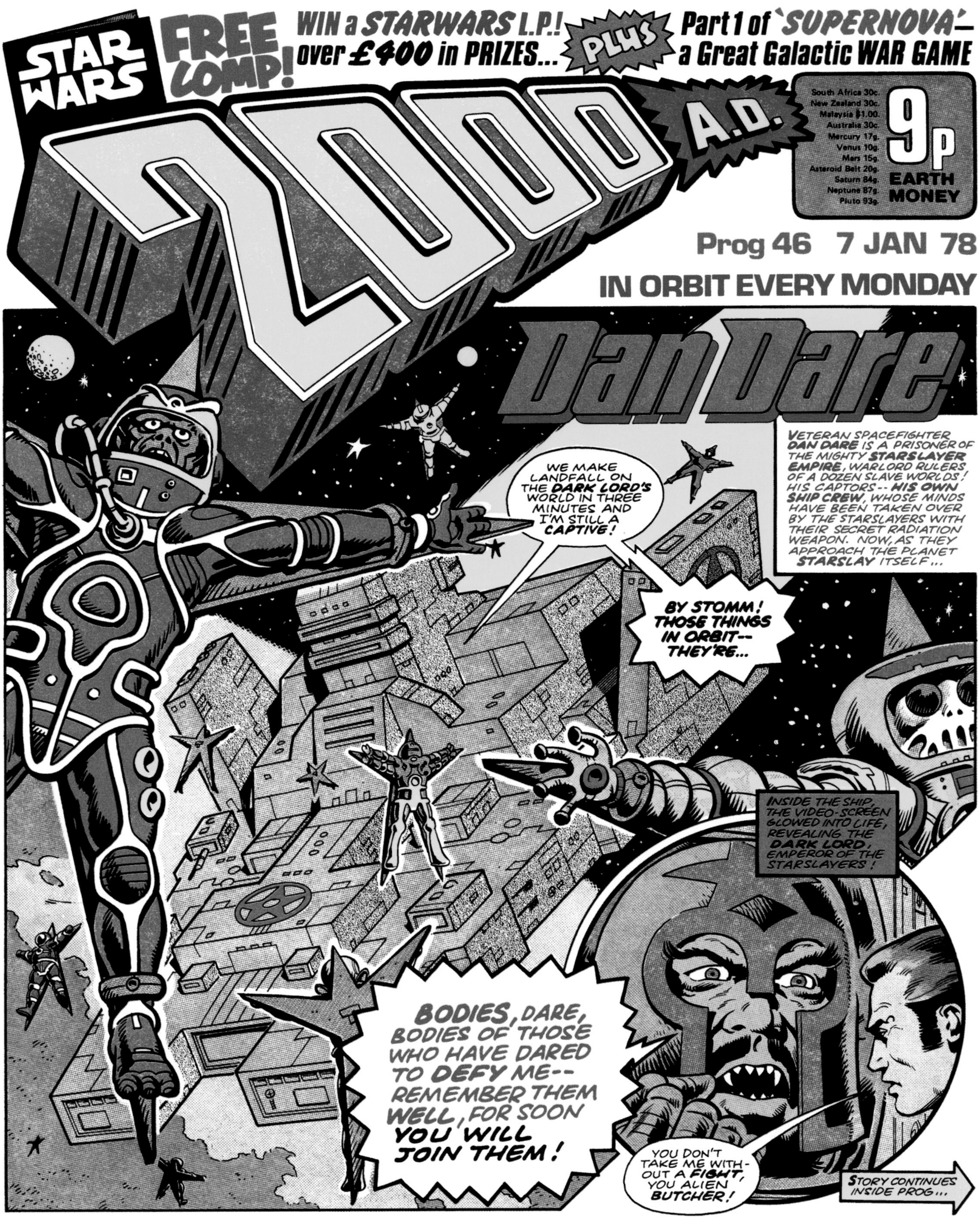
STAR WARS
FREE COMP!
WIN a STARWARS L.P.! over £400 in PRIZES...
PLUS
Part 1 of 'SUPERNOVA'– a Great Galactic WAR GAME
2000 A.D.
South Africa 30c. New Zealand 30c. Malaysia $1.00. Australia 30c. Mercury 17g. Venus 10g. Mars 15g. Asteroid Belt 20g. Saturn 84g. Neptune 87g. Pluto 93g.
9p EARTH MONEY
Prog 46 7 JAN 78
IN ORBIT EVERY MONDAY
Dan Dare
VETERAN SPACEFIGHTER DAN DARE IS A PRISONER OF THE MIGHTY STARSLAYER EMPIRE, WARLORD RULERS OF A DOZEN SLAVE WORLDS! HIS CAPTORS -- HIS OWN SHIP CREW, WHOSE MINDS HAVE BEEN TAKEN OVER BY THE STARSLAYERS WITH THEIR SECRET RADIATION WEAPON. NOW, AS THEY APPROACH THE PLANET STARSLAY ITSELF...
WE MAKE LANDFALL ON THE DARK LORD'S WORLD IN THREE MINUTES AND I'M STILL A CAPTIVE!
BY STOMM! THOSE THINGS IN ORBIT-- THEY'RE...
INSIDE THE SHIP, THE VIDEO-SCREEN GLOWED INTO LIFE, REVEALING THE DARK LORD, EMPEROR OF THE STARSLAYERS!
BODIES, DARE, BODIES OF THOSE WHO HAVE DARED TO DEFY ME-- REMEMBER THEM WELL, FOR SOON YOU WILL JOIN THEM!
YOU DON'T TAKE ME WITH-OUT A FIGHT, YOU ALIEN BUTCHER!
STORY CONTINUES INSIDE PROG...

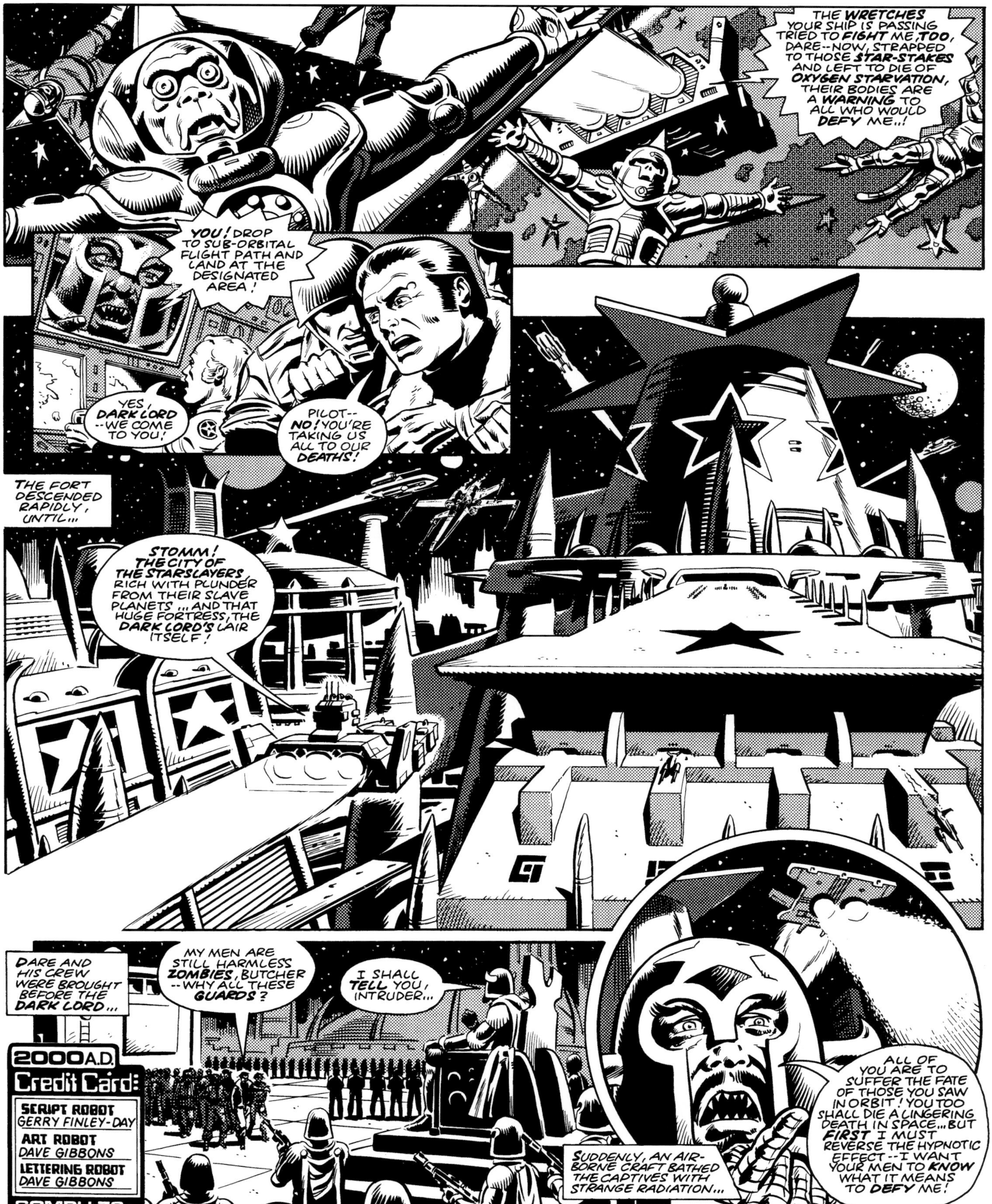
THE WRETCHES YOUR SHIP IS PASSING TRIED TO FIGHT ME, TOO, DARE--NOW, STRAPPED TO THOSE STAR-STAKES AND LEFT TO DIE OF OXYGEN STARVATION, THEIR BODIES ARE A WARNING TO ALL WHO WOULD DEFY ME..!
YOU! DROP TO SUB-ORBITAL FLIGHT PATH AND LAND AT THE DESIGNATED AREA!
YES, DARK LORD --WE COME TO YOU!
PILOT-- NO! YOU'RE TAKING US ALL TO OUR DEATHS!
THE FORT DESCENDED RAPIDLY, UNTIL...
STOMM! THE CITY OF THE STARSLAYERS, RICH WITH PLUNDER FROM THEIR SLAVE PLANETS ... AND THAT HUGE FORTRESS, THE DARK LORD'S LAIR ITSELF!
DARE AND HIS CREW WERE BROUGHT BEFORE THE DARK LORD...
MY MEN ARE STILL HARMLESS ZOMBIES, BUTCHER --WHY ALL THESE GUARDS?
I SHALL TELL YOU, INTRUDER...
SUDDENLY, AN AIR-BORNE CRAFT BATHED THE CAPTIVES WITH STRANGE RADIATION...
ALL OF YOU ARE TO SUFFER THE FATE OF THOSE YOU SAW IN ORBIT! YOU TOO SHALL DIE A LINGERING DEATH IN SPACE...BUT FIRST I MUST REVERSE THE HYPNOTIC EFFECT--I WANT YOUR MEN TO KNOW WHAT IT MEANS TO DEFY ME!
2000 A.D. Credit Card:
SCRIPT ROBOT GERRY FINLEY-DAY
ART ROBOT DAVE GIBBONS
LETTERING ROBOT DAVE GIBBONS
COMPU-73E

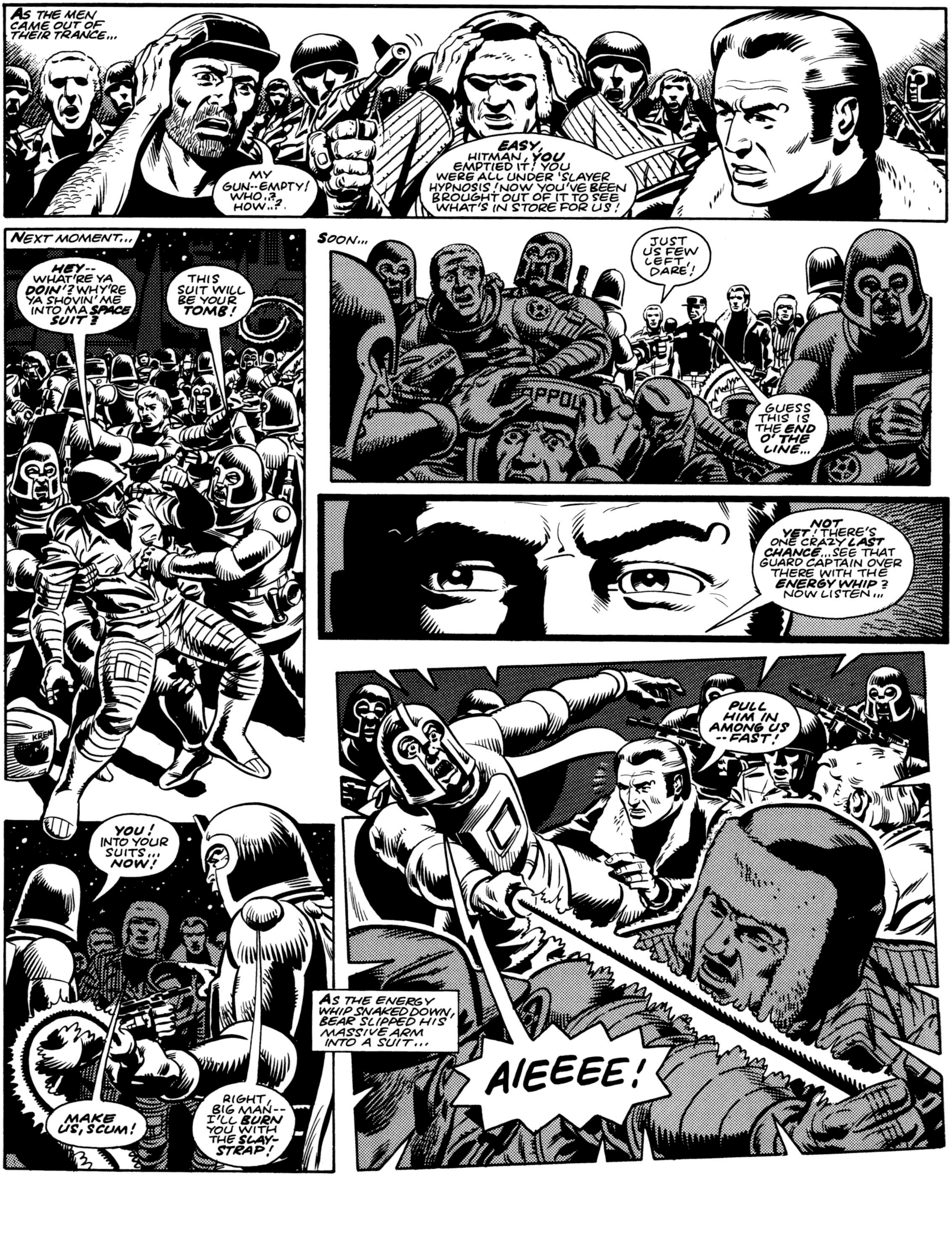

AS THE MEN CAME OUT OF THEIR TRANCE...
MY GUN--EMPTY! WHO..? HOW..?.
EASY, HITMAN, YOU EMPTIED IT! YOU WERE ALL UNDER 'SLAYER HYPNOSIS! NOW YOU'VE BEEN BROUGHT OUT OF IT TO SEE WHAT'S IN STORE FOR US!
NEXT MOMENT...
HEY-- WHAT'RE YA DOIN'? WHY'RE YA SHOVIN' ME INTO MA SPACE SUIT?
THIS SUIT WILL BE YOUR TOMB!
SOON...
JUST US FEW LEFT DARE!
GUESS THIS IS THE END O' THE LINE...
NOT YET! THERE'S ONE CRAZY LAST CHANCE... SEE THAT GUARD CAPTAIN OVER THERE WITH THE ENERGY WHIP? NOW LISTEN...
YOU! INTO YOUR SUITS... NOW!
MAKE US, SCUM!
RIGHT, BIG MAN-- I'LL BURN YOU WITH THE SLAY-STRAP!
PULL HIM IN AMONG US --FAST!
AS THE ENERGY WHIP SNAKED DOWN, BEAR SLIPPED HIS MASSIVE ARM INTO A SUIT...
AIEEEE!

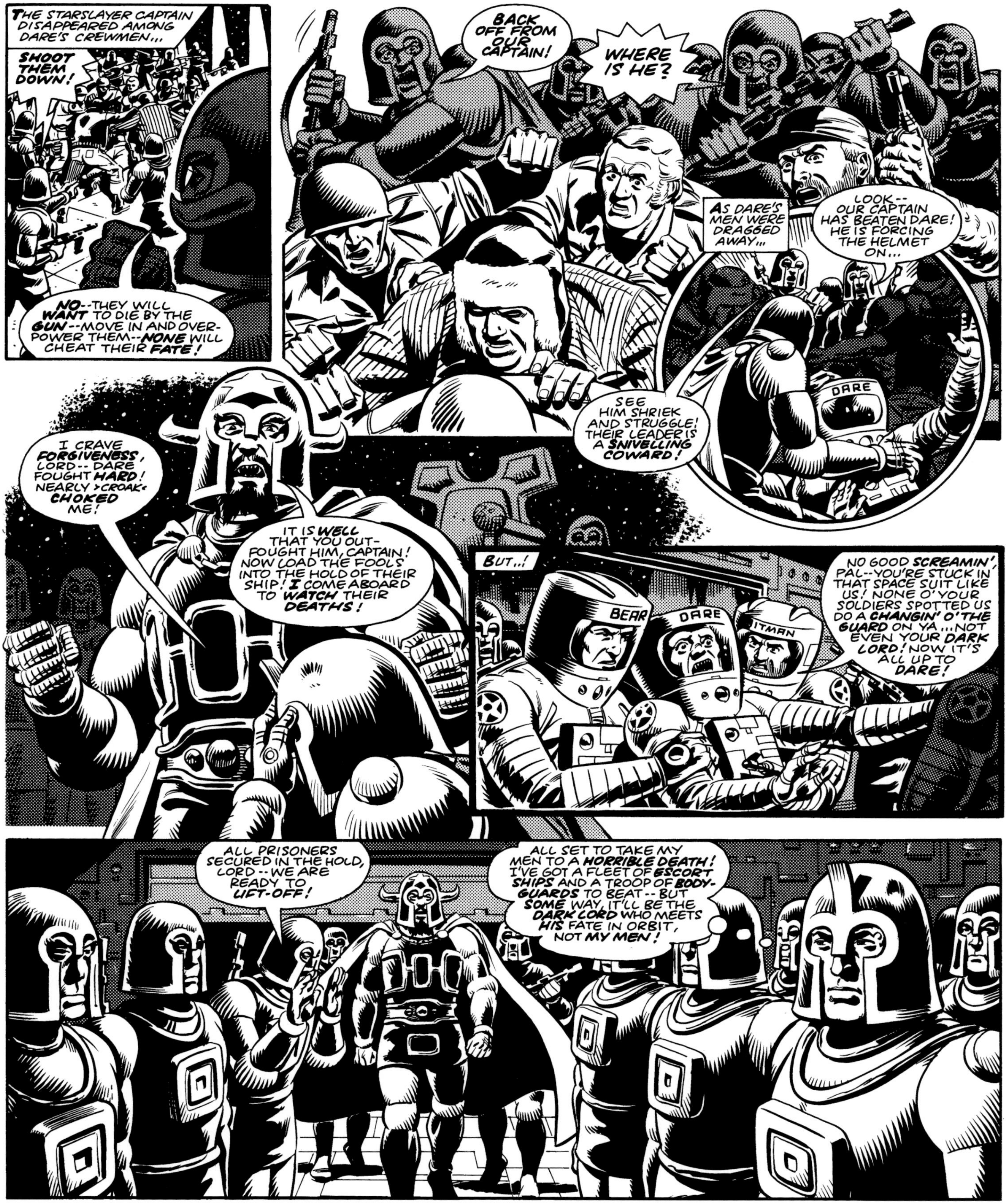
THE STARSLAYER CAPTAIN DISAPPEARED AMONG DARE'S CREWMEN...
SHOOT THEM DOWN!
NO--THEY WILL WANT TO DIE BY THE GUN--MOVE IN AND OVER-POWER THEM--NONE WILL CHEAT THEIR FATE!
BACK OFF FROM OUR CAPTAIN!
WHERE IS HE?
AS DARE'S MEN WERE DRAGGED AWAY...
LOOK--OUR CAPTAIN HAS BEATEN DARE! HE IS FORCING THE HELMET ON...
SEE HIM SHRIEK AND STRUGGLE! THEIR LEADER IS A SNIVELLING COWARD!
DARE
I CRAVE FORGIVENESS, LORD--DARE FOUGHT HARD! NEARLY >CROAK< CHOKED ME!
IT IS WELL THAT YOU OUT-FOUGHT HIM, CAPTAIN! NOW LOAD THE FOOLS INTO THE HOLD OF THEIR SHIP! I COME ABOARD TO WATCH THEIR DEATHS!
BUT..!
BEAR
DARE
ITMAN
NO GOOD SCREAMIN', PAL--YOU'RE STUCK IN THAT SPACE SUIT LIKE US! NONE O' YOUR SOLDIERS SPOTTED US DO A CHANGIN' O' THE GUARD ON YA...NOT EVEN YOUR DARK LORD! NOW IT'S ALL UP TO DARE!
ALL PRISONERS SECURED IN THE HOLD, LORD--WE ARE READY TO LIFT-OFF!
ALL SET TO TAKE MY MEN TO A HORRIBLE DEATH! I'VE GOT A FLEET OF ESCORT SHIPS AND A TROOP OF BODY-GUARDS TO BEAT--BUT SOME WAY, IT'LL BE THE DARK LORD WHO MEETS HIS FATE IN ORBIT, NOT MY MEN!

IN THIS PROG → PART 2 of 'SUPERNOVA' the Game to End it all!
PART 2 of our Great Free STAR WARS Comp!

Prog 47 14 JAN 78

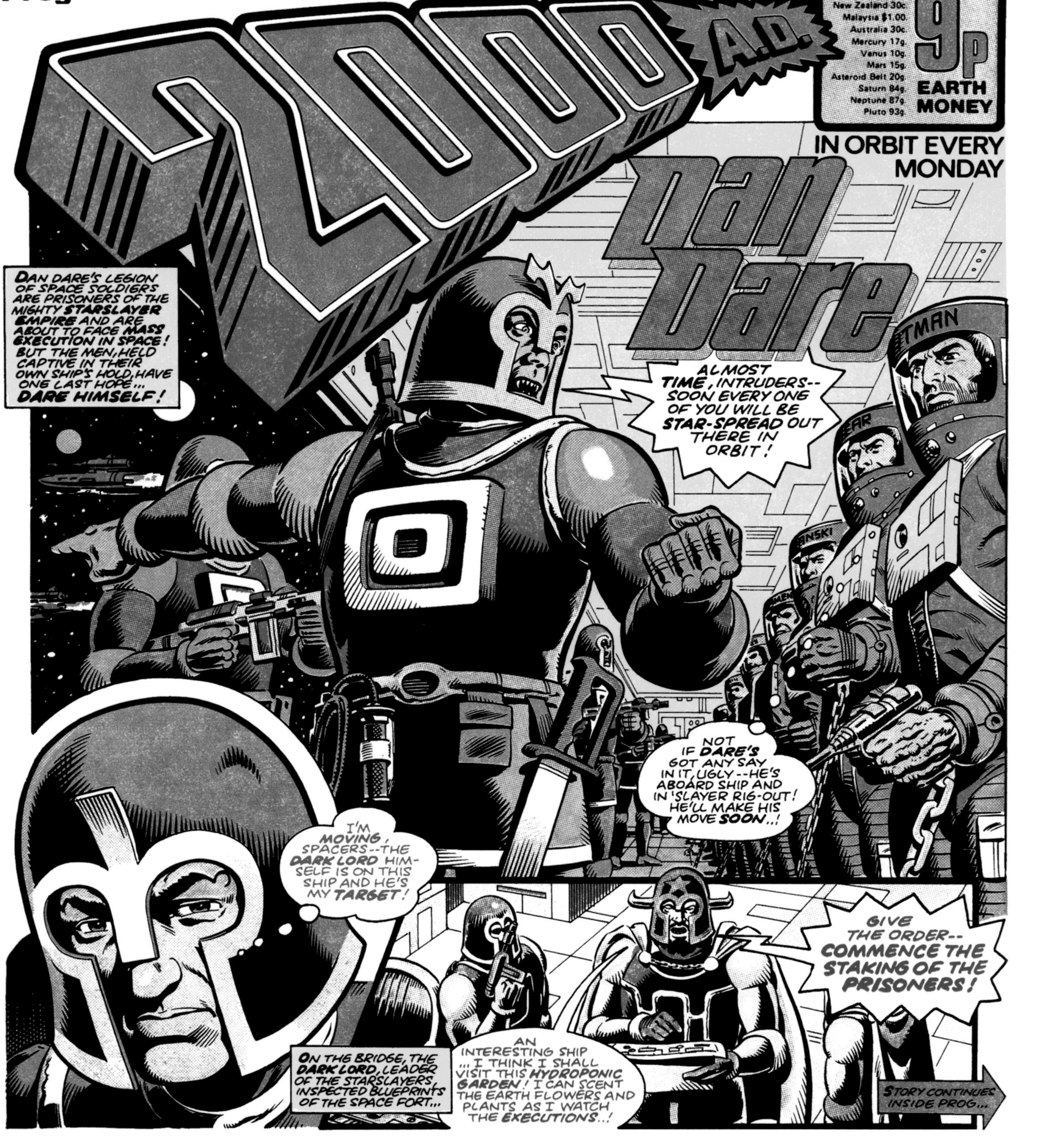

2000 A.D.
South Africa 30c. New Zealand 30c. Malaysia $1.00. Australia 30c. Mercury 17g. Venus 10g. Mars 15g. Asteroid Belt 20g. Saturn 84g. Neptune 87g. Pluto 93g.
9p EARTH MONEY
IN ORBIT EVERY MONDAY
Dan Dare
DAN DARE'S LEGION OF SPACE SOLDIERS ARE PRISONERS OF THE MIGHTY STARSLAYER EMPIRE AND ARE ABOUT TO FACE MASS EXECUTION IN SPACE! BUT THE MEN, HELD CAPTIVE IN THEIR OWN SHIP'S HOLD, HAVE ONE LAST HOPE... DARE HIMSELF!
ALMOST TIME, INTRUDERS-- SOON EVERY ONE OF YOU WILL BE STAR-SPREAD OUT THERE IN ORBIT!
NOT IF DARE'S GOT ANY SAY IN IT, UGLY--HE'S ABOARD SHIP AND IN 'SLAYER RIG-OUT! HE'LL MAKE HIS MOVE SOON..!
I'M MOVING, SPACERS--THE DARK LORD HIMSELF IS ON THIS SHIP AND HE'S MY TARGET!
GIVE THE ORDER-- COMMENCE THE STAKING OF THE PRISONERS!
ON THE BRIDGE, THE DARK LORD, LEADER OF THE STARSLAYERS, INSPECTED BLUEPRINTS OF THE SPACE FORT...
AN INTERESTING SHIP ...I THINK I SHALL VISIT THIS HYDROPONIC GARDEN! I CAN SCENT THE EARTH FLOWERS AND PLANTS AS I WATCH THE EXECUTIONS..!
STORY CONTINUES INSIDE PROG...

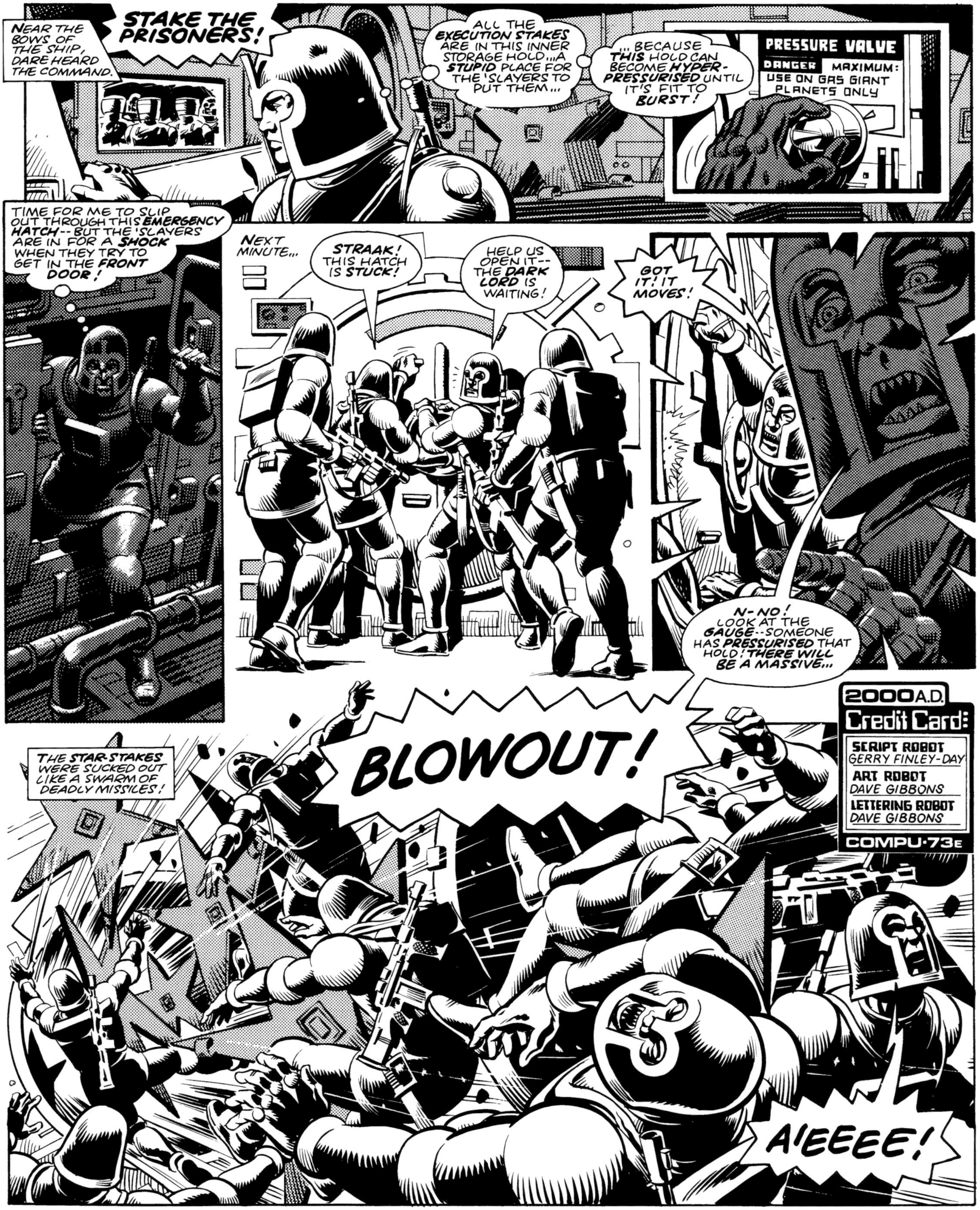
NEAR THE BOWS OF THE SHIP, DARE HEARD THE COMMAND.
STAKE THE PRISONERS!
ALL THE EXECUTION STAKES ARE IN THIS INNER STORAGE HOLD...A STUPID PLACE FOR THE 'SLAYERS TO PUT THEM...
...BECAUSE THIS HOLD CAN BECOME HYPER-PRESSURISED UNTIL IT'S FIT TO BURST!
PRESSURE VALVE
DANGER MAXIMUM: USE ON GAS GIANT PLANETS ONLY
TIME FOR ME TO SLIP OUT THROUGH THIS EMERGENCY HATCH--BUT THE 'SLAYERS ARE IN FOR A SHOCK WHEN THEY TRY TO GET IN THE FRONT DOOR!
NEXT MINUTE...
STRAAK! THIS HATCH IS STUCK!
HELP US OPEN IT--THE DARK LORD IS WAITING!
GOT IT! IT MOVES!
N-NO! LOOK AT THE GAUGE--SOMEONE HAS PRESSURISED THAT HOLD! THERE WILL BE A MASSIVE...
BLOWOUT!
THE STAR-STAKES WERE SUCKED OUT LIKE A SWARM OF DEADLY MISSILES!
2000 A.D. Credit Card:
SCRIPT ROBOT GERRY FINLEY-DAY
ART ROBOT DAVE GIBBONS
LETTERING ROBOT DAVE GIBBONS
COMPU-73E
AIEEEE!

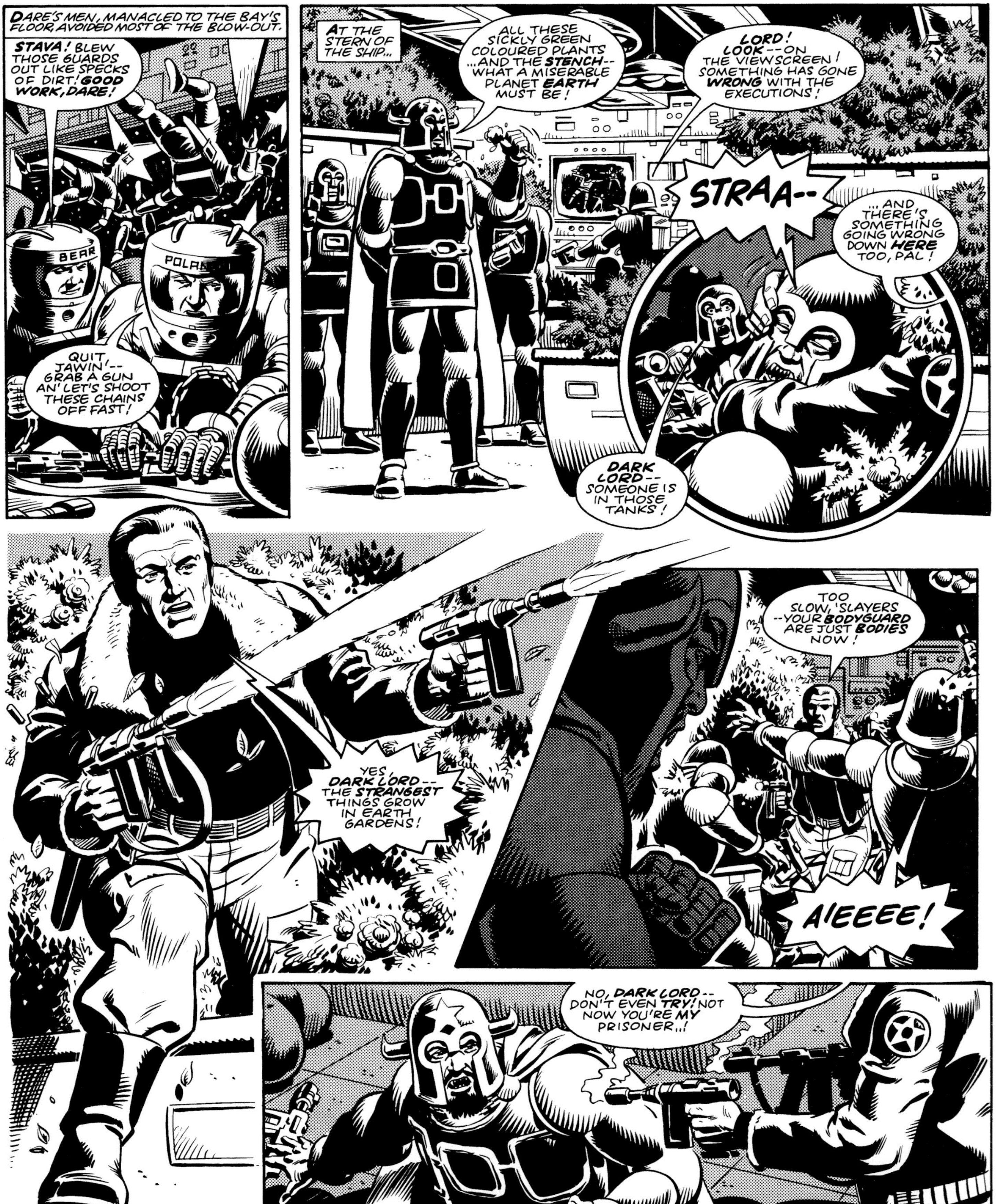

DARE'S MEN, MANACLED TO THE BAY'S FLOOR, AVOIDED MOST OF THE BLOW-OUT.
STAVA! BLEW THOSE GUARDS OUT LIKE SPECKS OF DIRT! GOOD WORK, DARE!
BEAR
POLAR
QUIT JAWIN'-- GRAB A GUN AN' LET'S SHOOT THESE CHAINS OFF FAST!
AT THE STERN OF THE SHIP...
ALL THESE SICKLY GREEN COLOURED PLANTS ...AND THE STENCH-- WHAT A MISERABLE PLANET EARTH MUST BE!
LORD! LOOK--ON THE VIEWSCREEN! SOMETHING HAS GONE WRONG WITH THE EXECUTIONS!
STRAA--
...AND THERE'S SOMETHING GOING WRONG DOWN HERE TOO, PAL!
DARK LORD-- SOMEONE IS IN THOSE TANKS!
YES, DARK LORD-- THE STRANGEST THINGS GROW IN EARTH GARDENS!
TOO SLOW, 'SLAYERS --YOUR BODYGUARD ARE JUST BODIES NOW!
AIEEEE!
NO, DARK LORD-- DON'T EVEN TRY! NOT NOW YOU'RE MY PRISONER..!

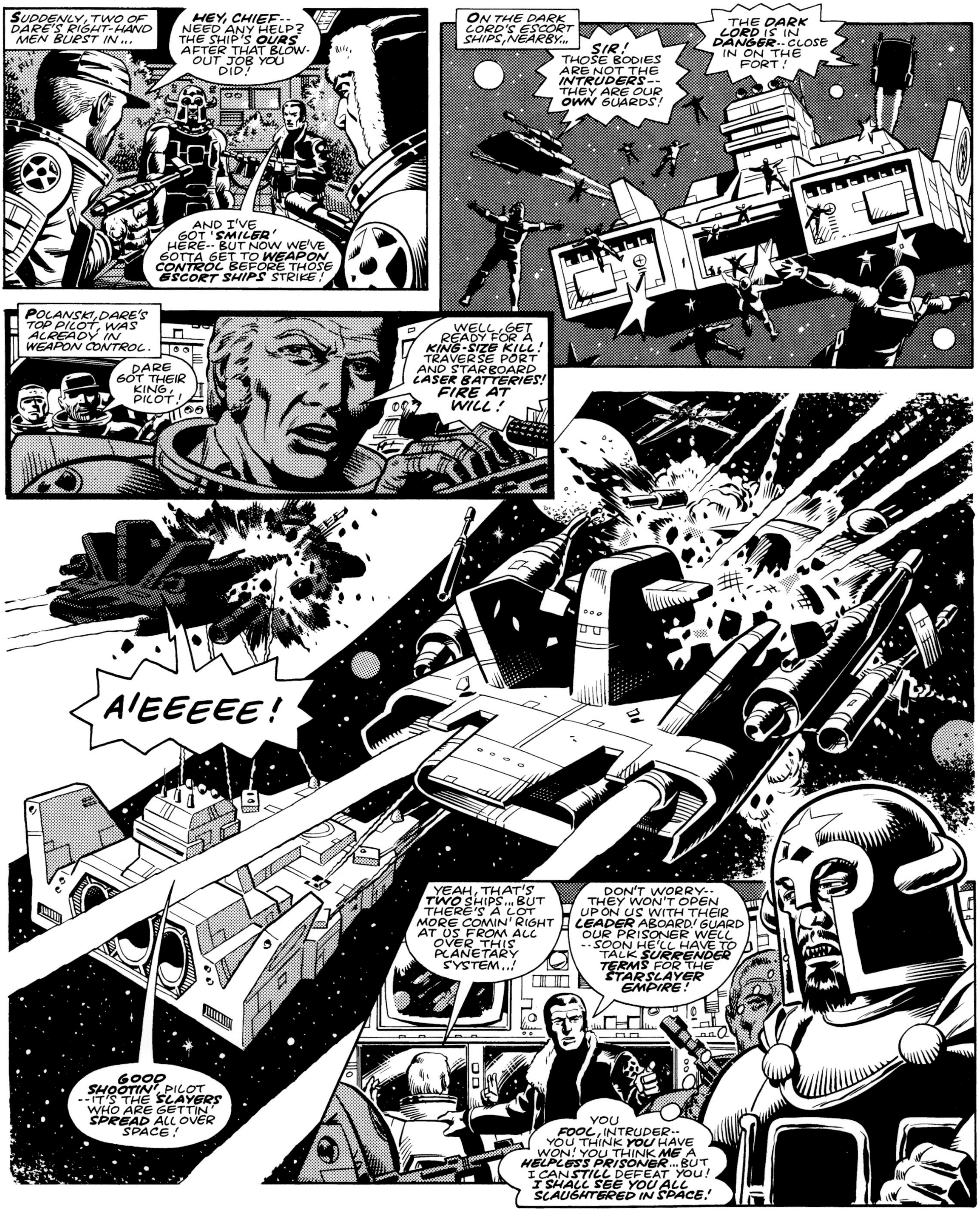

SUDDENLY, TWO OF DARE'S RIGHT-HAND MEN BURST IN...
HEY, CHIEF-- NEED ANY HELP? THE SHIP'S OURS AFTER THAT BLOW-OUT JOB YOU DID!
AND I'VE GOT 'SMILER' HERE-- BUT NOW WE'VE GOTTA GET TO WEAPON CONTROL BEFORE THOSE ESCORT SHIPS STRIKE!
ON THE DARK LORD'S ESCORT SHIPS, NEARBY...
SIR! THOSE BODIES ARE NOT THE INTRUDERS-- THEY ARE OUR OWN GUARDS!
THE DARK LORD IS IN DANGER-- CLOSE IN ON THE FORT!
POLANSKI, DARE'S TOP PILOT, WAS ALREADY IN WEAPON CONTROL.
DARE GOT THEIR KING, PILOT!
WELL, GET READY FOR A KING-SIZE KILL! TRAVERSE PORT AND STARBOARD LASER BATTERIES! FIRE AT WILL!
AIEEEEE!
GOOD SHOOTIN', PILOT --IT'S THE SLAYERS WHO ARE GETTIN' SPREAD ALL OVER SPACE!
YEAH, THAT'S TWO SHIPS... BUT THERE'S A LOT MORE COMIN' RIGHT AT US FROM ALL OVER THIS PLANETARY SYSTEM...!
DON'T WORRY-- THEY WON'T OPEN UP ON US WITH THEIR LEADER ABOARD! GUARD OUR PRISONER WELL --SOON HE'LL HAVE TO TALK SURRENDER TERMS FOR THE STARSLAYER EMPIRE!
YOU FOOL, INTRUDER-- YOU THINK YOU HAVE WON! YOU THINK ME A HELPLESS PRISONER... BUT I CAN STILL DEFEAT YOU! I SHALL SEE YOU ALL SLAUGHTERED IN SPACE!

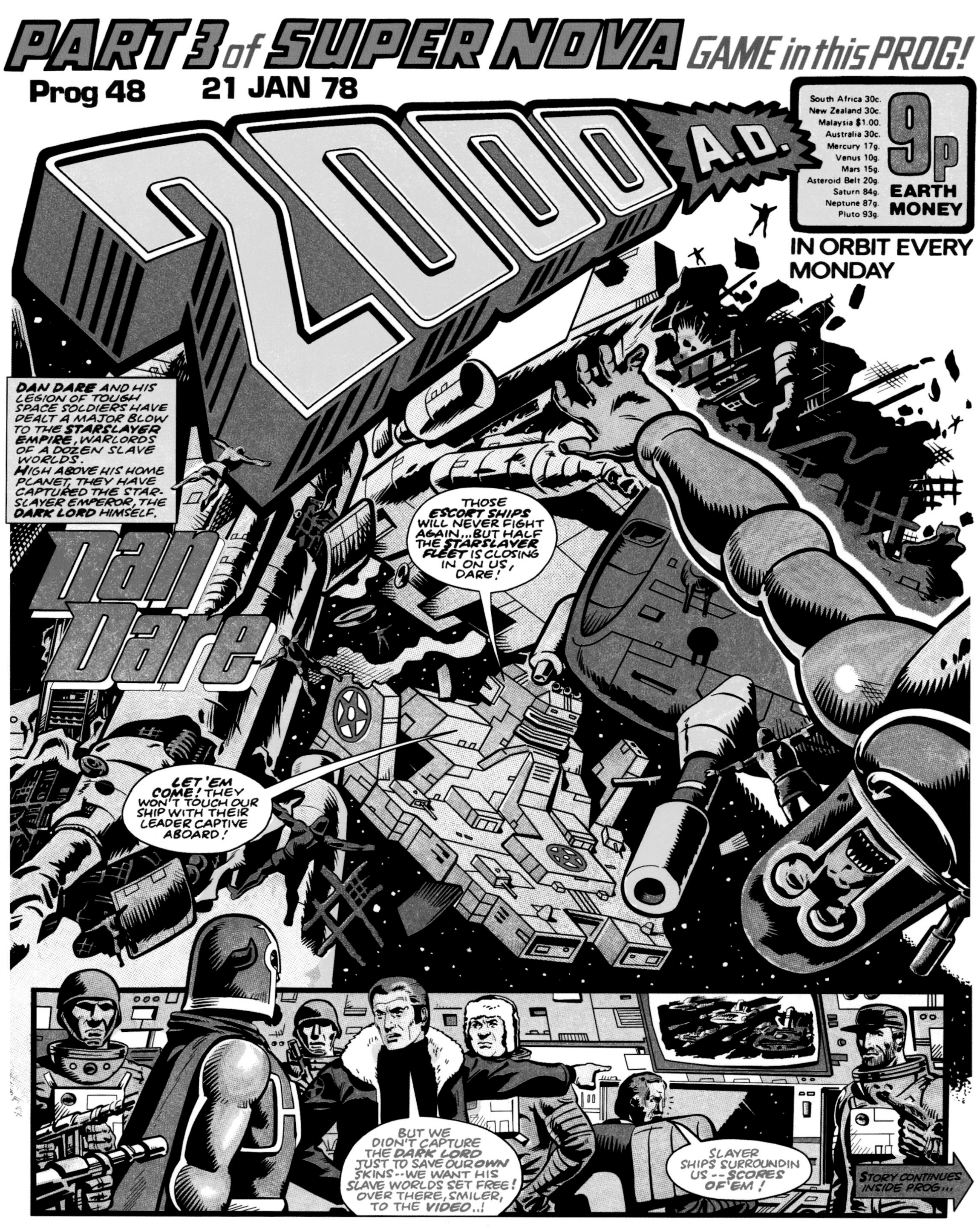

PART 3 of SUPER NOVA GAME in this PROG!
Prog 48
21 JAN 78
2000 A.D.
South Africa 30c. New Zealand 30c. Malaysia $1.00. Australia 30c. Mercury 17g. Venus 10g. Mars 15g. Asteroid Belt 20g. Saturn 84g. Neptune 87g. Pluto 93g.
9p EARTH MONEY
IN ORBIT EVERY MONDAY
DAN DARE AND HIS LEGION OF TOUGH SPACE SOLDIERS HAVE DEALT A MAJOR BLOW TO THE STARSLAYER EMPIRE, WARLORDS OF A DOZEN SLAVE WORLDS. HIGH ABOVE HIS HOME PLANET, THEY HAVE CAPTURED THE STAR-SLAYER EMPEROR, THE DARK LORD HIMSELF.
Dan Dare
THOSE ESCORT SHIPS WILL NEVER FIGHT AGAIN...BUT HALF THE STARSLAYER FLEET IS CLOSING IN ON US, DARE!
LET'EM COME! THEY WON'T TOUCH OUR SHIP WITH THEIR LEADER CAPTIVE ABOARD!
BUT WE DIDN'T CAPTURE THE DARK LORD JUST TO SAVE OUR OWN SKINS--WE WANT HIS SLAVE WORLDS SET FREE! OVER THERE, SMILER, TO THE VIDEO..!
SLAYER SHIPS SURROUNDIN US--SCORES OF 'EM!
STORY CONTINUES INSIDE PROG...

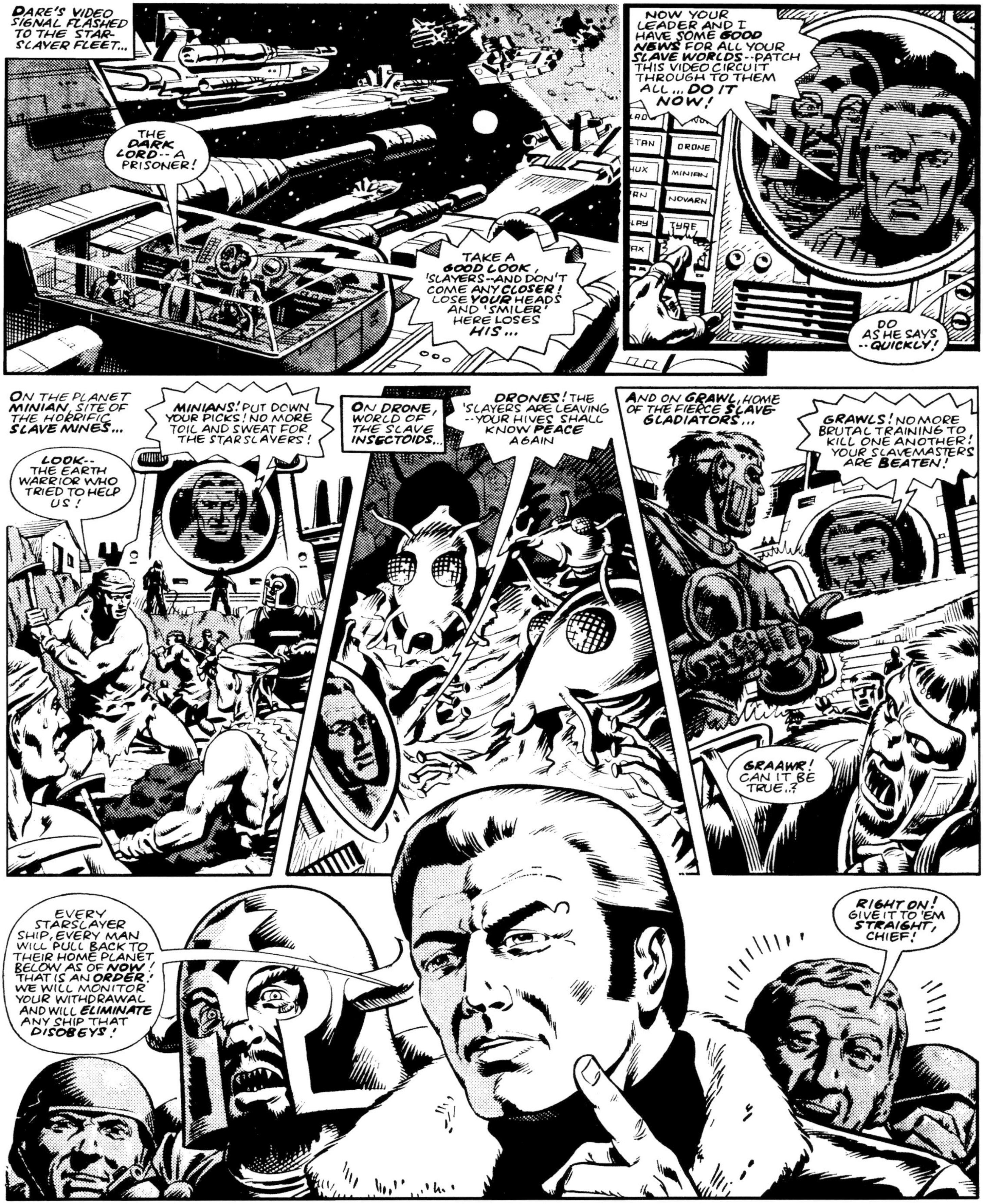

DARE'S VIDEO SIGNAL FLASHED TO THE STAR-SLAYER FLEET...
THE DARK LORD -- A PRISONER!
TAKE A GOOD LOOK, 'SLAYERS -- AND DON'T COME ANY CLOSER! LOSE YOUR HEADS AND 'SMILER' HERE LOSES HIS...
NOW YOUR LEADER AND I HAVE SOME GOOD NEWS FOR ALL YOUR SLAVE WORLDS -- PATCH THIS VIDEO CIRCUIT THROUGH TO THEM ALL... DO IT NOW!
DRONE
MINIAN
NOVARN
TYRE
DO AS HE SAYS -- QUICKLY!
ON THE PLANET MINIAN, SITE OF THE HORRIFIC SLAVE MINES...
MINIANS! PUT DOWN YOUR PICKS! NO MORE TOIL AND SWEAT FOR THE STARSLAYERS!
LOOK -- THE EARTH WARRIOR WHO TRIED TO HELP US!
ON DRONE, WORLD OF THE SLAVE INSECTOIDS...
DRONES! THE 'SLAYERS ARE LEAVING -- YOUR HIVES SHALL KNOW PEACE AGAIN
AND ON GRAWL, HOME OF THE FIERCE SLAVE-GLADIATORS...
GRAWLS! NO MORE BRUTAL TRAINING TO KILL ONE ANOTHER! YOUR SLAVEMASTERS ARE BEATEN!
GRAAWR! CAN IT BE TRUE..?
EVERY STARSLAYER SHIP, EVERY MAN WILL PULL BACK TO THEIR HOME PLANET BELOW AS OF NOW! THAT IS AN ORDER! WE WILL MONITOR YOUR WITHDRAWAL AND WILL ELIMINATE ANY SHIP THAT DISOBEYS!
RIGHT ON! GIVE IT TO 'EM STRAIGHT, CHIEF!

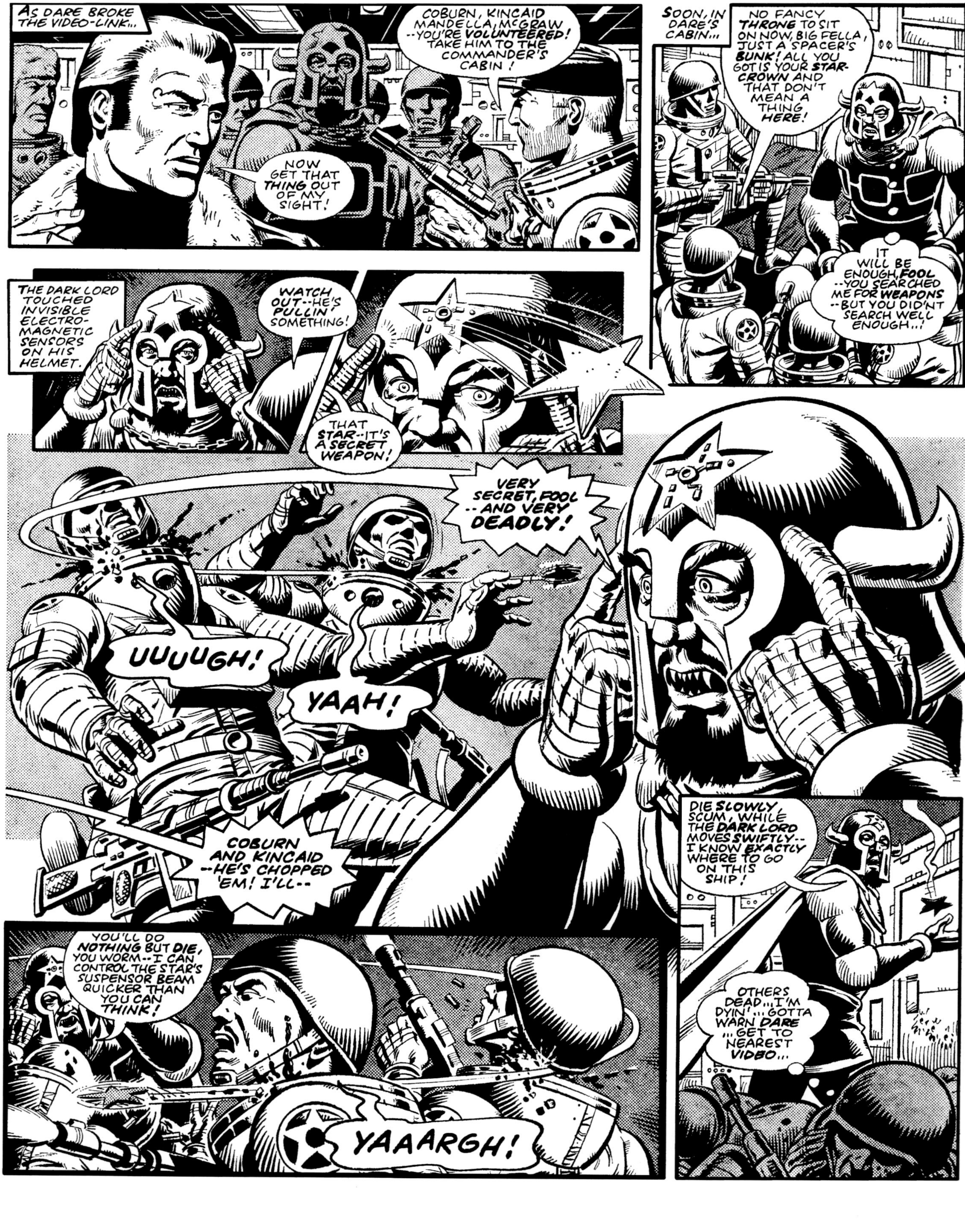
AS DARE BROKE THE VIDEO-LINK...
COBURN, KINCAID MANDELLA, McGRAW --YOU'RE VOLUNTEERED! TAKE HIM TO THE COMMANDER'S CABIN!
NOW GET THAT THING OUT OF MY SIGHT!
SOON, IN DARE'S CABIN...
NO FANCY THRONE TO SIT ON NOW, BIG FELLA, JUST A SPACER'S BUNK! ALL YOU GOT IS YOUR STAR-CROWN AND THAT DON'T MEAN A THING HERE!
IT WILL BE ENOUGH, FOOL --YOU SEARCHED ME FOR WEAPONS --BUT YOU DIDN'T SEARCH WELL ENOUGH...!
THE DARK LORD TOUCHED INVISIBLE ELECTRO-MAGNETIC SENSORS ON HIS HELMET.
WATCH OUT--HE'S PULLIN' SOMETHING!
THAT STAR--IT'S A SECRET WEAPON!
VERY SECRET, FOOL --AND VERY DEADLY!
UUUUGH!
YAAH!
COBURN AND KINCAID --HE'S CHOPPED 'EM! I'LL--
DIE SLOWLY, SCUM, WHILE THE DARK LORD MOVES SWIFTLY-- I KNOW EXACTLY WHERE TO GO ON THIS SHIP!
YOU'LL DO NOTHING BUT DIE, YOU WORM--I CAN CONTROL THE STAR'S SUSPENSOR BEAM QUICKER THAN YOU CAN THINK!
YAAARGH!
OTHERS DEAD...I'M DYIN'...GOTTA WARN DARE ...GET TO NEAREST VIDEO...

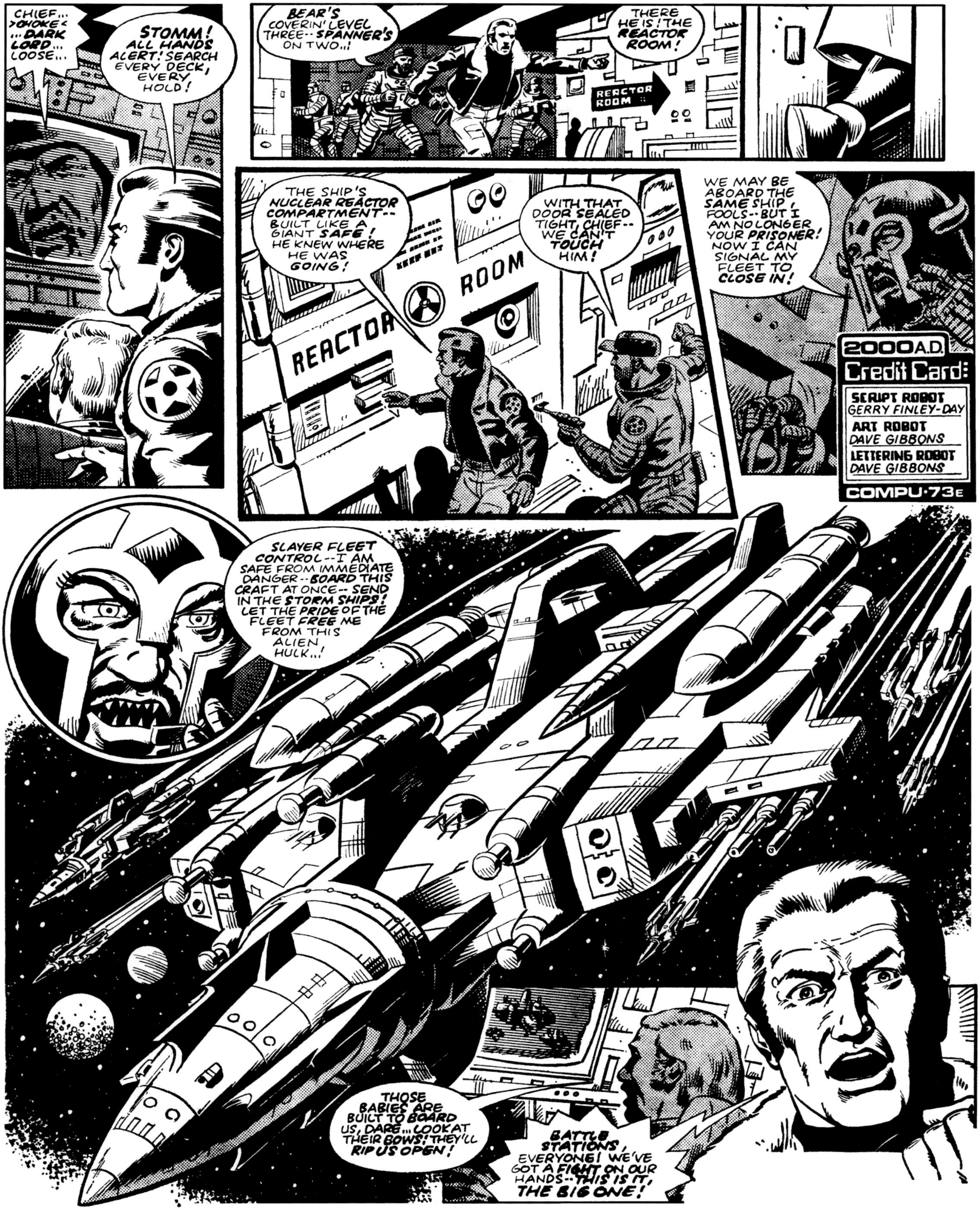

CHIEF... >CHOKE< ...DARK LORD... LOOSE...
STOMM! ALL HANDS ALERT! SEARCH EVERY DECK, EVERY HOLD!
BEAR'S COVERIN' LEVEL THREE-- SPANNER'S ON TWO...!
THERE HE IS! THE REACTOR ROOM!
REACTOR ROOM
THE SHIP'S NUCLEAR REACTOR COMPARTMENT-- BUILT LIKE A GIANT SAFE! HE KNEW WHERE HE WAS GOING!
WITH THAT DOOR SEALED TIGHT, CHIEF-- WE CAN'T TOUCH HIM!
REACTOR ROOM
WE MAY BE ABOARD THE SAME SHIP, FOOLS-- BUT I AM NO LONGER YOUR PRISONER! NOW I CAN SIGNAL MY FLEET TO CLOSE IN!
2000 A.D. Credit Card:
SCRIPT ROBOT GERRY FINLEY-DAY
ART ROBOT DAVE GIBBONS
LETTERING ROBOT DAVE GIBBONS
COMPU·73E
SLAYER FLEET CONTROL-- I AM SAFE FROM IMMEDIATE DANGER-- BOARD THIS CRAFT AT ONCE-- SEND IN THE STORM SHIPS! LET THE PRIDE OF THE FLEET FREE ME FROM THIS ALIEN HULK...!
THOSE BABIES ARE BUILT TO BOARD US, DARE... LOOK AT THEIR BOWS! THEY'LL RIP US OPEN!
BATTLE STATIONS, EVERYONE! WE'VE GOT A FIGHT ON OUR HANDS-- THIS IS IT, THE BIG ONE!

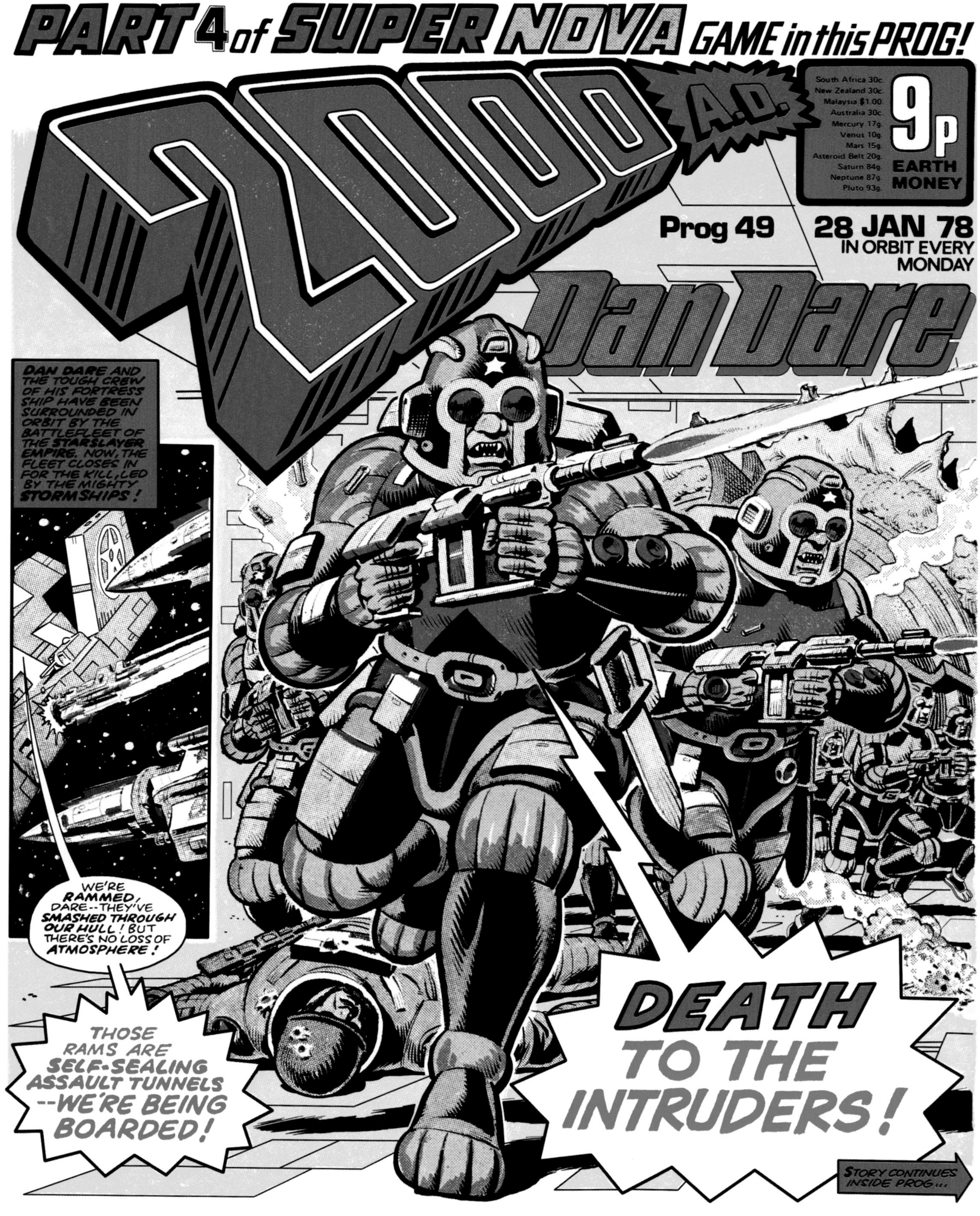

PART 4 of SUPER NOVA GAME in this PROG!
2000 A.D.
South Africa 30c. New Zealand 30c. Malaysia $1.00 Australia 30c. Mercury 17g. Venus 10g. Mars 15g. Asteroid Belt 20g. Saturn 84g. Neptune 87g. Pluto 93g.
9p EARTH MONEY
Prog 49
28 JAN 78 IN ORBIT EVERY MONDAY
Dan Dare
DAN DARE AND THE TOUGH CREW OF HIS FORTRESS SHIP HAVE BEEN SURROUNDED IN ORBIT BY THE BATTLEFLEET OF THE STARSLAYER EMPIRE. NOW, THE FLEET CLOSES IN FOR THE KILL, LED BY THE MIGHTY STORMSHIPS!
WE'RE RAMMED, DARE--THEY'VE SMASHED THROUGH OUR HULL! BUT THERE'S NO LOSS OF ATMOSPHERE!
THOSE RAMS ARE SELF-SEALING ASSAULT TUNNELS --WE'RE BEING BOARDED!
DEATH TO THE INTRUDERS!
STORY CONTINUES INSIDE PROG...

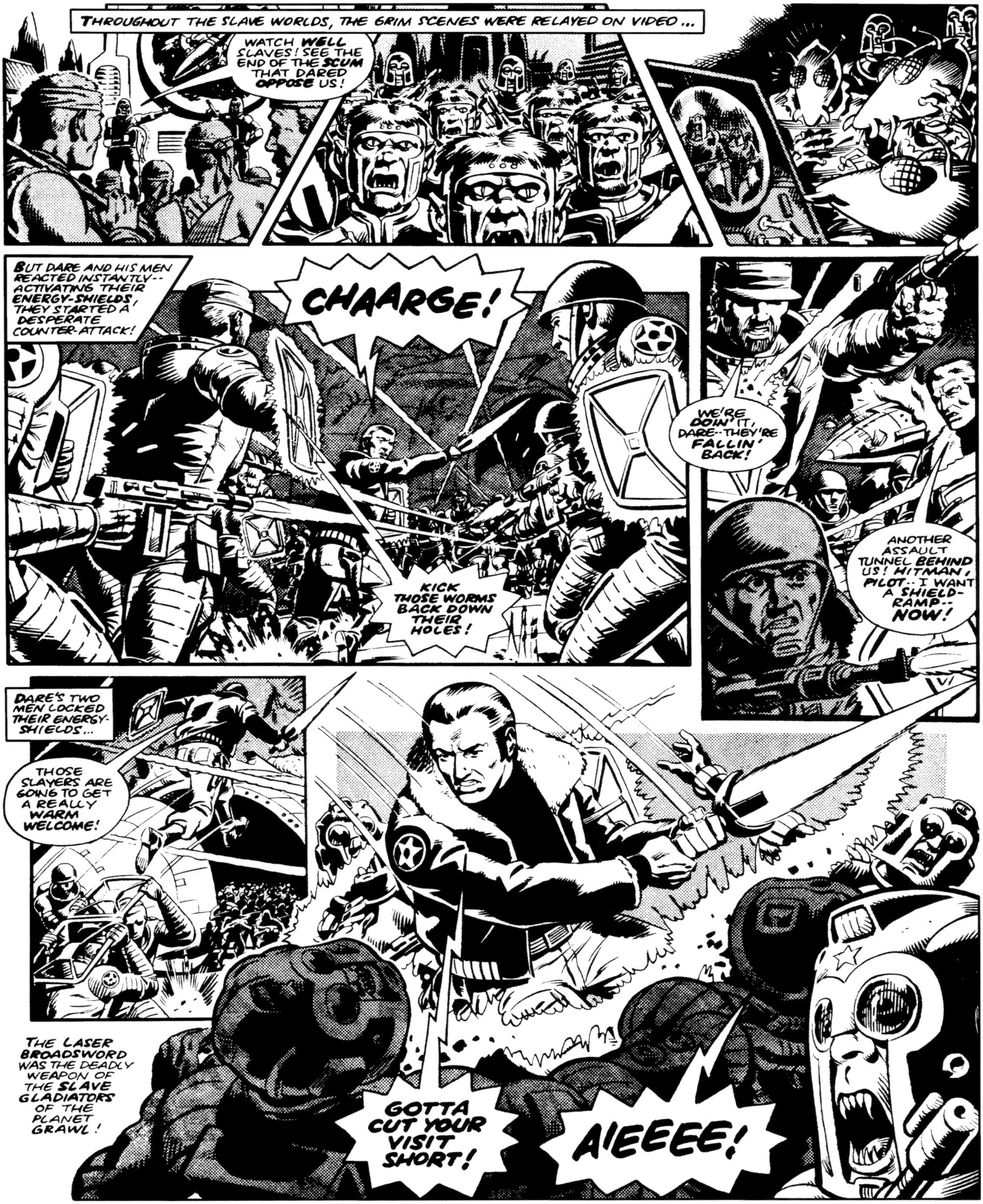
THROUGHOUT THE SLAVE WORLDS, THE GRIM SCENES WERE RELAYED ON VIDEO ...
WATCH WELL SLAVES! SEE THE END OF THE SCUM THAT DARED OPPOSE US!
BUT DARE AND HIS MEN REACTED INSTANTLY -- ACTIVATING THEIR ENERGY-SHIELDS, THEY STARTED A DESPERATE COUNTER-ATTACK!
CHAARGE!
KICK THOSE WORMS BACK DOWN THEIR HOLES!
WE'RE DOIN' IT, DARE-- THEY'RE FALLIN' BACK!
ANOTHER ASSAULT TUNNEL BEHIND US! HITMAN, PILOT-- I WANT A SHIELD-RAMP-- NOW!
DARE'S TWO MEN LOCKED THEIR ENERGY-SHIELDS...
THOSE SLAYERS ARE GOING TO GET A REALLY WARM WELCOME!
THE LASER BROADSWORD WAS THE DEADLY WEAPON OF THE SLAVE GLADIATORS OF THE PLANET GRAWL!
GOTTA CUT YOUR VISIT SHORT!
AIEEEE!

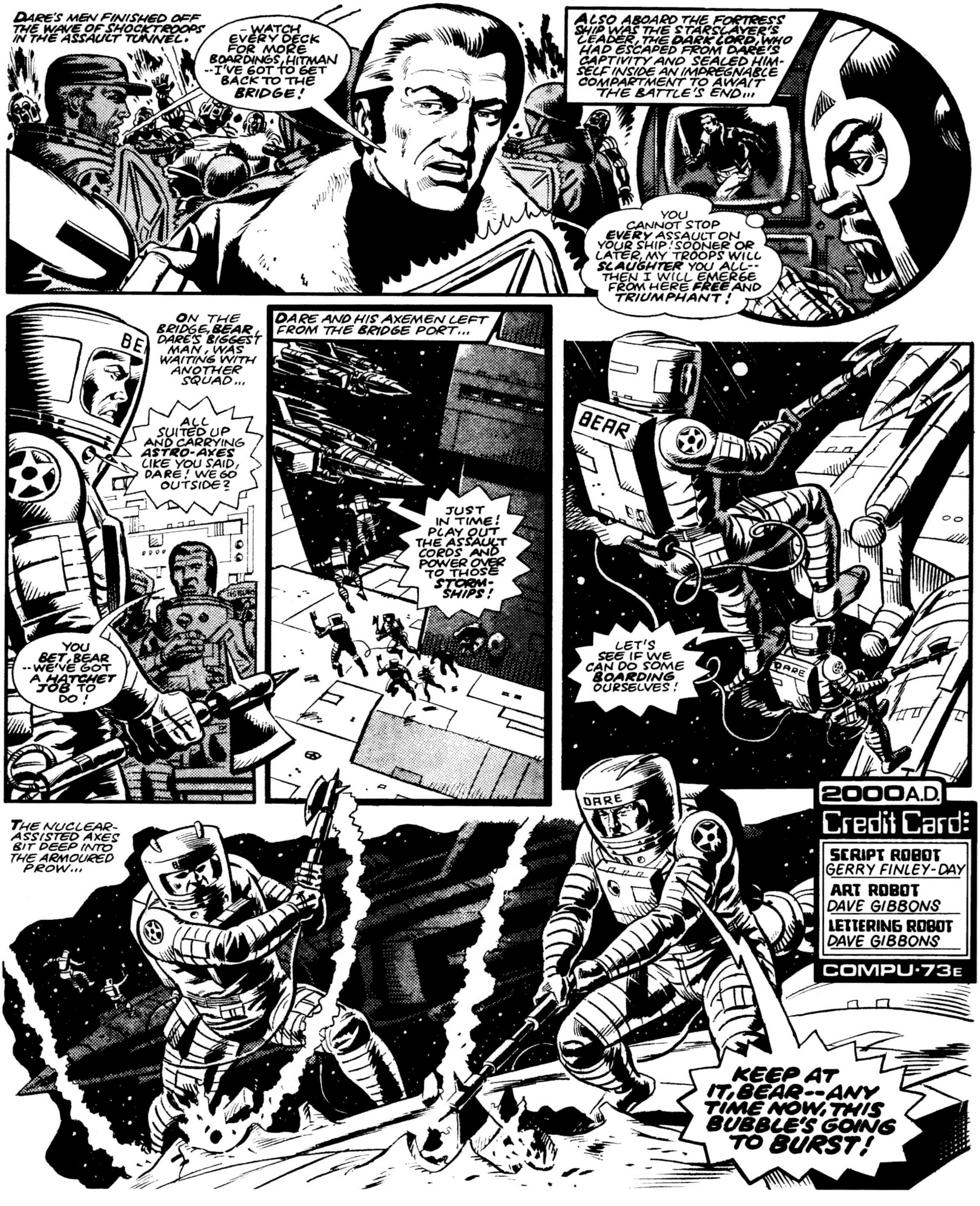
DARE'S MEN FINISHED OFF THE WAVE OF SHOCKTROOPS IN THE ASSAULT TUNNEL.
- WATCH EVERY DECK FOR MORE BOARDINGS, HITMAN -- I'VE GOT TO GET BACK TO THE BRIDGE!
ALSO ABOARD THE FORTRESS SHIP WAS THE STARSLAYER'S LEADER, THE DARK LORD, WHO HAD ESCAPED FROM DARE'S CAPTIVITY AND SEALED HIMSELF INSIDE AN IMPREGNABLE COMPARTMENT TO AWAIT THE BATTLE'S END...
YOU CANNOT STOP EVERY ASSAULT ON YOUR SHIP! SOONER OR LATER, MY TROOPS WILL SLAUGHTER YOU ALL -- THEN I WILL EMERGE FROM HERE FREE AND TRIUMPHANT!
ON THE BRIDGE, BEAR, DARE'S BIGGEST MAN, WAS WAITING WITH ANOTHER SQUAD...
BEAR
ALL SUITED UP AND CARRYING ASTRO-AXES LIKE YOU SAID, DARE! WE GO OUTSIDE?
YOU BET, BEAR -- WE'VE GOT A HATCHET JOB TO DO!
DARE AND HIS AXEMEN LEFT FROM THE BRIDGE PORT...
JUST IN TIME! PLAY OUT THE ASSAULT CORDS AND POWER OVER TO THOSE STORM-SHIPS!
BEAR
LET'S SEE IF WE CAN DO SOME BOARDING OURSELVES!
DARE
THE NUCLEAR-ASSISTED AXES BIT DEEP INTO THE ARMOURED PROW...
DARE
KEEP AT IT, BEAR -- ANY TIME NOW, THIS BUBBLE'S GOING TO BURST!
2000 A.D.
Credit Card:
SCRIPT ROBOT
GERRY FINLEY-DAY
ART ROBOT
DAVE GIBBONS
LETTERING ROBOT
DAVE GIBBONS
COMPU-73E

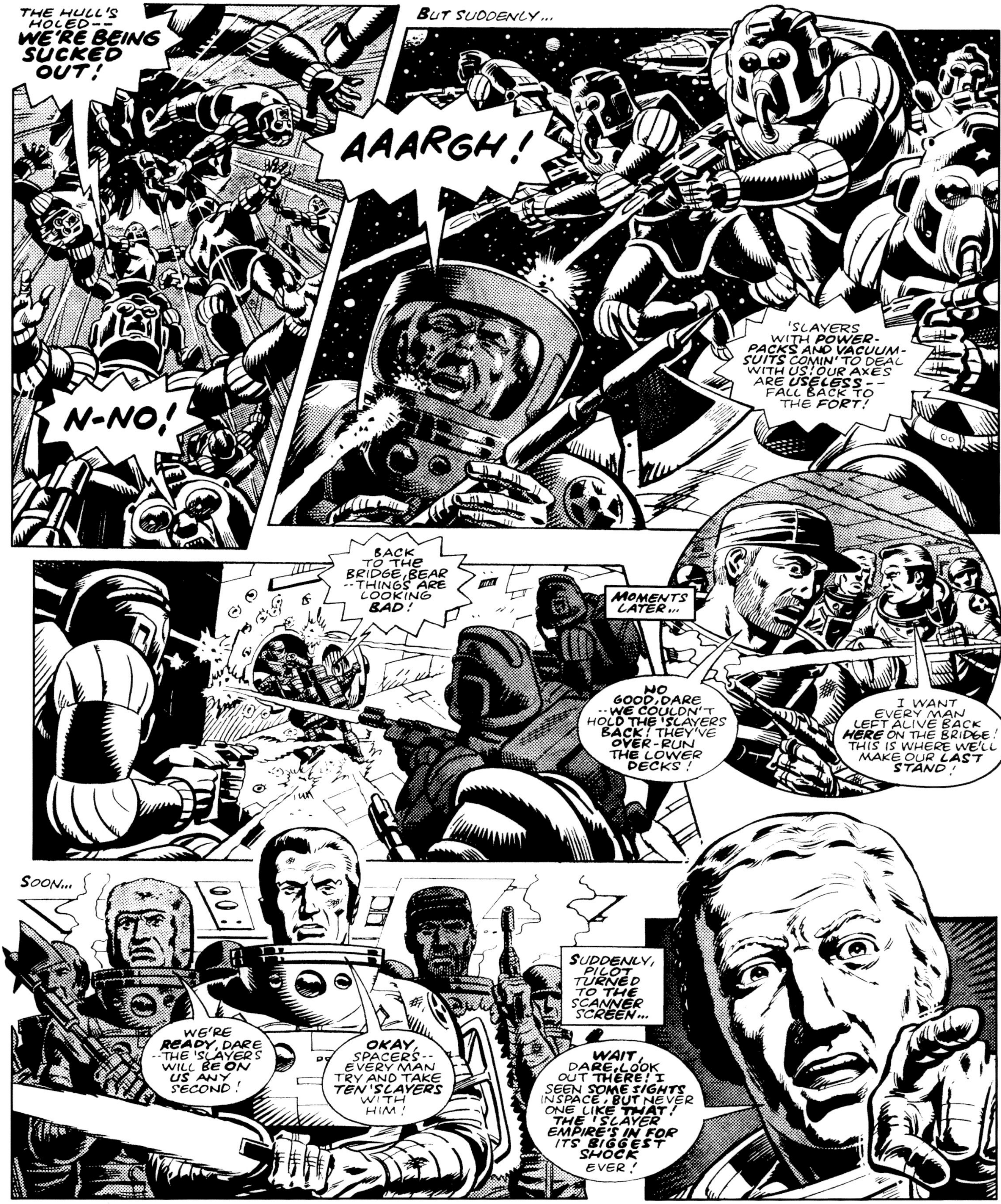
THE HULL'S HOLED-- WE'RE BEING SUCKED OUT!
N-NO!
BUT SUDDENLY...
AAARGH!
'SLAYERS WITH POWER-PACKS AND VACUUM-SUITS COMIN' TO DEAL WITH US! OUR AXES ARE USELESS-- FALL BACK TO THE FORT!
BACK TO THE BRIDGE, BEAR --THINGS ARE LOOKING BAD!
MOMENTS LATER...
NO GOOD, DARE --WE COULDN'T HOLD THE 'SLAYERS BACK! THEY'VE OVER-RUN THE LOWER DECKS!
I WANT EVERY MAN LEFT ALIVE BACK HERE ON THE BRIDGE! THIS IS WHERE WE'LL MAKE OUR LAST STAND!
SOON...
WE'RE READY, DARE --THE 'SLAYERS WILL BE ON US ANY SECOND!
OKAY, SPACERS-- EVERY MAN TRY AND TAKE TEN 'SLAYERS WITH HIM!
SUDDENLY, PILOT TURNED TO THE SCANNER SCREEN...
WAIT, DARE, LOOK OUT THERE! I SEEN SOME SIGHTS IN SPACE, BUT NEVER ONE LIKE THAT! THE 'SLAYER EMPIRE'S IN FOR ITS BIGGEST SHOCK EVER!

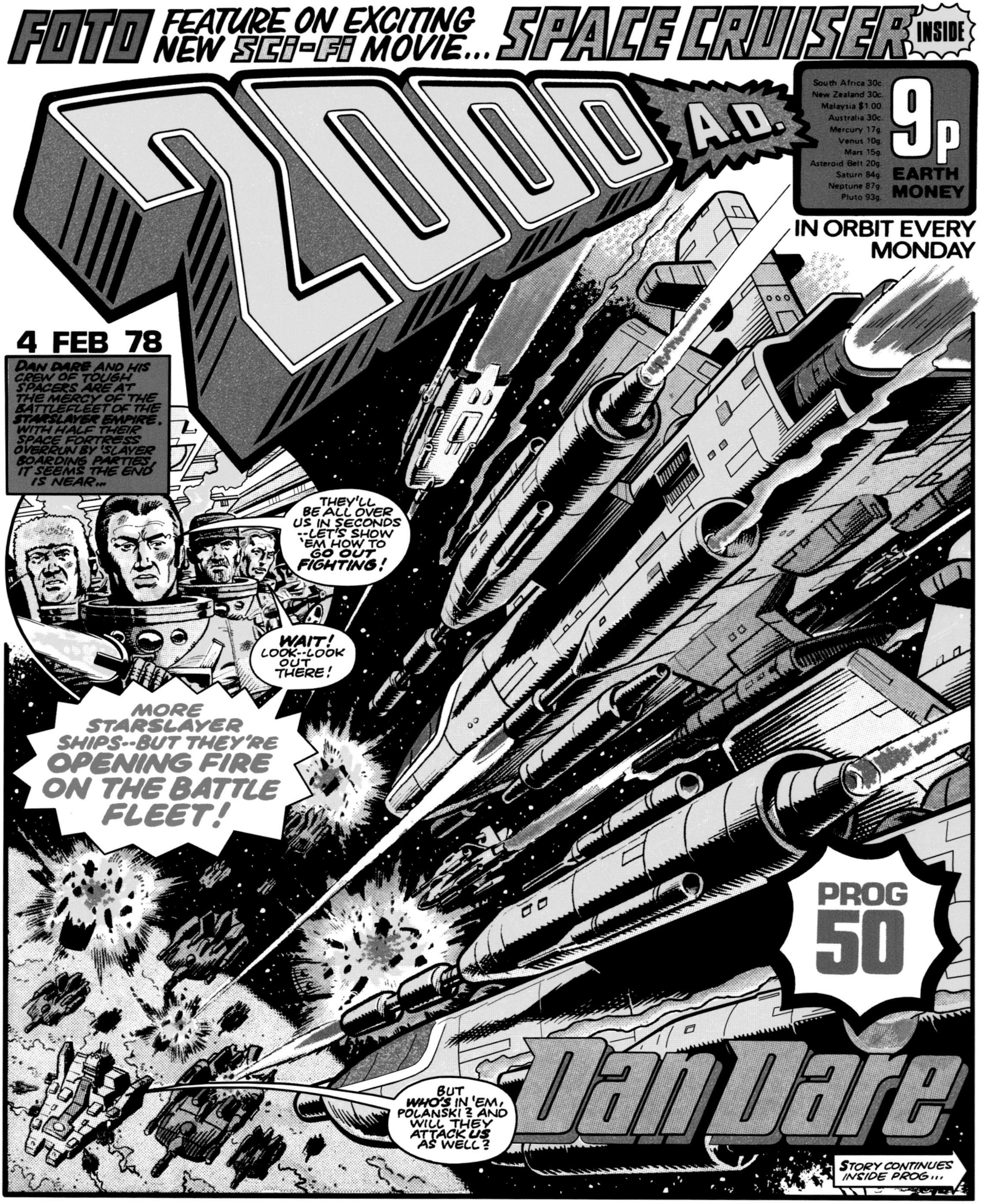

FOTO FEATURE ON EXCITING NEW SCI-FI MOVIE... SPACE CRUISER INSIDE
2000 A.D.
South Africa 30c. New Zealand 30c. Malaysia $1.00. Australia 30c. Mercury 17g. Venus 10g. Mars 15g. Asteroid Belt 20g. Saturn 84g. Neptune 87g. Pluto 93g.
9p EARTH MONEY
IN ORBIT EVERY MONDAY
4 FEB 78
DAN DARE AND HIS CREW OF TOUGH SPACERS ARE AT THE MERCY OF THE BATTLEFLEET OF THE STARSLAYER EMPIRE. WITH HALF THEIR SPACE FORTRESS OVERRUN BY 'SLAYER BOARDING PARTIES, IT SEEMS THE END IS NEAR...
THEY'LL BE ALL OVER US IN SECONDS --LET'S SHOW 'EM HOW TO GO OUT FIGHTING!
WAIT! LOOK--LOOK OUT THERE!
MORE STARSLAYER SHIPS--BUT THEY'RE OPENING FIRE ON THE BATTLE FLEET!
PROG 50
Dan Dare
BUT WHO'S IN 'EM, POLANSKI? AND WILL THEY ATTACK US AS WELL?
STORY CONTINUES INSIDE PROG...

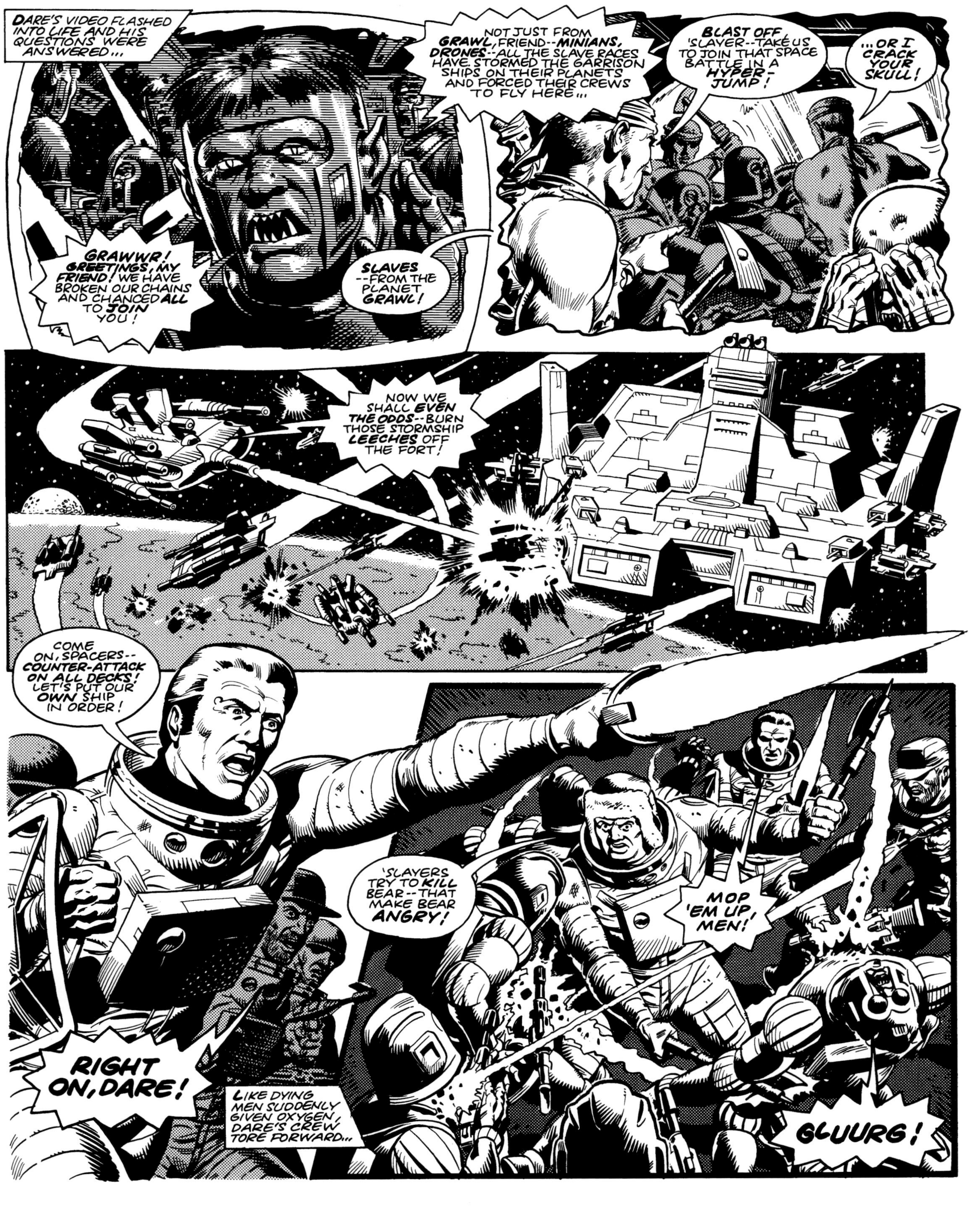

DARE'S VIDEO FLASHED INTO LIFE AND HIS QUESTIONS WERE ANSWERED...
GRAWWR! GREETINGS, MY FRIEND! WE HAVE BROKEN OUR CHAINS AND CHANCED ALL TO JOIN YOU!
SLAVES --FROM THE PLANET GRAWL!
NOT JUST FROM GRAWL, FRIEND--MINIANS, DRONES--ALL THE SLAVE RACES HAVE STORMED THE GARRISON SHIPS ON THEIR PLANETS AND FORCED THEIR CREWS TO FLY HERE...
BLAST OFF 'SLAYER--TAKE US TO JOIN THAT SPACE BATTLE IN A HYPER-JUMP!
...OR I CRACK YOUR SKULL!
NOW WE SHALL EVEN THE ODDS--BURN THOSE STORMSHIP LEECHES OFF THE FORT!
COME ON, SPACERS--COUNTER-ATTACK ON ALL DECKS! LET'S PUT OUR OWN SHIP IN ORDER!
'SLAYERS TRY TO KILL BEAR--THAT MAKE BEAR ANGRY!
MOP 'EM UP, MEN!
RIGHT ON, DARE!
LIKE DYING MEN SUDDENLY GIVEN OXYGEN, DARE'S CREW TORE FORWARD...
GLUURG!

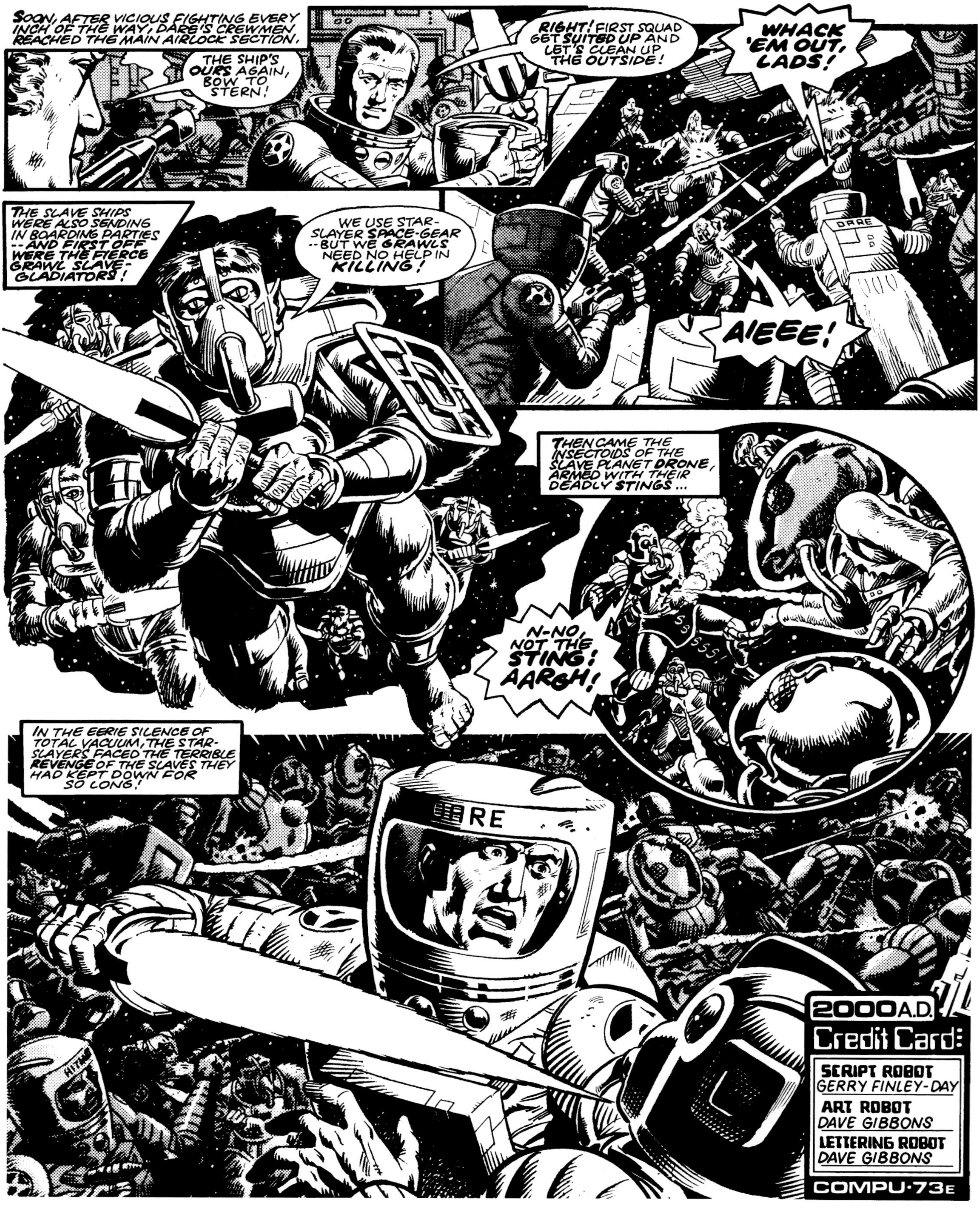
SOON, AFTER VICIOUS FIGHTING EVERY INCH OF THE WAY, DARE'S CREWMEN REACHED THE MAIN AIRLOCK SECTION.
THE SHIP'S OURS AGAIN, BOW TO STERN!
RIGHT! FIRST SQUAD GET SUITED UP AND LET'S CLEAN UP THE OUTSIDE!
WHACK 'EM OUT, LADS!
DARE
AIEEE!
THE SLAVE SHIPS WERE ALSO SENDING IN BOARDING PARTIES -- AND FIRST OFF WERE THE FIERCE GRAWL SLAVE-GLADIATORS!
WE USE STAR-SLAYER SPACE-GEAR -- BUT WE GRAWLS NEED NO HELP IN KILLING!
THEN CAME THE INSECTOIDS OF THE SLAVE PLANET DRONE, ARMED WITH THEIR DEADLY STINGS...
N-NO, NOT THE STING! AARGH!
IN THE EERIE SILENCE OF TOTAL VACUUM, THE STAR-SLAYERS FACED THE TERRIBLE REVENGE OF THE SLAVES THEY HAD KEPT DOWN FOR SO LONG!
RE
2000 A.D.
Credit Card:
SCRIPT ROBOT
GERRY FINLEY-DAY
ART ROBOT
DAVE GIBBONS
LETTERING ROBOT
DAVE GIBBONS
COMPU-73E

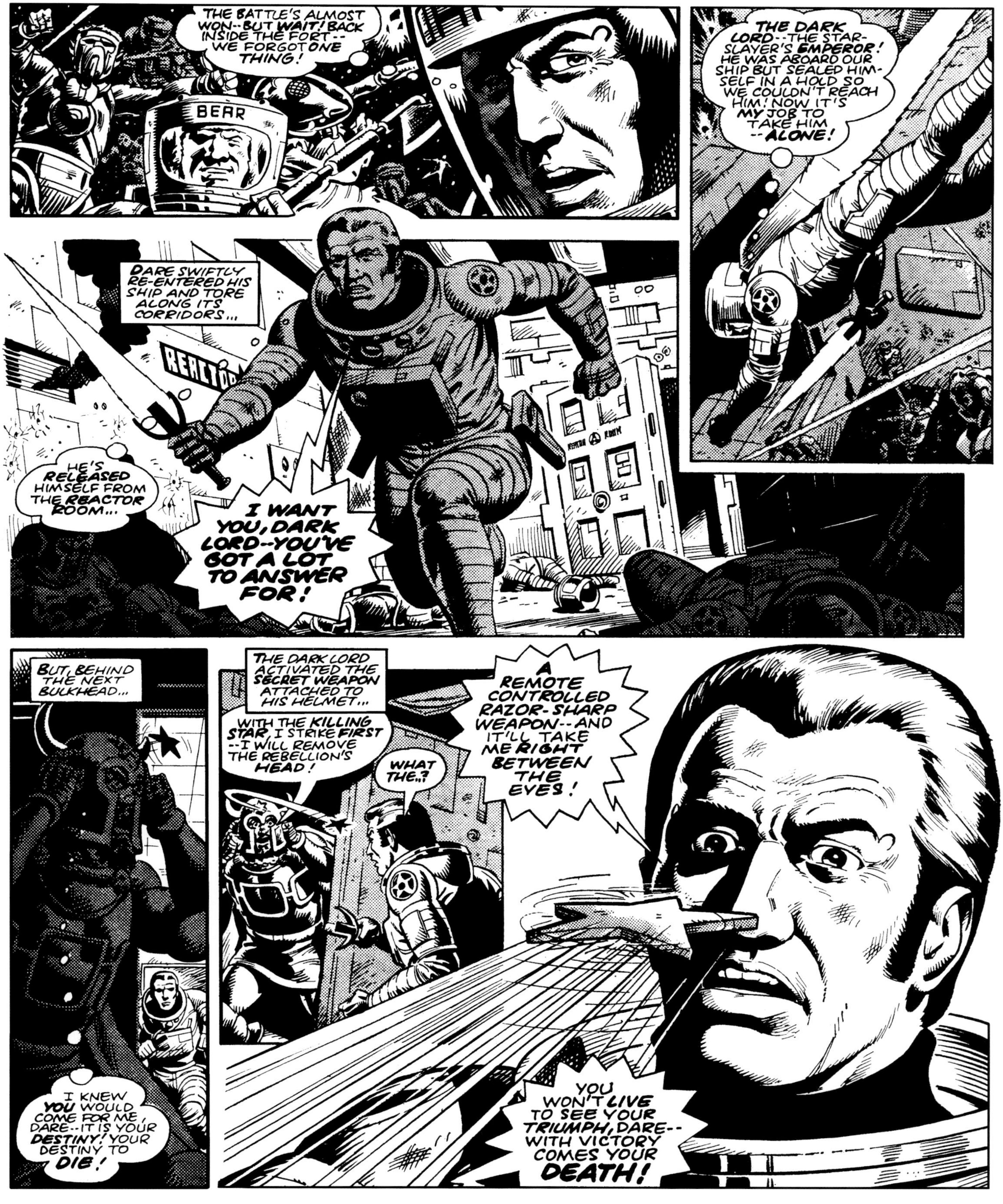

THE BATTLE'S ALMOST WON--BUT WAIT! BACK INSIDE THE FORT--WE FORGOT ONE THING!
BEAR
THE DARK LORD--THE STAR-SLAYER'S EMPEROR! HE WAS ABOARD OUR SHIP BUT SEALED HIMSELF IN A HOLD SO WE COULDN'T REACH HIM! NOW IT'S MY JOB TO TAKE HIM--ALONE!
DARE SWIFTLY RE-ENTERED HIS SHIP AND TORE ALONG ITS CORRIDORS...
REACTOR
HE'S RELEASED HIMSELF FROM THE REACTOR ROOM...
I WANT YOU, DARK LORD--YOU'VE GOT A LOT TO ANSWER FOR!
BUT, BEHIND THE NEXT BULKHEAD...
I KNEW YOU WOULD COME FOR ME, DARE--IT IS YOUR DESTINY! YOUR DESTINY TO DIE!
THE DARK LORD ACTIVATED THE SECRET WEAPON ATTACHED TO HIS HELMET...
WITH THE KILLING STAR, I STRIKE FIRST--I WILL REMOVE THE REBELLION'S HEAD!
WHAT THE..?
A REMOTE CONTROLLED RAZOR-SHARP WEAPON--AND IT'LL TAKE ME RIGHT BETWEEN THE EYES!
YOU WON'T LIVE TO SEE YOUR TRIUMPH, DARE--WITH VICTORY COMES YOUR DEATH!

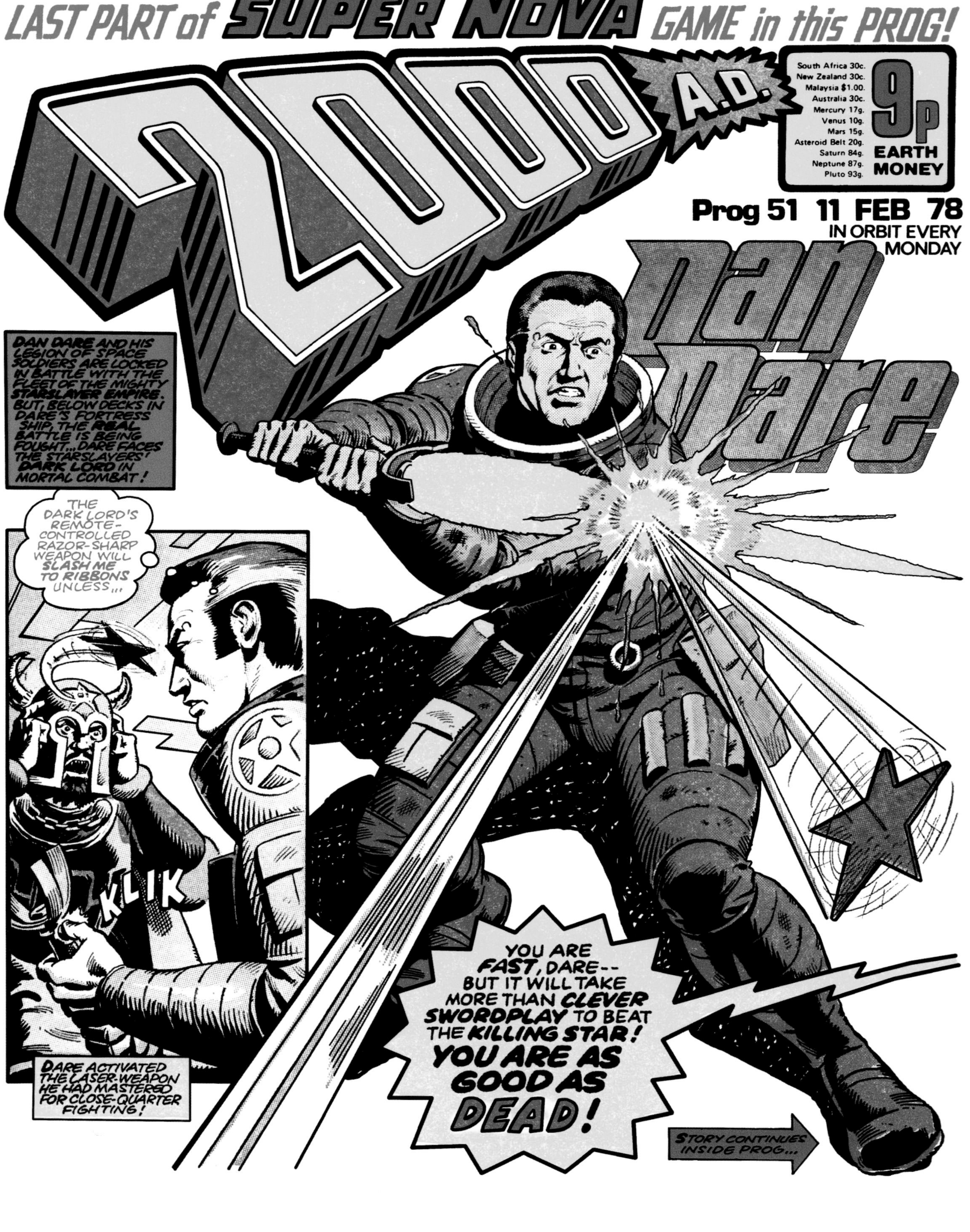

LAST PART of SUPER NOVA GAME in this PROG!
2000 A.D.
South Africa 30c. New Zealand 30c. Malaysia $1.00. Australia 30c. Mercury 17g. Venus 10g. Mars 15g. Asteroid Belt 20g. Saturn 84g. Neptune 87g. Pluto 93g.
9p EARTH MONEY
Prog 51 11 FEB 78
IN ORBIT EVERY MONDAY
Dan Dare
DAN DARE AND HIS LEGION OF SPACE SOLDIERS ARE LOCKED IN BATTLE WITH THE FLEET OF THE MIGHTY STARSLAYER EMPIRE. BUT, BELOW DECKS IN DARE'S FORTRESS SHIP, THE REAL BATTLE IS BEING FOUGHT... DARE FACES THE STARSLAYERS' DARK LORD IN MORTAL COMBAT!
THE DARK LORD'S REMOTE-CONTROLLED RAZOR-SHARP WEAPON WILL SLASH ME TO RIBBONS UNLESS...
KLIK
DARE ACTIVATED THE LASER-WEAPON HE HAD MASTERED FOR CLOSE-QUARTER FIGHTING!
YOU ARE FAST, DARE-- BUT IT WILL TAKE MORE THAN CLEVER SWORDPLAY TO BEAT THE KILLING STAR! YOU ARE AS GOOD AS DEAD!
STORY CONTINUES INSIDE PROG...

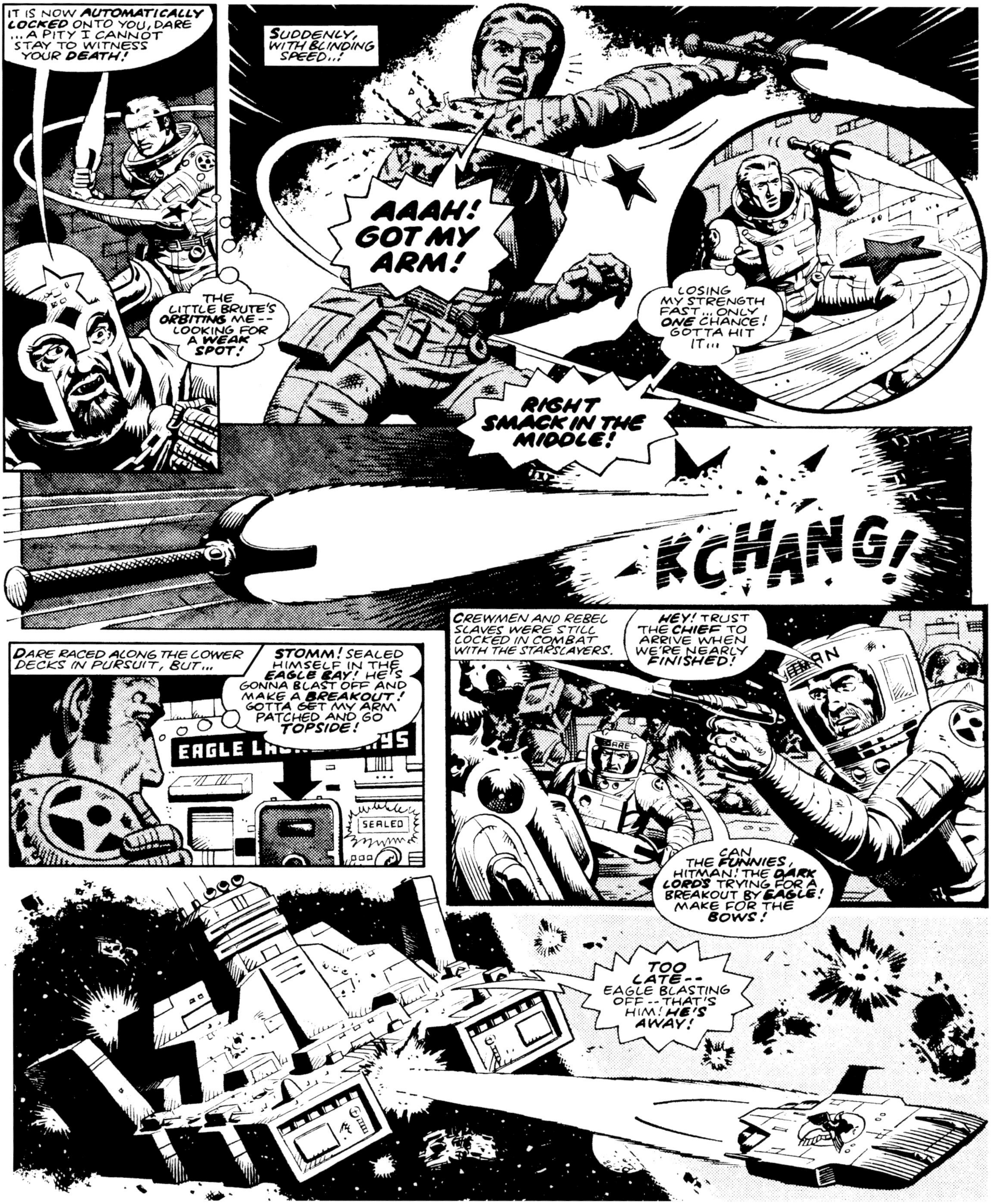
IT IS NOW AUTOMATICALLY LOCKED ONTO YOU, DARE ...A PITY I CANNOT STAY TO WITNESS YOUR DEATH!
THE LITTLE BRUTE'S ORBITING ME -- LOOKING FOR A WEAK SPOT!
SUDDENLY, WITH BLINDING SPEED..!
AAAH! GOT MY ARM!
LOSING MY STRENGTH FAST... ONLY ONE CHANCE! GOTTA HIT IT...
RIGHT SMACK IN THE MIDDLE!
KCHANG!
DARE RACED ALONG THE LOWER DECKS IN PURSUIT, BUT...
STOMM! SEALED HIMSELF IN THE EAGLE BAY! HE'S GONNA BLAST OFF AND MAKE A BREAKOUT! GOTTA GET MY ARM PATCHED AND GO TOPSIDE!
SEALED
CREWMEN AND REBEL SLAVES WERE STILL LOCKED IN COMBAT WITH THE STARSLAYERS.
HEY! TRUST THE CHIEF TO ARRIVE WHEN WE'RE NEARLY FINISHED!
CAN THE FUNNIES, HITMAN! THE DARK LORD'S TRYING FOR A BREAKOUT BY EAGLE! MAKE FOR THE BOWS!
TOO LATE -- EAGLE BLASTING OFF -- THAT'S HIM! HE'S AWAY!

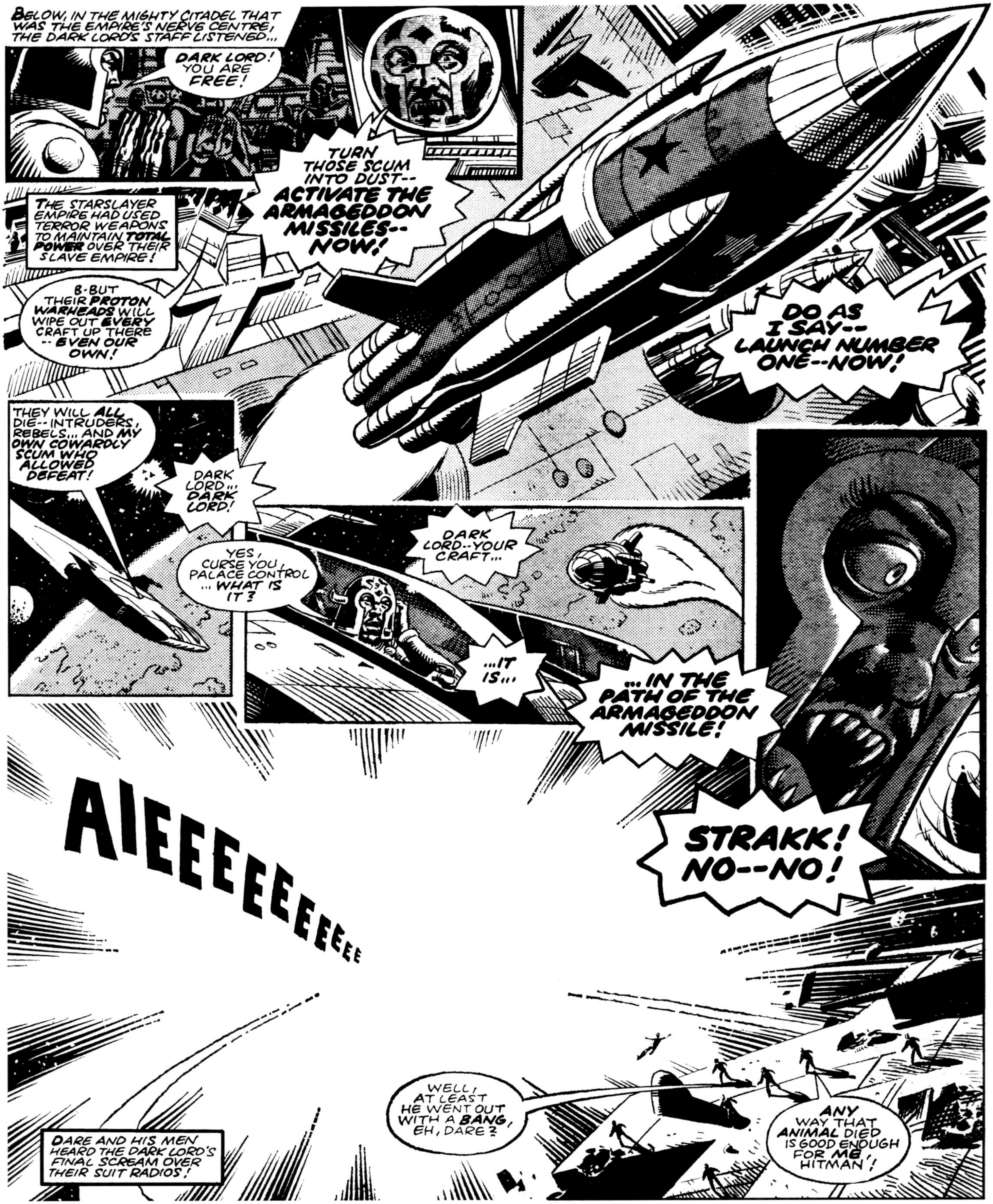

BELOW, IN THE MIGHTY CITADEL THAT WAS THE EMPIRE'S NERVE CENTRE, THE DARK LORD'S STAFF LISTENED...
DARK LORD! YOU ARE FREE!
TURN THOSE SCUM INTO DUST-- ACTIVATE THE ARMAGEDDON MISSILES-- NOW!
THE STARSLAYER EMPIRE HAD USED TERROR WEAPONS TO MAINTAIN TOTAL POWER OVER THEIR SLAVE EMPIRE!
B-BUT THEIR PROTON WARHEADS WILL WIPE OUT EVERY CRAFT UP THERE -- EVEN OUR OWN!
DO AS I SAY-- LAUNCH NUMBER ONE--NOW!
THEY WILL ALL DIE-- INTRUDERS, REBELS... AND MY OWN COWARDLY SCUM WHO ALLOWED DEFEAT!
DARK LORD... DARK LORD!
YES, CURSE YOU, PALACE CONTROL ... WHAT IS IT?
DARK LORD--YOUR CRAFT...
...IT IS...
...IN THE PATH OF THE ARMAGEDDON MISSILE!
STRAKK! NO--NO!
AIEEEEEEEEEE
WELL, AT LEAST HE WENT OUT WITH A BANG, EH, DARE?
ANY WAY THAT ANIMAL DIED IS GOOD ENOUGH FOR ME, HITMAN!
DARE AND HIS MEN HEARD THE DARK LORD'S FINAL SCREAM OVER THEIR SUIT RADIOS!

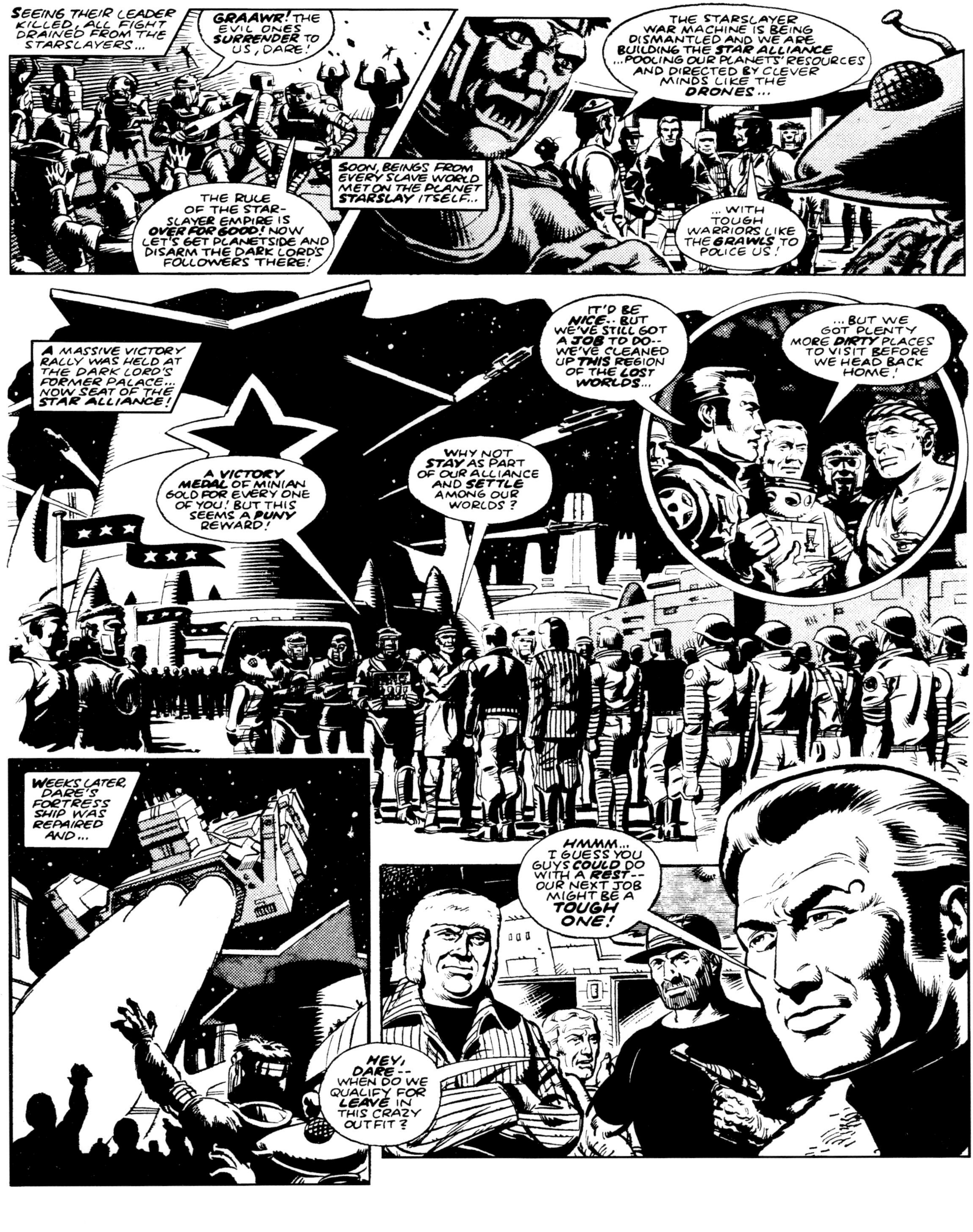
SEEING THEIR LEADER KILLED, ALL FIGHT DRAINED FROM THE STARSLAYERS...
GRAAWR! THE EVIL ONES SURRENDER TO US, DARE!
THE RULE OF THE STAR-SLAYER EMPIRE IS OVER FOR GOOD! NOW LET'S GET PLANETSIDE AND DISARM THE DARK LORD'S FOLLOWERS THERE!
SOON, BEINGS FROM EVERY SLAVE WORLD MET ON THE PLANET STARSLAY ITSELF...
THE STARSLAYER WAR MACHINE IS BEING DISMANTLED AND WE ARE BUILDING THE STAR ALLIANCE ...POOLING OUR PLANETS' RESOURCES AND DIRECTED BY CLEVER MINDS LIKE THE DRONES...
...WITH TOUGH WARRIORS LIKE THE GRAWLS TO POLICE US!
A MASSIVE VICTORY RALLY WAS HELD AT THE DARK LORD'S FORMER PALACE... NOW SEAT OF THE STAR ALLIANCE!
A VICTORY MEDAL OF MINIAN GOLD FOR EVERY ONE OF YOU! BUT THIS SEEMS A PUNY REWARD!
WHY NOT STAY AS PART OF OUR ALLIANCE AND SETTLE AMONG OUR WORLDS?
IT'D BE NICE.. BUT WE'VE STILL GOT A JOB TO DO-- WE'VE CLEANED UP THIS REGION OF THE LOST WORLDS...
...BUT WE GOT PLENTY MORE DIRTY PLACES TO VISIT BEFORE WE HEAD BACK HOME!
WEEKS LATER, DARE'S FORTRESS SHIP WAS REPAIRED AND...
HEY, DARE-- WHEN DO WE QUALIFY FOR LEAVE IN THIS CRAZY OUTFIT?
HMMM... I GUESS YOU GUYS COULD DO WITH A REST-- OUR NEXT JOB MIGHT BE A TOUGH ONE!

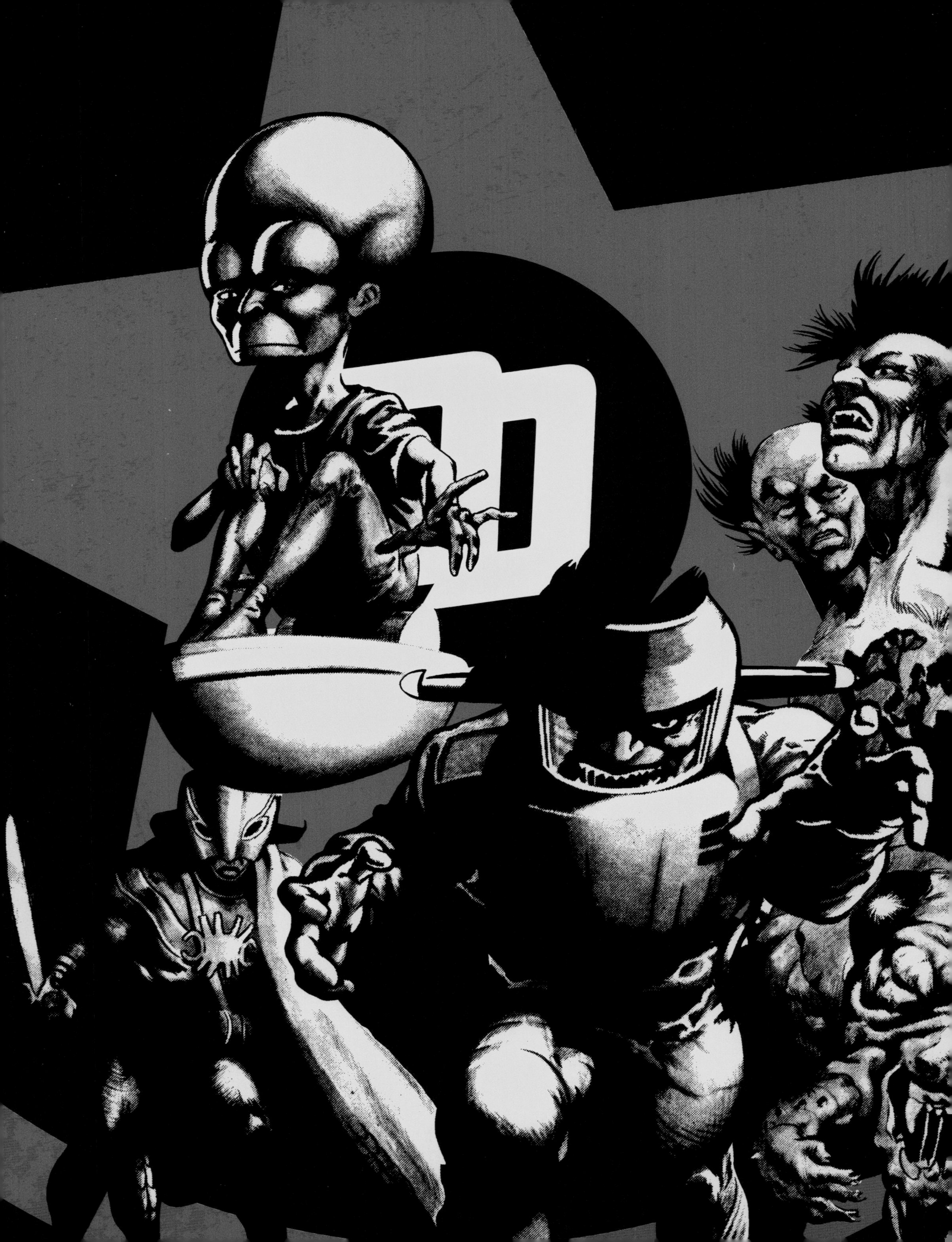

BONUS STRIPS

DAN DARE: UNTITLED

Script: Unknown
Art: Unknown
Letters: Unknown

Originally published in *2000 AD* Summer Special 1977

THE CURSE OF MYTAX

Script: Unknown
Art: Massimo Belardinelli
Letters: Unknown

Originally published in *2000 AD* Annual 1978

VISCO

Script: Garry Leach
Art: Garry Leach
Letters: John Aldrich

Originally published in *2000 AD* Sci-Fi Special 1978

DAN DARE: UNTITLED

Script: Unknown
Art: Ian Kennedy
Letters: Unknown

Originally published in the *Dan Dare* Annual 1979

DAN DARE: THE 2000 AD ORIGIN

Script: Unknown
Art: Unknown
Letters: Unknown

Originally published in the *Dan Dare* Annual 1979

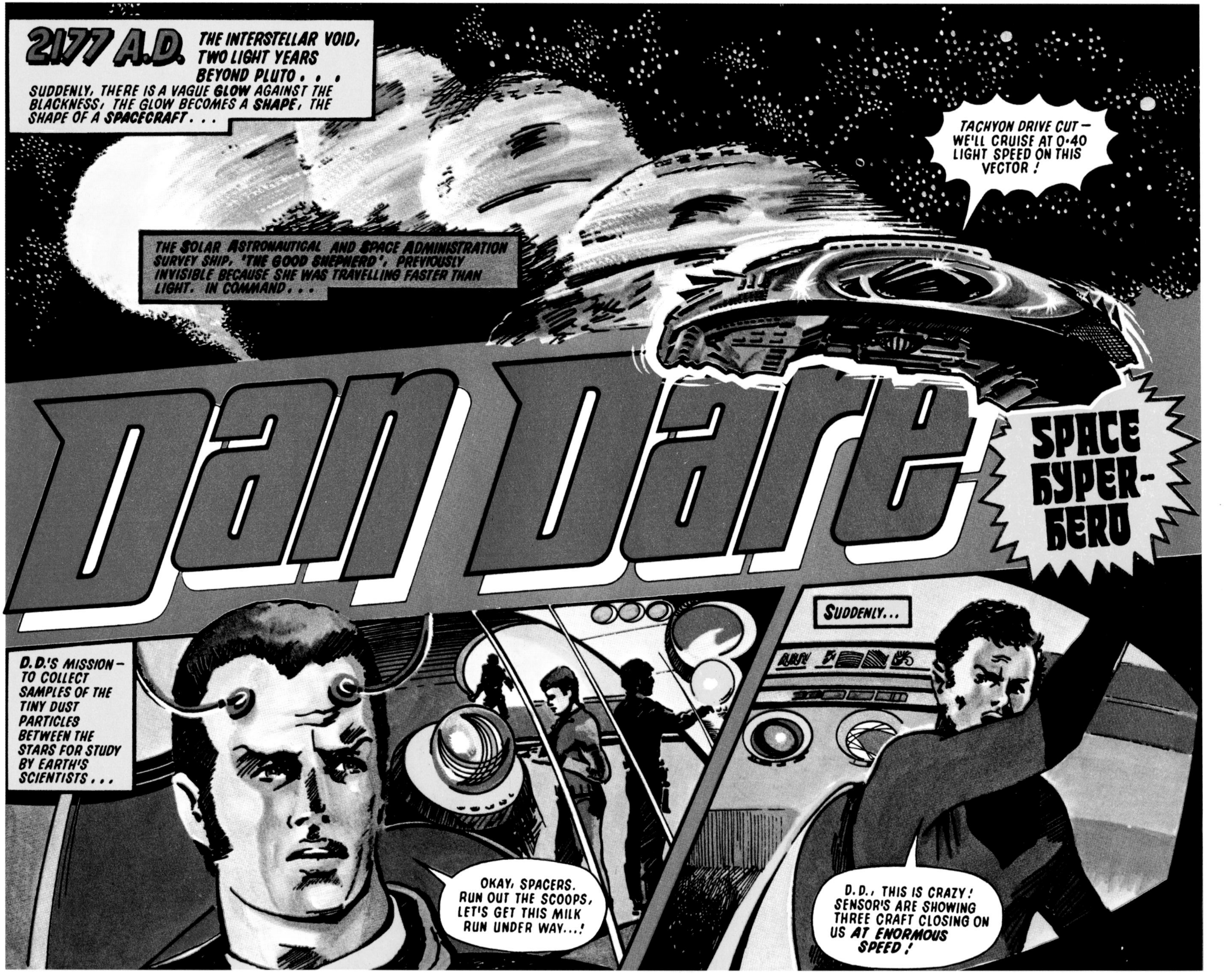
2177 A.D. THE INTERSTELLAR VOID, TWO LIGHT YEARS BEYOND PLUTO . . .
SUDDENLY, THERE IS A VAGUE GLOW AGAINST THE BLACKNESS, THE GLOW BECOMES A SHAPE, THE SHAPE OF A SPACECRAFT . . .
TACHYON DRIVE CUT — WE'LL CRUISE AT 0·40 LIGHT SPEED ON THIS VECTOR !
THE SOLAR ASTRONAUTICAL AND SPACE ADMINISTRATION SURVEY SHIP, 'THE GOOD SHEPHERD', PREVIOUSLY INVISIBLE BECAUSE SHE WAS TRAVELLING FASTER THAN LIGHT. IN COMMAND . . .
DAN DARE
SPACE HYPER-HERO
D.D.'S MISSION — TO COLLECT SAMPLES OF THE TINY DUST PARTICLES BETWEEN THE STARS FOR STUDY BY EARTH'S SCIENTISTS . . .
OKAY, SPACERS. RUN OUT THE SCOOPS, LET'S GET THIS MILK RUN UNDER WAY...!
SUDDENLY...
D. D., THIS IS CRAZY ! SENSOR'S ARE SHOWING THREE CRAFT CLOSING ON US AT ENORMOUS SPEED !

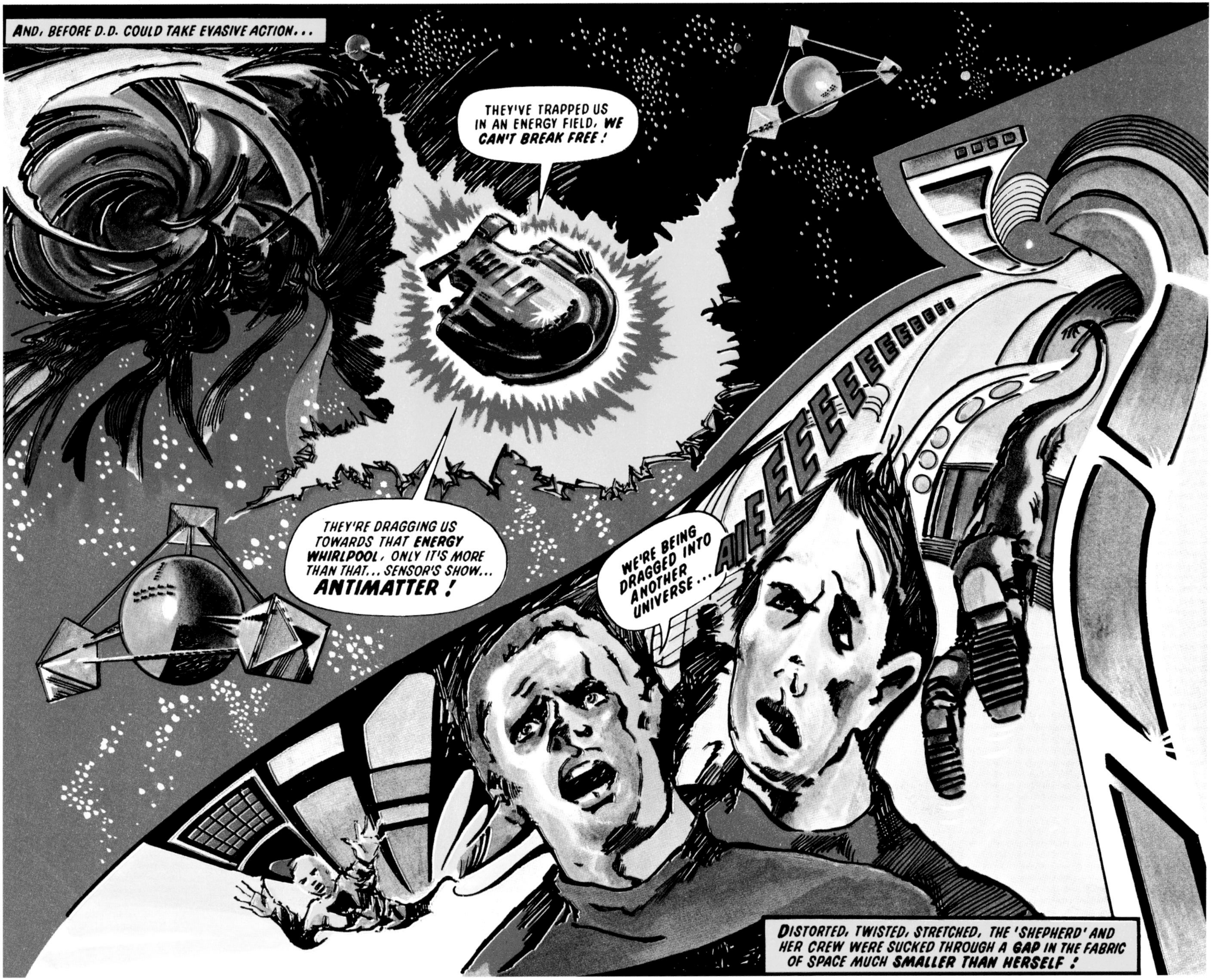
AND, BEFORE D.D. COULD TAKE EVASIVE ACTION...
THEY'VE TRAPPED US IN AN ENERGY FIELD, WE CAN'T BREAK FREE!
THEY'RE DRAGGING US TOWARDS THAT ENERGY WHIRLPOOL, ONLY IT'S MORE THAN THAT... SENSOR'S SHOW... ANTIMATTER!
WE'RE BEING DRAGGED INTO ANOTHER UNIVERSE...
AIEEEEEEEEEEEEEE
DISTORTED, TWISTED, STRETCHED, THE 'SHEPHERD' AND HER CREW WERE SUCKED THROUGH A GAP IN THE FABRIC OF SPACE MUCH SMALLER THAN HERSELF!

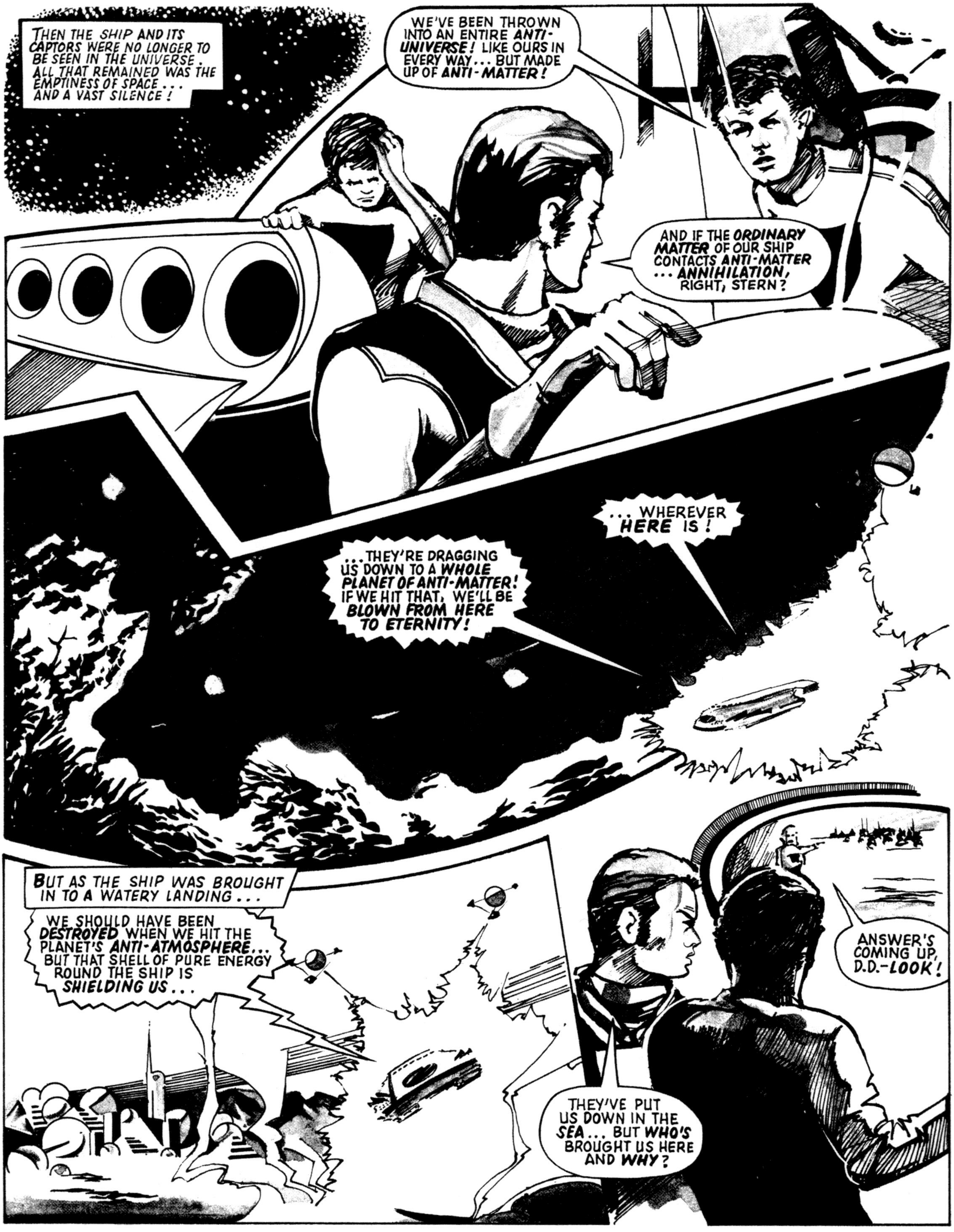
THEN THE SHIP AND ITS CAPTORS WERE NO LONGER TO BE SEEN IN THE UNIVERSE. ALL THAT REMAINED WAS THE EMPTINESS OF SPACE... AND A VAST SILENCE!
WE'VE BEEN THROWN INTO AN ENTIRE ANTI-UNIVERSE! LIKE OURS IN EVERY WAY... BUT MADE UP OF ANTI-MATTER!
AND IF THE ORDINARY MATTER OF OUR SHIP CONTACTS ANTI-MATTER ... ANNIHILATION, RIGHT, STERN?
...THEY'RE DRAGGING US DOWN TO A WHOLE PLANET OF ANTI-MATTER! IF WE HIT THAT, WE'LL BE BLOWN FROM HERE TO ETERNITY!
...WHEREVER HERE IS!
BUT AS THE SHIP WAS BROUGHT IN TO A WATERY LANDING...
WE SHOULD HAVE BEEN DESTROYED WHEN WE HIT THE PLANET'S ANTI-ATMOSPHERE... BUT THAT SHELL OF PURE ENERGY ROUND THE SHIP IS SHIELDING US...
THEY'VE PUT US DOWN IN THE SEA... BUT WHO'S BROUGHT US HERE AND WHY?
ANSWER'S COMING UP, D.D.-LOOK!

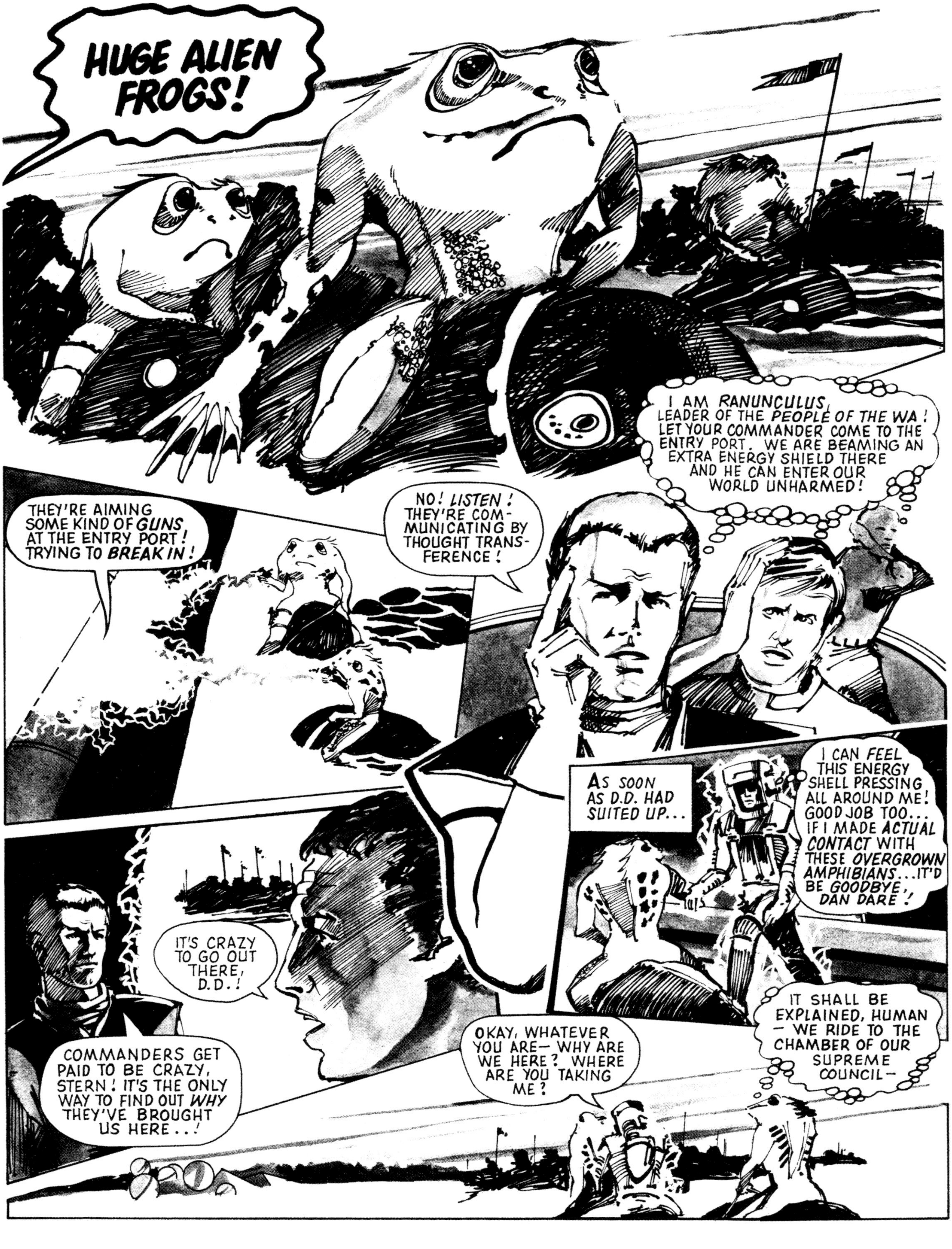
HUGE ALIEN FROGS!
I AM RANUNCULUS, LEADER OF THE PEOPLE OF THE WA! LET YOUR COMMANDER COME TO THE ENTRY PORT. WE ARE BEAMING AN EXTRA ENERGY SHIELD THERE AND HE CAN ENTER OUR WORLD UNHARMED!
THEY'RE AIMING SOME KIND OF GUNS AT THE ENTRY PORT! TRYING TO BREAK IN!
NO! LISTEN! THEY'RE COMMUNICATING BY THOUGHT TRANSFERENCE!
IT'S CRAZY TO GO OUT THERE, D.D.!
COMMANDERS GET PAID TO BE CRAZY, STERN! IT'S THE ONLY WAY TO FIND OUT WHY THEY'VE BROUGHT US HERE..!
AS SOON AS D.D. HAD SUITED UP...
I CAN FEEL THIS ENERGY SHELL PRESSING ALL AROUND ME! GOOD JOB TOO... IF I MADE ACTUAL CONTACT WITH THESE OVERGROWN AMPHIBIANS...IT'D BE GOODBYE, DAN DARE!
OKAY, WHATEVER YOU ARE— WHY ARE WE HERE? WHERE ARE YOU TAKING ME?
IT SHALL BE EXPLAINED, HUMAN — WE RIDE TO THE CHAMBER OF OUR SUPREME COUNCIL—

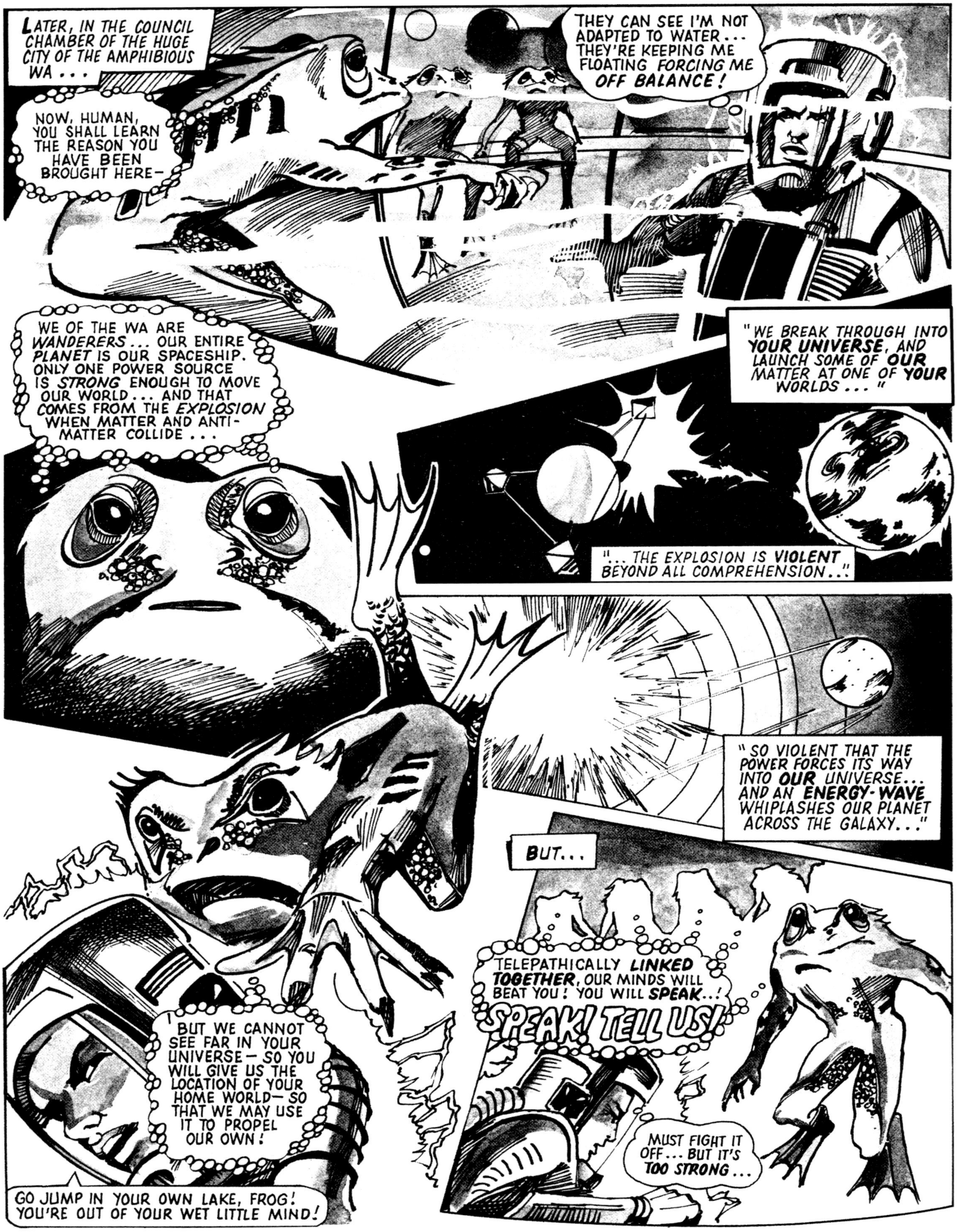
LATER, IN THE COUNCIL CHAMBER OF THE HUGE CITY OF THE AMPHIBIOUS WA . . .
NOW, HUMAN, YOU SHALL LEARN THE REASON YOU HAVE BEEN BROUGHT HERE–
THEY CAN SEE I'M NOT ADAPTED TO WATER . . . THEY'RE KEEPING ME FLOATING FORCING ME OFF BALANCE!
WE OF THE WA ARE WANDERERS . . . OUR ENTIRE PLANET IS OUR SPACESHIP. ONLY ONE POWER SOURCE IS STRONG ENOUGH TO MOVE OUR WORLD . . . AND THAT COMES FROM THE EXPLOSION WHEN MATTER AND ANTI-MATTER COLLIDE . . .
"WE BREAK THROUGH INTO YOUR UNIVERSE, AND LAUNCH SOME OF OUR MATTER AT ONE OF YOUR WORLDS . . ."
". . . THE EXPLOSION IS VIOLENT BEYOND ALL COMPREHENSION . ."
"SO VIOLENT THAT THE POWER FORCES ITS WAY INTO OUR UNIVERSE . . . AND AN ENERGY-WAVE WHIPLASHES OUR PLANET ACROSS THE GALAXY . . ."
BUT . . .
BUT WE CANNOT SEE FAR IN YOUR UNIVERSE– SO YOU WILL GIVE US THE LOCATION OF YOUR HOME WORLD– SO THAT WE MAY USE IT TO PROPEL OUR OWN!
GO JUMP IN YOUR OWN LAKE, FROG! YOU'RE OUT OF YOUR WET LITTLE MIND!
TELEPATHICALLY LINKED TOGETHER, OUR MINDS WILL BEAT YOU! YOU WILL SPEAK . .!
SPEAK! TELL US!
MUST FIGHT IT OFF . . . BUT IT'S TOO STRONG . . .

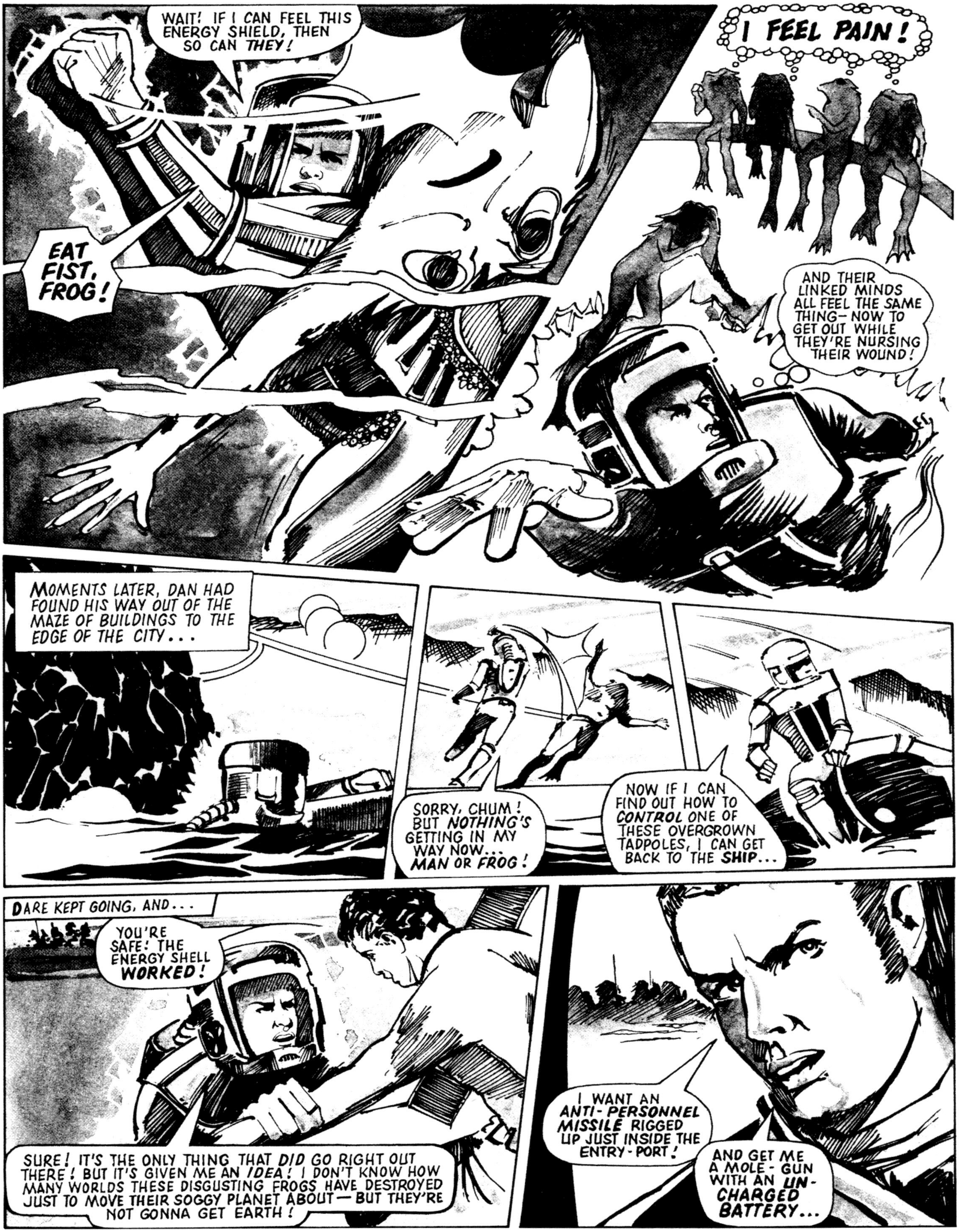
WAIT! IF I CAN FEEL THIS ENERGY SHIELD, THEN SO CAN THEY!
EAT FIST, FROG!
I FEEL PAIN!
AND THEIR LINKED MINDS ALL FEEL THE SAME THING– NOW TO GET OUT WHILE THEY'RE NURSING THEIR WOUND!
MOMENTS LATER, DAN HAD FOUND HIS WAY OUT OF THE MAZE OF BUILDINGS TO THE EDGE OF THE CITY...
SORRY, CHUM! BUT NOTHING'S GETTING IN MY WAY NOW... MAN OR FROG!
NOW IF I CAN FIND OUT HOW TO CONTROL ONE OF THESE OVERGROWN TADPOLES, I CAN GET BACK TO THE SHIP...
DARE KEPT GOING, AND...
YOU'RE SAFE: THE ENERGY SHELL WORKED!
SURE! IT'S THE ONLY THING THAT DID GO RIGHT OUT THERE! BUT IT'S GIVEN ME AN IDEA! I DON'T KNOW HOW MANY WORLDS THESE DISGUSTING FROGS HAVE DESTROYED JUST TO MOVE THEIR SOGGY PLANET ABOUT— BUT THEY'RE NOT GONNA GET EARTH!
I WANT AN ANTI-PERSONNEL MISSILE RIGGED UP JUST INSIDE THE ENTRY-PORT!
AND GET ME A MOLE-GUN WITH AN UN-CHARGED BATTERY...

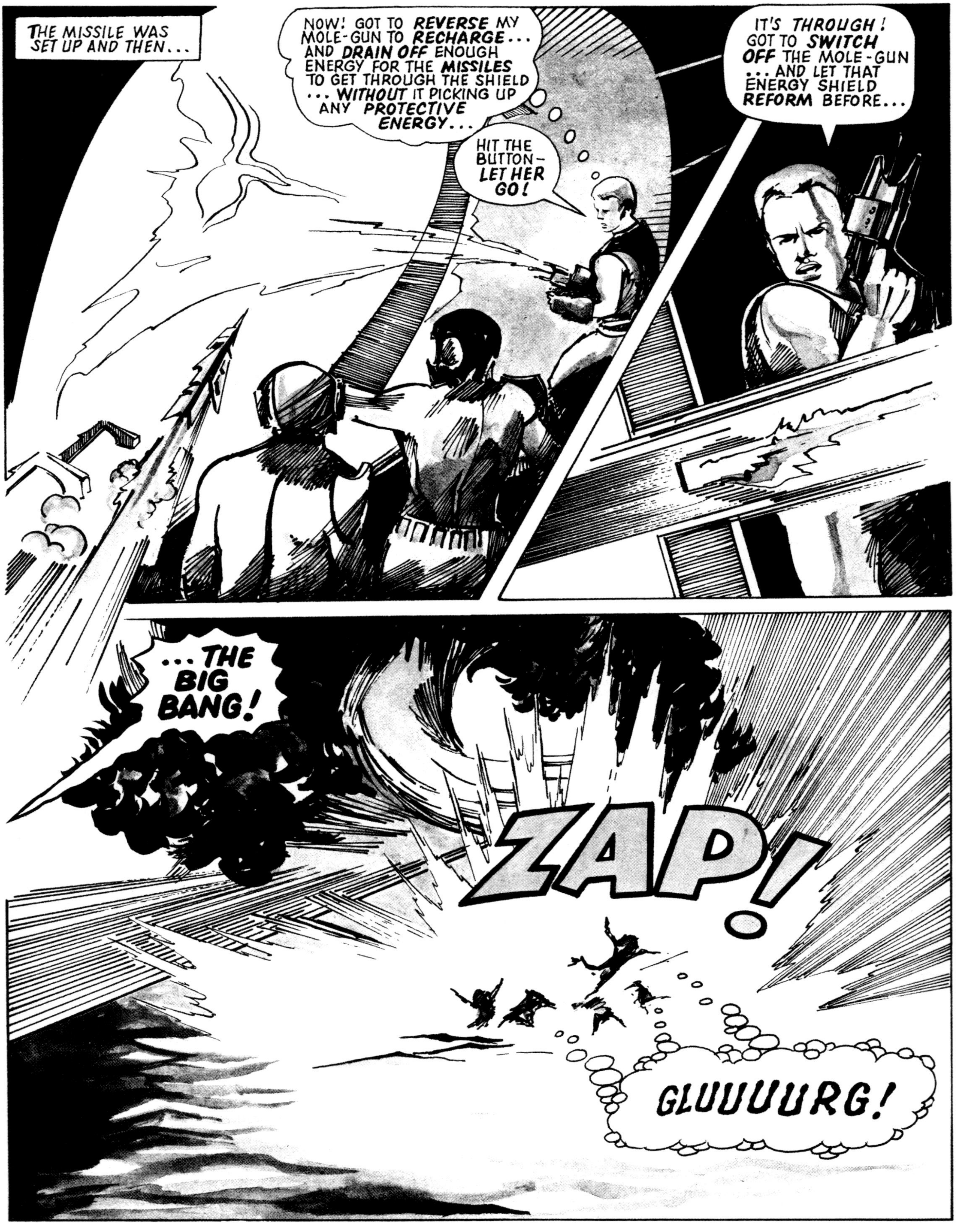

THE MISSILE WAS SET UP AND THEN...
NOW! GOT TO REVERSE MY MOLE-GUN TO RECHARGE... AND DRAIN OFF ENOUGH ENERGY FOR THE MISSILES TO GET THROUGH THE SHIELD ... WITHOUT IT PICKING UP ANY PROTECTIVE ENERGY...
HIT THE BUTTON– LET HER GO!
IT'S THROUGH! GOT TO SWITCH OFF THE MOLE-GUN ... AND LET THAT ENERGY SHIELD REFORM BEFORE...
... THE BIG BANG!
ZAP!
GLUUUURG!

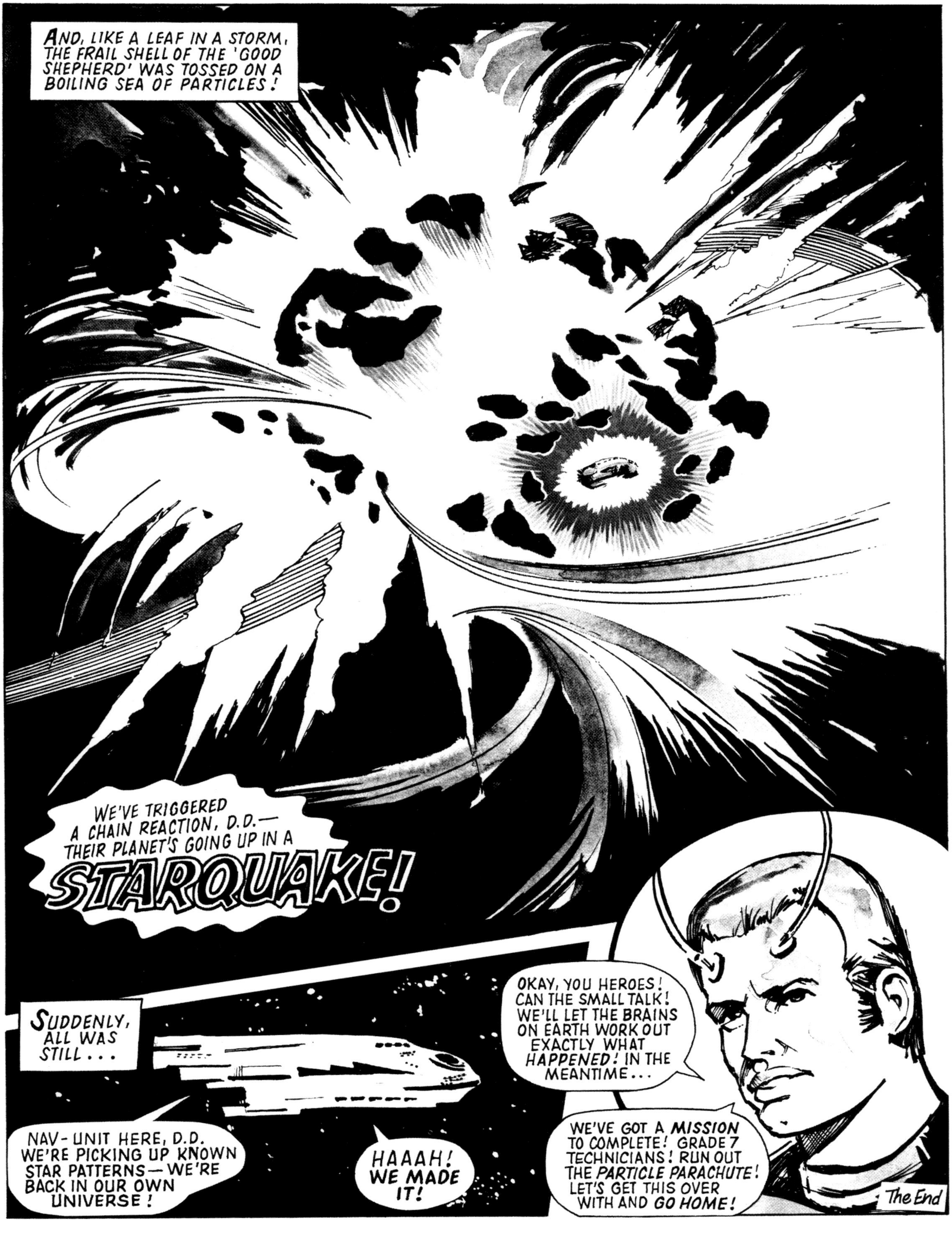

AND, LIKE A LEAF IN A STORM, THE FRAIL SHELL OF THE 'GOOD SHEPHERD' WAS TOSSED ON A BOILING SEA OF PARTICLES!
WE'VE TRIGGERED A CHAIN REACTION, D.D.— THEIR PLANET'S GOING UP IN A STARQUAKE!
SUDDENLY, ALL WAS STILL...
NAV-UNIT HERE, D.D. WE'RE PICKING UP KNOWN STAR PATTERNS— WE'RE BACK IN OUR OWN UNIVERSE!
HAAAH! WE MADE IT!
OKAY, YOU HEROES! CAN THE SMALL TALK! WE'LL LET THE BRAINS ON EARTH WORK OUT EXACTLY WHAT HAPPENED! IN THE MEANTIME...
WE'VE GOT A MISSION TO COMPLETE! GRADE 7 TECHNICIANS! RUN OUT THE PARTICLE PARACHUTE! LET'S GET THIS OVER WITH AND GO HOME!
The End

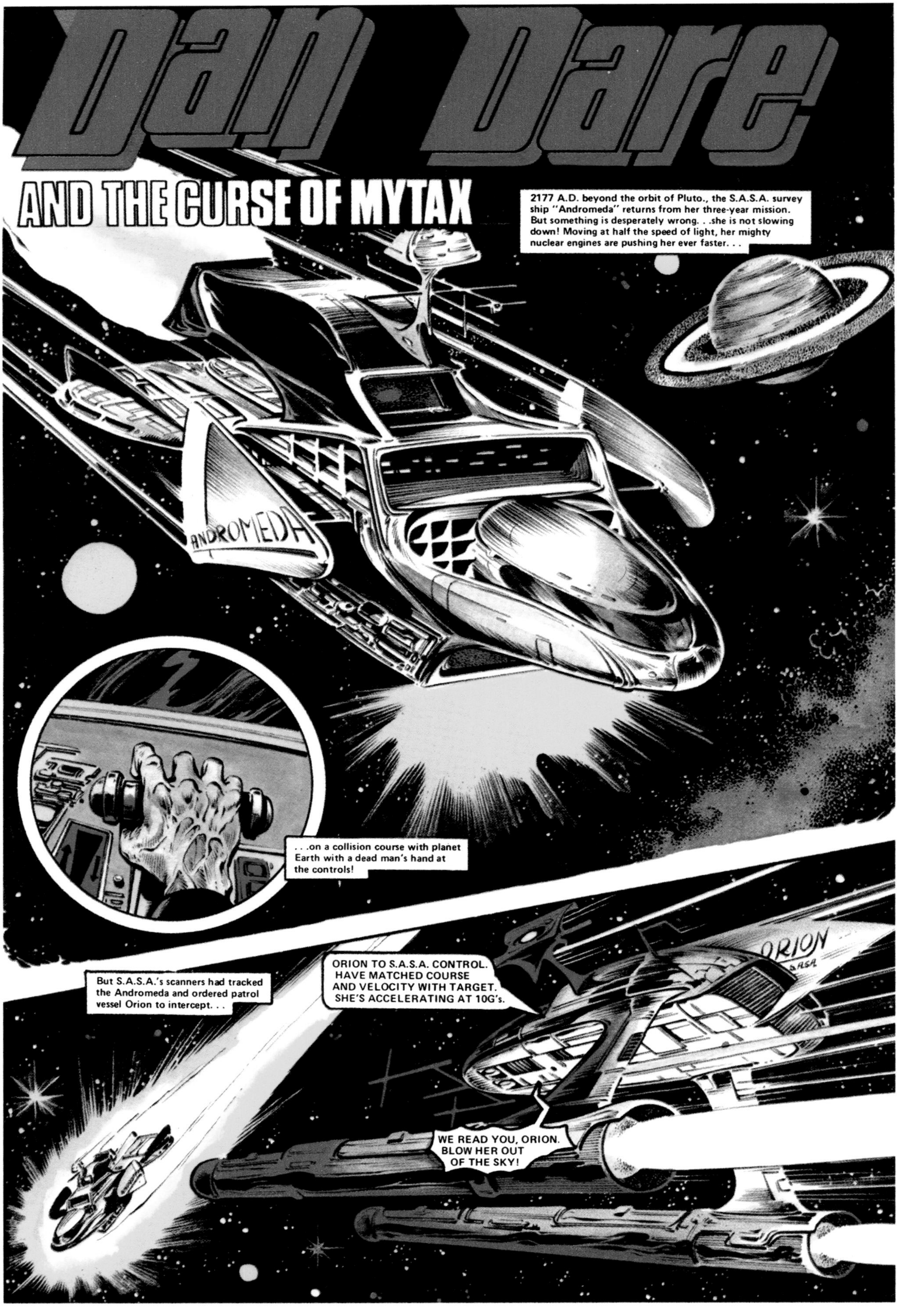
DAN DARE
AND THE CURSE OF MYTAX
2177 A.D. beyond the orbit of Pluto., the S.A.S.A. survey ship "Andromeda" returns from her three-year mission. But something is desperately wrong. . .she is not slowing down! Moving at half the speed of light, her mighty nuclear engines are pushing her ever faster. . .
ANDROMEDA
. . .on a collision course with planet Earth with a dead man's hand at the controls!
But S.A.S.A.'s scanners had tracked the Andromeda and ordered patrol vessel Orion to intercept. . .
ORION TO S.A.S.A. CONTROL. HAVE MATCHED COURSE AND VELOCITY WITH TARGET. SHE'S ACCELERATING AT 10G's.
ORION
WE READ YOU, ORION. BLOW HER OUT OF THE SKY!

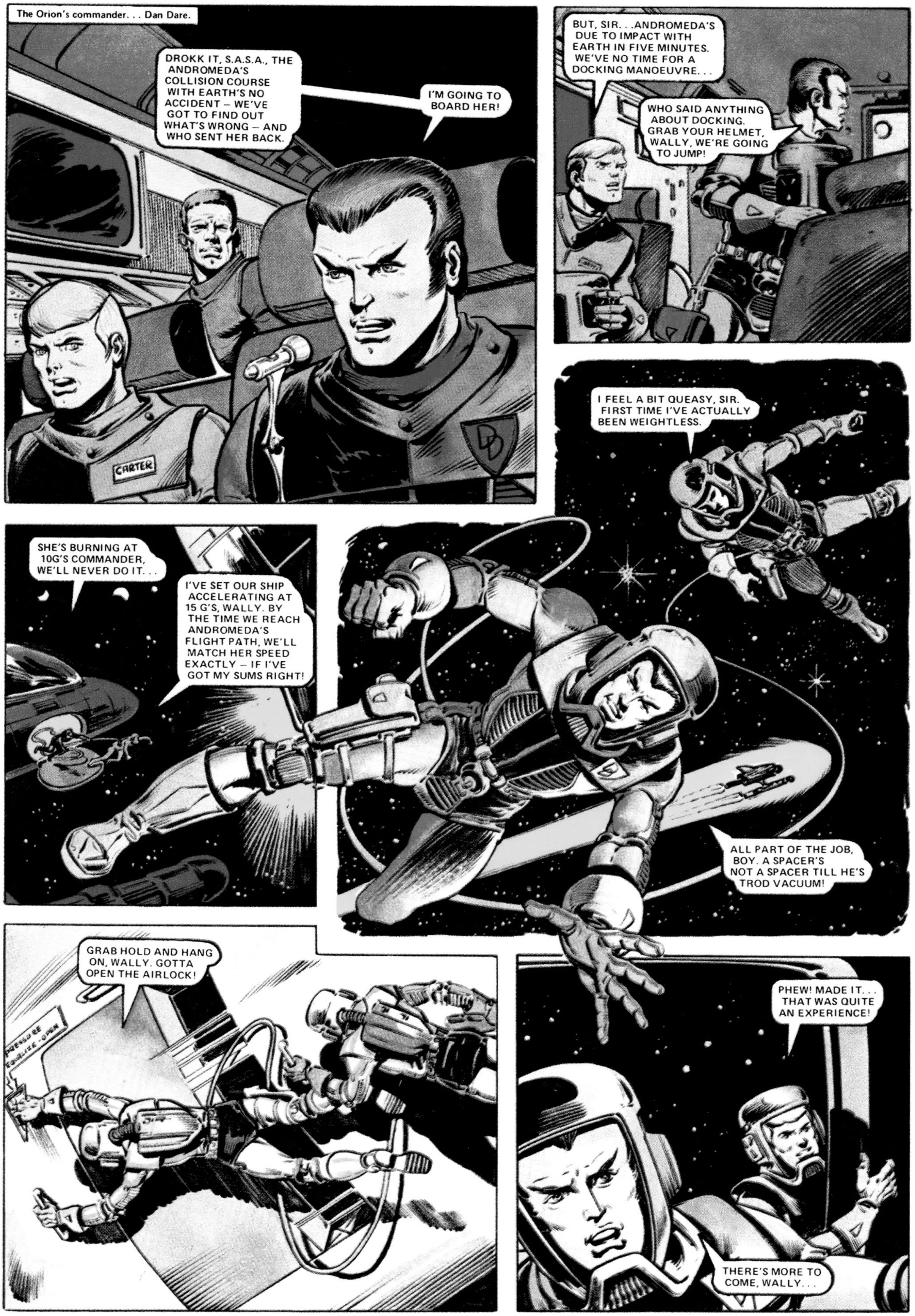
The Orion's commander. . . Dan Dare.
DROKK IT, S.A.S.A., THE ANDROMEDA'S COLLISION COURSE WITH EARTH'S NO ACCIDENT – WE'VE GOT TO FIND OUT WHAT'S WRONG – AND WHO SENT HER BACK.
I'M GOING TO BOARD HER!
CARTER
BUT, SIR. . .ANDROMEDA'S DUE TO IMPACT WITH EARTH IN FIVE MINUTES. WE'VE NO TIME FOR A DOCKING MANOEUVRE. . .
WHO SAID ANYTHING ABOUT DOCKING. GRAB YOUR HELMET, WALLY, WE'RE GOING TO JUMP!
SHE'S BURNING AT 10G'S COMMANDER, WE'LL NEVER DO IT. . .
I'VE SET OUR SHIP ACCELERATING AT 15 G'S, WALLY. BY THE TIME WE REACH ANDROMEDA'S FLIGHT PATH, WE'LL MATCH HER SPEED EXACTLY – IF I'VE GOT MY SUMS RIGHT!
I FEEL A BIT QUEASY, SIR. FIRST TIME I'VE ACTUALLY BEEN WEIGHTLESS.
ALL PART OF THE JOB, BOY. A SPACER'S NOT A SPACER TILL HE'S TROD VACUUM!
GRAB HOLD AND HANG ON, WALLY. GOTTA OPEN THE AIRLOCK!
PHEW! MADE IT. . . THAT WAS QUITE AN EXPERIENCE!
THERE'S MORE TO COME, WALLY. . .

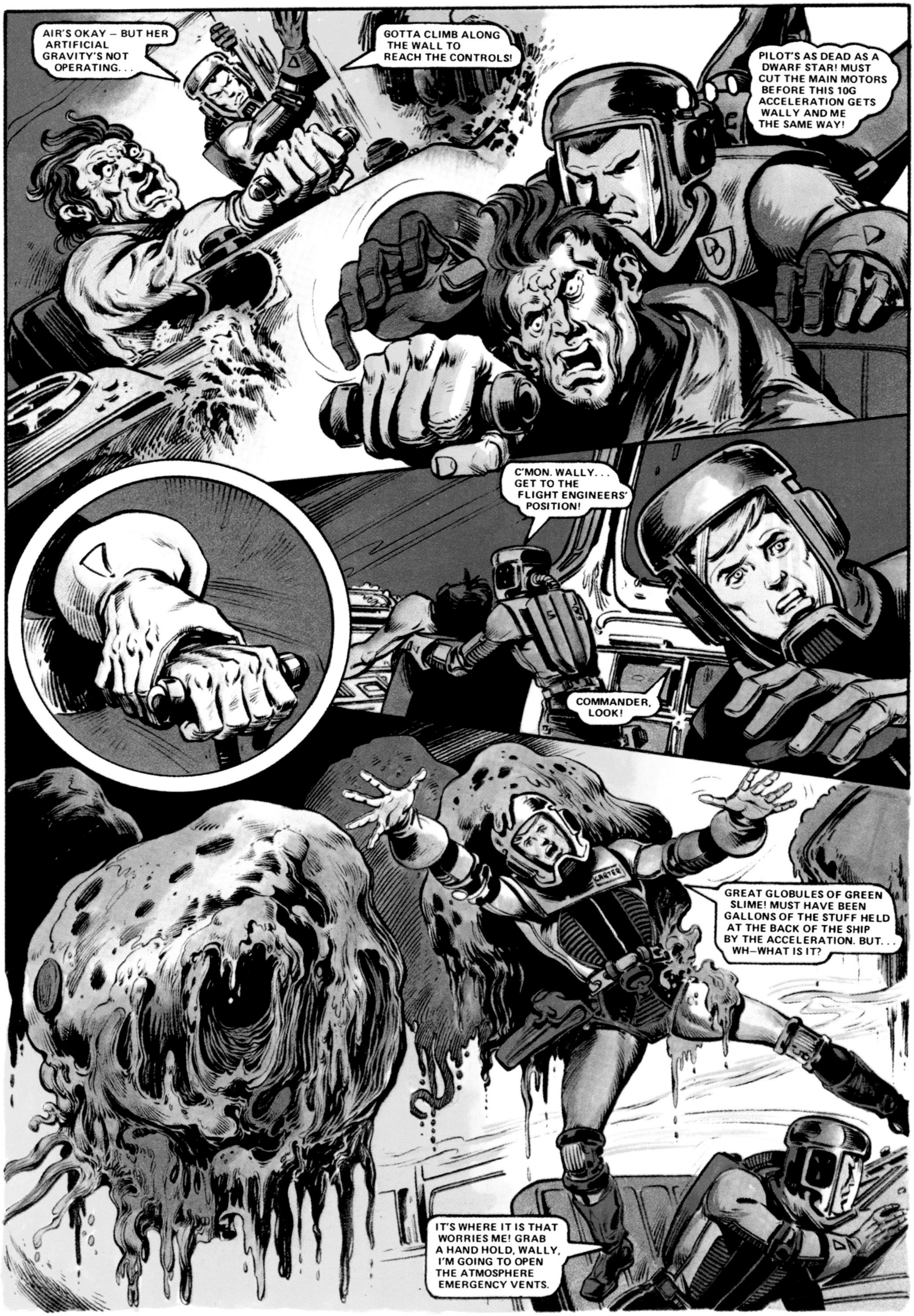
AIR'S OKAY – BUT HER ARTIFICIAL GRAVITY'S NOT OPERATING. . .
GOTTA CLIMB ALONG THE WALL TO REACH THE CONTROLS!
PILOT'S AS DEAD AS A DWARF STAR! MUST CUT THE MAIN MOTORS BEFORE THIS 10G ACCELERATION GETS WALLY AND ME THE SAME WAY!
C'MON. WALLY. . . GET TO THE FLIGHT ENGINEERS' POSITION!
COMMANDER, LOOK!
GREAT GLOBULES OF GREEN SLIME! MUST HAVE BEEN GALLONS OF THE STUFF HELD AT THE BACK OF THE SHIP BY THE ACCELERATION. BUT. . . WH–WHAT IS IT?
IT'S WHERE IT IS THAT WORRIES ME! GRAB A HAND HOLD, WALLY, I'M GOING TO OPEN THE ATMOSPHERE EMERGENCY VENTS.

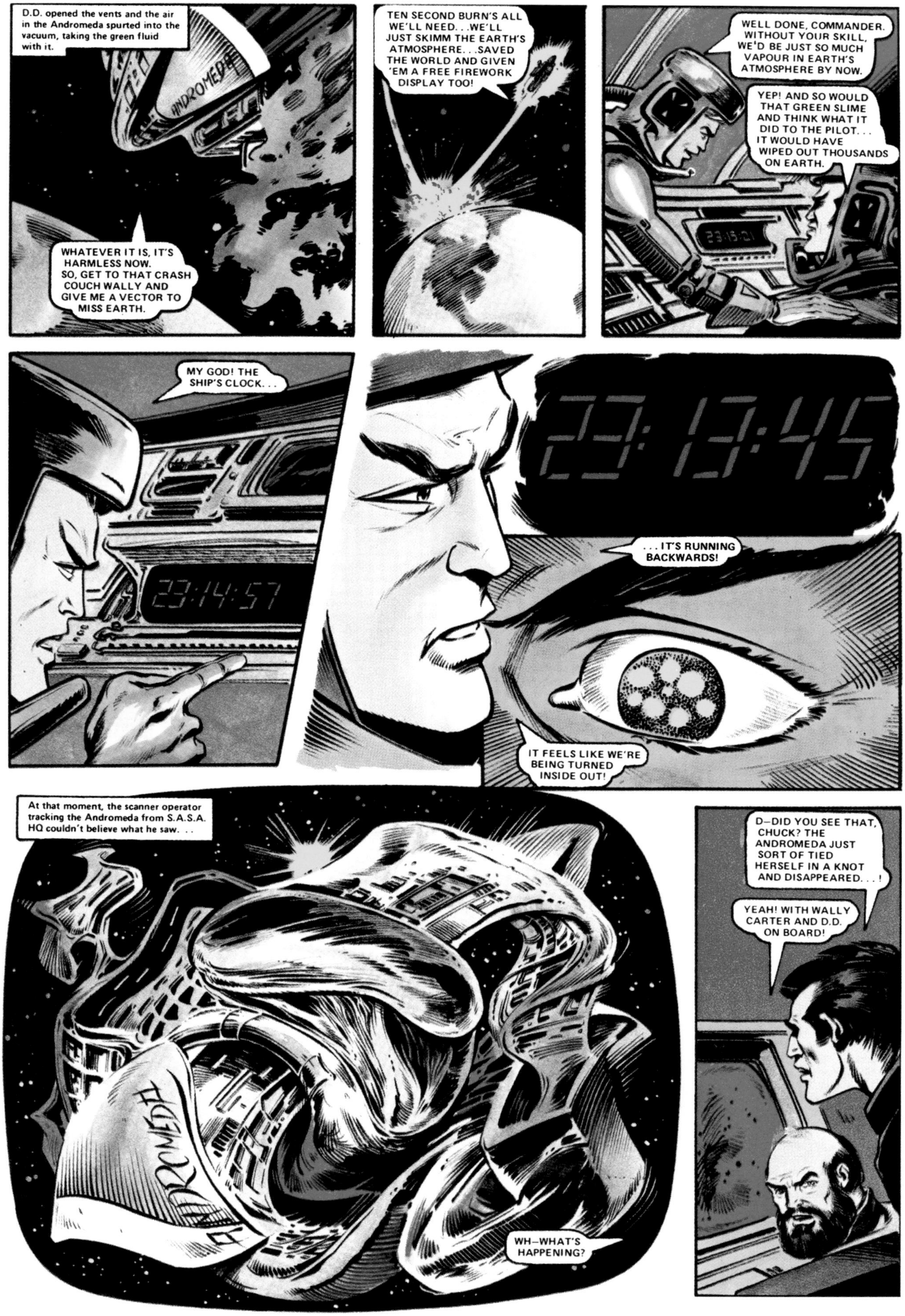

D.D. opened the vents and the air in the Andromeda spurted into the vacuum, taking the green fluid with it.
ANDROMEDA
WHATEVER IT IS, IT'S HARMLESS NOW. SO, GET TO THAT CRASH COUCH WALLY AND GIVE ME A VECTOR TO MISS EARTH.
TEN SECOND BURN'S ALL WE'LL NEED. . .WE'LL JUST SKIMM THE EARTH'S ATMOSPHERE. . .SAVED THE WORLD AND GIVEN 'EM A FREE FIREWORK DISPLAY TOO!
WELL DONE, COMMANDER. WITHOUT YOUR SKILL, WE'D BE JUST SO MUCH VAPOUR IN EARTH'S ATMOSPHERE BY NOW.
YEP! AND SO WOULD THAT GREEN SLIME AND THINK WHAT IT DID TO THE PILOT. . . IT WOULD HAVE WIPED OUT THOUSANDS ON EARTH.
23:15:21
MY GOD! THE SHIP'S CLOCK. . .
23:14:57
23:13:45
. . . IT'S RUNNING BACKWARDS!
IT FEELS LIKE WE'RE BEING TURNED INSIDE OUT!
At that moment, the scanner operator tracking the Andromeda from S.A.S.A. HQ couldn't believe what he saw. . .
ANDROMEDA
WH–WHAT'S HAPPENING?
D–DID YOU SEE THAT, CHUCK? THE ANDROMEDA JUST SORT OF TIED HERSELF IN A KNOT AND DISAPPEARED. . .!
YEAH! WITH WALLY CARTER AND D.D. ON BOARD!

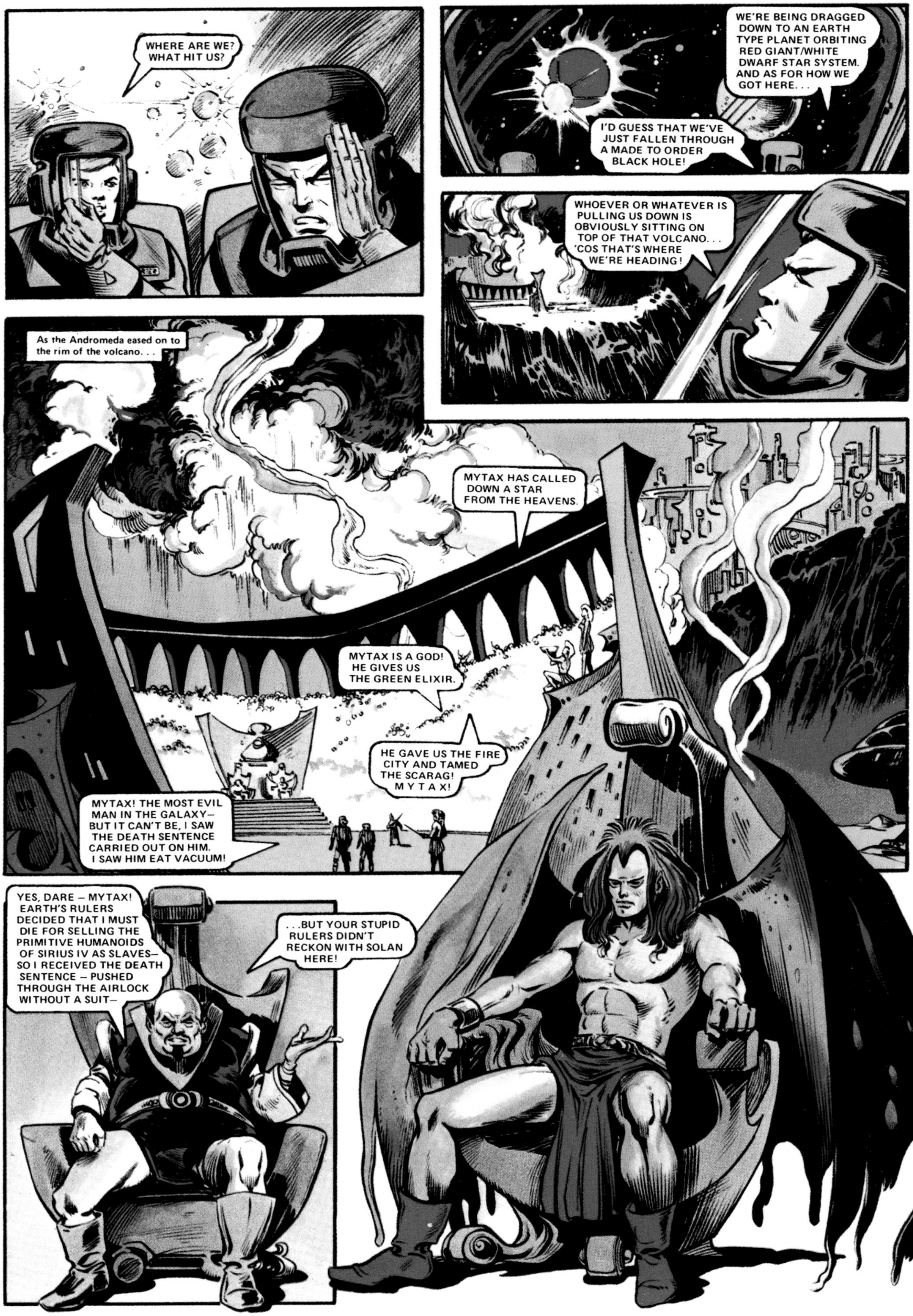
WHERE ARE WE? WHAT HIT US?
WE'RE BEING DRAGGED DOWN TO AN EARTH TYPE PLANET ORBITING RED GIANT/WHITE DWARF STAR SYSTEM. AND AS FOR HOW WE GOT HERE. . .
I'D GUESS THAT WE'VE JUST FALLEN THROUGH A MADE TO ORDER BLACK HOLE!
WHOEVER OR WHATEVER IS PULLING US DOWN IS OBVIOUSLY SITTING ON TOP OF THAT VOLCANO. . . 'COS THAT'S WHERE WE'RE HEADING!
As the Andromeda eased on to the rim of the volcano. . .
MYTAX HAS CALLED DOWN A STAR FROM THE HEAVENS.
MYTAX IS A GOD! HE GIVES US THE GREEN ELIXIR.
HE GAVE US THE FIRE CITY AND TAMED THE SCARAG! M Y T A X!
MYTAX! THE MOST EVIL MAN IN THE GALAXY— BUT IT CAN'T BE, I SAW THE DEATH SENTENCE CARRIED OUT ON HIM. I SAW HIM EAT VACUUM!
YES, DARE – MYTAX! EARTH'S RULERS DECIDED THAT I MUST DIE FOR SELLING THE PRIMITIVE HUMANOIDS OF SIRIUS IV AS SLAVES— SO I RECEIVED THE DEATH SENTENCE – PUSHED THROUGH THE AIRLOCK WITHOUT A SUIT—
. . .BUT YOUR STUPID RULERS DIDN'T RECKON WITH SOLAN HERE!

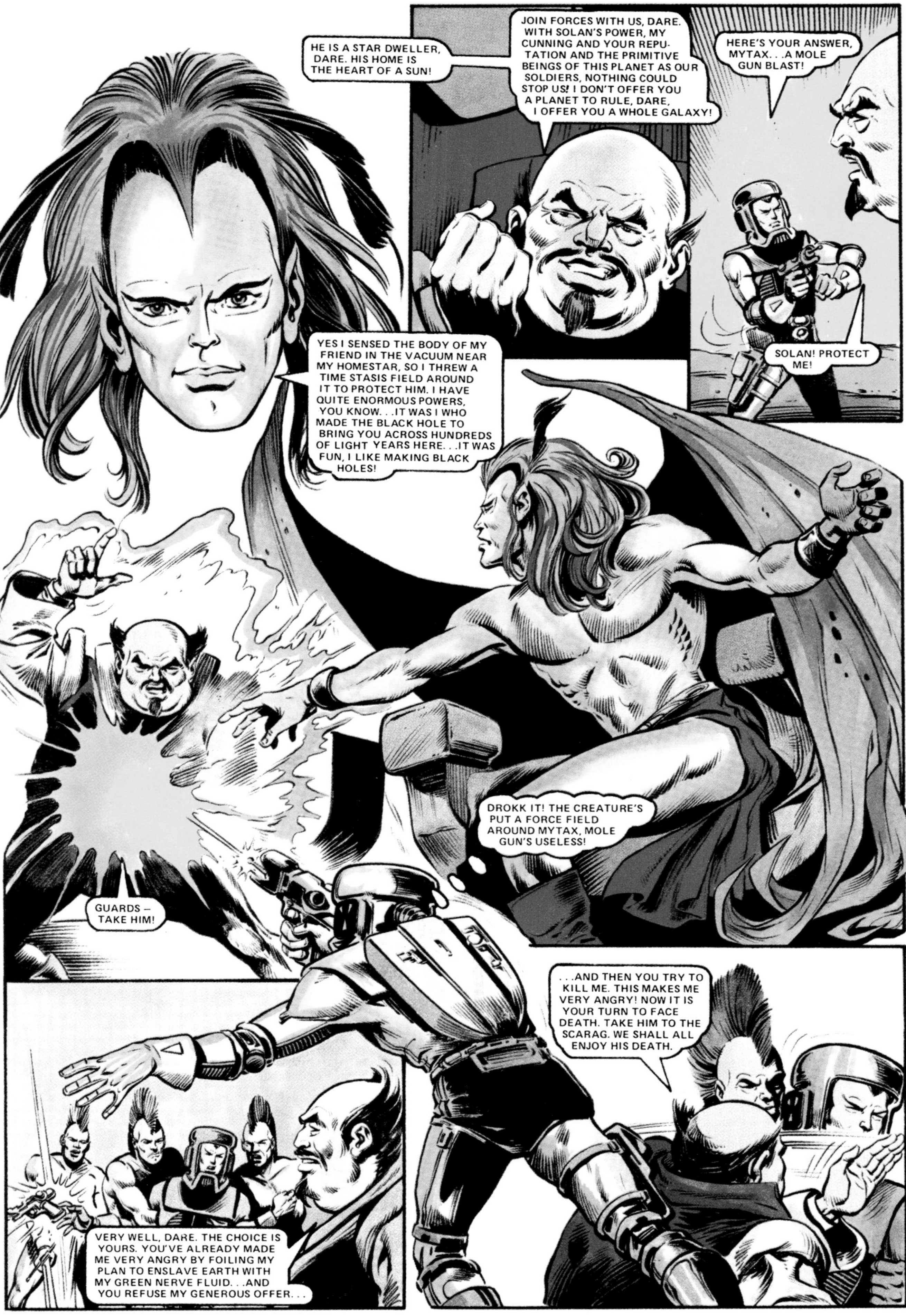

HE IS A STAR DWELLER, DARE. HIS HOME IS THE HEART OF A SUN!
JOIN FORCES WITH US, DARE. WITH SOLAN'S POWER, MY CUNNING AND YOUR REPU-TATION AND THE PRIMITIVE BEINGS OF THIS PLANET AS OUR SOLDIERS, NOTHING COULD STOP US! I DON'T OFFER YOU A PLANET TO RULE, DARE, I OFFER YOU A WHOLE GALAXY!
HERE'S YOUR ANSWER, MYTAX. . .A MOLE GUN BLAST!
SOLAN! PROTECT ME!
YES I SENSED THE BODY OF MY FRIEND IN THE VACUUM NEAR MY HOMESTAR, SO I THREW A TIME STASIS FIELD AROUND IT TO PROTECT HIM. I HAVE QUITE ENORMOUS POWERS, YOU KNOW. . .IT WAS I WHO MADE THE BLACK HOLE TO BRING YOU ACROSS HUNDREDS OF LIGHT YEARS HERE. . .IT WAS FUN, I LIKE MAKING BLACK HOLES!
DROKK IT! THE CREATURE'S PUT A FORCE FIELD AROUND MYTAX, MOLE GUN'S USELESS!
GUARDS – TAKE HIM!
VERY WELL, DARE. THE CHOICE IS YOURS. YOU'VE ALREADY MADE ME VERY ANGRY BY FOILING MY PLAN TO ENSLAVE EARTH WITH MY GREEN NERVE FLUID. . .AND YOU REFUSE MY GENEROUS OFFER. . .
. . .AND THEN YOU TRY TO KILL ME. THIS MAKES ME VERY ANGRY! NOW IT IS YOUR TURN TO FACE DEATH. TAKE HIM TO THE SCARAG. WE SHALL ALL ENJOY HIS DEATH.

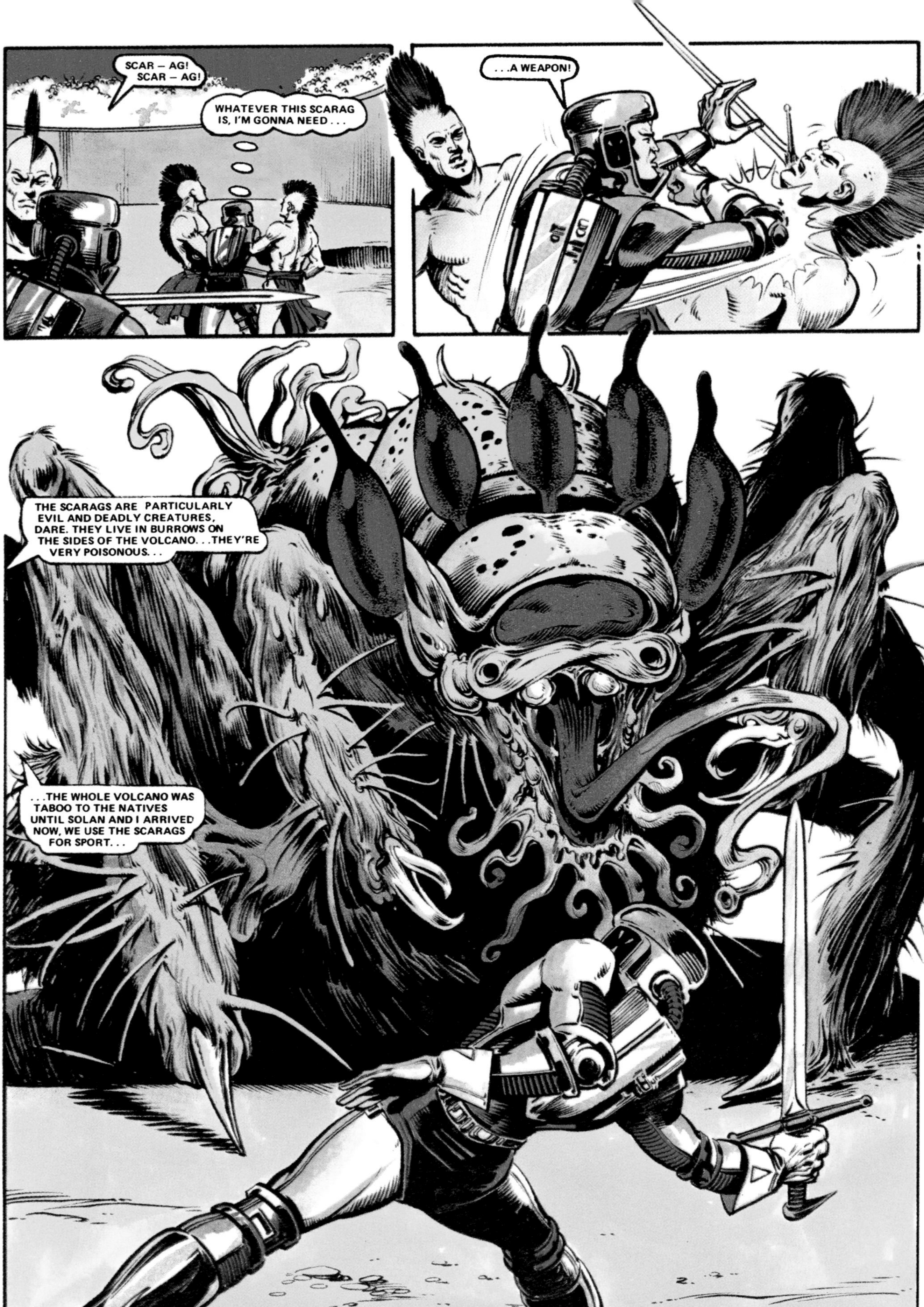
SCAR – AG!
SCAR – AG!
WHATEVER THIS SCARAG IS, I'M GONNA NEED . . .
. . . A WEAPON!
THE SCARAGS ARE PARTICULARLY EVIL AND DEADLY CREATURES, DARE. THEY LIVE IN BURROWS ON THE SIDES OF THE VOLCANO. . . THEY'RE VERY POISONOUS. . .
. . . THE WHOLE VOLCANO WAS TABOO TO THE NATIVES UNTIL SOLAN AND I ARRIVED. NOW, WE USE THE SCARAGS FOR SPORT. . .

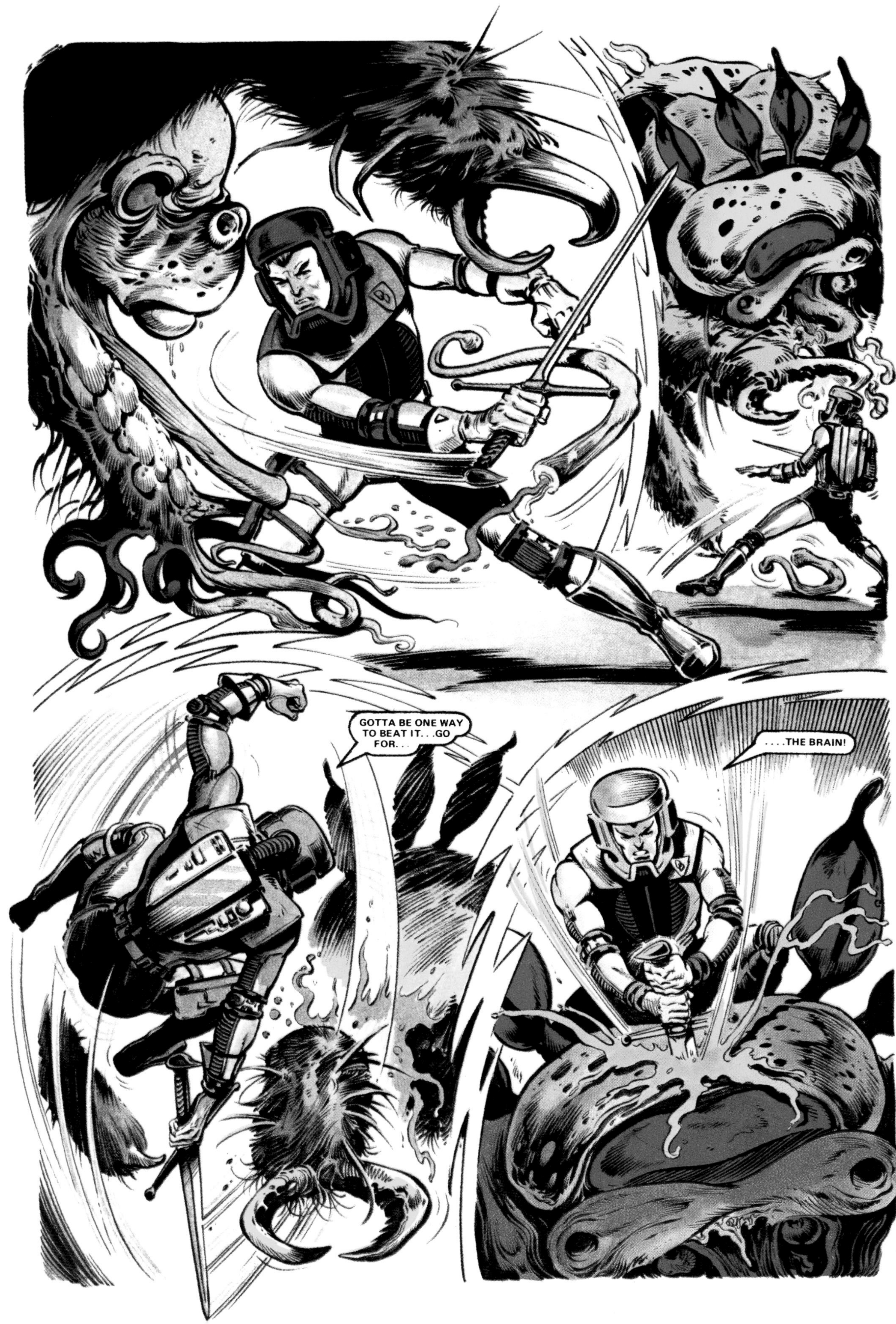
GOTTA BE ONE WAY TO BEAT IT. . .GO FOR. . .
. . . .THE BRAIN!

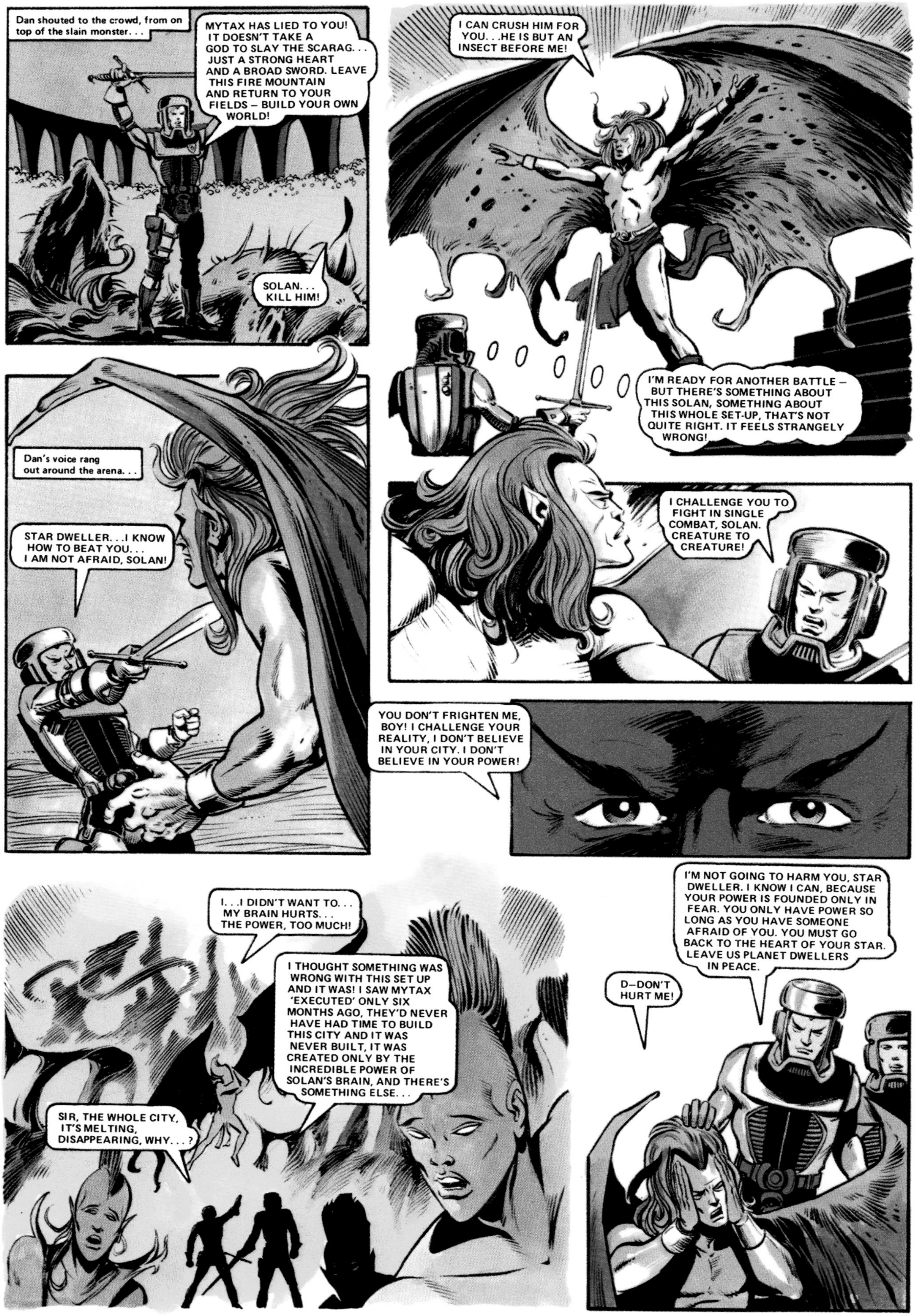

Dan shouted to the crowd, from on top of the slain monster...
MYTAX HAS LIED TO YOU! IT DOESN'T TAKE A GOD TO SLAY THE SCARAG... JUST A STRONG HEART AND A BROAD SWORD. LEAVE THIS FIRE MOUNTAIN AND RETURN TO YOUR FIELDS – BUILD YOUR OWN WORLD!
SOLAN... KILL HIM!
I CAN CRUSH HIM FOR YOU... HE IS BUT AN INSECT BEFORE ME!
I'M READY FOR ANOTHER BATTLE – BUT THERE'S SOMETHING ABOUT THIS SOLAN, SOMETHING ABOUT THIS WHOLE SET-UP, THAT'S NOT QUITE RIGHT. IT FEELS STRANGELY WRONG!
Dan's voice rang out around the arena...
STAR DWELLER... I KNOW HOW TO BEAT YOU... I AM NOT AFRAID, SOLAN!
I CHALLENGE YOU TO FIGHT IN SINGLE COMBAT, SOLAN. CREATURE TO CREATURE!
YOU DON'T FRIGHTEN ME, BOY! I CHALLENGE YOUR REALITY, I DON'T BELIEVE IN YOUR CITY. I DON'T BELIEVE IN YOUR POWER!
I... I DIDN'T WANT TO... MY BRAIN HURTS... THE POWER, TOO MUCH!
I THOUGHT SOMETHING WAS WRONG WITH THIS SET UP AND IT WAS! I SAW MYTAX 'EXECUTED' ONLY SIX MONTHS AGO, THEY'D NEVER HAVE HAD TIME TO BUILD THIS CITY AND IT WAS NEVER BUILT, IT WAS CREATED ONLY BY THE INCREDIBLE POWER OF SOLAN'S BRAIN, AND THERE'S SOMETHING ELSE...
SIR, THE WHOLE CITY, IT'S MELTING, DISAPPEARING, WHY...?
I'M NOT GOING TO HARM YOU, STAR DWELLER. I KNOW I CAN, BECAUSE YOUR POWER IS FOUNDED ONLY IN FEAR. YOU ONLY HAVE POWER SO LONG AS YOU HAVE SOMEONE AFRAID OF YOU. YOU MUST GO BACK TO THE HEART OF YOUR STAR. LEAVE US PLANET DWELLERS IN PEACE.
D–DON'T HURT ME!

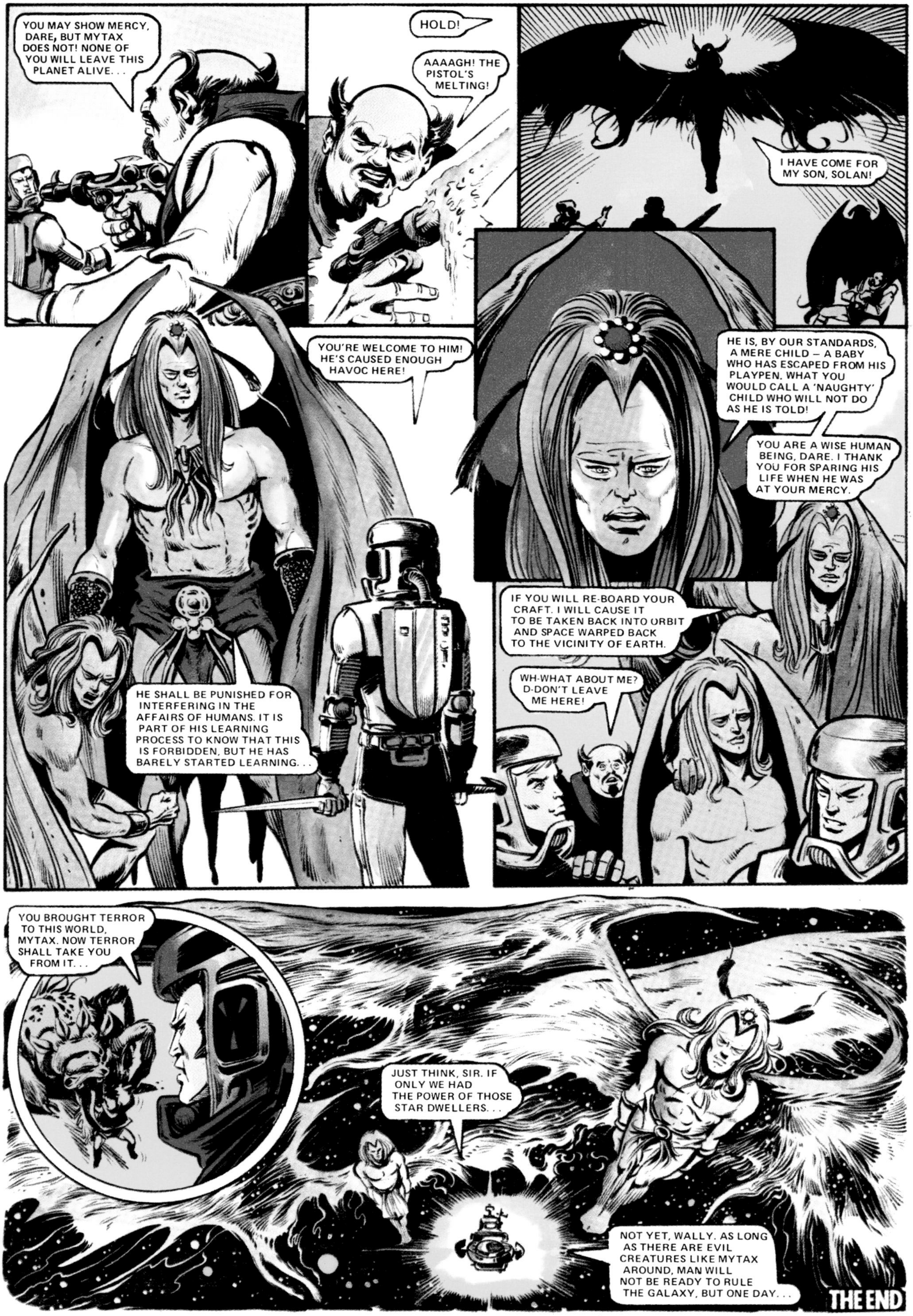

YOU MAY SHOW MERCY, DARE, BUT MYTAX DOES NOT! NONE OF YOU WILL LEAVE THIS PLANET ALIVE...
HOLD!
AAAAGH! THE PISTOL'S MELTING!
I HAVE COME FOR MY SON, SOLAN!
YOU'RE WELCOME TO HIM! HE'S CAUSED ENOUGH HAVOC HERE!
HE SHALL BE PUNISHED FOR INTERFERING IN THE AFFAIRS OF HUMANS. IT IS PART OF HIS LEARNING PROCESS TO KNOW THAT THIS IS FORBIDDEN, BUT HE HAS BARELY STARTED LEARNING...
HE IS, BY OUR STANDARDS, A MERE CHILD – A BABY WHO HAS ESCAPED FROM HIS PLAYPEN. WHAT YOU WOULD CALL A 'NAUGHTY' CHILD WHO WILL NOT DO AS HE IS TOLD!
YOU ARE A WISE HUMAN BEING, DARE. I THANK YOU FOR SPARING HIS LIFE WHEN HE WAS AT YOUR MERCY.
IF YOU WILL RE-BOARD YOUR CRAFT, I WILL CAUSE IT TO BE TAKEN BACK INTO ORBIT AND SPACE WARPED BACK TO THE VICINITY OF EARTH.
WH-WHAT ABOUT ME? D-DON'T LEAVE ME HERE!
YOU BROUGHT TERROR TO THIS WORLD, MYTAX. NOW TERROR SHALL TAKE YOU FROM IT...
JUST THINK, SIR. IF ONLY WE HAD THE POWER OF THOSE STAR DWELLERS...
NOT YET, WALLY. AS LONG AS THERE ARE EVIL CREATURES LIKE MYTAX AROUND, MAN WILL NOT BE READY TO RULE THE GALAXY, BUT ONE DAY...
THE END

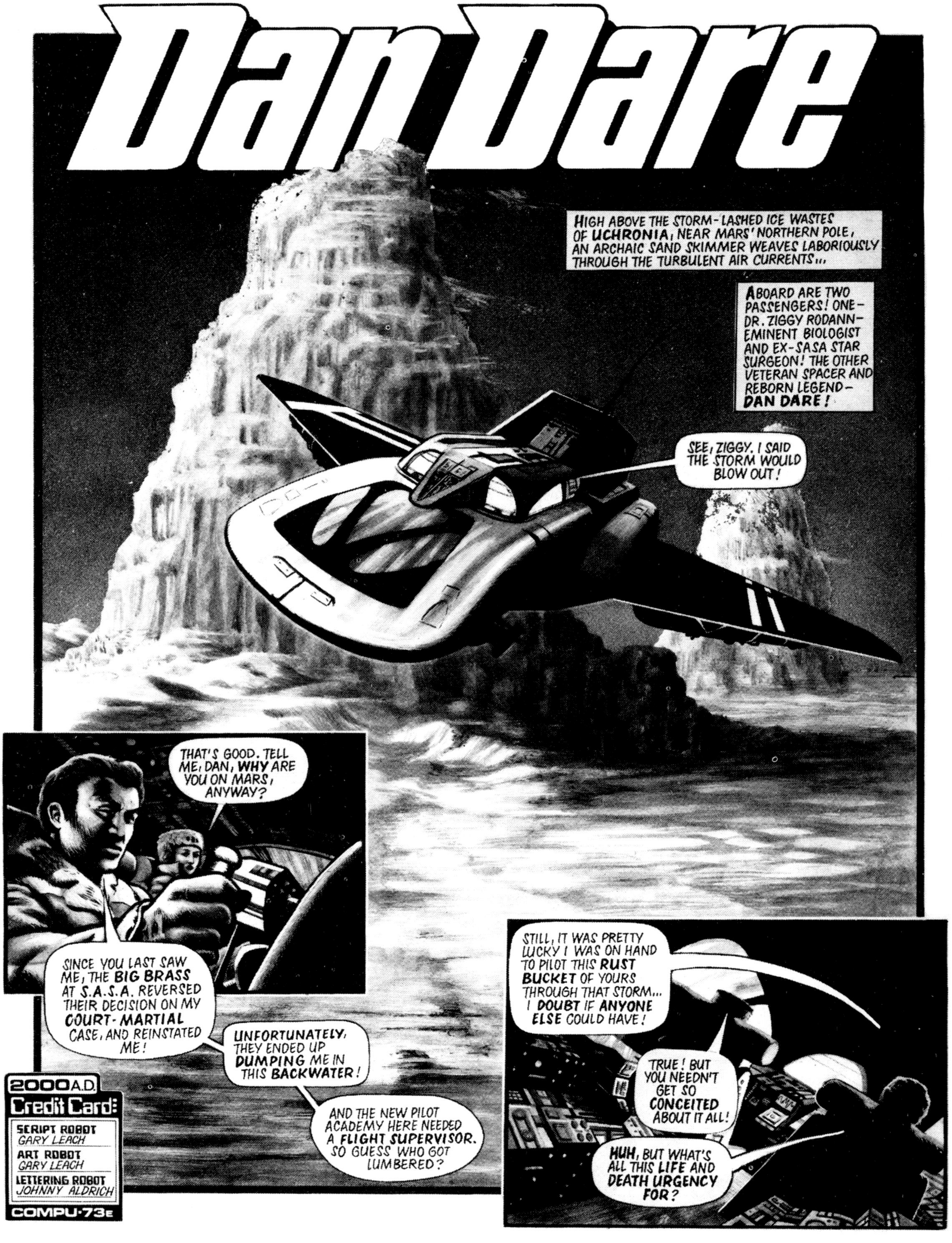

Dan Dare
HIGH ABOVE THE STORM-LASHED ICE WASTES OF UCHRONIA, NEAR MARS' NORTHERN POLE, AN ARCHAIC SAND SKIMMER WEAVES LABORIOUSLY THROUGH THE TURBULENT AIR CURRENTS...
ABOARD ARE TWO PASSENGERS! ONE- DR. ZIGGY RODANN- EMINENT BIOLOGIST AND EX-SASA STAR SURGEON! THE OTHER VETERAN SPACER AND REBORN LEGEND- DAN DARE!
SEE, ZIGGY, I SAID THE STORM WOULD BLOW OUT!
THAT'S GOOD. TELL ME, DAN, WHY ARE YOU ON MARS, ANYWAY?
SINCE YOU LAST SAW ME, THE BIG BRASS AT S.A.S.A. REVERSED THEIR DECISION ON MY COURT-MARTIAL CASE, AND REINSTATED ME!
UNFORTUNATELY, THEY ENDED UP DUMPING ME IN THIS BACKWATER!
AND THE NEW PILOT ACADEMY HERE NEEDED A FLIGHT SUPERVISOR. SO GUESS WHO GOT LUMBERED?
STILL, IT WAS PRETTY LUCKY I WAS ON HAND TO PILOT THIS RUST BUCKET OF YOURS THROUGH THAT STORM... I DOUBT IF ANYONE ELSE COULD HAVE!
TRUE! BUT YOU NEEDN'T GET SO CONCEITED ABOUT IT ALL!
HUH, BUT WHAT'S ALL THIS LIFE AND DEATH URGENCY FOR?
2000 A.D. Credit Card:
SCRIPT ROBOT GARY LEACH
ART ROBOT GARY LEACH
LETTERING ROBOT JOHNNY ALDRICH
COMPU-73E

AH YES... WELL... THAT'S THE AWKWARD BIT!

HEY, YOU **TRUST ME,** DON'T YOU?

OF COURSE I DO, DAN! BUT THERE'RE OTHERS INVOLVED! THE PROJECT'S SUPPOSED TO BE **SECRET.** IF SASA **EVER** DISCOVERED..!

PROJECT? **WHAT** PROJECT?

LOOK, DAN, **PLEASE** DON'T PRESS ME!

ALRIGHT! ALRIGHT! I'LL TELL YOU, BUT **IF** YOU SO MUCH AS...

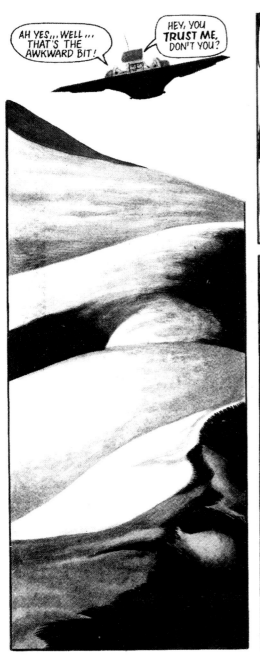

MY LIPS ARE SEALED...

WHAAA!

AM I SEEING THINGS? IS THAT A PURPLE LAKE OUT THERE?

ER, DAN, THAT'S THE BIG SECRET!

THAT SO-CALLED "**LAKE**" HAPPENS TO BE A TOTALLY **UNIQUE** LIFE-FORM, OR SO WE BELIEVE. YOU SEE, THREE YEARS AGO AN OLD PROFESSOR DISCOVERED IT.

EVENTUALLY HE SOLD IT TO A LARGE INDUSTRIAL COMPANY WHO DECIDED IT MIGHT POSSESS SOME **COMMERCIAL POTENTIAL!**

THIS COMPANY-SPONSORED A TEAM OF **FREELANCE SCIENTISTS** TO EXTENSIVELY ANALYSE THEIR **NEW** APPROPRIATION!

I WAS PART OF THAT TEAM!

VISCO, AS WE NAMED IT, IS ACTUALLY ONE SINGLE, VAST, SEMI-INTELLIGENT ORGANISM! WOULD YOU BELIEVE WE EVEN TAUGHT IT **ELEMENTARY** MATHS?

SAY, THOSE WEAPONS AREN'T TOO HEAVY FOR YOU?

IN THIS LOW GRAVITY? GIVE ME SOME CREDIT, GIRL!

ANYWAY, VISCO ALSO CAUSED ALL OUR TEST PLANTS TO GROW TO **ABNORMAL PROPORTIONS!**

SO, WE CONSTRUCTED A TRITON SEA LAB ON THE LAKE BED TO STUDY IT. THEN SUDDENLY LAST MONTH FOR **NO REASON** VISCO STARTED **ATTACKING** US!

SINCE THEN, WE'VE BEEN LIVING IN A STATE OF TERROR. THE **FINAL BLOW** CAME WHEN THREE OF OUR TEAM VANISHED WITHOUT TRACE!

BUT WE COULDN'T LEAVE, DAN. THINK OF ALL THE KNOWLEDGE WE MIGHT BE FORSAKING!

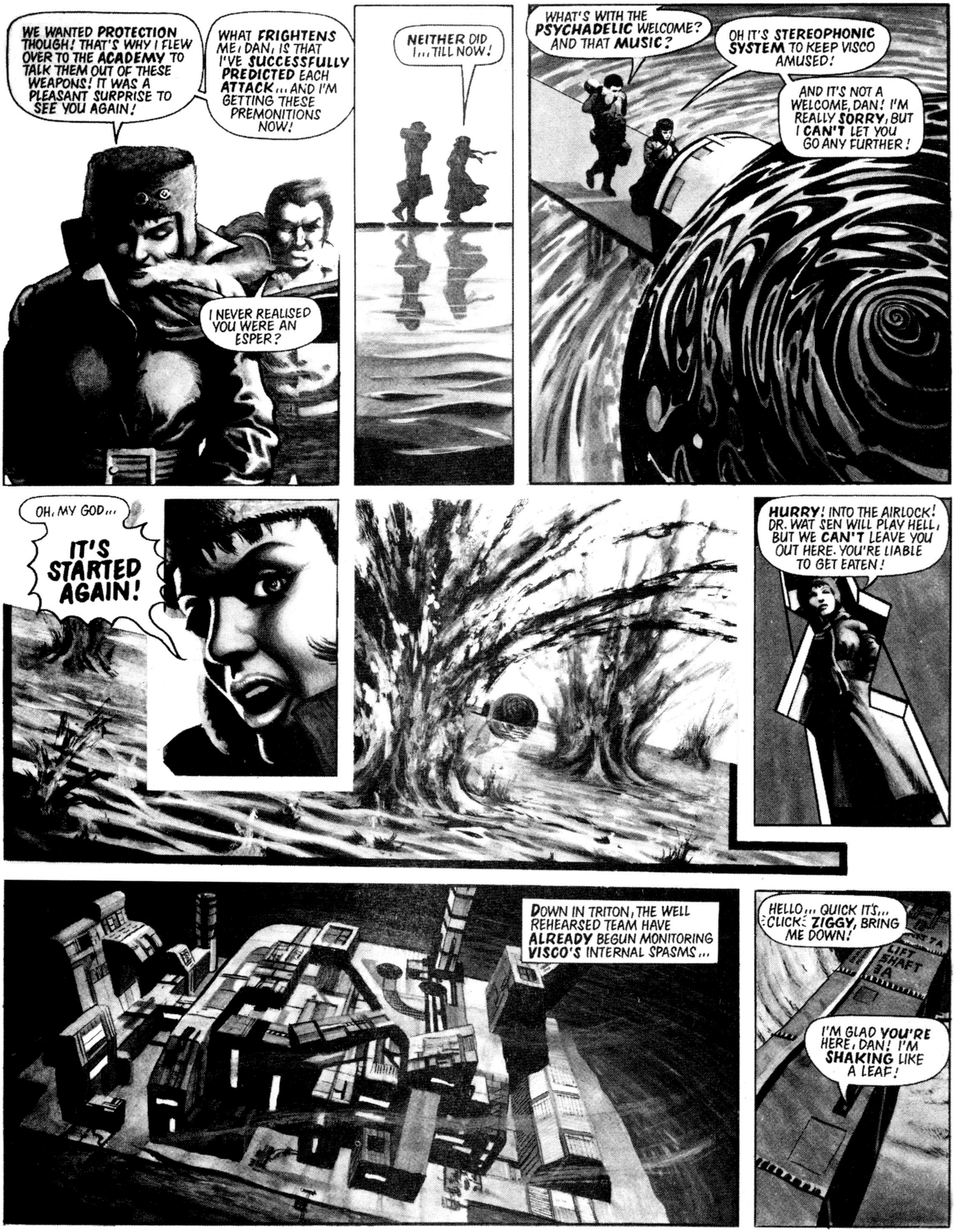
WE WANTED PROTECTION THOUGH! THAT'S WHY I FLEW OVER TO THE ACADEMY TO TALK THEM OUT OF THESE WEAPONS! IT WAS A PLEASANT SURPRISE TO SEE YOU AGAIN!
WHAT FRIGHTENS ME, DAN, IS THAT I'VE SUCCESSFULLY PREDICTED EACH ATTACK... AND I'M GETTING THESE PREMONITIONS NOW!
I NEVER REALISED YOU WERE AN ESPER?
NEITHER DID I... TILL NOW!
WHAT'S WITH THE PSYCHADELIC WELCOME? AND THAT MUSIC?
OH IT'S STEREOPHONIC SYSTEM TO KEEP VISCO AMUSED!
AND IT'S NOT A WELCOME, DAN! I'M REALLY SORRY, BUT I CAN'T LET YOU GO ANY FURTHER!
OH, MY GOD...
IT'S STARTED AGAIN!
HURRY! INTO THE AIRLOCK! DR. WAT SEN WILL PLAY HELL, BUT WE CAN'T LEAVE YOU OUT HERE. YOU'RE LIABLE TO GET EATEN!
DOWN IN TRITON, THE WELL REHEARSED TEAM HAVE ALREADY BEGUN MONITORING VISCO'S INTERNAL SPASMS...
HELLO... QUICK IT'S... CLICK ZIGGY, BRING ME DOWN!
LIFT SHAFT 7A
I'M GLAD YOU'RE HERE, DAN! I'M SHAKING LIKE A LEAF!

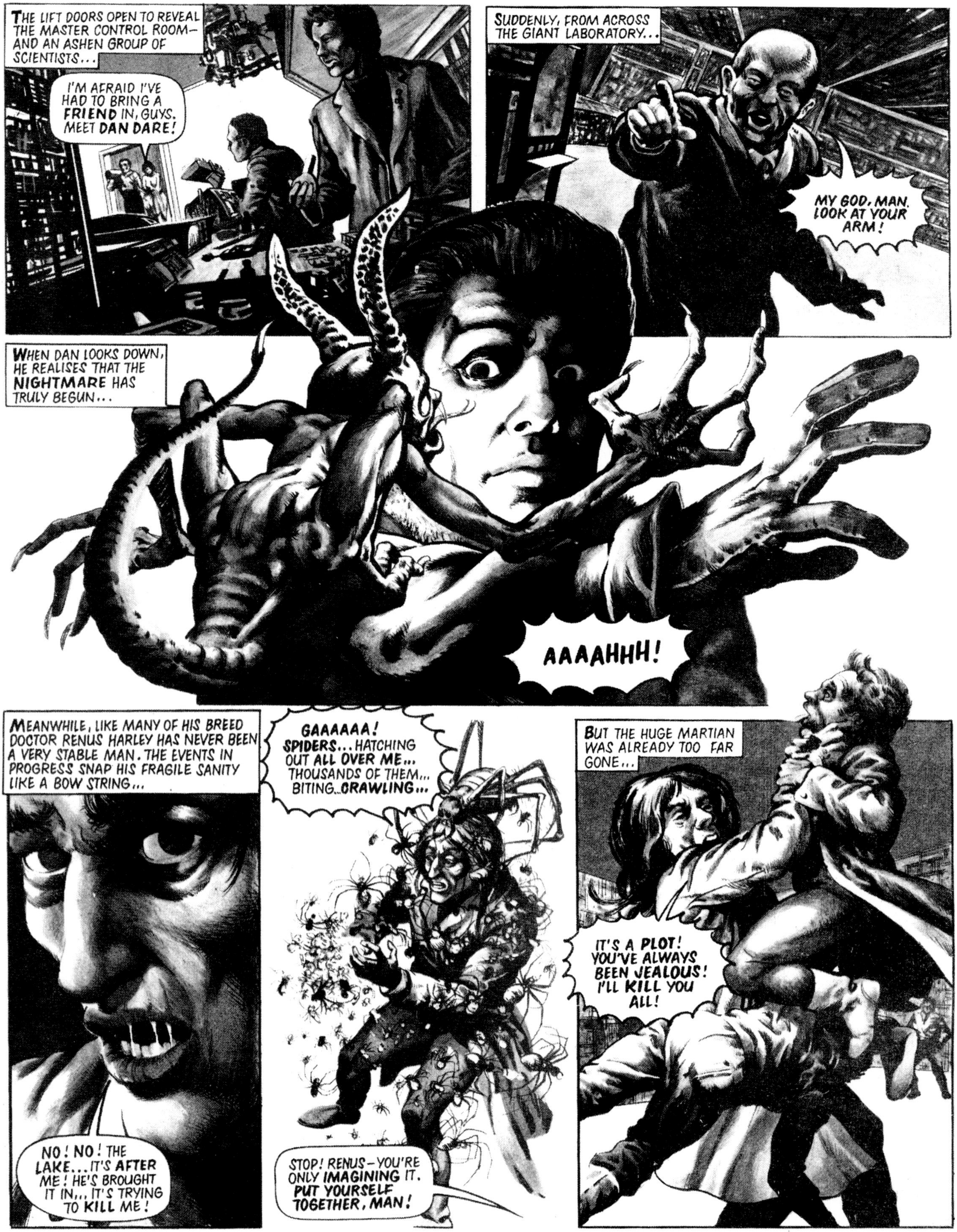

THE LIFT DOORS OPEN TO REVEAL THE MASTER CONTROL ROOM— AND AN ASHEN GROUP OF SCIENTISTS...
I'M AFRAID I'VE HAD TO BRING A FRIEND IN, GUYS. MEET DAN DARE!
SUDDENLY, FROM ACROSS THE GIANT LABORATORY...
MY GOD, MAN. LOOK AT YOUR ARM!
WHEN DAN LOOKS DOWN, HE REALISES THAT THE NIGHTMARE HAS TRULY BEGUN...
AAAAHHH!
MEANWHILE, LIKE MANY OF HIS BREED DOCTOR RENUS HARLEY HAS NEVER BEEN A VERY STABLE MAN. THE EVENTS IN PROGRESS SNAP HIS FRAGILE SANITY LIKE A BOW STRING...
NO! NO! THE LAKE... IT'S AFTER ME! HE'S BROUGHT IT IN,,, IT'S TRYING TO KILL ME!
GAAAAAA! SPIDERS... HATCHING OUT ALL OVER ME... THOUSANDS OF THEM... BITING... CRAWLING...
STOP! RENUS—YOU'RE ONLY IMAGINING IT. PUT YOURSELF TOGETHER, MAN!
BUT THE HUGE MARTIAN WAS ALREADY TOO FAR GONE...
IT'S A PLOT! YOU'VE ALWAYS BEEN JEALOUS! I'LL KILL YOU ALL!

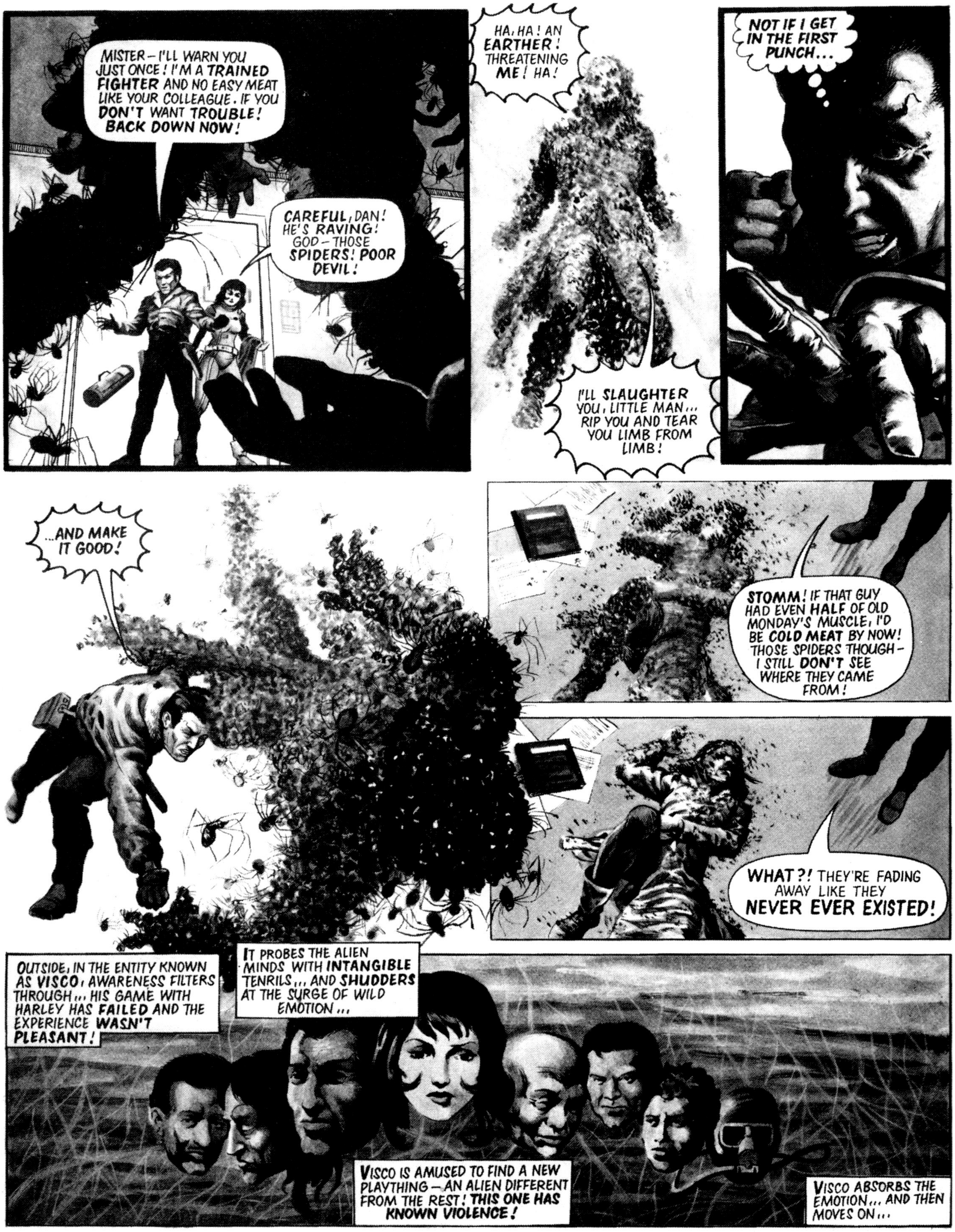
MISTER — I'LL WARN YOU JUST ONCE! I'M A TRAINED FIGHTER AND NO EASY MEAT LIKE YOUR COLLEAGUE. IF YOU DON'T WANT TROUBLE! BACK DOWN NOW!
CAREFUL, DAN! HE'S RAVING! GOD — THOSE SPIDERS! POOR DEVIL!
HA, HA! AN EARTHER! THREATENING ME! HA!
I'LL SLAUGHTER YOU, LITTLE MAN... RIP YOU AND TEAR YOU LIMB FROM LIMB!
NOT IF I GET IN THE FIRST PUNCH...
...AND MAKE IT GOOD!
STOMM! IF THAT GUY HAD EVEN HALF OF OLD MONDAY'S MUSCLE, I'D BE COLD MEAT BY NOW! THOSE SPIDERS THOUGH — I STILL DON'T SEE WHERE THEY CAME FROM!
WHAT?! THEY'RE FADING AWAY LIKE THEY NEVER EVER EXISTED!
OUTSIDE, IN THE ENTITY KNOWN AS VISCO, AWARENESS FILTERS THROUGH... HIS GAME WITH HARLEY HAS FAILED AND THE EXPERIENCE WASN'T PLEASANT!
IT PROBES THE ALIEN MINDS WITH INTANGIBLE TENRILS... AND SHUDDERS AT THE SURGE OF WILD EMOTION...
VISCO IS AMUSED TO FIND A NEW PLAYTHING — AN ALIEN DIFFERENT FROM THE REST! THIS ONE HAS KNOWN VIOLENCE!
VISCO ABSORBS THE EMOTION... AND THEN MOVES ON...

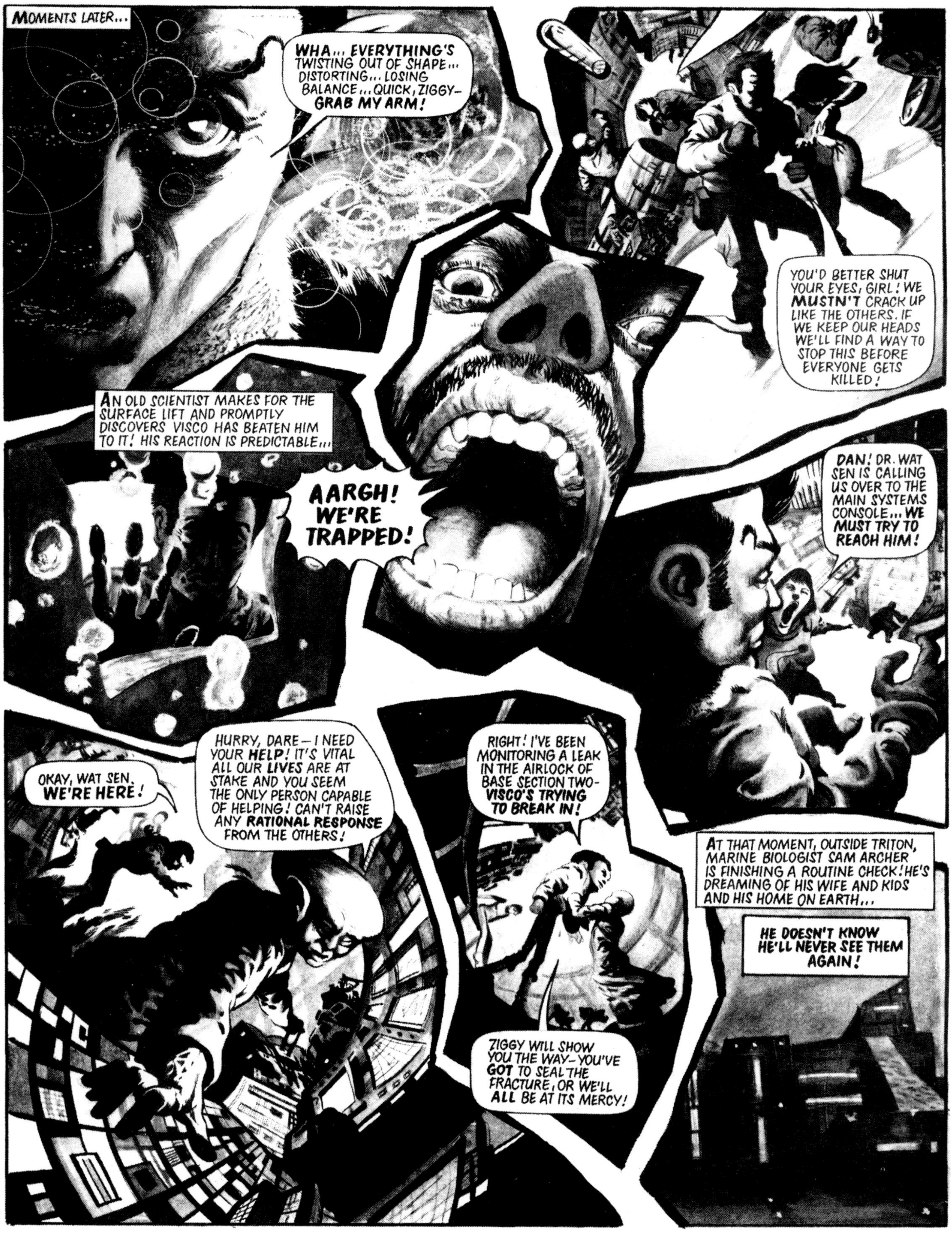
MOMENTS LATER...
WHA... EVERYTHING'S TWISTING OUT OF SHAPE... DISTORTING... LOSING BALANCE... QUICK, ZIGGY– GRAB MY ARM!
YOU'D BETTER SHUT YOUR EYES, GIRL! WE MUSTN'T CRACK UP LIKE THE OTHERS. IF WE KEEP OUR HEADS WE'LL FIND A WAY TO STOP THIS BEFORE EVERYONE GETS KILLED!
AN OLD SCIENTIST MAKES FOR THE SURFACE LIFT AND PROMPTLY DISCOVERS VISCO HAS BEATEN HIM TO IT! HIS REACTION IS PREDICTABLE...
AARGH! WE'RE TRAPPED!
DAN! DR. WAT SEN IS CALLING US OVER TO THE MAIN SYSTEMS CONSOLE... WE MUST TRY TO REACH HIM!
OKAY, WAT SEN, WE'RE HERE!
HURRY, DARE– I NEED YOUR HELP! IT'S VITAL ALL OUR LIVES ARE AT STAKE AND YOU SEEM THE ONLY PERSON CAPABLE OF HELPING! CAN'T RAISE ANY RATIONAL RESPONSE FROM THE OTHERS!
RIGHT! I'VE BEEN MONITORING A LEAK IN THE AIRLOCK OF BASE SECTION TWO– VISCO'S TRYING TO BREAK IN!
ZIGGY WILL SHOW YOU THE WAY– YOU'VE GOT TO SEAL THE FRACTURE, OR WE'LL ALL BE AT ITS MERCY!
AT THAT MOMENT, OUTSIDE TRITON, MARINE BIOLOGIST SAM ARCHER IS FINISHING A ROUTINE CHECK! HE'S DREAMING OF HIS WIFE AND KIDS AND HIS HOME ON EARTH...
HE DOESN'T KNOW HE'LL NEVER SEE THEM AGAIN!

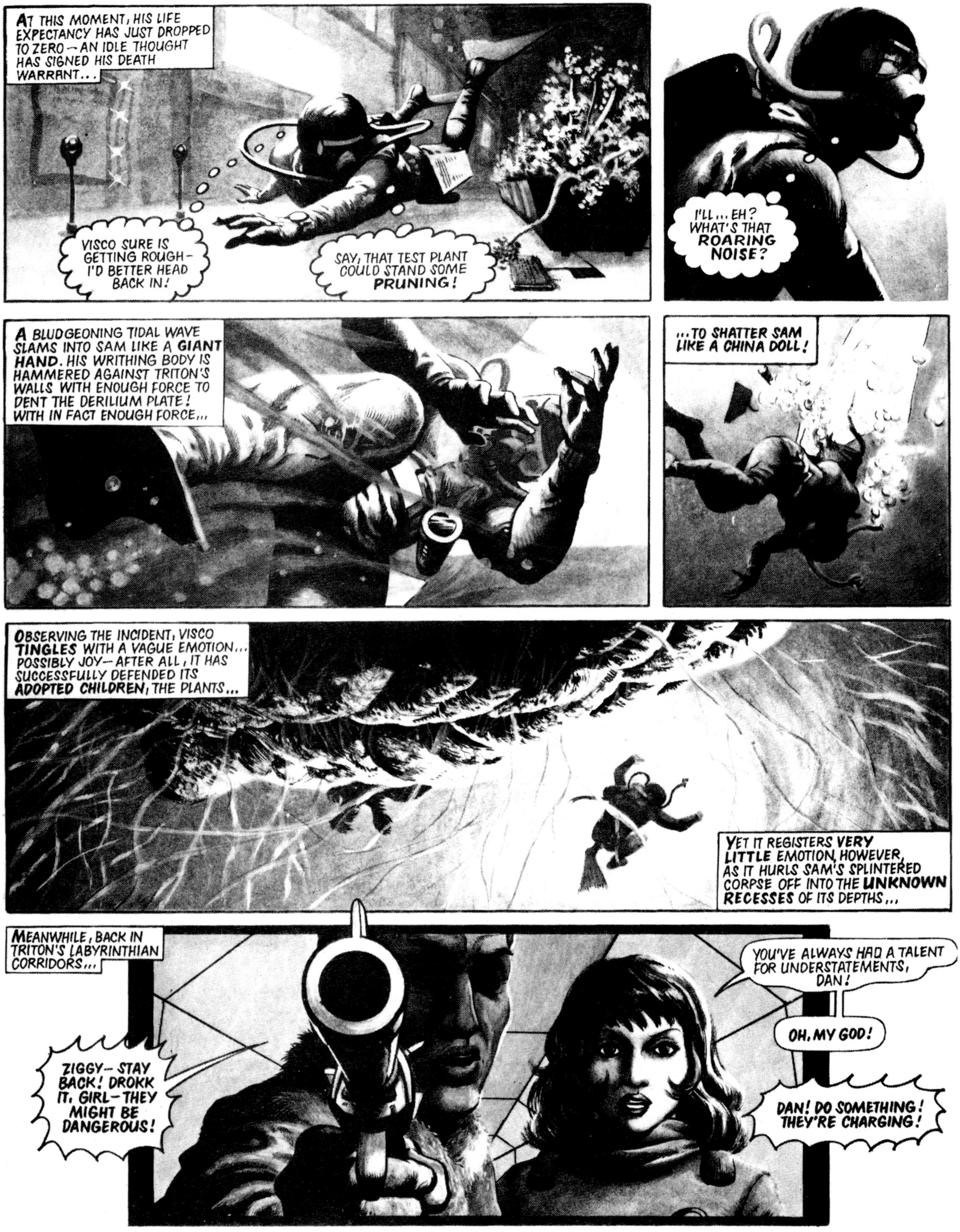

AT THIS MOMENT, HIS LIFE EXPECTANCY HAS JUST DROPPED TO ZERO — AN IDLE THOUGHT HAS SIGNED HIS DEATH WARRANT...
VISCO SURE IS GETTING ROUGH— I'D BETTER HEAD BACK IN!
SAY, THAT TEST PLANT COULD STAND SOME PRUNING!
I'LL... EH? WHAT'S THAT ROARING NOISE?
A BLUDGEONING TIDAL WAVE SLAMS INTO SAM LIKE A GIANT HAND. HIS WRITHING BODY IS HAMMERED AGAINST TRITON'S WALLS WITH ENOUGH FORCE TO DENT THE DERILIUM PLATE! WITH IN FACT ENOUGH FORCE...
...TO SHATTER SAM LIKE A CHINA DOLL!
OBSERVING THE INCIDENT, VISCO TINGLES WITH A VAGUE EMOTION... POSSIBLY JOY— AFTER ALL, IT HAS SUCCESSFULLY DEFENDED ITS ADOPTED CHILDREN, THE PLANTS...
YET IT REGISTERS VERY LITTLE EMOTION, HOWEVER, AS IT HURLS SAM'S SPLINTERED CORPSE OFF INTO THE UNKNOWN RECESSES OF ITS DEPTHS...
MEANWHILE, BACK IN TRITON'S LABYRINTHIAN CORRIDORS...
ZIGGY— STAY BACK! DROKK IT, GIRL— THEY MIGHT BE DANGEROUS!
YOU'VE ALWAYS HAD A TALENT FOR UNDERSTATEMENTS, DAN!
OH, MY GOD!
DAN! DO SOMETHING! THEY'RE CHARGING!

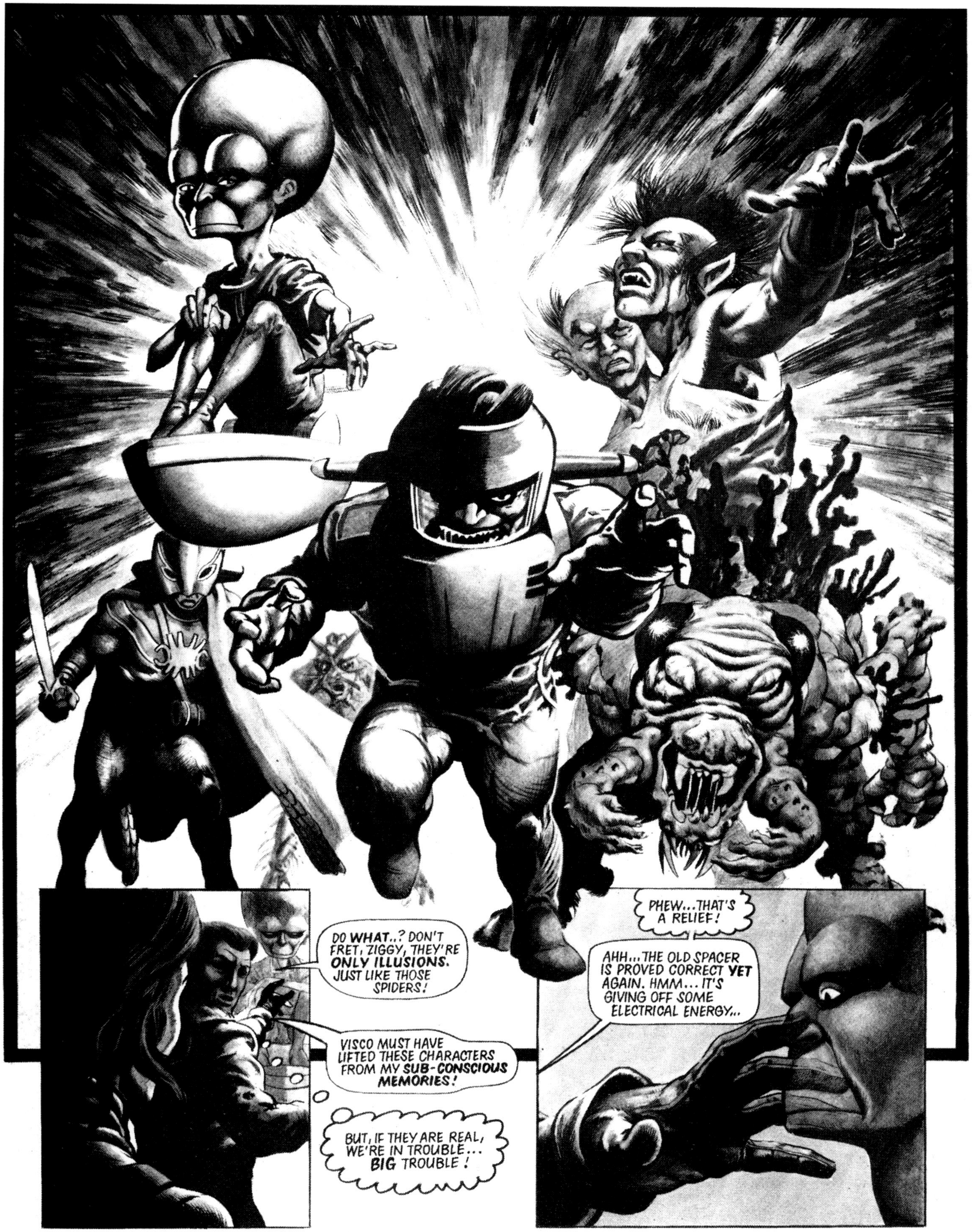

DO WHAT..? DON'T FRET, ZIGGY, THEY'RE ONLY ILLUSIONS. JUST LIKE THOSE SPIDERS!
VISCO MUST HAVE LIFTED THESE CHARACTERS FROM MY SUB-CONSCIOUS MEMORIES!
BUT, IF THEY ARE REAL, WE'RE IN TROUBLE... BIG TROUBLE!
PHEW... THAT'S A RELIEF!
AHH... THE OLD SPACER IS PROVED CORRECT YET AGAIN. HMM... IT'S GIVING OFF SOME ELECTRICAL ENERGY...

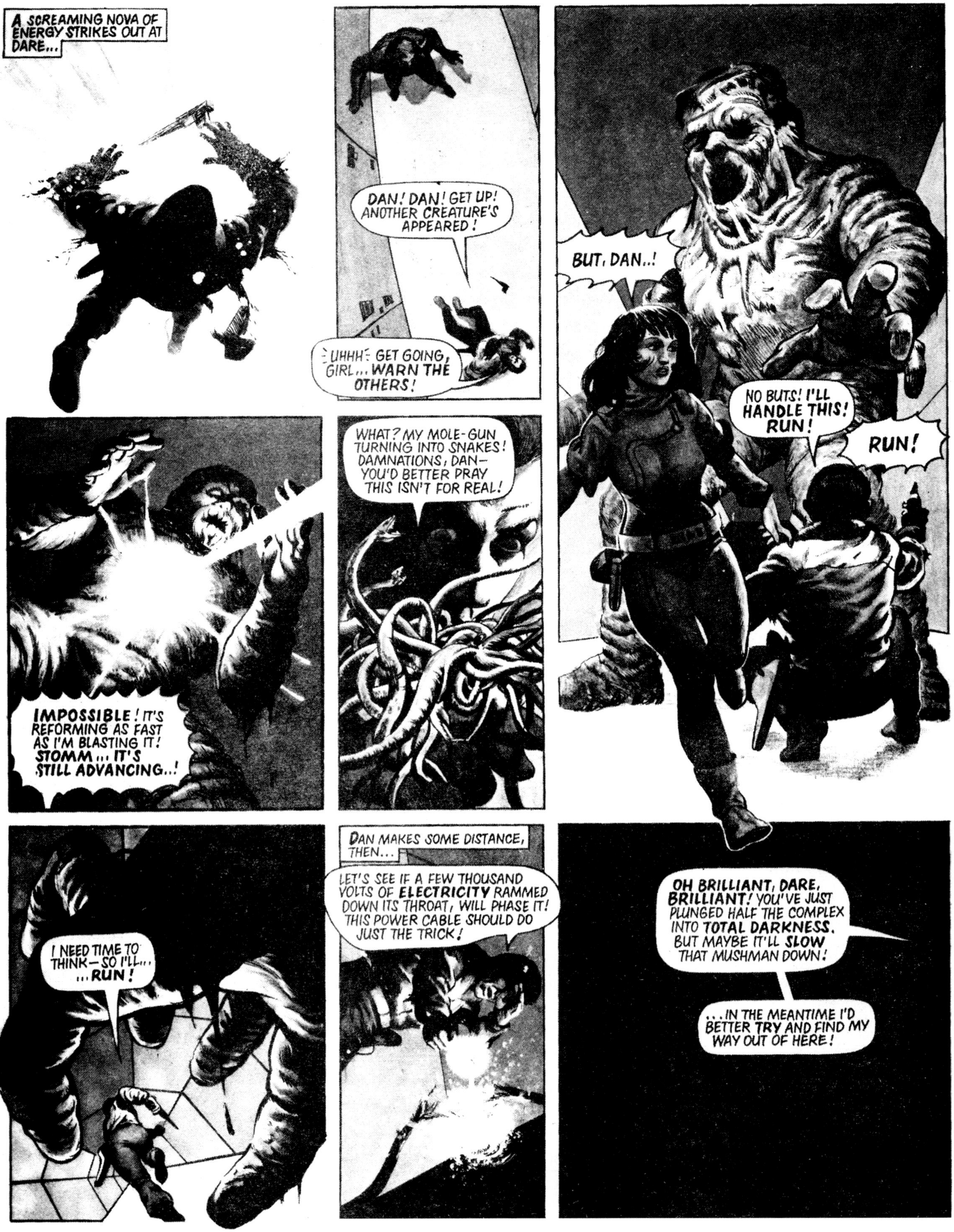
A SCREAMING NOVA OF ENERGY STRIKES OUT AT DARE...
DAN! DAN! GET UP! ANOTHER CREATURE'S APPEARED!
UHHH! GET GOING, GIRL... WARN THE OTHERS!
BUT, DAN..!
NO BUTS! I'LL HANDLE THIS! RUN!
RUN!
IMPOSSIBLE! IT'S REFORMING AS FAST AS I'M BLASTING IT! STOMM... IT'S STILL ADVANCING..!
WHAT? MY MOLE-GUN TURNING INTO SNAKES! DAMNATIONS, DAN-YOU'D BETTER PRAY THIS ISN'T FOR REAL!
I NEED TIME TO THINK-SO I'LL... ...RUN!
DAN MAKES SOME DISTANCE, THEN...
LET'S SEE IF A FEW THOUSAND VOLTS OF ELECTRICITY RAMMED DOWN ITS THROAT, WILL PHASE IT! THIS POWER CABLE SHOULD DO JUST THE TRICK!
OH BRILLIANT, DARE, BRILLIANT! YOU'VE JUST PLUNGED HALF THE COMPLEX INTO TOTAL DARKNESS. BUT MAYBE IT'LL SLOW THAT MUSHMAN DOWN!
...IN THE MEANTIME I'D BETTER TRY AND FIND MY WAY OUT OF HERE!

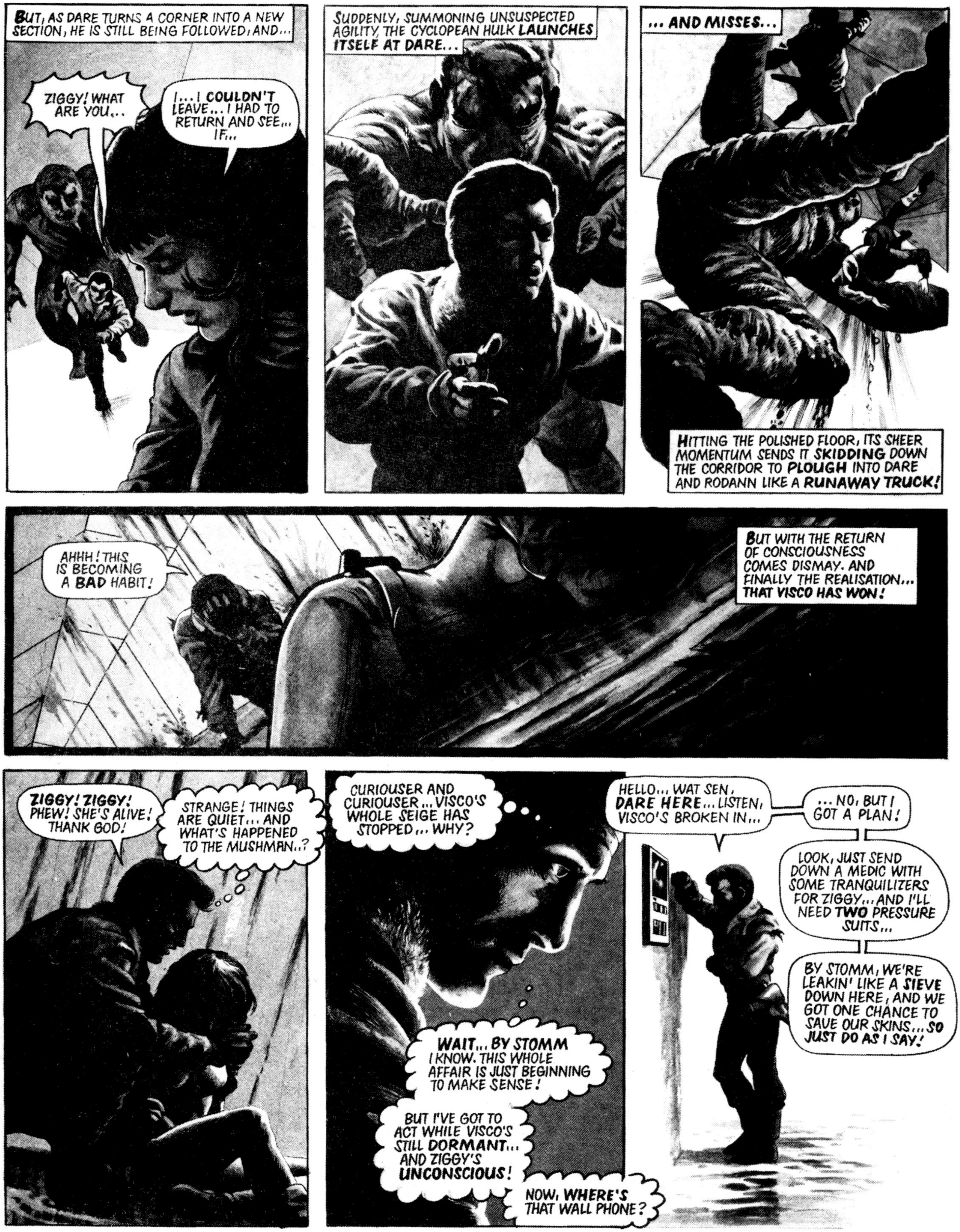

BUT, AS DARE TURNS A CORNER INTO A NEW SECTION, HE IS STILL BEING FOLLOWED, AND...
ZIGGY! WHAT ARE YOU...
I... I COULDN'T LEAVE... I HAD TO RETURN AND SEE... IF...
SUDDENLY, SUMMONING UNSUSPECTED AGILITY, THE CYCLOPEAN HULK LAUNCHES ITSELF AT DARE...
... AND MISSES...
HITTING THE POLISHED FLOOR, ITS SHEER MOMENTUM SENDS IT SKIDDING DOWN THE CORRIDOR TO PLOUGH INTO DARE AND RODANN LIKE A RUNAWAY TRUCK!
AHHH! THIS IS BECOMING A BAD HABIT!
BUT WITH THE RETURN OF CONSCIOUSNESS COMES DISMAY. AND FINALLY THE REALISATION... THAT VISCO HAS WON!
ZIGGY! ZIGGY! PHEW! SHE'S ALIVE! THANK GOD!
STRANGE! THINGS ARE QUIET... AND WHAT'S HAPPENED TO THE MUSHMAN..?
CURIOUSER AND CURIOUSER... VISCO'S WHOLE SEIGE HAS STOPPED... WHY?
WAIT... BY STOMM I KNOW. THIS WHOLE AFFAIR IS JUST BEGINNING TO MAKE SENSE!
BUT I'VE GOT TO ACT WHILE VISCO'S STILL DORMANT... AND ZIGGY'S UNCONSCIOUS!
NOW, WHERE'S THAT WALL PHONE?
HELLO... WAT SEN, DARE HERE... LISTEN, VISCO'S BROKEN IN...
... NO, BUT I GOT A PLAN!
LOOK, JUST SEND DOWN A MEDIC WITH SOME TRANQUILIZERS FOR ZIGGY... AND I'LL NEED TWO PRESSURE SUITS...
BY STOMM, WE'RE LEAKIN' LIKE A SIEVE DOWN HERE, AND WE GOT ONE CHANCE TO SAVE OUR SKINS... SO JUST DO AS I SAY!

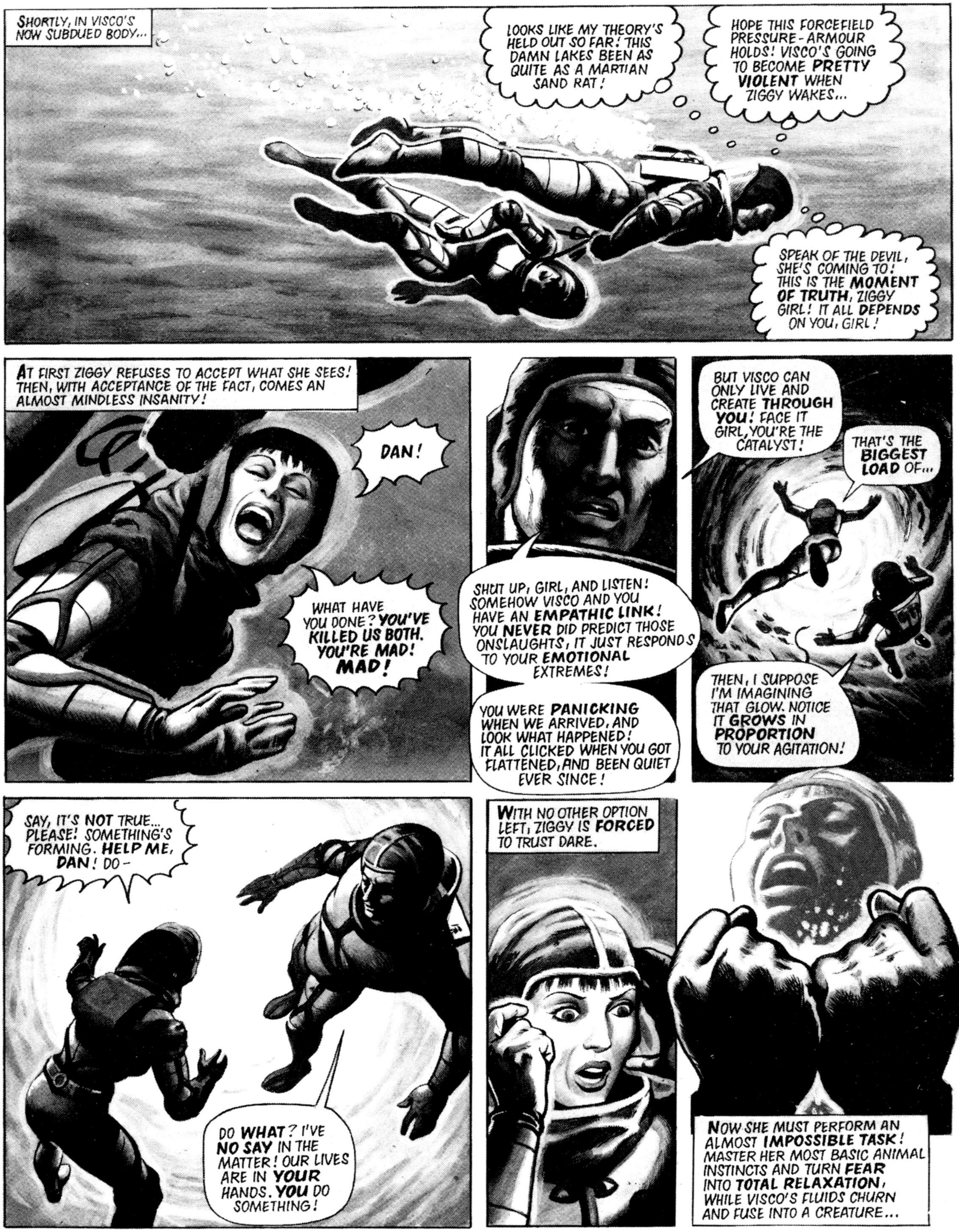

SHORTLY, IN VISCO'S NOW SUBDUED BODY...
LOOKS LIKE MY THEORY'S HELD OUT SO FAR! THIS DAMN LAKES BEEN AS QUITE AS A MARTIAN SAND RAT!
HOPE THIS FORCEFIELD PRESSURE-ARMOUR HOLDS! VISCO'S GOING TO BECOME PRETTY VIOLENT WHEN ZIGGY WAKES...
SPEAK OF THE DEVIL, SHE'S COMING TO! THIS IS THE MOMENT OF TRUTH, ZIGGY GIRL! IT ALL DEPENDS ON YOU, GIRL!
AT FIRST ZIGGY REFUSES TO ACCEPT WHAT SHE SEES! THEN, WITH ACCEPTANCE OF THE FACT, COMES AN ALMOST MINDLESS INSANITY!
DAN!
WHAT HAVE YOU DONE? YOU'VE KILLED US BOTH. YOU'RE MAD! MAD!
SHUT UP, GIRL, AND LISTEN! SOMEHOW VISCO AND YOU HAVE AN EMPATHIC LINK! YOU NEVER DID PREDICT THOSE ONSLAUGHTS, IT JUST RESPONDS TO YOUR EMOTIONAL EXTREMES!
YOU WERE PANICKING WHEN WE ARRIVED, AND LOOK WHAT HAPPENED! IT ALL CLICKED WHEN YOU GOT FLATTENED, AND BEEN QUIET EVER SINCE!
BUT VISCO CAN ONLY LIVE AND CREATE THROUGH YOU! FACE IT GIRL, YOU'RE THE CATALYST!
THAT'S THE BIGGEST LOAD OF...
THEN, I SUPPOSE I'M IMAGINING THAT GLOW. NOTICE IT GROWS IN PROPORTION TO YOUR AGITATION!
SAY, IT'S NOT TRUE... PLEASE! SOMETHING'S FORMING. HELP ME, DAN! DO-
DO WHAT? I'VE NO SAY IN THE MATTER! OUR LIVES ARE IN YOUR HANDS. YOU DO SOMETHING!
WITH NO OTHER OPTION LEFT, ZIGGY IS FORCED TO TRUST DARE.
NOW SHE MUST PERFORM AN ALMOST IMPOSSIBLE TASK! MASTER HER MOST BASIC ANIMAL INSTINCTS AND TURN FEAR INTO TOTAL RELAXATION, WHILE VISCO'S FLUIDS CHURN AND FUSE INTO A CREATURE...

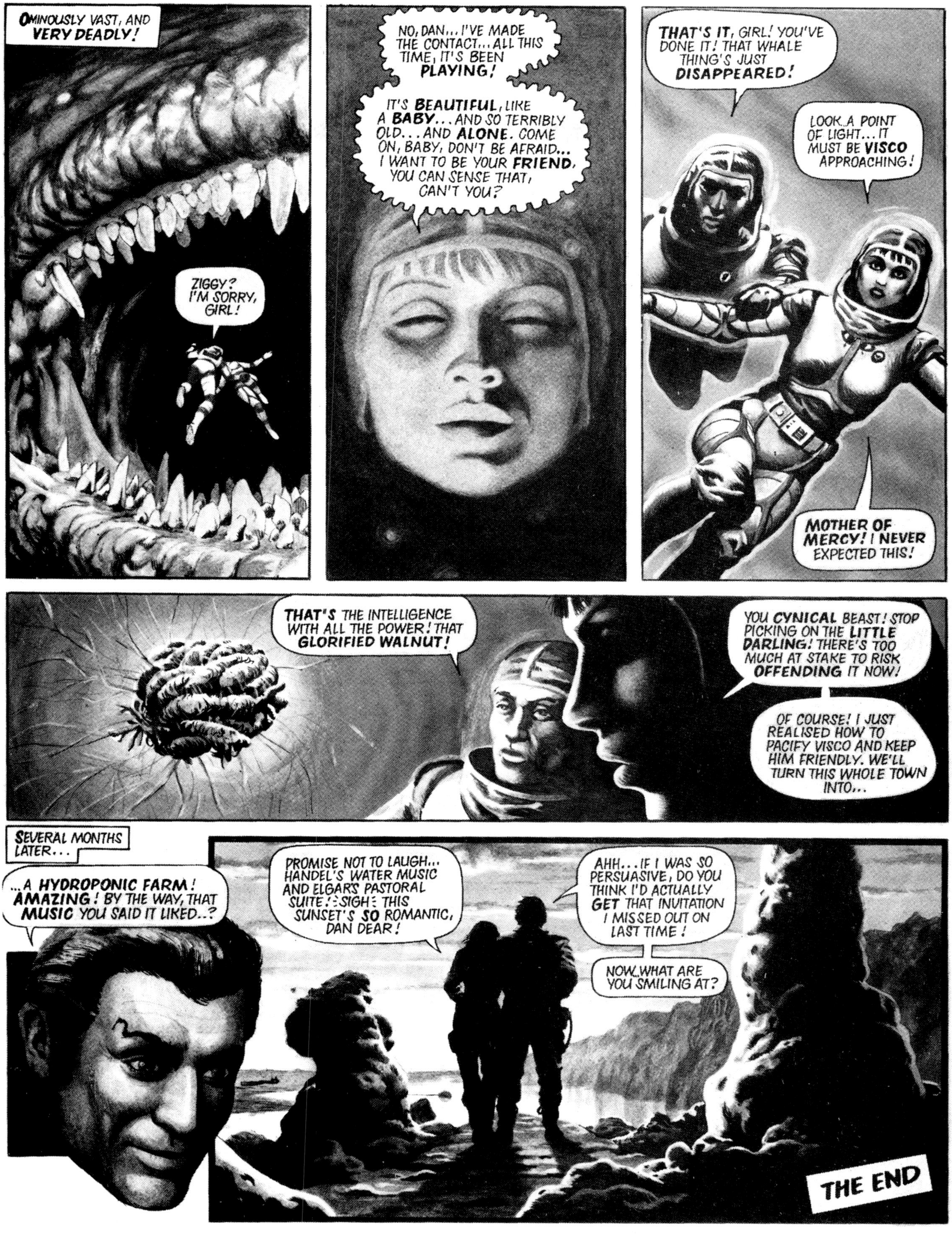
OMINOUSLY VAST, AND VERY DEADLY!
ZIGGY? I'M SORRY, GIRL!
NO, DAN... I'VE MADE THE CONTACT... ALL THIS TIME, IT'S BEEN PLAYING!
IT'S BEAUTIFUL, LIKE A BABY... AND SO TERRIBLY OLD... AND ALONE. COME ON, BABY, DON'T BE AFRAID... I WANT TO BE YOUR FRIEND, YOU CAN SENSE THAT, CAN'T YOU?
THAT'S IT, GIRL! YOU'VE DONE IT! THAT WHALE THING'S JUST DISAPPEARED!
LOOK..A POINT OF LIGHT... IT MUST BE VISCO APPROACHING!
MOTHER OF MERCY! I NEVER EXPECTED THIS!
THAT'S THE INTELLIGENCE WITH ALL THE POWER! THAT GLORIFIED WALNUT!
YOU CYNICAL BEAST! STOP PICKING ON THE LITTLE DARLING! THERE'S TOO MUCH AT STAKE TO RISK OFFENDING IT NOW!
OF COURSE! I JUST REALISED HOW TO PACIFY VISCO AND KEEP HIM FRIENDLY. WE'LL TURN THIS WHOLE TOWN INTO...
SEVERAL MONTHS LATER...
...A HYDROPONIC FARM! AMAZING! BY THE WAY, THAT MUSIC YOU SAID IT LIKED..?
PROMISE NOT TO LAUGH... HANDEL'S WATER MUSIC AND ELGAR'S PASTORAL SUITE! :SIGH: THIS SUNSET'S SO ROMANTIC, DAN DEAR!
AHH... IF I WAS SO PERSUASIVE, DO YOU THINK I'D ACTUALLY GET THAT INVITATION I MISSED OUT ON LAST TIME!
NOW..WHAT ARE YOU SMILING AT?
THE END

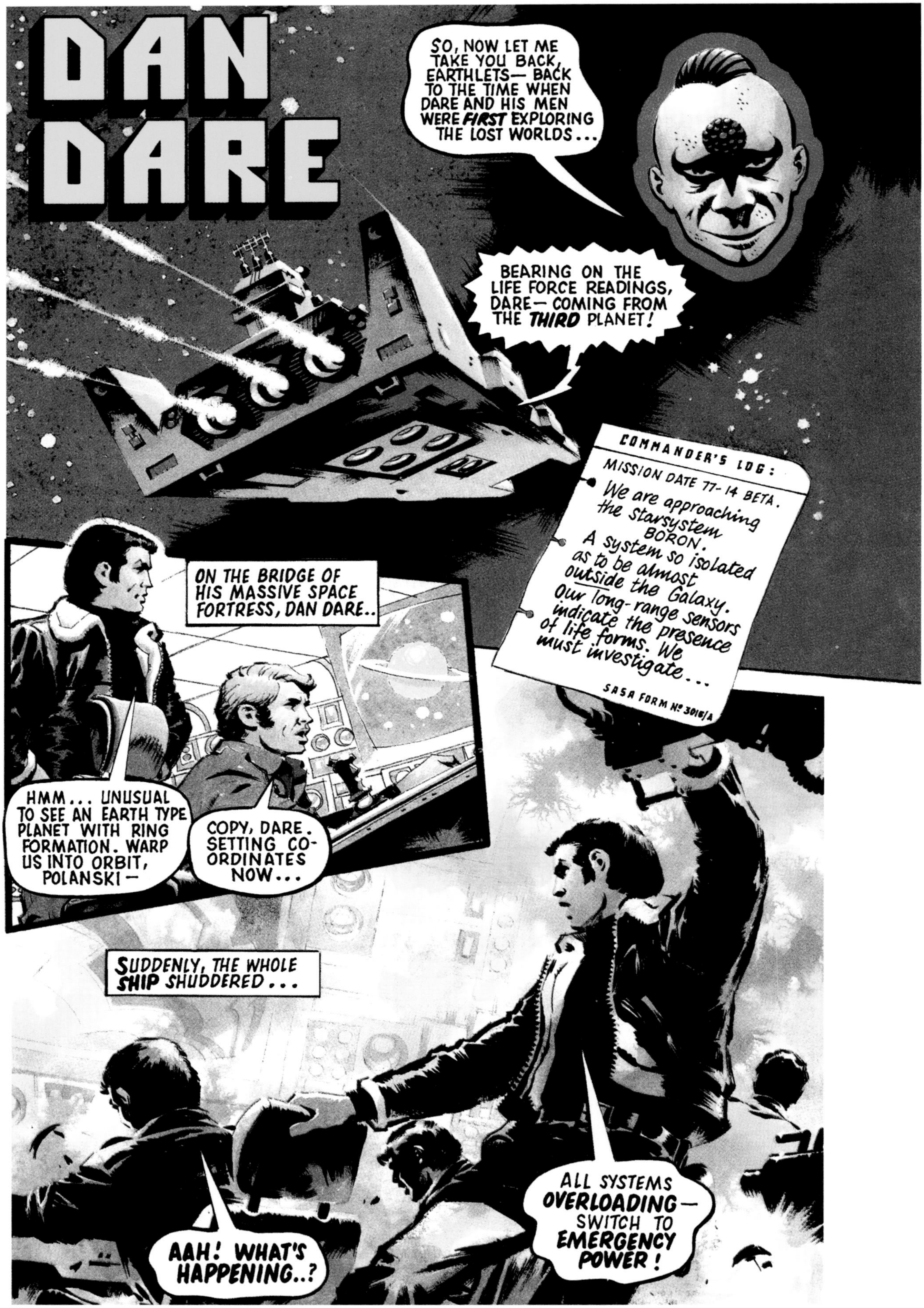
DAN DARE
SO, NOW LET ME TAKE YOU BACK, EARTHLETS— BACK TO THE TIME WHEN DARE AND HIS MEN WERE FIRST EXPLORING THE LOST WORLDS...
BEARING ON THE LIFE FORCE READINGS, DARE— COMING FROM THE THIRD PLANET!
COMMANDER'S LOG:
MISSION DATE 77-14 BETA.
We are approaching the Starsystem BORON.
A system so isolated as to be almost outside the Galaxy.
Our long-range sensors indicate the presence of life forms. We must investigate...
SASA FORM Nº 3018/A
ON THE BRIDGE OF HIS MASSIVE SPACE FORTRESS, DAN DARE..
HMM... UNUSUAL TO SEE AN EARTH TYPE PLANET WITH RING FORMATION. WARP US INTO ORBIT, POLANSKI—
COPY, DARE. SETTING CO-ORDINATES NOW...
SUDDENLY, THE WHOLE SHIP SHUDDERED...
AAH! WHAT'S HAPPENING..?
ALL SYSTEMS OVERLOADING— SWITCH TO EMERGENCY POWER!

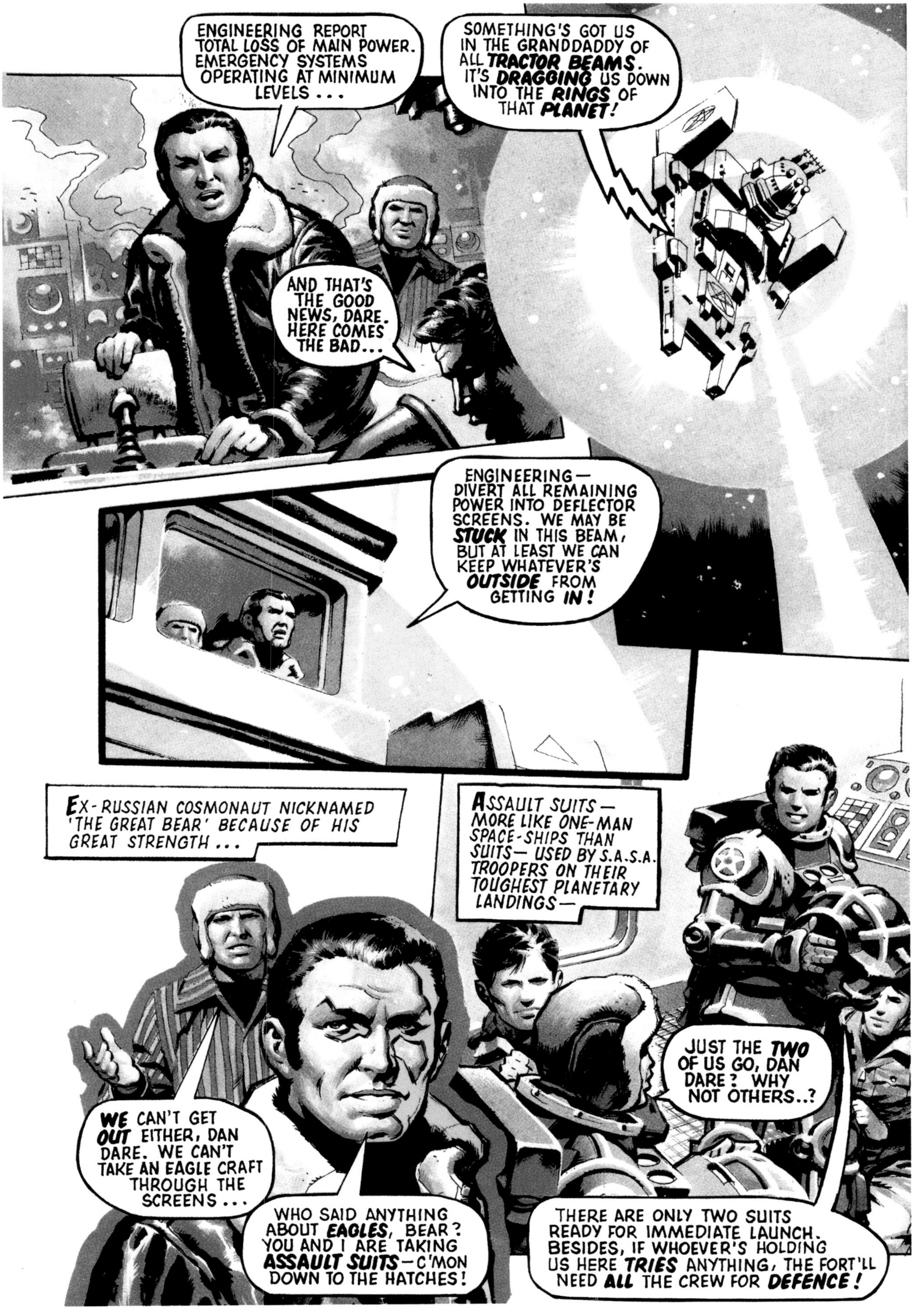

ENGINEERING REPORT TOTAL LOSS OF MAIN POWER. EMERGENCY SYSTEMS OPERATING AT MINIMUM LEVELS . . .
SOMETHING'S GOT US IN THE GRANDDADDY OF ALL TRACTOR BEAMS. IT'S DRAGGING US DOWN INTO THE RINGS OF THAT PLANET!
AND THAT'S THE GOOD NEWS, DARE. HERE COMES THE BAD...
ENGINEERING— DIVERT ALL REMAINING POWER INTO DEFLECTOR SCREENS. WE MAY BE STUCK IN THIS BEAM, BUT AT LEAST WE CAN KEEP WHATEVER'S OUTSIDE FROM GETTING IN!
EX-RUSSIAN COSMONAUT NICKNAMED 'THE GREAT BEAR' BECAUSE OF HIS GREAT STRENGTH . . .
ASSAULT SUITS— MORE LIKE ONE-MAN SPACE-SHIPS THAN SUITS— USED BY S.A.S.A. TROOPERS ON THEIR TOUGHEST PLANETARY LANDINGS—
WE CAN'T GET OUT EITHER, DAN DARE. WE CAN'T TAKE AN EAGLE CRAFT THROUGH THE SCREENS . . .
WHO SAID ANYTHING ABOUT EAGLES, BEAR? YOU AND I ARE TAKING ASSAULT SUITS— C'MON DOWN TO THE HATCHES!
JUST THE TWO OF US GO, DAN DARE? WHY NOT OTHERS..?
THERE ARE ONLY TWO SUITS READY FOR IMMEDIATE LAUNCH. BESIDES, IF WHOEVER'S HOLDING US HERE TRIES ANYTHING, THE FORT'LL NEED ALL THE CREW FOR DEFENCE!

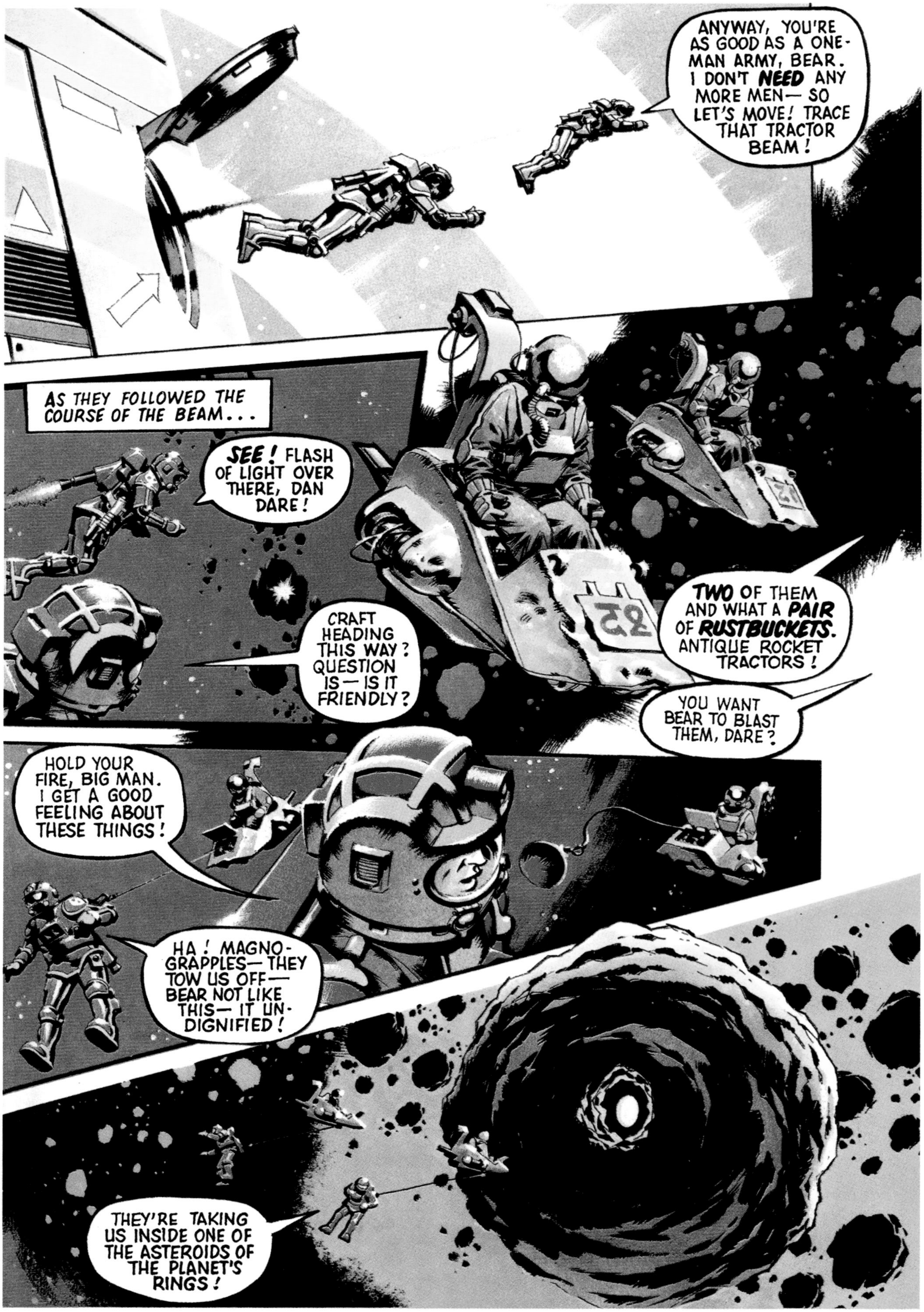

ANYWAY, YOU'RE AS GOOD AS A ONE-MAN ARMY, BEAR. I DON'T **NEED** ANY MORE MEN— SO LET'S MOVE! TRACE THAT TRACTOR BEAM!
AS THEY FOLLOWED THE COURSE OF THE BEAM...
SEE! FLASH OF LIGHT OVER THERE, DAN DARE!
CRAFT HEADING THIS WAY? QUESTION IS— IS IT FRIENDLY?
TWO OF THEM AND WHAT A **PAIR** OF **RUSTBUCKETS**. ANTIQUE ROCKET TRACTORS!
YOU WANT BEAR TO BLAST THEM, DARE?
HOLD YOUR FIRE, BIG MAN. I GET A GOOD FEELING ABOUT THESE THINGS!
HA! MAGNO-GRAPPLES— THEY TOW US OFF— BEAR NOT LIKE THIS— IT UNDIGNIFIED!
THEY'RE TAKING US INSIDE ONE OF THE ASTEROIDS OF THE PLANET'S RINGS!

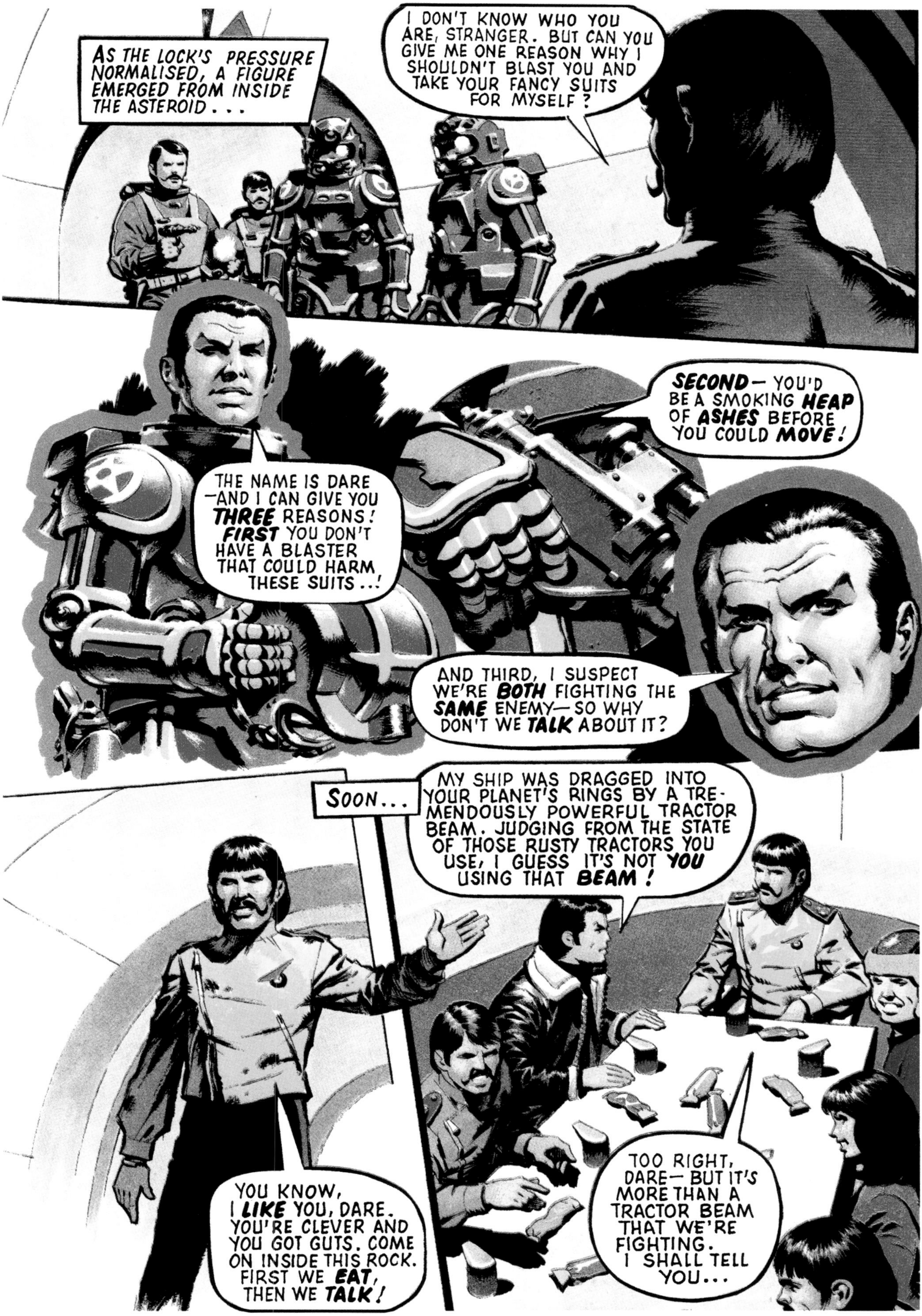
AS THE LOCK'S PRESSURE NORMALISED, A FIGURE EMERGED FROM INSIDE THE ASTEROID . . .
I DON'T KNOW WHO YOU ARE, STRANGER. BUT CAN YOU GIVE ME ONE REASON WHY I SHOULDN'T BLAST YOU AND TAKE YOUR FANCY SUITS FOR MYSELF ?
THE NAME IS DARE —AND I CAN GIVE YOU THREE REASONS! FIRST YOU DON'T HAVE A BLASTER THAT COULD HARM THESE SUITS ..!
SECOND— YOU'D BE A SMOKING HEAP OF ASHES BEFORE YOU COULD MOVE!
AND THIRD, I SUSPECT WE'RE BOTH FIGHTING THE SAME ENEMY— SO WHY DON'T WE TALK ABOUT IT?
SOON . . .
YOU KNOW, I LIKE YOU, DARE. YOU'RE CLEVER AND YOU GOT GUTS. COME ON INSIDE THIS ROCK. FIRST WE EAT, THEN WE TALK!
MY SHIP WAS DRAGGED INTO YOUR PLANET'S RINGS BY A TREMENDOUSLY POWERFUL TRACTOR BEAM. JUDGING FROM THE STATE OF THOSE RUSTY TRACTORS YOU USE, I GUESS IT'S NOT YOU USING THAT BEAM !
TOO RIGHT, DARE— BUT IT'S MORE THAN A TRACTOR BEAM THAT WE'RE FIGHTING. I SHALL TELL YOU...

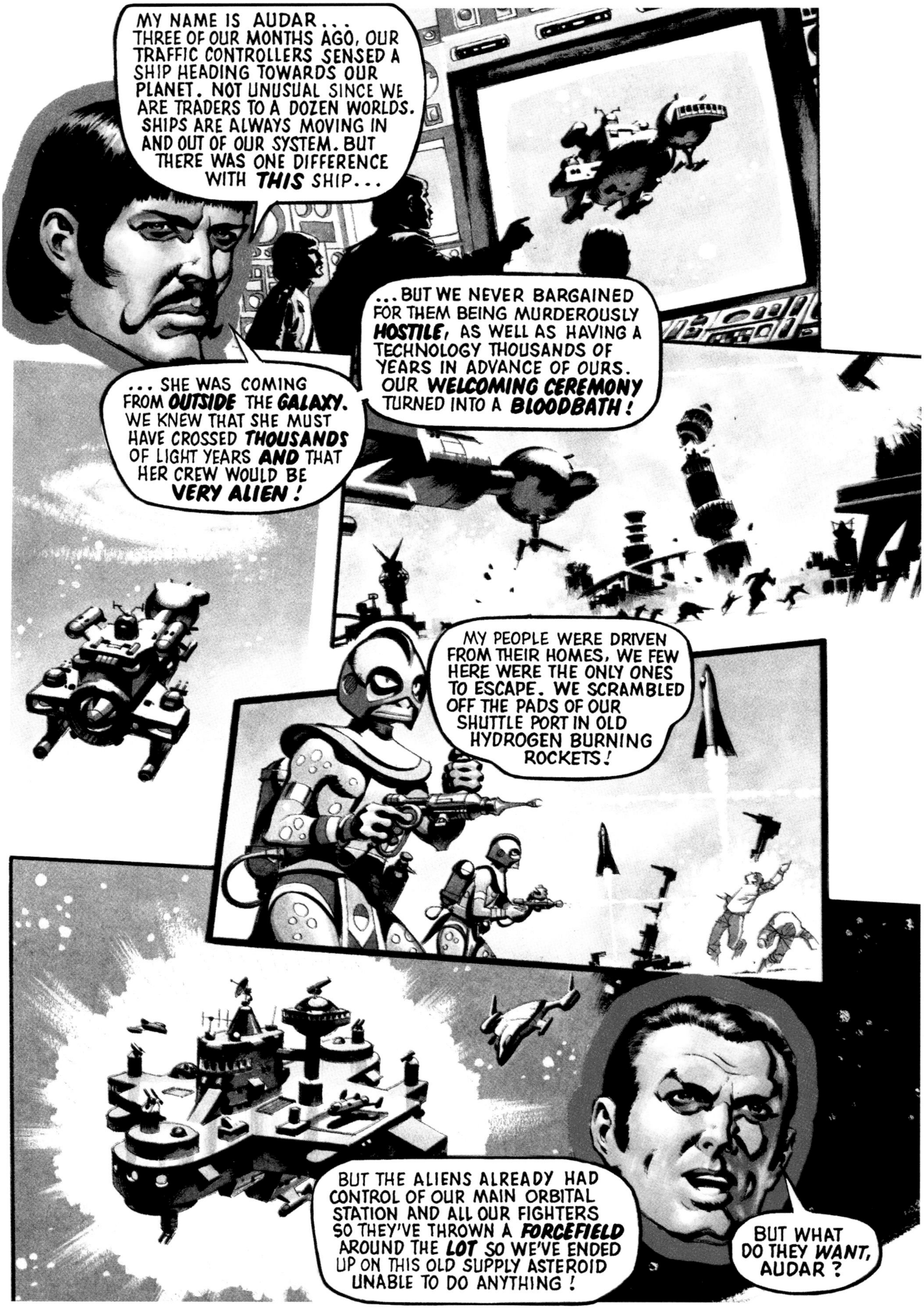
MY NAME IS AUDAR... THREE OF OUR MONTHS AGO, OUR TRAFFIC CONTROLLERS SENSED A SHIP HEADING TOWARDS OUR PLANET. NOT UNUSUAL SINCE WE ARE TRADERS TO A DOZEN WORLDS. SHIPS ARE ALWAYS MOVING IN AND OUT OF OUR SYSTEM. BUT THERE WAS ONE DIFFERENCE WITH THIS SHIP...
...SHE WAS COMING FROM OUTSIDE THE GALAXY. WE KNEW THAT SHE MUST HAVE CROSSED THOUSANDS OF LIGHT YEARS AND THAT HER CREW WOULD BE VERY ALIEN!
...BUT WE NEVER BARGAINED FOR THEM BEING MURDEROUSLY HOSTILE, AS WELL AS HAVING A TECHNOLOGY THOUSANDS OF YEARS IN ADVANCE OF OURS. OUR WELCOMING CEREMONY TURNED INTO A BLOODBATH!
MY PEOPLE WERE DRIVEN FROM THEIR HOMES, WE FEW HERE WERE THE ONLY ONES TO ESCAPE. WE SCRAMBLED OFF THE PADS OF OUR SHUTTLE PORT IN OLD HYDROGEN BURNING ROCKETS!
BUT THE ALIENS ALREADY HAD CONTROL OF OUR MAIN ORBITAL STATION AND ALL OUR FIGHTERS SO THEY'VE THROWN A FORCEFIELD AROUND THE LOT SO WE'VE ENDED UP ON THIS OLD SUPPLY ASTEROID UNABLE TO DO ANYTHING!
BUT WHAT DO THEY WANT, AUDAR?

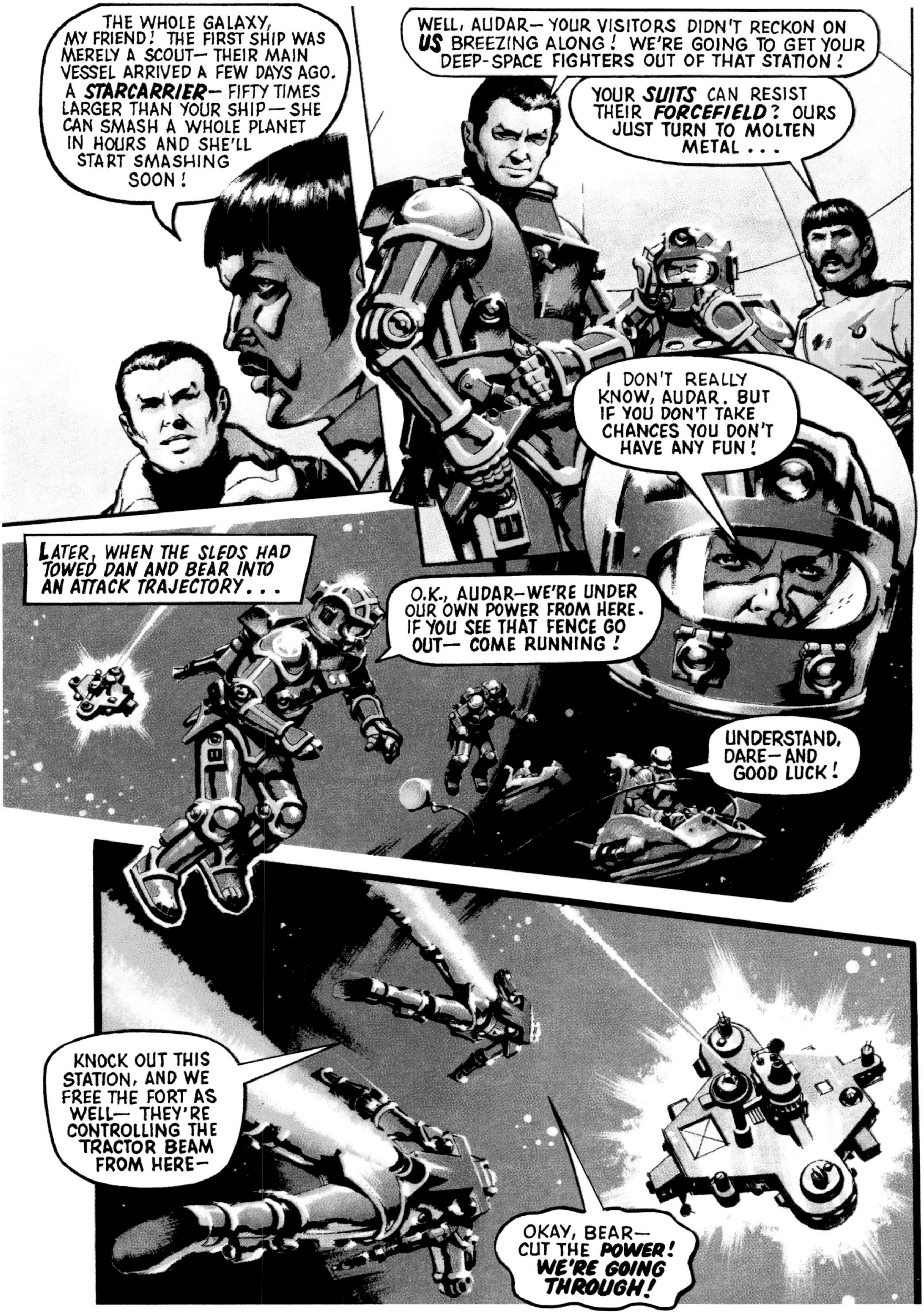
THE WHOLE GALAXY, MY FRIEND! THE FIRST SHIP WAS MERELY A SCOUT— THEIR MAIN VESSEL ARRIVED A FEW DAYS AGO. A STARCARRIER— FIFTY TIMES LARGER THAN YOUR SHIP— SHE CAN SMASH A WHOLE PLANET IN HOURS AND SHE'LL START SMASHING SOON!
WELL, AUDAR— YOUR VISITORS DIDN'T RECKON ON US BREEZING ALONG! WE'RE GOING TO GET YOUR DEEP-SPACE FIGHTERS OUT OF THAT STATION!
YOUR SUITS CAN RESIST THEIR FORCEFIELD? OURS JUST TURN TO MOLTEN METAL...
I DON'T REALLY KNOW, AUDAR. BUT IF YOU DON'T TAKE CHANCES YOU DON'T HAVE ANY FUN!
LATER, WHEN THE SLEDS HAD TOWED DAN AND BEAR INTO AN ATTACK TRAJECTORY...
O.K., AUDAR—WE'RE UNDER OUR OWN POWER FROM HERE. IF YOU SEE THAT FENCE GO OUT— COME RUNNING!
UNDERSTAND, DARE—AND GOOD LUCK!
KNOCK OUT THIS STATION, AND WE FREE THE FORT AS WELL— THEY'RE CONTROLLING THE TRACTOR BEAM FROM HERE—
OKAY, BEAR— CUT THE POWER! WE'RE GOING THROUGH!

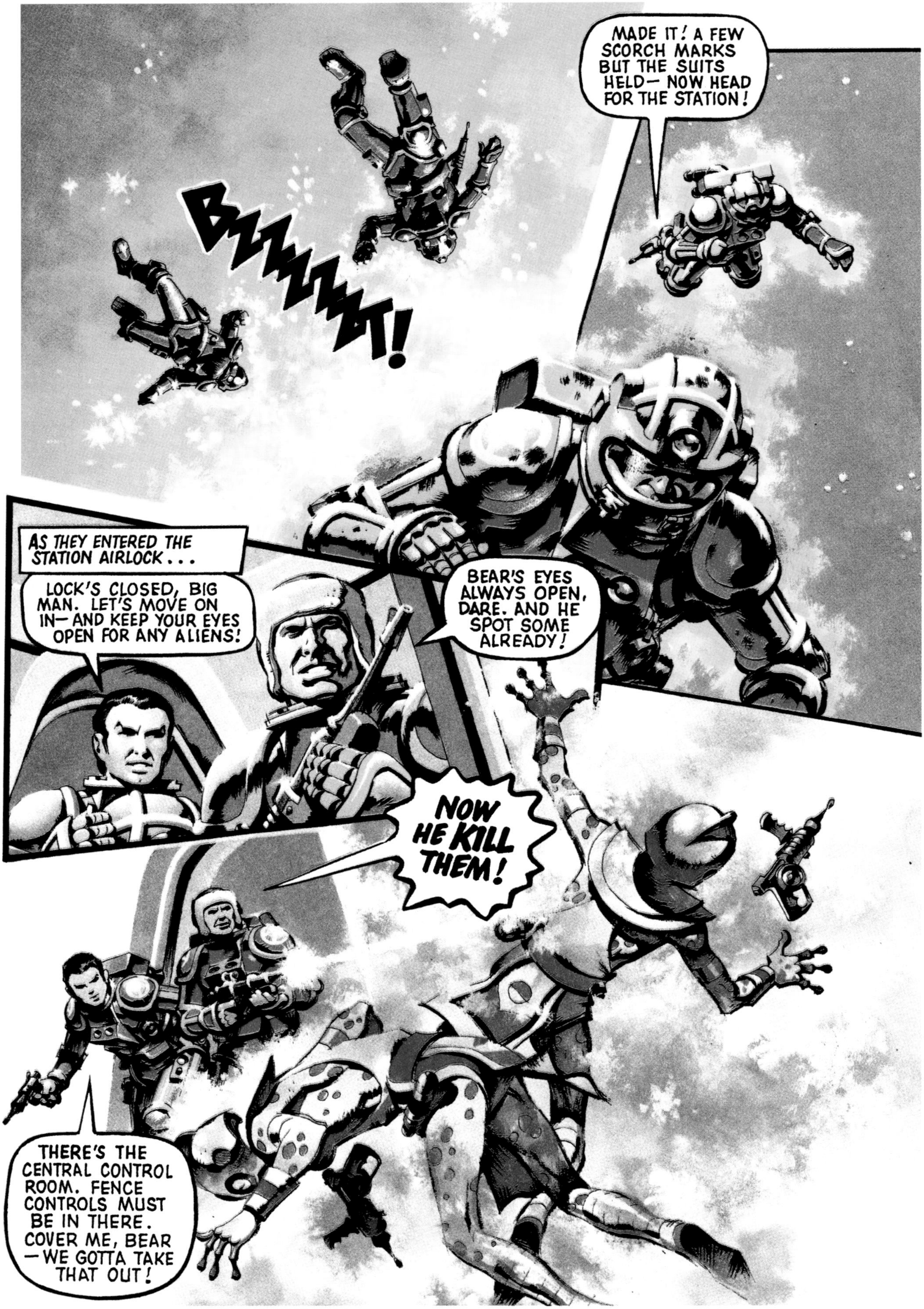
BZZZZZZT!
MADE IT! A FEW SCORCH MARKS BUT THE SUITS HELD— NOW HEAD FOR THE STATION!
AS THEY ENTERED THE STATION AIRLOCK...
LOCK'S CLOSED, BIG MAN. LET'S MOVE ON IN— AND KEEP YOUR EYES OPEN FOR ANY ALIENS!
BEAR'S EYES ALWAYS OPEN, DARE. AND HE SPOT SOME ALREADY!
NOW HE KILL THEM!
THERE'S THE CENTRAL CONTROL ROOM. FENCE CONTROLS MUST BE IN THERE. COVER ME, BEAR —WE GOTTA TAKE THAT OUT!

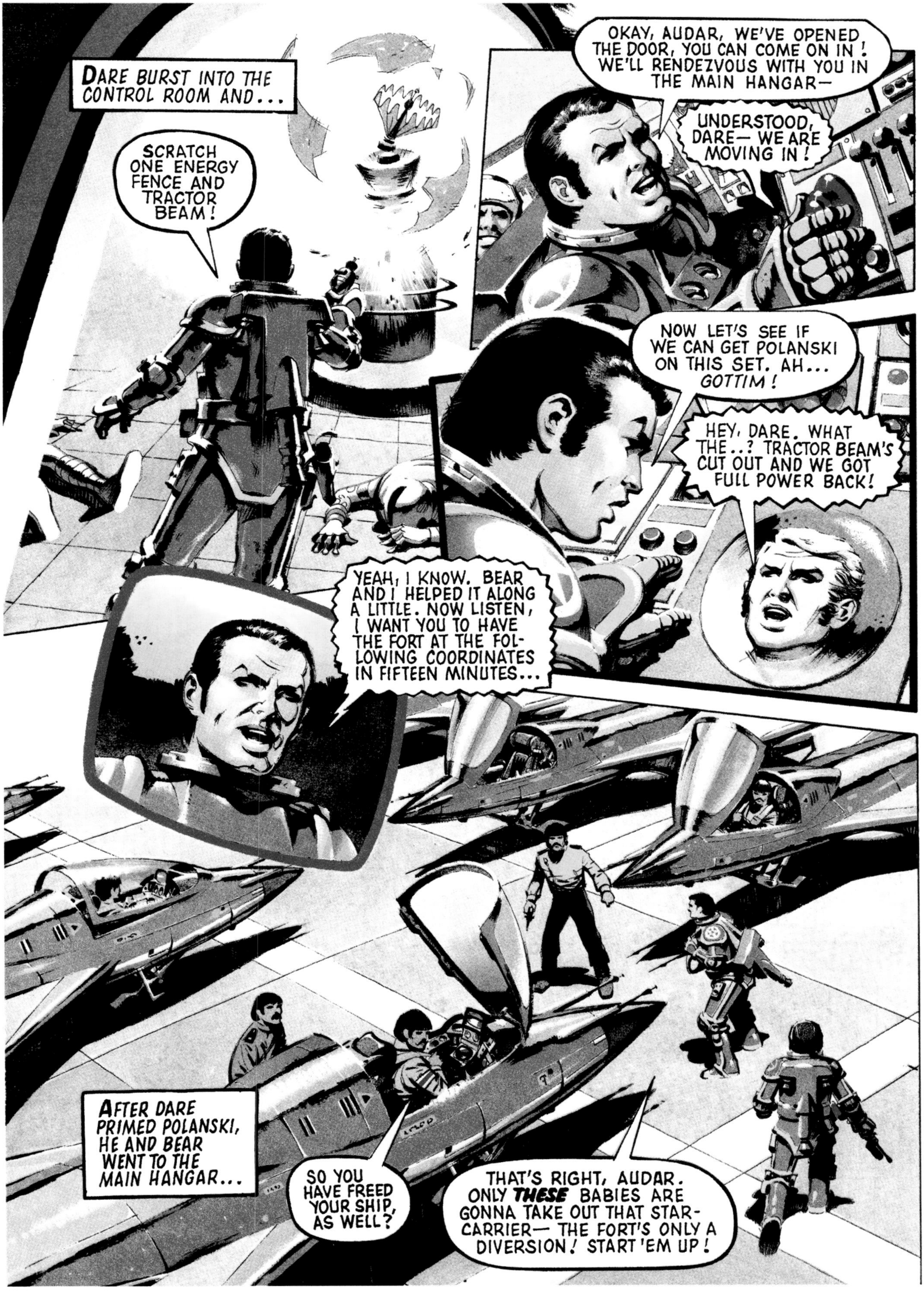
DARE BURST INTO THE CONTROL ROOM AND...
SCRATCH ONE ENERGY FENCE AND TRACTOR BEAM!
OKAY, AUDAR, WE'VE OPENED THE DOOR, YOU CAN COME ON IN! WE'LL RENDEZVOUS WITH YOU IN THE MAIN HANGAR—
UNDERSTOOD, DARE— WE ARE MOVING IN!
NOW LET'S SEE IF WE CAN GET POLANSKI ON THIS SET. AH... GOTTIM!
HEY, DARE. WHAT THE..? TRACTOR BEAM'S CUT OUT AND WE GOT FULL POWER BACK!
YEAH, I KNOW. BEAR AND I HELPED IT ALONG A LITTLE. NOW LISTEN, I WANT YOU TO HAVE THE FORT AT THE FOL-LOWING COORDINATES IN FIFTEEN MINUTES...
AFTER DARE PRIMED POLANSKI, HE AND BEAR WENT TO THE MAIN HANGAR...
SO YOU HAVE FREED YOUR SHIP, AS WELL?
THAT'S RIGHT, AUDAR. ONLY THESE BABIES ARE GONNA TAKE OUT THAT STAR-CARRIER— THE FORT'S ONLY A DIVERSION! START 'EM UP!

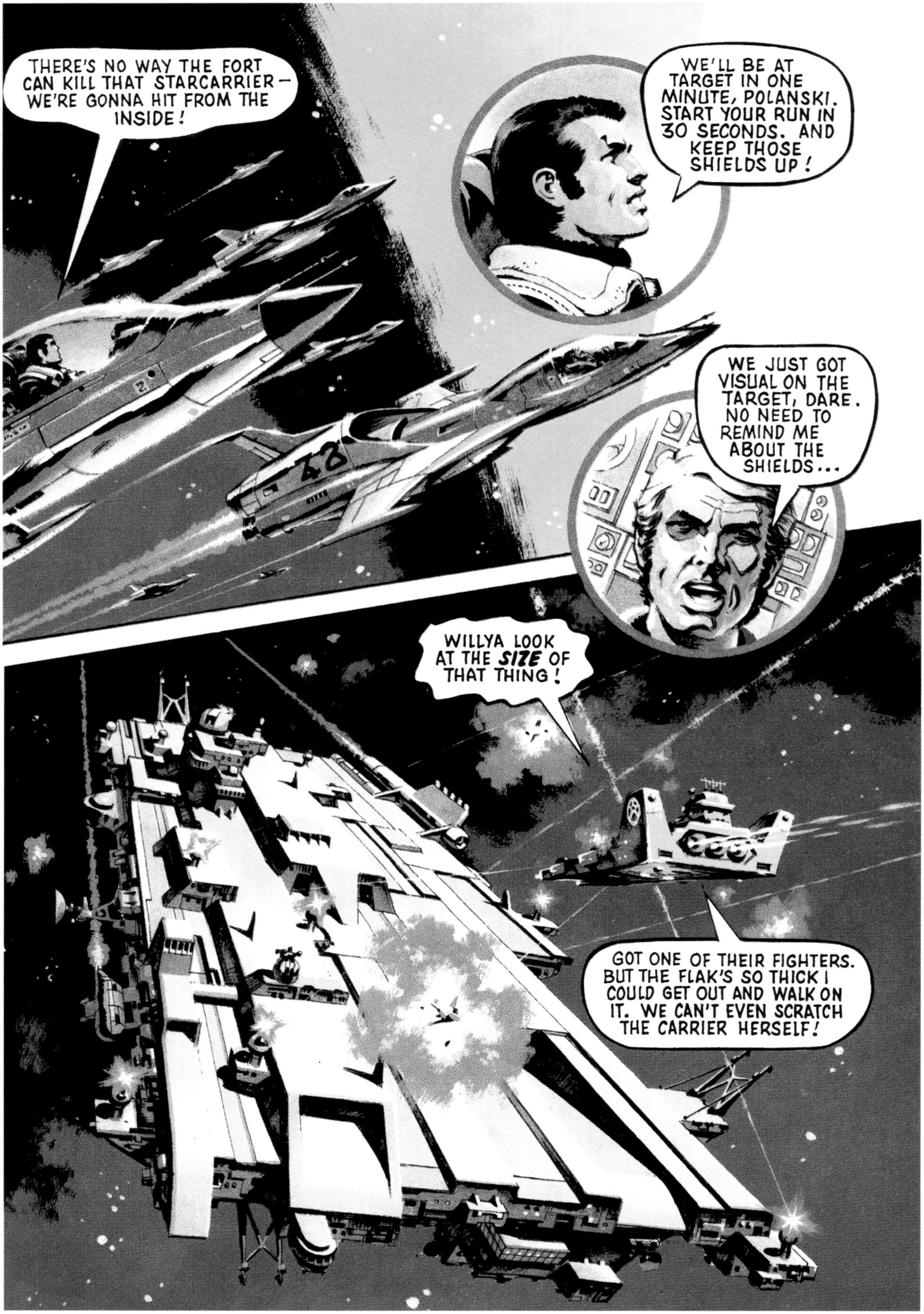
THERE'S NO WAY THE FORT CAN KILL THAT STARCARRIER— WE'RE GONNA HIT FROM THE INSIDE!
WE'LL BE AT TARGET IN ONE MINUTE, POLANSKI. START YOUR RUN IN 30 SECONDS. AND KEEP THOSE SHIELDS UP!
WE JUST GOT VISUAL ON THE TARGET, DARE. NO NEED TO REMIND ME ABOUT THE SHIELDS...
WILLYA LOOK AT THE SIZE OF THAT THING!
GOT ONE OF THEIR FIGHTERS. BUT THE FLAK'S SO THICK I COULD GET OUT AND WALK ON IT. WE CAN'T EVEN SCRATCH THE CARRIER HERSELF!

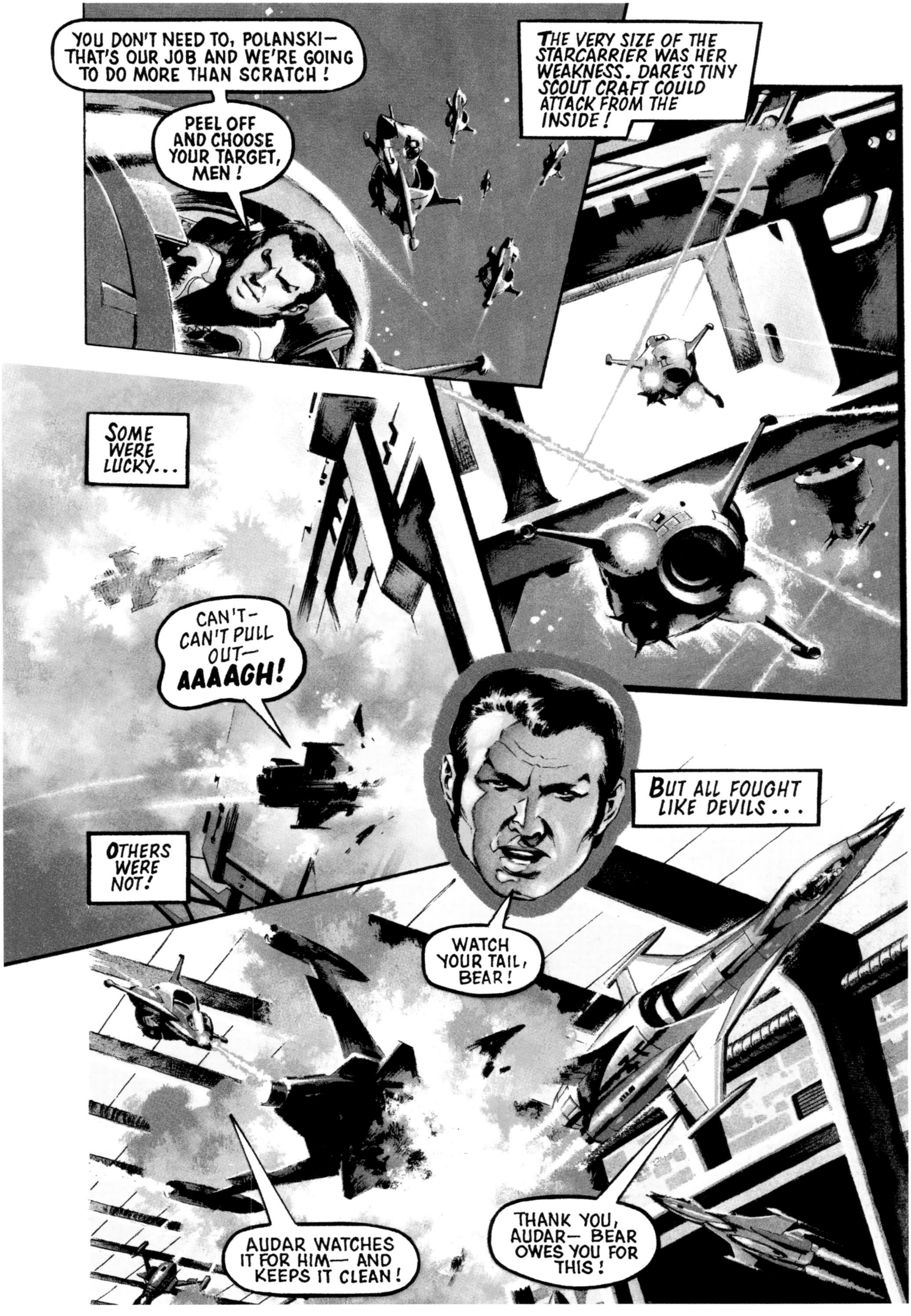
YOU DON'T NEED TO, POLANSKI— THAT'S OUR JOB AND WE'RE GOING TO DO MORE THAN SCRATCH!
PEEL OFF AND CHOOSE YOUR TARGET, MEN!
THE VERY SIZE OF THE STARCARRIER WAS HER WEAKNESS. DARE'S TINY SCOUT CRAFT COULD ATTACK FROM THE INSIDE!
SOME WERE LUCKY...
CAN'T— CAN'T PULL OUT— AAAAGH!
OTHERS WERE NOT!
BUT ALL FOUGHT LIKE DEVILS...
WATCH YOUR TAIL, BEAR!
AUDAR WATCHES IT FOR HIM— AND KEEPS IT CLEAN!
THANK YOU, AUDAR— BEAR OWES YOU FOR THIS!

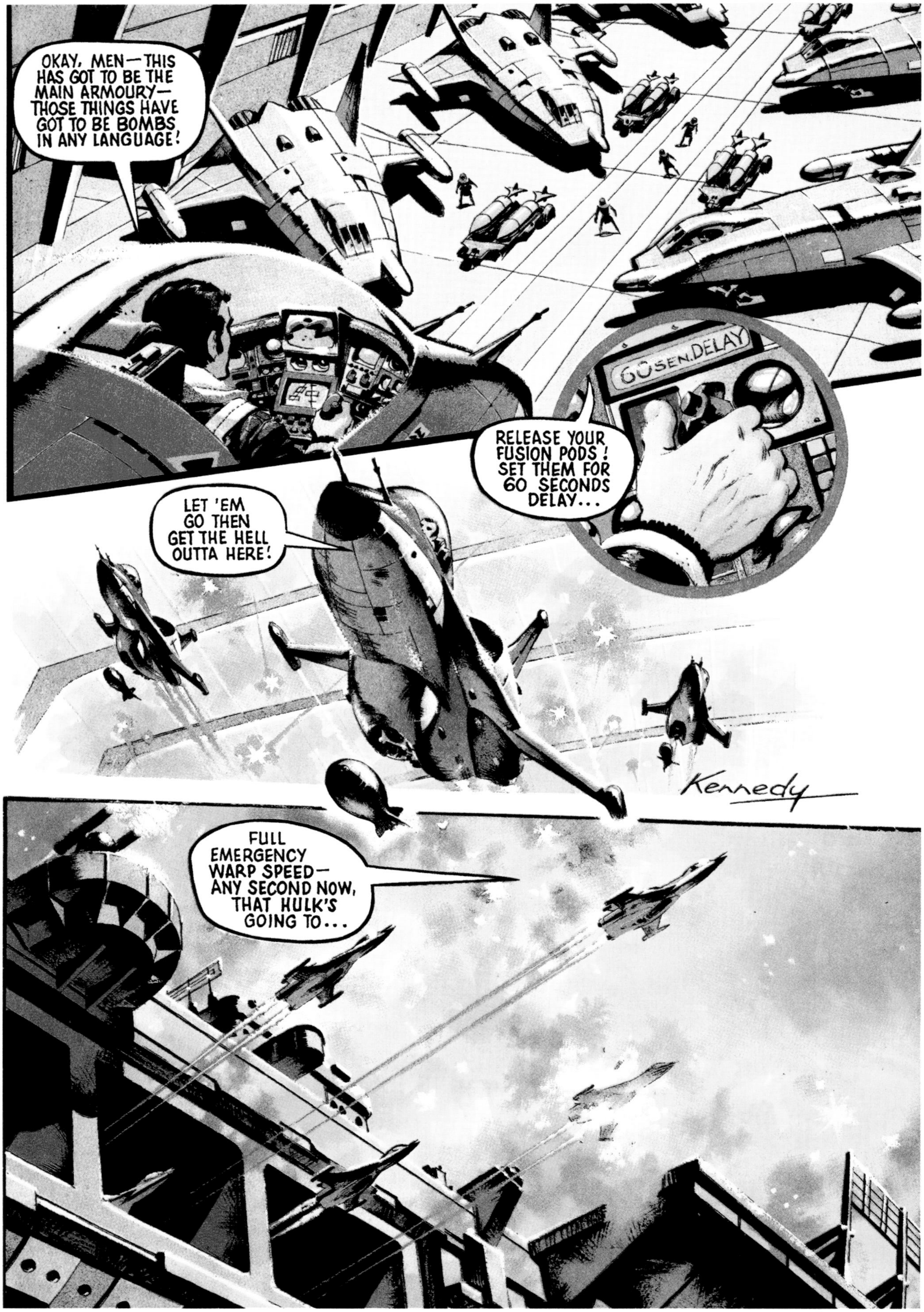
OKAY, MEN—THIS HAS GOT TO BE THE MAIN ARMOURY—THOSE THINGS HAVE GOT TO BE BOMBS IN ANY LANGUAGE!
GO SEN. DELAY
RELEASE YOUR FUSION PODS! SET THEM FOR 60 SECONDS DELAY...
LET 'EM GO THEN GET THE HELL OUTTA HERE!
Kennedy
FULL EMERGENCY WARP SPEED—ANY SECOND NOW, THAT HULK'S GOING TO...

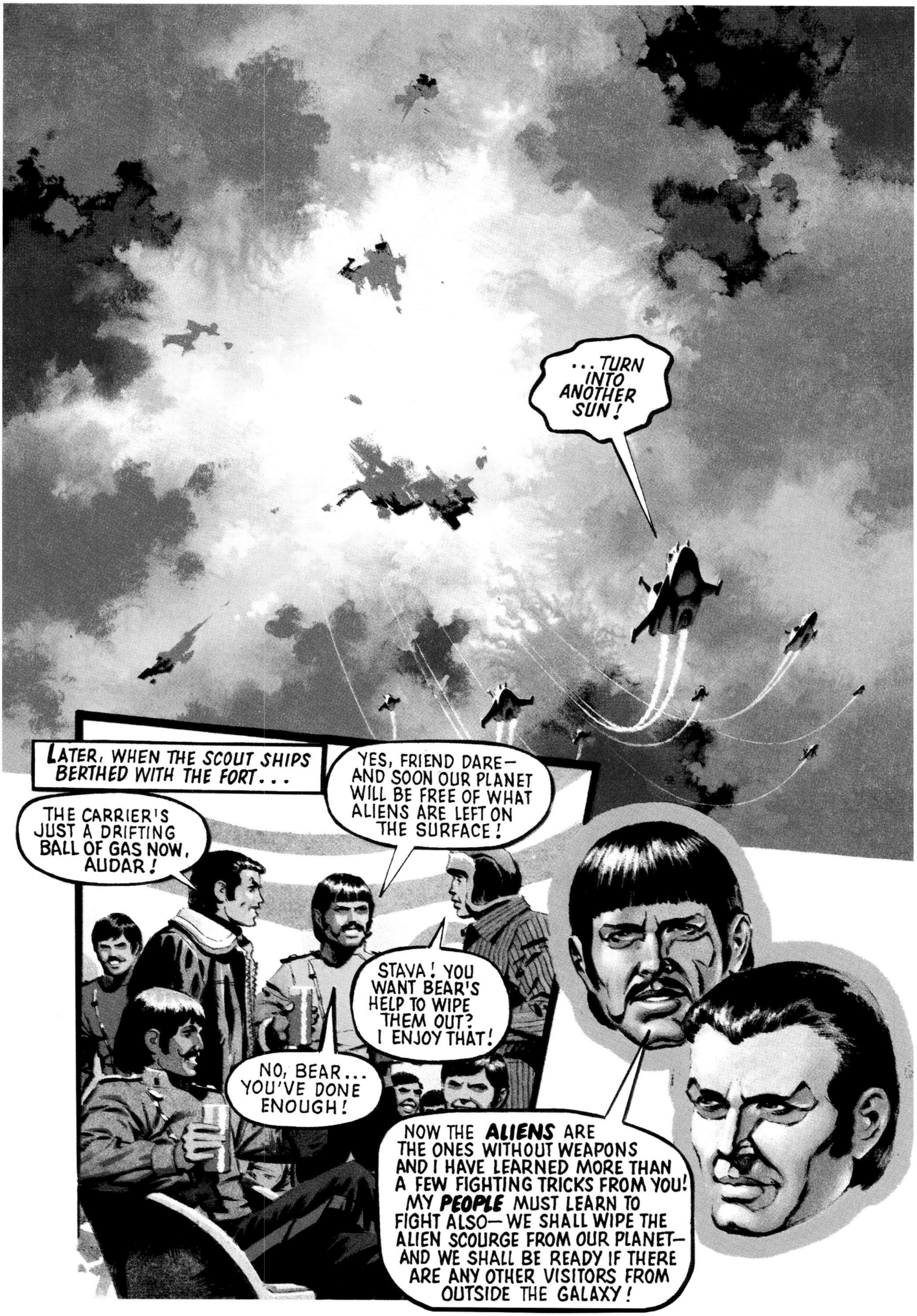
...TURN INTO ANOTHER SUN!
LATER, WHEN THE SCOUT SHIPS BERTHED WITH THE FORT...
THE CARRIER'S JUST A DRIFTING BALL OF GAS NOW, AUDAR!
YES, FRIEND DARE— AND SOON OUR PLANET WILL BE FREE OF WHAT ALIENS ARE LEFT ON THE SURFACE!
STAVA! YOU WANT BEAR'S HELP TO WIPE THEM OUT? I ENJOY THAT!
NO, BEAR... YOU'VE DONE ENOUGH!
NOW THE ALIENS ARE THE ONES WITHOUT WEAPONS AND I HAVE LEARNED MORE THAN A FEW FIGHTING TRICKS FROM YOU! MY PEOPLE MUST LEARN TO FIGHT ALSO— WE SHALL WIPE THE ALIEN SCOURGE FROM OUR PLANET— AND WE SHALL BE READY IF THERE ARE ANY OTHER VISITORS FROM OUTSIDE THE GALAXY!

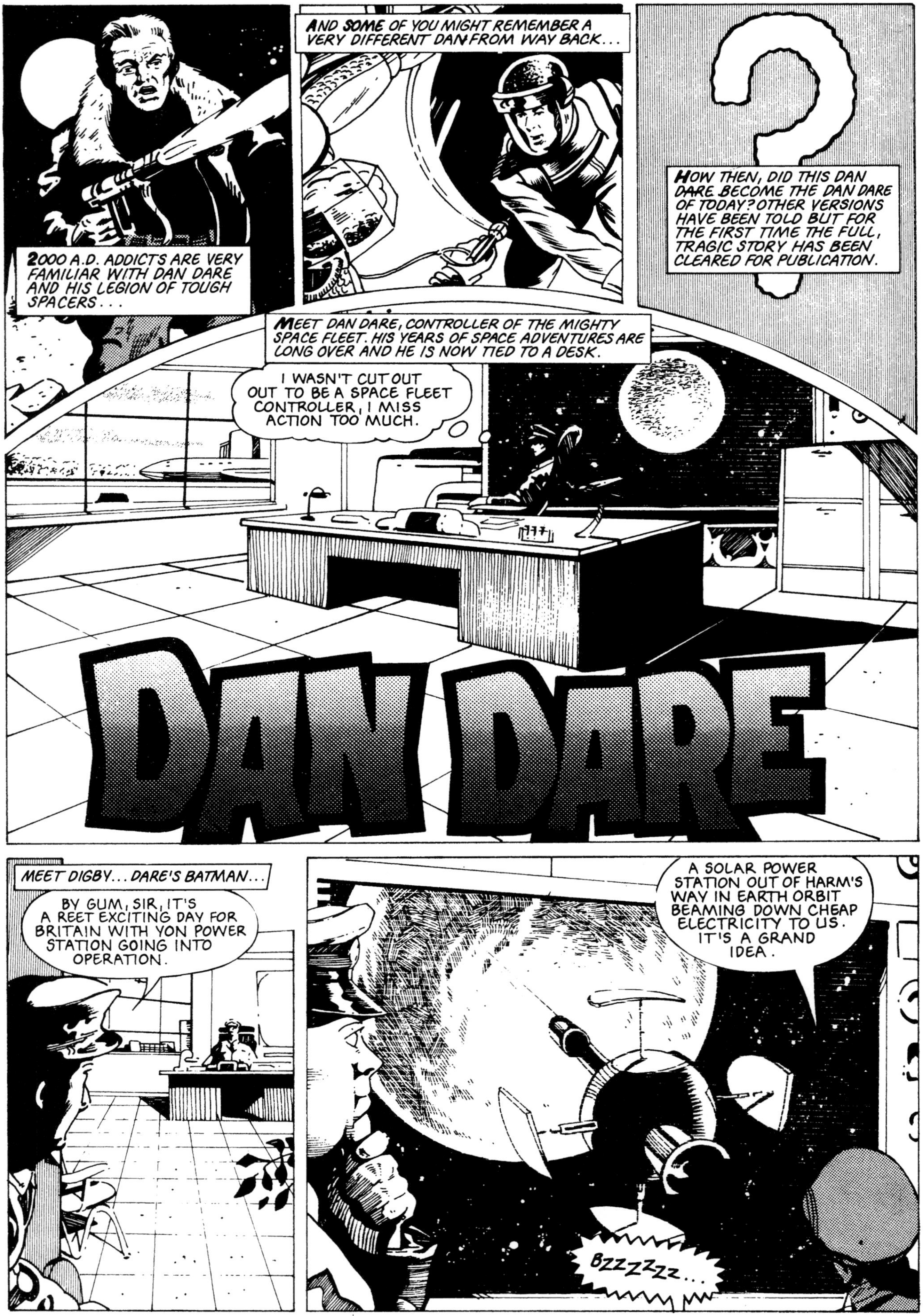
2000 A.D. ADDICTS ARE VERY FAMILIAR WITH DAN DARE AND HIS LEGION OF TOUGH SPACERS...
AND SOME OF YOU MIGHT REMEMBER A VERY DIFFERENT DAN FROM WAY BACK...
HOW THEN, DID THIS DAN DARE BECOME THE DAN DARE OF TODAY? OTHER VERSIONS HAVE BEEN TOLD BUT FOR THE FIRST TIME THE FULL, TRAGIC STORY HAS BEEN CLEARED FOR PUBLICATION.
MEET DAN DARE, CONTROLLER OF THE MIGHTY SPACE FLEET. HIS YEARS OF SPACE ADVENTURES ARE LONG OVER AND HE IS NOW TIED TO A DESK.
I WASN'T CUT OUT OUT TO BE A SPACE FLEET CONTROLLER, I MISS ACTION TOO MUCH.
DAN DARE
MEET DIGBY... DARE'S BATMAN...
BY GUM, SIR, IT'S A REET EXCITING DAY FOR BRITAIN WITH YON POWER STATION GOING INTO OPERATION.
A SOLAR POWER STATION OUT OF HARM'S WAY IN EARTH ORBIT BEAMING DOWN CHEAP ELECTRICITY TO US. IT'S A GRAND IDEA.
BZZZZZZ...

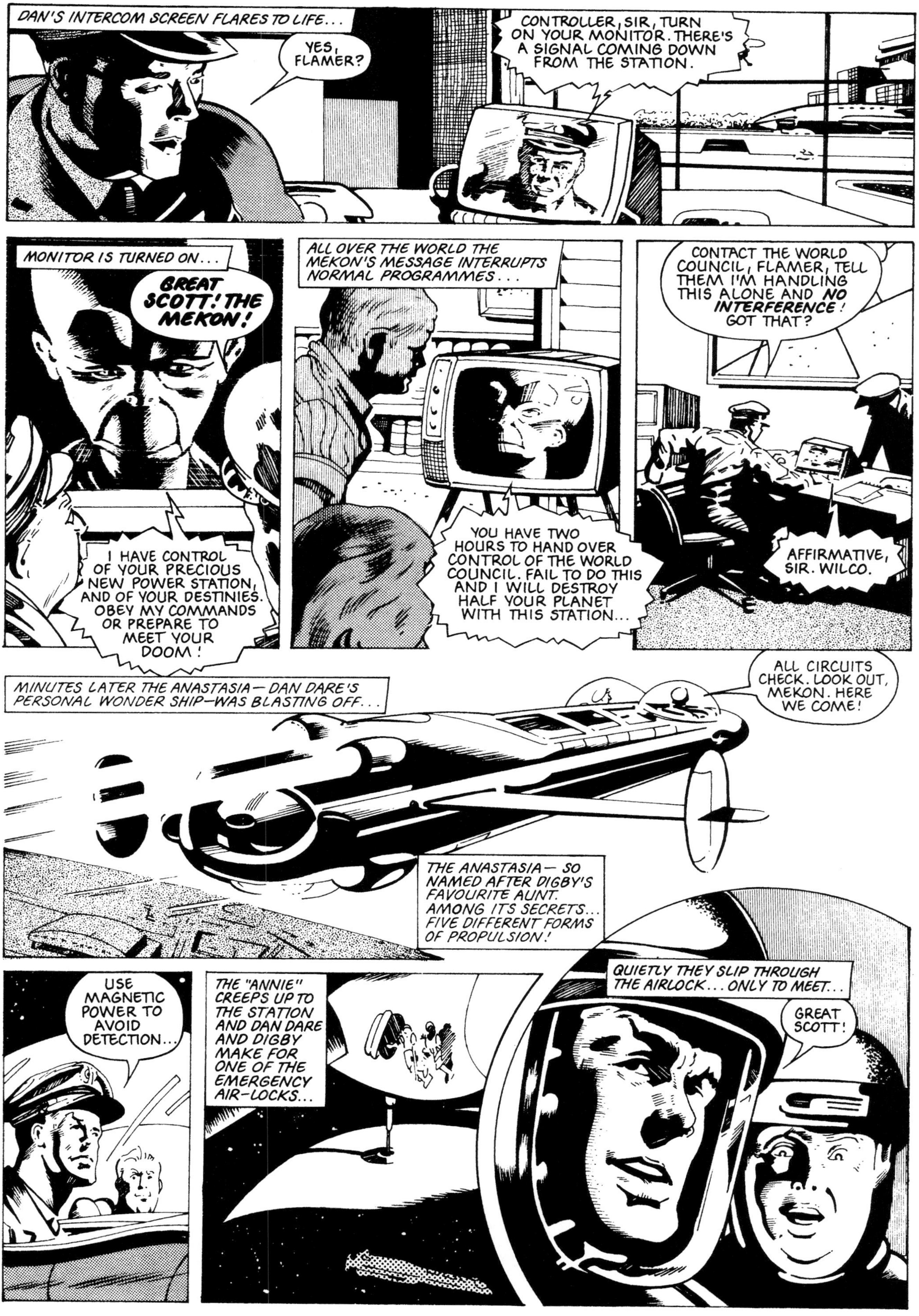
DAN'S INTERCOM SCREEN FLARES TO LIFE...
YES, FLAMER?
CONTROLLER, SIR, TURN ON YOUR MONITOR. THERE'S A SIGNAL COMING DOWN FROM THE STATION.
MONITOR IS TURNED ON...
GREAT SCOTT! THE MEKON!
I HAVE CONTROL OF YOUR PRECIOUS NEW POWER STATION, AND OF YOUR DESTINIES. OBEY MY COMMANDS OR PREPARE TO MEET YOUR DOOM!
ALL OVER THE WORLD THE MEKON'S MESSAGE INTERRUPTS NORMAL PROGRAMMES...
YOU HAVE TWO HOURS TO HAND OVER CONTROL OF THE WORLD COUNCIL. FAIL TO DO THIS AND I WILL DESTROY HALF YOUR PLANET WITH THIS STATION...
CONTACT THE WORLD COUNCIL, FLAMER, TELL THEM I'M HANDLING THIS ALONE AND NO INTERFERENCE! GOT THAT?
AFFIRMATIVE, SIR. WILCO.
MINUTES LATER THE ANASTASIA—DAN DARE'S PERSONAL WONDER SHIP—WAS BLASTING OFF...
ALL CIRCUITS CHECK. LOOK OUT, MEKON. HERE WE COME!
THE ANASTASIA— SO NAMED AFTER DIGBY'S FAVOURITE AUNT. AMONG ITS SECRETS... FIVE DIFFERENT FORMS OF PROPULSION!
USE MAGNETIC POWER TO AVOID DETECTION...
THE "ANNIE" CREEPS UP TO THE STATION AND DAN DARE AND DIGBY MAKE FOR ONE OF THE EMERGENCY AIR-LOCKS...
QUIETLY THEY SLIP THROUGH THE AIRLOCK... ONLY TO MEET...
GREAT SCOTT!

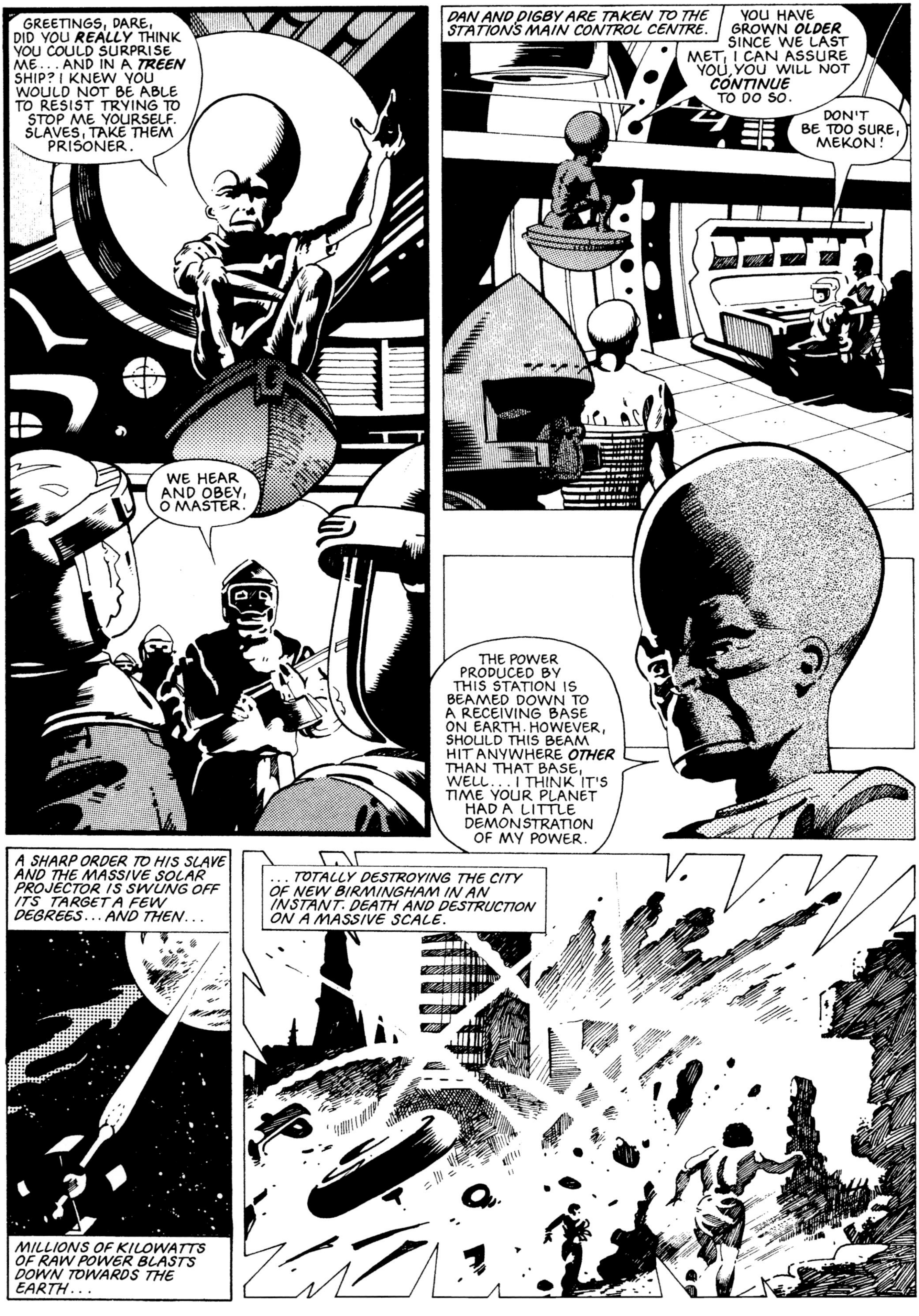
GREETINGS, DARE, DID YOU REALLY THINK YOU COULD SURPRISE ME... AND IN A TREEN SHIP? I KNEW YOU WOULD NOT BE ABLE TO RESIST TRYING TO STOP ME YOURSELF. SLAVES, TAKE THEM PRISONER.
WE HEAR AND OBEY, O MASTER.
DAN AND DIGBY ARE TAKEN TO THE STATION'S MAIN CONTROL CENTRE.
YOU HAVE GROWN OLDER SINCE WE LAST MET, I CAN ASSURE YOU, YOU WILL NOT CONTINUE TO DO SO.
DON'T BE TOO SURE, MEKON!
THE POWER PRODUCED BY THIS STATION IS BEAMED DOWN TO A RECEIVING BASE ON EARTH. HOWEVER, SHOULD THIS BEAM HIT ANYWHERE OTHER THAN THAT BASE, WELL... I THINK IT'S TIME YOUR PLANET HAD A LITTLE DEMONSTRATION OF MY POWER.
A SHARP ORDER TO HIS SLAVE AND THE MASSIVE SOLAR PROJECTOR IS SWUNG OFF ITS TARGET A FEW DEGREES... AND THEN...
MILLIONS OF KILOWATTS OF RAW POWER BLASTS DOWN TOWARDS THE EARTH...
... TOTALLY DESTROYING THE CITY OF NEW BIRMINGHAM IN AN INSTANT. DEATH AND DESTRUCTION ON A MASSIVE SCALE.

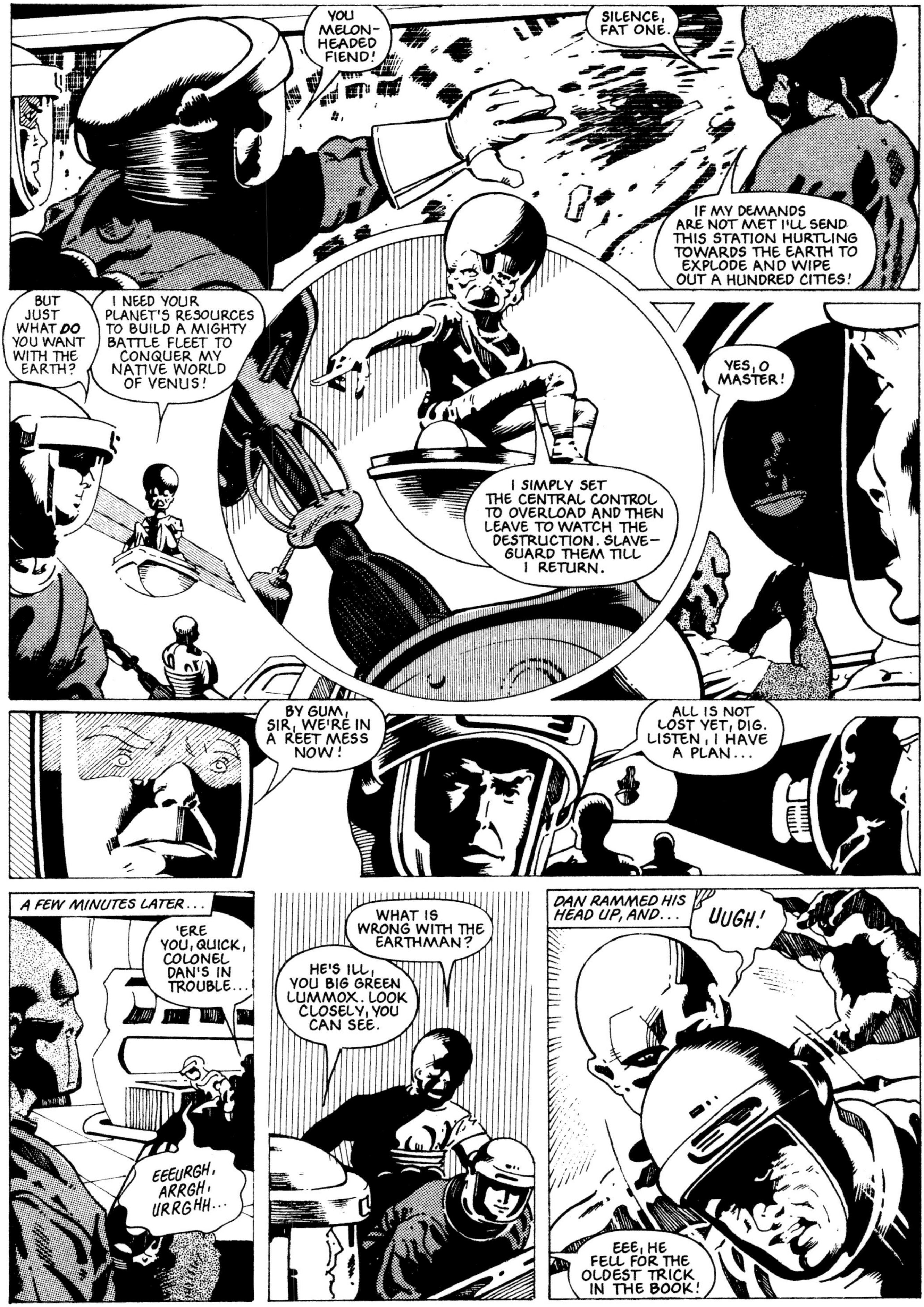
YOU MELON-HEADED FIEND!
SILENCE, FAT ONE.
IF MY DEMANDS ARE NOT MET I'LL SEND THIS STATION HURTLING TOWARDS THE EARTH TO EXPLODE AND WIPE OUT A HUNDRED CITIES!
BUT JUST WHAT DO YOU WANT WITH THE EARTH?
I NEED YOUR PLANET'S RESOURCES TO BUILD A MIGHTY BATTLE FLEET TO CONQUER MY NATIVE WORLD OF VENUS!
I SIMPLY SET THE CENTRAL CONTROL TO OVERLOAD AND THEN LEAVE TO WATCH THE DESTRUCTION. SLAVE-GUARD THEM TILL I RETURN.
YES, O MASTER!
BY GUM, SIR, WE'RE IN A REET MESS NOW!
ALL IS NOT LOST YET, DIG. LISTEN, I HAVE A PLAN...
A FEW MINUTES LATER...
'ERE YOU, QUICK, COLONEL DAN'S IN TROUBLE...
EEEURGH, ARRGH, URRGHHH...
WHAT IS WRONG WITH THE EARTHMAN?
HE'S ILL, YOU BIG GREEN LUMMOX. LOOK CLOSELY, YOU CAN SEE.
DAN RAMMED HIS HEAD UP, AND...
UUGH!
EEE, HE FELL FOR THE OLDEST TRICK IN THE BOOK!

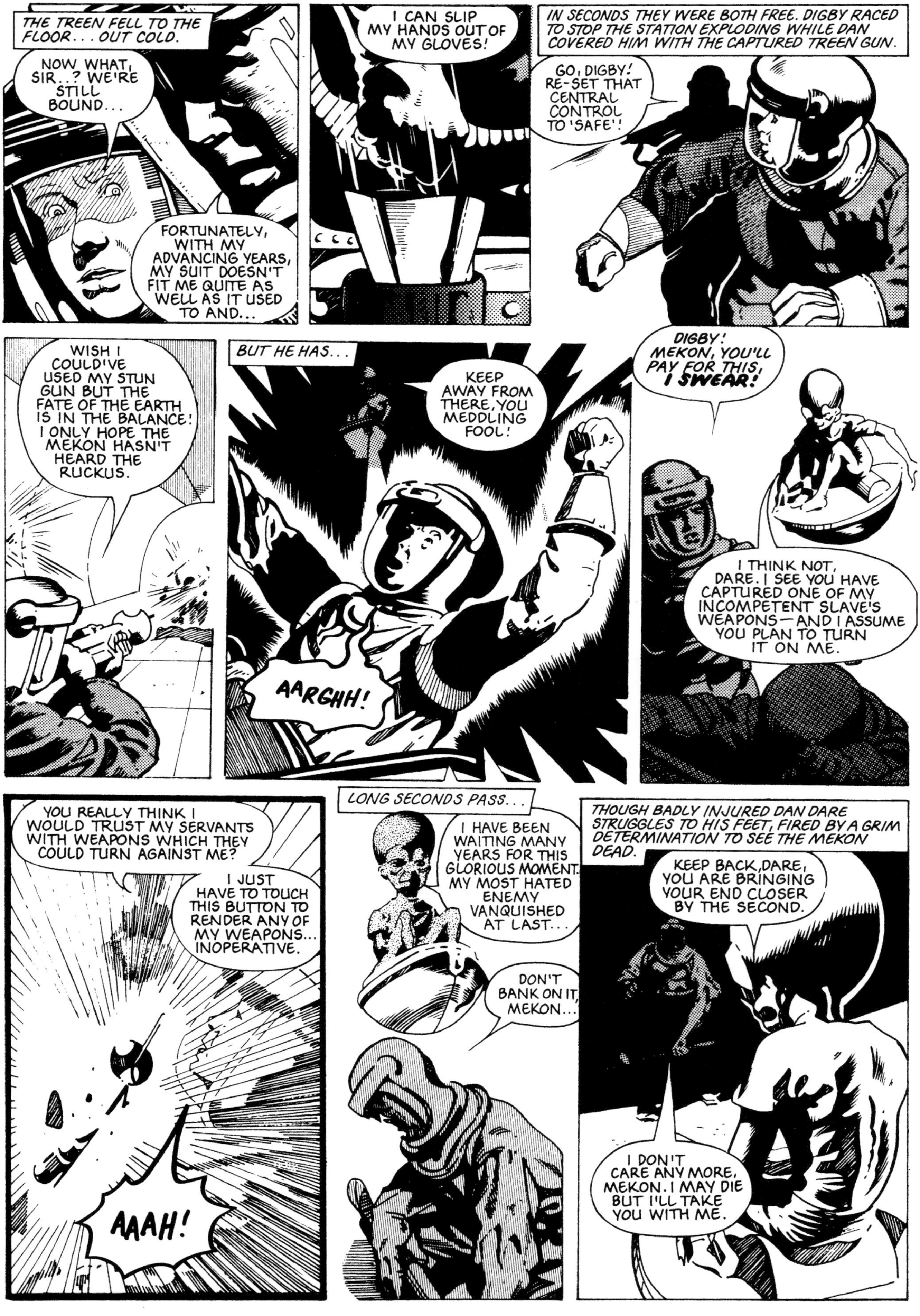
THE TREEN FELL TO THE FLOOR... OUT COLD.
NOW WHAT, SIR..? WE'RE STILL BOUND...
FORTUNATELY, WITH MY ADVANCING YEARS, MY SUIT DOESN'T FIT ME QUITE AS WELL AS IT USED TO AND...
I CAN SLIP MY HANDS OUT OF MY GLOVES!
IN SECONDS THEY WERE BOTH FREE. DIGBY RACED TO STOP THE STATION EXPLODING WHILE DAN COVERED HIM WITH THE CAPTURED TREEN GUN.
GO, DIGBY! RE-SET THAT CENTRAL CONTROL TO 'SAFE'!
WISH I COULD'VE USED MY STUN GUN BUT THE FATE OF THE EARTH IS IN THE BALANCE! I ONLY HOPE THE MEKON HASN'T HEARD THE RUCKUS.
BUT HE HAS...
KEEP AWAY FROM THERE, YOU MEDDLING FOOL!
AARGHH!
DIGBY! MEKON, YOU'LL PAY FOR THIS, I SWEAR!
I THINK NOT, DARE. I SEE YOU HAVE CAPTURED ONE OF MY INCOMPETENT SLAVE'S WEAPONS—AND I ASSUME YOU PLAN TO TURN IT ON ME.
YOU REALLY THINK I WOULD TRUST MY SERVANTS WITH WEAPONS WHICH THEY COULD TURN AGAINST ME?
I JUST HAVE TO TOUCH THIS BUTTON TO RENDER ANY OF MY WEAPONS... INOPERATIVE.
AAAH!
LONG SECONDS PASS...
I HAVE BEEN WAITING MANY YEARS FOR THIS GLORIOUS MOMENT. MY MOST HATED ENEMY VANQUISHED AT LAST...
DON'T BANK ON IT, MEKON...
THOUGH BADLY INJURED DAN DARE STRUGGLES TO HIS FEET, FIRED BY A GRIM DETERMINATION TO SEE THE MEKON DEAD.
KEEP BACK, DARE, YOU ARE BRINGING YOUR END CLOSER BY THE SECOND.
I DON'T CARE ANY MORE, MEKON. I MAY DIE BUT I'LL TAKE YOU WITH ME.

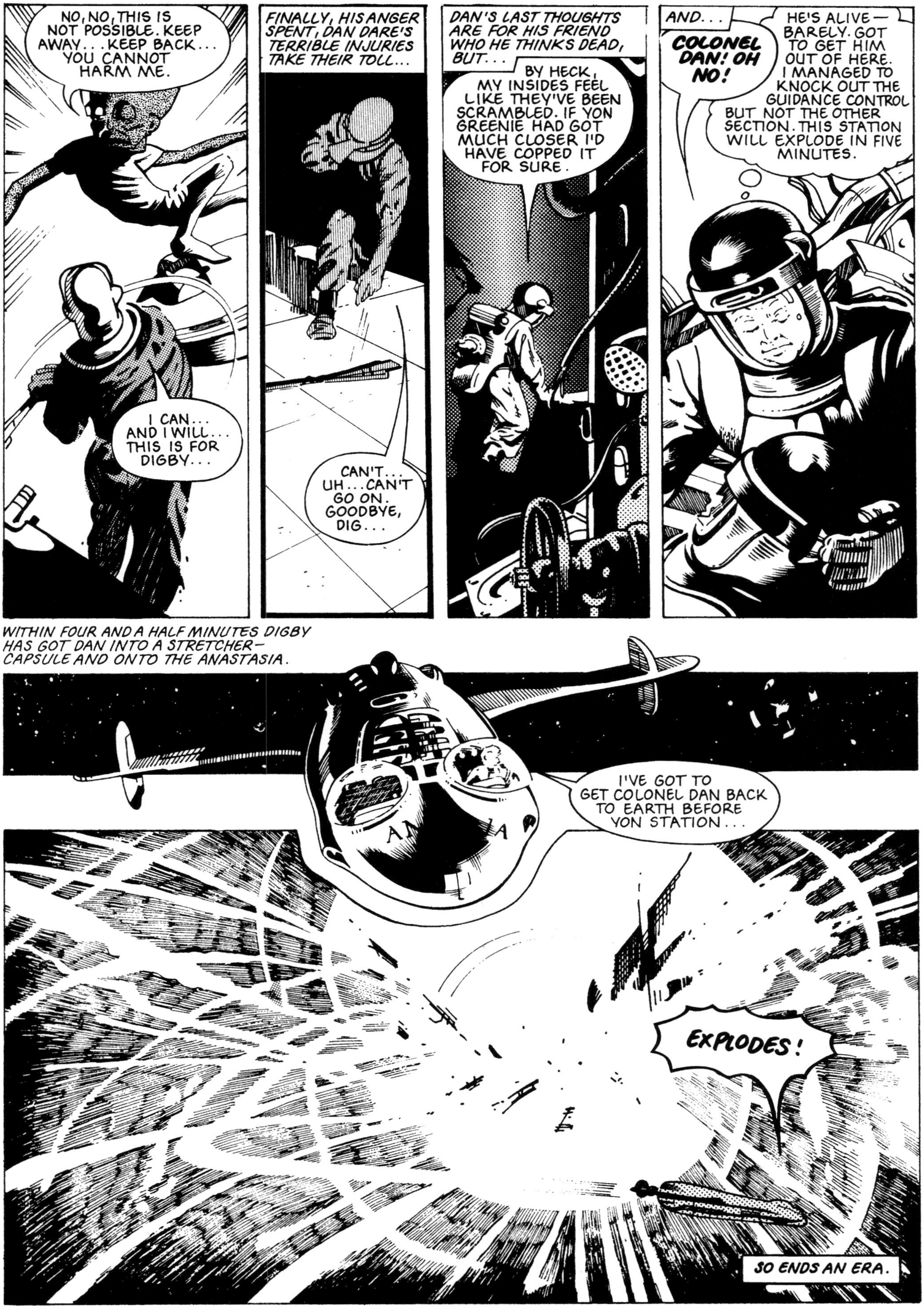
NO, NO, THIS IS NOT POSSIBLE. KEEP AWAY... KEEP BACK... YOU CANNOT HARM ME.
I CAN... AND I WILL... THIS IS FOR DIGBY...
FINALLY, HIS ANGER SPENT, DAN DARE'S TERRIBLE INJURIES TAKE THEIR TOLL...
CAN'T... UH... CAN'T GO ON. GOODBYE, DIG...
DAN'S LAST THOUGHTS ARE FOR HIS FRIEND WHO HE THINKS DEAD, BUT...
BY HECK, MY INSIDES FEEL LIKE THEY'VE BEEN SCRAMBLED. IF YON GREENIE HAD GOT MUCH CLOSER I'D HAVE COPPED IT FOR SURE.
AND...
COLONEL DAN! OH NO!
HE'S ALIVE — BARELY. GOT TO GET HIM OUT OF HERE. I MANAGED TO KNOCK OUT THE GUIDANCE CONTROL BUT NOT THE OTHER SECTION. THIS STATION WILL EXPLODE IN FIVE MINUTES.
WITHIN FOUR AND A HALF MINUTES DIGBY HAS GOT DAN INTO A STRETCHER-CAPSULE AND ONTO THE ANASTASIA.
I'VE GOT TO GET COLONEL DAN BACK TO EARTH BEFORE YON STATION...
EXPLODES!
SO ENDS AN ERA.

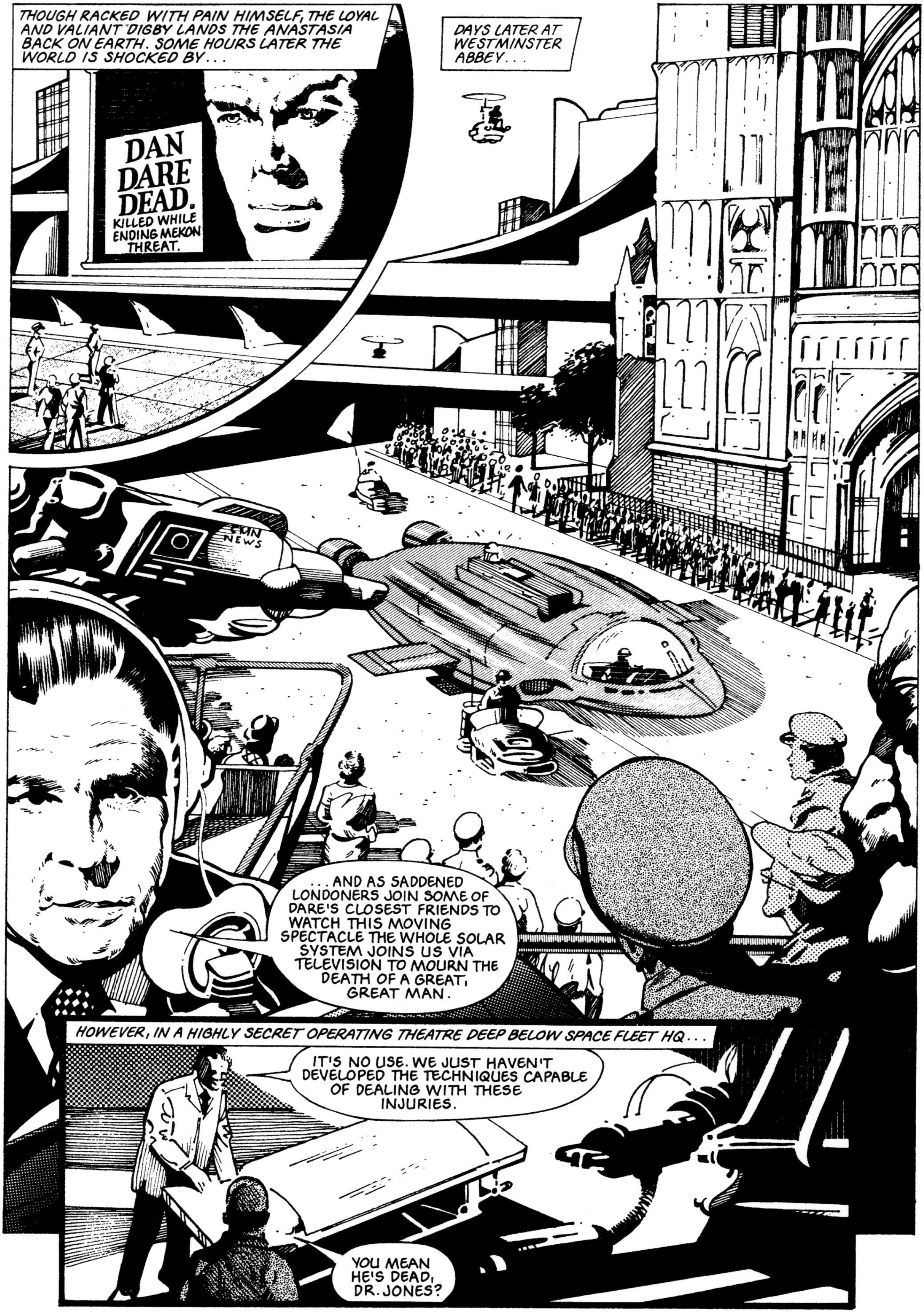
THOUGH RACKED WITH PAIN HIMSELF, THE LOYAL AND VALIANT DIGBY LANDS THE ANASTASIA BACK ON EARTH. SOME HOURS LATER THE WORLD IS SHOCKED BY...
DAN DARE DEAD. KILLED WHILE ENDING MEKON THREAT.
DAYS LATER AT WESTMINSTER ABBEY...
SMN NEWS
...AND AS SADDENED LONDONERS JOIN SOME OF DARE'S CLOSEST FRIENDS TO WATCH THIS MOVING SPECTACLE THE WHOLE SOLAR SYSTEM JOINS US VIA TELEVISION TO MOURN THE DEATH OF A GREAT, GREAT MAN.
HOWEVER, IN A HIGHLY SECRET OPERATING THEATRE DEEP BELOW SPACE FLEET HQ...
IT'S NO USE. WE JUST HAVEN'T DEVELOPED THE TECHNIQUES CAPABLE OF DEALING WITH THESE INJURIES.
YOU MEAN HE'S DEAD, DR. JONES?

NO, DOCTOR. BUT WE JUST CAN'T DEAL WITH HIS WOUNDS! AND AS FOR HIS FACE... WELL...

I SUGGEST WE PLACE HIM IN SUSPENDED ANIMATION UNTIL MEDICAL SCIENCE HAS DEVELOPED BETTER SKILLS AND TRY AGAIN.

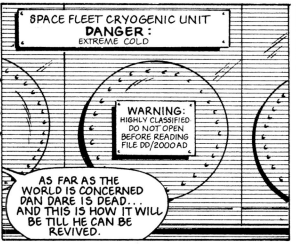

SPACE FLEET CRYOGENIC UNIT
DANGER:
EXTREME COLD

WARNING:
HIGHLY CLASSIFIED.
DO NOT OPEN
BEFORE READING
FILE DD/2000 AD

AS FAR AS THE WORLD IS CONCERNED DAN DARE IS DEAD... AND THIS IS HOW IT WILL BE TILL HE CAN BE REVIVED.

THE DECADES PASSED—MORE THAN A FULL CENTURY. THE GALAXY BECAME A MORE SAVAGE PLACE AS MAN PUSHED EVER OUTWARDS IN SEARCH OF SPACE TO LIVE.

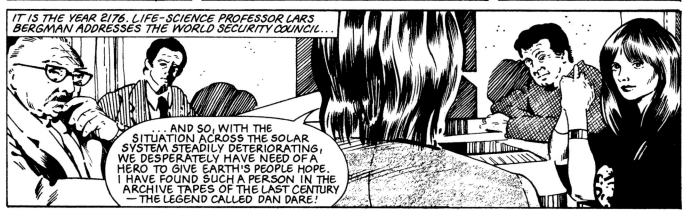

IT IS THE YEAR 2176. LIFE-SCIENCE PROFESSOR LARS BERGMAN ADDRESSES THE WORLD SECURITY COUNCIL...

...AND SO, WITH THE SITUATION ACROSS THE SOLAR SYSTEM STEADILY DETERIORATING, WE DESPERATELY HAVE NEED OF A HERO TO GIVE EARTH'S PEOPLE HOPE. I HAVE FOUND SUCH A PERSON IN THE ARCHIVE TAPES OF THE LAST CENTURY — THE LEGEND CALLED DAN DARE!

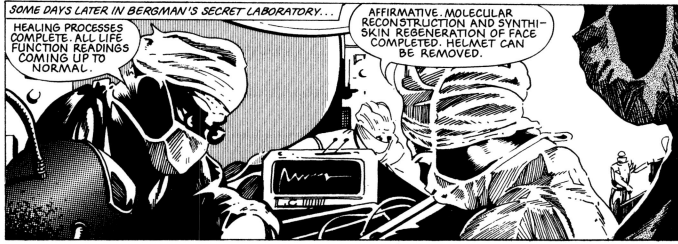

SOME DAYS LATER IN BERGMAN'S SECRET LABORATORY...

HEALING PROCESSES COMPLETE. ALL LIFE FUNCTION READINGS COMING UP TO NORMAL.

AFFIRMATIVE. MOLECULAR RECONSTRUCTION AND SYNTHI-SKIN REGENERATION OF FACE COMPLETED. HELMET CAN BE REMOVED.

GOOD, LET'S SEE WHAT THE "NEW" DAN DARE LOOKS LIKE.

...THIS IS THE FACE OF THE DAN DARE FOR TODAY, A MAN FOR OUR OWN DANGEROUS TIMES...

AFTER MONTHS OF RETRAINING AND GETTING USED TO HIS NEW WORLD, DAN DARE JOINED THE S.A.S.A. AND BEGAN A WHOLE NEW SERIES OF FANTASTIC ADVENTURES IN SPACE...

LOOK TO THE STARS— DAN DARE IS BACK!!

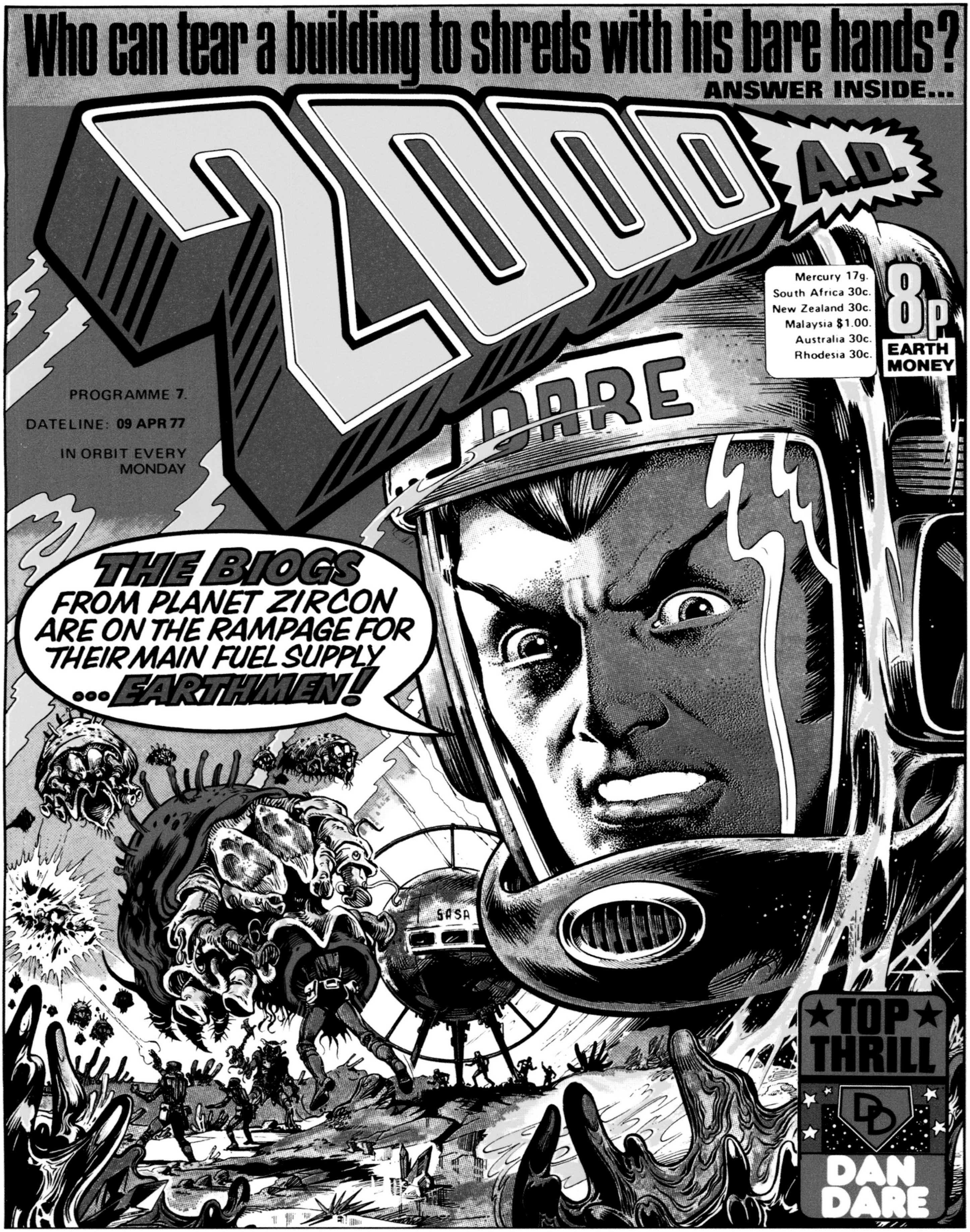
Who can tear a building to shreds with his bare hands?
ANSWER INSIDE...
2000 A.D.
Mercury 17g.
South Africa 30c.
New Zealand 30c.
Malaysia $1.00.
Australia 30c.
Rhodesia 30c.
8p
EARTH MONEY
PROGRAMME 7.
DATELINE: 09 APR 77
IN ORBIT EVERY MONDAY
DARE
THE BIOGS FROM PLANET ZIRCON ARE ON THE RAMPAGE FOR THEIR MAIN FUEL SUPPLY ...EARTHMEN!
SASA
TOP THRILL
DD
DAN DARE

2000 AD Prog 07: Cover by **Massimo Belardinelli**

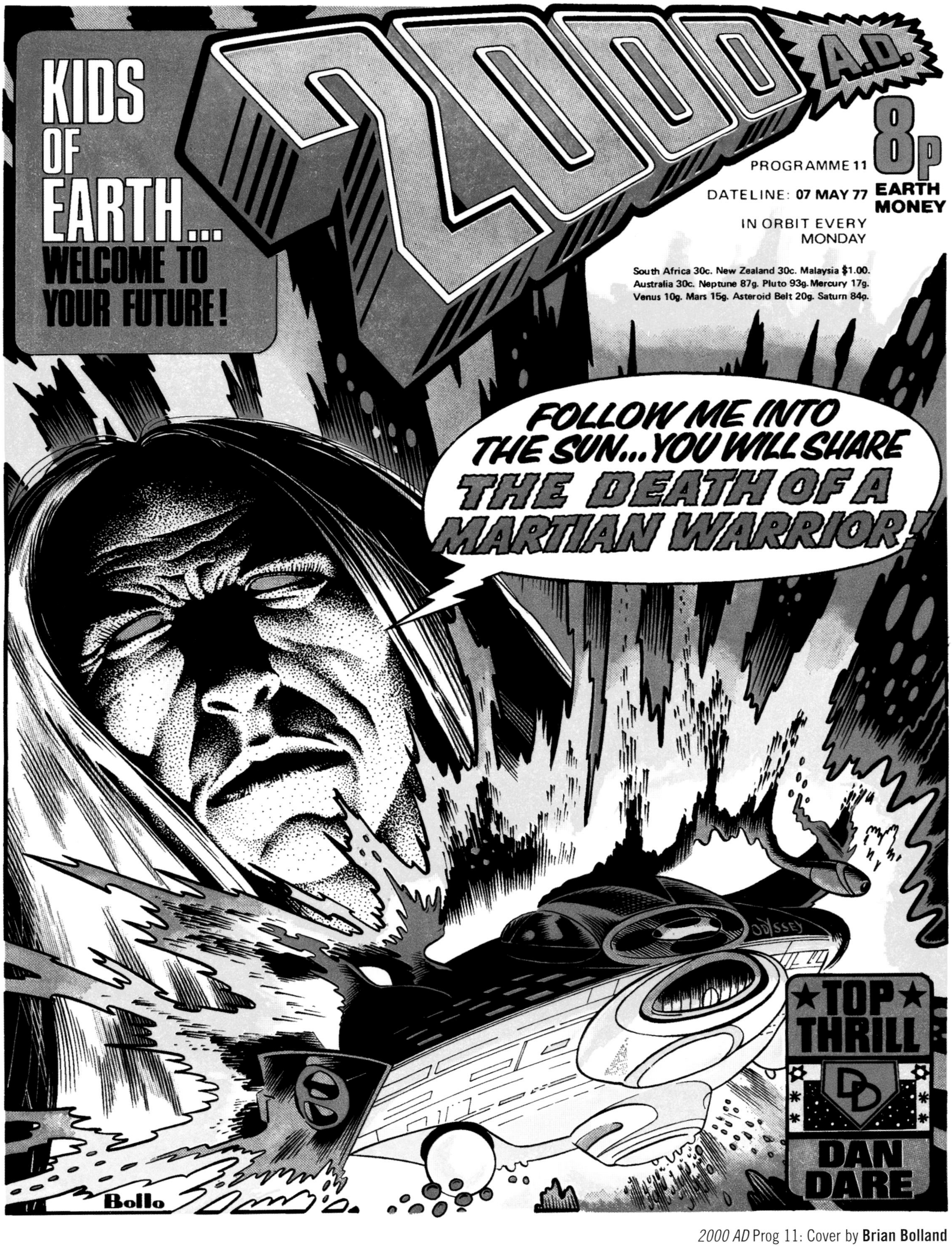
KIDS OF EARTH... WELCOME TO YOUR FUTURE!
2000 A.D.
8p EARTH MONEY
PROGRAMME 11
DATELINE: 07 MAY 77
IN ORBIT EVERY MONDAY
South Africa 30c. New Zealand 30c. Malaysia $1.00. Australia 30c. Neptune 87g. Pluto 93g. Mercury 17g. Venus 10g. Mars 15g. Asteroid Belt 20g. Saturn 84g.
FOLLOW ME INTO THE SUN... YOU WILL SHARE THE DEATH OF A MARTIAN WARRIOR!
ODYSSEY
TOP THRILL
DD
DAN DARE
Bollo

2000 AD Prog 11: Cover by **Brian Bolland**

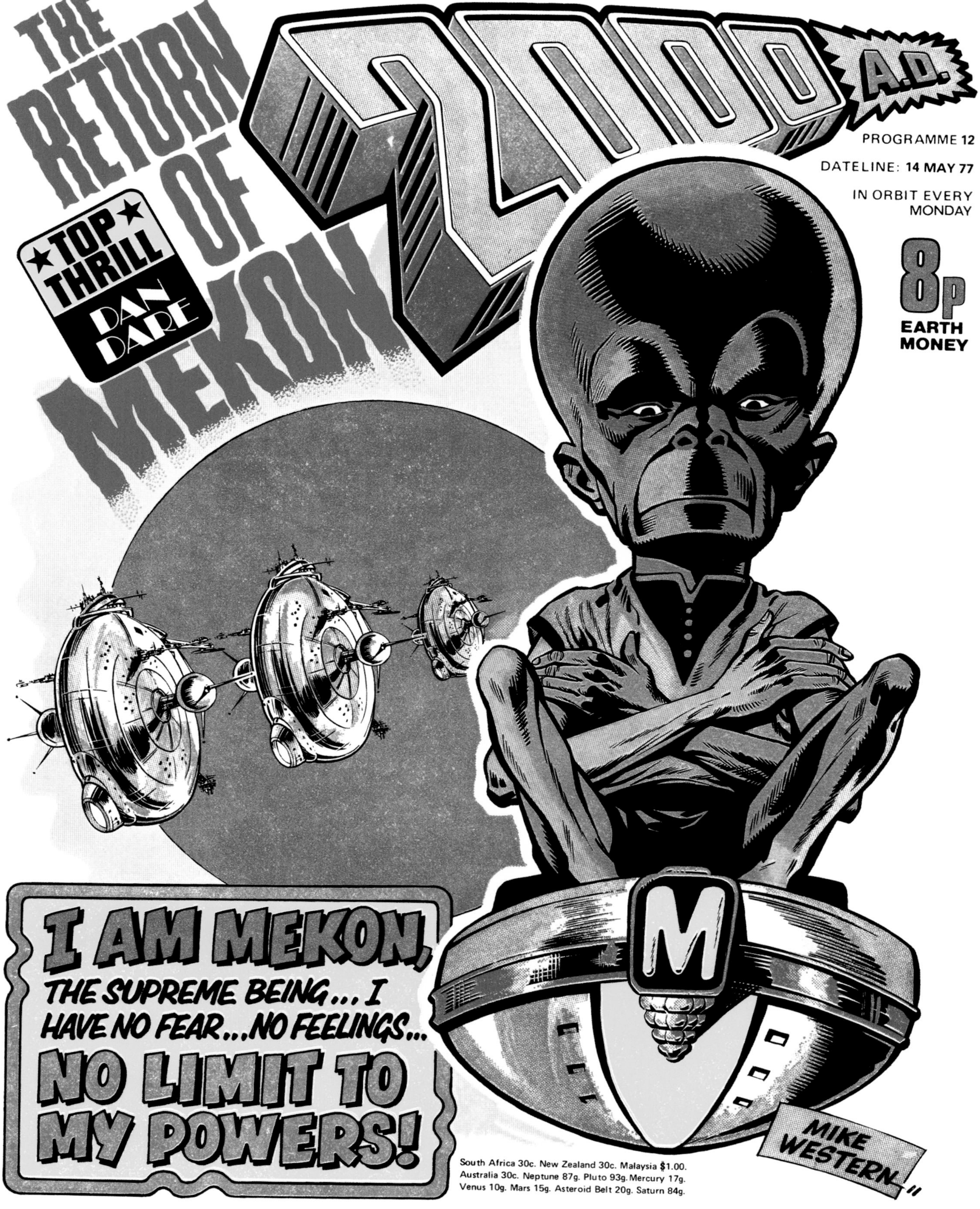
THE RETURN OF MEKON
2000 A.D.
PROGRAMME 12
DATELINE: 14 MAY 77
IN ORBIT EVERY MONDAY
8p EARTH MONEY
TOP THRILL
DAN DARE
I AM MEKON, THE SUPREME BEING... I HAVE NO FEAR...NO FEELINGS... NO LIMIT TO MY POWERS!
M
MIKE WESTERN
South Africa 30c. New Zealand 30c. Malaysia $1.00. Australia 30c. Neptune 87g. Pluto 93g. Mercury 17g. Venus 10g. Mars 15g. Asteroid Belt 20g. Saturn 84g.

2000 AD Prog 12: Cover by **Mike Western**

WRITERS

Pat Mills is the creator and first editor of *2000 AD*. For the Galaxy's Greatest Comic, he is the writer and co-creator of *ABC Warriors*, *Finn*, *Flesh*, *Nemesis the Warlock*, *Sláine*, *M.A.C.H 1*, *Harlem Heroes*, *Savage*, *Defoe* and *Greysuit*. He also developed *Judge Dredd* and wrote one of the early *Dredd* serials – *The Cursed Earth*. He wrote *Third World War* for *Crisis!*, a politically-charged spin-off from *2000 AD*, and *Black Siddha* for the *Judge Dredd Megazine*.
Outside *2000 AD* he is the writer and co-creator of the long-running classic anti-war story *Charley's War*, as well as *Marshal Law*. He has also written *Batman*, *Star Wars* and the *Zombie World* series for the US market. He co-created the best-selling series *Requiem – Vampire Knight* for Editions Nickel of France with artist Olivier Ledroit, and a spin-off series, *Claudia – Vampire Knight*, with artist Frank Tacito.

One of the most prolific writers in the comic's history, **Gerry Finley-Day** holds a special place in many *2000 AD* fans' hearts as the creator of classics like *Rogue Trooper*, *Fiends of the Eastern Front* and *The V.C.s*, as well as *Harry 20 on the High Rock* and *Ant Wars*.
A keen "ideas man", Finley-Day's concepts of the horrors future warfare had in store were key to both Rogue and *The V.C.s'* continuing popularity, ensuring that their recent return to the Galaxy's Greatest Comic was well-received.
Finley-Day also scripted episodes of *Judge Dredd* and *Dan Dare*, and co-scripted much of *Invasion!* (and entirely scripted the prequel story, *'Disaster 1990!'*).

A lifelong fan of comics and SF, **Steve Moore** was a notable participant within early fandom groups, where he met several stalwart creators, including Alan Moore. Having published several fanzines in the sixties, such as one of the first to cover British comics (*Ka-Pow*), Moore was also heavily involved in setting up Britain's first comics' convention – Comicon '68.
When *2000 AD* began in 1977, Steve was on hand to write the new *Dan Dare* strip. An extremely prolific and talented writer, Moore's greatest contribution towards *2000 AD* was undoubtedly the creation of *Tharg's Future Shocks*.

Ken Armstrong scripted an episode of *Dan Dare* and several episode of *Flesh* for *2000 AD*.

Kelvin Gosnell served as *2000 AD*'s second editor, from Progs 17 to 85. He also wrote *Blackhawk*, *Dan Dare*, *A Joe Black Adventure*, *Judge Dredd*, *One-Offs*, *Project Overkill*, *Ro-Jaws' Robo-Tales*, *The Stainless Steel Rat* and *Tharg's Future Shocks*, as well as co-writing the first series of *Flesh*.

ARTISTS

Dave Gibbons is one of 2000 AD's most popular artists, having co-created *Harlem Heroes* and *Rogue Trooper*. He has also pencilled *A.B.C. Warriors*, *Dan Dare*, *Judge Dredd*, *Mega-City One*, *Ro-Busters*, *Tharg the Mighty*, *Tharg's Future Shocks* and *Time Twisters*, as well as having scripted several *Rogue Trooper* stories – making Gibbons one of the few *2000 AD* creators to have served as writer, artist and letterer! Beyond *2000 AD*, Gibbons is unquestionably best known for his work on the award-winning classic *Watchmen* (with Alan Moore), but he has also drawn *Batman*, *Doctor Who*, *Give Me Liberty*, *Green Lantern*, *Superman*, *Star Wars* and his graphic novel, *The Originals*.

Massimo Belardinelli's career started with painting the backgrounds for animated cartoons for Rosi Studio in Rome. In 1977 he started working for *2000 AD* where his distinctive style graced many strips including *Dan Dare*, *Sláine*, *Meltdown Man* and *Ace Trucking Co.* Belardinelli has been much praised for his delicate brushwork and intricate representations of the fantastic. Massimo died in March 2007.

Perhaps the most popular *2000 AD* artist of all time, **Brian Bolland**'s clean-line style and meticulous attention to detail ensure that his artwork on strips including *Dan Dare*, *Future Shocks*, *Judge Dredd* and *Walter the Wobot* looks as fresh today as it did when first published. Co-creator of both *Judge Anderson* and *The Kleggs*, Bolland's highly detailed style unfortunately precluded him from doing many sequential strips — although he found the time to pencil both *Camelot 3000* and *Batman: The Killing Joke* for DC Comics.

Ian Kennedy provided the art for various *2000 AD* strips including *Invasion!*, *Judge Dredd*, *Tharg's Future Shocks* and *M.A.C.H. 1*.

Garry Leach is a highly-respected artist who has pencilled *Dan Dare*, *Judge Dredd*, *Tharg's Future Shocks* and *The V.C.'s*. His career beyond *2000 AD* is highly notable for his work on the legendary *Miracleman*, which he effectively co-created with Alan Moore.